Lecture Notes in Computer Science 8824

Commenced Publication in 1973
Founding and Former Series Editors:
Gerhard Goos, Juris Hartmanis, and Jan van Leeuwen

T0212826

Eric Yu   Gillian Dobbie   Matthias Jarke
Sandeep Purao (Eds.)

Conceptual Modeling

33rd International Conference, ER 2014
Atlanta, GA, USA, October 27-29, 2014
Proceedings

 Springer

Volume Editors

Eric Yu
University of Toronto
Faculty of Information
Toronto, ON, M5S 3G6, Canada
E-mail: eric.yu@utoronto.ca

Gillian Dobbie
University of Auckland
Department of Computer Science
Auckland 1142, New Zealand
E-mail: gill@cs.auckland.ac.nz

Matthias Jarke
RWTH Aachen University
Lehrstuhl Informatik 5
52056 Aachen, Germany
E-mail: jarke@dbis.rwth-aachen.de

Sandeep Purao
Penn State University
University Park
PA 16802, USA
E-mail: spurao@ist.psu.edu

ISSN 0302-9743   e-ISSN 1611-3349
ISBN 978-3-319-12205-2   e-ISBN 978-3-319-12206-9
DOI 10.1007/978-3-319-12206-9
Springer Cham Heidelberg New York Dordrecht London

Library of Congress Control Number: 2014950401

LNCS Sublibrary: SL 3 – Information Systems and Application, incl. Internet/Web
and HCI

Typesetting: Camera-ready by author, data conversion by Scientific Publishing Services, Chennai, India

Printed on acid-free paper

Springer is part of Springer Science+Business Media (www.springer.com)

Preface

The 33rd edition of the International Conference on Conceptual Modeling (ER), held this year in Atlanta, Georgia, USA, continued the long tradition of the ER conference series as the leading international forum for presenting research results and discussing emerging trends in conceptual modeling.

Since the seminal work of Peter Chen on the entity relationship (ER) model, the field of conceptual modeling has had profound impact on many areas of computing and information systems, including databases, software, business processes, and Internet systems and services. Conceptual modeling consists of the creation of foundational elements of intended information systems and applications that can serve as communication vehicles among stakeholders, blueprints for developers, as well as long-term preservation of designer intent. Conceptual models, therefore, serve a critical role in the design and deployment of new technologies and applications. As a set of languages, tools and techniques, conceptual models and modeling provide a rich arena for researchers with immediate applications to practice.

This foundational role of conceptual models was evident in this year's program, which included research papers addressing many contemporary topics such as big data, city informatics, policy compliance, enterprise architecture, data-intensive ecosystems, and open source software strategies. In addition, the research community continues to investigate fundamental concerns of conceptual modeling such as pragmatics, deployment paths, and modeling primitives.

The call for papers this year included a focus on fundamental concerns as well as contemporary application areas. The international research community responded by submitting a total of 123 abstracts, which resulted in 80 full paper submissions. With the use of an online review system, each paper was reviewed by at least three reviewers. On the basis of these reviews, we selected 23 submissions as full papers (an acceptance rate of 28.75%). The authors of a further 15 papers were invited to present their papers based on the contemporary nature of these research efforts and the promise for future impact. These papers are included as short papers in the proceedings.

The technical program at the conference consisted of a number of sessions covering the aforementioned papers. In addition, the program consisted of panels related to modeling for extreme events, conceptual models related to security concerns, and other fundamental concerns. There were two tutorials, one devoted to meta-models and meta-execution models, and a second related to creating new requirements modeling languages.

In addition to these, the conference included a number of workshops related to contemporary application areas. Papers from these workshops and papers describing research software demonstrations are included in a companion volume to these proceedings.

Finally, three highly interesting keynote presentations addressed important current topics in the theory and practice of conceptual modeling. Financial data mining pioneer Vasant Dhar (New York University, USA) pointed out critical issues in predictive modeling in the context of big data and data science, including the quest for an additional set of skills that students and practitioners in the field will need to acquire. Giancarlo Guizzardi (Federal University of Espirito Santo, Brazil, and University of Trento, Italy) emphasized quality control of conceptual modeling using real-world semantics. Antonio Furtado (Pontifical Catholic University of Rio de Janeiro, Brazil) emphasized the advantages of a semiotic perspective as another important foundation of formally supported database design and usage.

We would like to thank all those who helped put this program together. We would especially like to thank the individuals who have spearheaded a number of activities. This includes Workshop Chair Marta Indulska; Doctoral Consortium Chair Carson Woo; Tutorial Chair Cecil Chua; Panel Chair Sham Navathe; Demonstrations Chair Akhilesh Bajaj; and Educational Symposium Chair Lois Delcambre. In addition, Matti Rossi helped us in publicizing the conference; Jon Becker kept the website updated regularly. Antoni Olivé, ER Steering Committee Chair, and Veda Storey, ER Steering Committee Liaison, were always generous with their time in answering questions and providing guidance. We also thank Stuart Madnick and Colette Rolland, who provided valuable guidance as honorary chairs. Finally, Richard Welke was instrumental in ensuring that the logistics ran smoothly, as the local arrangements chair. Special thanks to Greg O'Dillon, who made a major contribution to making everything happen in and around the conference venue.

We are grateful for the support from all the sponsors of the conference. Major support for the conference was provided by Penn State University and Singapore Management University. We wish to express our appreciation for Georgia State University as the local organizing partner.

We sincerely thank the members of the Program Committee and external reviewers who provided thoughtful reviews on time. Their reviews provided feedback as well as suggestions that have significantly improved the technical program as well as each individual paper.

Most importantly, we thank the authors for submitting their work and for participating in the conference.

July 2014

Eric Yu
Gill Dobbie
Matthias Jarke
Sandeep Purao

Conference Organization

Honorary Chairs

Stuart Madnick   MIT, Boston, MA, USA
Colette Rolland   Université Paris 1 Panthéon – Sorbonne, France

Conference Chair

Sandeep Purao   Penn State University, State College, PA, USA

Technical Program Co-chairs

Eric Yu   University of Toronto, Canada
Gill Dobbie   University of Auckland, New Zealand
Matthias Jarke   RWTH Aachen University and Fraunhofer FIT, Germany

Workshop Chair

Marta Indulska   University of Queensland, Australia

Publicity Chair

Matti Rossi   Aalto University, Finland

Panel Chair

Sham Navathe   Georgia Tech, USA

Tutorial Chair

Cecil Chua   Auckland University, New Zealand

Poster / Demo Chair

Akhilesh Bajaj   University of Tulsa, USA

PhD Symposium Chair

Carson Woo   University of British Columbia, Canada

Local Organization Chair

Richard Welke   Georgia State University, USA

Sponsorships Co-chairs

Sandeep Purao   Penn State University, USA
Aditya Ghose   University of Wollongong, Australia
Wolfgang Maass   Universität des Saarlandes, Germany

Finance Chair

Anna Squicciarini   Penn State University, State College, USA

Webmaster

Jon Becker   Penn State University, State College, USA

Steering Committee Liaison

Veda Storey   Georgia State University, USA

Program Committee

Jacky Akoka   CNAM and TEM, France
Yuan An   Drexel University, USA
Joao Araujo   Universidade Nova de Lisboa, Portugal
Zhifeng Bao   University of Singapore, Singapore
Sandro Bimonte   IRSTEA, France
Shawn Bowers   Gonzaga University, USA
Stephane Bressan   National University of Singapore, Singapore
Stefano Ceri   Politecnico di Milano, Italy
Roger Chiang   University of Cincinnati, USA
Dickson Chiu   University of Hong Kong, SAR China

Isabel F. Cruz	University of Illinois, USA
Alfredo Cuzzocrea	ICAR-CNR and University of Calabria, Italy
Fabiano Dalpiaz	Universiteit Utrecht, The Netherlands
Karen Davis	University of Cincinnati, USA
Valeria De Antonellis	University of Brescia, Italy
Lois Delcambre	Portland State University, USA
Joerg Evermann	Memorial University of Newfoundland, Canada
Xavier Franch	UniversitatPolitècnica de Catalunya, Spain
Avigdor Gal	Technion-Israel Institute of Technology, Israel
Aditya Ghose	University of Wollongong, Australia
Paolo Giorgini	University of Trento, Italy
Georg Grossmann	University of Australia, Australia
Giancarlo Guizzardi	Federal University of Espirito Santo, Brazil
Arantza Illarramendi	Basque Country University, Spain
Hemant Jain	University of Wisconsin-Milwaukee, USA
Manfred Jeusfeld	Tilburg University, The Netherlands
Ivan Jureta	University of Namur, Belgium
Dimitris Karagiannis	University of Vienna, Austria
David Kensche	Thinking Networks AG, Germany
Alberto Laender	Federal University of Minas Gerais, Brazil
Sang-Goo Lee	Seoul National University, Korea
Mong Li Lee	National University of Singapore, Singapore
Dik Lun Lee	Hong Kong University of Science and Technology, SAR China
Wolfgang Lehner	Technische Universität Dresden, Germany
Julio Cesar Leite	PUC Rio de Janeiro, Brazil
Stephen Liddle	Brigham Young University, USA
Tok Wang Ling	National University of Singapore, Singapore
Sebastian Link	The University of Auckland, New Zealand
Mengchi Liu	Carleton University, Canada
Fred Lochovsky	The Hong Kong University of Science and Technology, SAR China
Pericles Loucopoulos	Loughborough University, UK
Hui Ma Victoria	University of Wellington, New Zealand
Heinrich C. Mayr	Alpen-Adria-Universität Klagenfurt, Austria
Jan Mendling	Wirtschafts Universität Wien, Austria
Haralambos Mouratidis	University of Brighton, UK
John Mylopoulos	University of Trento, Italy
Antoni Olivé	Universitat Politècnica de Catalunya, Spain
Andreas L. Opdahl	University of Bergen, Norway
José Palazzo M. De Oliveira	Universidade Federal do Rio Grande do Sul, Brazil
Jeffrey Parsons	Memorial University of Newfoundland, Canada

Oscar Pastor Lopez	University of Valencia, Spain
Zhiyong Peng	Wuhan University, China
Barbara Pernici	Politecnico di Milano, Italy
Geert Poels	Ghent University, Belgium
Henderik Proper	Public Research Centre Henri Tudor, Luxembourg
Christoph Quix	RWTH Aachen University, Germany
Jolita Ralyté	University of Geneva, Switzerland
Sudha Ram	University of Arizona, USA
Iris Reinhartz-Berger	University of Haifa, Israel
Stefano Rizzi	University of Bologna, Italy
Colette Rolland	Université Paris 1 Panthéon – Sorbonne, France
Antonio Ruiz-Cortés	University of Seville, Spain
Bernhard Rumpe	RWTH Aachen University, Germany
Mehrdad Sabetzadeh	University of Luxembourg, Luxembourg
Motoshi Saeki	Tokyo Institute of Technology, Japan
Camille Salinesi	Université Paris 1 Panthéon – Sorbonne, France
Peretz Shoval	Ben-Gurion University, Israel
Il-Yeol Song	Drexel University, USA
Steffen Staab	University of Koblenz-Landau, Germany
Veda Storey	Georgia State University, USA
Arnon Sturm	Ben-Gurion University of the Negev, Israel
David Taniar	Monash University, Australia
Ernest Teniente	Universitat Politècnica de Catalunya, Spain
James Terwilliger	Microsoft Corporation, USA
Bernhard Thalheim	University of Kiel, Germany
Juan Trujillo	University of Alicante, Spain
Panos Vassiliadis	University of Ioannina, Greece
Ramesh Venkataraman	Indiana University, USA
Gerd Wagner	Brandenburg University of Technology at Cottbus, Germany
Barbara Weber	University of Innsbruck, Austria
Roel Wieringa	University of Twente, The Netherlands
Carson Woo	University of British Columbia, Canada
Huayu Wu	Agency for Science, Technology and Research, Singapore
Esteban Zimányi	Université Libre de Bruxelles, Belgium

Additional Reviewers

Bertossi, Leopoldo	Cappiello, Cinzia
Bianchini, Devis	De Kinderen, Sybren
Bjekovic, Marija	Fernandez, Pablo
Bork, Domenik	Guarino, Nicola

Horst, Andreas
Kim, Hyun Joon
Kim, Meenv Chul
Koehler, Henning
Lee, Hanbit
Ling, Yuan
Liu, Mengwen
Manousis, Petros
Marosin, Diana
Mascaro, Christopher
Mate, Alejandro
Melchiori, Michele
Mir Seyed Nazari, Pedram

Navarro Perez, Antonio
Palmonari, Matteo
Peña, Joaquín
Plataniotis, Georgios
Resinas, Manuel
Sagi, Tomer
Shin, Youhyun
Sugumaran, Vijayan
Visic, Niksa
Wu, Feng
Yu, Ting
Zang, Yizhou
Zhu, Yongjun

Sponsors

Gold Sponsors

Silver Sponsors

Bronze Sponsors

Keynotes (Abstracts)

Data Science and Prediction

Vasant Dhar

Professor and Director
Center for Business Analytics
New York University
vdhar@stern.nyu.edu

Abstract. Data Science is the study of the generalizable extraction of knowledge from data. A common epistemic requirement in assessing whether new knowledge is actionable for decision making is its predictive power, not just its ability to explain the past. The heterogeneity and scale of data and diversity of analytical methods require data scientists to have an integrated skill set, as well as a deep understanding of the craft of problem formulation and the science required to engineer effective solutions. I shall talk about the key issues that arise in industrial strength predictive modeling, including the implications for education in this fast emerging field.

A Semiotic Approach to Conceptual Modelling

Antonio L. Furtado, Marco A. Casanova, and Simone D.J. Barbosa

Departmento de Informática
Pontifícia Universidade Católica do Rio de Janeiro (PUC-Rio)
Rio de Janeiro, Brazil
{furtado,casanova,simone}@inf.puc-rio.br

Abstract. The work on Conceptual Modelling performed by our group at PUC-Rio is surveyed, covering four mutually dependent research topics. Regarding databases as a component of information systems, we extended the scope of the Entity-Relationship model, so as to encompass facts, events and agents in a three-schemata specification method employing a logic programming formalism. Next we proceeded to render the specifications executable, by utilizing backward-chaining planners to satisfy the agents' goals through sequences of fact-modification events. Thanks to the adoption of this plan-recognition / plan-generation paradigm, it became possible to treat both business-oriented and fictional narrative genres. To guide our conceptual modelling approach, we identified four semiotic relations, associated with the four master tropes that have been claimed to provide a system to fully grasp the world conceptually.

Keywords: Entity-Relationship Model, Information Systems, Planning, Logic Programming, Narrative Genres, Semiotics.

Ontological Patterns, Anti-Patterns and Pattern Languages for Next-Generation Conceptual Modeling

Giancarlo Guizzardi

Ontology and Conceptual Modeling Research Group (NEMO),
Computer Science Department,
Federal University of Espírito Santo (UFES), Vitória - ES, Brazil
gguizzardi@inf.ufes.br

Abstract. This paper addresses the complexity of conceptual modeling in a scenario in which semantic interoperability requirements are increasingly present. It elaborates on the need for developing sound ontological foundations for conceptual modeling but also for developing complexity management tools derived from these foundations. In particular, the paper discusses three of these tools, namely, ontological patterns, ontological anti-patterns and pattern languages.

Keywords: Conceptual Modeling, Formal Ontology, Patterns, Anti-Patterns and Pattern Languages

Table of Contents

New Modeling Languages and Applications

Software Concepts and Strategies

Patterns and Narratives

Data Management for Enterprise Architecture

City and Urban Applications

A Semiotic Approach to Conceptual Modelling

Antonio L. Furtado, Marco A. Casanova, and Simone Diniz Junqueira Barbosa

Departmento de Informática
Pontifícia Universidade Católica do Rio de Janeiro (PUC-Rio)
Rio de Janeiro, Brazil
{furtado,casanova,simone}@inf.puc-rio.br

Abstract. The work on Conceptual Modelling performed by our group at PUC-Rio is surveyed, covering four mutually dependent research topics. Regarding databases as a component of information systems, we extended the scope of the Entity-Relationship model, so as to encompass facts, events and agents in a three-schemata specification method employing a logic programming formalism. Next we proceeded to render the specifications executable, by utilizing backward-chaining planners to satisfy the agents' goals through sequences of fact-modification events. Thanks to the adoption of this plan-recognition / plan-generation paradigm, it became possible to treat both business-oriented and fictional narrative genres. To guide our conceptual modelling approach, we identified four semiotic relations, associated with the four master tropes that have been claimed to provide a system to fully grasp the world conceptually.

Keywords: Entity-Relationship Model, Information Systems, Planning, Logic Programming, Narrative Genres, Semiotics.

1 Introduction

Our understanding of information systems comprises facts, events and agents. Everywhere the Entity-Relationship model is used. The existing entity instances and their properties, i.e., their attributes and the relationships among them, are the *facts* that characterize a state of the world. States are changed by the occurrence of *events* caused by operations defined by pre-conditions and post-conditions that are in turn expressed in terms of such facts. The event-producing operations are performed by certain *agents*, in an attempt to satisfy their goals, once again expressed by facts. Accordingly, our specifications are divided into three schemas to introduce, respectively, the classes of facts (static schema), events (dynamic schema) and agents (behavioural schema).

It so happens that the pre-conditions to bring about an event may need to be first fulfilled as part of the effect (post-conditions) of other events. This partial-order dependence immediately suggests the recursive application of backward-chaining *plan-generators* in order to find one or more sequences of operations (plans) able to perform a transition from the current state to a state wherein the goals of an agent hold. By using a logic programming notation to represent the three schemas and

E. Yu et al. (Eds.): ER 2014, LNCS 8824, pp. 1–12, 2014.

having developed in Prolog a plan-generation algorithm, we gained the benefit of executable specifications, enabling to simulate and helping to gradually produce a running system. Moreover, plans previously generated by the algorithm, or originated from regulations or from customary practice, can be converted into patterns and kept in libraries from which they can be retrieved by a *plan-recognition* algorithm and reused, after the necessary adaptations, to reach similar goals.

Besides business information systems domains, we soon realized that our specification method was applicable to narrative genres in general, ranging from "serious" applications, such as maintenance procedures for an oil company, to fictional sword-and-dragon stories. Indeed plot composition can be conveniently achieved via interactive plan-generation. Alternatively, narrative *motifs* can serve as patterns to be retrieved from a library and combined to compose the plots, thus providing another opportunity to utilize plan-recognition.

When specifying any system, and when using it as well, some guidelines should be available. What properties are relevant to characterize an object? What events should be observed? How do agents interact, either collaborating or competing? Is it possible to attain modularity, by setting the focus to different degrees of detail? Which integrity constraints should be enforced? We found that four *semiotic relations* establish and delimit the information space, covering the need for helpful reasoning principles to a comprehensive extent. The *syntagmatic relations* determine – employing semiotic terminology [53] – a horizontal axis expressing the notion of connectivity between information components. Another notion is similarity expressed by *paradigmatic relations*, along a vertical axis. A depth axis, expressing granularity, results from *meronymic relations*. Finally, topological limits are imposed to this three-dimensional space by *antithetic relations*, which express negation and opposition. The four semiotic relations are associated with the so-called *four master tropes* (metonym, metaphor, synecdoche, and irony) [9], thought to constitute "a system, indeed *the* system, by which the mind comes to grasp the world conceptually in language" [23].

Our research work on conceptual modelling, motivated by the considerations above, is briefly surveyed as follows. Section 2 refers to the separate but consistently adjusted specification of facts, events and agents. Section 3 covers plan-generation and plan-recognition. Section 4 addresses application domains and narrative genres. Section 5, the longest one, discusses the semiotic relations. Section 6 presents the concluding remarks.

2   Three-Schemata Specifications

We have been working with the conceptual modeling of information systems with a database component, considering their static, dynamic and behavioral aspects.

The static aspect concerns what *facts* hold at some database state, conveniently described in terms of the entity-relationship model.

The dynamic aspect corresponds to events that can produce state transitions. Events result from the execution of operations, defined in a declarative style by their pre-conditions and post-conditions, according to the STRIPS proposal [25].

Pre-conditions involve the presence or absence of facts, whereas post-conditions comprise the sets of facts added or deleted as the effect of the operation. Adopting the notion of abstract data types, implicit in object-oriented approaches, we require that facts can only be modified through the execution of such operations, whose pre- and post-conditions are adjusted so as to preserve all integrity constraints.

The behavioural aspect refers to the agents authorized to cause events by performing the operations. To model this aspect we mainly use goal-inference rules, which indicate what facts should hold, or cease to hold, at a target state that an agent will be motivated to bring about in view of a situation, again expressed in terms of facts holding or not holding, prevailing at the current state [22]. In order to reach the desired target state, an agent would execute – or ask the authorized agents to execute – some appropriate plan, composed of one or more pre-defined operations. As a further development, we have started to look at agent profiles involving three kinds of personality factors, from which a decision-making process could operate: drives for the emergence of goals from situations, attitudes for the choice of plans to achieve the preferred goal, and emotions to decide whether or not to commit to the execution of the chosen plan, depending on the expected emotional gain when passing from the current to the target state [4,40]. As an inducement to revise individual decisions, we included competition and collaboration interferences, as prescribed for multi-agent contexts [54].

3   The Plan-Recognition / Plan-Generation Paradigm

The three aspects treated in the preceding section were integrated through the application of a plan-recognition / plan-generation paradigm [35,38].

In order to make our conceptual specifications executable [32], we created an environment where entity and relationship classes, operations, and goal-inference rules and agent profiles are all represented as Prolog clauses. Also written in Prolog, algorithms were provided for planning and for the simulated execution of the generated plans [17,18,19,29]. Moreover it was noted that simulation can become a useful resource to support learning or training [20].

The plan-recognition side of the paradigm is relevant, after the system has been made operational, as a means to extend conventional query facilities towards truly cooperative responses. Cooperation, as discussed in section 5, is most effective when one can detect what the user is trying to accomplish. The plan-recognition algorithm, which we adapted from [46], matches a few observed actions of the user against a library of previously recorded typical plans. The observed actions can be taken from the execution log, which is updated whenever each operation of a transaction of the user's initiative is executed. As we explained in [39], the library of typical plans, in turn, can be constructed by inspecting the log and extracting and filtering sequences of executed operations, whereby the transition indicated in some goal-inference rule has been achieved.

4   Application Domains and Narrative Genres

Treating databases as a component of information systems encompassing facts, events and agents permits a shift from a purely descriptive to a *narrative context* [27]. Indeed in a workshop devoted to the application of natural languages to information systems, we showed how to generate template-based natural language text, by inspecting the plot-structured execution log and analyzing it against our three-level conceptual schemas [37]. It is therefore not surprising that all the discussion in this section applies in essentially the same way to literary genres [15,28,36], whenever the fictional events can be equally attributed to a pre-defined repertoire of operations performed by agents (cf. the functions and *dramatis personae* in [50]). Recognizing that literary genres ruled by identifiable conventions can thus be treated as one more kind of application domain, we have adopted plan-based plot composition, coupled with several dramatization techniques and visual media, within an ongoing digital storytelling project [16,21].

The application of the plan-recognition / plan-generation paradigm to the narrative domain [28] was presented at the XIX Brazilian Symposium on Data Bases as an invited talk, on which occasion the author received a prize from the Brazilian Computer Society, acknowledging his contributions to database research.

Having started in the fictional genres with folktale sword-and-dragon stories, we have recently moved to genres where, besides action events, communicative events must be specified and play a decisive role, such as detective stories [5].

5   Semiotic Completeness

Based on studies [9,12,51,55] asserting the completeness as reasoning processes of the so-called four master tropes – metonymy, metaphor, irony and synecdoche, we identified four types of semiotic relations that can exist not only between facts, but also between events and between agents, which we denominated, respectively, syntagmatic, paradigmatic, antithetic and meronymic relations. Informally speaking, syntagmatic relations refer to connectivity, paradigmatic relations to similarity and analogy, antithetic relations to negation, and meronymic relations to hierarchy.

Meronymy was, curiously, treated in our very first participation in Entity-Relationship events [52], when we proposed to include semantic is-a and part-of hierarchies into the ER model. Not much later we learned about the seminal contribution of [56], where six types of part-of were distinguished.

The paradigmatic relations were the next to attract our attention. In a SIGPLAN Notices paper [26], belonging to logic programming rather than to the database area, we argued that a powerful kind of reasoning by analogy is provided by combining unification with most specific generalization. We presented a revised version of an existing algorithm to compute the most specific generalization of terms, which correctly decides whether or not new variables should be introduced in each case. We also provided programs to perform unification and most specific generalization over frames, a data structure which would be of major importance for the practical application of our ideas, as will be repeatedly stressed in the sequel.

Our paper presented at SBBD 2007 [2] can be regarded as a first attempt to deal with paradigmatic relations in the context of databases. The motivating problem was that databases, particularly when storing heterogeneous, sparse semi-structured data, tend to provide incomplete information and information which is difficult to categorize. The paper first considers how to classify entity instances as members of entity classes organized in a lattice-like generalization/specialization hierarchy. Then, it describes how the frame representation employed for instances and classes, as well as the closeness criterion involved in the classification method, favors the practical use of similarity and analogy, where similarity refers to instances within the same class, and analogy involves different classes. Finally, the paper argues that similarity and analogy facilitate querying semi-structured data.

A more in-depth investigation of classification methods based on frames was the object of a more recent work [48]. In fact, the problem of data classification goes back to the definition of taxonomies covering knowledge areas. With the advent of the Web, the amount of data available increased several orders of magnitude, making manual data classification impossible. The paper presents a tool to automatically classify semi-structured data, represented by frames, without any previous knowledge about structured classes. The tool uses a variation of the K-Medoid algorithm and organizes a set of frames into classes, structured as a strict hierarchy.

The next step, still focusing on paradigmatic relations and the corresponding trope, metaphor, was to promote a reuse strategy, whereby new conceptual specifications might be partly derived from previous ones. A paper along this line was presented at CIKM [8]. Metaphor is not merely a rhetorical device, characteristic of language alone, but rather a fundamental feature of the human conceptual system. A metaphor is understood by finding an analogy mapping between two domains. The paper argued that analogy mappings facilitate conceptual modeling by allowing the designer to reinterpret fragments of familiar conceptual models in other contexts. The contributions of the paper were expressed within the tradition of the ER model, the Description Logic framework and as extensions of the OWL.

This reuse strategy was further examined in [7,30]. These papers argued in favor of a database conceptual schema and Semantic Web ontology design discipline that explores analogy mappings to reuse the structure and integrity constraints of conceptual models, stored in a repository. We presupposed that a team of expert conceptual designers would build a standard repository of source conceptual models, which less experienced designers would use to create new target conceptual models in other domains. The target models will then borrow the structure and the integrity constraints from the source models by analogy. The concepts were once again expressed in the contexts of Description Logic, the RDF model and OWL to reinforce the basic principles and explore additional questions, such as the consistency of the target model.

Reusing a conceptual schema is of course a multi-phase process. After finding a suitable source schema, adaptations will often be needed in view of conflicts with the target schema being designed. The notion of *blending* [24] was exploited for this objective in [10]. To support the generation of database schemas of information systems, the paper proposed a five-step design process that explores the notions of generic and blended spaces and favors the reuse of predefined schemas. The use of generic and blended spaces is essential to achieve the passage from the source space into the target space in such a way that differences and conflicts can be detected and, whenever possible, conciliated. The convenience of working with multiple source schemas to cover distinct aspects of a target schema, as well as the possibility of creating schemas at the generic and blended spaces, was also considered. Notice that, as we would indicate more explicitly in later articles, the presence of conflicts already suggests the need to deal with antithetic relations.

As mentioned before, since our already referred SBBD paper [2], we have been using frames and frame-sets as a more flexible data structure than relational tuples and tables. At the 27th ER Conference [33], as we proceeded to show how to extend the reuse strategy to the design of dynamic schemas, we employed *plots*, also defined as a frame-like data structure. A plot is a partially ordered set of events. Plot analysis is a relevant source of knowledge about the agents' behavior when accessing data stored in the database. It relies on logical logs, which register the actions of individual agents. The paper proposed techniques to analyze and reuse plots based on the concepts of similarity and analogy. The concept of similarity was applied to organize plots as a library and to explore the reuse of plots in the same domain. By contrast, the concept of analogy helps reuse plots across different domains. The techniques proposed in the paper find applications in areas such as digital storytelling and emergency response information system, as well as some traditional business applications.

Our first study wherein all four semiotic relations were explicitly discussed was indeed presented at a digital storytelling conference, namely SBGames [14]. In that paper, the process of plot composition in the context of interactive storytelling was considered under a fourfold perspective, in view of syntagmatic, paradigmatic, antithetic and meronymic relations between the constituent events. These relations were then shown to be associated with the four major tropes of semiotic research. A conceptual model and set of facilities for interactive plot composition and adaptation dealing with the four relations was described. To accommodate antithetic relations, corresponding to the irony trope, our plan-based approach leaves room for the unplanned. A simple storyboarding prototype tool has been implemented to conduct experiments. In another paper [4], already mentioned in Section 2, we utilized the semiotic relations to characterize classes of characters (agents, in the context of business information systems) according to their mutually interfering behavior in decision-making processes.

As remarked earlier, frames and plots became increasingly important to our research projects. The ER model is arguably today's most widely accepted basis for the conceptual specification of information systems. A further common practice is to use the relational model at an intermediate logical stage, in order to adequately prepare for physical implementation. Although the relational model still works well in contexts relying on standard databases, it imposes certain restrictions, not inherent in ER specifications, which make it less suitable in Web environments. Our 28th ER Conference invited paper [34], mentioned at the end of Section 3, recommends frames as an alternative to move from ER specifications to logical stage modeling, and treats frames as an abstract data type equipped with a Frame Manipulation Algebra. It is argued that frames, with a long tradition in AI applications, are able to accommodate the irregularities of semi-structured data, and that frame-sets generalize relational tables, allowing to drop the strict homogeneity requirement. The paper includes examples to help describe the use of the operators.

Likewise, a Plot Manipulation Algebra was proposed to handle plots in an ICEC conference [45]. The seven basic operators, equally named in both the Frame Manipulation Algebra and in the Plot Manipulation Algebra, and working respectively on frames and plots, were introduced in view of the four fundamental semiotic relations, as indicated below:

- syntagmatic relations - product, projection
- paradigmatic relations - union, selection
- antithetic relations - difference
- meronymic relations - combination, factoring

The operators in the first three lines above encompass the equivalent to the five basic operators of Codd's relational algebra (product, projection, union, selection, difference). The additional two operators (combination, factoring) handle the hierarchical structures induced by the meronymic relations, a notion that would correspond to non-first-normal form (NF2) relations in the relational model (cf. our algebra of quotient relations [41]). Thus, it seems fair to claim that our algebras are *semiotically complete*, a notion that covers an ampler scope than that of Codd's relational algebra. Prototype logic-programming tools have been developed to experiment with the Frame Manipulation Algebra and the Plot Manipulation Algebra.

The pragmatic aspects of information systems constitute the main thrust of our present work, strongly influenced by the fundamental semiotic concepts exposed in this section. At the Second Workshop of the Brazilian Institute for Web Science Research [3], we argued for this orientation, which becomes increasingly relevant with the transition from the closed world of the old proprietary databases to the open world of the Web. Our view of information systems recognizes that, in order to serve as a basis for an effective communication process, their conceptual specification is comparable to the definition of a specialized language. Accordingly, it must pass through four levels: lexical, syntactic, semantic, and pragmatic [47]. At the semantic level, the correspondence between the stored data and real world facts is considered, but to design systems of practical usefulness, one still needs to investigate what purposes they will serve, which falls in the scope of the pragmatic level.

This pragmatic orientation, as we soon realized, is fully consistent with our conceptual design method that, as gradually exposed in the preceding sections, encompasses not only facts, but also events and agents. Motivated by their goals, defined in terms of database facts, agents try to cause the occurrence of events whereby a database state is reached where the goals are satisfied. And our plan-recognition / plan-generation paradigm puts together all these aspects and leads to executable specifications, which allow simulation experiments to effectively test the usability of the proposed conceptual design.

6   Concluding Remarks

An early proposal on the subject of database modelling [1] introduced an architecture that puzzled both theoreticians and practitioners. What could be a "conceptual schema"? None of the existing models seemed to offer an adequate basis to formulate what was intended, namely the *semantic* contents of the stored data. As we all know, this gap was appropriately filled by the Entity-Relationship model. Recognizing the wise orientation taken by the model of describing the application domains in their own language, our group proceeded to extend this direct and highly intuitive way to characterize factual information to events and agents.

In the present time, the Web gives access to a continuously growing number of information sources and once again the word "navigation" is employed, no longer in the sense of traversing an intricate network of physical pointers, but to designate the novel opportunities opened by connectivity across linked Web pages. We are convinced that detecting semiotic relations helps to guide navigation, not only exploring connectivity but enriching the quest for information with similarity and inter-domain analogy, allowing to zoom in and out to alternate between summaries and details, and limiting excessive recall, in favour of precision, by negative directives purporting to exclude irrelevant responses. With the objective of meeting the Semantic Web standards, some new formalisms have been proposed, but they clearly keep supporting the conceptual modelling principles. Peter Chen himself has endorsed the statement that "...RDF can be viewed as a member of the Entity-Relationship model family" [13].

Another contribution of the ANSI/X3/SPARC report that will continue to receive close attention in our research project is the identification of *external schemas*, whereby the participation of the different *users* should be duly taken into consideration. By making the external schemas branch from the conceptual schema, the report implicitly imposes, as a consequence, that they cannot be simply confused with views extracted from relational tables. Conceptual modelling should first be applied to their specification, which extends in one more direction the scope of the Entity-Relationship model family.

A crucial semiotic notion applies whenever users, as human – rather than supposedly tightly-controlled software agents – are concerned: to the *signifier-signified* correspondence between an object and its representation [53], an *interpretant* [49] must be interposed as a third component to stress that the correspondence is subject to each person's understanding, which may be faulty or incomplete. Conceptual modelling at the individual users' level must then deal with *beliefs*, as a correct or incorrect rendering of facts. When specifying an information system meeting, not only semantic, but also *pragmatic* requirements, serious efforts should be invested in the design of adequate interfaces that, as much as possible, avoid misconceptions and misconstruals [42,43], and seek to identify the users' goals and plans [11], to maximize their satisfaction while pursuing activities in consonance with ethical conduct and the adopted procedural norms.

In Web environments, the possibility to tackle multiple sources raises to an especially critical level the problem of dealing with conflicting information. Examining the process of *communication* as described in [44], showing a *sender* in the act of delivering a *message* expressed in some *code* to a *receiver*, we get a feeling of how many are the chances of mistranslation or misunderstanding. Recalling Peirce's notion of interpretant, those who act as senders, installing information on a Web page, may have failed when observing, or interpreting, or "coding" the reality in terms of the adopted models. Moreover, the stored "message" is subject to the same sorts of failures from users on the receiver side. Choosing the most likely version among conflicting data requires suitable heuristic criteria, such as the reputation of the source (*provenance*), but no easy solution seems attainable at the present state of the art. With the continuation of our project, we intend to investigate to what extent our semiotic approach can be further developed to cope with this very relevant issue.

References

1. ANSI/X3/SPARK Study Group on Data Base Management Systems. Interim Report. FDT - Bulletin of ACM SIGMOD 7(2) (1975)
2. Barbosa, S.D.J., Breitman, K.K., Casanova, M.A., Furtado, A.L.: Similarity and Analogy over Application Domains. In: Proceedings of the Brazilian Symposium on Data Bases, João Pessoa, Brazil, pp. 238–254 (2007)
3. Barbosa, S.D.J., Breitman, K.K., Casanova, M.A., Furtado, A.L.: The Semiotic Web. In: Proceedings of the Second Workshop of the Brazilian Institute for Web Science Research. Rio de Janeiro, Brazil (2011)
4. Barbosa, S.D.J., Furtado, A.L., Casanova, M.A.: A decision-making process for digital storytelling. In: Proceedings of the IX Brazilian Symposium on Games and Digital Entertainment. Florianópolis, Brazil, pp. 1–11 (2010)
5. Barbosa, S.D.J., Lima, E.S., Furtado, A.L., Feijó, B.: Early Cases of Bertillon, the Logic Programming Sleuth. In: Proceedings of the XII Brazilian Symposium on Games and Digital Entertainment, pp. 7–16 (2013)
6. Barbosa, S.D.J., Silva, B.S.: Interação Humano-Computador. Rio de Janeiro, Campus/Elsevier (2010)
7. Breitman, K.K., Barbosa, S.D.J., Casanova, M.A., Furtado, A.L.: Using analogy to promote conceptual modeling reuse. In: Proceedings of the Workshop on Leveraging Applications of Formal Methods, Verification and Validation, Poitiers, France, pp. 111–122 (2007a)
8. Breitman, K.K., Barbosa, S.J., Casanova, M.A., Furtado, A.L.: Conceptual Modeling by Analogy and Metaphor. In: Proceedings of the ACM Conference on Information and Knowledge Management, Lisbon, Portugal, pp. 865–868 (2007b)
9. Burke, K.: A Grammar of Motives. University of California Press (1969)
10. Casanova, M.A., Barbosa, S.D.J., Breitman, K.K., Furtado, A.L.: Generalization and blending in the generation of entity-relationship schemas by analogy. In: Proceedings of the International Conference on Enterprise Information Systems, Barcelona, Spain, pp. 43–48 (2008)
11. Casanova, M.A., Furtado, A.L.: An Information System Environment based on Plan Generation. In: Proceedings of the Working Conference on Cooperating Knowledge Based Systems. Keele, UK (1990)
12. Chandler, D.: Semiotics: The Basics. Routledge, London (2002)
13. Chen, P.P.: Entity-Relationship Modeling: Historical Events, Future Trends, and Lessons Learned. In: Software Pioneers. Springer (2002)

14. Ciarlini, A.E.M., Barbosa, S.D.J., Casanova, M.A., Furtado, A.L.: Event relations in plot-based plot composition. In: Proceedings of the Brazilian Symposium on Computer Games and Digital Entertainment, Belo Horizonte, Brazil, pp. 31–40 (2008)
15. Ciarlini, A.E.M., Casanova, M.A., Furtado, A.L., Veloso, P.A.S.: Modeling interactive storytelling genres as application domains. Journal of Intelligent Information Systems 35(3), 31–40 (2010)
16. Ciarlini, A.E.M., Feijo, B., Furtado, A.L.: An Integrated Tool for Modelling, Generating and Exhibiting Narratives. In: Proceedings of the AI, Simulation and Planning in High Autonomy Systems, Lisboa, Portugal, pp. 150–154 (2002)
17. Ciarlini, A.E.M., Furtado, A.L.: Simulating the Interaction of Database Agents. In: Proceedings of the Database and Expert Systems Applications Conference, Florence, Italy, pp. 499–510 (1999a)
18. Ciarlini, A.E.M., Furtado, A.L.: Interactive multistage simulation of goal-driven agents. Journal of the Brazilian Computer Society 2(6), 21–32 (1999b)
19. Ciarlini, A.E.M., Furtado, A.L.: Understanding and Simulating Narratives in the Context of Information Systems. In: Spaccapietra, S., March, S.T., Kambayashi, Y. (eds.) ER 2002. LNCS, vol. 2503, pp. 291–306. Springer, Heidelberg (2002)
20. Ciarlini, A.E.M., Furtado, A.L.: Towards a Plan-based Learning Environment. In: Proceedings of the PGL Database Research Conference, Rio de Janeiro, Brazil (2003)
21. Ciarlini, A.E.M., Pozzer, C.T., Furtado, A.L., Feijo, B.: A logic-based tool for interactive generation and dramatization of stories. In: Proceedings of the ACM-SIGCHI International Conference on Advances in Computer Entertainment Technology, Valencia, Spain, pp. 133–140 (2005)
22. Ciarlini, A.E.M., Veloso, P.A.S., Furtado, A.L.: A formal framework for modelling at the behavioural level. In: Information Modeling and Knowledge Bases XII, pp. 107–122. IOS Press (2000)
23. Culler, J.: The Pursuit of Signs: Semiotics, Literature, Deconstruction. Routledge (1981)
24. Fauconnier, G., Turner, M.: Conceptual projection and middle spaces. Tech. Rep. 9401, Univ. California, San Diego (1994)
25. Fikes, R., Nilsson, N.: STRIPS: A new approach to the application of theorem proving to problem solving. Artificial Intelligence 2(3-4), 189–208 (1971)
26. Furtado, A.L.: Analogy by generalization and the quest of the grail. ACM SIGPLAN Notices 27(1), 105–113 (1992)
27. Furtado, A.L.: Narratives and temporal databases: An interdisciplinary perspective. In: Chen, P.P., Akoka, J., Kangassalu, H., Thalheim, B. (eds.) Conceptual Modeling. LNCS, vol. 1565, pp. 73–86. Springer, Heidelberg (1999)
28. Furtado, A.L.: Narratives over real-life and fictional domains. In: Proceedings of the Brazilian Symposium on Data Bases, Brasília, Brazil, pp. 4–12 (2004)
29. Furtado, A.L.: IDB - "An environment for experimenting with intelligent database-resident information systems". T.R. 11, Pontifícia Universidade Católica (2011)
30. Furtado, A.L., Breitman, K.K., Casanova, M.A., Barbosa, S.D.J.: Applying Analogy to Schema Generation. Revista Brasileira de Sistemas de Informação 1, 1–8 (2008)
31. Furtado, A.L., Casanova, M.A.: Updating Relational Views. In: Query Processing in Database Systems. Springer, New York (1985)
32. Furtado, A.L., Casanova, M.A.: Plan and Schedule Generation over Temporal Databases. In: Proceedings of the International Conference on Entity-Relationship Approach, Lausanne, Switzerland, pp. 235–248 (1990)

33. Furtado, A.L., Casanova, M.A., Barbosa, S.D.J., Breitman, K.K.: Analysis and Reuse of Plots Using Similarity and Analogy. In: Proceedings of the International Conference on Conceptual Modeling, Barcelona, Spain, pp. 355–368 (2008)
34. Furtado, A.L., Casanova, M.A., Breitman, K.K., Barbosa, S.D.J.: A Frame Manipulation Algebra for ER Logical Stage Modeling. In: Proceedings of the International Conference on Conceptual Modeling, Gramado, Brazil, pp. 9–24 (2009)
35. Furtado, A.L., Ciarlini, A.E.M.: Plots of Narratives over Temporal Databases. In: Proceedings of the International Conference and Workshop on Database and Expert Systems Applications, Toulouse, France, pp. 590–595 (1997)
36. Furtado, A.L., Ciarlini, A.E.M.: Operational Characterization of Genre in Literary and Real-life Domains. In: Proceedings of the Conceptual Modeling Conference, Paris, France, pp. 460–474 (1999)
37. Furtado, A.L., Ciarlini, A.E.M.: Generating Narratives from Plots using Schema Information. In: Proceedings of the International Workshop on Applications of Natural Language for Information Systems, Versailles, France, pp. 17–29 (2000a)
38. Furtado, A.L., Ciarlini, A.E.M.: The plan recognition / plan generation paradigm. In: Information Engineering: State of the Art and Research Themes. Springer, London (2000b)
39. Furtado, A.L., Ciarlini, A.E.M.: Constructing Libraries of Typical Plans. In: Proceedings of the Conference on Advanced Information Systems Engineering, Interlaken, Switzerland, pp. 124–139 (2001)
40. Furtado, A.L., Ciarlini, A.E.M.: Cognitive and affective motivation in conceptual modelling. Revista Colombiana de Computación 3(2) (2002)
41. Furtado, A.L., Kerschberg, L.: An Algebra of Quotient Relations. In: Proceedings of the ACM SIGMOD International Conference on Management of Data, Toronto, Canada, pp. 1–8 (1977)
42. Hemerly, A.S., Casanova, M.A., Furtado, A.L.: Cooperative behaviour through request modification. In: Proceedings of the International Conference on Entity-Relationship Approach, San Mateo, CA, USA, pp. 607–621 (1991)
43. Hemerly, A.S., Casanova, M.A., Furtado, A.L.: Exploiting User Models to Avoid Misconstruals. In: Nonstandard Queries and Nonstandard Answers: Studies in Logic and Computation, pp. 73–97. Oxford University Press (1994)
44. Jakobson, R.: Closing statements: Linguistics and poetics. In: Sebeok, T.A. (ed.) Style in Language. MIT Press (1960)
45. Karlsson, B., Barbosa, S.D.J., Furtado, A.L., Casanova, M.A.: A plot-manipulation algebra to support digital storytelling. In: Proceedings of the International Conference on Entertainment Computing, Paris, France, pp. 132–144 (2009)
46. Kautz, H.A.: A formal theory of plan recognition and its implementation. In: Reasoning about Plans. Morgan-Kaufmann (1991)
47. Morris, C.W.: Foundations of the Theory of Signs. Chicago University Press, Chicago (1938/1970)
48. Nunes, B.P., Casanova, M.A.: A Frame-Based System for Automatic Classification of Semi-Structured Data. Revista de Informática Teórica e Aplicada 16, 87–92 (2010)
49. Peirce, C.S.: The Essential Peirce, vol. 2. Peirce edition Project. Indiana University Press (1998)
50. Propp, V.: Morphology of the Folktale. Laurence, S. (trans.). University of Texas Press (1968)
51. Ramus, P.: Rhetoricae Distinctiones in Quintilianum. In: Murphy, J.J. (ed.) C. Newlands (trans.). Southern Illinois University, Carbondale (2010)

52. Santos, C.S., Neuhold, E.J., Furtado, A.L.: A Data Type Approach to the Entity-Relationship Model. In: Proceedings of the International Conference on the Entity-Relationship Approach to Systems Analysis and Design, Los Angeles, USA, pp. 103–119 (1979)
53. Saussure, F.: Cours de Linguistique Générale. In: Bally, C., et al. (eds.) Payot (1995)
54. Willensky, R.: Planning and Understanding–a Computational Approach to Human Reasoning. Addison-Wesley (1983)
55. Vico, G.: The New Science. T.G. Bergin, M.H. Finch (trans). Cornell University Press, Ithaca (1968)
56. Winston, M.E., Chaffin, R., Herrmann, D.: A taxonomy of part-whole relations. Cognitive Science 11(4) (1987)

Ontological Patterns, Anti-Patterns and Pattern Languages for Next-Generation Conceptual Modeling

Giancarlo Guizzardi

Ontology and Conceptual Modeling Research Group (NEMO), Computer Science Department, Federal University of Espírito Santo (UFES), Vitória - ES, Brazil
gguizzardi@inf.ufes.br

Abstract. This paper addresses the complexity of conceptual modeling in a scenario in which semantic interoperability requirements are increasingly present. It elaborates on the need for developing sound ontological foundations for conceptual modeling but also for developing complexity management tools derived from these foundations. In particular, the paper discusses three of these tools, namely, ontological patterns, ontological anti-patterns and pattern languages.

Keywords: Conceptual Modeling, Formal Ontology, Patterns, Anti-Patterns and Pattern Languages.

"To begin on a philosophical plane, let us note that we usually behave as if there were three realms of interest in data processing: the real world itself, ideas about it existing in the minds of men, and symbols on paper or some other storage medium. The latter realms are, in some sense, held to be models of the former. Thus, we might say that data are fragments of a theory of the real world, and data processing juggles representations of these fragments of theory...The issue is ontology, or the question of what exists." (G.H. Mealy, Another Look at Data, 1967) [1].

1 Introduction

Information is the foundation of all rational decision-making. Without the proper information, individuals, organizations, communities and governments can neither systematically take optimal decisions nor understand the full effect of their actions. In the past decades, information technology has played a fundamental role in automating an increasing number of information spaces. Furthermore, in the past decades, there has been a substantial improvement in information access. This was caused not only by the advances in communication technology but also, more recently, by the demands on transparency and public access to information.

Despite these advances, most of these automated spaces remained as independent components in large and increasingly complex silo-based architectures. The problem with this is that several of the critical questions we have nowadays in large corporations, government and even professional communities (e.g., scientific communities) can only be answered by precisely connecting pieces of information distributed over

E. Yu et al. (Eds.): ER 2014, LNCS 8824, pp. 13–27, 2014.

these silos. Take for example the following question: from all the outsourcing contracts signed by a government organizational unit with private parties, which ones include parties that made a donation to the political campaign of any individual with power of decision over that contract? The information needed to answer this question typically exists *"in the ether"*, i.e., in the set of information represented by an existing set of information systems. Moreover, given the current requirements for data transparency, this information is typically even public. However, it usually only exists in dispersed form in a number of autonomous information silos. As consequence, despite the increasing amount of information produced and acquired by the entities, as well as the improvements in information access, answering critical questions such as this one is still extremely hard. In practice, they are still answered in a case-by-case fashion and still require a significant amount of human effort, which is slow, costly and error-prone. The problem of combining independently conceived information spaces and providing unified analytics over them is termed the problem of *Semantic Interoperability*. As reflected in OMG's SIMF RFP [2]: *"the overall human and financial cost to society from our failure to share and reuse information is many times the cost of the systems' operation and maintenance"*.

I use the term Information System here in a broader sense that includes also *Sociotechnical Systems*. Moreover, I subscribe here to the so-called *representation view* of information systems [3]. Following this view, an information system is a representation of a certain *conceptualization* of reality. To be more precise, an information system contains information structures that represent *abstractions* over certain portions of reality, capturing aspects that are relevant for a class of problems at hand. There are two direct consequences of this view. Firstly, the quality of an information system directly depends on how truthful are its information structures to the aspects of reality it purports to represent. Secondly, in order to connect two information systems A and B, we first need to understand the precise relation between the abstractions of entities in reality represented in A and B. For instance, suppose A and B are two different systems recording city indicators for two different cities, and that we have to compare the student/teacher ratios in these two cities. In order to do that, we must understand what is the relation between the terms *Student* and *Teacher* as represented in A versus these two terms as represented in B. Understanding this relation requires precisely understanding the relation between the referents in a certain conceptualization of reality represented by these terms. Even a simple indicator such as this one can hide a number of subtle meaning distinctions as explained in [4]: *"One problem is whether "student" refers to full time students, or part time students...it is also difficult to compare an indicator for a single city across time if the definition of student changes. For example, today the educational system includes students with special needs, but 60 years ago they may not have been enrolled."*

In his ACM Turing Award Lecture entitled *"The Humble Programmer"* [5], E. W. Dijkstra discusses the sheer complexity one has to deal with when programming large computer systems. His article represented an open call for an acknowledgement of the complexity at hand and for the need of more sophisticated techniques to master this complexity. Dijkstra's advice is timely and even more insightful in our current scenario, in which semantic interoperability becomes a pervasive force driving and constraining the process of creating information systems in increasingly complex combinations of domains. More and more, information systems are created either by combining existing autonomously developed subsystem, or are created to eventually serve as components in multiple larger yet-to-be-conceived systems. In this scenario, information systems engineering, in particular, and rational governance, in general, cannot succeed without the support of a particular type of discipline. A discipline devoted to establish well-founded theories, principles, as well as methodological and computational tools for supporting us in the tasks of understanding, elaborating and precisely representing the nature of conceptualizations of reality, as well as in tasks of negotiating and safely establishing the correct relations between different conceptualizations of reality. On one hand, this discipline should help us in producing representations of these conceptualizations that are *ontologically consistent*, i.e., that represent a worldview that aggregates a number of abstractions that are consistent with each other. On the other hand, it should help to make explicit our *ontological commitments*, i.e., to make explicit what exactly is the worldview to which we are committing. In summary, this discipline should help to produce concrete representation artifacts (models) of conceptualizations of reality that achieve the goals of *intra-worldview consistency* and *inter-worldview interoperability*.

The discipline to address the aforementioned challenges is the discipline of *Conceptual Modeling*. However, in order to do that, conceptual modeling languages, methodologies and tools must be informed by another discipline, namely, the discipline of *Ontology*, in philosophy. *Formal Ontology* has exactly the objective of developing domain-independent theories and systems of categories and their ties that could then be used to articulate conceptualizations in different domains in reality. More recently, the discipline of *Applied Ontology* has developed systematic and repeatable techniques for applying these theories in solving problems in concrete domains[1][6]. Given this essential role played by Ontology in this view of the discipline of Conceptual Modeling, we have termed it elsewhere *Ontology-Driven Conceptual Modeling* [7]. However, exactly due to this dependence, it occurred to us that the term is actually pleonastic. To put bluntly: if conceptual modeling is about representing aspects of the physical and social world and for promoting a shared understanding of this reality among human users [8], then all conceptual modeling should be ontology-driven!

The importance of Ontology as a foundation for Conceptual Modeling is not new in this discipline. There is an established tradition and a growing interest in using ontological theories for analyzing conceptual modeling languages as well as for proposing methodological guidelines for using these languages in the production of ontologically consistent models [3,9]. However, not until much more recently, Ontology has been used not only as an analysis tool but also in the development of engineering tools such as conceptual modeling languages with explicitly defined and properly axiomatized metamodels [10], as well as computational environments supporting automated model verification, validation and transformation [11,12]. These are complexity management tools that are fundamental for addressing the challenge hig-

---

[1] The relation between Formal and Applied Ontology can be understood in analogy to the relation between Pure and Applied Mathematics.

hlighted by Dijkstra's advice. In this paper, I would like to concentrate on a different (albeit complementary and intimately related) set of complexity management tools. The set includes three of these tools, all related to the notion of patterns, namely: *Ontological Conceptual Patterns*, *Ontological Anti-Patterns*, and *Ontology Pattern Languages*.

The remainder of the paper is organized as follows. In section 2, I briefly discuss the notion of ontological commitment of a language, as well as the notion of foundational ontologies to which general conceptual modeling languages should commit. Section 3 discusses the notion of *Ontological Conceptual Patterns (OCPs)* as methodological mechanisms for encoding basic ontological micro-theories. In that section, I also briefly elaborate on the idea of *Ontology Pattern Languages (OPLs)*, as systems of representation that take OCPs as higher-granularity modeling primitives. In section 4, I elaborate on *Ontological Anti-Patterns (OAP)* as structures that can be used to systematically identify recurrent possible deviations between the set of valid state of affairs admitted by a model and the set of state of affairs actually intended by the stakeholders. In particular, I illustrate here these tools from the point of view of one particular language and ontology. Finally, section 5 presents some final considerations.

2   Ontological Foundations for Conceptual Modeling

Figure 1 below depicts the well-known *Semiotic Triangle*. The dotted line in the base of this triangle between language and reality highlights the fact that the relation between them is always intermediated by a certain *conceptualization*.

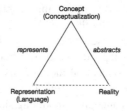

Fig. 1. The Semiotic Triangle

The *represents* relation in Figure 1 stands for the so-called *real-world semantics* of the language, i.e., the function that assigns meaning to the language constructs in terms of elements constituting a conceptualization. This relation also represents the *ontological commitment* of the language [13]. In other words, any representation system that has *real-world semantics* (i.e., which is not limited to purely mathematical formal semantics) has an ontological commitment. As discussed in depth in [13], given this ontological commitment we can systematically evaluate the ontology adequacy of the language, i.e., the adequacy of the language to represent phenomena in reality according to that conceptualization. On one hand, it informs the expected *expressivity* of the language, i.e., that the language should have a maximally economic set of constructs that allows it to represent the distinctions put forth by that conceptualization. On the other hand, it informs the expect *clarity* of the language, i.e., that the language should be such that any valid combination of its constructs should have a univocal interpretation in terms of that conceptualization [3]. However, this ontological commitment does something else of uttermost importance: it informs the set of formal constraints that should be included in the language metamodel to restrict the set of grammatically *valid models of the language* to exact those models that are compatible with that ontological commitment, i.e., those models that represent state of affairs that are deemed acceptable according to that conceptualization. These are named the *intended models of the language* according to that ontological commitment [13].

As discussed in depth in a number of papers [3, 13], in the case of general conceptual modeling, the ontological commitment of this language should be to a domain independent system of categories and their ties that can be used to articulate conceptualizations of reality in different domains, i.e., a *Foundational Ontology*.

Since our first paper on this topic in this very conference [9], we have engaged in a research program to develop a philosophically sound, formally axiomatized and empirically informed foundational ontology that could serve as a foundation for conceptual modeling. This ontology later termed *UFO (Unified Foundational Ontology)* aggregates results from disciplines such as Analytical Philosophy, Cognitive Science, Philosophical Logics and Linguistics. This ontology is composed of a number of theories addressing the foundation of all classical conceptual modeling constructs including Object Types and Taxonomic Structures, Part-Whole Relations, Intrinsic and Relational Properties, Events, Weak Entities, Attributes and Datatypes, etc. [10, 14-17].

In [10], we have proposed a conceptual modeling language that ontologically commits to this foundational ontology. As we have produced this language through the analysis and redesign of the UML 2.0 metamodel (more specifically, the fragment of UML class diagrams), it later came to be dubbed *OntoUML*. As demonstrated in [10], UML contained many problems of ontological adequacy that needed to be addressed and, in one sense it would have been easier to just define a new conceptual modeling language from scratch. However, UML presented some important features (besides its significant base of users), namely, it had an explicitly defined metamodel coded in a standard metamodeling framework. Building OntoUML by redesigning this metamodel then allowed the language to be used by computational tools that could process implemented metamodels based on MOF (Meta-Object Facility), as well as enable formal verification of OntoUML models with available OCL (Object Constraint Language) tools. We leveraged on this features when building a model-based editor for this language ([11] and, more recently, with continuous updates in http://nemo.inf.ufes.br).

3   OntoUML as an Ontology Pattern Language

Due to the ontological commitment to UFO, the metamodel of OntoUML includes: (i) modeling primitives that reflect ontological distinctions put forth by this ontology; (ii) formal constraints that govern how these constructs can be combined, which are derived from the axiomatization of the ontology. As a result of (ii), we have that the only grammatically correct models that can be produced using OntoUML are those that are consistent with the axiomatization of UFO. However, another consequence of (ii) is that modeling elements of OntoUML never occur freely. In contrast, they only appear in certain modeling configurations and combined with other modeling elements, thus forming certain *modeling patterns*. These patterns are higher-granularity modeling primitives that can be said to represent micro-theories constituting UFO. We term these *Ontology Conceptual Patterns* [18]. In the sequel, I illustrate this idea with some of OntoUML distinctions among different categories of types and relations.

In UFO's theory of types, we have a fundamental distinction between what are named *Sortal* and *Non-Sortal types*. A sortal is a type whose instances obey a uniform principle of identity. A principle of identity, in turn, is a principle with which we can judge if two individuals are the same or, as a special case, what changes an individual can undergo and still be the same. A stereotypical example is the type Person. Contrast it with the type Insurable Item. Whilst in the former case all instance of that type obey the same principle of identity, in the latter case, the type classifies instances of differcent kinds (e.g., cars, boats, people, houses, body parts, works of art) and that obey different principles of identity. A *Kind* is a sortal which is rigid. Rigidity can be characterized as follows: a type T is rigid iff all instances of that type are necessarily (in the modal sense) instances of that type, i.e., the instances of T cannot cease to be an instance of T without ceasing to exist. In contrast with rigidity, we have the notion of anti-rigidity: a type T' is anti-rigid iff every instance of that type can cease to be an instance of that type (again, in the modal sense), i.e., instances of T' can move in an out of the extension of T' in different possible worlds while maintaining their identity. As formally shown in [10], every object in a conceptual model must obey a unique principle of identity and, hence, must be an instance of a unique kind. As consequence, a sortal T is either a kind or specialize (directly or indirectly) a unique kind.

Among the anti-rigid sortal types, we have again two subcatetories: *Phases* and *Roles*. In both cases, we have that the instances can move in and out of the extension of these types without any effect on their identity. However, while in the case of phases these changes occur due to a change in the intrinsic properties of these instances, in the cases of roles, they occur due to a change in their relational properties. Contrast the types Child, Adolescent, Adult as phases of Person with the roles Student, Husband or Wife. In the former cases, it is a change in intrinsic properties of a person that causes her to move in and out of the extension of these phases. In contrast, a student is a role that a person plays when related to an education institution, and it is the establishment (or termination) of this relation that alters the instantiation relation between an instance of person and the type Student. Analogously, a husband is a role played by a person when married to a (person playing the role of) wife. Thus, besides being anti-rigid, the Role category possesses another meta-property (absent in phases) named *Relational Dependence* [10]. As a consequence, we have that the following constraints must apply to Roles: every Role in an OntoUML conceptual model must be connected to an association representing this relational dependence condition. Moreover, the association end connected to the depended type (e.g., Education Institution for the case of Student, Wife for the case of Husband) in this relation must have a minimum cardinality ≥ 1 [10]. In contrast, phases always occur in the so-called

Phase Partition of a type T obeying the following constraints: (i) a phase Partition ⟨P₁...Pₙ⟩ defines an actual partition of sortal S , i.e., (i.a) in every situation, every instance of P_i is an instance of S; Moreover, (i.b) in every situation, every instance of S is an instance of exactly one P_i; (ii) for every instance of type S and for every phase P_i in a Phase Partition specializing S, there is a possible world w in which x is not an instance of P_i. This implies that, in w, x is an instance of another Phase P_j in the same partition [10].

The aforementioned ontological constraints defining Roles cause the manifestation of its constructs in OntoUML to obey necessarily the pattern of Figure 2.a: (i) all roles must specialize (directly or indirectly) a unique kind and, hence, must be a directly specialization of a sortal S; (ii) roles must be connected to a characterizing relation with an opposite association having a minimum cardinality higher or equal to one (symbolizing the relational dependence condition). Likewise, the ontological axioms defining phases cause the manifestation of its construct in OntoUML to obey necessarily the pattern of fig. 2.b.

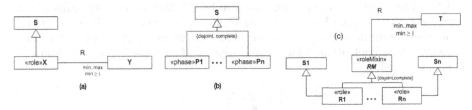

Fig. 2. Role Pattern (a), Phase Partition Pattern (b) and the RoleMixin Pattern (c)

Distinctions generated by the variation of these ontological meta-properties can also be found among non-sortals. One example is the notion of a *RoleMixin*. A RoleMixin is a non-sortal, which is anti-rigid and relationally dependent. In other words, the RoleMixin category is similar to and, hence, is subject to many of the same constraints of the Role category. However, unlike a role, a RoleMixin classify entities that instantiate different kinds (and that obey different principles of identity). Once more, the ontological axioms defining a RoleMixin cause it to manifest in OntoUML necessarily following a particular pattern depicted in Figure 2.c. Like Roles, Role-Mixins must be connected to a characterizing relation with an opposite association having a minimum cardinality higher or equal to one (symbolizing the relational dependence condition). However, since RoleMixins classify entities of different kinds, they must be partitioned in a series of specializing sortals (roles), each of which classify entities of a particular kind [10].

Finally, in UFO, we have a fundamental distinction between the so-called *formal* and *material relations*. A formal relation is a relation that holds directly between its relata and that is reducible to intrinsic properties of these relata. Take, for instance, the relation of being-taller-than between people. If John is taller than Paul then this relation is established by the mere existence of John and Paul. Moreover, in this case, there is no real connection between John and Paul, but the relation is reducible to intrinsic properties of these two individuals, namely, John is taller than Paul iff John's height is bigger than Paul's height. Now, take the case of relations such as being-married-to, being-enrolled-at, being-employed-by, being-a-customer-of, etc.

These relations are not reducible to intrinsic properties of their relata. In contrast, in order for these relations to hold, something else needs to exist connecting their relata, namely, particular instances of marriages, enrollments, employments and purchases. These mediating entities can be thought as aggregations of relational properties and are termed *relators* [10]. Relations that are founded on these relators are termed *material relations*. As discussed in [10], the explicit representation of relators solves a number of conceptual modeling problems, including the classical problem of the *collapse of cardinality constraints*. Furthermore, as demonstrated in [16], relators also play a decisive role in providing precise methodological guidelines for systematically choosing between the constructs of *association specialization, subsetting* and *redefinition*. Once more, in OntoUML, a material relation appears in a model connected to a relator from which it is derived forming the pattern depicted in Figure 3. In this pattern, the dashed relation is termed derivation and connects a material relation with the relator from which it is derived; the mediation relation is a relation of existential dependence connecting an instance of a relator with multiple entities of which a relator depends (e.g., the marriage between Paul and Mary existentially depends on Paul and Mary; the employment between John and the UN likewise can only exist whilst John and the UN exist). Moreover, the cardinality constraints of the derived material relation and of the derivation relation are constrained by the cardinality constraints of these (otherwise implicit) mediation relations (some of these constraints are illustrated in Figure 3) [10].

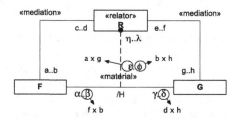

Fig. 3. Relator and Material Relations Pattern

Since the formal modeling primitives of this language can only appear following these patterns, these patterns end up being the *actual* modeling primitives of the language. As a consequence, modeling in OntoUML is done by the chained application of these ontological patterns [19]. This idea is illustrated in Figure 4. We start by modeling the type Customer. We first identify that a Customer is a RoleMixin: instances of Customer can be different kinds (people and organizations); Customer is an anti-rigid type (no Customer is necessity a Customer); in order for someone to be a Customer, she has to purchase something from a Supplier. In applying the RoleMixin pattern of Figure 2.c, we identify the presence of two phases (Living Person and Active Organization), a role (Supplier, which is assumed to be played by entities of the unique kind Organization) and a relation (purchases from). We then expand this model by applying to phases and roles the patterns of Figure 2.a and 2.b, respectively. Finally, we apply the pattern of Figure 3 to the material relation *purchases from*.

This strategy of building models by the successive instantiation of these patterns has been implemented in the new version of the OntoUML editor. This approach can bring several benefits to conceptual modeling. Firstly, since these patterns are the representation of ontological theories, the construction of models by instantiating these patterns preserves ontological consistency *by construction*. This can also facilitate the process of model building, especially to novice users. The hypothesis is that in each step of the modeling activity, the solution space that characterizes the possible choices of modeling primitives to be adopted is reduced. This strategy, in turn, reduces the cognitive load of the modeler and, consequently, the complexity of model building using this language [19]. Moreover, this strategy also brings more uniformity to the models (which become described in terms of known patterns) and provides for a natural unit of conceptually breaking down the models in cognitive manageable pieces. However, there is an additional aspect that I would like to highlight here. As previously mentioned, each of these ontological patterns embodies an ontological micro-theory. This means that each application of these patterns implies to the inclusion of a predefined set of formal axioms in the logical rendering of the resulting model (see, for instance, [17]).

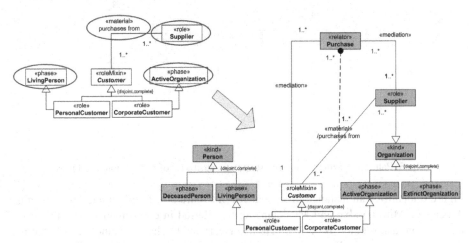

Fig. 4. Model expansion by iterative application of ontological patterns

Up to now, I have focused on patterns that organize the possible manifestations of the modeling primitives of an ontology-based modeling language. Now, I would like to highlight the existence of a second class of conceptual patterns, termed *Analysis Patterns*. These patterns can contribute to conceptual modeling by offering a systematic way of analyzing certain ontological properties of the models. Take for example the much-discussed problem of deciding on the transitivity of part-whole relations. Parthood is non-transitive (i.e., transitive in certain cases and intransitive in others) [10]. This issue is of great importance since transitivity plays a fundamental role both conceptually (e.g., to afford inferences in problem-solving) and computationally (e.g., to afford propagations of properties and events in a transitive chains, as well as automated reasoning with parts). As discussed in [10], precisely identifying the scope of transitivity of part-whole relations requires solving fundamental ontological problems. In [10], using UFO's theory of relations, I have formally proved a number of situations in which part-whole relations should be taken as transitive. Now, the proof presented there demands for its full understanding at least a basic notion of logics and an advanced understanding of formal ontology. Since this obviously compromises the scalability of the proposed solution, [10] also advances a number of *visual patterns* derived from the underlying theory, and that can be directly applied to diagrams to isolate the scope of transitivity of functional part-whole relations (Figure 5). It is important to emphasize that these patterns can be used to isolate the contexts of transitivity in a diagram *regardless of the content of what is being represented there*. As a consequence, fully automated tool support can be built for this task in a relatively simple way, since the underlying algorithm merely has to check structural (topological) properties of the graph and not the content of the involved nodes. In fact, the automatic identification of these patterns has also been implemented in the OntoUML editor.

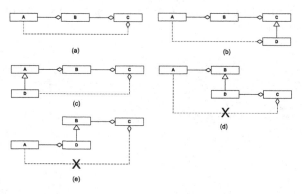

Fig. 5. Patterns for identifying the scope of transitivity of Part-Whole Relations

Figure 6 identifies an instance of the pattern of Figure 5.b. In this model, the relation **A** between Mitral Valve and Musician can be inferred in conformance with this pattern. In contrast, relation **B** between Human Heart and Orchestra cannot be asserted in the model since it actually amounts to a case of the anti-pattern of Figure 5.d.

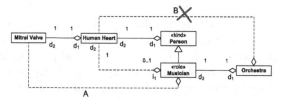

Fig. 6. Example (A) and Counterexample (B) of warranted inference of part-whole relation

4   Ontological Anti-Patterns

By incorporating the ontological constraints of a foundational theory, a modeling language such as the one discussed in the previous section prevents the representation of ontologically non-admissible states of affair in conceptual models represented in that language. However, it cannot guarantee that the produced conceptual models will have as instances only those that represent intended state of affairs. This is because the admissibility of *domain-specific states of affairs* depends on domain-specific rules, not on ontological ones. To illustrate this point, suppose a conceptual model representing a transplant. In this case, we have domain concepts such as Person, Transplant Surgeon, Transplant, Transplanted Organ, Organ Donor, Organ Donee, etc. The model fragment of Figure 7, which models aspects of this domain, does not violate any ontological rule. In fact, this model can be assembled by instantiating instances of the aforementioned *role modeling* and *relator patterns*. However, there are still unintended states of affairs (according to a conceptualization assumed here) that are represented by valid instances of this model. Examples include a state of affairs in which the Donor, the Donee and the Transplant Surgeon are one and the same Person (Figure 8.a), but also the state of affairs in which the same person plays the roles of Donor and Surgeon (Figure 8.b) or Donor and Donee. Please note that: (a) the model instances of Figures 8a-b are valid instances of the model of Figure 7; (b) these model instances do not represent intended state of affairs according to our assumed conceptualization of the domain of transplants; (c) the state of affairs represented by these model instances are only considered inadmissible (unintended) due to domain-specific knowledge of social and natural laws. Consequently, they cannot be ruled out a priori by a domain independent system of ontological categories.

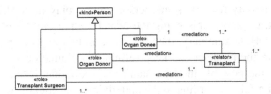

Fig. 7. A fragment of a conceptual model in the domain of organ transplants

Guaranteeing the exclusion of unintended states of affairs without a computational support is a practically impossible task for any relevant domain. In particular, given that many fundamental ontological distinctions are modal in nature, in order to validate a model, one would have to take into consideration the possible valid instances of that model in all possible worlds. In [12], we have proposed an approach for OntoUML that offers a contribution to this problem by supporting conceptual model validation via visual simulation. On the one hand, it aims at proving the finite satisfiability of a given ontology by presenting a valid instance (logical model) of that ontology. On the other hand, it attempts to exhaustively generate instances of the model in a finite scope. The generated model instances confront a modeler with states of affairs that are deemed admissible by the model's current axiomatization. This enables modelers to detect unintended states of affairs and to take the proper measures to rectify the model.

Fig. 8. Examples of valid but unintended instances of the Organ Transplant Model

After running simulations of the model of Figure 7, the conceptual modeler is presented with the consequences of her specification. The set of possible instances of this model, produced automatically by this simulator, includes the two models presented in Figure 8. When faced with a situation in which the Donor, Donee and Surgeon roles are played by the same person, the modeler can realize that the model at hand has been *underconstrained*, and then include a constraint in the model to exclude this unintended situation. Now, suppose the situation in which the modeler tries to rectify this model by declaring the types Transplant Surgeon, Organ Donor and Organ Donee as mutually disjoint. In a follow up execution of simulating this ontology, she then realizes that it is not possible, for example, for an Organ Donor to receive an organ in a different transplant, and for a Transplant Surgeon to be either an Organ Donor or an Organ Donee in different transplants. When facing this new simulation results, the modeler can realize that the model has been *overconstrained*. After all, there is no problem in having the same person as Organ Donor and Donee, or as Surgeon and Donor (Donee), it is only that the same person cannot play more than one of these roles in the same transplant! (this being the actual formal constraint that should be included in the model). In summary, the idea is that in this multi-step interaction with the model simulator, the modeler can keep refining the domain constraints to increasingly approximate the possible model instances of the model to those that represent admissible states of affairs according to the underlying conceptualization.

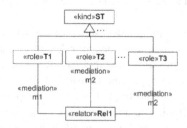

Fig. 9. The RWOR anti-pattern

In [7], we have employed this validation strategy over a benchmark of 52 OntoUML models. In this empirical investigation, we managed to identify model structures that would systematically create deviations between the sets of valid and intended model instances. When these structures appeared in at least roughly 1/3 of the models, we catalogued them as *anti-patterns*. In [7], we have identified 7 of these anti-patterns.

In the OntoUML editor, we have implemented a strategy for the automatic detection of these anti-patterns as well as for systematically correcting them via the inclusion of proper formal constraints. For instance, in Figure 7, the problem of model *underconstraining* identified is caused by the manifestation of an anti-pattern termed *RWOR (Relator with Overlaping Roles)*. This anti-pattern (Figure 9) is characterized by a Relator (Rel_1) mediating two or more Roles (T_1, T_2...T_n) whose extensions overlap, i.e., these roles have their identity principle provided by a common Kind as a supertype (ST). In addition, the roles are not explicitly declared disjoint. This modeling structure is prone to be overly permissive, since there are no restrictions for an instance to act as multiples roles for the same relator. The possible commonly identified intended interpretations are that: (i) the roles are actually disjoint (disjoint roles), i.e., no instance of ST may act as more than one role for the same instance of a relator Rel_1 (mutually exclusive roles); (ii) some roles may be played by the same instance of ST, while others may not (partially exclusive roles). An alternative case is: (iii) one in which all or a subset of the roles in question are mutually exclusive but across different relators. An example of this anti-pattern may also be found in the model of Figure 4: a possible instance of that model is one involving more than one supplier, and having the same organization playing both the roles of Customer and Supplier within the scope of the same purchase.

5   Final Considerations

Semantic interoperability will more and more be a pervasive force driving and constraining the development of Information Systems (including Sociotechnical Systems). Information Systems will need to be constructed out of the interconnection of different autonomously developed subsystems and/or will need to be conceived as potential subsystem in multiple yet-to-be conceived larger systems. In this scenario, *conceptual modeling* plays a fundamental role, helping us to understand, elaborate, negotiate and precisely represent subtle distinctions in our multiple conceptualizations of reality. In other words, conceptual modeling should help us to represent proper *"theories of the real-world"* (to use Mealy's expressions) that are both *ontologically consistent* and maximally explicit with respect to their *ontological commitments*. However, in order to successfully play this role, conceptual modeling must rely on sound foundations. Developing these foundations is necessarily an exercise in *Ontology*. Furthermore, since conceptual models are meant to support humans in increasingly complex and interconnected domains, from these foundations, we must develop a number of tools for complexity management. In this paper, I have briefly discussed a particular set of these tools including *Patterns*, *Anti-Patterns* and *Pattern Languages*. There is of course an extensive body of literature on these three topics. However, I focused here on: (i) *Ontological Conceptual Patterns (OCPs)*, i.e., patterns that emerge from the ontological distinctions and axiomatization of foundational ontologies; (ii) *Ontological Pattern Languages (OPLs)*, i.e., systems of representation that take these OCPs as modeling primitives; (iii) *Ontological Anti-Patterns*, i.e., recurrent configurations that potentially make a particular model accept as *valid* some instances that are not *intended* (or, in other words, that are not compatible with its ontological commitment).

I have conducted the discussion here focusing on a particular foundational ontology (UFO) and a particular language based on it (OntoUML). Due to space limitations, I have illustrated my argument using only a very small subset of the patterns and anti-patterns comprising this approach. Additional examples can be found in: [15], in which we present an ontological pattern for decoupling the representation of qualities from the multiple quality spaces on which they can be projected; [17], in which we present a number of patterns derived from a foundational ontology of events. Furthermore, in [14], I formally show how in classical derivation patterns such as *derivation by union* or *derivation by exclusion,* the ontological meta-properties of the derived types can be inferred from the meta-properties of the types participating in the derivation rules.

Finally, there is a very important topic related to ontological patterns and pattern languages that I did not have the chance to discuss here. The modeling patterns discussed in this article are all domain-independent as they are all derived from a domain-independent ontological theory. However, *Domain-Related Ontological Patterns (DROPs)* can also be derived from the so-called *Domain and Core Ontologies.* In particular, as discussed in [20], patterns derived from Core Ontologies can typically be organized in *Domain-Related Ontology Pattern Languages (DROPL).* In that paper, for instance, we illustrate this approach by developing a DROPL in the domain of Software Processes.

Acknowledgements. I am grateful to G. Wagner, N. Guarino, R. Falbo, R.S.S. Guizzardi, J.P.A. Almeida, J. Mylopoulos and the members of NEMO for many years of fruitful collaboration. This research was partially supported by the Lucretius ERC Advanced Grant # 267856.

References

1. Mealy, G.H.: Another Look at Data, AFIPS Conference Proceedings, vol. 31, pp. 525–534. Thompson Books, Academic Press, Washington, London (1967)
2. Object Management Group, Semantic Information Modeling for Federation (SIMF) Request for Proposals (2011)
3. Weber, R.: Ontological Foundations of Information Systems. Coopers & Lybrand, Melbourne (1997)
4. Fox, M.: A Foundational Ontology for Global City Indicators, Global Cities Institute Working Papers no. 3 (2013)
5. Dijkstra, E.W.: The Humble Programmer. Communications of the ACM 15, 10 (1972)
6. Guarino, N., Musen, M.: Applied Ontology: Focusing on Content, Applied Ontology, vol. 1, pp. 1–5. IOS Press (2005)
7. Guizzardi, G., Sales, T.P.: Detection, Simulation and Elimination of Semantic Anti-Patterns in Ontology-Driven Conceptual Models. In: Proc. of 33rd International Conf. on Conceptual Modeling, ER 2014, Atlanta (2014)

8. Mylopoulos, J.: Conceptual modeling and Telos. In: Loucopoulos, P., Zicari, R. (eds.) Conceptual Modeling, Databases, and CASE, ch. 2, pp. 49–68. Wiley (1992)

9. Guizzardi, G., Herre, H., Wagner, G.: On the General Ontological Foundations of Conceptual Modeling. In: Spaccapietra, S., March, S.T., Kambayashi, Y. (eds.) ER 2002. LNCS, vol. 2503, pp. 65–78. Springer, Heidelberg (2002)

10. Guizzardi, G.: Ontological foundations for structural conceptual models. Centre for Telematics and Information Technology, University of Twente (2005)

11. Benevides, A.B., Guizzardi, G.: A Model-Based Tool for Conceptual Modeling and Domain Ontology Engineering in OntoUML. In: 11th International Conf. on Enterprise Information Systems (ICEIS), Milan (2009)

12. Benevides, A.B., et al.: Validating Modal Aspects of OntoUML Conceptual Models Using Automatically Generated Visual World Structures. Journal of Universal Computer Science 16, 2904–2933 (2010)

13. Guizzardi, G.: On Ontology, ontologies, Conceptualizations, Modeling Languages, and (Meta) Models. In: Frontiers in Artificial Intelligence and Applications, Databases and Information Systems IV. IOS Press, Amsterdam (2007)

14. Guizzardi, G.: Ontological Meta-Properties of Derived Object Types. In: Ralyté, J., Franch, X., Brinkkemper, S., Wrycza, S. (eds.) CAiSE 2012. LNCS, vol. 7328, pp. 318–333. Springer, Heidelberg (2012)

15. Guizzardi, G., Masolo, C., Borgo, S.: In the Defense of a Trope-Based Ontology for Conceptual Modeling: An Example with the Foundations of Attributes, Weak Entities and Datatypes. In: Embley, D.W., Olivé, A., Ram, S. (eds.) ER 2006. LNCS, vol. 4215, pp. 112–125. Springer, Heidelberg (2006)

16. Costal, D., Gómez, C., Guizzardi, G.: Formal Semantics and Ontological Analysis for Understanding Subsetting, Specialization and Redefinition of Associations in UML. In: Jeusfeld, M., Delcambre, L., Ling, T.-W. (eds.) ER 2011. LNCS, vol. 6998, pp. 189–203. Springer, Heidelberg (2011)

17. Guizzardi, G., Wagner, G., de Almeida Falbo, R., Guizzardi, R.S.S., Almeida, J.P.A.: Towards Ontological Foundations for the Conceptual Modeling of Events. In: Ng, W., Storey, V.C., Trujillo, J.C. (eds.) ER 2013. LNCS, vol. 8217, pp. 327–341. Springer, Heidelberg (2013)

18. Falbo, R., et al.: Ontology Patterns: Clarifying Concepts and Terminology. In: 4th International Workshop on Ontologies and Semantic Patterns (WOP 2013), Sydney (2013)

19. Guizzardi, G., et al.: Design Patterns and Inductive Modeling Rules to Support the Construction of Ontologically Well-Founded Conceptual Models in OntoUML. In: 3rd International Workshop on Ontology-Driven Information Systems (ODISE 2011), London, UK (2011)

20. de Almeida Falbo, R., Barcellos, M.P., Nardi, J.C., Guizzardi, G.: Organizing Ontology Design Patterns as Ontology Pattern Languages. In: Cimiano, P., Corcho, O., Presutti, V., Hollink, L., Rudolph, S. (eds.) ESWC 2013. LNCS, vol. 7882, pp. 61–75. Springer, Heidelberg (2013)

A Computer-Guided Approach to Website Schema.org Design

Albert Tort and Antoni Olivé

Department of Service and Information System Engineering
Universitat Politècnica de Catalunya – Barcelona Tech
{atort,olive}@essi.upc.edu

Abstract. Schema.org offers to web developers the opportunity to enrich a website's content with microdata and schema.org. For large websites, implementing microdata can take a lot of time. In general, it is necessary to perform two main activities, for which we lack methods and tools. The first consists in designing what we call the *website schema.org*, which is the fragment of schema.org that is relevant to the website. The second consists in adding the corresponding microdata tags to the web pages. In this paper, we describe an approach to the design of a website schema.org. The approach consists in using a human-computer task-oriented dialogue, whose purpose is to arrive at that design. We describe a dialogue generator that is domain-independent, but that can be adapted to specific domains. We propose a set of six evaluation criteria that we use to evaluate our approach, and that could be used in future approaches.

Keywords: Schema.org, Microdata, Ontologies, Conceptual Modeling.

1 Introduction

Google, Bing and Yahoo's initiative to create schema.org for structured data markup has offered an opportunity and at the same time has posed a threat to many web developers. The opportunity is to transform the website's content to use HTML microdata and schema.org, so that search engines can understand the information in web pages and, as a consequence, they can improve the accuracy and the presentation of search results, which can translate to better click through rates and increased organic traffic [1,15]. The threat of not doing that transformation is just the opposite: not reaping the above benefits that other websites may gain. This is the reason why many web developers are considering, or will consider in the near future, the schema.org markup of their web pages.

For large websites, implementing microdata can take a lot of time and require some big changes in the HTML source code [1]. In general, that implementation requires two main activities. The first consists in designing what we call the *website schema.org*, which is the fragment of schema.org that is relevant to the website. The second consists in adding the microdata tags to the web pages, using the previously designed website schema.org.

E. Yu et al. (Eds.): ER 2014, LNCS 8824, pp. 28–42, 2014.

In this paper, we describe an approach to website schema.org design. Our approach consists in a human-computer task-oriented dialogue, whose purpose is to design a website schema.org. The dialogue uses the directive mode, in which the computer has complete control. In each dialogue step, the computer asks a question to the web developer about the website content. Depending on the answer, a fragment of schema.org is or is not added to the website schema.org. The dialogue continues until the design is finished.

The methodology of our research is that of design science [2]. The problem we try to solve is the design of a website schema.org. The problem is significant because it is (or will be) faced by many developers and, due to the novelty of the problem, they lack the knowledge and the tools required for solving it. In this paper we present an approach to the solution of that problem. As far as we know, this is the first work that explores the problem of website schema.org design.

The structure of the paper is as follows. Next section describes schema.org and presents its metamodel. Section 3 defines the problem of website schema.org design and reviews the relevant previous work for its solution. Section 4 explains our approach to the solution of the problem. The approach has been implemented in a tool that has been very useful for testing and experimentation[1]. Section 5 presents the evaluation of the approach. Finally, section 6 summarizes the conclusions and points out future work.

2   Schema.org

In this section, we briefly review schema.org and introduce its UML [3] metamodel, which is shown in Fig. 1. As far as we know, this metamodel has not been published before (in any formal language).

Schema.org is a large conceptual schema (or ontology) [4] comprising a set of types. A type may be an object type or a property[2]. Each type has a name and a description. An object type may be an entity type, a data type or an enumeration. An enumeration consists of a set of literals.

A property may have one or more entity types as its domain and one or more object types as its range. For example, the property *creator* has as its domain *CreativeWork* and *UserComments*, and its range may be an *Organization* or a *Person*.

Types are arranged in a multiple specialization/generalization hierarchy where each type may be a *subtype* of multiple *supertypes*. For example, the entity type *LocalBusiness* is a subtype of both *Organization* and *Place*. The top of the hierarchy is the entity type *Thing*. All other object types are a direct or indirect subtype of it. A property may also be a subtype of another one, although this is used only in user extensions to schema.org. Enumerations may have subtypes. For example, *MedicalSpecialty* is a subtype of *Specialty*.

---

[1] A public preliminary version of the tool can be found at http://genweb.upc.edu/mpi/gmc-grup/eines/schemaorg/introduction

[2] At the time of writing, there are 428 object types and 581 properties, with a significant increase over time.

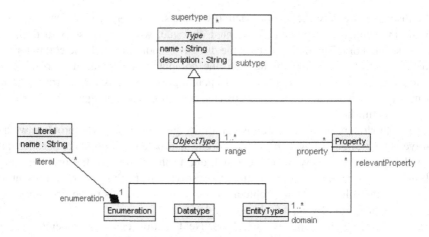

Fig. 1. The UML metamodel of Schema.org

3   Website Schema.org Design

In this section, we formalize the concept of website schema.org (3.1), we define the problem of designing that schema (3.2), and we review the relevant previous work (3.3). Our approach to the solution of that problem will be presented in the next section.

3.1   Website Schema.org

In general, the web pages of a website include the representation of many facts, some of which are an instance of concepts defined in schema.org while others are an instance of concepts that are not defined in schema.org. We call *website schema.org* of a website the set of concepts of schema.org that have (or may have) instances represented in its web pages.

However, a website schema.org is not simply a subset of the schema.org concepts, because there are facts of a concept that are represented in a context of the website, but not represented in another one of the same website. For example, consider a website that represents instances of the entity type *Offer*, including values for the properties *seller* and *itemOffered*, among others. The value of *seller* is an *Organization*, for which the website shows only its *name*, *address* an *email*. On the other hand, the value of *itemOffered* is a *Product*, for which the website may show its *manufacturer*, which is also an *Organization*. However, for manufacturing organizations the website only shows their name, and not their address and email. The website schema.org of this example must indicate that the address and email of an organization are shown only for sellers.

Figure 2 shows the metamodel in UML of a website schema.org. As far as we know, this metamodel has not been published before (in any language). A website schema.org has one or more roots, which are instances of *Item*. We use here the term

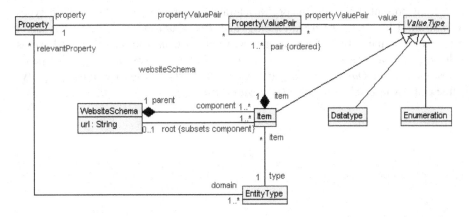

Fig. 2. The UML metamodel of a *website schema.org*

item with the same meaning as in the microdata model: a group of name-value pairs (that we call property-value pairs). An *Item* has a type, which is an *EntityType*. For example, the root of a restaurant website schema.org is an *Item* whose type is the *EntityType Restaurant*. An *Item* consists of an ordered set of at least one *PropertyValuePairs*.

Each instance of a *PropertyValuePair* has a *property* and a *value*. The property is an instance of *Property* and it must be one of the direct or indirect relevant properties of the type of the item. The value is an instance of the abstract class *ValueType*, which is an *Item*, a *Datatype* or an *Enumeration*. If the value is an *Item* then its *type* must be an *EntityType* that is in the range of the property, or a subtype of one of the ranges of the property.

We use a textual notation for defining a website schema.org (that is, an instance of the metamodel shown in Fig. 2). Figure 3 shows the example corresponding to the

```
<Restaurant,name,Text>
<Restaurant, aggregateRating, AggregateRating>
    <AggregateRating, ratingValue,Text>
    <AggregateRating, reviewCount,Number>
<Restaurant, address, PostalAddress>
    <PostalAddress, streetAddress,Text>
    <PostalAddress, addressLocality,Text>
    <PostalAddress, addressRegion,Text>
<Restaurant, telephone,Text>
<Restaurant, url,Text>
<Restaurant, openingHours, Duration>
<Restaurant, servesCuisine,Text>
<Restaurant, priceRange,Text>
```

Fig. 3. A website schema.org example, using a textual notation

restaurant presented in "schema.org/Restaurant". There are three *Items*, with types *Restaurant* (the root), *AggregateRating* and *PostalAddress*. The first, has eight property-value pairs, two of which have as value an *Item*, and the other six have as value a *Datatype* (*Text* or *Duration*). *AggregateRating* has two property-value pairs, whose values are *Datatypes* (*Text* and *Number*). *PostalAddress* has three property-value pairs, whose values are also *Datatypes* (*Text*).

```
<div itemscope itemtype="http://schema.org/Restaurant">
  <span itemprop="name">GreatFood</span>

  <div itemprop="aggregateRating" itemscope itemtype="http://schema.org/AggregateRating">
    <span itemprop="ratingValue">4</span> stars -
    based on <span itemprop="reviewCount">250</span> reviews
  </div>
...
  Hours:
  <meta itemprop="openingHours" content="Mo-Sa 11:00-14:30">Mon-Sat 11am - 2:30pm
  <meta itemprop="openingHours" content="Mo-Th 17:00-21:30">Mon-Thu 5pm - 9:30pm
  <meta itemprop="openingHours" content="Fr-Sa 17:00-22:00">Fri-Sat 5pm - 10:00pm
..
</div>
```

Fig. 4. Example of microdata markup using the website schema.org of Figure 3

Once the website schema.org is known, the web developer can add the corresponding microdata to the webpages. Figure 4 shows an example (an excerpt from the example shown in schema.org/Restaurant).

3.2   Problem Definition

Once we have defined what we mean by website schema.org, we can now state the problem we try to solve in this paper: the design of the website schema.org of a given website. The problem can be formally defined as follows:

Given:
− A website W consisting of a set of web pages. The website W may be fully operational or under design.
− The current version S of schema.org
  Design:
− The *website schema.org WS* of W.
  A variant of the problem occurs when the input includes a database D that is the source of the data displayed in W. A subvariant occurs when the database is not fully operational yet, and only its schema DS is available. Usually, DS will be relational.

All web developers that want to markup the web pages with schema.org microdata are faced with this problem. Once WS is known, the developers can add the corresponding markup in the web pages. Tools that illustrate how to add microdata once WS is known start to appear in the market[3].

---

[3] For example http://schema-creator.org/ or
  http://www.microdatagenerator.com/

3.3   Related Work

The task of web information extraction (WIE) could be seen as similar to website schema.org design, and therefore the work done on WIE systems [5] could be relevant to our problem. However, there are a few differences that make WIE systems inappropriate for website schema.org design. The input to a WIE system is a set of online documents that are semi-structured and usually generated by a server-side application program. The extraction target can be a relation tuple or a complex object with hierarchically organized data. In our case, the target is a fragment of a schema, without the facts, and if the website is under design, the online documents are not available. On the other hand, in these systems users must program a wrapper to extract the data (as in W4F [6] or DEQA [7]) or to show (examples of) the data to be extracted (as in Thresher [8]). In our case, this is unfeasible because web developers do not know what to extract.

The table interpretation problem is a specialization of WIE focused on extracting data from HTML tables [9]. [10] describes one of the more recent systems, which is an example of the ontology-guided extraction approach. In this case, the ontology is the universal probabilistic taxonomy called Probase, which contains over 2.7 million concepts. The system uses that ontology to determine the concepts corresponding to the rows of a table, and to its columns, from the names of the table headers and the values of the columns. This approach cannot be used in our case because in general web pages display many facts in a non-table format, and on the other hand the web pages may not be available.

Another related problem is schema matching, which deals with finding semantic correspondences between elements of two schemas or ontologies [11, 12]. Schema matching may be relevant to our problem when the source of the website is a database and we know its schema [13]. Assuming the database is relational, in our context the correspondences are between table attributes and schema.org properties. There exist a large spectrum of possible matchers (see [14] for a recent review) but in our context they would require the involvement of users who know both the database schema and schema.org.

4   Our Approach to Website Schema.org Design

In this section we describe our approach to the design of a *website schema.org*. We start with an overview of the approach (sect. 4.1) and then we continue with a detailed explanation of its main components (sect. 4.2-4.4). Throughout this section we use examples from the websites *allrecipes.com* and *food.com*, which deal with cooking recipes [15]. Users publish their recipes in those websites, including for each of them its name, a description, the ingredients, nutritional information, cooking time, preparation videos, and so on.

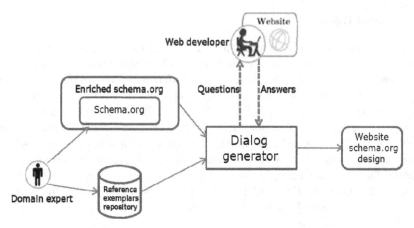

Fig. 5. A dialog approach to *website schema.org* design

4.1   Overview

Our approach to the design of a website schema.org is based on a computer-controlled dialogue (see Fig. 5). The dialogue is automatically generated (see sect. 4.4) from schema.org, enriched with domain knowledge by domain experts (as indicated in sections 4.2 and 4.3). In most cases, the dialog asks simple yes/no questions in natural language to the web developer. Figure 6 shows a fragment of that dialogue in our example. The answer to a question requires the web developer to know only the contents of the website. Prior knowledge on schema.org is not needed. Note that in our approach the website could be under design and that we do not need to know the schema of the website source database (if it exists).

4.2   Enriching Schema.org

The dialogue generator can generate dialogues from the content of schema.org. However, if domain experts can provide additional knowledge then the generated dialogues can be more understandable (by improving the phrasing of the questions) and more selective (by asking only the most relevant questions). Figure 7 shows the enrichment of the metamodel of schema.org that allows defining that additional knowledge.

The dialog generator deals with a property P always in a context. The context is an entity type that has P as a direct or indirect relevant property. In absence of additional knowledge, the dialog generator deals with P taking into account only the "official" names and descriptions of the involved types.

However, domain experts may add new knowledge by means of instances of *PropertyInContext* (*PIC*). An instance of that type has a few attributes and links that are useful when the dialog generator deals with a property in a particular context.

A *PIC* contextualizes a property (*contextualizedProperty*). The context in which a *PIC* is applicable is a set of one or more *EntityTypes* (*type*). If there is only one type and it is *Thing*, then the context is any entity type. For any given pair of *contextualizedProperty* and *type* there must be at most one *PIC*.

The three first attributes of a *PIC* are the specific name form, normalized name and description of the contextualized property. The specific name form indicates the grammatical form of the name, which may be a noun in singular form or a verb in third-person singular form. By default, it is assumed to be a noun. The specific normalized name and description may be used in the cases where the original name and description defined in schema.org can be improved in a given context. Such improvements allow the dialog generator to generate "better" questions. For example, *CreativeWork* includes the property *inLanguage*. A *PIC* could specify a better name for this *contextualizedProperty*. The specific name form could be *verb*, and the

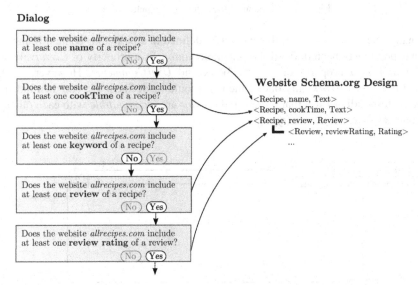

Fig. 6. Fragment of a dialogue in the allrecipes.com example

specific name could be *"isWrittenInTheLanguage"*. In this case, the *type* would be *Thing*.

The last attribute of a *PIC* is *isApplicable*. The attribute may be used to indicate that a property is not applicable in a given context. For example, a domain expert can define that the property *genre* of *CreativeWork* is non-applicable for *Recipe*.

The *applicableRange* of a *PIC* may be used to restrict the set of ranges for the contextualized property. For example, the property *author* of *CreativeWork* has as range {*Organization, Person*}. If we want to specify that for *Recipes* the *author* must be a *Person*, then we create a link between the corresponding *PIC* and *Person* as its *applicableRange*.

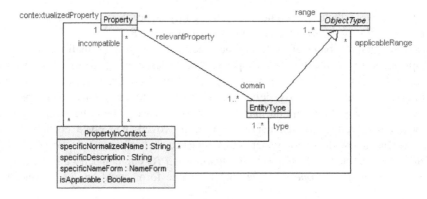

Fig. 7. Enrichment of the schema.org metamodel

Finally, there are properties that cannot be defined in a particular context if another one has previously been defined. For example, *author* is a property of *CreativeWork*, and *creator* is a property of *CreativeWork* and *UserComments*. However, in the context of *CreativeWork* only one of the two should be defined. We can then indicate in the corresponding *PICs* that *author* and *creator* are *incompatible* with each other in the context of *CreativeWork* (*type*).

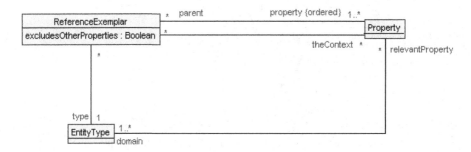

Fig. 8. Schema of reference exemplars

4.3   Reference Exemplars

A basic approach to website schema.org design could be that the web developer first defines the root of the website (such as *Recipe*), then the dialogue generator automatically determines the schema.org properties that could be relevant, and finally the system asks the web developer which of those properties are relevant for the website.

However, that approach would not be practical, for two main reasons. The first is that there can be many schema.org properties for a given root, but not all of them are actually used in practice. For example, *Recipe* (a subtype of *CreativeWork*, which in turn is a subtype of *Thing*) has 67 properties (7 for *Thing*, 50 for *CreativeWork* and 10 for *Recipe*), but a representative website such as *allrecipes.com* only shows 13 of those properties. Clearly, if the dialog generator were able to select the subset of properties that might be of interest for a given website, the system would ask much less questions to the web developer.

The second reason why the simple approach described above would not be practical is that the system would ask questions without any particular order, mixing questions belonging to different topics. For example, the system could ask about the presence of property *prepTime* (of *Recipe*), followed by *aggregateRaing* (of *CreativeWork*), *name* (of *Thing*) and then *cookTime* (again of *Recipe*). Clearly, such approach would confuse the web developer. Ideally, the questions posed by the system should be grouped by topic and unfold in a logical order, as required in, for example, questionnaire design [16].

Our solution to those problems is what we propose to call *reference exemplars*. Figure 8 shows their schema. There are two kinds of reference exemplars: root and dependent. A root reference exemplar of a given *type* (which is an *EntityType*) is an ordered set of one or more properties that are shown in recommended websites of the given root. The order of the properties of the set is the order in which those properties are usually displayed in those websites. A root reference exemplar can be seen as a recommended practice for the schema.org markup of websites of a given root.

There must be a reference exemplar for the type *Thing*, which is used when other more specific exemplars are not available.

Root reference exemplars are defined by domain experts. In the simplest case, a domain expert indicates a recommended website, from which the properties and their order can be automatically extracted using tools such as the Google Rich Snippet tool[4]. Another possibility is to just adopt the recommendations from search engines[5]. An even better possibility, not explored further here, is to integrate the properties shown in several recommended websites. For example, if a domain expert recommends *food.com* as a reference exemplar for *Recipe*, the root reference exemplar of *Recipe* would comprise 16 properties in a given order. The properties shown by *allrecipes.com* are 12 of those, and only one new (*video*).

A dependent reference exemplar of a given type *E* and property *P* (*theContext*) is an ordered set of one or more properties that are usually shown in current websites of the given type *E* when it is the value of the property *P*. As before, the order of the properties of the set is the order in which those properties are usually displayed in recommended websites. A dependent reference exemplar can also be seen as a recommended practice. The same dependent reference exemplar can have several properties in its *context* meaning that it applies to any of them.

For example, *food.com* includes the property *nutrition* of *Recipe*, whose value is the entity type *NutritionInformation*. For this type, nine properties are shown (*calories*, etc.).

---

[4] https://www.google.com/webmasters/tools/richsnippets

[5] For example. Google suggests the properties of *Recipe* indicated in
https://support.google.com/webmasters/answer/173379?hl=
en&ref_topic=1088474

Reference exemplars have the boolean attribute *excludesOtherProperties*. We use it to indicate whether or not the dialog generator should consider other properties of the *type* beyond those indicated by the reference exemplar. For example, *Energy* has seven properties (all of *Thing*), but when used as a property of *calories*, only one of those properties are likely to be used (a text of the form <Number> <Energy unit of measure>). We could define a dependent reference exemplar for the type *Energy* and property *calories*, consisting of a single property (*name*) and excluding other properties. In this way, the dialogs can be highly simplified.

4.4   Dialog Generation and Execution

In the following, we describe the main steps of the process needed to design the schema of a website using our approach (see Fig. 5). The starting point is the creation of an instance *w* of *WebsiteDesign* (see Fig. 2), followed by the determination (by the web developer) of a root entity type *e* of *w*, and the invocation of the procedure *designSchema* indicated in Algorithm 1. As can be seen, the procedure creates a root item *i* of *w* and then invokes (in line 5) the procedure *designSchemaForItem i*.

Algorithm 1. designSchema

input: An instance *w* of *WebsiteDesign*; an instance *e* of *EntityType*.

output: The complete design of website schema.org for *w*.

1. i := new Item;
2. i.root :=w;
3. i.parent := w;
4. i.type := e;
5. designSchemaForItem(i);
6. if i.pair -> isEmpty() then destroy i; end;

Note that in line 6 of the above algorithm, the item is deleted if no property-value pairs have been found for it. This may happen when the website does not represent any fact about the schema.org properties of the root entity type *e*.

The procedure for the design of the schema for an item *i* is indicated in Algorithm 2. We first determine the (root) reference exemplar *ref* for *i* (there is always one), and then we generate and execute two dialogs: the reference and the complementary dialogs. The first (lines 1-4) is based on the reference exemplar *ref* and considers only the properties of *ref*, and in their order. The second (lines 6-8) is performed only if *ref* does not exclude other properties and the web developer wants to consider all remaining properties. These properties are presented in the order of their position in the hierarchy of schema.org.

Algorithm 2. designSchemaForItem

input: An instance *i* of *Item*.

output: The complete design of the fragment corresponding to *i*.

1. ref:= determineReferenceExemplarForItem(i);
2. for each p in ref.property do

3.   generatePairsForProperty(i,p);

4. end;

5. if not ref.excludesOtherProperties and userWantsAllProperties then

6.   for each p in
                              (i.type.hasProperty() - ref.property->asSet()) ->sortedBy(positionInHierarchy) do
7.   generatePairsForProperty(i,p);

8.   end

9. end

The procedure *generatePairsForProperty* (algorithm 3) generates the property-values pairs of a property, if it is applicable and it is not incompatible with previously defined ones (see Fig. 7). In line 2, the system asks the user whether or not the property *p* of item *i* is shown in the website, as illustrated in the examples of Fig. 6. The paraphrasing of the question uses the name and description indicated in the corresponding property in context, if it exists. If the property is present in the website, the system determines its possible ranges, taking into account what is indicated in the corresponding *PropertyInContext* (Fig.7) or, if any, the definition of the property in schema.org (Fig. 1). If the range is not unique, then the operation asks the user the possible ranges of the property (one or more). If one of the possible ranges of *p* is an instance *E* of *EntityType*, then that operation asks whether the range of *p* is *E* or one of its subtypes. For example, the possible ranges of *author* are *Person* and *Organization*. If the user selects *Organization* as a possible range, then the system asks whether the range is *Organization* or one of its subtypes (there are no subtypes of *Person* in schema.org).

Algorithm 3. generatePairsForProperty

input: An instance *i* of *Item;* a property *p*

output: The property value pairs of *p* for item *i*.

1. if isApplicable(i,p) and not incompatible(i,p)

2.   ranges := askQuestion(i,p);

3.   for each r in ranges do

4.   pvp := new PropertyValuePair;

5.   pvp.property := p;

6.   pvp.item := i;

7.   if r is an EntityType then

8.   inew := new Item;

9.   pvp.value := inew;

10.   inew.parent := i.parent;

11.   inew.type := r;

12.   designSchemaForItem(inew);

13.   if inew.pair -> isEmpty() then destroy inew; end;

14.   else

15.   pvp.value = r;

16.   end;

17.   end

For each range, a property value pair is created (line 4), and if its value is an instance of *EntityType*, then the corresponding instance of *Item* is created (*inew*, line 8), and it is requested to generate its design by recursively invoking the operation *designSchemaForItem* in line 12. The execution of this operation now uses dependent reference exemplars. The process always ends because the depth of the compositions (Fig. 2) is finite in all practical websites.

5   Evaluation

As far as we know, ours is the first approach that has been proposed in the literature for solving the problem of website schema.org design, and therefore we cannot evaluate our proposal with respect to others. We propose in the following a set of six evaluation criteria that could be used to evaluate future new approaches to that problem, and we provide an evaluation of our approach with respect to those criteria. The criteria are: generality, precision, recall, human effort, cohesiveness and computation time.

Solutions may be general or domain specific. A general solution is applicable to any website, while a domain specific one is applicable to only one or more domains such as, for example, ecommerce or tourism. The approach presented in this paper is general.

Precision and recall are two classical criteria used in information retrieval contexts, which can be used here also. Now, instead of documents, we deal with schema.org properties that are relevant to a website and the properties that have been found. In our case, precision is the number of properties relevant to the website that have been found (true positives) divided by the total number of properties that have been found. Similarly, recall is the number of true positives, divided by the total number of relevant properties. Ideally, both precision and recall should have the value one.

In our approach, assuming that the web developer correctly identifies the root entity types (such as *Recipe*) of a website, the value of precision is always one, because the approach only considers those properties that are relevant and, therefore, all properties found are necessarily relevant. The value of recall is also one if the web developer chooses the complementary dialog and he correctly identifies the properties proposed by the system that are relevant to the website. The value of recall is less than one only when the web developer indicates that one or more proposed properties are not relevant to the website when, in fact, they are.

The human effort criterion evaluates the amount of effort the use of the approach requires to the web developers. That effort would be null if an approach were completely automated, but it is difficult to see that such approach is possible and, if it were, it would not be applicable when the website is under design. In our approach, web developers have to answer one question for each potentially relevant property. Questions are simple, and their answer should be easy in most cases.

Approaches that, like ours, are based on a human-computer dialog in a directive mode face the problem of dialog cohesiveness. Intuitively, we define cohesiveness as the degree in which the questions posed by the system are grouped by topic and unfold in a logical order, as required in questionnaire design [16]. The lowest value would correspond to dialogs in which questions are randomly selected.

In our approach, we achieve maximum cohesiveness when the dialog is based only on reference exemplars, because then the order of the questions is the same as (or based on) the order used in recommended practices. However, if the web developer chooses a complementary dialog, then the overall cohesiveness may decrease, because the additional properties considered are presented in a top-down order, which should be better than random, but not necessarily the most logical.

The computation time criterion evaluates the amount of time required by the computer. We conjecture that this time will normally be small and insignificant, because the number of schema properties relevant to a website is normally small, and the design must be performed only once. In our tool, the computation time has been less than one second per question.

In summary, we believe that our approach gets reasonable good results in the six proposed evaluation criteria.

6   Conclusions

We have seen that the creation of schema.org for structured data markup has posed a problem to the (many) developers of websites that want to implement it in their web pages. We have formally defined that problem, which we call the problem of designing the *website schema.org* of a given website.

We have presented an approach to that design, consisting in a human-computer dialogue. The dialogue is automatically generated from schema.org, possibly enriched with domain knowledge. In the dialogue, the system asks simple questions in natural language to the web developer. The answer to a question requires the web developer to know only the contents of the website. Prior knowledge on schema.org is not needed. In our approach the website could be under design, and we do not need to know the schema of the website source database (if it exists). For the purposes of testing and experimentation, we have implemented our approach in a prototype tool.

We have proposed a set of six criteria for the evaluation of possible solutions to the design of website schema.org, and we have evaluated our approach with respect to those criteria. Due to the novelty of the problem, there are not comparable alternative solutions yet. We believe that our approach will be useful to web developers because –among other things- it is easy to use, and it provides a systematic method to discover all schema.org microdata that could be added to the web pages.

The work reported here can be extended in several directions. First, the approach should be tested in the development of industrial websites in order to experimentally confirm its usefulness in practice. The experiment should be performed using our tool (or a professional version of it), fully loaded with relevant domain knowledge (properties in context and reference exemplars). Second, the approach could be extended to automatically generate examples of microdata markup from the design. Those examples could be useful to the web developers. Third, when the website is operational, it could be interesting to analyze the existing web pages in order to guess the presence of potential schema.org properties, which could then be suggested to the web developer. Finally, it would be interesting to develop a (semi-) automatic way of obtaining reference exemplars by integrating several recommended websites.

Acknowledgments. This work has been partly supported by the Ministerio de Economía y Competitividad and FEDER under project TIN2008-00444, Grupo Consolidado.

References

1. Seochat: Schema.org and microdata markups for SEO (May 2013), http://www.seochat.com/c/a/search-engine-optimization-help/schema-org-and-microdata-markups-for-seo/
2. Hevner, A.R., March, S.T., Park, J., Ram, S.: Design science in information systems research. MIS Quarterly, 75–105 (2004)
3. OMG. UML Superstructure v.2.4.1 (2011), http://www.omg.org/spec/UML
4. Olive, A.: Conceptual Modeling of Information Systems. Springer, Berlin (2007)
5. Chang, C.H., Kayed, M., Girgis, R., Shaalan, K.F.: A survey of web information extraction systems. IEEE Transactions on Knowledge and Data Engineering 18(10), 1411–1428 (2006)
6. Sahuguet, A., Azavant, F.: Building intelligent web applications using lightweight wrappers. Data & Knowledge Engineering 36(3), 283–316 (2001)
7. Lehmann, J., et al.: DEQA: Deep web extraction for question answering. In: Cudré-Mauroux, P., et al. (eds.) ISWC 2012, Part II. LNCS, vol. 7650, pp. 131–147. Springer, Heidelberg (2012)
8. Hogue, A., Karger, D.: Thresher: Automating the unwrapping of semantic content from the World Wide Web. In: WWW 2005, pp. 86–95. ACM (2005)
9. Embley, D.W., Hurst, M., Lopresti, D., Nagy, G.: Table-processing paradigms: A research survey. IJDAR Journal 8(2-3), 66–86 (2006)
10. Wang, J., Wang, H., Wang, Z., Zhu, K.Q.: Understanding tables on the web. In: Atzeni, P., Cheung, D., Ram, S. (eds.) ER 2012 Main Conference 2012. LNCS, vol. 7532, pp. 141–155. Springer, Heidelberg (2012)
11. Rahm, E., Bernstein, P.A.: A survey of approaches to automatic schema matching. VLDB Journal 10(4), 334–350 (2001)
12. Bellahsene, Z.: Schema Matching and Mapping. Springer (2011)
13. An, Y., Borgida, A., Mylopoulos, J.: Discovering the semantics of relational tables through mappings. Journal on Data Semantics VII, 1–32 (2006)
14. Shvaiko, P., Euzenat, J.: Ontology matching: State of the art and future challenges. IEEE Transactions on Knowledge and Data Engineering 25(1), 158–176 (2013)
15. Krutil, J., Kudelka, M., Snasel, V.: Web page classification based on schema.org collection. In: CASoN, pp. 356–360. IEEE (2012)
16. Pew Research Center. Question Order, http://www.people-press.org/methodology/questionnaire-design/question-order/

On Designing Archiving Policies for Evolving RDF Datasets on the Web

Kostas Stefanidis, Ioannis Chrysakis, and Giorgos Flouris

Institute of Computer Science, FORTH, Heraklion, Greece
{kstef,hrysakis,fgeo}@ics.forth.gr

Abstract. When dealing with dynamically evolving datasets, users are often interested in the state of affairs on previous versions of the dataset, and would like to execute queries on such previous versions, as well as queries that compare the state of affairs across different versions. This is especially true for datasets stored in the Web, where the interlinking aspect, combined with the lack of central control, do not allow synchronized evolution of interlinked datasets. To address this requirement the obvious solution is to store all previous versions, but this could quickly increase the space requirements; an alternative solution is to store adequate deltas between versions, which are generally smaller, but this would create the overhead of generating versions at query time. This paper studies the trade-offs involved in these approaches, in the context of archiving dynamic RDF datasets over the Web. Our main message is that a hybrid policy would work better than any of the above approaches, and describe our proposed methodology for establishing a cost model that would allow determining when each of the two standard methods (version-based or delta-based storage) should be used in the context of a hybrid policy.

1 Introduction

DBpedia, Freebase, and YAGO are, among many others, examples of large data repositories that are available to a wide spectrum of users through the Web. These data repositories store information about various entities, such as persons, movies, organizations, cities and countries, as well as their relationships. Typically, data in such datasets are represented using the RDF model [6], in which information is stored in triples of the form (*subject, predicate, object*), meaning that *subject* is related to *object* via *predicate*. By exploiting the advances of methods that automatically extract information from Web sites [16], such datasets became extremely large and grow continuously. For example, the Billion Triples Challenge dataset of 2012[1] contains about 1.44B triples, while DBPedia v3.9, Freebase and Yago alone feature 25M, 40M and 10M entities, and 2.46B, 1.9B and 120M triples, respectively [12].

Dynamicity is an indispensable part of the current Web, because datasets are constantly evolving for a number of reasons, such as the inclusion of new

---

[1] http://km.aifb.kit.edu/projects/btc-2012/

E. Yu et al. (Eds.): ER 2014, LNCS 8824, pp. 43–56, 2014.

experimental evidence or observations, or the correction of erroneous conceptualizations [14]. The evolution of datasets poses several research problems, which are related to the identification, computation, storage and management of the evolving versions. In this paper, we are focusing on the *archiving problem*, i.e., the problem of efficiently storing the evolving versions of a dataset, with emphasis on datasets stored on the Web.

Datasets on the Web are interlinked; this is promoted by the recent hype of the Linked Open Data (LOD) cloud[2], which encourages the open publication of interrelated RDF datasets to encourage reusability and allow the exploitation of the added value generated by these links. Currently, the LOD cloud contains more that 60B triples and more than 500 million links between datasets.

The interlinking of evolving datasets causes problems in the Web context. The open and chaotic nature of the Web makes impossible to keep track of who uses (i.e., links to) a given dataset, or what are the effects of a given change to interrelated datasets; this is in contrast to closed settings, where every change in a dataset is automatically propagated to all related parties. As a result, access to previous versions should be allowed to guarantee that all related applications will be able to seamlessly continue operations and upgrade to the new version at their own pace, if at all. In addition, even in a non-interlinked setting, experiments or other data may refer to a particular state of the dataset and may be non-understandable when viewed under the new version. Finally, certain applications may require access to previous versions of the dataset to support *historical* or *cross-version* queries, e.g., to identify past states of the dataset, to understand the evolution/curation process, or to detect the source of errors in the current modeling.

Supporting the functionality of accessing and querying past versions of an evolving dataset is the main challenge behind archiving systems. The obvious solution to the problem is to store all versions, but this can quickly become infeasible, especially in settings where the dataset is too large and/or changes are too frequent, as is the case in the Web of data [12]. To avoid this, several works (e.g., [9,5,17]) have proposed the use of *deltas*, which essentially allow the on-the-fly generation of versions, given any version and the deltas that lead to it. Even though this approach generally reduces space requirements, it causes an overhead at query time, because versions need to be reconstructed before being queried.

Given that RDF is the de-facto standard language for publishing and exchanging structured information on the Web, the main objective of this paper is to present our work towards designing a number of archiving policies for evolving RDF datasets. To do this, we study the trade-offs between the above two, basic archiving policies. In fact, we are proposing to use a cost model that employs the time and space overheads that are imposed by them in order to support *hybrid policies*, where some of the versions and some of the deltas are stored. Such policies could enjoy the best of both worlds by identifying which versions and which deltas should be stored to achieve optimal performance in terms of

---

[2] http://linkeddata.org/

both space requirements and query efficiency. To our knowledge this is the first work studying this problem for RDF datasets on the Web.

The rest of this paper is organized as follows. Section 2 presents a classification of the queries we are interested in, and Section 3 defines deltas between versions of datasets. Section 4 describes the basic archiving policies. Section 5 introduces the hybrid archiving policies, while Section 6 discusses a number of extensions. Section 7 focuses on different implementation strategies by considering different aspects of the archiving problem. Section 8 presents related work, and finally, Section 9 concludes the paper.

2   Query Types

We consider 3 types of queries, namely *modern*, *historical* and *cross-version*. These differ on the version(s) that they require access to, in order to be answered. *Modern queries* are queries referring to the current version of a dataset. For instance, in a social network scenario, one may want to pose a query about the (current) average number of friends of a certain group of subscribers. *Historical queries* are queries posed on a (single) past version of the dataset. In the example above, one could be interested to know the average number of friends for the same group at a given past version. Finally, *cross-version queries* are posed on several versions of the dataset, thereby retrieving information residing in multiple versions. For example, one may be interested in assessing how the number of friends of a certain person evolved over the different versions of the dataset. Such queries are important for performing different types of analytics across versions or for monitoring and understanding the evolution process.

From a different perspective, and motivated by [4] that focuses on storing and querying large graphs, we distinguish between *global* and *targeted* queries. Abstractly, to answer a global query, we need the entire version of a dataset. In contrast, targeted queries require accessing only parts of the version. For example, the average number of friends, at a given version, of all subscribers of a social network is a global query, while the average number of friends for a specific group of subscribers is a targeted query.

Finally, we distinguish queries as *version-centered* and *delta-centered* queries. Version-centered queries require the versions themselves for the computation of results. On the other hand, delta-centered queries manage to work only with deltas. For instance, retrieving the difference in the number of friends of a group of subscribers in a social network between two versions, represents a delta-centered query. We generalize the notion of delta-centered queries, so as to include queries that need for evaluation, along with deltas, stored versions, while dictating no versions reconstructions.

3   Changes and Deltas

The option of storing deltas, rather than versions, was proposed as an alternative archiving strategy to reduce storage space requirements. To implement this, one has to develop a *language of changes*, which is a formal specification of the changes that the system understands and detects, as well as *change detection and application algorithms* that allow the computation of deltas, and their subsequent on-demand application upon versions [9].

One way to do this, is to use *low-level deltas*, which amount to identifying the RDF triples added and deleted to get from one version to the other (e.g., [15,17]). Many approaches however, employ more complex languages, resulting to *high-level deltas*, which produce more concise deltas that are closer to human perception and understanding, and capture changes from a semantical (rather than syntactical) perspective (e.g., [9,8]).

Languages are coupled with appropriate change detection algorithms, which, given two versions V_i, V_j, produce a delta δ that describes the changes that lead from V_i to V_j; obviously, said delta is expressed using the language of changes that the corresponding tool understands and detects. Moreover, languages are coupled with change application algorithms, which take a version, say V_i, and a delta, δ, in the input and return the result of applying δ on V_i. Note that both algorithms should abide by the semantics of the language of changes that they implement. In addition, the change detection and application algorithms should be *compatible*, in the sense that the output of change detection between V_i and V_j, when applied upon V_i, should return V_j (this is called *consistent detection and application semantics* in [9]).

Also it often makes sense to store V_j, rather than V_i. This gives more flexibility to the archiving system, as it allows the storage of intermediate versions (or the current one), rather than necessarily the first one only. To support this feature, the change detection algorithm should be able to compute the *inverse delta*, denoted by δ^{-1}, either from the original input (V_i, V_j) or from the delta itself; moreover, the change application algorithm should be able to use it to correctly produce V_i, when V_j and δ^{-1} are available. This property is called *reversibility* [9].

In this work, we are not restricting ourselves to any particular language and change detection/application algorithm. We only have two requirements: first, that such algorithms exist and they are *compatible*, and, second, that such algorithms satisfy the *reversibility* property.

4   Basic Archiving Policies

In this section, we elaborate on the pros and cons of the two main archiving approaches, namely *full materialization* and *materialization using deltas* (a high level representation is depicted in Fig. 1). In addition, we present a third basic approach that materializes exhaustively both versions and deltas.

Full Materialization. The most obvious solution to evaluate queries of any type involves maintaining all the different versions of a dataset. Under this archiving policy, every time a new version of a dataset is available, such version is stored in the archive. The advantages of this approach is that the archiving task comes

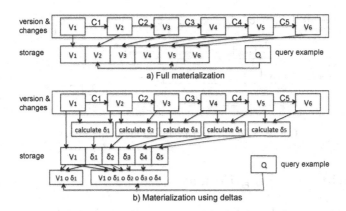

Fig. 1. Visualizing the a) *full materialization* and b) *materialization using deltas* archiving policies

with no processing cost, as the version is stored as-is. Moreover, since all versions are materialized, the full materialization policy allows efficient query processing (in general, for all types of queries). The main drawback of this policy is that the space overhead may become enormous, especially in cases where the stored versions are large and/or too many versions need to be stored (e.g., due to the fact that the dataset evolves too often). Under this policy, even the slightest change in the dataset between two versions would force the full replication and storage of the new version in the archive, resulting in large space requirements.

Materialization Using Deltas. A feasible alternative to the full materialization policy is the storage of deltas. Under this policy, only one of the versions of the dataset needs to be fully materialized (e.g., the first or the last one); to allow access to the other versions, deltas that describe the evolution of the versions from the materialized version should be computed and stored. Clearly, in this case, space requirements are small. However, the evaluation of queries would require the on-the-fly reconstruction of one or more of the non-materialized versions, which introduces an overhead at query time. Furthermore, storing the deltas introduces an overhead at storage time (to compute the deltas).

Materialization Using Versions and Deltas. From another extreme, the materialization using versions and deltas policy maintains both all different versions of a dataset, as well as all deltas between any two consecutive versions. That is, for each new published version of the dataset, we store in the archive the version along with its delta from the previous version. The main advantage of this approach is that allows for efficient query processing, even for delta-centered queries. However, computing deltas, at storage time, introduces an overhead. The obvious drawback of the policy is its vast space requirements.

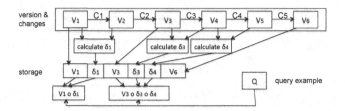

Fig. 2. Visualizing the *hybrid* archiving policy

5   Hybrid Archiving Policies

The main motivation behind our paper is that a *hybrid solution*, where some of the versions are stored under the *full materialization* policy, while others are stored using the *materialization using deltas* policy, would work best. Thus, a hybrid policy would materialize only *some* of the versions (which could include the first, last and/or intermediate versions), as well as deltas for reconstructing the non-materialized versions (Fig. 2). The objective of a hybrid policy is to strike a balance between query performance and storage space; applied correctly, it would allow us to enjoy the best of both worlds, by leading to modest space requirements, while not introducing a large overhead at storage and query time, according to the specific needs and peculiarities of the corresponding application domain.

The challenge in this direction is to determine what to materialize at each step, i.e., a version or a delta, by employing an appropriate cost model. Each of the two policies would introduce a specific time and space overhead, which need to be quantified and compared via the cost model. To make this more specific, let's assume that an existing version V_{i-1} evolves into V_i, and we need to decide whether to store V_i itself, or the appropriate delta δ_i.

5.1   Storing a Version

At storage time, the policy of full materialization (fm) causes a time overhead to store V_i, namely $t_{store}^{fm}(V_i) = |V_i| \cdot g$, where $|V_i|$ is the size of V_i (#triples), and g is the cost of storing a triple in the disk[3]. At query time, given a specific query q_j, there is a time overhead for executing q_j over V_i, that is, $t_{query}^{fm}(V_i, q_j) = c(V_i, q_j)$, where c reflects the complexity of executing q_j over V_i and depends on $|V_i|$ and the size of the result $res(q_j)$ of q_j. Assuming that p_{V_i} is an estimation on the number of the set of upcoming queries Q that refer to V_i, the time overhead for executing all Q queries is expressed as:

$$t_{query}^{fm}(V_i, Q) = p_{V_i} \cdot avg_Q(t_{query}^{fm}(V_i, q_j))$$

---

[3] In general, there may be other factors affecting the storage time (e.g., caching effects, storage method, disk technology, etc.), which may cause small deviations from this time estimate; however this paper aims to provide an approximation of the various costs, and minor deviations are acceptable.

Then, the overall time overhead when storing a version V_i is defined, taking into consideration the estimated upcoming queries for the version, using an aggregation function $\mathcal{F}$:

$$t^{fm}(V_i, Q) = \mathcal{F}(t^{fm}_{store}(V_i), t^{fm}_{query}(V_i, Q))$$

The corresponding space overhead of storing V_i is denoted by $s^{fm}(V_i)$ and is equal to $|V_i|$.

5.2   Storing a Delta

When storing the delta δ_i instead of V_i, in order to compute it, we need both versions V_{i-1} and V_i. Next, we distinguish between two cases, namely, V_{i-1} was stored during the previous step, or not.

V_{i-1} is Stored

Assuming the scenario in which V_{i-1} is stored, there is a time overhead for computing and storing δ_i, at storage time, and for reconstructing V_i and executing a set of queries Q over it, at query time.

Specifically, we formulate the overhead to compute δ_i as $t^{\delta, V_{i-1}}_{compute}(V_i, V_{i-1}, \delta_i) = d_c(V_i, V_{i-1}, \delta_i)$, where d_c reflects a function expressing the difficulty of computing δ_i with respect to the size and form of V_{i-1}, V_i and δ_i. As when storing a version, the overhead to store δ_i is $t^{\delta, V_{i-1}}_{store}(\delta_i) = |\delta_i| \cdot g$, where $|\delta_i|$ is the size of δ_i (#triples).

At query time, the overhead for reconstructing the version V_i is given by:

$$t^{\delta, V_{i-1}}_{reconstruct}(V_{i-1}, \delta_i) = p_{V_i} \cdot d_a(V_{i-1}, \delta_i)$$

where d_a defines the difficulty of applying δ_i to V_{i-1} taking into account the size and form of V_{i-1} and δ_i. Similarly to t^{fm}_{query}, the overhead of executing a set of p_{V_i} queries Q over V_i is:

$$t^{\delta, V_{i-1}}_{query}(V_i, Q) = p_{V_i} \cdot avg_Q(t^{\delta, V_{i-1}}_{query}(V_i, q_j))$$

where $t^{\delta, V_{i-1}}_{query}(V_i, q_j)$ is the specific overhead for computing the results of q_j over V_i.

The overall time overhead in this policy is defined, using an aggregation function $\mathcal{G}$, as follows:

$$t^{\delta, V_{i-1}}(V_i, Q) = \mathcal{G}(t^{\delta, V_{i-1}}_{compute}(V_i, V_{i-1}, \delta_i), t^{\delta, V_{i-1}}_{store}(\delta_i), t^{\delta, V_{i-1}}_{reconstruct}(V_{i-1}, \delta_i), t^{\delta, V_{i-1}}_{query}(V_i, Q))$$

Finally, the space overhead for storing the delta, denoted by $s^{\delta, V_{i-1}}(\delta_i)$, equals to $|\delta_i|$.

V_{i-1} is not Stored

When V_{i-1} is not stored, it must be somehow created to allow computing the delta; towards this aim, we propose two alternative policies. The former reconstructs sequentially all previous versions, starting from the latest stored one, in order to manage to reconstruct V_{i-1}. The latter just maintains temporarily the current version of a dataset (until the next "new version" appears), independently of the decision regarding the storage of the version or its delta.

Reconstruct V_{i-1}

Assume that V_j is the latest stored version. Then, we should first reconstruct V_{j+1}. Using V_{j+1}, we reconstruct V_{j+2}, and so forth. At the final step, we use V_{i-2} to reconstruct V_{i-1}. This way, the time overhead to reconstruct V_{i-1} is:

$$t^{\delta, \neg V_{i-1}}_{prev\_reconstruct}(V_{j+1}, V_{i-1}) = (i - 1 - j) \cdot avg_{j \ to \ (i-1)}(d_a(V_x, \delta_{x+1}))$$

while the overhead to store $V_{j+1}, V_{j+2}, \ldots, V_{i-1}$ is:

$$t^{fm, \neg V_{i-1}}_{prev\_store}(V_{j+1}, V_{i-1}) = t^{fm}_{store}(V_{j+1}) + t^{fm}_{store}(V_{j+2}) + \ldots + t^{fm}_{store}(V_{i-1})$$

Having reconstructed V_{i-1}, the additional time overhead is defined as in the case in which V_{i-1} is stored. In overall, given an aggregation function $\mathcal{H}$, the time overhead of this policy is:

$$t^{\delta, \neg V_{i-1}}(V_i, Q) = \mathcal{H}(t^{\delta, \neg V_{i-1}}_{prev\_reconstruct}(V_{j+1}, V_{i-1}), t^{fm, \neg V_{i-1}}_{prev\_store}(V_{j+1}, V_{i-1}), t^{\delta, V_{i-1}}(V_i, Q))$$

Finally, the space overhead $s^{\delta, \neg V_{i-1}}(\delta_i)$ in this policy is $max\{|V_{j+1}| + |V_{j+2}| + \ldots + |V_{i-1}|\} + |\delta_i|$.

Maintain temporarily V_{i-1}

The *reconstruct V_{i-1}* policy exhaustively reconstructs, from the latest stored version, all intermediate versions in order to catch V_{i-1}. Differently, we propose maintaining temporarily the current version. Using this heuristic, when the new version arrives, i.e., V_i, we can directly compare it with the previous one, i.e., V_{i-1}. Then, we drop the version that has been assigned as current, i.e., V_{i-1}, and maintain the new version, i.e., V_i. Abstractly speaking, the *maintain temporarily V_{i-1}* policy reduces both the time and space overheads, compared to the *reconstruct V_{i-1}* policy, since it only requires the maintenance of one additional version.

Following this approach, the time and space overheads are defined as follows:

$$t^{\delta, +V_{i-1}}(V_i, Q) = t^{\delta, V_{i-1}}(V_i, Q) + t^{fm}_{store}(V_{i-1})$$

$$s^{\delta, +V_{i-1}}(\delta_i) = s^{\delta, V_{i-1}}(\delta_i) + |V_{i-1}|$$

5.3   On Selecting a Hybrid Archiving Policy

To generalize, the decision on which policy is optimal, when a new version arrives, depends on the relative importance given to the time and space overheads for the application at hand. For example, a time-critical application might not care too much about the space overheads, whereas other applications could be more balanced in their requirements.

A simple way to model this, is by using the weighted summation of the time and space overheads of our hybrid policies, and select the best choice per case. In particular, assume a function $\mathcal{I}$ defined as:

$$\mathcal{I}^{\alpha} = w_t \cdot t^{\alpha} + w_s \cdot s^{\alpha}$$

where w_t, w_s are weights in $[0,1]$, t^{α} corresponds to $t^{fm}(V_i, Q)$, $t^{\delta, V_{i-1}}(V_i, Q)$, $t^{\delta, \neg V_{i-1}}(V_i, Q)$ or $t^{\delta, +V_{i-1}}(V_i, Q)$, and s^{α} corresponds to $s^{fm}(V_i)$, $s^{\delta, V_{i-1}}(\delta_i)$,

$s^{\delta,\neg V_{i-1}}(\delta_i)$ or $s^{\delta,+V_{i-1}}(\delta_i)$ for the *storing a version, storing a δ, storing a δ & reconstruct V_{i-1}* or *storing a δ & maintain V_{i-1}* policy, respectively. Typically, the policy with the minimum cost, i.e., the minimum value for $\mathcal{I}^\alpha$, is the one that will be used. Although more sophisticated functions can be designed, this function is simple and intuitive, and allows directly comparing the policies costs.

6 Extending Hybrid Archiving Policies

Clearly, the process of version reconstruction appears to be costly. In this section, we study different ways for, whenever possible, i.e., for specific query types, either avoiding reconstructions, or reconstructing only parts of versions. This way, we manage to reduce the time overhead when processing queries.

6.1 Use Only Deltas

Given a delta-centered query, i.e., a query that can be evaluated directly on deltas without accessing any versions, when following the *use only deltas* policy, no version reconstruction is required. As an example, consider a query that targets at retrieving the difference in the number of friends of a specific group of subscribers in a social network between two versions. For computing the answer of this query, we count the number of triples in the delta, added or deleted, that involve at least one subscriber in the given group and reflect friendships between subscribers.

This way for a delta-centered query, the corresponding overall time overheads for the *storing a δ, storing a δ & reconstruct V_{i-1}* and *storing a δ & maintain V_{i-1}* policies, reduce to:

$$t_{only\ \delta}^{\delta,V_{i-1}}(V_i,Q) = \mathcal{G}(t_{compute}^{\delta,V_{i-1}}(V_i,V_{i-1},\delta_i), t_{store}^{\delta,V_{i-1}}(\delta_i), t_{query}^{\delta,V_{i-1}}(\delta_i,Q))$$

$$t_{only\ \delta}^{\delta,\neg V_{i-1}}(V_i,Q) = \mathcal{H}(t_{prev\_reconstruct}^{\delta,\neg V_{i-1}}(V_{j+1},V_{i-1}), t_{prev\_store}^{fm,\neg V_{i-1}}(V_{j+1},V_{i-1}), t_{only\ \delta}^{\delta,V_{i-1}}(V_i,Q))$$

and

$$t_{only\ \delta}^{\delta,+V_{i-1}}(V_i,Q) = t_{only\ \delta}^{\delta,V_{i-1}}(V_i,Q) + t_{store}^{fm}(V_{i-1})$$

where $t_{query}^{\delta,V_{i-1}}(V_i,\delta_i)$ defines the cost of executing p_{V_i} queries over δ_i.

6.2 Use Deltas and Stored Versions

Alternatively, one can assume a scenario in which both stored versions and deltas can be used for answering a query, instead of reconstructing versions referring to this query. For example, for computing the average number of friends of a specific user in a set of versions, we count first the number of friends in the stored version, and while accessing the deltas that correspond to the other versions of the query, we calculate the average requested value. As motivated by the example, this policy is applicable only to delta-centered queries.

The overall time overheads, denoted as $t_{\delta,V_i}^{\delta,V_{i-1}}(V_i,Q)$, $t_{\delta,V_i}^{\delta,\neg V_{i-1}}(V_i,Q)$ and $t_{\delta,V_i}^{\delta,+V_{i-1}}(V_i,Q)$ are defined as in Section 6.1. The only difference is on the cost $t_{query}^{\delta,V_{i-1}}(\delta_i,Q)$, which is replaced by $t_{query}^{\delta,V_{i-1}}(V_i,(\delta_i,\delta_{i-1},\ldots,\delta_x),Q)$, since one query in Q is evaluated over the version V_i, while the rest over the deltas $\delta_i,\delta_{i-1},\ldots,\delta_x$.

6.3   Partial Version Reconstruction

However, there are cases in which version reconstruction cannot be avoided. To improve the efficiency of such scenarios, we propose the partial version reconstruction policy. Specifically, when queries access only parts of a dataset, like the targeted queries, we may construct only those parts required for the query execution.

Let's assume that an existing version V_{i-1} evolves into V_i. Let also V_i' be the needed part of V_i for query answering, and δ_i' be the part of δ_i that when applied to V_{i-1} constructs V_i'. Then, the overall time overheads for the *storing a δ*, *storing a δ & reconstruct V_{i-1}* and *storing a δ & maintain V_{i-1}* policies are defined as:

$$t_{partial}^{\delta,V_{i-1}}(V_i,Q) = \mathcal{G}(t_{compute}^{\delta,V_{i-1}}(V_i,V_{i-1},\delta_i),t_{store}^{\delta,V_{i-1}}(\delta_i),t_{reconstruct}^{\delta,V_{i-1}}(V_{i-1},\delta_i'),t_{query}^{\delta,V_{i-1}}(V_i',Q))$$

$$t_{partial}^{\delta,\neg V_{i-1}}(V_i,Q) = \mathcal{H}(t_{prev\_reconstruct}^{\delta,\neg V_{i-1}}(V_{j+1},V_{i-1}),t_{prev\_store}^{fm,\neg V_{i-1}}(V_{j+1},V_{i-1}),t_{partial}^{\delta,V_{i-1}}(V_i,Q))$$

$$t_{partial}^{\delta,+V_{i-1}}(V_i,Q) = t_{partial}^{\delta,V_{i-1}}(V_i,Q) + t_{store}^{fm}(V_{i-1})$$

where $t_{reconstruct}^{\delta,V_{i-1}}(V_{i-1},\delta_i')$ includes as well the cost for computing δ_i'.

7   Implementation Strategies

Above, we studied a number of policies for storing evolving datasets, each of which has different pros and cons and is suitable for a different usage scenario. In particular, full materialization policies are good when versions are not too large or not too many, or when the storage space required for storing the evolving datasets is not an issue compared to the access time (which is optimal in this policy). On the contrary, delta-based strategies are on the other end of the spectrum, optimizing storage space consumption but causing overheads at query time for most types of queries. The intermediate policies considered in this paper (hybrid policies, partial reconstruction of versions, temporary storage of the latest version) aim to strike a balance between these extremes. Table 1 presents a summary of the various policies, while next we focus on different implementation strategies by considering different aspects of the problem of what to store.

To decide which policy to follow, one needs to somehow "predict" the future behavior of the dataset, e.g., the number, type and difficulty of queries that will be posed upon the new or already existing versions. Even though an experienced curator may be able to do such a prediction with a reasonable accuracy (e.g., based on past queries or on the importance of the new version), predictions may need to be revised. Based on this idea, we discriminate three different ways to take decisions regarding the policy to follow for the storage of each new version.

Table 1. Archiving policies

Archiving policy		Short Description	Applicability
Basic policies (store all versions, one version and deltas between versions, or all versions and all deltas)	*full materialization*	maintain all the different versions of a dataset	all query types
	materialization using deltas	maintain only one version of a dataset and deltas describing the evolution from the stored version	all query types
	materialization using versions and deltas	maintain all versions of a dataset and all deltas between consecutive versions	all query types
Hybrid policies (given that an existing V_{i-1} evolves into V_i, decide whether to store V_i or δ_i)	*store a version*	store V_i	all query types
	store a delta	store δ_i (V_{i-1} is stored)	all query types
	store a delta & reconstruct V_{i-1}	store δ_i (V_{i-1} is not stored) V_{i-1} is reconstructed via a set of reconstructions from the latest stored version	all query types
	store a delta & maintain V_{i-1}	store δ_i (V_{i-1} is not stored) maintain V_{i-1}, until V_i arrives	all query types
Extensions (special cases for avoiding (full) reconstructions)	*use only deltas*	query evaluation on deltas, i.e., no version reconstruction is required	delta-centered queries
	use deltas & stored versions	query evaluation on deltas and stored versions, i.e., no version reconstruction is required	delta-centered queries
	partial version reconstruction	reconstruct only the parts needed for query evaluation	targeted queries

In general, when deciding if a new version will be materialized or not at the time of its publication, we care for achieving a feasible and efficient solution at local level. This notion of *locality* resembles a greedy approach that targets at decisions taking into account only the recent history of materializations, for example, by comparing the current version with only the previous one (possibly, by using materialized deltas). In other words, the locality implementation strategy takes a decision on the storage policy based on the current data/curator knowledge, and does not revise or reconsider such decision later.

Following a different implementation strategy, we may judge about what to materialize periodically. In particular, *periodicity* uses periods defined as sets, of specific size, of consecutive versions or versions published within specific time intervals. Then, decisions about which versions and deltas to store, within a period, are taken with respect to the versions published in the period. Periodicity succeeds in extending the local behavior of the previous approach. However, it wrongly assumes that updates are uniformly distributed over periods, leading sometimes to maintaining versions with very few changes.

Alternatively, one may be interested in decisions that aim to store those versions that offer global potentials to the storage and query processing model. The *globality* implementation strategy works towards this direction. It resembles a more exhaustive approach targeting at storing decisions based on comparisons between the current version and all the previously materialized ones, i.e., taking into account the whole history of materializations. Note that globality could also lead to the re-evaluation of the decisions to keep/drop some of the previous versions, as new versions appear, which is not the case for the locality and periodicity strategies that do not reconsider past decisions. This way, globality typically comes at the cost of a huge number of comparisons between versions.

Clearly, a strategy that combines characteristics of the above approaches, in order to achieve efficient and effective storing schemes, is a challenge worth studying. In our current work, for bounding the number of the comparisons executed when the globality strategy, i.e., the strategy with the best quality, is employed, we focus on tuning the number of versions to be examined with respect to the estimated frequencies and types of the upcoming queries, and the frequencies and amounts of changes between consecutive versions.

8   Related Work

In the context of XML data, [7] presents a delta-based method for managing a sequence of versions of XML documents. Differences, representing deltas, between any two consecutive versions are computed, and only one version of the document is materialized. To achieve efficiency, [1] merges all versions of the XML data into one hierarchy; an element, associated with a timestamp, appears in multiple versions and is stored only once. Clearly, our work does not target at hierarchical models for archiving, but on graph-organized data on the Web.

[5] presents, in the context of social graphs, a solution for reconstructing only the part of a version that is required to evaluate a historical query, instead of the whole version, similar to our partial version reconstruction policy. However, the main focus of this work is different, since it considers time with respect to graph evolution. [3] considers as well the addition of time. Specifically, it enhances RDF triples with temporal information, thus yielding temporal RDF graphs, and presents semantics for these graphs, including a way for incorporating temporal aspects into standard RDF graphs by adding temporal labels. Our approach is different in that it does not consider temporal-aware query processing. [11] proposes a graph model for capturing relationships between evolving datasets and changes applied on them, where both versions and deltas are maintained. From a different perspective, [13] supports versioning by proposing the use of an index for all versions.

Recently, several commercial approaches that support archiving come up. To do so, for example, Dropbox uses deltas between different versions [2], Googledrive[4] stores the entire versions, while, to our knowledge, none of them employs a hybrid approach. In general, it should be noted that adding timestamps to the triples in

---

[4] drive.google.com/

the datasets could partly solve the archiving problem, as versions could be generated on-the-fly using temporal information [1]. However, encoding temporal information in RDF triples often resorts to cumbersome approaches, such as the use of reification [3], which create overheads during querying. Furthermore, timestamps are generally absent in the context of Web data [10], which makes such a solution infeasible in practice. Studying this alternative is beyond the scope of this paper.

9   Conclusions

In this paper, we discuss the problem of archiving multiple versions of an evolving dataset. This problem is of growing importance and applies in many areas where data are dynamic and users need to perform queries not only on a single (possibly the current) dataset version, but also on a set of previous versions. The problem becomes more difficult in the context of the Web, where large, interconnected datasets of a dynamic nature appear.

Towards addressing the archiving requirements of data on the Web, we focus on designing different policies that, taking into consideration time and space overheads, aim to determine the versions of a dataset that should be materialized, as opposed to those that should be created on-the-fly at query time using deltas. We consider various parameters affecting such a decision, related to the type, frequency and complexity of queries, and size and frequency of changes.

Clearly, there are many directions for future work. As a first step, our plans include the evaluation of the cost model to experimentally verify whether the actual overheads appearing in practice are consistent with the theoretically expected ones. Moreover, it is our purpose to study methods for appropriately selecting the input parameters of our cost functions, algorithms for query evaluation and implementations in specific contexts. We peer a two-phase algorithm; in the first phase, the algorithm locates or reconstructs the version(s) required, in the second phase, for the query execution.

To further increase the efficiency of archiving, we envision building indexes on the materialized versions and deltas. In general, indexing could improve performance significantly, by enabling faster access of the data required for versions reconstructions and query executions. Specifically, we examine specific index structures suitable for specific query types and policies. For example, when assuming a *targeted query*, one option is to use an index for efficiently identifying only the part of a version or delta that the query targets at. Such an index appears to be of high importance when using, for example, the *partial version reconstruction* policy.

Interestingly, specific parts of versions or deltas that are not stored in the archive, but have been reconstructed to satisfy various query requirements, can be indexed in order to be re-used either as they are, or after being combined with each other. Our goal in this direction is to define a policy that exploits previous reconstructions, as well as their combinations, to minimize the number of reconstructions needed for new queries. To do this, properties such as *applicability*, expressing whether a part of a version can be used for evaluating a specific query, and *combining ability*, expressing whether two parts of a version can be combined to produce a new one, need to be appropriately defined.

Acknowledgments. This work was partially supported by the European project DIACHRON (IP, FP7-ICT-2011.4.3, #601043).

References

1. Buneman, P., Khanna, S., Tajima, K., Tan, W.C.: Archiving scientific data. TODS 29, 2–42 (2004)
2. Drago, I., Mellia, M., Munafò, M.M., Sperotto, A., Sadre, R., Pras, A.: Inside Dropbox: understanding personal cloud storage services. In: Internet Measurement Conference (2012)
3. Gutierrez, C., Hurtado, C.A., Vaisman, A.A.: Temporal RDF. In: Gómez-Pérez, A., Euzenat, J. (eds.) ESWC 2005. LNCS, vol. 3532, pp. 93–107. Springer, Heidelberg (2005)
4. Kang, U., Tong, H., Sun, J., Lin, C.-Y., Faloutsos, C.: Gbase: A scalable and general graph management system. In: KDD (2011)
5. Koloniari, G., Souravlias, D., Pitoura, E.: On graph deltas for historical queries. In: WOSS (2012)
6. Manola, F., Miller, E., McBride, B.: RDF primer (2004), http://www.w3.org/TR/rdf-primer
7. Marian, A., Abiteboul, S., Cobena, G., Mignet, L.: Change-centric management of versions in an XML warehouse. In: VLDB (2001)
8. Noy, N., Musen, M.: PromptDiff: A fixed-point algorithm for comparing ontology versions. In: AAAI (2002)
9. Papavasileiou, V., Flouris, G., Fundulaki, I., Kotzinos, D., Christophides, V.: High-level change detection in RDF(S) KBs. TODS 38(1) (2013)
10. Rula, A., Palmonari, M., Harth, A., Stadtmüller, S., Maurino, A.: On the diversity and availability of temporal information in Linked Open Data. In: Cudré-Mauroux, P., et al. (eds.) ISWC 2012, Part I. LNCS, vol. 7649, pp. 492–507. Springer, Heidelberg (2012)
11. Stavrakas, Y., Papastefanatos, G.: Supporting complex changes in evolving inter-related web databanks. In: OTM Conferences (1) (2010)
12. Stefanidis, K., Efthymiou, V., Herchel, M., Christophides, V.: Entity resolution in the Web of data. In: WWW (2014)
13. Tzitzikas, Y., Theoharis, Y., Andreou, D.: On storage policies for semantic Web repositories that support versioning. In: Bechhofer, S., Hauswirth, M., Hoffmann, J., Koubarakis, M. (eds.) ESWC 2008. LNCS, vol. 5021, pp. 705–719. Springer, Heidelberg (2008)
14. Umbrich, J., Hausenblas, M., Hogan, A., Polleres, A., Decker, S.: Towards dataset dynamics: Change frequency of Linked Open Data sources. In: LDOW (2010)
15. Volkel, M., Winkler, W., Sure, Y., Kruk, S., Synak, M.: SemVersion: A versioning system for RDF and ontologies. In: ESWC (2005)
16. Weikum, G., Theobald, M.: From information to knowledge: harvesting entities and relationships from Web sources. In: PODS (2010)
17. Zeginis, D., Tzitzikas, Y., Christophides, V.: On computing deltas of RDF(S) knowledge bases. In: TWEB (2011)

Ontology-Based Spelling Suggestion
for RDF Keyword Search

Sheng Li[1], Junhu Wang[1], and Xin Wang[2]

[1] School of Information and Communication Technology, Griffith University,
Gold Coast Campus, Australia
sheng.li@griffithuni.edu.au, j.wang@griffith.edu.au
[2] School of Computer Science and Technology, Tianjin University, Tianjin, China
wangx@tju.edu.cn

Abstract. We study the spelling suggestion problem for keyword search over RDF data, which provides users with alternative queries that may better express users' search intention. In order to return the suggested queries more efficiently, we utilize the ontology information to reduce the search space of query candidates and facilitate the generation of suggested queries. Experiments with real datasets show the effectiveness and efficiency of our approach.

Keywords: RDF, Keyword Search, Spelling Suggestion, Ontology.

1   Introduction

With the growing interest in the research and application of Semantic Web, accessing the Resource Description Framework (RDF) data has become a hot topic. Keyword search provides a user-friendly information discovery mechanism for people to access data without the need of understanding a structured query language or possibly complex and evolving data schemas [5]. Keyword search over RDF data has been studied in the recent years, and most works [3,7,10,12,16,17] focus on how to find the results by the keyword query.

For a query issued by a user, it is likely to return empty or low-quality results when typographical errors or incorrect keywords exist in the query. In order to alleviate this problem, *query suggestion (QS)*, a.k.a. *spelling suggestion* or *query cleaning*, has been proposed, which provides users with alternative keyword queries that better express users' search intention.

Most of previous works on QS are designed for Web queries and plain text data. Besides, most of them rely solely on the query log. As a result, the quality of the suggested queries relies on the quantity and quality of the log, and this approach has biases towards popular queries. Different from previous work, recently [13] tackles the query cleaning problem for relational databases. Later, works [9] and [8] focus on the spelling suggestion problem for XML Keyword Search. These methods generate the suggested queries based on the data content itself, avoiding the biases caused by the query log.

E. Yu et al. (Eds.): ER 2014, LNCS 8824, pp. 57–70, 2014.

In this work, we study the QS problem over RDF data. Previous methods designed for plain text or XML data cannot be directly applied to RDF data because of its different data model. Thus, we group the RDF triples into entities, and build inverted list for the evaluation of query candidates. Besides, the large volume of RDF data makes it challenging to generate the query candidates efficiently. Therefore, we use the concept information to reduce the search space so that better performance can be achieved.

To the best of our knowledge, this paper is the first work on QS over RDF data. The contributions of our work can be summarized as:

1. We analyze and rank the related concepts of an input query, and use the concepts to reduce the search space of query candidates and avoid computation of non-related records in the inverted list.
2. We implement a mechanism where a user can choose his/her desired concept to generate query candidates with better quality.

The rest of the paper is organized as follows: we begin with a review of the previous work in Section 2. Section 3 elaborates on our approach to generating query candidates by exploring the ontology and data content. In Section 4 experiments and analysis are presented. Section 5 is the conclusion of the paper.

2   Previous Work

In this section, we will discuss related definitions and previous works.

2.1   Spelling Suggestion

Spelling suggestion is defined as: given a dataset and a keyword query Q containing keywords $t_1, t_2, ..., t_q$, we return the top-k candidate queries C_i ($1 \leq i \leq k$) with the highest score that represent the most likely queries intended by users.

Previous studies, such as [13] and [9], generate the candidate queries in the following two steps:

1. For each keyword t_i in the query Q, a list of variants, denoted as $var_\epsilon(t_i)$, is generated. Each variant is a keyword in the vocabulary of the document, and has no more than ϵ edit errors from t_i.
2. The query candidate space C is the Cartesian product of the lists, namely $C = \prod_{i=1}^{q} var_\epsilon(t_i)$.

For example, consider the data fragment from DBpedia[1] shown in Fig. 1 and a dirty input query $Q =\{neutal,\ brain\}$. Suppose $\epsilon = 1$, step 1 generates the variants for keywords in Q based on the vocabulary of the database, $var_1(neutal) = \{neutal,\ neural,\ neutral\}$ and $var_1(brain) =\{brain\}$. Then step 2 generates the candidate space from the lists of variants, which contains $\{neutal,\ brain\}$, $\{neural,\ brain\}$ and $\{neutral,\ brain\}$.

---

[1] DBpedia, http://dbpedia.org

Basically, a query Q is meaningful for a dataset if it has high quality results from the dataset [19]. Let $rel(Q)$ be the relevance of the query Q to a dataset, $rel(Q)$ can be computed as the total score of all its results. However, this approach could overestimate queries that have numerous results over other queries that have fewer but meaningful results. To be balanced, $rel(Q)$ is often evaluated as the total score of its top-k results [19], where k is a selected parameter. $rel(Q)$ can be computed using the following formula:

$$rel(Q) = \sum_{i=1}^{k} score(R_i, Q) \tag{1}$$

where R_i is the i-th top result of Q, and $score(R_i, Q)$ is the relevant score of R_i to Q.

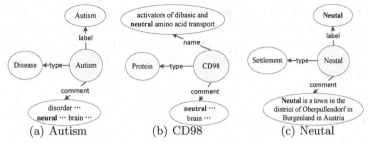

(a) Autism   (b) CD98   (c) Neutal

Fig. 1. Fragments of three RDF documents in DBpedia dataset

2.2 RDF Entity

RDF is a generic, graph-based data model with which to structure and link data that describe things in the world [2]. The model encodes data in the form of SPO triples (s, p, o) that stand for a *subject*, a *predicate*, and an *object*.

For example, the triple in Fig. 2 describes the fact that *Autism* is a *type* of *Disease*.

<http://dbpedia.org/resource/Autism> **<http://www.w3.org/1999/02/22-rdf-syntax-ns#type>** <http://dbpedia.org/ontology/Disease>
Subject   **Predicate**   Object

Fig. 2. An example of RDF triple

A large number of RDF triples form a Knowledge Base (KB), such as DBpedia [1], YAGO [15], which typically contains a large number of triples, describing millions of *entities* [16]. An *entity* is basically an object in the real world, as shown in Fig. 1. The definition of *entity* is given as follows:

Definition 1 (Entity). *Given the KB, we define an entity as all the triples that share the same subject s, denoted as $S(s)$. For simplicity, we refer to the entity as s.*

The work on keyword search over structured data, such as XML and RDF, can be classified into two categories [7]: (1) mapping the keyword query into one or more structured queries [12,17]; (2) directly retrieving results from data. Methods in category (2) can be further divided into two groups based on the results they return. One is to retrieve entities each of which contains the keywords [3,10,16]. The other is to find subgraphs each of which contains the keywords [7,18]. The subgraph-retrieval algorithm (SR) [7] builds the inverted list of triples for each keyword, and each triple (s, p, o) is viewed as an edge connecting two nodes s and o. First, SR retrieves all the triples that match the query keywords, namely inverted list l_i for keyword w_i in query Q. All the retrieved triples can be viewed as a disconnected graph. Then SR adapts the backtracking algorithm to retrieve the subgraphs, which utilizes adjacency list for edges. Given edge t_i from inverted list l_i, its adjacency list $A(t_i)$ consists of all the neighboring edges t_j from all other inverted list l_j. Finally, SR loops over all edges and generate all unique subgraphs. Though SR may be efficient for keyword search for a single query, it is not applicable to the QS problem which requires to evaluate all the query candidates. Finding the adjacency lists of the edges and looping over all the edges for every single query candidate could be highly time-consuming.

In this paper, our QS for RDF keyword search method is mainly designed for keyword search approaches that retrieve entities. How to extend our work to approaches that are designed to retrieve subgraphs or more general methods is our further work.

2.3 Ontology

The ontology in RDF KB provides information that describes the *concepts* (or classes) of the entities in the world and the relationships between the entities.

A *concept* represents a collection or class of entities. Relations describe the interactions between concepts and ways in which classes and entities are related to one another. The concepts in an ontology are usually organized into hierarchical structures, where a concept may have sub-concepts and/or super-concepts. In this work, we consider the simplified and common case where the concepts form a tree structure (i.e., a taxonomy). However, our approach can be easily extended to the general case. For example, the ontology in DBpedia describes that *PopulatedPlace* is a sub-class of *Place* and *Place* is a sub-class of *owl:Thing* which is at the top of the concept hierarchy. We encode the concepts by a type of Dewey code ORDPATH [11], so that the hierarchical relationships between two concepts can be easily captured and allows extra space for further addition, as shown in Fig. 3.

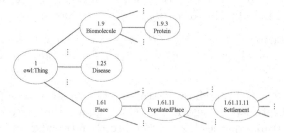

Fig. 3. A fragment of the concept tree in DBpedia

Note that the concept of *Autism* is *Disease*, but also could be its super-concept *owl:Thing*. However, in our work, when we discuss the concept of an entity s, we only refer to the direct concept c that s belongs to, ignoring the super-concepts of c. We use $Class(s)$ to denote the set of *concepts* that s directly belongs to.

In our work, we exploit the concept information of entities and keywords to reduce the search space, as will be discussed in the following section.

3   QS Model

The main idea of our approach is to locate the concepts that users are interested in, implemented by one of the following two mechanisms:

1. Based on the input query, we provide users with a list of concepts organized in a tree structure, so that users can navigate and choose the intended concepts.
2. By default, if a user does not choose any concept, the concepts will be ranked and the top-k concepts are selected by the system.

Based on the selected concepts, we propose a method to reduce the space of the query candidates. Before discussion of our method, we need to define some indices and definitions.

3.1   Indexes

In order to adapt to the BM25F ranking [14,16] for RDF entities related to a query, the predicates in an entity are divided into four fields *label, comment, type* and *others*, and assigned with different weights. The term frequencies in each field along with the field's weight are used in the calculation of BM25F. Thus, we define our entity inverted list as:

Definition 2 (Entity inverted list). *The inverted list of a term t is a list of tuples $(s, info)$, where s represents an entity that contains the term t, and info contains the term frequencies in different fields in s.*

Definition 3. *A term (keyword) t is said to be directly related to a concept c (denoted as $t \overset{d}{\sim} c$) if t exists in an entity s, and s directly belongs to concept c, namely, $c \in Class(s)$. For a list of concepts C, if for every $c \in C$ we have $t \overset{d}{\sim} c$, then we say t directly relates to C, denoted as $t \overset{d}{\sim} C$.*

For example, term *neural* is in entity *Autism* whose concept is *Disease* in Fig. 1, thus *neural*$\overset{d}{\sim}$*Disease*. Similarly, we have *neutral*$\overset{d}{\sim}$*Protein*, and *brain*$\overset{d}{\sim}${*Disease, Protein*}.

Definition 4 (Term-Concepts index). *For each term t in the database, suppose C is the set of concepts that directly relate to t in the database. The index contains a set of tuples (c, tf_t^c), where $c \in C$ and tf_t^c is the frequency of term t that directly relates to concept c. The term frequency (tf_t^c) is calculated as $\frac{f_t^c}{f_t}$, where f_t^c is the number of occurrences of t directly relate to concept c and f_t is the total number of occurrences of t.*

For example in Fig. 1, the Term-Concepts index of term "brain" contains concepts Disease and Protein, along with $tf_{brain}^{Disease} = 0.5$ and $tf_{brain}^{Protein} = 0.5$ respectively.

The index will be used to to rank and select concepts (see Section 3.2).

Definition 5. *For each concept c in the ontology, and a set of terms T in the database, if for every $t \in T$ we have $t \overset{d}{\sim} c$, then we say c directly relates to T (T is directly related to c), denoted as $c \overset{d}{\sim} T$.*

For example in Fig. 1, entity *Neutal* is a type of *Settlement*, so every term in *Neutal* is directly related to the concept *Settlement*. Therefore, *Settlement* directly relates to all the terms in entity *Neutal*.

Definition 6 (Concept-Terms index/Concept-related vocabulary). *For each concept c in the ontology, let C be the union of sub-concepts of c (descendants of c in the concept tree) and c itself. For each $c_i \in C$, let T_i be the set of all the terms directly related to c_i ($c_i \overset{d}{\sim} T_i$). Let vocabulary $T = \bigcup_{c_i \in C} T_i$, we say c relates to the vocabulary T, denoted as $c \sim T$. Then we say T is the Concept-Terms index of c (or c-related vocabulary), denoted as $T(c)$*

For example, let T_1 and T_2 be the lists of all the terms directly related to concept *Settlement* and *Place* in DBpedia respectively, and T is the *Place*-related vocabulary ($T(Place)$). We have term *neutal*$\in T_1$ and *neutal*$\notin T_2$. However, since *Place* is the super-concept of Settlement, T is the union of T_1 and T_2; as a result, *neutal*$\in T$.

This index will be used when generating query candidates (see Section 3.3). The index for every concept in the ontology can be easily generated in two steps: (1) traverse the Term-Concepts index to create a list T for each concept c, where $c \overset{d}{\sim} T$; (2) c-related vocabulary can be generated by merging the vocabularies of c's descendants by traversing the concept tree in a recursive way.

When a query Q is issued by a user, we retrieve a list of concepts related to the query Q, and use the top-k ranked concepts as the default concepts that users are interested in. If needed, users can even choose the specific concepts that he/she is interested in. Then we use the vocabulary related to the default or chosen concepts to generate the variants of keywords in the query and reduce the search space.

3.2   Concept Selection

When a user inputs a query $Q = t_1, t_2, ..., t_q$, for each keyword $t_i \in Q$, we retrieve its related concepts C_{t_i} from the Term-Concepts Index. Let $C_Q = \cup_{t_i \in Q} C_{t_i}$, we provide users with C_Q along with the super-concepts of each concept organized in a tree structure, so that users can choose the concepts that they are interested in at different levels. For example, suppose a user inputs a query $\{neutal\}$, only one concept *Settlement* is directly related to the term *neutal*. However, the super-concepts of *Settlement* and itself are presented to users in a tree structure, as shown in Fig. 4, so users can choose the concepts that are easy to understand and interesting to them. In this case, users may choose a more general concept *Place*, instead of the more specific concept *Settlement*.

Algorithm 1. Retrieve the concepts and calculate the scores

Input: keyword query Q;
Output: a list of concepts with scores;
1. create Map; //create a new hash table to store concept and its score.
2. **for** each keyword $t \in Q$ **do**
3.   list of concepts $C \leftarrow$ the Term-Concepts index of t;
4.   **for** each concept $c \in C$ **do**
5. $score \leftarrow tf_t^c \cdot icf_t^c$;
6.   **if** Map contains c **then**
7. $score \leftarrow score+$Map.get(c);
8.   **end if**
9.   update c and its $score$ to Map;
10.   **end for**
11. **end for**
12. return Map;

Fig. 4. Returned Concepts for query $\{neutal\}$

If a user does not choose any concepts, we rank the concepts and use the top-k concepts to speed up the process. In order to rank the concepts, we adopt the $tf \cdot idf$ model in the IR world, to measure the content relevance of a concept to a keyword query. The score of a concept to the input query Q can be calculated as:

$$CScore(c, Q) = \sum_{t \in Q} tf_t^c \cdot icf_t \tag{2}$$

The term frequency (tf_t^c) is calculated as $\frac{f_t^c}{f_t}$, as discussed in Definition 4. Instead of idf, *inverse concept frequency* of a term t (icf_t) is employed, which is the total number N of concepts over the number N_t of concepts that term t is directly related to, calculated as $icf_t = \log \frac{1+N}{1+N_t}$.

Consider the data in Fig. 1, we calculate the scores for related concepts based on input query $Q_1 = \{neutal, brain\}$. In this case, C_{Q_1} includes concepts $Disease(c_1)$, $Protein(c_2)$ and $Settlement(c_3)$, their relevance to Q are:

$$CScore(c_1, Q_1) = tf_{neutal}^{c_1} \cdot icf_{neutal} + tf_{brain}^{c_1} \cdot icf_{brain}$$
$$= 0 + 0.5 \times \log \frac{1+3}{1+2} \approx 0.06$$

, $CScore(c_2, Q_1) = 0 + 0.5 \times \log \frac{1+3}{1+2} \approx 0.06$ and $CScore(c_3, Q_1) = 1 \times \log \frac{1+3}{1+1} + 0 \approx 0.3$.

Similarly, for query $Q_2 = \{neutral, brain\}$, we have $CScore(c_1, Q_2) = 0 + 0.5 \times \log \frac{1+3}{1+2} \approx 0.06$, $CScore(c_2, Q_2) = 1 \times \log \frac{1+3}{1+1} + 0.5 \times \log \frac{1+3}{1+2} \approx 0.36$ and $c_3 \notin C_{Q_2}$.

Note that in the QS scenario, Q may be a dirty query, as a result, the user-intended concepts may not be always in the top-k ranked list with a relatively small k. In the worst case, if none of the keywords in Q is correct, it is likely that the intended concepts are not even in C_Q. However, in practice this case is rare. Even if Q is a dirty query, it is the only source that could be used to guess the intention of a user. Thus, we assume that input query Q at least preserve some intended information. Further study and experiments are given in Section 4 regarding dirty queries with no intended information preserved.

To generate the concepts list and calculate the score of each concept, we use the Term-Concepts Index. The details of this process are shown in Algorithm 1. After this step, we can rank the concepts and select top-k concepts based on the scores. Also, we build a tree-structured interface for users to choose concepts, as shown in Fig. 4.

3.3   Generating Query Candidates

Algorithm 2. Generate query candidates

Input: keyword query Q, a concept list C, ϵ,
Output: query candidates QC;
1. new hash table Map; //create a new hash table to entity and its related queries
2. **for** each variant $v \in var_\epsilon(t_1)$ **do**
3. $l_v \leftarrow$ inverted list of v;
4.   **for** each entity s in l_v **do**
5.   **if** any concept in $Class(s)$ is a sub-concept of any concept in C **then**
6. $info \leftarrow$ the local distribution information of v in s;
7.   create a new query object o, and $o.add(v, info)$;
8.   create a new list I, and add o into I;
9. $Map.put(s, I)$;
10.   **end if**
11.   **end for**
12. **end for**
13. **for** i from 2 to q **do**
14.   new hash table $cMap$; //create a new temperate hash table
15.   **for** each variant $v \in var_\epsilon(t_i)$ **do**
16. $l_v \leftarrow$ inverted list of v;
17.   **for** each entity $s \in Map.keySet()$ **do**
18.   **if** l_v contains s **then**
19. $info \leftarrow$ the local distribution information of v in s;
20.   create a new list I';
21.   **for** each o in Map.get(s) **do**
22.   create $o' \leftarrow o.add(v, info)$
23. $I'.add(o')$
24.   **end for**
25. $cMap.put(s, I')$;
26.   **end if**
27.   **end for**
28.   **end for**
29.   Map $\leftarrow$ cMap;
30. **end for**
31. return $QC \leftarrow$ traverse Map to get each query candidate and calculate its score.

Previous works on QS [9,8] use the entire vocabulary of the dataset to generate the variants for each keyword in the query. In this work, let C be the set of the top-k ranked concepts or chosen concepts by users, $T_C = \bigcup_{c \in C} T(c)$ is the vocabulary related to C, we use T_C as the vocabulary to generate the variants. We use a version of FastSS method [4] to generate variants for a keyword t within edit distance ϵ.

Given a query $Q = \{t_1, t_2, ..., t_q\}$, suppose that $t_1, ..., t_q$ have been rearranged in such a way that $L_1 \leq L_2 \leq \cdots \leq L_q$, where L_i is the total size of the inverted lists of the variants of term t_i, namely, $L_i = \sum_{v \in var_e(t_i)} |l_v|$, where l_v is the inverted list of variant v. The details of the generation of the candidates are given in Algorithm 2. When generating query candidates, we use C to filter the search space (Lines 5-10). We use a hash table (Map created in Line 1) to keep track of the entities and the queries they match. The key of the Map is the id of the entity s. For simplicity, we use entity s to present its id. The value of the Map is a list of *query objects*, recording the keywords (variants of every keywords in Q) s matches; for each keyword (variant) v in the query object o, it relates to its local distribution information $info$ (Lines 7, 22).

3.4 Ranking Query Candidates

In Algorithm 2, the Map records entities and the matching queries. By traversing the Map, we can get every valid query candidate and the entities matching the candidate, as well as the score of the results (entities) of the candidate (Line 31).

Given a query candidate Q' and a result (entity) s matching Q', the relevant score of s to Q' ($score(s, Q')$) is estimated by the BM25F [14,3,16] ranking model. The BM25F ranking model sets several boost factors and parameters. In our paper, the factors and parameters are set to the values as in previous work [16]. Then the relevant score of query candidate Q', namely, $rel(Q')$, can be calculated by Equation (1).

Finally, we combine the factor of edit distance of Q' to input query Q with $rel(Q')$ to rank the candidate Q', calculated as:

$$Score(Q') = e^{-ed(Q', Q)} \cdot rel(Q') \tag{3}$$

where $ed(Q', Q)$ is the edit distance between query candidate Q' and the input query Q.

3.5 Complexity Analysis

Given a query $Q = \{t_1, t_2, ..., t_q\}$, let $L_i = \sum_{v \in var_e(t_i)} |l_v|$, where l_v is the inverted list of variant v, the complexity of Algorithm 2 of is:

$$L_1 + \sum_{i=2}^{q-1} \sum_{v \in var_e(t_i)} M_i \cdot \log |l_v|$$

where M_i is the number of entities in Map during the iteration of different i in Algorithm 2, and $L_1 \geq M_1 \geq M_2 \geq \cdots \geq M_{q-1}$. As we can see, M_i plays an important role in the time complexity, especially M_1. When no concept constraint is applied, $M_1 = L_1$; besides, for each keyword in the input query, there would be more variants generated from the whole vocabulary of the database, causing larger L_1 and M_i. When concept constraint is applied, $M_1 < L_1$; in practice, M_1 is usually much smaller than L_1.

4   Experiments

In this section, we present the experimental results and analyze the effectiveness and efficiency of our approach.

4.1   Experimental Setup

All our experiments were carried out on a PC with Intel Core i5 CPU and 3.7GB RAM. The operating system was Ubuntu 12.04 64-bit, and we used the Cassandra[2] as the database. The algorithms were implemented with JDK 1.7.

We used DBpedia 3.7 as the dataset in our experiment. DBpedia is one of the largest real-world RDF datasets extracted from Wikipedia, containing more than 40 million triples. Although we only use one dataset in the experiment, our approach is applicable for other RDF datasets.

For query cleaning, finding the *ground truth* is difficult [6,9]. We first designed a set of initial clean queries, as the *ground truth*, from keywords that occur in the entities. We then used random edit operations ($\epsilon = 1$) to obtain dirty queries from them. We randomly generated 50 clean queries and 50 dirty queries on the dataset, some query samples are given in Table 1. All the queries can be found at http://www.ict.griffith.edu.au/~jw/ER14/query.xls. Like previous work [9], to ensure enough information is preserved for the input query, we do not introduce random edit operations to very short keywords whose length is no larger than 4.

Table 1. Sample Queries

	Clean		Dirty
Q1	disorder neural brain	Q2	diserder neutal brain
Q3	optics laser	Q4	optice laser
Q5	australia gold coast	Q6	austalia gold foast
Q7	sichuan earthquake china	Q8	sicuan earthqiake china
Q9	titanic james cameron	Q10	titaic james camaron

4.2   Algorithms and Measures

To the best of our knowledge, our approach is the first work on QS on RDF keyword search. Thus, in our paper, we compared the effectiveness and efficiency between methods with and without concept constraint; We implemented the following three configurations: **NoConcept** does not use any concept constraint in generating the candidates; **Top-k** uses the top-k ($k = 5$ by default) concepts to reduce the search space; **UserSelect** generates the candidates based on the concept that users choose. For comparison, we use the following measurements:

MRR (Mean Reciprocal Rank) is defined as MRR $= \frac{1}{|Q|} \cdot \sum_{Q \in \mathcal{Q}} \frac{1}{rank(Q_g)}$, where $\mathcal{Q}$ is a set of queries, and $rank(Q_g)$ is the rank of the ground truth Q_g [9]. The larger the value of MRR is, the better the quality is.

Precision@N is defined as $precision@N = \frac{A}{|Q|}$, where A is the number of queries whose top-N suggestions contain the ground truth, which indicates what percentage of given queries that users will be satisfied if they are presented with

---

[2] Cassandra, http://cassandra.apache.org

at most N suggestions for each query [9]. The higher Precision@N is, the better the quality.

Time We record the execution time of the generation of query candidates.

4.3 Analysis

Effectiveness. To compare the effectiveness, we first measured the MRR for the three spelling suggestion algorithms on clean and dirty datasets, as shown in Fig. 5. As we can see, the three configurations achieved a close-to-1 MRR for clean queries. However, NoConcept and Top-k did not reach the MRR of value 1. For some clean queries, they suggested other queries with "better quality". For example, for query Q={neutal, austria}, the search intention of which may be to find a town in Austria called Neutal in this case, NoConcept and Top-k ranked the query Q' ={neutral, austria} as first and Q as second. Apparently there are more entities matching Q', and only one entity matching Q. While UserSelect returned Q as the most relevant query candidate when selecting *Place* as related concept. For dirty queries, UserSelect had the best quality of suggested queries out of the three. NoConcept and Top-k achieved similar MRR on the dirty queries.

Then we measured the Precision@N under the three configurations to see what percentage of given queries that users will be satisfied if they are presented with at most N suggestions for each query. As we can see in Fig. 6, UserSelect outperformed the other two, and NoConcept and Top-k had the similar quality based on Precision@N. For Top-k, we set k to 5; for some queries, the default top-k concepts did not contain the intended concept of users, causing the generated query candidates to miss the ground truth. Thus, the Precision@N for Top-k did

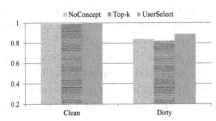

Fig. 5. MRR

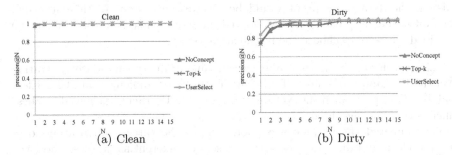

(a) Clean   (b) Dirty

Fig. 6. Precision@N with clean and dirty queries

not reach a close-to-1 value, as shown in Fig. 6(B). However, this problem could be largely avoided by assigning a larger value to k.

For example, for the input dirty query Q_D ={neutral, austra}, the concept Settlement is not in the top-k related concepts when $k = 5$. As a result, the variant "neutal" is missed and the intended query Q ={neutal austria} is not returned, causing Top-k approach not reaching a close-to-1 Precision@N in Fig. 6(B). However when k is set to 8 in this case, Q is in the suggested candidates.

Table 2. Experiments on 50 dirty queries with no intended information preserved

	# exist in concept tree	# exist in top-15 ranked concepts	# return ground truth
50 queries	35	29	38

The previous experiments were under the assumption that some intended information is preserved in the query when generating the dirty queries, and k is set to 5. To further study how our work response to the situation when none of the keywords is correct in a dirty query, we ran the experiments on another 50 dirty queries in this situation and analyzed the results, as shown in Table 2. The intended concepts of 35 queries (70%) were still returned to the users by concept tree, so users would be able to manually choose the intended concept.

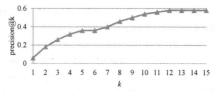

Fig. 7. Precison@k for top-k ranked concepts

For Top-k approach, we used the Precision@k (similar to Precision@N) here to measure the satisfaction of top-k ranked concepts, as shown in Fig. 7. As we can see, when $k = 15$, the intended concepts of 58% of dirty queries were in the top-k ranked list. Furthermore, when $k = 15$, the ground truth of 76% dirty queries were returned by the Top-k approach according to Table 2. The Precision@k can be further improved by introducing the popularity of concepts, which can be implemented by recording users' preference of concepts in the log. Combining the popularity of concepts to rank the concepts for the input query is in our future work.

Note that in some cases when none of the keyword from the input query exist in the data, no concept would be returned. However, in this situation, the NoConcept approach can be adopted, and the whole concept tree can be provided for users to choose the intended concepts.

Efficiency. Figure 8 shows the execution time of query candidate generation over the 10 example queries in Table 1 under the three configurations. UserSelect and Top-k outperformed the NoConcept approach; UserSelect achieved the best efficiency among the three.

We compared the average execution time of the three configurations over the 100 clean and dirty queries with datasets of different sizes, to see how the execution time increased with the growth of data, as shown in Fig. 9. In the

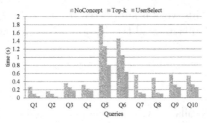

Fig. 8. Execution time over the example queries

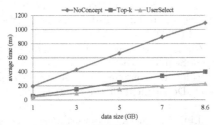

Fig. 9. Average execution time of 100 queries over different sizes of data

experiment, we extracted datasets of different sizes from DBpedia 3.7 (8.64GB), and use all the clean and dirty queries as test queries. As we can see, UserSelect outperformed the other two approaches in generating query candidates, and the execution time of Top-k and UserSelect grew more smoothly compared with NoConcept.

Note that, for the execution time of UserSelect, the time for users to choose concepts was not taken into consideration. We admit that allowing users to choose concepts takes considerable time, nevertheless the UserSelect approach does achieve better effectiveness, and require less execution time for generating query candidates. UserSelect is particularly useful when the keywords in the query are all dirty.

To summarize, by exploring ontology and using concepts to reduce the search space, our query suggestion approach of RDF keyword search achieves better efficiency. For Top-k approach, it maintains high quality of suggested queries, while achieves much better efficiency. UserSelect provides users with a mechanism to choose the intended concepts, so that query candidates with better quality can be generated and less execution time is needed for the generation of query candidates.

5   Conclusion

This paper studies the query suggestion problem for keyword search over RDF data. We utilize the ontology information to reduce the search space to achieve better performance. However, our model is designed for RDF keyword search approaches that return entities as results, and is not yet applicable to subgraph-based keyword search approaches. How to extend our work to subgraph-based approaches and further use log information and ontology is our future work.

Acknowledgement. This work is supported by the Australian Research Council Discovery Grant DP1093404 and the National Natural Science Foundation of China (61100049).

References

1. Auer, S., Bizer, C., Kobilarov, G., Lehmann, J., Cyganiak, R., Ives, Z.: Dbpedia: A nucleus for a web of open data. In: Aberer, K., et al. (eds.) ISWC/ASWC 2007. LNCS, vol. 4825, pp. 722–735. Springer, Heidelberg (2007)
2. Bizer, C., Heath, T., Berners-Lee, T.: Linked data - the story so far. Int. J. Semantic Web Inf. Syst. 5(3), 1–22 (2009)
3. Blanco, R., Mika, P., Zaragoza, H.: Entity search track submission by Yahoo! research barcelona. In: SemSearch (2010)
4. Bocek, T., Hunt, E., Stiller, B.: Fast similarity search in large dictionaries. Technical Report ifi-2007.02, Department of Informatics, University of Zurich (April 2007)
5. Chen, Y., Wang, W., Liu, Z., Lin, X.: Keyword search on structured and semi-structured data. In: SIGMOD Conference, pp. 1005–1010 (2009)
6. Cucerzan, S., Brill, E.: Spelling correction as an iterative process that exploits the collective knowledge of web users. In: EMNLP, pp. 293–300 (2004)
7. Elbassuoni, S., Blanco, R.: Keyword search over RDF graphs. In: CIKM, pp. 237–242 (2011)
8. Li, S., Wang, J., Wang, K., Li, J.: A distance-based spelling suggestion method for XML keyword search. In: Atzeni, P., Cheung, D., Ram, S. (eds.) ER 2012 Main Conference 2012. LNCS, vol. 7532, pp. 176–189. Springer, Heidelberg (2012)
9. Lu, Y., Wang, W., Li, J., Liu, C.: XClean: Providing valid spelling suggestions for XML keyword queries. In: ICDE, pp. 661–672 (2011)
10. Nie, Z., Ma, Y., Shi, S., Wen, J.-R., Ma, W.-Y.: Web object retrieval. In: WWW, pp. 81–90 (2007)
11. O'Neil, P.E., O'Neil, E.J., Pal, S., Cseri, I., Schaller, G., Westbury, N.: ORDPATHs: Insert-friendly XML node labels. In: SIGMOD Conference, pp. 903–908 (2004)
12. Pound, J., Ilyas, I.F., Weddell, G.E.: Expressive and flexible access to web-extracted data: A keyword-based structured query language. In: SIGMOD Conference, pp. 423–434 (2010)
13. Pu, K.Q., Yu, X.: Keyword query cleaning. PVLDB 1(1), 909–920 (2008)
14. Robertson, S.E., Zaragoza, H.: The probabilistic relevance framework: BM25 and beyond. Foundations and Trends in Information Retrieval 3(4), 333–389 (2009)
15. Suchanek, F.M., Kasneci, G., Weikum, G.: YAGO: A large ontology from wikipedia and wordnet. J. Web Sem. 6(3), 203–217 (2008)
16. Tang, X., Wang, X., Feng, Z., Jiang, L.: Ontology-based semantic search for large-scale RDF data. In: Wang, J., Xiong, H., Ishikawa, Y., Xu, J., Zhou, J. (eds.) WAIM 2013. LNCS, vol. 7923, pp. 570–582. Springer, Heidelberg (2013)
17. Tran, T., Wang, H., Rudolph, S., Cimiano, P.: Top-k exploration of query candidates for efficient keyword search on graph-shaped (RDF) data. In: ICDE, pp. 405–416 (2009)
18. Yee, K.-C.: Keyword search on huge RDF graph. PhD thesis, The University of Hong Kong (2010)
19. Yu, B., Li, G., Sollins, K.R., Tung, A.K.H.: Effective keyword-based selection of relational databases. In: SIGMOD Conference, pp. 139–150 (2007)

Schema-Independence in XML Keyword Search

Thuy Ngoc Le[1], Zhifeng Bao[2], and Tok Wang Ling[1]

[1] National University of Singapore
{ltngoc,lingtw}@comp.nus.edu.sg
[2] University of Tasmania & HITLab Australia
zhifeng.bao@utas.edu.au

Abstract. XML keyword search has attracted a lot of interests with typical search based on lowest common ancestor (LCA). However, in this paper, we show that meaningful answers can be found beyond LCA and should be independent from schema designs of the same data content. Therefore, we propose a new semantics, called CR (Common Relative), which not only can find more answers beyond LCA, but the returned answers are independent from schema designs as well. To find answers based on the CR semantics, we propose an approach, in which we have new strategies for indexing and processing. Experimental results show that the CR semantics can improve the recall significantly and the answer set is independent from the schema designs.

1 Introduction

Since XML has become a standard for information exchange over the Internet, more and more data are represented as XML. At the same time, there is increasing recognition of the importance of flexible query mechanisms including keyword queries. Therefore, XML keyword search has been studied extensively based on lowest common ancestors such as SLCA [15], VLCA [10], MLCA [13] and ELCA [17].

Keyword search is a user-friendly way so that users can issue keyword queries without or with little knowledge about the schema of the underlying data. However, they often know what the data is about. Therefore, when they issue a query, they often have some expectations about the answers in mind. Since they may not know which schema is being used, their expectations are independent from schema designs. If they already got some answers for this schema, it could be surprised if different answers are returned when they try another schema which represents the same data content. Thus, different schemas of the same data content should provide them the same answers. However, this is not the case for the existing LCA-based approaches as shown in Example 1.

Running database: Consider the database with the ER diagram in Figure 1. There are many ways to represent this database in XML. Figure 2 shows five possible XML schema designs for this database. For simplicity, we do not show attributes and values in these schemas. Each edge in the schemas corresponds to a *many-to-many* relationship types between the two object classes.

Example 1 (Schema dependence). *Users may know a university database about courses, lecturers, teaching assistants (TAs), students, and research groups (R_group)[1],*

---

[1] R_group can be an object class with attributes: name, topics, leader, etc.

E. Yu et al. (Eds.): ER 2014, LNCS 8824, pp. 71–85, 2014.
© Springer International Publishing Switzerland 2014

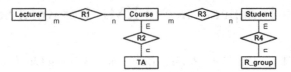

Fig. 1. ER diagram of a database

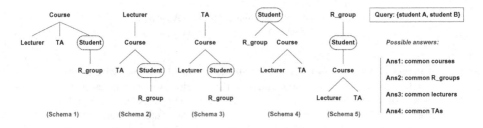

Fig. 2. Equivalent XML schemas of the database in Figure 1

but they do not know what the schema looks like, i.e., which of the five schema designs in Figure 2 is used. When they ask for two students *(e.g., Q = {StudentA, StudentB}), beside information about the two students, they may want to know some of the below:*

- *Ans1: the common* courses *that they both take,*
- *Ans2: the common* research groups (R_groups) *that they both belong to,*
- *Ans3: the common* lecturers *who teach both of them,*
- *Ans4: the common* teaching assistants (TAs) *who teach and mark both of them.*

They are common ancestors in some schema(s): Ans1 in Schema 1, Schema 2 and Schema 3; Ans2 in Schema 5; Ans3 in Schema 2; and Ans4 in Schema 3. Therefore, they are all meaningful answers (probably with different ranking scores). Different users may have different expectations. However, expectations of a user should be independent from schema designs because he does not know which schema is used. However, all five different schema designs provide five different sets of answers by the LCA semantics. Particularly:

- *for Schema 1: only Ans1 could be returned;*
- *for Schema 2: Ans1 and Ans3 could be returned;*
- *for Schema 3: Ans1 and Ans4 could be returned;*
- *for Schema 4: no answer;*
- *for Schema 5: only Ans2 could be returned.*

The above example provides a strong evidence for our two following arguments:

Firstly, meaningful answers can be found beyond common ancestors because all kinds of answers Ans1, Ans2, Ans3 and Ans4 are meaningful. However, if relying only on the common ancestor techniques, none of the five schemas can provide all the above meaningful answers. For some schema, answers from common ancestors may be better than the others, but returning more meaningful answers would be better than missing meaningful ones.

A final answer obtained by LCA-based approaches includes two parts: a returned node (LCA node) and a presentation of the answer, e.g., a subtree or paths. Arguably, the presentation of an answer as a subtree may contain other answers. For instance, for Schema 1, the subtree rooted at the common courses (Ans1) that both students take may contain other kinds of answers (Ans2, Ans3, Ans4). However, the LCA-based approaches do not explicitly identify them and it may be hard for users to identify them because this presentation contains a great deal of irrelevant information. Thus, it is necessary to identify and separate them clearly.

Secondly, answers of XML keyword search should be independent from the schema designs, e.g., Ans1, Ans2, Ans3 and Ans4 should be returned regardless which schema is used to capture data. However, as can be seen, the LCA-based approaches return different answer sets for different schema designs in Figure 2.

In practice, many real XML datasets have different schema designs such as IMDb[2] and NBA[3]. In IMDb, there are many ways to capture relationships among actors, actresses, movies, and companies. In NBA, relationships among coaches, teams, and players can also be captured in different ways. Moreover, due to the flexibility and exchangeability of XML, many relational datasets can be transformed to XML [6], and each relational database can correspond to several XML schemas by picking up different entities as the root for the resulting XML document.

Therefore, it necessitates to consider the above two arguments when processing XML keyword search. However, to the best of our knowledge, no current system satisfies the above two arguments, including keyword search over XML graph.

Challenges. To determine what should be returned beside common ancestors is a great challenge. First, the new answers must be reasonably meaningful. That they must also cover possible answers returned by other alternative schemas is even harder. After such kinds of answers are defined, another challenge is how to construct an efficient index and how to find answers efficiently. Finding common ancestors is efficient because the computation can be based on node labels. However, this technique cannot be easily applied for finding other types of answers.

Our Approach and Contributions. We make the following contributions.

- *New semantics*. We propose a new semantics for XML keyword search, called CR (Common Relative), which provides common relatives as answers. A common relative corresponds to a common ancestor in some equivalent schema(s). The CR semantics not only improves the effectiveness by providing more meaningful answers beyond common ancestors, but also returns the same answer set regardless of different schemas backing the same data content. So it is more reliable and stable to users (Section3).
- *Indexing techniques*. Unlike conventional inverted index where each keyword has a set of matching nodes, to find common relatives efficiently, we need to maintain a set of relatives for each keyword, which is much more difficult to construct. To accomplish this index, we propose some properties and an algorithm to identify relatives of a node effectively and efficiently (Section 4).
- *Processing techniques*. Unlike a common ancestor which appears at only one node, a common relative may be referred by multiple nodes. Therefore, we model data as a so-called *XML IDREF graph* by using *virtual IDREF* mechanism, in which we assign a *virtual object node* to connect all instances of the same object. We also

---

[2] http://www.imdb.com/interfaces
[3] http://www.nba.com

discover the hierarchical structure of the XML IDREF graph and exploit it to find common relatives efficiently (Section 4).

– *Experiment.* The experimental results show the completeness, the soundness, and the independence from schema designs of our CR semantics. They also show our approach can find answers based on the CR semantics efficiently (Section 5).

2 Preliminary

A *reasonable schema* is a schema in which an implicit relationship type must be represented by adjacent object classes, i.e., there is nothing between object classes of a relationship type. The same data content can have different reasonable *schema designs* (or *schemas* in short). For example, to transform from a relational database to XML, there are different schema designs, each of which corresponds to a way that XML organizes the data. These schemas are *equivalent* in the sense that they capture the same information in different ways. We call databases corresponding to these equivalent schemas and represent the same data content as *equivalent databases*.

An *object* is identified by *object class* and *object identifier* (OID). In XML, it occurs as object instances, each of which is represented by a group of nodes, rooted at the object class tagged node, followed by a set of attributes and their associated values to describe its properties. In this paper, we refer to the root of this group as an *object node* and the other nodes as *non-object nodes*. Hereafter, in unambiguous contexts, we use object node as the representative for a whole object instance, and nodes are object nodes by default. For example, matching node means matching object nodes.

In an XML document with IDREFs, an object node which is referred by some other object node(s) by IDREFs is called a *referred object node*. In other words, a referred object node is an object node having IDREFs as its incoming edges.

In an XML data tree, the path of a node u, denoted as $path(u)$, is the path from the root to u.

3 The CR Semantics

This section introduces our proposed semantics, called CR (<u>Com</u>mon <u>R</u>elative), which can return more meaningful answers beyond LCAs of matching nodes and the returned answer set is independent from schema designs. For ease of comprehension, we first present intuitive analysis about the CR semantics by example.

3.1 Intuitive Analysis

We analyze the problem in Example 1 and discuss how to find all types of answers with only one particular schema. For simplicity, figures used for illustration in this section provide intuitive information and only contain object nodes, without attributes and values. For example, for the left most figure in Figure 3, StudentA means that this node together with the corresponding attributes and values represent information about studentA; or common R_group represents the research group that both StudentA and StudentB belong to.

Example 2 (Using one schema to find all types of answers). *Recall that in Example 1, there are four types of meaningful answers for a query about two students (e.g., StudentA and StudentB). Each type of answers can be returned by the LCA semantics for some schema(s) in Figure 2. They are: Ans1 (common courses) from*

Schema 1, Schema 2 and Schema 3, Ans2 (common R_groups) from schema 5, Ans3 (common `lecturers`) *from Schema 2, and Ans4 (common* `TAs`) *from Schema 3. Now we discuss how a database w.r.t. a given schema can return all the above answers. We take the data of Schema 1 for illustration.*

For Ans1 (common `courses`): *this is a common ancestor of the two students and Schema 1 can provide it.*

For Ans2 (common `R_groups`): *Schema 1 cannot provide it, but Schema 5 can provide it. Figure 3 shows that in Schema 1, common* `R_groups` *appear as descendants of the two students. If these descendants are connected by a referred object node via IDREFs, Ans2 can be found at that referred object node. We call that referred object node as a common descendant.*

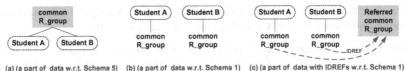

(a) (a part of data w.r.t. Schema 5)   (b) (a part of data w.r.t. Schema 1)   (c) (a part of data with IDREFs w.r.t. Schema 1)

Fig. 3. Illustration for Ans2 (common R_groups)

For Ans3 (common `lecturers`): *Schema 1 cannot provide it, but Schema 2 can provide it. Figure 4 shows that in Schema 1, common* `lecturers` *appear as relatives of the two students (formal definition of relative is given in Section 3.2). If these relatives are connected by a referred object node via IDREFs, Ans3 can be found at that referred object node. We call that referred object node as a common relative.*

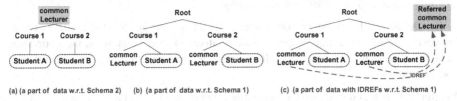

(a) (a part of data w.r.t. Schema 2)   (b) (a part of data w.r.t. Schema 1)   (c) (a part of data with IDREFs w.r.t. Schema 1)

Fig. 4. Illustration for Ans3 (common lecturers)

Ans4 (common `TAs`) *is similar to Ans3 (common* `lecturers`).*

As can be seen, all types of answers can be found at common ancestors, common descendants, or common relatives. Although we only take the data of Schema 1 for illustration, the data of other schemas have similar results when analyzed.

3.2 The CR Semantics

Before introducing the new semantics, let us present some properties which makes the semantics meaningful. Consider a chain C: $< u_1, u_2, \ldots, u_n >$ of object nodes, where u_i and u_{i+1} have parent-child or child-parent relationship in an XML data D. We have the following properties related to C.

Property 1. *If C is a parent-child chain of object nodes, i.e., u_i is the parent of u_{i+1} $\forall i$, then all nodes on the chain C have different node paths.*

The above property is obvious. Recall that node path (or the path of a node) presented in Section 2 is the path from the root to that node. If an object class has multiple occurrences in XML schema, its instances may corresponds to different node paths.

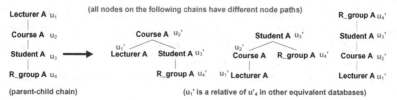

Fig. 5. The "same" chain w.r.t. different equivalent databases

Property 2. *The chain C has a corresponding chain C': $< u'_1, u'_2, \ldots, u'_n >$ of object nodes in a database D' equivalent to D, where u'_i refers to the same object with u_i.*

Property 2 can be illustrated in Figure 5, in which the data chain $< u_1, u_2, u_3, u_4 >$ (in the most left) has three corresponding chains $< u'_1, u'_2, u'_3, u'_4 >$ in its equivalent databases. Combining Property 1 and Property 2, we have Property 3.

Property 3. *If C is a <u>parent-child chain</u>, then there always exists a corresponding chain C': $< u'_1, u'_2, \ldots, u'_n >$ of object nodes in another database D' equivalent to D, where u'_i refers to the same object with u_i $\forall i$, such that all object nodes u'_i's in the chain C' have <u>different node paths</u>.*

We call nodes u'_i's in the chain C' in Property 3 are *relatives* of each other. It has different meanings from relatives in family relationship and it is defined as follows.

Definition 1 (Relative). *In an XML data tree, an object node u is a relative of an object node v if there is a chain of object nodes from u to v where all object nodes on that chain (including u and v) have different node paths.*

By Definition 1, ancestors and descendants of a node u are also relatives of u. However, siblings of u may or may not be relatives of u, depending on the node path of u and that of its siblings. The following properties are inferred from Definition 1 and Property 3.

Property 4. *If u is a <u>relative</u> of v in an XML database D, then there exists some XML database D' equivalent to D such that u' is an <u>ancestor</u> of v', where u' and v' refer to the same object with u and v respectively.*

Property 5. *If w is a <u>common relative</u> of u and v in an XML database D, then there exists some XML database D' equivalent to D such that w' is a <u>common ancestor</u> of u' and v', where w', u' and v' refer to the same object with w, u and v respectively.*

By Property 4, a relative corresponds to an ancestor in some equivalent database(s). More generally, a common relative corresponds to a common ancestor in some equivalent database(s) as stated in Property 5. Since a common ancestor can provide a meaningful answer, a common relative should correspond to an answer. Based on all discussions above, we propose the novel semantics for XML keyword search as follows.

Definition 2 (The CR (Common Relative) semantics). *Given a keyword query $Q = \{k_1, \ldots, k_n\}$ to an XML database, an answer to Q is a pair $\langle c, \mathbb{K} \rangle$ where:*
- $\mathbb{K} = \bigcup_1^n u_i$ *where object node u_i matches k_i.*
- *c is a common relative of $\mathbb{K}$.*

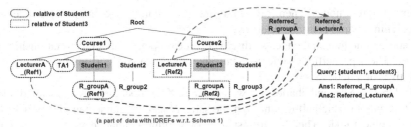

Fig. 6. Illustration for query {Student1, Student3}

When the XML document contains IDREFs, the referred node and its referrer(s) refer to the same object. For such documents, the two definitions above are still valid with the following extensions: (1) for the condition in Definition 1, the referred object node is not considered if its referrer(s) are already considered, and (2) a relative of a referring object node is also a relative of its referred object node.

Example 3. *Consider query {Student1, Student3} to the data in Figure 6, in which we use ID/IDREFs to connect all instances of the same object. Since Referred_LecturerA are referred by LecturerA_(Ref1) and LecturerA_(Ref2) by IDREFs, it is considered as a relative of nodes which its two referrers are relatives. It is similar for Referred_R_groupA. As a result, we have:*

- *Relatives of Student1: Student1, Course1, TA1, LecturerA_(Ref1), Referred_LecturerA, R_groupA_(Ref1), and Referred R_groupA.*
- *Relatives of Student3: Student3, Course2, LecturerA_(Ref2), Referred_LecturerA, R_groupA_(Ref2), and Referred R_groupA.*

Therefore, the common relatives of the two students are Referred_LecturerA, and Referred_R_groupA which provide two answers for the query.

Although the number of relatives of an object node may be large, the number of relatives which is potential to be common relatives is much fewer as will be discussed in Property 6. We only index such potential relatives, not all relatives. This saves index space dramatically.

We consider all common ancestors (common ancestors are a part of common relatives) of matching nodes instead of filtering out common ancestors which are less relevant as the LCA semantics and its extensions such as SLCA, ELCA do. This is because in many cases, this filter loses many meaningful answers. For example, consider a query about two students. For Schema 2 in Figure 2, if two students take the same course, then the lecturer teaches that course cannot be returned as an answer. However, common lecturer of two students is meaningful to users.

4   Our Schema-Independent Approach

Our approach is to find answers for a query under our proposed CR semantics, which returns common relatives for a set of matching object nodes. Finding common relatives is much more challenging than finding common ancestors. Firstly, while the set of ancestors of a node can be easily identified based on the hierarchical structure of XML, the set of relatives of a node are difficult to identify. Secondly, given a set of matching nodes, unlike a common ancestor which appears as only one node, a common relative may be referred by many different nodes. Therefore, it requires more complex techniques for indexing and searching to find common relatives.

To address the first challenge, we discover some properties about the relationships of relatives. These properties enable us to introduce an effective algorithm to pre-compute all relatives of a node (Section 4.2).

To address the second challenges, we model an XML document as a so-called *XML IDREF graph*, in which all instances of the same object are connected via IDREFs by a referred object node. Thereby, all instances of a common relative are also connected by a referred object node (Section 4.1). Another challenge appears when searching over an XML IDREF graph. Searching over graph-structured data has been known to be equivalent to the group Steiner tree problem, which is NP-Hard [3]. In contrast, keyword search on XML tree is much more efficient based on the hierarchical structure of XML tree. This is because the search in an XML tree can be reduced to find LCAs of matching nodes, which can be efficiently computed based on the longest common prefix of node labels.

To solve the above challenge, we discover that XML IDREF graph is a special graph. Particularly, it is an XML tree (with parent-child (PC) edges) plus a portion of *reference edges*. A reference edge is an IDREF from a referring node to a referred node. Although these nodes refer to the same object, we can treat them as having a parent-child relationship, in which the parent is the referring node and the child is the referred node. This shows that XML IDREF graph still has hierarchy, which enables us to generalize efficient techniques of LCA-based approaches (based on the hierarchy) for searching over an XML IDREF graph. Particularly, we use ancestor-descendant relationships among nodes for indexing (Section 4.2 and Section 4.3). Thereby, we do not have to traverse the XML IDREF graph when processing a query (Section 4.4).

4.1   Data Modeling

We propose virtual ID/IDREF mechanism, in which we assign a virtual referred object node as a hub to connect all instances of the same object by using virtual IDREF edges. The resulting model is called an XML IDREF graph. Intuitively, it is ID/IDREF mechanism, but we do not modify XML documents and IDREFs are virtually created just for finding common relatives. In the XML IDREF graph, there may co-exist both real and virtual IDREFs. For example, in the XML IDREF graph in Figure 6, LecturerA_(Ref1) and LecturerA_(Ref2) are instances of the same object and there are two virtual IDREFs to connect them with the virtual object node Referred_Lecturer_A.

To generate an XML IDREF graph from an XML document, we need to detect object instances of the same object. Since an object is identified by object class and OID, two object instances (object nodes as their representatives) are considered as the same object if they belong to the same *object class* and have the same *OID* value. In many cases, object classes (e.g., Lecturer, Course, Student, TA and R_group in Figure 2) and OIDs are directly available, because XML was initially designed based on them. When this is not the case, these values can be discovered from XML by our previous work [12], which achieve high accuracy (greater than 98% for object classes and greater than 93% for OIDs). Thus, we assume object classes and OIDs are available.

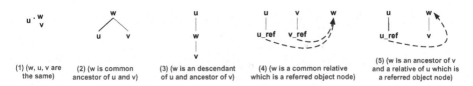

Fig. 7. Cases which w is a common relative of u and v

4.2 Identifying Relatives of a Node

To facilitate the search, we identify the set of relatives of a node in advance and maintain an index for the set of relatives for each object node. To solve challenges of identifying such sets, we propose the following properties about the relationships of relatives. Note that, as discussed in Section 4.1, the data is modeled as an XML IDREF graph which still has hierarchy. Thus, it contains ancestor-descendant relationships among nodes.

Property 6. *Among relatives of an object node u, potential common relatives of u and other object node(s) can only be ancestors of u or relatives of u which are also referred object nodes, i.e., object nodes with IDREFs as incoming edges.*

We discover that not all relatives can become common relatives. A common relative of more than one node must be able to connect multiple nodes. Thus, it can only fall into cases in Figure 7. We can ignore Case 3 because u is already the common ancestor of u and v in this case. Therefore, to be a potential common relative, a relative of a matching object node u must be u, or an ancestor of u, or a relative of u which is also a referred object node. Thereby, this saves index space significantly and therefore improves the efficiency of the search as well.

Example 4. *Recall Example 3 with Figure 6 to find answers for query {Student1, Student3}. By Property 6, the set of relatives of the keywords which can be potential common relatives are:*
- *For Student1: Student1, Course1, Referred_LecturerA and Referred_R_groupA*
- *For Student3: Student3, Course2, Referred_LecturerA and Referred_R_groupA*

where Student1 and Student3 are matching object nodes; Course1 and Course2 are ancestors of matching nodes; and Referred_LecturerA and Referred_R_groupA are referred object nodes. The common relatives are Referred_LecturerA and Referred_R_groupA. As can be seen, we can get the same answers as in Example 3 while the sets of relatives of keywords is much fewer. TA1, LecturerA_(Ref1) and R_groupA_(Ref1) (relatives of Student1); and LecturerA_(Ref2) and R_groupA_(Ref2) (relatives of Student3) are not considered because they cannot be a common relative.

Property 7. *Consider two sets $\mathbb{S}_1$ and $\mathbb{S}_2$ where (1) each set contains all object nodes of the same node path, (2) the node paths w.r.t. these two sets are different, and (3) these sets do not contain referred object nodes and are sorted by document order. If $u_i \in \mathbb{S}_1$ is a relative of $v_{j-1} \in \mathbb{S}_2$, but not a relative of $v_j \in \mathbb{S}_2$, then u_i will not be a relative of $v_k \in \mathbb{S}_2 \ \forall k > j$.*

This is because node $u_i \in \mathbb{S}_1$ can have many relatives in $\mathbb{S}_2$, but these relatives are continuous in $\mathbb{S}_2$ because the sets are sorted by document order as illustrated in Figure 8. Thus, instead of checking all nodes in $\mathbb{S}_2$, we can proactively stop the checking soon thanks to Property 7.

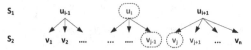

(if u_i is a relative of v_{j-1} but not a relative of v_j,
then it will not be a relative of v_{j+1} afterwards)

Fig. 8. Illustration for Property 7

Property 8. *In XML data, two nodes u and v are relative if and only if the path of their LCA corresponds to the path of the LCA of their schema nodes in XML schema. In other words, we have:*

$$path(LCA(u,v)) = path(LCA(schema(u), schema(v))) \leftrightarrow relative(u,v) = true$$

where schema(u) is the corresponding node in XML schema of node u.

This property is used to construct the set of relatives of a node efficiently. It is proved in [7] and is illustrated as follows. In Figure 6, we have: path(Course1) = path(Course2) = root/Course; and path(Student1) = root/Course/Student. Therefore, we have:

- path(LCA(Student1, Course 1)) = root/Course = path(LCA(schema(Student1), schema(Course 1))). Thus, Student1 and Course 1 are relatives.
- path(LCA(Student1, Course 2)) = root $\neq$ path(LCA(schema(Student1), schema(Course 2))) = root/Course. Thus, Student1 and Course 2 are not relatives.

Based on all the discussions above, we design an algorithm for constructing of the set of relatives of object nodes in Algorithm 1, for an object node u, we only consider nodes having different node path with $path(u)$ thank to Definition 1.

Algorithm 1: Find relatives of object nodes

   Input: All object nodes in an XML data
   Output: The set of relatives $Rel(u)$ of each object node u
1 **for** *each object node u in the data* **do**
2   **for** *each node path $p \neq path(u)$* (//Def.1) **do**
3          $v_{first} \leftarrow$ find the first relative of u
4   **for** *each node v after v_{first} having node path p* **do**
5   **if** $path(LCA(u,v))$ is $path(LCA(schema(u), schema(v)))$ (//Prop 8) **then**
6   flag = 1;
7   **if** *v is an ancestor of u* (//Prop 6) **then**
8   Add v to $Rel(u)$
9   **else**
10   (//Prop 6)
11                  $ref(v) \leftarrow$ object node referred by v
12   **if** $ref(v)$ *is not in $Rel(u)$* **then**
13   Add $ref(v)$ to $Rel(u)$
14   **else**
15   **if** *flag = 1* **then**
16   flag = 0;
17   break (for non-referred nodes) //Prop7

Space complexity. The space complexity for index is $N \times (H + R)$ where N is the number of *real object nodes* in the XML IDREF graph; H is the maximum number of *ancestors* of a real object nodes, which is equal to the height of the XML IDREF graph (XML IDREF graph still has hierarchy); and R is the maximum number of *referred object nodes* which are referred by the relatives of a real object node. N is much smaller than the number of nodes (including attributes and values) in an XML data. H is usually a very small number. Thus, the space for indexing is reasonable.

4.3   Labeling and Indexing

Labeling. We only label *object nodes*. All *non-object nodes* are assigned the same label with their corresponding object nodes. Thereby, the number of labels is largely reduced. We use *number* instead of Dewey for labeling because in XML IDREF graph, a node can have multiple parents. In addition, computation on number is faster than on Dewey since a Dewey label has multiple components to be accessed and computed. Each virtual node is also assigned a label which succeeds labels of real nodes.

Indexing. Each keyword k has a set $Rel(k)$ of relatives of *real object nodes* matching k. We have $Rel(k) = \bigcup Rel(u_i)$ where u_i is an object node matching k and $Rel(u_i)$ is the set of relatives of u_i. u_i must be an object node because of our labeling scheme, which helps reduce the index size dramatically. u_i is a real node because virtual nodes, which are created only for connecting instances of the same object, do not contain contents. To identify $Rel(u_i)$, we follow the properties and algorithm introduced in Section 4.2.

4.4 Processing

Thanks to the index where we already have the set of relatives of each keyword, the processing of our approach is very efficient as follows. Consider a query $Q = \{k_1, \ldots, k_n\}$. Let $CR(Q)$ denote the set of common relatives of Q. We have $CR(Q) = \bigcap_1^n Rel(k_i)$, where $Rel(k_i)$ denotes the set of relatives of nodes matching keyword k_i. Therefore, to find $CR(Q)$, we compute the intersection of sets $Rel(k_i)$'s;

The computation for set intersection can leverage any existing fast set intersection algorithms. The computation of set intersection has been used to find SLCA and ELCA in [16] and has been shown to be more efficient than the traditional computation based on common prefix of labels when dealing with XML tree.

5 Experiment

In this section, we evaluate the completeness, the soundness, the independence from schemas of our proposed CR semantics. We also make a comparison between our semantics and common ancestors, SLCAs and ELCAs [16]. Finally, we compare the efficiency of our approach with an LCA-based approach. The experiments were performed on an Intel(R) Core(TM) i7 CPU 3.4GHz with 8GB of RAM.

5.1 Experimental Setup

Dataset. We pre-processed two real datasets including **IMDb**[4], and **Basketball**[5]. We used the subsets with the sizes of 150MB and 86MB for IMDb and Basketball respectively. In IMDb, there are many ways to capture relationships between actors, actresses, movies, and companies. In Basketball, relationships between coaches, teams, and players also can be captured in different ways.

Creating Equivalent Databases. For each dataset, we manually designed all possible schemas. For example, there are three equivalent schemas for Basketball, corresponding to picking up three different object classes (Coach, Team, Player) as the root of the schema (Figure 9). Because of more equivalent schema designs for IMDb and due to space constraints, we do not show these schemas of IMDb. From the original databases, we automatically created the corresponding database for each schema of each dataset.

Query Set. We randomly generated 50 queries from document keywords. To avoid meaningless queries, we filtered out generated queries which do not contain any value keyword, such as queries contains only tags, or prepositions, or articles, e.g., query

---

[4] http://www.imdb.com/interfaces
[5] http://www.databasebasketball.com/stats_download.htm

Fig. 9. Three equivalent schema designs of Basketball dataset

{and, the, to}. 35 remaining queries include 20 and 12 queries for Basketball and IMDb datasets respectively.

Compared Algorithms. We compared our approach with an LCA-based approach to show the advantages of our approach over the LCA-based approaches. We chose Set-intersection [16] because it processes two popular semantics: SLCA and ELCA, because it is one of the most recent works, and because it outperforms other LCA-based approaches in term of efficiency.

5.2 Completeness

The completeness describes whether our semantics can return all common ancestors from all equivalent databases by using only one equivalent database. To study the completeness, for each query, we calculated the ratio of the number of CAs from all equivalent databases found in CRs from the original database over the total number of CAs from all equivalent databases, i.e., $\frac{A \cap B}{B}$, where A is the number of answers by our proposed CR semantics from only the original database, and B is the number of all common ancestors (CAs) for all equivalent databases. The checking has been done both automatically and with user study.

Automatically. We based on Definition 3 to check whether the two answers from equivalent databases are the same or not. We achieved the result of 100% for Basketball and 100% for IMDb. This is because based on the properties and definitions in Section 3.2, given a query Q to a database D, for any common ancestor of Q in some database equivalent to D, there always exists a common relative of Q in D.

Definition 3 (Answer-equivalent). *Given an n-keyword query Q, two answers of Q a_1 = $\langle c_1, \mathbb{K}_1 \rangle$ in schema S_1 where $\mathbb{K}_1 = \{u_1, \ldots, u_n\}$, and $a_2 = \langle c_2, \mathbb{K}_2 \rangle$ in schema S_2 where $\mathbb{K}_2 = \{v_1, \ldots, v_n\}$ are equivalent w.r.t. Q, denoted as $a_1 \equiv_Q a_2$ if*
- *c_1 and c_2 refer to the same object and*
- *u_i and v_i refer to the same object for all i.*

User Study. We asked 15 students in major of computer science to compare answers from different equivalent databases. Although the information for these answers are exactly the same by our Definition 3, they are represented in different ways due to different schemas such as two answers in Figure 3(a) and 3(c) or two answers in Figure 4(a) and 4(c). Thus, some users might think they are different. Therefore, we would like to study how users think about them. Surprisingly, we got the results of 100% for Basketball and 100% for IMDb from users. This implies that users share the same opinions with us on the similarity of answers.

5.3 Soundness

The soundness describes whether all answers (CRs) returned from our semantics can be common ancestors in other equivalent database(s). To study the soundness, for each query, we calculated the ratio of the number of CRs from the original database found in all CAs from all equivalent databases over the total number of CRs from the original database, i.e., $\frac{A \cap B}{A}$, where A and B have the same meanings in Section 5.2. The checking was also done both automatically and with user study. We compared the two answers in the same manner with the discussion in Section 5.2.

We got the result of 100% for both Basketball and IMDb for automatical checking. This is because based on the discussions in Section 3.2, for any common relative of a query Q to a database D, there exists a common ancestor of Q in some database equivalent to D. For user study, we also got the surprising results of 100% for both Basketball and IMDb. This implies the agreements of users on our theories.

5.4 Schema-Independence

To study the independence of our CR semantics from schemas, we checked whether the answer sets returned by the CR semantics from all equivalent databases are the same or not. The result is the ratio of the number of answers returned from all equivalent databases over the total number of distinct answers from all equivalent databases. We also performed this checking both automatically and with user study.

We achieved the result of 100% for Basketball and 100% for IMDb. This can be explained because the completeness and the soundness of our semantics are both 100%. This implies that for a query Q and two equivalent databases D and D'. If Ans is an answer of Q in D, then there exists an answer Ans' for Q in D' such that Ans' $\equiv_Q Ans'$ and vice versa. For user study, once again we got the result of 100% for Basketball and 100% for IMDb.

5.5 Comparing with SLCA and ELCA

For a given query Q, We have $CR(Q) \supseteq CA(Q) \supseteq ELCA(Q) \supseteq SLCA(Q)$. We ran our approach to find CAs and CRs while we ran Set-intersection [16] to find SLCAs and ELCAs. Figure 10 shows the percentages of $CA(Q)$, $ELCA(Q)$ and $SLCA(Q)$ in $CR(Q)$ for the original databases. The results are similar for the two datasets. As can be seen, CAs is just around one third of CRs, and SLCAs and ELCAs are around 15% to 20% of CRs. This implies that

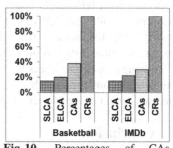

Fig. 10. Percentages of CAs, ELCAs, SLCAs in CRs

our CR semantics improves the recall significantly by providing much more meaningful answers.

5.6 Efficiency Evaluation

The response time of our approach and Set-intersection [16] is shown in Figure 11, in which we varied the number of query keywords and the number of matching nodes. Although our approach has to process more matching nodes because of the relatives, its response time is faster than the Set-intersection because of two reasons. Firstly, by

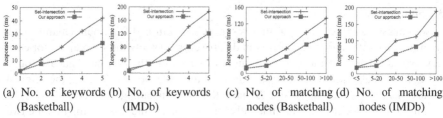

(a) No. of keywords (b) No. of keywords   (c) No. of matching (d) No. of matching
    (Basketball)   (IMDb)   nodes (Basketball)   nodes (IMDb)

Fig. 11. Efficiency evaluation

only labeling object nodes and assign all non-objects nodes the same labels with the corresponding object nodes, the number of matching nodes for a keyword query is reduced. Secondly, Set-intersection has two phases for finding CAs and filtering some CAs to find SLCAs and ELCAs. In contrast, the processing of our approach is only similar to the first phase of Set-intersection.

6   Related Work

LCA-based approaches. XKSearch [15] defines Smallest LCAs (SLCAs) to be the LCAs that do not contain other LCAs. Meaningful LCA (MLCA) [13] incorporates SLCA into XQuery. VLCA [10] and ELCA [17] introduces the concept of valuable/ exclusive LCA to improve the effectiveness of SLCA. XReal [1] proposes an approach based on Information Retrieval techniques. MESSIAH [14] handles cases of missing values in optional attributes. Recently, XRich [8] takes common descendants into account of answers.

Graph-based approaches. Graph-based approaches can be classified based on the semantics such as the Steiner tree [2], distinct root [4] and subgraph [11,5]. Later, [9] propose an approach to model XML data as a so-called OR graph. For an XML document with ID/IDREF, graph-based approaches such as [11,5] can provide more answers by following IDREFs. However, those graph-based approaches can do that only if XML documents contain ID/IDREF. Otherwise, those graph-based approaches do not recognize instances of the same object and may still miss meaningful answers.

Although extensive works have been done on improving the effectiveness, no work can provides answers which are independent from schema designs, and their returned answers cannot cover answers which can be found from other schema designs.

7   Conclusion

We have argued that meaningful answers can be found beyond common ancestors and when users issue a query, their expectations are independent from the schema designs. Based on these arguments, we proposed a novel semantics called CR (Common Relative), which returns all common relatives of matching nodes as answers. Our proposed CR semantics not only provides more meaningful answers than common ancestors, but these answers are independent from schema designs of the same data content as well. We proposed an approach to find answers based on the CR semantics in which we introduced properties of relatives and designed an algorithm to find relatives of a node effectively and efficiently. Experimental results showed that our semantics possesses the properties of completeness, soundness and independence from schema designs while the response time is faster than an LCA-based approach because we only work with object nodes.

References

1. Bao, Z., Ling, T.W., Chen, B., Lu, J.: Efficient XML keyword search with relevance oriented ranking. In: ICDE (2009)
2. Ding, B., Yu, J.X., Wang, S., Qin, L., Zhang, X., Lin, X.: Finding top-k min-cost connected trees in database. In: ICDE (2007)
3. Dreyfus, S.E., Wagner, R.A.: The steiner problem in graphs. Networks (1971)
4. He, H., Wang, H., Yang, J., Yu, P.S.: BLINKS: ranked keyword searches on graphs. In: SIGMOD (2007)
5. Kargar, M., An, A.: Keyword search in graphs: finding r-cliques. PVLDB (2011)
6. Kim, J., Jeong, D., Baik, D.-K.: A translation algorithm for effective RDB-to-XML schema conversion considering referential integrity information. Journal Inf. Sci. Eng. (2009)
7. Le, T.N., Bao, Z., Ling, T.W.: Schema-independent XML keyword search. TRA6/14, Technical Report, School of Computing, National University of Singapore (2014)
8. Le, T.N., Ling, T.W., Jagadish, H.V., Lu, J.: Object semantics for XML keyword search. In: Bhowmick, S.S., Dyreson, C.E., Jensen, C.S., Lee, M.L., Muliantara, A., Thalheim, B. (eds.) DASFAA 2014, Part II. LNCS, vol. 8422, pp. 311–327. Springer, Heidelberg (2014)
9. Le, T.N., Wu, H., Ling, T.W., Li, L., Lu, J.: From structure-based to semantics-based: Effective XML keyword search. In: Ng, W., Storey, V.C., Trujillo, J.C. (eds.) ER 2013. LNCS, vol. 8217, pp. 356–371. Springer, Heidelberg (2013)
10. Li, G., Feng, J., Wang, J., Zhou, L.: Effective keyword search for valuable LCAs over XML documents. In: CIKM (2007)
11. Li, G., Ooi, B.C., Feng, J., Wang, J., Zhou, L.: EASE: Efficient and adaptive keyword search on unstructured, semi-structured and structured data. In: SIGMOD (2008)
12. Li, L., Le, T.N., Wu, H., Ling, T.W., Bressan, S.: Discovering semantics from data-centric XML. In: Decker, H., Lhotská, L., Link, S., Basl, J., Tjoa, A.M. (eds.) DEXA 2013, Part I. LNCS, vol. 8055, pp. 88–102. Springer, Heidelberg (2013)
13. Li, Y., Yu, C., Jagadish, H.V.: Schema-free XQuery. In: VLDB (2004)
14. Truong, B.Q., Bhowmick, S.S., Dyreson, C.E., Sun, A.: MESSIAH: missing element-conscious SLCA nodes search in XML data. In: SIGMOD (2013)
15. Xu, Y., Papakonstantinou, Y.: Efficient keyword search for smallest LCAs in XML databases. In: SIGMOD (2005)
16. Zhou, J., Bao, Z., Wang, W., Ling, T.W., Chen, Z., Lin, X., Guo, J.: Fast SLCA and ELCA computation for XML keyword queries based on set intersection. In: ICDE (2012)
17. Zhou, R., Liu, C., Li, J.: Fast ELCA computation for keyword queries on XML data. In: EDBT (2010)

Mapping Heterogeneous XML Document Collections to Relational Databases

Prudhvi Janga and Karen C. Davis

Department of Electrical Engineering and Computing Systems
University of Cincinnati, Cincinnati, Ohio, USA
jangapi@mail.uc.edu, karen.davis@uc.edu

Abstract. XML web data is heterogeneous in terms of content and tagging of information. Integrating, querying, and presenting heterogeneous collections presents many challenges. The structure of XML documents is useful for achieving these tasks; however, not every XML document on the web includes a schema. We propose and implement a framework for efficient schema extraction, integration, and relational schema mapping from heterogeneous XML documents collected from the web. Our approach uses the Schema Extended Context Free Grammar (SECFG) to model XML schemas and transform them into relational schemas. Unlike other implementations, our approach is also able to identify and transform many XML constraints into relational schema constraints while supporting multiple XML schema languages, e.g., DTD or XSD, or no XML schema, as input. We compare our approach with other proposed approaches and conclude that we offer better functionality more efficiently and with greater flexibility.

Keywords: XML schema, schema mapping, XML to relational schema mapping, schema integration, schema extraction, schema discovery.

1 Introduction

The wide range and volume of web data available in tabular and semi-structured formats motivates creation of techniques for efficient and flexible integration and exchange of this data. The overall goal of our research is integrating tabular and semi-structured web data so that it can be published in a uniform format. Our focus is on extracting schemas from web tables [11] and XML data [12], integrating the results, and publishing the integrated data in either relational or XML formats. In this paper, we illustrate how heterogeneous XML document collections, with or without schemas, can be integrated and then mapped to a relational representation that preserves constraints inherent in the XML data using relational constraints.

We utilize a context-free grammar to represent an XML schema. This has several advantages. One, we can extract an XML schema (as a grammar) from a schema-less document or we can represent any XML schema (e.g., DTD or XSD) as a grammar so that our approach is source format independent. Two, we can transform the grammar to any XML schema language, so our results are also target XML format independent.

E. Yu et al. (Eds.): ER 2014, LNCS 8824, pp. 86–99, 2014.
© Springer International Publishing Switzerland 2014

Three, since the approach supports generalization of a grammar through similarity matching of non-terminal symbols, grammars from heterogeneous (non-identical) sources can be merged using the same techniques we use to create a grammar from an XML document [12]. Four, the grammar can be used to effectively map XML documents and their inherent constraints to a relational schema with constraints. Previously proposed techniques for XML to relational mapping [1, 2, 3, 4, 6, 7, 8, 15, 16, 18, 19, 22, 24, 25, 26] do not address any/all of the constraints we do, and only a few of these techniques are language independent [18, 19]. In addition, only a few techniques handle recursion [2, 3] and do not require schema simplification [6, 7, 8, 18, 22, 26]; our approach has both of these advantages as well. Previous approaches to XML schema integration [5, 9, 13, 14, 17, 20, 30] do not consider heterogeneous collections; i.e., all of the documents to be merged must have the same or highly similar structures. We compare the time and schema quality of our mapping approach to other related techniques and demonstrate that our approach is more flexible, captures more semantics, and has better performance.

The reminder of this paper is organized as follows. Section 2 reviews how an XML document (or schema) is represented as a grammar and how this also accomplishes merging of heterogeneous XML schemas. Section 3 describes XML to relational schema mapping algorithms and provides an example. Section 4 presents experimental results. We conclude with a discussion of future work in Section 5.

2   Merging XML Schemas

XML schema generation for a given XML document normally involves three main steps: extraction of XML elements, simplification/generalization to obtain the structure of the document, and transformation of the structure into an XML schema definition. Simplification or generalization of elements to generate good DTDs using regular expressions [9, 14] only works with DTDs and does not address complete schema generation. Simplification or generalization of elements using tree construction has been proposed [13, 20], but there are no individual XML document schemas available except for the merged final schema after the process is complete. Some research efforts [5, 21, 28] use grammars for modeling XML document structure. However, these efforts do not produce a complete XML schema that represents the XML document collection, and the extraction and integration of XML schemas are combined into a single stage. Min et al. [17] propose a schema extraction system that supports the generation of a DTD and XSD from XML documents, but it does not guarantee the completeness of the generated schema. Xing et al. [30] focus on schema extraction from a large collection of XML documents, but the approach does not support complete XML schema generation, heterogeneous collections, and multiple schema languages.

We leverage the extraction process to merge generated schemas. Our approach offers the following advantages. Our technique works well with large collections of both homogenous and heterogeneous data and produces an integrated view of the XML data by clustering similar XML document data together. Our integration technique produces one or more merged schemas from a given collection of XML documents based on the structure of documents present in a given collection. This helps to avoid over-fitting the given collection or failing to represent all the documents. Our approach also separates the extraction and integration of XML schemas into two different stages to achieve better real-time performance and guarantee reusability.

2.1   Schema Generation

The three main steps for XML schema generation are (1) structured example creation, (2) generation of a corresponding context-free grammar, and (3) generalizing the grammar [12]. Since this grammar is also used here for XML schema integration and generation of relational schemas, the definition and an example are provided below.

We model an XML schema by creating a grammar called the Schema Extended Context-Free Grammar (SECFG), an extension of ECFG [5]. The SECFG grammar addresses features such as attribute detection, order of child elements, number of child elements and detection of default, fixed, and substitution group values for elements and attributes, along with all other features already addressed using ECFG modeling.

Formally, a Schema Extended Context Free Grammar is defined by a 5-tuple $G = (T, N, P, \delta, start)$ where T, N, and P are disjoint sets of terminals, non-terminals, and properties, respectively. Each property in P is defined over an empty set (any value) or an enumeration or a range of values it can accept. The symbol $start$ is an initial non-terminal and δ is a finite set of production rules of the form $A \rightarrow \alpha$ for $A \in N$, where α is an extended regular expression over terms, where each term is a terminal-properties-nonterminal-terminal sequence such as $tpBt'$ where t, t' are a pair of opening and closing tags, respectively, and $t, t' \in T$, $B \in N$ and $p \in P$. The expression $tpBt'$ can be abbreviated as $tp:B$ without loss of information. The properties inside a properties tag are defined as a semicolon-delimited list of strings where each string is denoted by $P=a$, where P represents the name of the property (attribute name) and a represents the value of the property. A properties tag that accompanies a terminal symbol summarizes features such as order, number of child elements, data type, default value, and fixed values.

We represent an XML document as a structured example [5] and induce an SECFG from this structured example by traversing the tree in a depth-first approach. Every time we encounter an unknown node in the structured example tree, we add a production to the SECFG being generated and traverse the unknown node under consideration to complete the right side of the production. Since the grammar represents the complete document structure, there are numerous productions that are structurally identical. To achieve conciseness, generalization removes duplicate productions and merges productions with similar content and context [5].

2.2   Schema Integration

The XML schema integration step aims at generating a schema that is adequate to describe the collection of XML documents under consideration but not too generic such that it could describe many other XML documents not under consideration. The XML schema integration technique involves merging multiple individual schemas into a final schema. We merge multiple grammars to produce an integrated SECFG by utilizing the generalization process introduced above as the final step of schema generation. Any grammars that could not be merged in this stage are marked as independent grammars. An overview of our process is shown in Fig. 1. A schema (grammar) is created for each document in a heterogeneous collection, then this set of grammars is further generalized to create a merged schema (grammar). The resulting merged schema can then be used to produce XML schemas (e.g., DTD or XSD) or relational schemas with constraints.

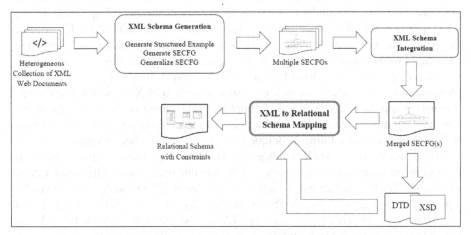

Fig. 1. XML Schema Extraction, Integration and Relational Mapping Framework

3   XML to Relational Schema Mapping

There are four main steps in our XML to relational schema mapping process shown in Fig. 2. Once a merged SECFG is obtained, the schema mapping from SECFG to a relational schema is performed. This mapping starts by generating element ancestry followed by an inlining operation on the SECFG. Inlining is the process that merges child productions with parent productions to reduce the number of relations obtained in the final relational schema. After inlining, relations and relational constraints are generated from the grammar. Each of the steps in the process is explained below.

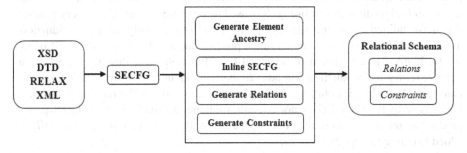

Fig. 2. Overview of XML to Relational Schema Mapping Process

3.1   Inlining an SECFG

Generate Element Ancestry recursively iterates through every production of the SECFG grammar to create a list of parent-child pairs of non-terminal elements. The non-terminal ancestry is useful for deciding if a given non-terminal can be inlined into its parent. Nested elements are flattened rather than having each element generate a new relational table.

The idea behind our inlining approach is similar to the hybrid inlining mechanism proposed by Shanmugasundaram et al. [24]. We select the hybrid approach among other approaches such as basic inlining, shared inlining, and ODTDMap [2] because the hybrid approach combines the join reduction properties of basic inlining with the advantages of the shared inlining approach such as a lower number of relations. Although our approach is inspired by the hybrid technique, it is different from an implementation perspective as we utilize a grammar instead of XML schema languages. The hybrid approach [24] works on a simplified DTD, therefore it cannot translate a schema without information loss, and it does not handle recursion and relational constraints. However, our inlining technique provides all of those improvements.

The algorithm *Inline SECFG* inlines a non-terminal production into its parent if none of its parent production(s) contain more than one occurrence of the non-terminal production. To illustrate an inlined schema, consider the DTD and XSD examples for a product catalog given in Fig. 3. The Product Catalog DTD or XSD can have at most one occurrence of *OPTIONS* and *NOTES* in the element *PRODUCT*. Hence, *OPTIONS* and *NOTES* can be inlined into the non-terminal production representing *PRODUCT*. The non-inlined productions and the corresponding inlined SECFG are shown in Fig. 4. The highlighted part shows that all the attributes of *OPTIONS* and *NOTES* have been inlined into the *ProductType* non-terminal production representing the element *PRODUCT* and their non-terminal productions have been removed from the inlined grammar. The properties of the attributes of *OPTIONS* and *NOTES* have not been shown in Fig. 4 due to space constraints. The result of inlining an SECFG is a generalized grammar with fewer productions.

3.2   Generating Relations and Constraints from an Inlined SECFG

The last step of our XML to relational schema mapping process involves the generation of relations and constraints from the inlined SECFG. The *Generate Relations and Constraints* algorithm shown in Fig. 5 is used to generate a relation for every production in the inlined grammar. It takes a production *Prod* (initially the *start* production) as input and for every non-terminal in the production, the algorithm calls itself recursively. If *Prod* is not visited (determined by a function call), then it creates a new relation *rel* for the production and adds to the relation an *ID* column with unique key constraint. We add this column to make sure that every row in the relation is uniquely identifiable even if *Prod* does not contain a unique attribute. If *Prod* has a parent production and occurs more than once in the parent then another column, *ParentID,* is added to enforce referential integrity.

```
<?xml version="1.0" encoding="utf-8"?>
<xs:schema xmlns:xs="http://www.w3.org/2001/XMLSchema" xmlns="Product Catalog.dtd"
xmlns:wmh="http://www.wmhelp.com/2003/eGenerator" elementFormDefault="qualified"
targetNamespace="Product Catalog.dtd">
  <xs:element name="CATALOG">
    <xs:complexType>
      <xs:sequence>
        <xs:element ref="PRODUCT" maxOccurs="unbounded"/>
      </xs:sequence>
    </xs:complexType>
  </xs:element>
  <xs:element name="PRODUCT">
    <xs:complexType>
      <xs:sequence>
        <xs:element ref="SPECIFICATIONS" maxOccurs="unbounded"/>
        <xs:element ref="OPTIONS" minOccurs="0"/>
        <xs:element ref="PRICE" maxOccurs="unbounded"/>
        <xs:element ref="NOTES" minOccurs="0"/>
      </xs:sequence>
      <xs:attribute name="NAME" type="xs:string"/>
      <xs:attribute name="CATEGORY" default="HandTool">
        <xs:simpleType>
          <xs:restriction base="xs:NMTOKEN">
            <xs:enumeration value="HandTool"/>
            <xs:enumeration value="Table"/>
            <xs:enumeration value="Shop-Professional"/>
          </xs:restriction>
        </xs:simpleType>
      </xs:attribute>
      <xs:attribute name="PARTNUM" type="xs:string"/>
      <xs:attribute name="PLANT" default="Chicago">
        <xs:simpleType>
          <xs:restriction base="xs:NMTOKEN">
            <xs:enumeration value="Pittsburgh"/>
            <xs:enumeration value="Milwaukee"/>
            <xs:enumeration value="Chicago"/>
          </xs:restriction>
        </xs:simpleType>
      </xs:attribute>
```

```
<!ELEMENT CATALOG (PRODUCT+)>

<!ELEMENT PRODUCT (SPECIFICATIONS+,OPTIONS?,PRICE+,NOTES?)>
<!ATTLIST PRODUCT NAME CDATA #IMPLIED>
<!ATTLIST PRODUCT CATEGORY (HandTool|Table|Shop-Professional) "HandTool">
<!ATTLIST PRODUCT PARTNUM CDATA #IMPLIED>
<!ATTLIST PRODUCT PLANT (Pittsburgh|Milwaukee|Chicago) "Chicago">
<!ATTLIST PRODUCT INVENTORY (InStock|Backordered|Discontinued) "InStock">

<!ELEMENT SPECIFICATIONS (#PCDATA)>
<!ATTLIST SPECIFICATIONS WEIGHT CDATA #IMPLIED>
<!ATTLIST SPECIFICATIONS POWER CDATA #IMPLIED>

<!ELEMENT OPTIONS (#PCDATA)>
<!ATTLIST OPTIONS FINISH (Metal|Polished|Matte) "Matte">
<!ATTLIST OPTIONS ADAPTER (Included|Optional|NotApplicable) "Included">
<!ATTLIST OPTIONS CASE (HardShell|Soft|NotApplicable) "HardShell">

<!ELEMENT PRICE (#PCDATA)>
<!ATTLIST PRICE MSRP CDATA #IMPLIED>
<!ATTLIST PRICE WHOLESALE CDATA #IMPLIED>
<!ATTLIST PRICE STREET CDATA #IMPLIED>
<!ATTLIST PRICE SHIPPING CDATA #IMPLIED>

<!ELEMENT NOTES (#PCDATA)>
```

Fig. 3. Product Catalog Example

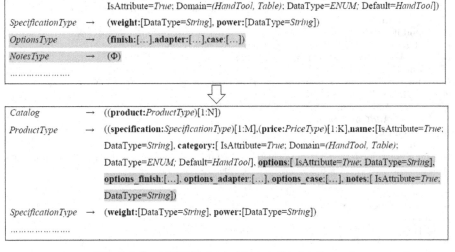

Fig. 4. Inlined SECFG for the Product Catalog Example

If the production *Prod* has multiple parents then another column is added, *Parent-Type*, to detect to which parent type a row belongs. The *ParentType* column contains the full name of the XML elements that the current *Prod* is a child of. For example, *ParentType* of a row in a *paragraph* table can be *section.subsection* or *article.body.abstract*. In the next step, a column/attribute for every terminal *T* in the production is generated and added to the relation *rel*. All the constraints that can be applied to this column are determined from the properties tag of the terminal symbol using the *AddConstraints* algorithm and added to the relation. After this step, the algorithm iterates through every non-terminal production to add a column to the relation *rel* and also call the *AddConstraints* algorithm again to find constraints and add them to the relation. Once all the steps are complete, the relation with its constraints *rel* is added to the relational schema *R*.

The algorithm *Add Constraints* (not shown due to space constraints) adds relational constraints and also generates some columns if the current item *I* (non-terminal or terminal) contains any attributes in the properties tag. If the properties of the item *I* contain an *IsNullable* property for the item, then a column-level *null* constraint is

---

Algorithm : *GenerateRelationsandConstraints(Prod, R)*

Input: Non-terminal production: *Prod*

Output: Relational schema with constraints: *R*

```
 1: BEGIN
 2: for every non-terminal, N in production, Prod do
 3:     GenerateRelationsandConstraints(N_{production}, R)
 4: end for
 5: if Prod is not Visited then                              ▷ Visted is a function call
 6:     Initialize a new relation, rel
 7:     rel.Name=Prod.Name
 8:     Add ID column to relation, rel
 9:     if Prod has parent(s) then
10:         Add ParentID column to relation, rel
11:         if Prod occurs multiple times in parent(s) then
12:             Add column level foreign key constraint on column ParentID, refering parent type ID
13:         end if
14:     end if
15:     if Prod has more than one parent then
16:         Add ParentType column to relation, rel
17:     end if
18:     for every terminal, T in production, Prod do
19:         if not T.Name =ID then
20:             Add column with name, T.Name to relation, rel
21:             AddConstraints(T, rel)
22:         end if
23:     end for
24:     for every non-terminal, I in production, Prod do    ▷ considers only inlined non-terminals
25:         Add column with name, I.Name to relation, rel
26:         AddConstraints(I, rel)
27:     end for
28:     Add the relation with constraints, rel to R
29: end if
30: END
```

Fig. 5. Algorithm to Generate Relations and Constraints from Inlined SECFG

added; similarly for default or fixed values, unique key constraints, and domain constraints. In the same way, if the attributes inside the properties tag contain any such metadata then constraints are generated from that information and added to the relation. The properties tag of a terminal or a non-terminal present in an SECFG grammar is populated with all this information such as *IsNullable, IsUnique,* and *DefaultOrFixValue* when a grammar is generated and generalized for a given DTD or XSD [12]. Table 1 summarizes XML DTD and XSD constraint constructs, and how they are represented in an SECFG and translated to relational schema constraints.

Table 1. Mapping XML Constraints from an SECFG to the Relational Model

DTD Construct	XSD Construct	SECFG	Relational Schema
* versus +	minOccurs	Properties.IsNullable	NULL Constraint
CDATA "*default_value*"	default="*default_value*"	Properties.IsDefaultorFixValue	Default Constraint
#FIXED "fixed_value"	fixed="*fixed_value*"	Properties.IsDefaultorFixValue Properties.DomainValues	Default & Domain Constraints
ID	ID	Properties.IsUnique	Unique Constraint
attribute-name *(en1|en2|..)*	<xs:restriction/>	Properties.DomainValues	Domain Constraint
IDREF, IDREFS, *, +	IDREF, IDREFS, minOccurs, maxOccurs	Non-terminal and Terminal Symbols	Foreign Key Constraint
CDATA, PCDATA	String, Date, Numeric etc.	Properties.DataType	Column Data Type

The output of the XML to relational schema mapping process contains relations and constraints. Fig. 6 shows an excerpt of the output generated from our application after the mapping process is complete. It can be observed from Figures 3, 4 and 6 that some XML elements such as CATALOG and PRODUCT have been translated into separate relations while some elements such as OPTIONS have been inlined under other relations (e.g, PRODUCT). Fig. 6 also shows relational constraints such as Entity Integrity, Domain, NULL, and CHECK on different attributes of the PRODUCT relation that have been generated by identifying and translating related XML constraints.

CATALOG

ID	Info/Name

CONSTRAINTS
EntityIntegrity:: [Column:ID] [Expression:PRIMARY KEY] [ColumnLevel:True]
NULLVal:: [Column:Info/Name] [Expression:NULLABLE] [ColumnLevel:True]

PRODUCT

ID	ParentID	NAME	CATEGORY	PARTNUM	PLANT	INVENTORY	OPTIONS	OP

CONSTRAINTS
EntityIntegrity:: [Column:ID] [Expression:PRIMARY KEY] [ColumnLevel:True]
ReferentialIntegrity:: [Column:ParentID] [Expression:FOREIGN KEY REFERENCES (CATALOG)] [Co
NULLVal:: [Column:NAME] [Expression:NULLABLE] [ColumnLevel:True]
NULLVal:: [Column:CATEGORY] [Expression:NULLABLE] [ColumnLevel:True]
DefaultVal:: [Column:CATEGORY] [Expression:DEFAULT ((HandTool))] [ColumnLevel:True]
Check:: [Column:CATEGORY] [Expression:DOMAIN VALUES WITHIN (HandTool|Table|Shop-Profes

Fig. 6. Mapping XML Constraints from an SECFG to the Relational Model

4   Experimental Results

In this section we discuss results of experiments carried out to test the validity and efficiency of our approach. We quantitatively evaluate our schema mapping technique using 15 DTDs that are obtained from the XBench XML Benchmark [23], World Wide Web Consortium [27], and XML cover pages [29]. We ran the schema mapping process 1000 times on every DTD. For evaluation purposes, the counts of * and + operators have been obtained along with the number of relations/tables present in each schema. Table 2 lists results for 10 of the DTD documents that are used subsequently for comparison to other approaches, including the size of the documents, running time for the algorithm, and counts of elements and attributes. Our schema mapping technique reduces the number of tables in comparison to the number of elements present in an XML schema. Sections 4.1 and 4.2 replicate previously published experimental results for our system compared to those in the literature.

Table 2. Experimental Results of Schema Mapping Technique for 10 DTDs

DTD File	File Size	# of Elements	# of Attributes	# of * Operators	# of + Operators	# of Tables	Running Time (ms)
Address.dtd	377	7	1	0	2	3	7
Article.dtd	1071	26	4	4	6	8	64
Book Catalog.dtd	2564	50	8	1	4	5	108
Countries.dtd	262	5	1	0	1	2	3
Customer.dtd	982	18	1	0	1	2	16
Item.dtd	942	19	1	0	2	3	18
News Paper.dtd	571	7	4	0	1	2	5
Order.dtd	1423	27	2	1	1	3	30
Product Catalog.dtd	1125	6	14	0	3	4	5
TV Schedule.dtd	581	10	5	0	4	5	12

4.1   Schema Mapping Performance

We compare the performance of our schema mapping technique with ODTDMap [2] as it is the only similar research effort providing experimental results, and they show that their technique outperforms other previously proposed techniques. We compare the two approaches for the same 6 DTDs selected by Atay et al. from the XBench XML Benchmark [23]. Since the platform used to develop and test our approach is different than theirs, we use a normalized time comparison. It can be observed from Fig. 7 that our approach performs on par with ODTDMap despite the fact that it performs an additional step to transform the DTD to an SECFG grammar. Similar to the ODTDMap results [2], the running time of the algorithm is proportional to the number of elements in the DTD (since each element is visited only once); this shows that our approach, like ODTDMap, is scalable.

Our approach generally produces fewer tables while preserving all the schema information after transformation (in addition to what the ODTDMap approach preserves) because it extends hybrid inlining, while ODTDMap uses shared inlining. Hence, we typically produce more compact schemas and require fewer joins to answer queries while preserving more schema information.

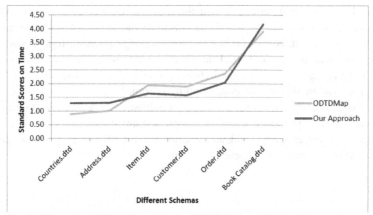

Fig. 7. Normalized Time Comparison of ODTDMap with Our Approach

4.2   Query Processing Capability and Efficiency

To evaluate the accuracy of the relational schema produced by our schema mapping technique we consider its ability to answer mapped queries as well as the efficiency of evaluating those queries. Shanmugasundaram et al. [24] present algorithms to translate XML path expressions into relational (SQL) queries and evaluate the accuracy and effectiveness of several inlining techniques for the mapped relational schemas over the mapped queries. The mapped SQL queries are either a single query or a union of single queries, each of which may contain one or more joins. For each algorithm, DTD, and path expression of length N, they measure: (1) q: the average number of SQL queries, (2) j: the average number of joins in each SQL query, and (3) tj: the total average number of joins ($q*j$). We compute the same metrics for selected DTDs, XPATH expressions (lengths 3 and 4) [24], and SQL queries (an example is shown in Table 3). Our results for XPATH expressions of length 3 are comparable to or better than results obtained using the original hybrid inlining approach [24]. The ability to answer the mapped queries with the mapped relational schemas indicates correctness (no information loss) of our XML to relational mapping approach. Since XML elements become tables, and the number of tables is always less than or equal to the number of XML elements in our approach, there is no information added. Redundancy is removed by the grammar generalization step.

Table 3. XPATH Expressions for an Example DTD and Equivalent SQL Queries

XPATH Expression	XPATH Expression Length	Equivalent SQL Query
Product Catalog		
/CATALOG/PRODUCT/[@PARTNUM='123']	3	select p.* from catalog c inner join product p on c.id=p.parentid where p.partnum='123'
/CATALOG/PRODUCT/[@PARTNUM='123']/SPECIFICATIONS	4	select s.* from catalog c inner join product p on c.id=p.parentid join specifications s on s.parentid=p.id where p.partnum='123'
/CATALOG/PRODUCT[PRICE>100]/NOTES	3	select p.notes from catalog c inner join product p on c.id=p.parentid join price pr on pr.parentid=p.id where pr.msrp>100

It can be observed from Fig. 8 that the average number of joins per SQL query (generated for expressions of length 3) is almost the same for both the approaches while the average number of queries and total average joins is slightly lower for our approach when compared to the hybrid. However, the differences are very minor. Our approach performs on par with the hybrid approach and also includes semantic constraint preservation after the schema mapping is complete.

The results obtained from replicating two published experiments indicate that the relational schemas produced using our approach are created at least as efficiently, generally have fewer tables, and are as effective for relational query processing as schemas produced by other mapping techniques.

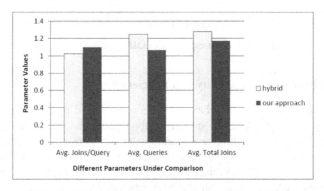

Fig. 8. SQL Query Comparison of the Hybrid Approach and Our Approach

5   Conclusions and Future Work

We introduce the problem of extraction, integration and relational mapping of XML schemas from heterogeneous collections of XML documents. The SECFG grammar that is used to generate DTDs or XSDs from XML documents and merge them [12] is used here to map an XML schema to the relational model. Unlike many other approaches that support XML to relational schema mapping for specific XML languages, our approach is adaptable to any XML schema language because of the intermediate form (SECFG) used to transform the schema language into the relational model. The schemas produced are also accurate as our approach generates relations and preserves semantic constraints present in XML schemas by generating equivalent relational constraints. We describe experimental studies that evaluate the efficiency and the quality of the relational schemas. We perform experiments using synthetic as well as real-world datasets and compare results from our approach to the ODTDMap and hybrid inlining approaches; we conclude that our approach performs on par with or better than all previous approaches.

As our research addresses web data where heterogeneous web data sources are integrated, we do not preserve the order of sub-elements in the merged schema. To make our approach useful for other applications we would like to develop an innovative approach to preserve the order of sub-elements. Existing techniques to track element order can be easily incorporated into the relations generated by adding columns to track element order [2, 24]. However, maintaining element order by adding extra columns for every inlined element doubles the size of the relation, thereby impacting query cost and performance. Hence, as future work, we would like to develop a solution to track element order while keeping the size of the relations the same by incorporating other element order schemes developed for schema oblivious XML to relational mapping [2, 3, 8]. A survey by Haw et al. [10] describes other research addressing storage of XML schemas in relational databases and reconstruction of the original XML from this mapping.

In our ongoing work, we are working on transforming relational schemas obtained from schema-less web data sources (tabular web data) [11] to XML schemas using the SECFG grammar towards achieving our goal of presenting heterogeneous web data in a uniform format.

References

1. Ahmad, K.: A comparative analysis of managing XML data in relational database. In: Nguyen, N.T., Kim, C.-G., Janiak, A. (eds.) ACIIDS 2011, Part I. LNCS, vol. 6591, pp. 100–108. Springer, Heidelberg (2011)
2. Atay, M., Chebotko, A., Liu, D., Lu, S., Fotouhi, F.: Efficient schema-based XML-to-Relational data mapping. Information Systems 32(3), 458–476 (2006)
3. Abdel-Aziz, A.A., Oakasha, H.: Mapping XML DTDs to relational schemas. In: Proceedings of the 3rd International Conference on Computer Systems and Applications (AICCSA 2005), Cairo, Egypt, January 3-6, pp. 47–50 (2005)
4. Bohannon, P., Freire, J., Roy, P., Siméon, J.: From XML schema to relations: A cost-based approach to XML storage. In: Proceedings of 18th International Conference on Data Engineering (ICDE 2002), San Jose, California, USA, February 26-March 1, pp. 64–75 (2002)
5. Chidlovskii, B.: Schema extraction from XML collections. In: Proceedings of the 2nd ACM/IEEE-CS Joint Conference on Digital Libraries, Portland, Oregon, USA, June 14-18, pp. 291–292 (2002)
6. Deutsch, A., Fernandez, M., Suciu, D.: Storing semistructured data with STORED. ACM SIGMOD Record 28(2) (1999)
7. Florescu, D., Kossmann, D.: Storing and Querying XML Data using an RDMBS. IEEE Data Engineering. Bull. 22(3), 27–34 (1999)
8. Fujimoto, K., Shimizu, T., DinhKha, D., Yoshikawa, M., Amagasa, T.: A Mapping Scheme of XML Documents into Relational Databases using Schema-based Path Identifiers. In: Proceedings of the International Workshop on Web Information Retrieval and Integration (WIRI 2005), Tokyo, Japan, April 8-9, pp. 82–90 (2005)
9. Garofalakis, M.N., Gionis, A., Rastogi, R., Seshadri, S., Shim, K.: XTRACT: A system for extracting document type descriptors from XML documents. In: Proceedings of the 2000 ACM SIGMOD International Conference on Management of Data, Dallas, Texas, USA, May 16-18, pp. 165–176 (2000)
10. Haw, S.-C., Lee, C.-S.: Data storage practices and query processing in XML databases: A survey. Knowledge-Based Systems 24(8), 1317–1340 (2011)
11. Janga, P., Davis, K.C.: Tabular web data: schema discovery and integration. In: Bellatreche, L., Mohania, M.K. (eds.) DaWaK 2013. LNCS, vol. 8057, pp. 26–33. Springer, Heidelberg (2013)

12. Janga, P., Davis, K.C.: Schema extraction and integration of heterogeneous XML document collections. In: Cuzzocrea, A., Maabout, S. (eds.) MEDI 2013. LNCS, vol. 8216, pp. 176–187. Springer, Heidelberg (2013)

13. Jung, J.-S., Oh, D.-I., Kong, Y.-H., Ahn, J.-K.: Extracting information from XML documents by reverse generating a DTD. In: Proceedings of the 1st EurAsian Conference on Information and Communication Technology (EurAsia ICT), Shiraz, Iran, October 29-31, pp. 314–321 (2002)

14. Leonov, A.V., Khusnutdinov, R.R.: Study and development of the DTD generationsystem for XML documents. Programming and Computer Software (PCS) 31(4), 197–210 (2005)

15. Lee, D., Chu, W.W.: CPI: constraints-preserving inlining algorithm for mapping XML DTD to relational schema. Data & Knowledge Engineering 39(1), 3–25 (2001)

16. Lee, D., Mani, M., Chu, W.W.: Schema conversion methods between XML and relational models. In: Knowledge Transformation for the Semantic Web, pp. 245–252. IOS (2003)

17. Min, J.-K., Ahn, J.-Y., Chung, C.-W.: Efficient extraction of schemas for XML documents. Information Processing Letters 85(1), 7–12 (2003)

18. Mani, M., Lee, D.: XML to relational conversion using theory of regular tree grammars. In: Proceedings of 28th International Conference on Very Large Databases (VLDB 2002), Hong Kong, China, August 20-23, pp. 81–103 (2002)

19. Mani, M., Lee, D., Muntz, R.R.: Semantic data modeling using XML schemas. In: Kunii, H.S., Jajodia, S., Sølvberg, A. (eds.) ER 2001. LNCS, vol. 2224, pp. 149–163. Springer, Heidelberg (2001)

20. Moh, C.-H., Lim, E.-P., Ng, W.K.: DTD-Miner: A tool for mining DTD from XML documents. In: Proceedings of the Second International Workshop on Advance Issues of E-Commerce and Web-Based Information Systems (WECWIS 2000), Milpitas, California, USA, June 8-9, pp. 144–151 (2000)

21. Papakonstantinou, Y., Vianu, V.: DTD Inference for Views of XML Data. In: Proceedings of the 19th ACM SIGMOD-SIGACT-SIGART Symposium on Principles of Database Systems (PODS), Dallas, Texas, USA, May 15-17, pp. 35–46 (2000)

22. Schmidt, A., Kersten, M.L., Windhouwer, M., Waas, F.: Efficient relational storage and retrieval of XML documents. In: Suciu, D., Vossen, G. (eds.) WebDB 2000. LNCS, vol. 1997, pp. 137–150. Springer, Heidelberg (2001)

23. Schmidt, A., Waas, F., Kersten, M., Carey, M.J., Manolescu, I., Busse, R.: XMark: A benchmark for XML data management. In: Proceedings of the 28th International Conference on Very Large Data Bases, Hong Kong SAR, China, August 20–23, pp. 974–985 (2002)

24. Shanmugasundaram, J., Tufte, K., Zhang, C., He, G., DeWitt, D.J., Naughton, J.F.: Relational databases for querying XML documents: limitations and opportunities. In: Proceedings of 25th International Conference on Very Large Data Bases (VLDB 1999), Edinburgh, Scotland, UK, September 7-10, pp. 302–314 (1999)

25. Hongwei, S., Shusheng, Z., Jingtao, Z., Jing, W.: Constraints-preserving mapping algorithm from XML-schema to relational schema. In: Han, Y., Tai, S., Wikarski, D. (eds.) EDCIS 2002. LNCS, vol. 2480, pp. 193–207. Springer, Heidelberg (2002)

26. Varlamis, I., Vazirgiannis, M.: Bridging XML-schema and relational databases: A system for generating and manipulating relational databases using valid XML documents. In: Proceedings of the 2001 ACM Symposium on Document Engineering, Atlanta, Georgia, USA, November 9-10, pp. 105–114 (2001)

27. http://www.w3schools.com/dtd/

28. Wood, D.: Standard generalized markup language: mathematical and philosophical issues. In: van Leeuwen, J. (ed.) Computer Science Today. LNCS, vol. 1000, pp. 344–365. Springer, Heidelberg (1995)
29. http://xml.coverpages.org/schemas.html
30. Xing, G., Parthepan, V.: Efficient schema extraction from a large collection of XML documents. In: Proceedings of the 49th Annual Southeast Regional Conference, Kennesaw, GA, USA, March 24-26, pp. 92–96 (2011)

MKStream: An Efficient Algorithm for Processing Multiple Keyword Queries over XML Streams

Evandrino G. Barros[1], Alberto H.F. Laender[2],
Mirella M. Moro[2], and Altigran S. da Silva[3]

[1] Centro Federal de Educação Tecnológica de Minas Gerais, Belo Horizonte, Brazil
ebarros@decom.cefetmg.br
[2] Universidade Federal de Minas Gerais, Belo Horizonte, Brazil
{laender,mirella}@dcc.ufmg.br
[3] Universidade Federal do Amazonas, Manaus, Brazil
alti@icomp.ufam.edu.br

Abstract. In this paper, we tackle the problem of processing *various* keyword-based queries over XML *streams* in a scalable way, improving recent *multi-query processing* approaches. We propose a customized algorithm, called MKStream, that relies on parsing stacks designed for simultaneously matching several queries. Particularly, it explores the possibility of adjusting the number of parsing stacks for a better trade-off between processing time and memory usage. A comprehensive set of experiments evaluates its performance and scalability against the state-of-the-art, and shows that MKStream is the most efficient algorithm for keyword search services over XML streams.

Keywords: Multi-query processing, keyword-based queries, XML streams.

1 Introduction

Applications involving online information (such as news and RSS feeds) have increased considerably in recent years. Hence, Web users explore more streaming data rather than archival data. In this context, XML is the standard for many of such applications, which disseminate their data in streaming fashion. Specifically, users and applications describe their information needs through XML query languages (e.g., XQuery and XPath). These languages allow querying on both the data structure and data values using predicates with exact semantics. Therefore, users formulating queries must have some knowledge of how the XML documents that compose the streams are structured. However, on the Web, XML documents that store values in a textual format are very common. Such a feature makes the retrieval of (text) values based on predicates with exact semantics extremely difficult. Both problems (knowledge of the structure and retrieval with exact semantics) are aggravated by the existence of many disparate data sources, since users have to know the exact structure of each data source to retrieve the desired information.

Intuitive keyword-based queries offer an alternative to XML query languages. Using keywords to express queries over archived XML documents has been successfully exploited in recent work [1,6,7,10]. The main advantage of this approach is to allow many users posing queries in an informal way, since they do not need to care for the

E. Yu et al. (Eds.): ER 2014, LNCS 8824, pp. 100–107, 2014.

document structure anymore. However, only very recently, this approach was adapted to the context of *XML streams*, in which there is no document storage, pre-processing, statistics, or indexing available [9].

Keyword-based queries can alleviate the issues of knowing the structure and using exact predicates. However, a third problem arises in the stream context: a large number of users and documents flowing on the Web. Here, processing *one query* per document traversal or *one query* per stream may not be efficient (as in [9]). There are two ways to process the queries: (*i*) traversing each document for each query on the fly or (*ii*) processing each query against local document indexes. Both strategies need to *locally store* the documents and are inefficient due to the repeated document parsing and expensive building index operation. Ideally, we would like to process *multiple* queries over *one* single traversal of each document on the stream. Recently, two algorithms, KStream and CKStream, emerged as alternatives to process *multiple* keyword-based queries over XML streams by adopting bitmap representations for the queries [5], being CKStream the current state-of-the-art.

Considering such context, in this paper we propose a new algorithm, called MK-Stream, for simultaneously processing XML streams against several keyword-based queries. This algorithm relies on parsing stacks designed for simultaneously matching several queries and explores the possibility of adjusting the number of parsing stacks for a better trade-off between processing time and memory usage. Through a thoroughly experimental evaluation, we show that our solution outperforms the state-of-the-art algorithm in terms of both processing time and memory usage.

The rest of this paper is organized as follows. Section 2 discusses related work. Next, Section 3 describes our algorithm and Section 4 presents its experimental evaluation. Finally, Section 5 concludes the paper.

2   Related Work

Traditionally, XML keyword search has been addressed in the context of stored databases. Current approaches model XML documents as labeled trees, consider a meaningful part of the XML document and retrieve nodes of the XML tree that contain the query terms. For example, XSeek [7] proposes a query processing strategy over the notion of entities inferred from DTDs, whereas the work in [6] proposes a semantics-based approach to process XML keyword queries. A recent and complementary part of keyword search is to find top-k results [4] or propose ranking strategies. Specifically, in [1], the authors propose an information retrieval approach that uses the statistics of underlying XML data to rank the individual matches of all possible search intentions. Finally, in [10], the authors propose approaches based on set operations, inverted lists and subtree structures for keyword-based query evaluation. We refer the reader to [8] for a survey on XML keyword-based search.

The work in [9], and the evaluation study in [3], took the first steps towards processing keyword-based queries over XML *streams* by evaluating *one single query* per time. To the best of our knowledge, Hummel et al. [5] are the first to address the problem of processing *multiple keyword-based queries* by proposing the SLCA-based[1] algorithms

---

[1] For a document d and a query q, SLCA semantics defines as a result the smallest XML subtrees in d that contain all q keywords.

KStream and CKStream. KStream employs a single bitmap for representing all queries and a query index to cope with this bitmap, but has unfeasible memory consumption. CKStream saves space by compacting the query index and the bitmap, and is our baseline. As we shall see, MKStream also processes multiple keyword-based queries according to the SLCA semantics, but improves significantly response time and memory consumption when compared with CKStream.

3   Processing Multiple Queries with MKStream

Supported Queries. Following [9], MKStream considers a keyword-based query q over an XML document stream as a list of query terms $\langle t_1, \ldots, t_m \rangle$. Each query term is of the form: ℓ::k, ℓ::, ::k, or k, where ℓ is an element label and k a keyword. Terms that involve labels are called *structural terms*. Thus, given a node n within a document d and considering that n is labelled t and has a content c, n satisfies a query term of the form: (*i*) ℓ::k, if $\ell = t$ and $k \subseteq c$; (*ii*) ℓ::, if $\ell = t$; (*iii*) ::k, if $k \subseteq c$; (*iv*) k, if $k = t$ or $k \subseteq c$. As an example, consider the following two query specifications based on the XML document represented in Fig. 1: (s_a) *New comedies starring "Lewis"* and (s_b) *New comedies having "Lewis" in their title*. Table 1 presents possible keyword-based query formulations that fulfill such specifications.

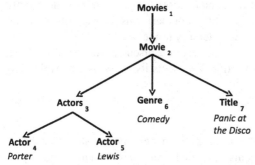

Fig. 1. Tree representation of an XML document

Table 1. Examples of keyword-based queries

Query	Formulation	Specification
q_1	Actor::Lewis Genre::Comedy	s_a
q_2	Actor::Lewis Comedy	s_a
q_3	Lewis Genre::Comedy	s_a, s_b
q_4	Lewis Comedy	s_a, s_b
q_5	Title::Lewis Genre::Comedy	s_b
q_6	Title::Lewis Comedy	s_b

General Multi-Query Procedure and MKStream. The algorithm in Figure 2 describes our general multi-query procedure for XML streams. We consider that a set of queries Q (from users' profiles) is processed against a stream D of XML documents. On arrival, each document d_j in D is individually processed (Lines 3 to 6). The results found within this document are collected and then returned in r_j (Lines 5 and 6). While being processed by a SAX parser (Line 5), each document d_j in D generates three types of event: $startElement(tag)$, $characters(text)$ and $endDocument()$. These events then trigger the respective *callback functions* that implement MKStream (Fig. 6).

Data Structures. MKStream is a multi stack-based algorithm that distributes the processing queries into different stacks, thus evaluating a smaller number of queries simultaneously. Furthermore, it improves performance by reducing the number of pushing and popping stack operations. The main data structures used by MKStream are: (*i*) a parsing stack S and (*ii*) a query index, named query_index.

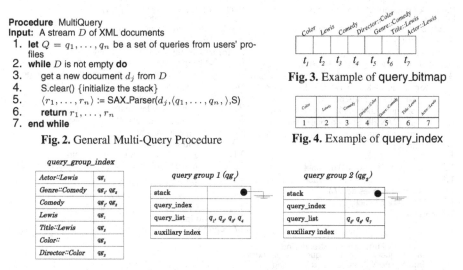

Procedure MultiQuery
Input: A stream D of XML documents
1. **let** $Q = q_1, \ldots, q_n$ be a set of queries from users' profiles
2. **while** D is not empty **do**
3.   get a new document d_j from D
4.   S.clear() {initialize the stack}
5. $\langle r_1, \ldots, r_n \rangle :=$ SAX_Parser($d_j, \langle q_1, \ldots, q_n, \rangle,$S)
6.   **return** $r_1, \ldots, r_n$
7. **end while**

Fig. 2. General Multi-Query Procedure

Fig. 3. Example of query_bitmap

Fig. 4. Example of query_index

Fig. 5. Configuration example of query_group_index and query_group for MKStream

The parsing stack S is used for keeping the XML nodes open during the SAX parser. Its top entry corresponds to a node v being processed and the previous entries correspond to ancestor nodes of v in the path from v to the document root. Each entry in the parsing stack stores the following information: (*i*) an XML node label; (*ii*) a set used_queries containing the queries that match any keyword in that node or in its descendants; (*iii*) a bitmap named CAN_BE_SLCA that keeps track of which queries can still match the corresponding node as an SLCA result; (*iv*) the list of keywords that have occurred in the corresponding node and its descendants; and (*v*) a second bitmap, named query_bitmap, that indicates which query terms (labels or keywords) occur in the XML node.

When a node matches any query term, its corresponding bit in the node's stack entry query_bitmap is set to true. Thus, if all query bits are true, the node matches all query terms. Fig. 3 illustrates the query_bitmap for distinct query terms in Table 1. MKStream also uses the query_index to identify in which bit position each query term occurs. This index is built directly from the set of queries Q and each of its entries represents a query term and refers to queries in which this term occurs in the query_bitmap, as illustrated in Fig. 4.

MKStream processes up to G stacks simultaneously, G being a user defined parameter. It separates the queries in Q into G query groups, each one controlling up to $\lceil |Q|/G \rceil$ by means of a single parsing stack and having its specific query_bitmap configuration. For example, considering the queries in Table 1 and $G=2$, the first parsing stack controls queries q_1, q_2, q_3 and q_4, and the second one queries q_5, q_6 and q_7, as illustrated by query groups qg_1 and qg_2 in Fig. 5. Each query_group includes the fields stack, query_index, query_list and auxiliary_index, which speeds up the search for queries that contain a certain term. MKStream identifies the correct parsing stack for each query by using the global index query_group_index, whose keys are query terms and entries are instances of query_group. For example, considering $G=2$ and the queries in Table 1, Fig. 5 illustrates the specific query_group_index configuration.

Callback Function MKStream.Start
Input: query_group_index
Input: e {the node being processed}
1. j := label(e)
2. node_path[$e.height$] := j
3. **for all** gr **in** query_group_index[j] **do**
4. N := # of distinct terms in queries of group gr
5.   **for** i := gr.stack.height+1 **to** $e.height$ **do**
6. sn_i.label := node_path[i]
7. sn_i.query_bitmap[0,. . .,N-1] := $false$
8. sn_i.CAN_BE_SLCA[gr.query_list]:= $true$
9.   gr.stack.push(sn_i)
10.   **end for**
11.   sn := *gr.stack.top()
12. q := gr.query_index[j].asLabel
13. L := gr.auxiliary_index[j].LabelOccurrences
14.   sn.used_queries.add(L)
15.   sn.query_bitmap[q] := $true$
16. **end for**

Callback Function MKStream.Text
Input: query_group_index
Input: e {the node being processed}
1. j := label(e)
2. **for all** k **in** set of text tokens in node e **do**
3.   **for all** gr **in** query_group_index[k] **do**
4. N := # of distinct terms in queries of group gr
5.   **for** i := gr.stack.height+1 **to** $e.height$ **do**
6. sn_i.label := node_path[i]
7. sn_i.query_bitmap[0,. . .,N-1] := $false$
8.   sn.CAN_BE_SLCA[gr.query_list]:= $true$
9.   gr.stack.push(sn_i)
10.   **end for**
11. q := gr.query_index[k].asKeyword
12. L := gr.auxiliary_index[k].KeywordOccurrences
13.   sn := *gr.stack.top ()
14.   sn.used_queries.add(L)
15.   sn.query_bitmap[q] := $true$
16.   **end for**
17. **end for**

Callback Function MKStream.End
Input: query group index query_group_index
Input: The XML node e that is ending
1. query_groups := query_group_index.values {gets all query groups}
2. **for all** gr **in** query_groups **do**
3.   **if** gr.stack.height $=$ $e.height$ **then**
4.   sn := group.stack.pop() {pops the top entry in the stack to sn}
5.   tn := *group.stack.top() {tn points to the top entry in the stack}
6.   tn.CAN_BE_SLCA:=tn.CAN_BE_SLCA **and** sn.CAN_BE_SLCA
7.   tn.used_queries.add(sn.used_queries)
8.   sn.query_bitmap := sn.query_bitmap **or** tn.query_bitmap
9.   **for all** q **in** sn.used_queries **do**
10.   **let** $\{j_1, \ldots, j_N\}$ be the bit positions corresponding to q terms in query_bitmap
11.   COMPLETE := sn.query_bitmap[j_1] **and** . . . **and** sn.query_bitmap[j_N]
12.   **if** sn.CAN_BE_SLCA[q] **and** COMPLETE **then**
13. q.results := q.results $\cup$ { sn }
14.   tn.CAN_BE_SLCA[q]:= $false$
15.   tn.used_queries.remove(q)
16.   **end if**
17.   **end for**
18.   **end if**
19. **end for**

Fig. 6. MKStream Callback Functions.

MKStream Callback Functions. Fig. 6 describes the three **MKStream** callback functions: MKStream.Start, MKStream.Text and MKStream.End.

MKStream.Start updates all parsing stacks whose queries include a node label as a term. It first assigns to j the node label (Line 1). Then, it processes each query group in query_group_index that contains j (Lines 3 to 16). Specifically, MKStream.Start pops up zeroed bitmaps into each query group parsing stack, corresponding to opened nodes not included into the stack (Lines 5 to 10). Then, it sets to $true$ the bit position associated with the label occurrence in the query_bitmap top entry and stores each query that must be evaluated when the node is finished (Lines 11 to 15).

MKStream.Text is similar to MKStream.Start in the sense that it updates all parsing stacks whose queries include text tokens as a term (terms such as k), eventually combined with its label (terms of the form $l::k$). Notice that MKStream.Text can handle terms of the form $l::k$ similarly to unlabeled terms such as k.

Finally, MKStream.End finishes the tree traversal by identifying which nodes match the specified queries, according to the SLCA semantics. First, it retrieves all query groups (Line 1) for processing its stacks. To be processed, the stack top entry must correspond to a node being finished, meaning that the stack height is equal to the height of the node being processed (Lines 3 to 8). For each one of these stacks, MKStream.End verifies if the stack top entry satisfies any query controlled by that stack (Lines 9 to 17). This evaluation process requires an auxiliary structure for testing which bits correspond to query terms controlled by the current stack (Line 10).

4 Experimental Results

We empirically evaluated MKStream efficiency in terms of processing time and memory space by comparing it to CKStream [5], the state-of-the-art algorithm for processing multiple keyword-based queries over XML streams. The experiments consisted in processing streams of XML documents against all posed queries simultaneously and measuring time spent and memory usage, using three different datasets, each one focusing on a different aspect of the algorithms. Due to lack of space, we report here only partial results of the experiments with the largest and more complex dataset, *ISFDB*, which consists of bibliographic data from fiction books available on the ISFDB Web site[2]. However, the experiments conducted with the other datasets show very similar results. For more details on the complete set of experiments, we refer the reader to [2].

For running the experiments, we split *ISFDB* into a stream of 10 different XML documents, corresponding to books published between 2000 and 2009. The resulting documents had on average 1.3 MB and 41,637 nodes. Then, from their contents, we randomly generated the sets of queries used in each specific experiment (e.g., "*Author*:: *Saramago Title*::*Blindness*"). In order to evaluate the performance of the algorithms, we measured the time spent for processing all XML documents on a given stream. Notice that this excludes the time spent to create the index structures, which is done only once by the time the operations start. The algorithms were implemented using Java and the SAX API from Xerces Java Parser. The query indexes and other data structures were kept entirely in memory. All experiments were performed on an Intel Dual Core 2.53 GHz computer with 4 GB of memory on Mac OS.

Figure 7 presents the results of the experiments conducted to analyze the impact of using structural terms (i.e., terms that include element labels) in the queries. For this experiment, we generated 50,000 queries with five query terms each and varied the number of structural terms from 0 to 3. These results highlight the significant impact of queries with structural terms to both algorithms. Such an impact happens because, usually, structural terms occur more frequently in XML documents, when compared to non-structural ones. Thus, the algorithms have to iterate over more queries. Note that this kind of term was present in each of the 50,000 queries to stress the performance of both algorithms. The large query set used in this experiment highlights the best processing time and memory usage of MKStream. Our algorithm is faster when using one or more stacks. When using five stacks, processing time is significantly reduced (54%) in comparison to CKStream. By using multiple stacks, MKStream processes smaller

---

[2] http://www.isfdb.org

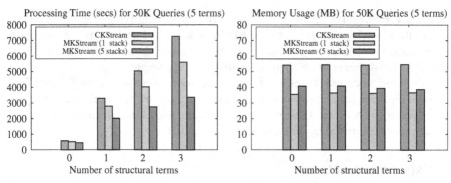

Fig. 7. Processing time (left) and memory usage (right) for 50,000 queries with up to 3 labels

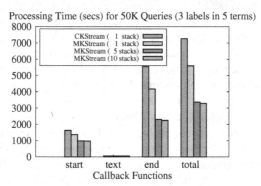

Fig. 8. Time spent by the callback functions when varying the number of queries

sets of queries when compared to CKStream that uses a single stack. Besides, since not all queries are evaluated by its End callback function, MKStream evaluates far fewer queries than the baseline, because such function only evaluates queries whose terms appear in the processed document.

Regarding memory consumption, Figure 7 (right) shows an almost constant memory usage by CKStream and MKStream algorithms for different number of terms, since the number of terms has a small impact on this resource for both algorithms. However, as we can see, MKStream presents a better memory performance due to the smaller number of stack pushing operations. This better performance is due to MKStream specific features that avoid unnecessary pushing operations, thus reducing stack entries. The figure also shows that, for MKStream, the use of more stacks degrade memory performance since they require additional memory space.

Finally, Figure 8 confirms the positive impact on the processing time of the callback functions when using multiple stacks for processing a large number of queries. Specifically, for the End callback function, MKStream presents a high processing time gain since its multiple stacks individually hold fewer queries to be evaluated. Note that Figure 8 also presents MKStream results for ten stacks which slightly improves processing time compared to MKStream with five stacks. We have also run MKStream with 15 and 20 stacks. However, there has been no performance gain. As a result, this experiment confirms that MKStream can be customized for a large number of queries, obtaining better results than the baseline. Figure 8 also shows the positive impact of the small number of stack pushing operations executed by the **MKStream.Start** callback function, even when a single stack is used.

5   Conclusions and Future Work

In this paper, we proposed a new algorithm, **MKStream**, for simultaneously process-ing several keyword-based queries over XML streams. This algorithm allows a large population of users with disparate interests to define their profiles by specifying queries in an informal way, since they do not have to worry about document structure, schema or even query language syntax. For evaluating its performance, we conducted a set of experiments comparing it to the state-of-the-art algorithm, which showed its superior behavior. **MKStream** reduces the number of pushing and popping stack operations and the number of query evaluations, thus improving response time and memory usage. Fur-thermore, MKStream can process several stacks simultaneously. This way, all queries can be distributed into different stacks, which means controlling a smaller number of queries if compared to a single parsing stack, used by the state-of-the-art algorithm. As future work, we plan to develop a complete framework for processing multiple queries over XML streams based on our algorithm, thus providing an environment for real ap-plications that would contribute with insights for its further improvement.

Acknowledgments. This work was partially funded by Project InWeb (grant MCT/CNPq 573871/2008-6) and individual grants from CNPq, FAPEAM and FAPEMIG.

References

1. Bao, Z., Lu, J., Ling, T.W., Chen, B.: Towards an Effective XML Keyword Search. IEEE TKDE 22(8), 1077–1092 (2010)
2. Barros, E.G.: Keyword-based Query Processing over XML Streams. PhD Thesis in Computer Science, UFMG (2012), http://www.bibliotecadigital.ufmg.br
3. Barros, E.G., Moro, M.M., Laender, A.H.F.: An Evaluation Study of Search Algorithms for XML Streams. JIDM 1(3), 487–502 (2010)
4. Chen, L.J., Papakonstantinou, Y.: Supporting Top-K Keyword Search in XML Databases. In: Proc. of ICDE, pp. 689–700 (2010)
5. da, F., Hummel, C., da Silva, A.S., Moro, M.M., Laender, A.H.F.: Multiple Keyword-based Queries over XML Streams. In: Proc. of CIKM, pp. 1577–1582 (2011)
6. Le, T.N., Wu, H., Ling, T.W., Li, L., Lu, J.: From Structure-Based to Semantics-Based: Towards Effective XML Keyword Search. In: Ng, W., Storey, V.C., Trujillo, J.C. (eds.) ER 2013. LNCS, vol. 8217, pp. 356–371. Springer, Heidelberg (2013)
7. Liu, Z., Chen, Y.: Identifying Meaningful Return Information for XML Keyword Search. In: Proc. of ACM SIGMOD, pp. 329–340 (2007)
8. Liu, Z., Chen, Y.: Processing Keyword Search on XML: A Survey. World Wide Web 14(5-6), 671–707 (2011)
9. Vagena, Z., Moro, M.M.: Semantic Search over XML Document Streams. In: Proc. of DataX (2008)
10. Zhou, J., Bao, Z., Wang, W., Zhao, J., Meng, X.: Efficient Query Processing for XML Keyword Queries based on the IDList Index. The VLDB Journal 23(1), 25–50 (2014)

Cardinality Constraints for Uncertain Data

Henning Koehler[1], Sebastian Link[2], Henri Prade[3], and Xiaofang Zhou[4]

[1] School of Engineering & Advanced Technology, Massey University, New Zealand
[2] Department of Computer Science, University of Auckland, New Zealand
[3] IRIT, CNRS and Université de Toulouse III, France
[4] School of Information Technology and Electrical Engineering,
The University of Queensland, Australia
{h.koehler@massey.ac.nz,s.link@auckland.ac.nz,
prade@irit.fr,zxf@itee.uq.edu.au}

Abstract. Modern applications require advanced techniques and tools to process large volumes of uncertain data. For that purpose we introduce cardinality constraints as a principled tool to control the occurrences of uncertain data. Uncertainty is modeled qualitatively by assigning to each object a degree of possibility by which the object occurs in an uncertain instance. Cardinality constraints are assigned a degree of certainty that stipulates on which objects they hold. Our framework empowers users to model uncertainty in an intuitive way, without the requirement to put a precise value on it. Our class of cardinality constraints enjoys a natural possible world semantics, which is exploited to establish several tools to reason about them. We characterize the associated implication problem axiomatically and algorithmically in linear input time. Furthermore, we show how to visualize any given set of our cardinality constraints in the form of an Armstrong instance, whenever possible. Even though the problem of finding an Armstrong instance is precisely exponential, our algorithm computes an Armstrong instance with conservative use of time and space. Data engineers and domain experts can jointly inspect Armstrong instances in order to consolidate the certainty by which a cardinality constraint shall hold in the underlying application domain.

Keywords: Armstrong database, Cardinality constraint, Data semantics, Possibility theory, Qualitative reasoning, Uncertain data.

1 Introduction

Background. The notion of cardinality constraints is fundamental for understanding the structure and semantics of data. In traditional conceptual modeling, cardinality constraints were introduced in Chen's seminal paper [2]. Here, a cardinality constraint consists of a finite set of attributes and a positive integer b, and holds in an instance if there are no $b + 1$ distinct objects in the instance that have matching values on all the attributes of the constraint. Cardinality constraints empower applications to control the occurrences of certain data, and have therefore significant applications in data cleaning, integration, modeling, processing, and retrieval.

E. Yu et al. (Eds.): ER 2014, LNCS 8824, pp. 108–121, 2014.

Table 1. RFID Readings for Indiana Bat

Zone	Time	Rfid	Conf.
Z0	07pm	B0	α_1
Z0	08pm	B1	α_1
Z0	09pm	B2	α_3
Z1	10pm	B3	α_1
Z2	10pm	B4	α_1

Zone	Time	Rfid	Conf.
Z3	11pm	B5	α_1
Z4	12am	B5	α_1
Z5	01am	B5	α_3
Z6	02am	B6	α_2
Z6	02am	B7	α_2

Zone	Time	Rfid	Conf.
Z7	03am	B8	α_3
Z7	04am	B8	α_3
Z8	05am	B9	α_3
Z9	05am	B9	α_3

Motivation. Traditional conceptual modeling was developed for applications with certain data, including accounting, inventory and payroll. Modern applications, such as information extraction, radio-frequency identification (RFID), scientific data management, data cleaning, and financial risk assessment produce large volumes of uncertain data. For example, RFID can track movements of endangered species of animals, such as the Indiana bat in Georgia, USA. For such an application data comes in the form of objects associated with some discrete level of confidence (*Conf.*) in the signal reading; for example, based on the quality of the signal received. More generally, uncertainty can be modeled qualitatively by associating objects with the degree of possibility that the object occurs in the instance. Table 1 shows such a possibilistic instance (p-instance), where each object is associated with an element from a finite scale of possibility degrees: $\alpha_1 > \ldots > \alpha_{k+1}$. The top degree α_1 is reserved for objects that are 'fully possible', the bottom degree α_{k+1} for objects that are 'impossible' to occur. Intermediate degrees are used as required and linguistic interpretations attached as preferred, such as 'quite possible' (α_2) and 'somewhat possible' (α_3).

As this scenario is typical for a broad range of applications, we ask how cardinality constraints can benefit from the possibility degrees assigned to objects. More specifically, we investigate cardinality constraints on uncertain data, where uncertainty is modeled qualitatively in the form of possibility degrees.

The degrees of possibility enable us to express classical cardinality constraints with different degrees of certainty. For example, to express that it is 'impossible' that the same bat is read more than three times we declare the cardinality constraint $card(Rfid) \leq 3$ to be 'fully certain', stipulating that no bat can feature in more than three objects that are at least 'somewhat possible'. Similarly, to say that it is only 'somewhat possible' that the same bat is read more than twice we declare the cardinality constraint $card(Rfid) \leq 2$ to be 'quite certain', stipulating that no bat can feature in more than two objects that are at least 'quite possible'. Finally, to say that it is only 'quite possible' that there are readings of different bats in the same zone at the same time we declare the cardinality constraint $card(Zone, Time) \leq 1$ to be 'somewhat certain', stipulating that there are no two distinct objects that are 'fully possible' and have matching values on *Zone* and *Time*. Our objective is to apply possibility theory from artificial intelligence to establish qualitative cardinality constraints (QCs) as a fundamental tool to control occurrences of uncertain data.

Contributions. (1) In Section 2 we point out the lack of qualitative approaches to constraints on uncertain data. (2) We define a semantics for cardinality

	Zone	Time	Rfid	Zone	Time	Rfid	Zone	Time	Rfid
w_1	Z0	07pm	B0	Z1	10pm	B3	Z3	11pm	B5
	Z0	08pm	B1	Z2	10pm	B4	Z4	12am	B5
w_2	Z6	02am	B6	Z6	02am	B7			
	Z0	09pm	B2	Z7	03am	B8	Z8	05am	B9
w_3	Z5	01am	B5	Z7	04am	B8	Z9	05am	B9

Fig. 1. Nested Possible Worlds of the p-Instance from Table 1

constraints on instances of uncertain data in Section 3. Here, uncertainty is modeled qualitatively by degrees of possibility. The degrees bring forward a nested chain of possible worlds, with each world being a classic relation that has some possibility. Hence, the more possible a world is the fewer objects it contains, and the sharper the bounds of cardinality constraints can become. For example, the possible worlds of the p-instance from Table 1 are shown in Figure 1. The cardinality constraint $card(Rfid) \leq 3$ is satisfied by the 'somewhat possible' world w_3, $card(Rfid) \leq 2$ is satisfied by the 'quite possible' world w_2 but not by w_3, and $card(Zone, Time) \leq 1$ is satisfied by the 'fully possible' world w_1 but not by w_2. (3) In Section 4 we establish axiomatic and linear-time algorithmic characterizations for the associated implication problem of QCs. (4) We show in Section 5 which QC sets can be visualized in the form of a finite Armstrong p-instance, and how such a p-instance is computed whenever it exists. That is, for any suitable QC set Σ we compute a p-instance that, for every given QC φ, satisfies φ iff φ is implied by Σ. While the problem of finding an Armstrong p-instance is precisely exponential, the size of our computed Armstrong p-instance is always at most the size of a minimum-sized Armstrong p-instance times the size of the given set of constraints. (5) In Section 6 we conclude and briefly discuss future work. Most proofs have been omitted to meet space requirements.

2   Related Work

Database constraints enforce the semantics of application domains in database systems [14]. Cardinality constraints are one of the most influential contributions conceptual modeling has made to the study of database constraints. They were already present in Chen's seminal paper [2] on conceptual database design. All major languages currently used for conceptual database design (say, the ER model, description logics, UML and ORM) come with means for specifying cardinality constraints. Cardinality constraints have been extensively studied in database design [3,7,8,10,12,13,17,19].

There are many quantitative approaches to uncertain data, foremost probability theory [18]. Research about constraints on probabilistic data is still in its infancy. Qualitative approaches to uncertain data deal with either query languages or extensions of functional dependencies [1]. *Qualitative approaches to cardinality constraints on uncertain data have not been studied yet to the best of our knowledge.* Our contributions extend results on cardinality constraints from classic conceptual modeling, covered by the special case of two possibility degrees. These include axiomatic and algorithmic solutions to their implication problem, as well as properties of Armstrong databases [8].

Possibilistic logic is a well-known framework for reasoning about uncertainty with numerous applications in AI [5], including approximate, non-monotonic and qualitative reasoning, belief revision, soft constraint satisfaction problems, decision-making, pattern classification and preferences. Our results show that possibilistic logic is suitable to extend the classic notion of cardinality constraints from certain to qualitatively uncertain data. The proposed treatment agrees with the idea of viewing the cardinality of a fuzzy set (here, a set of weighted tuples) as a fuzzy integer (here, an ordered set of possible cardinalities) [4].

3   Qualitative Cardinality Constraints

In this section we extend object types that model certain objects in traditional conceptual modeling to model uncertain objects qualitatively.

An object schema, denoted by O, is a finite non-empty set of *attributes*. Each attribute $A \in O$ has a *domain* $dom(A)$ of values. An *object* o over O is an element of the Cartesian product $\prod_{A \in O} dom(A)$. For $X \subseteq O$ we denote by $o(X)$ the *projection* of o on X. An *instance* over O is a set ι of objects over O. As example we use the object schema TRACKING with attributes *Zone*, *Time*, and *Rfid*. Objects either belong or do not belong to an instance. For example, we cannot express that we have less confidence for the bat identified by *Rfid* value $B5$ to be in *Zone* $Z5$ at $01am$ than for the same bat to be in $Z4$ at $12am$.

We model uncertain instances by assigning to each object some degree of possibility with which the object occurs in an instance. Formally, we have a *possibility scale*, or p-scale, that is, a strict linear order $\mathcal{S} = (S, <)$ with $k+1$ elements. We write $\mathcal{S} = \{\alpha_1, \ldots, \alpha_{k+1}\}$ to declare that $\alpha_1 > \cdots > \alpha_k > \alpha_{k+1}$. The elements $\alpha_i \in S$ are called *possibility degrees*, or p-degrees. Here, α_1 is reserved for objects that are 'fully possible' while α_{k+1} is reserved for objects that are 'impossible' to occur in an instance. Humans like to use simple scales in everyday life to communicate, compare, or rank. Here, the word "simple" means that items are classified qualitatively rather than quantitatively by putting precise values on them. Classical instances use two p-degrees, i.e. $k = 1$.

A *possibilistic object schema* $(O, \mathcal{S})$, or p-object schema, consists of an object schema O and a p-scale $\mathcal{S}$. A *possibilistic instance*, or p-instance, over $(O, \mathcal{S})$ consists of an instance ι over O, and a function $Poss$ that assigns to each object $o \in \iota$ a p-degree $Poss(o) \in \mathcal{S} - \{\alpha_{k+1}\}$. We sometimes omit $Poss$ when denoting a p-instance. Table 1 shows a p-instance over $(\text{TRACKING}, \mathcal{S} = \{\alpha_1, \ldots, \alpha_4\})$.

P-instances enjoy a possible world semantics. For $i = 1, \ldots, k$ let w_i consist of all objects in ι that have p-degree at least α_i, that is, $w_i = \{o \in \iota \mid Poss(o) \geq \alpha_i\}$. Indeed, we have $w_1 \subseteq w_2 \subseteq \cdots \subseteq w_k$. The possibility distribution π_ι for this linear chain of possible worlds is defined by $\pi_\iota(w_i) = \alpha_i$. Note that w_{k+1} is not a possible world, since its p-degree $\pi(w_{k+1}) = \alpha_{k+1}$ means 'impossible'. Vice versa,

$Poss(o)$ for an object $o \in \iota$ is the maximum p-degree $\max\{\alpha_i \mid o \in w_i\}$ of a world to which o belongs. If $o \notin w_k$, then $Poss(o) = \alpha_{k+1}$. Every object that is 'fully possible' occurs in every possible world, and is therefore also 'fully certain'. Hence, instances are a special case of uncertain instances. Figure 1 shows the possible worlds $w_1 \subsetneq w_2 \subsetneq w_3$ of the p-instance of Table 1.

We introduce qualitative cardinality constraints, or QCs, as cardinality constraints with some degree of certainty. As cardinality constraints are fundamental to applications with certain data, QCs will serve a similar role for applications with uncertain data. A *cardinality constraint* over object type O is an expression $card(X) \leq b$ where $X \subseteq O$, and b is a positive integer. The cardinality constraint $card(X) \leq b$ over O is satisfied by an instance w over O, denoted by $\models_w card(X) \leq b$, if there are no $b + 1$ distinct objects $o_1, \ldots, o_{b+1} \in w$ with matching values on all the attributes in X. For example, Figure 1 shows that $card(Zone) \leq 1$ is not satisfied by any instance w_1, w_2 or w_3; $card(Zone, Time) \leq 1$ is satisfied by w_1, but not by w_2 nor w_3; $card(Rfid) \leq 2$ is satisfied by w_1 and w_2, but not by w_3; and $card(Rfid) \leq 3$ is satisfied by w_1, w_2 and w_3.

The p-degrees of objects result in degrees of certainty by which QCs hold. As $card(Rfid) \leq 3$ holds in every possible world, it is fully certain to hold on ι. As $card(Rfid) \leq 2$ is only violated in a somewhat possible world w_3, it is quite certain to hold on ι. As the smallest world that violates $card(Zone, Time) \leq 1$ is the quite possible world w_2, it is somewhat certain to hold on ι. As $card(Zone) \leq 1$ is violated in the fully possible world w_1, it is not certain at all to hold on ι.

Similar to the scale $\mathcal{S}$ of p-degrees α_i for objects, we use a scale $\mathcal{S}^T$ of certainty degrees β_j, or c-degrees, for cardinality constraints. Formally, the correspondence between p-degrees in $\mathcal{S}$ and the c-degrees in $\mathcal{S}^T$ is defined by the mapping $\alpha_i \mapsto \beta_{k+2-i}$ for $i = 1, \ldots, k + 1$. Hence, the certainty $C_\iota(card(X) \leq b)$ by which the cardinality constraint $card(X) \leq b$ holds on the uncertain instance ι is either the top degree β_1 if $card(X) \leq b$ is satisfied by w_k, or the minimum amongst the c-degrees β_{k+2-i} that correspond to possible worlds w_i in which $card(X) \leq b$ is violated, that is,

$$C_\iota(card(X) \leq b) = \begin{cases} \beta_1 & , \text{ if } \models_{w_k} card(X) \leq b \\ \min\{\beta_{k+2-i} \mid \not\models_{w_i} card(X) \leq b\} & , \text{ otherwise} \end{cases}.$$

We can now define the semantics of qualitative cardinality constraints.

Definition 1. *Let $(O, \mathcal{S})$ denote a p-object schema. A qualitative cardinality constraint (QC) over $(O, \mathcal{S})$ is an expression $(card(X) \leq b, \beta)$ where $card(X) \leq b$ denotes a cardinality constraint over O and $\beta \in \mathcal{S}^T$. A p-instance $(\iota, Poss)$ over $(O, \mathcal{S})$ satisfies the QC $(card(X) \leq b, \beta)$ if and only if $C_\iota(card(X) \leq b) \geq \beta$.*

Example 1. Let Σ denote the set consisting of the following qualitative cardinality constraints: $(card(Zone) \leq 3, \beta_1)$, $(card(Time) \leq 2, \beta_1)$, $(card(Rfid) \leq 3, \beta_1)$, $(card(Zone, Rfid) \leq 2, \beta_1)$, $(card(Zone) \leq 2, \beta_2)$, $(card(Rfid) \leq 2, \beta_2)$, $(card(Zone, Rfid) \leq 1, \beta_2)$, $(card(Time, Rfid) \leq 1, \beta_2)$, $(card(Zone, Time) \leq 1, \beta_3)$. The p-instance ι from Table 1 satisfies all of these QCs. However, ι violates $(card(Rfid) \leq 2, \beta_1)$, $(card(Rfid) \leq 1, \beta_2)$, and $(card(Zone, Time) \leq 1, \beta_2)$.

4 Reasoning about Qualitative Cardinality Constraints

First, we establish a strong correspondence between the implication of QCs and traditional cardinality constraints. Let $\Sigma \cup \{\varphi\}$ denote a set of QCs over $(O, \mathcal{S})$. We say Σ *implies* φ, denoted by $\Sigma \models \varphi$, if every p-instance $(\iota, Poss)$ over $(O, \mathcal{S})$ that satisfies every QC in Σ also satisfies φ. We use $\Sigma^* = \{\varphi \mid \Sigma \models \varphi\}$ to denote the *semantic closure* of Σ. The *implication problem for QCs* is to decide, given any p-object schema, and any set $\Sigma \cup \{\varphi\}$ of QCs over the p-object schema, whether $\Sigma \models \varphi$ holds.

Example 2. Let Σ be as in Example 1. Further, let φ denote the QC $(card(Rfid) \leq 2, \beta_1)$. Then Σ does not imply φ as the following p-instance witnesses:

Zone	Time	Rfid	Poss. degree
Z3	11pm	B5	α_1
Z4	12am	B5	α_1
Z5	01am	B5	α_3

In particular, the certainty degree of $card(Rfid) \leq 2$ is β_2, which means that $(card(Rfid) \leq 2, \beta_1)$ is violated.

4.1 The Magic of β-Cuts

For a set Σ of QCs over $(O, \mathcal{S})$ and c-degree $\beta \in \mathcal{S}^T$ where $\beta > \beta_{k+1}$, let $\Sigma_\beta = \{card(X) \leq b \mid (card(X) \leq b, \beta') \in \Sigma$ and $\beta' \geq \beta\}$ be the β-*cut* of Σ. The following theorem can be shown by converting p-instances into traditional instances and vice versa.

Theorem 1. *Let* $\Sigma \cup \{(card(X) \leq b, \beta)\}$ *be a QC set over* $(O, \mathcal{S})$ *where* $\beta > \beta_{k+1}$. *Then* $\Sigma \models (card(X) \leq b, \beta)$ *if and only if* $\Sigma_\beta \models card(X) \leq b$.

Theorem 1 allows us to apply achievements from cardinality constraints for certain data to qualitative cardinality constraints. It is a major tool to establish the remaining results in this article.

Example 3. Let Σ be as in Example 1. Then Σ_{β_1} consists of the cardinality constraints $card(Zone) \leq 3$, $card(Time) \leq 2$, $card(Rfid) \leq 3$ and $card(Zone, Rfid) \leq 2$. Theorem 1 says that Σ_{β_1} does not imply $card(Rfid) \leq 2$. The possible world w_3 of the p-instance from Example 2:

Zone	Time	Rfid
Z3	11pm	B5
Z4	12am	B5
Z5	01am	B5

satisfies Σ_{β_1}, and violates $card(Rfid) \leq 2$.

Table 2. Axiomatization $\mathfrak{C}' = \{\mathcal{T}', \mathcal{R}', \mathcal{S}'\}$ of Cardinality Constraints

$\overline{card(O) \leq 1}$ (top, $\mathcal{T}'$)	$\dfrac{card(X) \leq b}{card(X) \leq b+1}$ (relax, $\mathcal{R}'$)	$\dfrac{card(X) \leq b}{card(XY) \leq b}$ (superset, $\mathcal{S}'$)

Table 3. Axiomatization $\mathfrak{C} = \{\mathcal{T}, \mathcal{R}, \mathcal{S}, \mathcal{B}, \mathcal{W}\}$ of Qualitative Cardinality Constraints

$\overline{(card(O) \leq 1, \beta)}$ (top, $\mathcal{T}$)	$\dfrac{(card(X) \leq b, \beta)}{(card(X) \leq b+1, \beta)}$ (relax, $\mathcal{R}$)	$\dfrac{(card(X) \leq b, \beta)}{(card(XY) \leq b, \beta)}$ (superset, $\mathcal{S}$)
$\overline{(card(X) \leq b, \beta_{k+1})}$ (bottom, $\mathcal{B}$)	$\dfrac{(card(X) \leq b, \beta)}{(card(X) \leq b, \beta')} \; \beta' \leq \beta$ (weakening, $\mathcal{W}$)	

4.2   Axiomatic Characterization

We determine the semantic closure by applying *inference rules* of the form $\dfrac{\text{premise}}{\text{conclusion}}$ condition. For a set $\mathfrak{R}$ of inference rules let $\Sigma \vdash_{\mathfrak{R}} \varphi$ denote the *inference* of φ from Σ by $\mathfrak{R}$. That is, there is some sequence $\sigma_1, \ldots, \sigma_n$ such that $\sigma_n = \varphi$ and every σ_i is an element of Σ or is the conclusion that results from an application of an inference rule in $\mathfrak{R}$ to some premises in $\{\sigma_1, \ldots, \sigma_{i-1}\}$. Let $\Sigma_{\mathfrak{R}}^+ = \{\varphi \mid \Sigma \vdash_{\mathfrak{R}} \varphi\}$ be the *syntactic closure* of Σ under inferences by $\mathfrak{R}$. $\mathfrak{R}$ is *sound* (*complete*) if for every set Σ over every $(O, \mathcal{S})$ we have $\Sigma_{\mathfrak{R}}^+ \subseteq \Sigma^*$ ($\Sigma^* \subseteq \Sigma_{\mathfrak{R}}^+$). The (finite) set $\mathfrak{R}$ is a (finite) *axiomatization* if $\mathfrak{R}$ is both sound and complete. Table 2 shows an axiomatization $\mathfrak{C}'$ for the implication of cardinality constraints. In these rules, it is assumed that O is an arbitrarily given object type, $X, Y \subseteq O$, and b is a positive integer. Theorem 1 and the fact that $\mathfrak{C}'$ forms an axiomatization for the implication of cardinality constraints [8] can be exploited to show directly that the set $\mathfrak{C}$ from Table 3 forms an axiomatization for the implication of QCs. Here, it is assumed that $(O, \mathcal{S})$ is an arbitrarily given p-object type, $X, Y \subseteq O$, b is a positive integer, and $\beta, \beta' \in \mathcal{S}^T$ are c-degrees. In particular, β_{k+1} denotes the bottom c-degree in $\mathcal{S}^T$.

Theorem 2. *The set $\mathfrak{C}$ forms a finite axiomatization for the implication of qualitative cardinality constraints.*

The application of inference rules in $\mathfrak{C}$ from Table 3 is illustrated on our running example.

Example 4. Let Σ be as in Example 1. The QC $(card(Zone, Rfid) \leq 4, \beta_2)$ is implied by Σ. Indeed, applying the *superset rule* $\mathcal{S}$ to $(card(Zone) \leq 3, \beta_1) \in \Sigma$ results in $(card(Zone, Rfid) \leq 3, \beta_1) \in \Sigma_{\mathfrak{C}}^+$. Applying the *relax rule* $\mathcal{R}$ to this QC results in $(card(Zone, Rfid) \leq 4, \beta_1) \in \Sigma_{\mathfrak{C}}^+$. Finally, an application of the *weakening rule* $\mathcal{W}$ to the last QC results in $(card(Zone, Rfid) \leq 4, \beta_2) \in \Sigma_{\mathfrak{C}}^+$.

4.3 Algorithmic Characterization

While $\mathfrak{C}$ enables us to enumerate all QCs that are implied by a QC set Σ, in practice it often suffices to decide whether a given QC φ is implied by Σ. Enumerating all implied QCs and checking whether φ is among them is neither efficient nor makes good use of φ.

Theorem 3. *Let $\Sigma \cup \{(card(X) \leq b, \beta)\}$ denote a set of QCs over $(O, \mathcal{S})$ with $|\mathcal{S}| = k+1$. Then Σ implies $(card(X) \leq b, \beta)$ if and only if $\beta = \beta_{k+1}$, or $X = O$, or there is some $(card(Y) \leq b', \beta') \in \Sigma$ such that $Y \subseteq X$, $b' \leq b$ and $\beta' \geq \beta$.*

Corollary 1. *An instance $\Sigma \models \varphi$ of the implication problem for qualitative cardinality constraints can be decided in time $\mathcal{O}(\|\Sigma \cup \{\varphi\}\|)$ where $\|\Sigma\|$ denotes the total number of symbol occurrences in Σ.*

Example 5. Let Σ be as in Example 1. Then the QC $(card(Zone, Rfid) \leq 4, \beta_2)$ is implied by Σ. Indeed, $(card(Zone) \leq 3, \beta_1) \in \Sigma$ and $Y = \{Zone\} \subseteq \{Zone, Rfid\} = X$, $b' = 3 \leq 4 = b$, and $\beta' = \beta_1 \geq \beta_2 = \beta$ shows this by Theorem 3.

5   Visualization of Cardinality Constraints

In this section, we develop a theory of Armstrong p-instances for sets of qualitative cardinality constraints. The concept of Armstrong databases is well established in database research [6]. They are widely regarded as an effective tool to visualize abstract sets of constraints in a user-friendly way [6,15,16]. As such data engineers exploit Armstrong databases as a communication tool in their interaction with domain experts in order to determine the set of constraints that are meaningful to the application domain at hand [9,11,15,16]. While finite Armstrong p-instances do not exist for all QC sets, we show how to compute such instances whenever they do exist.

5.1 Armstrong Instances

We first restate the original definition of an Armstrong database [6] in our context. A p-instance ι is said to be *Armstrong* for a given set Σ of QCs on a given p-object type $(O, \mathcal{S})$ if and only if for all QCs φ over $(O, \mathcal{S})$ it is true that ι satisfies φ if and only if Σ implies φ. Armstrong p-instances for Σ are exact visual representations of Σ, as illustrated on our running example.

Example 6. Table 4 shows an Armstrong p-instance ι for the QC set Σ from Example 1. Suitable substitutions yield the p-instance from Table 1.

Originally, an Armstrong instance ι for a set Σ of constraints in class $\mathcal{C}$ reduces the implication problem $\Sigma \models \varphi$ to the validation of φ in ι, for any $\varphi \in \mathcal{C}$. Armstrong p-instances ι for Σ go even further in our framework: they allow us to reduce the problem of inferring the highest c-degree β for which a QC (φ, β) is implied by Σ to the computation of the certainty degree $C_\iota(\varphi)$ of φ in ι,

Table 4. Armstrong p-Instance

Zone	Time	Rfid	p-degree
$c_{Z,1}$	$c_{T,1}$	$c_{R,1}$	α_1
$c_{Z,1}$	$c_{T,2}$	$c_{R,2}$	α_1
$c_{Z,1}$	$c_{T,3}$	$c_{R,3}$	α_3
$c_{Z,4}$	$c_{T,4}$	$c_{R,4}$	α_1
$c_{Z,5}$	$c_{T,4}$	$c_{R,5}$	α_1

Zone	Time	Rfid	p-degree
$c_{Z,6}$	$c_{T,6}$	$c_{R,6}$	α_1
$c_{Z,7}$	$c_{T,7}$	$c_{R,6}$	α_1
$c_{Z,8}$	$c_{T,8}$	$c_{R,6}$	α_3
$c_{Z,9}$	$c_{T,9}$	$c_{R,9}$	α_2
$c_{Z,9}$	$c_{T,9}$	$c_{R,10}$	α_2

Zone	Time	Rfid	p-degree
$c_{Z,11}$	$c_{T,11}$	$c_{R,11}$	α_3
$c_{Z,11}$	$c_{T,12}$	$c_{R,11}$	α_3
$c_{Z,13}$	$c_{T,13}$	$c_{R,13}$	α_3
$c_{Z,14}$	$c_{T,13}$	$c_{R,13}$	α_3

for all $\varphi \in \mathcal{C}$. For example, $C_\iota(card(Zone, Time) \leq 1) = \beta_3$ for the Armstrong p-instance ι in Table 1. Therefore, if $card(Zone, Time) \leq 1$ shall actually hold with a higher c-degree, then domain experts who inspect ι are likely to simply notice that $card(Zone, Time) \leq 1$ does not yet hold with the required certainty.

5.2   Structural Characterization

For characterizing the structure of Armstrong p-instances we define notions of agreement between objects of an instance. Cardinality constraints require us to compare any number of distinct objects. Let O be an object type, w an instance, and o_1, o_2 two objects of O. The *agree set* of o_1 and o_2 is defined as $ag(o_1, o_2) = \{A \in O \mid o_1(A) = o_2(A)\}$. The *agree set* of w is defined as $ag(w) = \{ag(o_1, o_2) \mid o_1, o_2 \in w \wedge o_1 \neq o_2\}$. For every $b \in \mathbb{N} \cup \{\infty\}$, $b > 1$ we define $ag_b(w) = \{\bigcap_{1 \leq i < j \leq b} ag(o_i, o_j) \mid \exists o_1, \ldots, o_b \in w (\forall i, j (1 \leq i < j \leq b \Rightarrow o_i \neq o_j))\}$, and $ag_1(w) = \{O\}$. If w is finite, $ag_\infty(w) = \emptyset$.

Example 7. For the worlds w_1, w_2 and w_3 from our running example in Figure 1 we obtain $ag_2(w_1) = \{\{Zone\}, \{Time\}, \{Rfid\}\}$ and $ag_b(w_1) = \emptyset$ for all $b > 2$, $ag_2(w_2) = \{\{Zone\}, \{Time\}, \{Rfid\}, \{Zone, Time\}\}$, $ag_b(w_2) = \emptyset$ for all $b > 2$, $ag_2(w_3) = \{\{Zone\}, \{Time\}, \{Rfid\}, \{Zone, Time\}, \{Zone, Rfid\}, \{Time, Rfid\}\}$, and $ag_3(w_3) = \{\{Zone\}, \{Rfid\}\}$ and $ag_b(w_3) = \emptyset$ for all $b > 3$.

An Armstrong p-instance ι violates all QCs not implied by the given QC set Σ. It suffices for any non-empty set X to have $card(X) \leq b_X^i - 1$ violated by w_{k+1-i} where b_X^i denotes the minimum positive integer for which $card(X) \leq b_X^i$ is implied by Σ_{β_i}. If there are implied $card(X) \leq b_X^i$ and $card(Y) \leq b_Y^i$ such that $b_X^i = b_Y^i$ and $Y \subseteq X$, then it suffices to have $card(X) \leq b_X^i - 1$ violated by w_{k+1-i}. Finally, if there are implied $card(X) \leq b_X^i$ and $card(X) \leq b_X^j$ such that $b_X^i = b_X^j$ and $i < j$, then it suffices to have $card(X) \leq b_X^j - 1$ violated by w_{k+1-j}. This motivates the following definition.

Let Σ be a set of QCs over p-object type $(O, \mathcal{S})$ with $|\mathcal{S}| = k + 1$. For $\emptyset \neq X \subset O$ and $i = 1, \ldots, k$, let

$$b_X^i = \begin{cases} \min\{b \in \mathbb{N} \mid \Sigma_{\beta_i} \models card(X) \leq b\} & \text{, if } \{b \in \mathbb{N} \mid \Sigma_{\beta_i} \models card(X) \leq b\} \neq \emptyset \\ \infty & \text{, else} \end{cases}.$$

The set $dup_{\Sigma_{\beta_i}}(O)$ of *duplicate sets with certainty* β_i is defined as $dup_{\Sigma_{\beta_i}}(O) = \{X \subseteq O \mid b_X^i > 1 \wedge (\forall A \in O - X (b_{XA}^i < b_X^i)) \wedge \forall j > i (b_X^j < b_X^i)\}$.

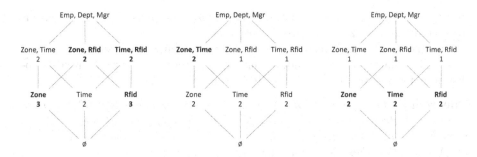

Fig. 2. Duplicate sets X in bold with cardinalities b_X^i for $i = 1, 2, 3$ from left to right

Example 8. Consider the set Σ over p-object type $(O, \mathcal{S})$ from Example 1. Figure 2 shows the non-trivial subsets X of O associated with their b_X^i values for $i = 1, 2, 3$ from left to right. Amongst these, the duplicate sets with certainty β_1 (left figure), β_2 (middle figure) and β_3 (right figure) are indicated in bold font. Here, $Y = \{Zone,\ Time\}$ is not a duplicate set with certainty β_1 as $b_Y^2 = 2 = b_Y^1$. Similarly, $Z = \{Rfid\}$ is not a duplicate set with certainty β_2 as $b_Z^3 = 2 = b_Z^2$.

Next we characterize the structure of Armstrong p-instances. A given p-instance satisfies $card(X) \leq b \in \Sigma_{\beta_i}$ if there are not $b + 1$ distinct objects in world w_{k+1-i} that have matching values on X. Also, a given p-instance violates all non-implied QCs if every duplicate set X with certainty β_i is contained by some attribute set on which b_X^i distinct objects in w_{k+1-i} agree.

Theorem 4. *Let Σ denote a set of QCs, and let $(\iota, Poss)$ denote a p-instance over $(O, \mathcal{S})$ with $|\mathcal{S}| = k + 1$. Then $(\iota, Poss)$ is Armstrong for Σ if and only if for all $i = 1, \ldots, k$, the world w_{k+1-i} is Armstrong for Σ_{β_i}. That is, for all $i = 1, \ldots, k$, for all $X \in dup_{\Sigma_{\beta_i}}(O)$ there is some $Z \in ag_{b_X^i}(w_{k+1-i})$ such that $X \subseteq Z$, and for all $card(X) \leq b \in \Sigma_{\beta_i}$ and for all $Z \in ag_{b+1}(w_{k+1-i})$, $X \nsubseteq Z$.*

Example 9. Consider the p-instance ι from Table 1 and the set Σ of QCs from Example 1. Example 7 and Example 8 show that ι satisfies the conditions of Theorem 4, and is therefore an Armstrong p-instance for Σ.

5.3 Computational Characterization

We now apply Theorem 4 to compute finite Armstrong p-instances for any given QC set Σ over any given p-object type $(O, \mathcal{S})$ where for all $A \in O$ there is some $(card(A) \leq b, \beta_1) \in \Sigma$. The latter condition is sufficient and necessary for the existence of a finite Armstrong p-instance, which can therefore be decided in linear time in the input. While the problem of finding an Armstrong p-instance is precisely exponential in the size of the given constraints we show that the size of our output Armstrong p-instance is always bounded by the product of the number of the given constraints and the size of a minimum-sized Armstrong p-instance. Finally, we show that there are Armstrong p-instances whose size is logarithmic in the size of the given constraints.

Our first result characterizes QC sets for which finite Armstrong p-instances exist. The characterization shows that the existence of finite Armstrong p-instances for a given QC set can be decided in linear time.

Theorem 5. *Let Σ be a set of QCs over some given p-object type $(O, \mathcal{S})$. Then there is a finite Armstrong p-instance for Σ if and only if for all $A \in O$ there is some $b \in \mathbb{N}$ such that $(card(A) \leq b, \beta_1) \in \Sigma$. It can therefore be decided in time $\mathcal{O}(\|\Sigma\|)$ whether there is a finite Armstrong p-instance for Σ.*

Proof. Suppose there is some $A \in O$ such that Σ does not imply $(card(A) \leq b, \beta_1)$ for any $b \in \mathbb{N}$. Consequently, there is some duplicate set X with certainty β_1 and $A \in X$ such that $b_X^1 = \infty$. Theorem 4 shows that every Armstrong p-instance for Σ must contain infinitely many objects that agree on X. Therefore, a finite Armstrong p-instance cannot exist for Σ. The sufficiency of the condition for the existence of finite Armstrong p-instances follows from the soundness of our algorithm that computes them in this case. This is presented next.

For a given QC set Σ over a given p-object type $(O, \mathcal{S})$ and $|\mathcal{S}| = k + 1$, which meets the condition of Theorem 5, we visualize Σ by computing an Armstrong p-instance ι for Σ. Theorem 4 provides us with a strategy for this computation. The main complexity goes into the computation of duplicate sets and their associated cardinalities. Here, we proceed in three stages. First, we compute for all $i = 1, \ldots, k$ and for all non-trivial $X \subset O$, b_X^i by starting with ∞ and setting b_X^i to b whenever there is some $card(Y) \leq b \in \Sigma_{\beta_i}$ such that $Y \subseteq X$ and $b < b_X^i$. Secondly, for all $i = 1, \ldots, k$ and starting with all non-trivial subsets X as the set of duplicate sets with certainty β_i, we remove X whenever $b_X^i = 1$ or there is some $A \in O - X$ such that $b_{XA}^i = b_X^i$. Finally, whenever there is some X in $dup_{\Sigma_{\beta_i}}(O)$ and $dup_{\Sigma_{\beta_j}}(O)$, with $b_X^i = b_X^j$ and $i < j$, then remove X from $dup_{\Sigma_{\beta_i}}(O)$. This procedure is called in lines 1-3 by Algorithm 1, which computes an Armstrong p-instance for a given QC set Σ over some given p-object type $(O, \mathcal{S})$ such that for all $A \in \mathcal{O}$ there is some $(card(A) \leq b, \beta_1) \in \Sigma$.

Algorithm 1 computes objects over O for each duplicate set X with certainty β_i, starting from $i = k$ down to 1. Before moving on to another duplicate set with certainty β_i, the algorithm processes all occurrences of X as a duplicate set with certainty $\beta_l \geq \beta_i$ (lines 8-9), introducing $b_X^l - b$ objects o_r (lines 10-19) with p-degree α_{k+1-l} (line 17), where b is the cardinality of the duplicate set X already processed in the previous step (line 20). Line 24 marks X as processed to exclude it from repeated computations in the future (line 6).

Theorem 6. *Let ι_{min} denote an Armstrong p-instance for Σ with a minimum number of objects, that is, there is no Armstrong p-instance for Σ with fewer objects than those in ι_{min}. Algorithm 1 computes an Armstrong p-instance ι for Σ such that $|\iota| \leq |\iota_{min}| \times |\Sigma|$.*

Not surprisingly, the problem of finding Armstrong p-instances is worst-case exponential in the input size. Indeed, this is to be expected as an Armstrong

---

Algorithm 1. Visualize

Require: QC set Σ over p-object type $(O, \{\beta_1, \ldots, \beta_k, \beta_{k+1}\})$ such that for every
    $A \in O$ there is some $(card(A) \leq b, \beta_1) \in \Sigma$ ▷ Necessary to guarantee existence
Ensure: Armstrong p-instance $(\iota, Poss_\iota)$ for Σ
  1: **for** $i = 1, \ldots, k$ **do**   ▷ Compute duplicate sets X with certainty β_i and b_X^i
  2:     Compute $(dup_{\Sigma_{\beta_i}}(O), \{b_X^i \mid X \in dup_{\Sigma_{\beta_i}}(O)\})$
  3: **end for**
  4: $r \leftarrow 0; \iota \leftarrow \emptyset; dup_\Sigma(O) \leftarrow \emptyset;$
  5: **for** $i = k$ downto 1 **do**
  6:     **for all** $X \in dup_{\Sigma_{\beta_i}}(O) - dup_\Sigma(O)$ **do**   ▷ Duplicate sets not processed yet
  7:         $b \leftarrow 0; j \leftarrow r + 1;$
  8:         **for** $l = i$ downto 1 **do**   ▷ Represent X in all possible worlds required
  9:             **if** $X \in dup_{\Sigma_{\beta_l}}(O)$ **then**   ▷ X requires more objects in world w_l
10:                 **for** $m = 1$ to $b_X^l - b$ **do**
11:                     $r \leftarrow r + 1;$
12:                     **for all** $A \in O$ **do**
13:                         **if** $A \in X$ **then** $o_r(A) \leftarrow c_{A,j};$ ▷ $\{c_{A,j} : A \in X\}$ represent X
14:                         **else** $o_r(A) \leftarrow c_{A,r};$ ▷ $c_{A,r}$ is a unique value in ι
15:                         **end if**
16:                     **end for**
17:                     $Poss_\iota(o_r) \leftarrow \alpha_{k+1-l};$ ▷ Add p-degree to new object
18:                     $\iota \leftarrow \iota \cup \{o_r\};$ ▷ Add new object to ι
19:                 **end for**
20:                 $b \leftarrow b_X^l;$ ▷ Book-keeping for cardinalities already represented
21:             **end if**
22:         **end for**
23:     **end for**
24:     $dup_\Sigma(O) \leftarrow dup_\Sigma(O) \cup dup_{\Sigma_{\beta_i}}(O);$ ▷ Mark duplicate set X as processed
25: **end for**
26: **return** $(\iota, Poss_\iota);$

---

p-instance ι_Σ for Σ represents the highest c-degree for which any cardinality constraint is implied by Σ.

Theorem 7. *Finding a finite Armstrong p-instance for a QC set Σ is precisely exponential in the size of Σ. That is, a finite Armstrong p-instance for Σ can be found in time at most exponential in the size of Σ whenever one exists, and there are QC sets Σ such that every finite Armstrong p-instance for Σ requires a number of objects that is exponential in the size of Σ.*

Proof. Algorithm 1 computes a finite Armstrong p-instance for Σ in time at most exponential in its size, whenever such an instance exists. Some QC sets Σ have only Armstrong p-instances with exponentially many objects in the size of Σ. For $O = \{A_1, \ldots, A_{2n}\}$, $\mathcal{S} = \{\alpha_1, \alpha_2\}$ and $\Sigma = \{(card(A_1, A_2) \leq 1, \beta_1), \ldots, (card(A_{2n-1}, A_{2n}) \leq 1, \beta_1)\} \cup \{(card(A_1) \leq 2, \beta_1), \ldots, (card(A_n) \leq 2, \beta_1)\}$ with size $2 \cdot n$, $dup_{\Sigma_{\beta_1}}(O)$ consists of the 2^n duplicate sets $\bigcup_{j=1}^n X_j$ where $X_j \in \{A_{2j-1}, A_{2j}\}$. $\square$

Armstrong p-instances for other QC sets Σ only require a size logarithmic in that of Σ. Such a set Σ is given by the following 2^n QCs: for all $i = 1, \ldots, n$, $(card(A_{2i-1}) \leq 3, \beta_1)$ and $(card(A_{2i}) \leq 3, \beta_1)$, and for all $X = X_1 \cdots X_n$ where $X_i \in \{A_{2i-1}, A_{2i}\}$, $(card(X) \leq 2, \beta_1)$. Then the size of Σ is in $\mathcal{O}(2^n)$ and there is no equivalent set for Σ of smaller size. Furthermore, $dup_{\Sigma_{\beta_1}}(O)$ consists of the n sets $O - \{A_{2i-1}, A_{2i}\}$ for $i = 1, \ldots, n$. Thus, Algorithm 1 computes a finite Armstrong p-instance for Σ whose size is in $\mathcal{O}(n)$.

For these reasons we recommend the use of abstract constraints sets and their Armstrong p-instances. Indeed, the constraint sets enable design teams to identify c-degrees of cardinality constraints that they currently perceive too high; and the Armstrong p-instances enable design teams to identify c-degrees of cardinality constraints that they currently perceive too low.

6   Conclusion and Future Work

Cardinality constraints occur naturally in most aspects of life. Consequently, they have received invested interest from the conceptual modeling community over the last three decades. We have introduced cardinality constraints to control the occurrences of uncertain data in modern applications, including big data. Uncertainty has been modeled qualitatively by applying the framework of possibility theory. Our cardinality constraints stipulate upper bounds on the number of occurrences of uncertain data, an ability that captures many real-world requirements. Our results show that cardinality constraints can be reasoned about efficiently. We have characterized which sets of cardinality constraints can be visualized perfectly in the form of a finite Armstrong instance. In such cases, our algorithm is always guaranteed to compute an Armstrong instance with conservative use of time and space. Armstrong instances embody the exact certainty by which any cardinality constraint is currently perceived to hold by the data analysts. The analysts can therefore show the small instances to domain experts in order to jointly consolidate the certainty by which cardinality constraints shall actually hold in a given application domain.

Our framework opens up several questions for future investigation, including the benefits of processing data with the help of cardinality constraints, more expressive cardinality constraints and their interaction with other constraints, as well as empirical evaluations for the usefulness of Armstrong p-instances. It is interesting to investigate whether infinite Armstrong p-instances can still be represented finitely in order to handle sets of cardinality constraints for which no finite Armstrong p-instance exists. Finally, constraints have not received much attention yet in probabilistic databases.

Acknowledgement. This research is supported by the Marsden fund council from Government funding, administered by the Royal Society of New Zealand.

References

1. Bosc, P., Pivert, O.: On the impact of regular functional dependencies when moving to a possibilistic database framework. Fuzzy Sets and Systems 140(1), 207–227 (2003)
2. Chen, P.P.: The Entity-Relationship model - toward a unified view of data. ACM Trans. Database Syst. 1(1), 9–36 (1976)
3. Currim, F., Neidig, N., Kampoowale, A., Mhatre, G.: The CARD system. In: Parsons, J., Saeki, M., Shoval, P., Woo, C., Wand, Y. (eds.) ER 2010. LNCS, vol. 6412, pp. 433–437. Springer, Heidelberg (2010)
4. Dubois, D., Prade, H.: Fuzzy cardinality and the modeling of imprecise quantification. Fuzzy Sets and Systems 16, 199–230 (1985)
5. Dubois, D., Prade, H.: Fuzzy set and possibility theory-based methods in artificial intelligence. Artif. Intell. 148(1-2), 1–9 (2003)
6. Fagin, R.: Horn clauses and database dependencies. J. ACM 29(4), 952–985 (1982)
7. Ferrarotti, F., Hartmann, S., Link, S.: Efficiency frontiers of XML cardinality constraints. Data Knowl. Eng. 87, 297–319 (2013)
8. Hartmann, S.: On the implication problem for cardinality constraints and functional dependencies. Ann. Math. Artif. Intell. 33(2-4), 253–307 (2001)
9. Hartmann, S., Kirchberg, M., Link, S.: Design by example for SQL table definitions with functional dependencies. VLDB J. 21(1), 121–144 (2012)
10. Jones, T.H., Song, I.Y.: Analysis of binary/ternary cardinality combinations in Entity-Relationship modeling. Data Knowl. Eng. 19(1), 39–64 (1996)
11. Langeveldt, W.D., Link, S.: Empirical evidence for the usefulness of Armstrong relations in the acquisition of meaningful functional dependencies. Inf. Syst. 35(3), 352–374 (2010)
12. Lenzerini, M., Nobili, P.: On the satisfiability of dependency constraints in entity-relationship schemata. Inf. Syst. 15(4), 453–461 (1990)
13. Liddle, S.W., Embley, D.W., Woodfield, S.N.: Cardinality constraints in semantic data models. Data Knowl. Eng. 11(3), 235–270 (1993)
14. Link, S.: Consistency enforcement in databases. In: Bertossi, L., Katona, G.O.H., Schewe, K.-D., Thalheim, B. (eds.) Semantics in Databases 2001. LNCS, vol. 2582, pp. 139–159. Springer, Heidelberg (2003)
15. Link, S.: Armstrong databases: Validation, communication and consolidation of conceptual models with perfect test data. In: Ghose, A., Ferrarotti, F. (eds.) Eighth Asia-Pacic Conference on Conceptual Modelling, APCCM 2012, pp. 3–20. Australian Computer Society, Melbourne (2012)
16. Mannila, H., Räihä, K.J.: Design by example: An application of Armstrong relations. J. Comput. Syst. Sci. 33(2), 126–141 (1986)
17. Queralt, A., Artale, A., Calvanese, D., Teniente, E.: OCL-Lite: Finite reasoning on UML/OCL conceptual schemas. Data Knowl. Eng. 73, 1–22 (2012)
18. Suciu, D., Olteanu, D., Ré, C., Koch, C.: Probabilistic Databases. Synthesis Lectures on Data Management. Morgan & Claypool Publishers (2011)
19. Thalheim, B.: Fundamentals of cardinality constraints. In: Pernul, G., Tjoa, A.M. (eds.) ER 1992. LNCS, vol. 645, pp. 7–23. Springer, Heidelberg (1992)

TopCrowd –

Efficient Crowd-enabled Top-k Retrieval on Incomplete Data

Christian Nieke[1], Ulrich Güntzer[2], and Wolf-Tilo Balke[1]

[1] IFIS, TU Braunschweig, Braunschweig, Germany
{nieke,balke}@ifis.cs.tu-bs.de
[2] Inst. f. Informatik, Universität Tübingen,Tübingen, Germany
ulrich.guentzer@informatik.uni-tuebingen.de

Abstract. Building databases and information systems over data extracted from heterogeneous sources like the Web poses a severe challenge: most data is incomplete and thus difficult to process in structured queries. This is especially true for sophisticated query techniques like Top-k querying where rankings are aggregated over several sources. The intelligent combination of efficient data processing algorithms with crowdsourced database operators promises to alleviate the situation. Yet the scalability of such combined processing is doubtful. We present TopCrowd, a novel crowd-enabled Top-k query processing algorithm that works effectively on incomplete data, while tightly controlling query processing costs in terms of response time and money spent for crowdsourcing. TopCrowd features probabilistic pruning rules for drastically reduced numbers of crowd accesses (up to 95%), while effectively balancing querying costs and result correctness. Extensive experiments show the benefit of our technique.

Keywords: Query processing, top-k queries, crowdsourcing, incomplete data.

1 Introduction

Bringing together peoples' cognitive abilities and efficient information processing algorithms is one of the hottest topics in database and information systems research [1–3]. The basic idea is simple, yet intriguing: let both, machines and people, do what they do best and combine their efforts! Machines and algorithms are perfect for fast and structured processing tasks over huge amounts of data, whereas humans are hard to beat in cognitive tasks or whenever flexible and intelligent decisions are needed. This combination is especially efficient where the classical structured databases are complemented by information derived from large collections of (semi-structured) data extracted in a 'schema later'-fashion from the Web. In particular, today's Web information management ties real world entities like consumer products, persons, or news items/media to additional information, thus boosting user experience.

Indeed, the usefulness of crowdsourced operators for query processing in databases has already been shown for tasks like the on-demand completion of missing values (CNULL values [2]), human-powered sorts and joins [4], human-guided similarity search [5], or entity linking and reconciliation [6]. However, the central question of

E. Yu et al. (Eds.): ER 2014, LNCS 8824, pp. 122–135, 2014.
© Springer International Publishing Switzerland 2014

query expressivity vs. processing costs remains. In the database world data accesses have to be minimized and the classical storage hierarchy is exploited for scalability. Now, crowdsourcing human intelligence tasks (HITs) adds another very expensive layer. Deploying HITs costs money and their completion via platforms like Amazon's Mechanical Turk (https://www.mturk.com), CrowdFlower (http://crowdflower.com/), or Samasource (http://samasource.org/) needs considerable time. Therefore, a careful balancing of a human intervention's usefulness with respective costs is necessary for all crowd-enabled query processing. *This paper focuses on exactly this problem: we introduce a new algorithm for crowd-enabled Top-k retrieval on incomplete data.*

Top-k retrieval, i.e. the aggregated ranking of database items according to user-provided preference functions, features a variety of efficient algorithms tailored to different scenarios. For example, a real world application of Top-k retrieval is support for purchases like buying a car or laptops for a company (which we will use as a running example in this paper). However, classical approaches to Top-k retrieval assume complete knowledge of all attributes for all objects in the database, which is not true in case of datasets aggregated from different sources like Open Linked Data or Web portals presenting offers from different vendors. For example, the average battery runtime of a laptop might be an important factor in decision making, but this piece of information might not be included in every vendor's description. In such scenarios, easily and reliably getting the best offers from an incomplete data set is well worth waiting a bit for the result and even investing a few dollars for crowdsourcing.

Looking at the challenges it is clear that a crowd-enabled Top-k algorithm should derive a correct and complete ranking at minimum cost in terms of response time and money spent. However, there is also some space for trade-offs: since crowd accesses are really expensive, can some of the result correctness be traded for better cost effectiveness? This question is valid, since Web sources generally do not claim completeness. They just collect all reasonably trustworthy pieces of information extracted from the Web (cf. DBPedia [7], Freebase [8], or the YAGO knowledge base [9]). Thus, our approach also has practical impact on Web information system engineering.

We present TopCrowd an innovative algorithm for crowd-enabled Top-k retrieval. In particular we investigate safe Top-k pruning rules, tuple selection heuristics for crowdsourcing, and probabilistic result set correctness. Thus, TopCrowd is able to balance crowdsourcing costs in terms of money and response times, HIT selection and batching, and result correctness. Our main contributions are:

- A sophisticated algorithmic framework for Top-k query processing over databases with missing values utilizing crowdsourcing techniques.
- Safe pruning rules for correct crowd-enabled Top-k retrieval enhanced by probabilistic rules for drastically reduced numbers of crowd accesses, and thus costs.
- Serious performance gains by an order of magnitude depending on the retrieval scenario
- Good prediction of either hard upper bound for costs (given a probability of result quality) or hard lower bound for probability of result quality (given a cost limit).
- Very good batch size optimization balancing financial cost and runtime.

2   Related Work

Due to the Web as a new information source Top-k retrieval in databases was investigated starting about a decade ago and now has reached a mature state. While the first applications focused on multimedia databases [10] and middleware solutions [11], it soon became clear that Top-k retrieval is important for a wide variety of scenarios like Web databases[12], mobile scenarios[13], or distributed retrieval settings [14].

Basically, for a database instance of N objects the model for Top-k queries on D attributes is a D-dimensional space usually restricted to $[0,1]^D$. Using a user-provided *utility* or *preference function,* numerical as well as categorical attributes can individually be transformed for each attribute into a total order [15]. Moreover, users provide a *monotonic scoring function totalscore*: $[0,1]^D \rightarrow [0,1]$ that allows the aggregation of individual attribute scores into a final score for subsequent ranking. Top-k algorithms usually distinguish two types of access: *sorted* and *random* access. While sorted accesses iterate over the objects in any list for some attribute in descending score order, random accesses directly retrieve some object's score value with respect to any attribute. Because the costs of these access types may strongly differ (usually random accesses are much more expensive than sorted accesses), algorithms that flexibly adapt to the respective usage scenario have been developed (see e.g. [13]).

Incomplete data sets create new problems: they contain CNULL values [2], which usually have a well-defined value (e.g. "5 hours" for some laptop's average battery runtime) that is however yet unknown to the system. In the presence of these CNULL values, conventional Top-k database algorithms will not work, as it is impossible to correctly rank objects with unknown attribute values with either kind of access (cf. failing access heuristics in [11, 13, 16]). We therefore need a way to either reliably estimate missing scores (see [17] and [18] for ranking in incomplete databases) or elicit the exact value using a new kind of access: the *crowd access*. The *crowd access* crowdsources the cognitive task of procuring adequate attribute values by e.g. performing Web searches to find the required information on a laptop in a vendor's specification or by calling the vendor of a used car and asking for additional details.

Of course, this leads to the question of the *quality* of information gathered by the crowd. Here typical safeguards can be used like blending in gold questions with previously established answers to detect malicious or incompetent users or performing majority votes over several users working on the same task (see. e.g. [2, 19]). Still, depending on the task there may be differing quality levels. For instance, for purely factual tasks like looking up movie genres on IMDB.com, experiments in [19] show a correctness of 95% at only 0.03 USD per tuple including gold questions. Similar results have been shown for labeling training data in the IR community. Hence, for simple attribute look-ups in Top-k query processing safeguarding with gold questions and banning malicious or incompetent workers works fine (see section 4.2).

It is obvious that due to the relatively high costs (especially in terms of response times ranging in the area of minutes for a crowdsourced HIT), the number of *crowd accesses* should be limited as much as possible. Especially for larger Web datasets, crowdsourcing every incomplete object up front to perform a classical Top-k retrieval is prohibitive. Thus, the most related work to our approach is [20] where approximate variants of the basic threshold algorithm to reduce run-time costs are presented. Top-k algorithms are basically considered as linear index scans over the descending score lists for each attribute. Based on probabilistic arguments, a point can be determined where it is safe to drop candidate items and to terminate the index scans. However, these approximation algorithms cannot cope with incomplete data, nor do they balance different access types or perform probabilistic selections of candidates for more complex score elicitation. Still, the probabilistic estimation of the final error in result correctness can to some degree be used in our scenario.

Another related problem is discussed in e.g. [21–23], which deal with Top-k requests over objects that need a crowd operator for comparison (e.g. comparing pictures). Here, the challenge is to find the Top-k objects without having to perform the (naïve) $O(n^2)$ comparisons of each object with each other, while we deal with the problem of reducing the $O(n)$ crowd lookups of missing attributes, whereas the order can be found algorithmically.

3   The TopCrowd Algorithm

In the following we will present our algorithm TopCrowd which allows performing Top-k retrieval on incomplete data while optimizing the cost of *crowd accesses* necessary to retrieve missing data.

3.1   Formal Definition

Given a D-dimensional dataset containing N objects, we will denote objects $o_i, 1 \leq i \leq N$ as tuples of attributes $o_i[1] \dots o_i[D]$ as $o_i \in ([0,1] \cup \{CNULL\})^D$.

Every attribute is assigned a score in $[0,1]$ or it is considered missing, but could be retrieved via crowdsourcing (CNULL). We further denote the set of all items A and define the set of incomplete items I as: $I := \{ o_i \in A | \exists_{1 \leq j \leq D} o_i[j] = CNULL \}$ and the set of complete items C as: $C := \{ o_i \in A | \nexists_{1 \leq j \leq D} o_i[j] = CNULL \}$.

For each complete object in C we can calculate its total score, representing how well it corresponds to a given query using any *monotonic* function $score : C \rightarrow [0,1]$. To avoid confusion, in the following we will refer to the score attributes simply as 'attributes' and 'score' always refers to the total score.

3.2   Basic Algorithm

The main optimization objective of our algorithm is to reduce the number of expensive crowd accesses. To achieve this, our algorithm performs the following 4 basic steps which will be discussed in detail in the following subsections:

1. Classic Top-k retrieval on complete objects
2. Optimal safe pruning of incomplete objects
3. Probabilistic ranking of incomplete objects
4. Crowd access cost control

In the first step we perform classical Top-k retrieval on all those objects that are completely known, resulting in a temporary Top-k result K_c and the remaining incomplete objects I that could not be handled by classical Top-k.

In the next step, we perform optimal safe pruning, i.e. we discard *exactly* those incomplete objects that could never reach the Top-k, independent of the actual value of all their CNULL values, to avoid all strictly unnecessary *crowd accesses*.

We then estimate the probability of all remaining incomplete objects to reach the Top-k after crowdsourcing, and rank them accordingly, so that the most promising ones will be crowdsourced first, which could allow further pruning.

We could now start crowdsourcing the incomplete objects one by one according to their rank and return to the pruning step after receiving any new result until no incomplete objects are left, which would minimize the number of crowd accesses to reach the *correct* result in an optimal way, assuming a correct rank estimation and correct results from the crowd accesses. However, in practice the user might have an interest in balancing financial costs (which depend on the number of crowd accesses) and processing time and might be willing to sacrifice some of the result quality to improve those costs.

We therefore added a fourth step that allows the user to control these costs by either letting her define an amount of money she is willing to spend and presenting her with a hard lower bound probability that the result will be correct (*P_target*), or letting her define the target probability she requires, and giving a hard upper bound for financial costs, while always trying to optimize processing time.

In the following, we will explain the single steps of the algorithm in more detail.

3.3   Optimal Safe Pruning

After receiving the temporary result K_c from the initial Top-k retrieval on the complete objects in the first step, or a previous iteration, we define the score of the worst object in this set as the minimal score, *min_topk,* which an incomplete object must at least surpass to replace any object in the temporary Top-k list.

Given an *upper bound* for each incomplete object as the score after replacing missing attributes with 1, we can then prune all incomplete objects whose upper bound is below or equal *min_topk*, as they will never replace any item in K_c. This makes the algorithm *correct*, as it prunes *only* items that cannot improve the Top-k result, but also *optimal*, as it prunes *all* items that, given our current knowledge, will never improve the Top-k. Objects with an upper bound of exactly *min_topk* will be pruned by our algorithm, as they might change, but not *improve* the result.   □

3.4   Ranking of Incomplete Objects

When crowdsourcing batches of incomplete objects, one should obviously start with the candidates that are most likely to actually be part of the Top-k, especially when following a probabilistic approach. In the following, we will first present two approaches used as lower and upper baseline during our evaluation, followed by a more sophisticated approach to estimate the ranking.

Lower Baseline: Naïve UpperLowerRatio. For our lower baseline, we developed the following, very intuitive way to predict if an incomplete object will be in the Top-k, by incorporating only its upper and lower bound score, where the lower bound is defined as the score of an incomplete object, with all missing attributes set to 0.

Assuming no knowledge of the scoring function and the data distribution, we assume a uniform distribution of scores, and define the probability of an incomplete object $I_i \in I$ to get into the current Top-k result set K_c as the probability of the objects score to reach above *min_topk*. Given its upper and lower bound, the conditional probability can therefore be defined as:

$$P(score(I_i) > min\_topk) = \frac{upperBound(I_i) - min\_topk}{upperBound(I_i) - lowerBound(I_i)}$$

Given these probabilities for each incomplete object, we can now select the most probable objects for crowdsourcing. In the following, we will refer to this ranking strategy as *UpperLowerRatio*. While this approach is very fast and intuitive, the underlying assumption of a uniform distribution of scores is of course very likely to be wrong, a problem that is addressed by our more sophisticated prediction approach presented later.

Upper Baseline: Perfect Ranking. For evaluation purposes, we define the upper baseline of what a prediction could possibly achieve as *perfect ranking*, i.e. a strategy that selects the objects ordered descending by their actual score, which is of course only known beforehand in our experimental setting, and not for real applications.

Probabilistic Prediction and Projection: KDEScorePrediction. This approach tries to predict the score probability distribution of an incomplete object, using the actual distribution of the complete objects.

A common approach for predicting the distribution of objects in a multidimensional space, given a sample of the distribution, is multivariate kernel density estimation (KDE), see e.g.,[24]. The KDE estimates a density function φ as:

$$\varphi_H(x) = \frac{1}{n}\sum_{i=1}^{n} K_H(x - x_i)$$

Here the x_i are the n sample vectors in the space, and K_H is a kernel function with a given bandwidth H for smoothing. In a nutshell, the idea of a KDE is to create a normalized histogram of the space and smooth it using the kernel.

For each incomplete item o with m missing attributes, an m-dimensional flat of that space F_o^m can be defined as:

$$F_o^m := \{ (f[1],\ldots,f[D]) \mid \forall_{1 \leq i \leq D} : \begin{cases} f[i] = o[i], o[i] \neq CNULL \\ f[i] \in [0,1], \quad else \end{cases} \}$$

F_o^m represents the sub area of the whole D-dimensional space, in which the real coordinates of o will be after crowdsourcing. This allows to calculate the probability of an incomplete object to be above *min_topk* by calculating the m-dimensional integral over the density in the area of F_o^m that would yield a score above *min_topk*, divided by the integral over the density in all of F_o^m.

Unfortunately, the complexity of calculating the discrete integral in a high dimensional space is exponential in terms of the number of dimensions. Assuming we used 100 steps per dimension to sample the space, we would have to calculate the density for 100^m points, which becomes computationally infeasible even for moderate m. Even though there are some computationally more efficient approaches of sampling, using Monte Carlo techniques or sparse grids (see e.g., [25] and [26]), they are still far from performing in real-time and our assumption of considering local computation as negligible would no longer hold. To avoid this problem (related to the *curse of dimensionality*) we propose the following approach, using a *localized sample* and the *projection* of multidimensional objects to a single score axis.

To understand our prediction method, it is essential to understand, that we are not actually interested in the *exact multidimensional coordinates* of the data, but only in their resulting *aggregated scores*. Thus, rather than predicting the distribution of coordinates in F_o^m, we will project all complete items in F_o^m to a one dimensional score axis reflecting only the objects' aggregated scores, and use their distribution to predict the score of the respective incomplete object.

To do this, we define a set of *support points* of the incomplete o, SP_o as the set of all complete items in F_o^m as: $SP_o := C \cap F_o^m$. As F_o^m will most likely be sparsely populated in higher dimensions, we will increase its size by a parameter $+/-\Delta$ along all known attributes of o, which we will call $F_{o,\Delta}^m$. This allows us to define the (larger or equal) set $SP_{o,\Delta}$ as: $SP_{o,\Delta} := C \cap F_{o,\Delta}^m$.

We can now use the scoring function to project the *support points* onto the one dimensional score axis, to receive a set of *support scores* $SS_{o,\Delta}$ as: $SS_{o,\Delta} := \{ ss \in [0,1] \mid \exists sp \in SP_{o,\Delta} : ss = score(sp) \}$.

Using these support scores as samples for a univariate KDE, we are able to create a score density function of o, $\varphi_o(score)$ which we finally use to predict the conditional probability of the incomplete object o to be above *min_topk* given its upper bound and lower bound as:

$$P(score(o) > min\_topk) = \frac{\int_{x=min\_topk}^{upperBound(o)} \varphi_o(x)}{\int_{x=lowerBound(o)}^{upperBound(o)} \varphi_o(x)}$$

Using this approach, rather than sampling a high dimensional space, we only need to perform a ranged query to retrieve the support points and then sample the one dimensional score density to calculate the discrete integral. During our experiments, we found that this calculation could be performed for all incomplete objects within a manner of seconds, and is thus negligible compared to crowdsourcing.

Note, that the choice of Δ can of course affect the performance of this approach. If chosen to small, there will not be enough *support points* for a good prediction, but if chosen to large, the prediction will lose its specificity for the incomplete object. This intuition was supported in a set of experiments, but for reasons of brevity we will simply set it to 0.02, which worked well in our experiments. We will refer to this estimation strategy as *KDEScorePrediction*.

3.5   Controlling Crowdsourcing Costs

In the following we will show how to balance the three major concerns of a user, namely result quality, processing time and financial cost, by giving the user full control over a tradeoff between result quality and financial costs and optimizing processing time in exchange for a potential, minor financial overhead.

As safe pruning must unfortunately be based on the upper bound score of incomplete objects, this often leads to crowdsourcing a long tail of objects which were estimated to be very unlikely to reach the Top-k but cannot be pruned *safely*. However, a user might be willing to trade a certain amount of result quality for lower costs, by accepting a probabilistic approach that ignores some of the unlikely candidates for crowdsourcing, as long as the result is *likely enough*, i.e. it is correct with a user defined probability P_target.

Since our ranking strategies UpperLowerRatio and KDEScorePrediction already yield a probability for each item to be a above the current threshold, and assuming these probabilities are independent, we can use these probabilities to calculate the probability of all incomplete items not being above threshold, P_{result}, as:

$$P_{result} := \prod_{o \in I}(1 - P(score(o) > min \_topk))$$

Using this formula, we can now predict the probability of a correct result and stop the algorithm when a user defined probability P_target is reached.

But while allowing a user to save financial costs in exchange for result quality is a good start, she needs a way to evaluate the trade-off between those two factors to make an informed decision. How much money would she save by reducing the probability from 95% to 90% and what would be the probability if she invested 3$?

Fortunately, we can make a prediction about this, using our probabilistic ranking strategies which define the rank r on which an item will be crowdsourced and its probability to reach the Top-k. The order of the incompletes is stable, assuming that a few crowdsourced objects do not influence the underlying probability distribution, and further crowdsourcing will only reduce the probability of an item becoming Top-k, by increasing the score needed to replace one of the temporary Top-k items. Using this information, we can a priori calculate a hard, lower bound probability that will be reached after any number t of ranked, incomplete objects o_r is crowdsourced as:

$$P_{result\_lowerbound}(t) := \prod_{r=t+1}^{R}\left(1 - P(score(o_r) > min \_topk)\right)$$

Here, o_r is the object at rank r and R is the maximal rank of incomplete items. Using this formula, we can now predict the minimal probability that will be reached for a given number of crowd requests t (and thus financial costs) or inversely calculate the maximal number of crowd requests (and therefore financial costs) needed to achieve an intended probability.

This leaves us with a well-defined set of objects that we would have to crowdsource if our pessimistic bounds were true and leads us to the problem of runtime optimization. While performing all the remaining *crowd accesses* one by one, could actually reduce the number of crowd accesses below our pessimistic estimate (by performing

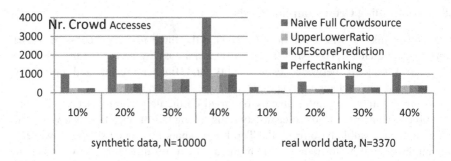

Fig. 1. TopCrowd for *P_target*=100% and different values of *missing_rate*

additional pruning whenever *min_topk* is increased), this is an extremely inefficient approach in praxis, as crowdsourcing jobs are best performed in large batches. For one, creating a batch with many HITs obviously allows a higher level of parallelization by dividing the tasks amongst several workers. Additionally, quality control usually tries to filter out incompetent or malicious workers by evaluating their agreement with other workers or by testing them using gold questions, which however creates an additional (also financial) overhead for each batch.

When we performed a set of experiments to evaluate the potential of performing small batches (see 4.2), we found that even when performing only one *crowd access* at a time we saved only between 1-2% of *crowd accesses*, and therefore decided to perform all requests in only one batch to optimize runtime. For similar reasons, we also decided to fetch all missing CNULL values of an object in one single *crowd access*, rather than splitting the attributes up into single tasks.

4   Evaluation

4.1   Datasets and Simulations

To test our algorithms under various conditions, we prepared a number of datasets consisting of both, real world data and synthetic data to allow larger experiments.

The real world data set consists of notebook offers crawled from linked data on the Web. We selected only suitable attributes to be used in Top-k requests. Since we needed a ground truth to assess our algorithms performance, we cleaned the data of all objects with actually missing attributes, and ended up with a set of 3370 notebooks, consisting of data for four dimensions: CPU frequency, hard drive size, memory size and screen size. All attribute values were scaled to an interval [0,1] and used as attribute scores.

For the synthetic data, we created a data set of 20 dimensions by creating pairs of attributes with attribute values in the interval [0,1]. Each pair follows either normal or uniform distribution and corresponds to a correlation factor of -0.8, -0.4, 0, 0.4 or 0.8 respectively. In total, this results in a dataset of over 10.000 objects with 20 dimensions of which *D* are picked randomly to represent either uniform or normal distribution and a certain chance that some of the dimensions will be correlated.

To test our algorithms in various conditions, we simulated several hundred different user queries per parameter set. A user query is characterized by a random selection of *D* attributes of the dataset combined via a scoring function representing the user's demands. Although our algorithm allows any monotonic scoring function, we used the arithmetic mean of all requested attributes for simplicity. We then randomly selected N objects from the data set and turned a given percentage of them into incomplete objects according to a *missing_rate*. Whenever an object was chosen to be turned into an incomplete object, each attribute had a chance of 50% to be deleted.

4.2   TopCrowd Evaluation

We will first evaluate the performance of the TopCrowd algorithm for Top-k query results with guaranteed correctness (*P_target* = 100%) using only safe pruning rules.

Figure 1 shows the results of our first experiment, in which we compared the performance of naïvely crowdsourcing all incomplete items to perform classical Top-k retrieval (Naïve Full Crowdsource) against our TopCrowd algorithm, using each of our three ranking strategies for P_target=100%. The result is shown for different values of *missing_rate*, which of course also defines the number of incomplete objects, and is averaged over at least 3000 samples with values of *D* between 2-4 and *k* ∈ (10,20,40). Here, we performed all crowd accesses one by one, followed by an additional pruning after a new Top-k item was found, but as mentioned before, this increased performance by only about 1-2%, so we decided to perform all accesses in one batch in the future. The overall result, however, is promising, and shows a reduction of crowd accesses to about 24% of the original number for the large synthetic data set, and a reduction to 32-34% for the real world data, while the *missing_rate* shows no influence on relative performance. Even more, our TopCrowd algorithm shows no significant difference in performance between all ranking strategies, including the theoretical upper bound *perfect ranking* which delivers optimal results.

To check whether this effect was due to the selection strategies performing similarly well or if there was another effect overshadowing the differences, we compared our proposed selection strategies to *perfect ranking*. To this end, we performed 500 runs for each value of *k* and *missing_rate* in 4 dimensions, performed the initial pruning, and then calculated Spearman's rank correlation coefficient between the predicted ranking for each ranking strategy and the *perfect ranking*. On average, we got a correlation coefficient of 0.31 for *UpperLowerRatio* and 0.43 for *KDEScorePrediction* on synthetic data, and scores about 0.02 lower for the real data. These results show that both algorithms tend towards a correct prediction, and our proposed algorithm *KDEScorePrediction* performs significantly better than our lower baseline *UpperLowerRatio*, but still leaves room for improvement.

As the selection strategies showed clear differences in prediction quality, we further investigated the problem and found that a better prediction strategy does indeed reach the correct Top-k set earlier, but the algorithm still needs to continue crowdsourcing to eliminate all the remaining incomplete items, even though they are very unlikely, to reach guaranteed correctness.

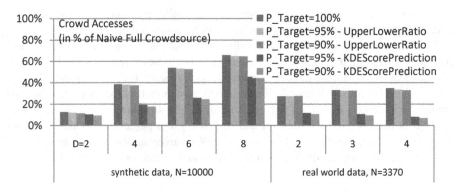

Fig. 2. TopCrowd for different values of *P_target* and *D*

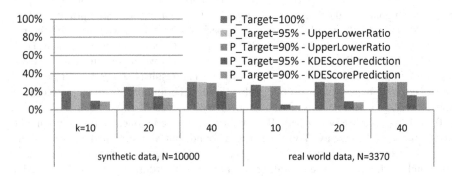

Fig. 3. TopCrowd for different values of *P_target* and *k*

This is exactly the problem which we tried to avoid with our probabilistic approach, so we performed another experiment comparing the ranking strategies for different values of *P_target* and *D*. Figure 2 shows the number of *crowd accesses* needed to achieve the given probability (in percentage of naïve crowdsourcing all incompletes), with each result averaged over at least 2400 samples with $missing\_rate \in (10\%, 20\%, 30\%, 40\%)$ and $k \in (10,20,40)$ while Figure 3 shows the same results for different values of k averaged over D from 2-4. The result clearly shows that the ranking strategy has a huge impact on our probabilistic approach, and while our lower baseline *UpperLowerRatio* improves performance by only about 1-2%, our strategy *KDEScorePrediction* allows to reduce the number of *crowd accesses* to 9-45% for synthetic data, and even more to 5-15% for our real world data set. While the performance for a higher number of dimensions decreases on the synthetic data set, it actually improves on the real world data set. We believe this effect is caused by the fact, that while in the synthetic data set most dimensions are actually unrelated, and therefore more dimensions simply increase the amount of information missing per object, the dimensions in the real world data set are related, which leads to a better prediction if it is based on more attributes (i.e. it is easier to predict A from B, C and D, rather than just from B).

When one uses a probabilistic approach to terminate the algorithm early, it is of course essential to evaluate if the prediction is indeed correct. To do this, we examined 16.000 simulations of TopCrowd with *KDEScorePrediction* for each target probability of 90% and 95% and counted the number of cases, where the result was actually correct when our algorithm terminated. We found that our algorithm actually found the correct result in 98.21% of all cases for a target probability of 90% and in 99.21% of all cases for a target probability of 95%, meaning that we are underestimating the probability of the result being correct. While these conservative estimations of our algorithm put us on the safe side when guaranteeing a lower bound probability, it also means that the intended probability was in fact reached earlier, meaning that a better prediction could lead to even better results.

In a final experiment, we performed the actual crowdsourcing operations for 10 runs of TopCrowd with 4 dimensions of the real dataset, a *missing_rate* of 20% and k=40. For quality control, we used gold questions and a majority vote of three workers per missing object. Per missing attribute we paid 0.01$ to look up the actual value, which we then transformed into the interval [0,1] the same way as for the original data. This led to a price of about 0.06$ per object including overhead for gold questions and fees to the portal *CrowdFlower*. On average, we paid 4$ for a probabilistic Top-k result with 90% probability and about 17.3$ for a correct result (probability 100%), while crowdsourcing *all* missing attributes would have cost about 40.44$ per experiment run. Our rudimentary safeguard mechanisms including gold questions and the majority vote of three crowd workers led to the correct result in 88% of all cases on average. The correctness could however likely be improved by employing some of the more advanced mechanisms as discussed before. In those cases where the result could not be reliably retrieved, we decided to exclude the object from the Top-k result, as we would rather risk a false negative than a false positive for Top-k scenarios.

5   Results and Discussion

Both, Web information management and retrieval, often face the problem of incomplete data, because information about central entities of interest may be distributed over several information sources. Hence, a new kind of query processing (including for instance data extraction, reference reconciliation, or entity ranking) is needed. As argued above for typical scenarios like product searches, individual recommendations, or decision support, this usually requires some intelligence to effectively perform the task. Fortunately the innovative combination of *efficient data processing algorithms* with new *crowdsourced database operators* promises to alleviate the situation.

In this paper we presented TopCrowd, a novel and efficient algorithm that shows the possibility of building sophisticated crowd-enabled query processing operators for Top-k query processing. Our extensive evaluations on synthetic, as well as real world Web data clearly show that the new TopCrowd operator can indeed be practical, although including human intervention. In particular, our *safe pruning rules* always deliver correct query results, while leading to immediate performance gains between 50-75% in terms of necessary crowd accesses, which indeed is valuable for such an expensive type of access. With individual response times and monetary query costs in mind, we then incorporated *probabilistic ranking strategies* allowing to sacrifice a bit of the result correctness for vast performance improvements in a user-guided fashion. Building on the basic idea of kernel density estimation enhanced by score projection, our approach already allows a tight prediction of either upper bounds for costs (given a desired probability or result quality), or lower bounds for the probability of a correct result, given the costs a user is willing to accept for each query. In fact we showed that our algorithm allows to reduce crowdsourcing costs by up to 95% while at the same time optimizing batch size and therefore runtime. In fact, it can be guaranteed to at least reach some desired probability with just a single batch paying only for slightly more crowd accesses than strictly necessary in a hypothetical optimal algorithm. For future work there is still room for in-detail optimization and a tighter estimation of error bounds. Moreover, our future work will investigate other sophisticated query processing operators and their potential for intelligent crowdsourcing. We believe that it is necessary to harness the benefits of human cognition, assessment, and validation to intelligently steer data management and query processing tasks in a vast variety of applications with growing complexity. Thus, crowdsourced database operators are bound to gain more momentum in future query processing scenarios.

References

1. Doan, A., Ramakrishnan, R., Halevy, A.Y.: Crowdsourcing systems on the World-Wide Web. Communications of the ACM, CACM (2011)
2. Franklin, M.J., Kossmann, D., Kraska, T., Ramesh, S., Xin, R.: CrowdDB. In: Proceedings of the 2011 International Conference on Management of Data (SIGMOD). ACM Press, New York (2011)
3. Parameswaran, A.: Answering Queries using Humans, Algorithms and Databases. Syst. Res., 160–166 (2011)
4. Marcus, A., Wu, E., Karger, D., Madden, S., Miller, R.: Human-powered Sorts and Joins. Proc. VLDB Endow. 5, 13–24 (2011)
5. Selke, J., Lofi, C., Balke, W.: Pushing the boundaries of crowd-enabled databases with query-driven schema expansion. Proc. VLDB Endow. (2012)
6. Demartini, G., Difallah, D.E., Cudré-Mauroux, P.: ZenCrowd. In: Proceedings of the 21st International Conference on World Wide Web (WWW). ACM Press, New York (2012)
7. Bizer, C., Lehmann, J., Kobilarov, G., Auer, S., Becker, C., Cyganiak, R., Hellmann, S.: DBpedia - A crystallization point for the Web of Data. Web Semant. Sci. Serv. Agents World Wide Web 7, 154–165 (2009)
8. Bollacker, K., Evans, C., Paritosh, P., Sturge, T., Taylor, J.: Freebase. In: Proceedings of the 2008 ACM SIGMOD International Conference on Management of Data (SIGMOD). ACM Press, New York (2008)
9. Suchanek, F.M., Kasneci, G., Weikum, G.: Yago. In: Proceedings of the 16th International Conference on World Wide Web (WWW). ACM Press, New York (2007)
10. Güntzer, U., Balke, W., Kießling, W.: Optimizing multi-feature queries for image databases. In: Proceedings of the 26th International Conference on Very Large Databases (VLDB), Cairo, Egypt (2000)
11. Fagin, R., Lotem, A., Naor, M.: Optimal aggregation algorithms for middleware. J. Comput. Syst. Sci. 66, 614–656 (2003)

12. Marian, A., Bruno, N., Gravano, L.: Evaluating top- k queries over web-accessible databases. ACM Trans. Database Syst. 29, 319–362 (2004)
13. Balke, W., Güntzer, U., Kießling, W.: On Real-Time Top k Querying for Mobile Services. In: Procs. of Int. Conf. on Cooperative Information Systems (CoopIS), Irvine, CA, USA, pp. 125–143 (2002)
14. Balke, W.-T., Nejdl, W., Siberski, W., Thaden, U.: Progressive Distributed Top-k Retrieval in Peer-to-Peer Networks. In: 21st International Conference on Data Engineering (ICDE), pp. 174–185. IEEE, Tokyo (2005)
15. Fishburn, P.: Preference structures and their numerical representations. Theor. Comput. Sci. 217, 359–383 (1999)
16. Guntzer, J., Balke, W.-T., Kiessling, W.: Towards efficient multi-feature queries in heterogeneous environments. In: Proceedings International Conference on Information Technology: Coding and Computing, pp. 622–628. IEEE Comput. Soc.
17. Wolf, G., Khatri, H., Chokshi, B., Fan, J., Chen, Y., Kambhampati, S.: Query processing over incomplete autonomous databases. In: Proceedings of the 33rd International Conference on Very Large Data Bases (VLDB), Vienna, Austria (2007)
18. Hua, M., Pei, J., Lin, X.: Ranking queries on uncertain data. VLDB J. 20, 129–153 (2010)
19. Lofi, C., Selke, J., Balke, W.-T.: Information Extraction Meets Crowdsourcing: A Promising Couple. Datenbank-Spektrum 12, 109–120 (2012)
20. Theobald, M., Weikum, G., Schenkel, R.: Top-k query evaluation with probabilistic guarantees. In: Proceedings of the Thirtieth International Conference on Very Large Data Bases (VLDB), Toronto, Canada, pp. 648–659 (2004)
21. Alfaro, L., De, D.J., Garcia-Molina, H., Polyzotis, N.: Human-Powered Top-k Lists. In: International Workshop on the Web and Databases (WebDB), New York, NY, USA (2013)
22. Davidson, S.B., Khanna, S., Milo, T., Roy, S.: Using the crowd for top-k and group-by queries. In: Proceedings of the 16th International Conference on Database Theory (ICDT). ACM Press, New York (2013)
23. Guo, S., Parameswaran, A., Garcia-Molina, H.: So who won?: dynamic max discovery with the crowd. In: Proceedings of the 2012 International Conference on Management of Data (SIGMOD), pp. 385–396 (2012)
24. Simonoff, J.S.: Smoothing Methods in Statistics. Springer (1996)
25. Jerrum, M., Sinclair, A.: The markov chain monte carlo method: An approach to approximate counting and integration. In: Hochbaum, D. (ed.) Approximation Algorithms for NP-Hard Problems. PWS Publishing Company (1996)
26. Griebel, M., Schneider, M., Zenger, C.: A combination technique for the solution of sparse grid problems. In: De Groen, P., Beauwens, R. (eds.) Iterative Methods in Linear Algebra, pp. 263–281. IMACS, Elsevier, North Holland (1992)

Web Services Composition
in the Presence of Uncertainty

Soumaya Amdouni[1], Mahmoud Barhamgi[1], Djamal Benslimane[1],
Rim Faiz[2], and Kokou Yetongnon[3]

[1] LIRIS Laboratory, Claude Bernard Lyon1 University 69622 Villeurbanne, France
[2] University of Carthage-IHEC 2016 Carthage, Tunisia
[3] Bourgogne University LE2I Laboratory 21078 Dijon France
{samdouni,barhamgi,dbenslim}@liris.cnrs.fr, Rim.Faiz@ihec.rnu.tn,
kokou@u-bourgogne.fr

Abstract. Recent years have witnessed a growing interest in using Web
Services as a powerful means for data publishing and sharing on top of
the Web. This class of services is commonly known as DaaS (Data-as-
a-Service), or also data services. The data returned by a data service is
often subject to uncertainty for various reasons (e.g., privacy constraints,
unreliable data collection instruments, etc. In this paper, we revisit the
basic activities related to (Web) data services that are impacted by uncertainty, including the service description, invocation and composition.
We propose a probabilistic approach to deal with uncertainty in all of
these activities.

Keywords: Data services, Uncertainty, Composition.

1 Introduction

In the last years, many organizations have started to provide a service-based access to their data on the Internet by puting their databases behind Web services.
This class of services is commonly known as DaaS (Data-as-a-Service) or *data
services* [6]. Data services and Web services in general have received a considerable attention in recent years [14]. Previous works have addressed the different
aspects of the Web service life-cycle, including service creation, selection, discovery, invocation and composition [14]. However, there are still many issues related
to the quality of data services themselves that need to be explored [8]. The uncertainty of the data returned by data services is one of the key issues that have
never been explored yet. Uncertainty is an inherent feature of the results returned by data services in many applications including Web data integration [9],
scientific data exploration [5], sensors networks [11], objects tracking, etc. We
refer to data services that return uncertain results as *uncertain data services* or
also *uncertain DaaSs*.

1.1 Motivating Scenario

The Table 1 below gives examples of uncertain data services from the eCommerce
domain. The service S_1 returns the information of a given product; S_2 returns

E. Yu et al. (Eds.): ER 2014, LNCS 8824, pp. 136–143, 2014.

the products ordered by a given customer; S_3 returns the customers at a given city; S_4 returns the sales representatives along with their phone numbers at a given city. Input parameters are proceeded by "$" and output parameters by "?" in the service signature.

The uncertainty of data services could have different origins. A data service may be uncertain because it integrates different data sources adopting different conventions for naming the same objects set. For example, S_1 provides complete information about products by integrating two Web data sources *cdiscount.com*, and *amazon.com*. S_1 joins products from these two sources over the product name. However, the name of the same product may be stored differently in the two sources, e.g., *computer* in *cdiscount.com* versus *laptop* in *amazon.com*. The uncertainty associated with S_2, S_3 and S_4 could come from the fact that the data sources accessed (or integrated) by these services contain conflicting information about customers and sales representatives.

The uncertainty associated with uncertain services must be explicitly modeled

Table 1. Examples of Data Web Services

Service	Semantics	Service Type
$S_1(\$p, ?pr, ?sh, ?cl)$	Returns informations (price pr, shape sh, color cl) about a given product p	Uncertain
$S_2(\$c, ?p, ?pr)$	Returns the products p along their prices pr which have been ordered by a given customer c.	Uncertain
$S_3(\$a, ?c, ?j)$	Returns the customers c and their jobs j at a given city a.	Uncertain
$S_4(\$a, ?s, ?t)$	Returns sales representatives s along with their phone t numbers at a given city a.	Uncertain

and described in order to ensure that service consumers can understand and interpret correctly the data returned by services and use them in the right way. For example, the consumer of S_2 should be advised about the probability of each retuned tuple so that he can make the right product choice. The need for a clear uncertainty model for uncertain services is further exacerbated when they are composed to provide value-added services.

1.2   Contributions

The objective of this article is to explore how uncertain database principles could be transposed to the service oriented data integration model. We revisited the basic activities related to data services that are impacted by uncertainty, including service description, invocation and composition, and proposed a probabilistic approach to deal with uncertainty in all of these activities. We identified a set of criteria under which a composition plan computes the correct probabilities of its returned results, which is very important for the correct interpretation of these results. The rest of the paper is organized as follows. In Section 2, we present our probabilistic models for uncertain data services and their invocation. We define our proposed composition model in Section 3 and we present some related works in Section 4. Finally we conclude the paper in Section 5.

2   A Probabilistic Model for Uncertain Data Services

2.1   The Description Model for Uncertain Data Services

Data uncertainty management has received a considerable attention from the database research community over the last decade. Two main challenges were addressed: uncertainty modeling and query processing over uncertain data. Different approaches were proposed to model data uncertainty [10]. Among these models, the probabilistic and the possibilistic models are the most adopted due to their simplicity. In the probabilistic data model, data uncertainty is modeled as a probability distribution over the possible tuple/attribute values [1]; i.e., each possible tuple/attribute value is assigned a degree of confidence, quantifying its probability. The probabilistic model is a numerical model that relies on an additive assumption and adopts the possible worlds semantics [9], where an uncertain relation is viewed as a set of possible instances (worlds). Each instance represents the real world with a confidence degree. The structure of these worlds could be governed by underlying generation rules (e.g., mutual exclusion of tuples that represent the same real-world entity). In the possibilistic data model, each possible tuple/attribute value is assigned a (normalized) degree representing how possible is that value.

In this section we give our model for representing uncertain data services. Our model adopts a probabilistic approach to describe the uncertainty associated with data services. An uncertain service may have one or more operations. Each operation may have one or more output parameters. The uncertainty associated with an operation may have two distinct levels: the individual output parameter and the whole output parameters set levels. These levels correspond to the attribute and the tuple levels in the relational model [10]. At the individual output parameter level, an output parameter may have multiple values from discrete or continuous domains [1], and each value has a given probability (that can be estimated by different techniques).

Definition: An uncertain data service is defined as follows: $S(\overline{I}, \overline{O^p})$, where

- $\overline{I}$ and $\overline{O^p}$ are respectively the input and output parameters of S.
- p represents the probability associated with output vector $\overline{O}$. p is in $[0, 1]$.

In this definition the input $\overline{I}$ represents only certain values. A certain service can be viewed as a particular uncertain service with probability $p = 1$.

The semantics of uncertain data service can be explained based on the possible worlds theory [10]. The probabilistic output tuples returned by the invocation can be interpreted as a set of possible worlds $(PW_1, ..., PW_n)$ and each possible world PW_i contains certain tuples and has a probability p_{PW_i} which is dependent on its contained tuples. In this present work we suppose that all returned outputs are independent events.

To correctly use an uncertain service, the probabilities and the correlations of its outputs should be modeled and integrated into service description standards. We exploited the extensibility feature of WSDL2.0 and defined two attributes: *"probability"* to specify the probability degree associated with each output, and

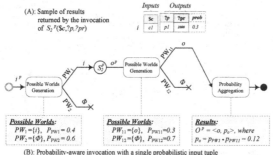

Fig. 1. Semantics of the probability-aware service invocation

"*Key*" to specify that an output parameter plays the role of an identifier (i.e. a primary key).

2.2 An Invocation Model for Uncertain Data Services

In this section we analyze the impact of data uncertainty on the service invocation process. Our objective is to define the invocation functionality and give insights on how its semantics should be extended to deal with uncertainty.
Notations: Let S^p be an uncertain data service, I denote certain inputs to the invocation process; I^p denote uncertain inputs: $I^p =< I, P >$, where P denotes the probability of I. Let O denote certain outputs of the invocation process; O^p denote uncertain outputs: $O^p =<O, P>$, where P denotes the probability of O.

Based on the input type (whether it is certain I or uncertain one I^p) we identify the following two invocation classes: conventional invocation and probabilistic invocation. If the input is certain I the invocation is conventional and O^p represents the set of returned outputs $\{O^p_1 =< O_1, P_1 >, ..., O^p_n =< O_n, P_n >\}$. The probabilistic invocation refers to the service invocation with uncertain inputs I^p. We use foundations of possible worlds semantics to explain the probabilistic invocation. Fig. 1 shows the results of the invocation of the service S^p_2 with the input $I^p = i$, where $i =< customer = $ "c_1"$, p_i = 0.4 >$

The probabilistic invocation is interpreted as follows: I^p can be represented as a set of possible worlds $\{PW_1, PW_2\}$ as $PW_1 = \{i\}$, and $PW_2 = \{\emptyset\}$. The probability of a possible world is derived from the probabilities of its involved tuples. For example PW_1 contains only one tuple i and thus its probability $p_{PW_1} = Prob(i) = 0.4$; PW_2 does not contain i thus $p_{PW_2} = 1 - Prob(i) = 0.6$. The probability of the output o is calculated as: $p_o = p_{PW_1} * p_{PW_{11}} = 0.4 * 0.3 = 0.12$ such as PW_{11} is a possible world of the interpretation of o and $PW_{11} = \{o\}, PW_{12} = \{\emptyset\}$.

Formally, the uncertain data service invocation can be defined in *extensional* manner (i.e., without materializing the possible worlds) as follows:
$$Invoke^p(S^p, I^p) = \{(O_1, P_{O_1} = P_1 * P_i), ..., (O_n, P_{O_n} = P_n * P_i)\} \qquad (1)$$

3   Uncertain Data Service Composition Model

While individual web services can provide interesting information, users queries often require the composition of multiple services. The existing web service

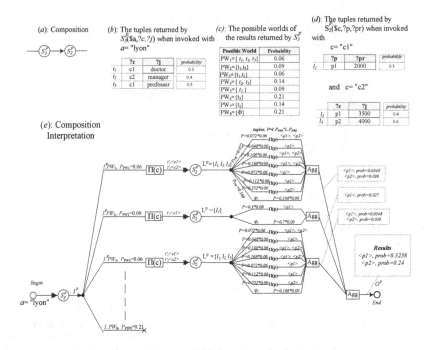

Fig. 2. Composition and Execution of uncertain Services

composition systems (e.g., [3]) don't address the problem of uncertainty. Data uncertainty is an important issue that must be taken into account in composition processes to allow for the right interpretation of returned results. In this section, we first define the semantics of uncertain services composition. Then we define a composition algebra that is aware of uncertainty and we present an algorithm which allows to find the correct orchestration plan.

3.1 Composition Semantics

In the case of uncertain data services, the interpretation of a composition is a bit harder than that of deterministic services. In this case, we are interested not only in computing the composition's results, but also in their probabilities. For example, assume that the uncertain services S_2^p and S_3^p are involved in a composition to find the products ordered in "lyon": The table in Fig.2(b) shows the results returned by S_3^p (along with their probabilities) when invoked with the value Lyon. The tables (c) and (d) in Fig. 2 give the results returned by S_2^p. S_3^p (t_1, t_2, and t_3 which are independent). These tuples are interpreted into eight possible worlds [10](Fig. 2(c)). For example, the world $PW1$ includes the tuples: t_1, t_2, and t_3; and hence the probability of that world is computed as follows: $P_{PW_1} = prob(t1) * prob(t2) * prob(t3) = 0.3 * 0.4 * 0.5 = 0.06$ (we assume that the returned tuples are independent). Fig. 2(e) shows the execution plan for the composition in Fig. 2(a). For each of the possible worlds corresponding to the results returned by S_3^p (denoted by I^p in the plan in Fig. 2(e)), there is an interpretation of the composition, each interpretation has a probability and is represented by a branch in the composition plan. Note that inside each branch we may use the conventional data processing operators (i.e., Projection, Selection, Join, etc.) as exchanged tuples are certain tuples. The results returned by the invocation of S_2^p in each branch are probabilistic (and are denoted by ^{p}), and are interpreted as a set of possible worlds. For example, the results $L^p = l_1, l_2, l_3$ returned by S_2^p in the first branch have eight possible worlds. The probabilities of these worlds depend on involved tuples and the considered world of I^p. For example, the probability of the first world in the first branch is computed as follows:

$P = I^p.P_{PW_1} * L^p.P_{PW_1} = 0.06 * [prob(l1) * prob(l2) * prob(l3)] = 0.06 * [0.3 * 0.4 * 0.6] = 0.06 * 0.072$.

The final aggregation operator computes the probability of tuples across the different worlds corresponding to I^p (i.e., across the different branches). The final probability of $p1$ added all probabilities where $p1$ exists so $p1 = 0.3238 = 0.0348 + 0.027 + 0.027 + 0.0812 + .0.027 + .0.063 + 0.056$.

3.2 An Algebra for Uncertain Data Services Composition

A composition may include multiple probabilistic Web services. When the outputs of these services are aggregated, the probabilities of the obtained results should be computed. These probabilities may be important for many reasons: computing the best results, to assess the quality of results, to take the right decisions, etc. Computing final results' probabilities requires exploring different combinations of possible worlds to assess the composition. Computing all possible worlds after the invocation of each service is ineffective as the number of these worlds is exponential with the number of tuples.

To solve this problem, we opt for an extensional approach (i.e., an approach that does not require the materialization of the possible worlds) and we define a set of composition operators that are needed to formulate the orchestration plans of services compositions [14] including probabilistic Web services. These operators assume that the processed tuples are uncorrelated (i.e., the processed tuples are independent from each others).

- $Invoke^p(S^p, I^p)$: The definition of this operator was given in Section 2.
- $Aggregate^p(\overline{I_1^p}, ..., \overline{I_n^p}, \overline{a})$: Let $\overline{I_i^p}$ (where $1 \leq i \leq n$) be a vector of probabilistic tuples outputted by a given service Si, and a set of attributes; the aggregate operator joins the vectors $\overline{I_1^p}, ..., \overline{I_n^p}$ over $\overline{a}$. The probability of an aggregated tuple t is computed as follows: $p(t) = p_{t_I1}*, , p_{t_Ii}*, ..., p_{t_In}$, where $t_{I_i} 1 \leq i \leq n$ are the tuples being aggregated from $Ii(1 \leq i \leq n)$.
- $Project^P(I_i^p, \overline{a})$: Let I_i^p be a vector of probabilistic tuples, and $\overline{a}$ a set of attributes. The project operator projects the vector over $\overline{a}$ and the probability of a tuple t in the outputted set is computed as follows:
$prob(t) = 1 - \prod_{t':\prod_{\overline{a}}(t')=t}(1 - prob(t'))$
- $Select(\overline{I^p}, \overline{c})$: Let $\overline{c}$ be a set of conditions; The probability of a tuple t in the outputted set is computed as follows: $prob(t) = \begin{cases} prob(t) \text{ if } \overline{c} = true \\ 0 \text{ if } \overline{c} = false \end{cases}$

3.3   The Correct Composition Plans

To answer a given query, uncertain data services must be arranged in an order that depends on their inputs and outputs. However, given a composition of services, different execution plans (a.k.a. orchestrations) may be possible. Not all of these plans are correct; i.e., different plans give different probabilities to the outputted final results. For example, S_3^p and S_2^p are involved in a composition to know the products ordered by the consumers in "Lyon" and the plan is $Project_p^p(Invoke(S_2^p, Invoke(S_3^p, "Lyon")))$. We notice that the probability of $p_1 = 0.437$ is incorrect, it should be 0.3238 as it is calculated using possible worlds' theory in Fig. 2. This observation is not surprising as it is already known in the literature that not all queries accept an execution plan that could correctly compute the probabilities. Such queries are called *hard queries* as they have a $\#P - complete$ data complexity under probabilistic semantics [7].

We define bellow a set of conditions under which a composition plan is correct. We call such compositions as safe compositions. We start by defining the dependency graph of a composition.

Dependency Graph: The dependency graph G of a composition is a directed acyclic graph in which nodes correspond to services and edges correspond to dependency constraints between component services. We say that there is a dependency constraint between two services S_i and S_j if one of the S_i's output parameters is an input parameter of S_j.

Correct composition plan p : We say that p is safe if:

- p respects G,
- all edges in p are joins that involve the primary key of at least one probabilistic service,
- $p$is tree,
- a probabilistic service appears in p at most once,
- the primary keys of services that are leaves in p appear at the p's output.

4   Related Works

Due to space limitation, in this section, we analyze only the closest works and discuss their limitations. Several works have focused on creating and modeling Data Web services [12]. Authors of [12] proposed an XML-based modeling for data Web services along with a platform (called AquaLogic) for building data Web services on top of heterogeneous data sources. Authors of [24] identified the different data quality aspects that a data Web service should specify in its description. Unfortunately, these works do not pay any attention to the uncertainty character that may be associated with the services accessed data, nor provide effective means for an automatic selection and composition of data Web services. A considerable body of works has addressed the services composition problem[2,13]. Most of these works are inspired by the Artificial Intelligence (AI) planning techniques; i.e., they are based on transforming the WS composition problem into an AI planning problem and on the use of AI planning techniques to automate the service composition. The authors of [13] proposed a Bayesian-based approach to select the services compositions. In[2], authors model Web services as automata executing actions and formalize the problem of computing Boolean formulas characterizing the conditions required for services to answer the client's request. Unfortunately, these composition approaches take into account only SaaS (Software-as-a-Service) Web services. They are inappropriate for the class of services we are targeting in this work, i.e., the Data Web services, which cannot be modeled as actions to apply the AI planning techniques[4]. Moreover, the uncertainty aspect was never looked at in these works.

5   Conclusion

In this paper, we proposed a probabilistic approach for modeling uncertain data services. Specifically, we showed how the uncertainty associated with a data service can be modeled, and proposed a composition algebra (i.e., a set of operators) that can compute the probabilities of the outputs of a composition. We also proposed an algorithm to find the correct execution plan of a composition. As a future work, we plan to address the ranking issue of uncertain output data based on their probabilities and their matching degrees with user' preferences.

References

1. Marian, A., Wu, M.: Corroborating Information from Web Sources. IEEE Data Engineering Bulletin 3, 11–17 (2011)
2. Balbiani, P., Cheikh, A.F., Heam, P.C., Kouchnarenko, O.: Composition of Services with Constraints. In: FACS, vol. 263, pp. 31–46 (2009)
3. Barhamgi, M., Benslimane, D., Amghar, Y.: Privcomp: A privacy-aware data service composition. In: EDBT, pp. 757–760 (2013)
4. Barhamgi, M., Benslimane, D., Medjahed, B.: A Query Rewriting Approach for Web Service Composition. IEEE Transactions on Services Computing 3, 206–222 (2010)
5. Buneman, P., Chapman, A., Cheney, J.: Provenance management in curated databases. In: SIGMOD, pp. 539–550 (2010)
6. Carey, J.C., Onose, N., Petropoulos, M.: Data services. Commun. ACM 55(6), 86–97 (2012)
7. Dalvi, N., Suciu, D.: Management of probabilistic data: foundations and challenges. In: ACM SIGMOD/PODS Conference (2007)
8. Dustdar, S., Pichler, R., Savenkov, V.: Quality aware service oriented data integration. SIGMOD Record 1(1), 1–9 (2012)
9. Agrawal, P., Sarma, A.D., Ullman, J., Widom, J.: Foundations of Uncertain-Data Integration. In: 36th International Conference on VLDB, pp. 1080–1090 (2010)
10. Sadri, F.: Modeling Uncertainty in Databases. In: International Conference on Data Engineering ICDE (1991)
11. Tatbul, N., Buller, M., Hoyt, R., Mullen, S., Zdonik, S.: Confidence-based Data Management for Personal Area Sensor Networks. In: DMSN (2004)
12. Truong, H.L., Dustdar, S.: On Analyzing and Specifying Concerns for Data as a Service. In: IEEE APSCC 2009, Singapore, pp. 7–11 (2009)
13. Wu, J., Liang, Q., Jian, H.: Bayesian network based services recommendation. In: Services Computing Conference, APSCC, Singapore, pp. 13–318 (2009)
14. Yu, Q., Liu, X., Bouguettaya, A., Medjahed, B.: Deploying and managing Web services: issues, solutions, and directions. VLDB Journal 17(3), 537–572 (2008)

Domain Ontology As Conceptual Model for Big Data Management: Application in Biomedical Informatics

Catherine Jayapandian[1], Chien-Hung Chen[1], Aman Dabir[2], Samden Lhatoo[2], Guo-Qiang Zhang[1], and Satya S. Sahoo[1]

[1]Division of Medical Informatics, Case Western Reserve University, Cleveland, USA
{catherine.jayapandian,chien-hung.chen,gq,satya.sahoo}@case.edu
[2]Department of Neurology, Case Western Reserve University, Cleveland, USA
{aman.dabir,samden.lhatoo}@uhhospitals.org

Abstract. The increasing capability and sophistication of biomedical instruments has led to rapid generation of large volumes of disparate data that is often characterized as biomedical "big data". Effective analysis of biomedical big data is providing new insights to advance healthcare research, but it is difficult to efficiently manage big data without a conceptual model, such as ontology, to support storage, query, and analytical functions. In this paper, we describe the Cloudwave platform that uses a domain ontology to support optimal data partitioning, efficient network transfer, visualization, and querying of big data in the neurology disease domain. The domain ontology is used to define a new JSON-based Cloudwave Signal Format (CSF) for neurology signal data. A comparative evaluation of the ontology-based CSF with existing data format demonstrates that it significantly reduces the data access time for query and visualization of large scale signal data.

Keywords: Domain Ontology, Biomedical Big Data, Cloud-based Data Management.

1 Introduction

The growing capability to collect, store, and analyze large volumes of data using "big data" infrastructure is providing us with an unprecedented opportunity to gain new insights through data-driven research [1, 2]. The scale of data generation requires development of new approaches to store, retrieve, and interpret data for real time decision making, deriving knowledge from data, and building predictive models. The increasing use of sophisticated sensors, imaging equipment, and recording instruments has led to generation of large volumes of multi-modal big data in many scientific domains, including biomedical research. The recent move towards the use of electronic health records (EHR), for storing patient information in the United States and Europe, has led to the development of big data applications to analyze this rich source of information while ensuring patient privacy and data security. Big data, which is characterized by large volume, high velocity (of data generation and analysis), and variety, usually do not have an associated schema that represents the domain

E. Yu et al. (Eds.): ER 2014, LNCS 8824, pp. 144–157, 2014.

semantics of the data. A conceptual model for big data applications can be used to represent terms, relations between terms, define constraints to support automated consistency checking, support efficient storage, and fast retrieval of data.

Ontologies as conceptual models can play an important role in big data applications by accurately representing domain knowledge using formal modeling languages such as the description logic-based Web Ontology Language (OWL) [3]. Ontologies can be integrated with data management workflows for big data applications to automate data processing, querying, and reconciling data heterogeneity [2]. Biomedical ontologies, such as the Gene Ontology (GO) [4] and the Foundational Model of Anatomy (FMA) [5], have played an important role in biomedical data management with application in data annotation and integration. OWL ontologies are used together with reasoning rules (based on OWL semantics [6] or user defined rules) to infer additional information from data in knowledge discovery applications [7]. Upper–level ontologies, such as the Descriptive Ontology for Linguistic and Cognitive Engineering (DOLCE) [8] and Basic Formal Ontology (BFO) [9], are usually extended to develop domain-specific ontologies. Domain ontologies can be integrated with cloud computing applications to query heterogeneous multi-modal big data in emerging bioinformatics projects, such as the new Brain Research through Advancing Innovative Neurotechnologies (BRAIN) initiative [10].

Biomedical "Big Data" in Healthcare Research. The BRAIN initiative was announced in 2013 by the US government to support the mapping of every neuron in human brain to help analyze how individual cells and complex neural networks interact [10]. The BRAIN initiative is expected to revolutionize the understanding of human brain and accelerate development of new drugs and treatment methods for neurological diseases, such as Epilepsy. Epilepsy is the most common serious neurological disease affecting 65 million persons worldwide with more than 200,000 new cases diagnosed each year. Epilepsy patients suffer from seizures due to abnormal electrical activity in brain that can be recorded as electrophysiological signal data from sensing devices called electrodes, which generate large volumes of multi-modal big data.

This signal big data consists of brain activity recordings (electroencephalogram, EEG), cardiac measurements (electrocardiogram, ECG), and other physiological measures (blood oxygen level), which is generated at high velocity. For example, a typical evaluation of a single epilepsy patient over 5 days generates 1.6GB of data and our medical collaborators at the University Hospitals of Cleveland have accumulated over 11 Terabytes (TB) of data over past 3 years. Each patient file consists of data from multiple *channels* where each channel corresponds to a single recording sensor, for example EEG or ECG are two distinct channels [11]. Similar to other categories of scientific big data, large scale epilepsy data are increasingly playing a critical role in advancing clinical research and improving patient care.

1.1   Motivation

Signal data is a critical component of epilepsy patient care and research. Signal data, such as EEG, is used to diagnose the type of epilepsy syndrome in patients, prescribe medication, and evaluate the suitability of patients for brain surgery. Existing signal data management platforms often do not support large volumes of data that is generated at high velocity and require fast analysis (e.g. Nihon Koden Neural Workbench [12]). An effective signal data management platform for big data needs to address multiple challenges, including:

1. Real time interactive visualization;
2. Efficient retrieval of data segments with clinical events (e.g. epilepsy seizures);
3. Reliable data storage with low disk space requirements for scalability; and
4. Optimal data partitioning scheme.

Meeting these challenges requires the development of a cloud-based platform that scales with high volume of heterogeneous data generated at high velocity. In addition, there is a clear need for a domain ontology to support ad-hoc querying, reasoning to automatically infer new knowledge, and define a suitable data partitioning scheme for distributed file systems, such as the Hadoop Distributed File System (HDFS) [13]. The data partitioning scheme can also be used for efficient network transfer to remote Web clients across collaborating institutions.

Existing signal data representation formats were not designed for use in cloud-based distributed file systems since their storage scheme does not support efficient data partitioning. For example, the European Data Format (EDF) is a widely used signal representation model that consists of: (a) metadata header field, and (b) signal data field with recorded values [14]. The EDF header field records the patient identification and recording details of the signal data, such as the number of recorded samples per data record, start time or duration of the data record. The EDF data segment stores the signal values in binary format that need to be converted into numeric values for use by signal query and visualization applications. In addition, many signal tools use data corresponding to a single channel (for example, EEG or ECG), but an EDF file stores data from all channels as interleaved segments [14].

An EDF file does not support ontology annotation of signal data, which makes it difficult to use ontology for querying and indexing EDF files. Ontology-driven query approaches have been successfully used to analyze large-scale multi-modal data [15]. Ontologies are used to expand query expressions to incorporate additional query terms based on the ontology class hierarchy and rules [6], which improves the quality of query results. A domain ontology can also be used for an optimal data partitioning scheme and query indexes for efficient data retrieval in a distributed computing environment. Hence, to address the challenges faced in signal big data management, we have developed the Cloudwave platform for scalable signal storage and real time analysis for supporting biomedical research in neurological disorders. In this paper, we describe the role of an epilepsy domain ontology as the conceptual model in Cloudwave to: (1) develop a new representation format for multi-modal data called Cloudwave Signal Format (CSF); (2) data partitioning for storage in a high performance distributed file system; and (3) querying complex clinical events in signal data.

1.2   Related Work

There has been limited work in the use of domain ontologies as conceptual models for big data management. Embley et al. discussed the role of conceptual modeling to facilitate querying of large volumes of data, integration of heterogeneous datasets, and developing automated tools to process data generated at high velocity [2]. This work provided a vision regarding the role of conceptual models in big data, but did not describe a concrete application. Column stores have been used to develop several big data applications for improving the performance of a specific category of queries [16]. An ontology-based approach has been proposed to develop "sliced column stores" (SCS) that partitions table columns representing attribute according to value of the attributes [17]. The SCS approach attempts to further optimize the column-based storage solution for queries that reference only particular attribute value, which is compared to row-based stores and existing column store approaches. We are not aware of any cloud-based application that uses OWL ontologies as conceptual model for biomedical "big data" management, which is similar to the Cloudwave approach. In the following sections, we describe the Cloudwave platform that uses an epilepsy domain ontology for storage and retrieval of multi-modal big data in the cloud (Section 2), results of our evaluation that demonstrate the effectiveness of using ontology as a conceptual model (Section 3), and discuss the broader role of ontology as knowledge models for big data applications (Section 4), and finally summarize our conclusions (Section 5).

2   Methods

Cloudwave is a big data application that aims to support real time access to large volumes of multi-modal biomedical data through an intuitive user interface. The Cloudwave platform consists of three modules: (1) a customized data processing module that can scale with increasing size of data generated at a rapid rate, (2) a middleware layer with customized Application Programming Interface (API) for signal data, and (3) a signal query and visualization interface accessible through a Web browser. Figure 1 illustrates the architecture of Cloudwave. In addition to query and visualization functionalities, Cloudwave extends various constituents of the open source Hadoop cloud computing technology stack, such as MapReduce implementation [18], to parallelize signal processing algorithms. The Cloudwave storage module is designed to efficiently store different types of signal data by extending the open source HDFS [13].

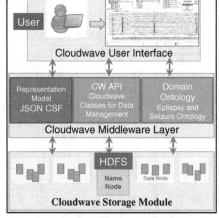

Fig. 1. The Cloudwave architecture with three components: User Interface, Middleware Layer, and Storage Module

HDFS is a read-optimized high performance distributed file system developed as part of Hadoop to reliably store extremely large volumes of different data types [13] for cloud computing applications. Similar to other Hadoop tools, HDFS is designed for horizontal scaling, which allows users to easily add new computing resources to increase the total available storage space without disrupting existing applications [13]. Cloudwave implements a middleware layer over HDFS to support standard file operations (e.g. create, read, update, and delete or CRUD) over signal data. The middleware layer consists of classes that extend the HDFS APIs to implement a data processing workflow to: (a) convert binary signal values into numeric data, (b) extract signal data corresponding to a single channel (e.g. ECG) from EDF file, and (c) extract and copy signal metadata, including clinical events, for each channel into HDFS. This middleware has been designed to facilitate third party signal processing applications to easily interface with Cloudwave storage module and develop new biomedical informatics tools using big data.

2.1   Cloudwave User Interface and Signal Montages

The Cloudwave query and visualization module is implemented in a Web browser to support access and real time interaction with signal data by multiple researchers across collaborating institutions. The query and visualization module features the following functionalities:

1. Visualization of single or multiple signal channels;
2. Real time application of signal filtering algorithms to reduce noise and improve signal quality;
3. Ad-hoc querying for data segments with specific clinical events; and
4. Composition of multiple signal channels into "montages" to visualize correlated signals (e.g. effect of epileptic seizure in EEG channel and heart rate in ECG channel).

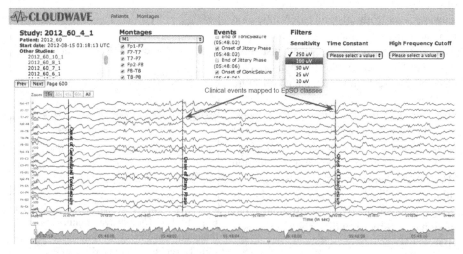

Fig. 2. The Cloudwave User Interface showing the signal visualization, signal filtering, and montage features

Figure 2 is a screenshot of the Cloudwave interface showing signals corresponding to the M1 montage channels (signal data from 19 channels). The primary challenge to render signals in real time is efficient transfer of signal data from the server to the Web browser client and conversion of data into an appropriate format for interactive visualization. The typical size of signal data per channel varies from 10 MB to 47 MB of data, which makes it difficult to transfer data efficiently over the network. In addition, as illustrated in Figure 2, users usually request for visualization of multiple channels constituting a "montage".

A montage is a composition of signal channels that are arranged in a logical series to provide an accurate localization of abnormal electrical activity to specific parts of the brain [19]. Visualization of signal data as montage helps neurologists to identify the brain regions that are responsible for start of seizures in patients and also help in diagnosis of specific category of epilepsy. The three major categories of montages are bipolar montage, referential montage, and Laplacian montage that are used in analysis of signal data in epilepsy [19]. There are six standard montages that are recommended for use in epilepsy center, which are supported as default montages in the Cloudwave user interface. These montages consist of multiple channels, which make it difficult to support interaction with signal data corresponding to these montages.

Cloudwave uses three-fold approach to support real time interaction with complex query functionality over signal data corresponding to each montage. First, signal data corresponding to each first channel is extracted from EDF files and converted to numeric values from the original binary format. Second, the signal data values are partitioned into "epoch" of 30 second durations based on the default visualization window size used in many existing signal visualization tools. These 30-second epochs are optimal for efficient transfer of data to Cloudwave query and visualization module. Third, Cloudwave uses an epilepsy domain ontology to define a new representation schema based on the Javascript Object Notation (JSON) called Cloudwave Signal Format (CSF). In contrast to the EDF schema, CSF is an extensible representation format that allows annotation of signal data with ontology terms, data partitioning, and querying. We describe the details of the epilepsy domain ontology in the next section.

2.2   Epilepsy and Seizure Ontology: Conceptual Modeling for Signal Big Data

The Epilepsy and Seizure Ontology (EpSO) was developed as a domain ontology to address multiple data management challenges in epilepsy research, including integration of heterogeneous data, querying, and data validation [20]. EpSO is already used in a patient information capture system, which is deployed at the Epilepsy Monitoring Unit (EMU) at University Hospitals of Cleveland, to ensure consistency in collection of patient information [21]. EpSO has also been used for development of a clinical text processing system called EpiDEA to extract structured information from patient discharge summaries [22]. In addition to these traditional roles of a domain ontology, EpSO is also used as a conceptual model for big data management in Cloudwave. EpSO uses the well-known "four-dimensional classification of epileptic seizures and epilepsies" [23, 24] to model concepts describing seizures (abnormal electrical activity in brain), location of the seizures in brain, cause of seizures, and other medical conditions.

EpSO re-uses concepts from many existing biomedical ontologies, such as the Foundational Model of Anatomy (FMA) [5] and RxNorm for medical drug classification [25].

EpSO uses OWL2 constructs, including existential quantifiers, to define classes, properties, and restrictions on class attributes. Epilepsy syndromes are complex concepts with specific values assigned to their attributes and EpSO models this information by defining appropriate restrictions on multiple OWL2 object properties. For example, Carbamazepine is asserted as the preferred medication for a specific category of epilepsy called ADNFLE using restriction on the *hasPreferredMedication* object property (Figure 3 illustrates the restrictions on ADNFLE). Similar ontology constructs in EpSO allows software applications to automatically distinguish and classify different types of epilepsy syndromes, for example mesial frontal epilepsy is a sub class of frontal lobe epilepsy. EpSO models the six standard montages (described earlier in Section 2.1) together with electrodes that constitute the montages. In addition, the specific brain region associated with each electrode, which generates the signal data corresponding to a channel, is defined using OWL2 class restrictions on object property *hasLocation*.

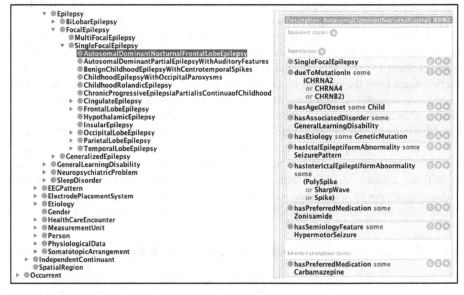

Fig. 3. EpSO defines the attribute values of complex epilepsy syndromes using OWL constructs, such as class level restrictions on object properties

In Cloudwave, EpSO classes are used to describe clinical events identified in signal data, which ensures commonality of clinical event descriptors across different EMUs. Signal data is manually analyzed to identify clinical events, such as abnormal electrical activity in EEG, and annotation tools are used to associate a text note with the signal data, which are automatically mapped to EpSO classes in Cloudwave. These ontology annotations on signal data are used to support efficient data query and retrieval in Cloudwave. Queries in the Cloudwave user interface are composed of EpSO classes, which allow Cloudwave to use EpSO as a query ontology (illustrated in Figure 3). Similar to traditional approaches to ontology-based query systems, Cloudwave uses EpSO to "expand" the user query with synonym and subclass information (using standard OWL2 semantics for reasoning [6]). This expanded query expression allows Cloudwave to support signal retrieval beyond "keyword matching" in signal data.

In addition to its role as a query ontology in Cloudwave, the EpSO schema has been used to define a new JSON-based representation model for signal data that supports optimal data partitioning for storage and efficient network transfer. This domain ontology-based signal representation model is described in the next section.

2.3   Cloudwave Signal Format (CSF): An Extensible JSON Model for Electrophysiological Signal Data

The two essential requirements for a representation model for signal data in Cloudwave are optimal data partitioning and efficient network transfer to remote Web clients implementing the user interface. The JavaScript Object Notation (JSON) is a lightweight, platform-independent, and extensible representation format that can be adapted to model valid data segments conforming to domain ontology. JSON was developed for efficient data transfer in client-server applications by using the Javascript programming language [26] and is defined by RFC 7159 as well as ECMA 404 standards. As compared to XML, JSON reduces the space requirements for datasets, but without constraining the expressivity or extensibility of the representation format.

JSON uses nested objects of "attribute-value" pairs with a set of standard syntactic elements that are easily parsed by JSON parsers, which are implemented in multiple languages [26]. Hence, Cloudwave uses JSON to define a signal representation format called Cloudwave Signal Format (CSF) that combines the flexibility of JSON with use of EpSO as reference schema.

The CSF is divided into two parts: (1) study metadata and annotations, and (2) data segments (Figure 4

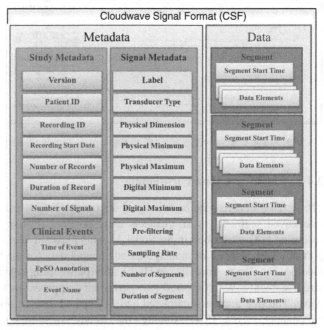

Fig. 4. The Cloudwave Signal Format consists of two segments storing the signal metadata and data values

illustrates the segments of the CSF). The study metadata segment of CSF is further sub-divided into two additional sections describing: (a) details of the experiment study, including the patient identifier, clinical events, recording timestamps, the total duration of recording, and (b) the instrument details of the recording, including the unit of measurement (e.g. microvolts) and transducer type. The second part of CSF consists of the signal data values, which have been divided into segments of specific duration. The signal data are stored as an array of text values after conversion from the original EDF file binary format in Cloudwave (discussed earlier in Section 1.1). The storage of data in CSF compliant text format reduces the computational workload on the Cloudwave user interface module to convert binary data into numeric format and improves the response time for signal visualization. Though, the storage of signal data in CSF file results in a moderate increase in total size of data as compared to the original EDF file binary format, there is a significant gain in user interface response time.

A key characteristic of CSF is the use of EpSO classes for describing clinical events across all channels in a given signal montage. CSF defines a composite "attribute-value" element consisting of the timestamp associated with the clinical event, the name of the clinical event, and the associated EpSO classes (Figure 5 shows a segment of the CSF with ontology annotation and the corresponding EpSO class). These CSF ontology annotations are used at multiple stages of signal management Cloudwave, including signal visualization, query execution, and data partitioning. In the next section, we describe the role of EpSO in Cloudwave data partitioning.

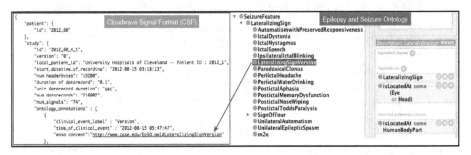

Fig. 5. The CSF ontology annotation segment illustrating the mapping to EpSO classes

2.4   Cloudwave Data Partitioning

The default storage schema for signal data in EDF files partitions signal values into interleaved segments of all channels corresponding to a specific time duration of a recording [14] (described in Section 1.1). This makes it very difficult to not only support efficient retrieval of montage-based channel data for the Cloudwave visualization module, but also to store data in HDFS after partitioning signal data into appropriately sized segments. We compared two partitioning approaches for signal data in Cloudwave. The first approach extracted and aggregated data corresponding to a single signal channel, such as ECG. Although the Cloudwave storage module could use the single channel dataset, they could not be efficiently transferred over the network to the visualization module (results of a comparative evaluation are discussed in Section 3).

Hence, we implemented a second approach, which partitions the data of each signal channel into "epochs" of 30 seconds duration.

The 30 seconds duration corresponds to the default "window size" of many existing signal processing tools, such as the Nihon Koden Neural Workbench [12], and is also implemented in the Cloudwave user interface. Hence, partitioning signal data into 30 seconds epochs, which are stored as CSF files, allows the Cloudwave user interface to visualize the signal data transferred from the server without additional processing. This approach significantly improves the response time of the user interface for visualization of complex signal montages consisting of multiple channels

3   Results

To demonstrate the advantages of using EpSO as a domain ontology in Cloudwave, we conducted a comparative evaluation of using CSF and epoch-based data partitioning techniques with existing EDF files. The comparative evaluation was performed on: (1) a desktop computer with Intel Core i7 2.93 GHz processor, 16GB main memory, and 8MB cache, and (2) a single node cluster implementation of Hadoop on the same desktop computer configuration. The objectives of the evaluations are to demonstrate that:

1. The time taken by the Cloudwave storage module to retrieve and transfer data to the user interface module is low as compared to existing approaches;
2. The access time for multiple signal channels in montages is significantly lower for Cloudwave epochs as compared to channel-based partitioning scheme; and
3. The CSF format improves the responsiveness of the Cloudwave user interface module for signal montages as compared to existing EDF file binary data format.

3.1   Cloudwave Storage Module Compared to Desktop File System

Figure 6 (a) shows that the time to retrieve and render signal data corresponding to a single ECG channel for increasing duration of signal recording time and Figure 6 (b) shows the access time for 20 signal channels. The results clearly demonstrate that the

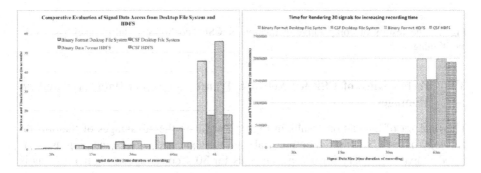

Fig. 6. The advantages of storing data in Cloudwave storage module as compared to a desktop file system for: (a) a single ECG channel, and (b) 20 signal channels

CSF file served from Cloudwave storage module requires less time required to re-trieve and render data in the user interface. The efficiency of the Cloudwave storage module is significantly higher as the size of the data (in terms of recording time) in-creases from 30 seconds to total of 6 hours as compared to desktop file systems.

3.2   Effectiveness of Cloudwave Data Partitioning Approach

Figure 7 shows that the Cloudwave approach to partitioning signal data into 30 seconds epochs leads to faster data retrieval and visualization as compared to simple channel-based data partitioning approach. The results demonstrate that the epoch-based partitioning approach is consistently faster as compared to channel-based parti-tioning for multiple signal channels corresponding to the six standard montages that are available as default choices for users in the Cloudwave user interface.

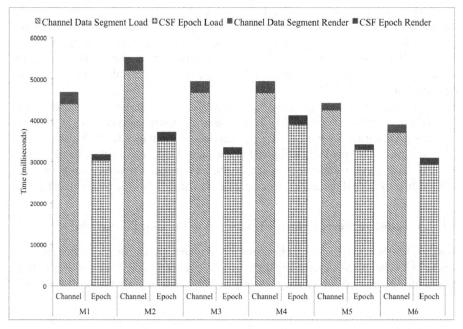

Fig. 7. The results of comparative evaluation of CSF epoch-based and channel-based data partitioning

3.3   Performance of CSF for Network Transfer of Signal Data for Standard Montages

The final set of evaluation results in Figure 8 validate the advantages of the domain ontology-based CSF file for both signal data retrieval and signal rendering as com-pared to existing binary format in EDF files for 30 seconds epoch segments. This is an important result that clearly demonstrates the advantage of using EpSO domain ontology as a conceptual model in Cloudwave.

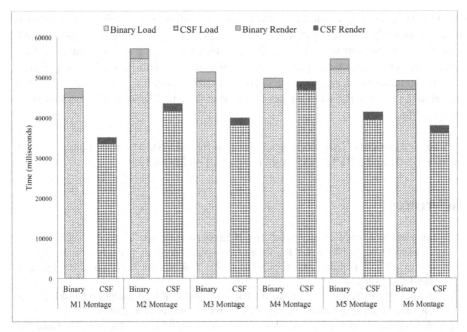

Fig. 8. The access time for CSF files is clearly less than the binary format EDF files for 30 seconds epoch data segments across all the six standard montages

4   Discussion

The results from the three comparative evaluations of using EpSO for data modeling (in form of CSF) and data partitioning clearly validate our hypothesis that domain ontologies have an important role in big data management. We believe that a domain ontology also have an essential role in implementing query indexes that effectively supports complex user queries over large volumes of big data. For example, as future work in Cloudwave we plan to build specific indexes for the six standard montages that will be updated for each new study data added to the Cloudwave storage module. Another index that can potentially improve the query performance in Cloudwave is a clinical event index that stores the specific timestamps associated with clinical events across all the studies stored in Cloudwave. The integration of an OWL reasoning tool, such as Pellet or Fact++, will allow Cloudwave to develop a clinical event index that can reason over query terms to expand the query expression and retrieve specific CSF files that contain signal data with appropriate clinical events.

5   Conclusions

In this paper we describe the role of an epilepsy domain ontology EpSO as a conceptual model in biomedical big data application called Cloudwave. EpSO is used not only as a query ontology in EpSO to efficiently retrieve specific data segments based on interesting clinical events, but also is used to define a new signal representation model called CSF. In comparison to existing signal representation formats, EpSO-based CSF supports efficient data access and data partitioning in Cloudwave for multiple signal channels. A comparative evaluation of CSF with EDF file binary format clearly demonstrates a significant reduction in data access time for increasing size of signal data for six standard montages implemented in the Cloudwave signal visualization module.

Acknowledgements. This work was supported by NIH/NINDS grant number 1-P20-NS076965-01 and NIH/NCATS grant number UL1TR000439.

References

[1] Madden, S.: From databases to big data. IEEE Internet Computing 16, 4–6 (2012)

[2] Embley, D.W., Liddle, S.W.: Big Data - Conceptual Modeling to the Rescue. In: Ng, W., Storey, V.C., Trujillo, J.C. (eds.) ER 2013. LNCS, vol. 8217, pp. 1–8. Springer, Heidelberg (2013)

[3] Hitzler, P., Krötzsch, M., Parsia, B., Patel-Schneider, P.F., Rudolph, S.: OWL 2 Web Ontology Language Primer. World Wide Web Consortium W3C (2009)

[4] Ashburner, M., et al.: Gene ontology: Tool for the unification of biology. The Gene Ontology Consortium. Nat. Genet. 25, 25–29 (2000)

[5] Rosse, C., Mejino Jr., J.L.: A reference ontology for biomedical informatics: The Foundational Model of Anatomy. Journal of Biomedical Informatics 36, 478–500 (2003)

[6] Motik, B., Patel-Schneider, P.F., Grau, B.C.: OWL 2 Web Ontology Language Direct Semantics, World Wide Web Consortium W3C December 11 (2012)

[7] Ferrucci, D., et al.: Building Watson: An Overview of the DeepQA Project. AI Magazine 31, 59–79 (2010)

[8] Gangemi, A., Guarino, N., Masolo, C., Oltramari, A., Schneider, L.: Sweetening Ontologies with DOLCE. In: 13th International Conference on Knowledge Engineering and Knowledge Management. Ontologies and the Semantic Web, Siguenza, Spain, pp. 166–181 (2002)

[9] Smith, B., Ceusters, W., Klagges, B., Kohler, J., Kumar, A., Lomax, J., Mungall, C., Neuhaus, F., Rector, A.L., Rosse, C.: Relations in biomedical ontologies. Genome Biol. 6, R46 (2005)

[10] Brain Research through Advancing Innovative Neurotechnologies (BRAIN), The White House, Washington, D.C. (2013)

[11] Schwartzkroin, P.A.: Cellular electrophysiology of human epilepsy. Epilepsy Research 17, 185–192 (1994)

[12] Koden, N.: Nihon Koden Neurology, http://www.nkusa.com/neurology_cardiology/

[13] Shvachko, K., Kuang, H., Radia, S., Chansler, R.: The Hadoop Distributed File System. Presented at the IEEE 26th Symposium on Mass Storage Systems and Technologies (MSST), NV (2010)

[14] Kemp, B., Olivan, J.: European data format 'plus' (EDF+), an EDF alike standard format for the exchange of physiological data. Clinical Neurophysiology 114, 1755–1761 (2003)

[15] Henson, C.A., Thirunarayan, K., Sheth, A.P.: An Efficient Bit Vector Approach to Semantics-Based Machine Perception in Resource-Constrained Devices. In: International Semantic Web Conference, Washington D.C, pp. 149–164 (2012)

[16] Stonebraker, M., Abadi, D.J., Batkin, A., Chen, X., Cherniack, M., Ferreira, M., Lau, E., Lin, A., Madden, S., O'Neil, E., O'Neil, P., Rasin, A., Tran, N., Zdonik, S.: C-store: A column-oriented DBMS. In: 31st International Conference on Very Large Data Bases (VLDB 2005), Trondheim, Norway, pp. 553–564 (2005)

[17] Sekhavat, Y.A., Parsons, J.: Sliced column-store (SCS): ontological foundations and practical implications. In: Atzeni, P., Cheung, D., Ram, S. (eds.) ER 2012. LNCS, vol. 7532, pp. 102–115. Springer, Heidelberg (2012)

[18] Dean, J., Ghemawat, S.: MapReduce: Simplified Data Processing on Large Clusters. In: OSDI 2004, San Francisco (2004)

[19] Hamer, H.M., Lüders, H.O.: Electrode montages and localization of potentials in clinical electroencephalography. In: Levin, K., Luders, H.O. (eds.) Comprehensive Clinical Neurophysiology, pp. 358–386. WB Saunders Company (2000)

[20] Sahoo, S.S., Lhatoo, S.D., Gupta, D.K., Cui, L., Zhao, M., Jayapandian, C., Bozorgi, A., Zhang, G.Q.: Epilepsy and seizure ontology: towards an epilepsy informatics infrastructure for clinical research and patient care. Journal of American Medical Association 21, 82–89 (2014)

[21] Sahoo, S.S., Zhao, M., Luo, L., Bozorgi, A., Gupta, A., Lhatoo, S.D., Zhang, G.Q.: OPIC: Ontology-driven Patient Information Capturing System for Epilepsy. In: The American Medical Informatics Association (AMIA) Annual Symposium, Chicago, pp. 799–808 (2012)

[22] Cui, L., Bozorgi, A., Lhatoo, S.D., Zhang, G.Q., Sahoo, S.S.: EpiDEA: Extracting Structured Epilepsy and Seizure Information from Patient Discharge Summaries for Cohort Identification. In: The American Medical Informatics Association (AMIA) Annual Symposium, Chicago, pp. 1191–1200 (2012)

[23] Loddenkemper, T., Kellinghaus, C., Wyllie, E., Najm, I.M., Gupta, A., Rosenow, F., Luders, H.O.: A proposal for a five-dimensional patient oriented epilepsy classification. Epileptic Disord 7, 308–316 (2005)

[24] Kellinghaus, C., et al.: Suggestion for a new, patient-oriented epilepsy classification. Nervenarzt 77, 961–969 (2006)

[25] Nelson, S.J., et al.: Normalized names for clinical drugs: RxNorm at 6 years. J. Am. Med. Inform. Assoc. 18, 441–448 (2011)

[26] Crockford, D.: Introducing JSON (1999), http://www.json.org/

Network Analytics ER Model –
Towards a Conceptual View of Network Analytics

Qing Wang

Research School of Computer Science, The Australian National University, Australia
qing.wang@anu.edu.au

Abstract. This paper proposes a conceptual modelling paradigm for network analysis applications, called the Network Analytics ER model (NAER). Not only data requirements but also query requirements are captured by the conceptual description of network analysis applications. This unified analytical framework allows us to flexibly build a number of topology schemas on the basis of the underlying core schema, together with a collection of query topics that describe topological results of interest. In doing so, we can alleviate many issues in network analysis, such as performance, semantic integrity and dynamics of analysis.

1 Introduction

Network analysis has proliferated rapidly in recent years, and it has useful applications across a wide range of fields, such as social science, computer science, biology and archaeology [2,3,10,13,15,16]. One key aspect of network analysis is to understand how entities and their interaction via various (explicit or implicit) relationships take place within a network that is often represented as a graph with possibly millions or even billions of vertices. In practice, network data are often managed in a database system, e.g., Facebook uses MySQL to store data like posts, comments, likes, and pages. Network analysis queries are performed by extracting data from the underlying database, then analyzing them using some software tools that incorporate data mining and machine learning techniques [11]. Since different fragments of data may be of interest for different analysis purposes, network analysis queries are usually performed in ad hoc and isolated environments. Therefore, there is a divorce of data models and query languages between managing network data and analyzing network data in many situations, and several questions may arise.

- *Semantic integrity*
  With more and more network analysis queries being performed, it becomes increasingly important to semantically align and mine their relationships. But how can we ensure that they are semantically relevant and consistent?

- *Analysis efficiency*
  Network analysis queries are often computationally expensive. Regardless of implementation details that different network analysis queries may have,

E. Yu et al. (Eds.): ER 2014, LNCS 8824, pp. 158–171, 2014.

the need to capture semantics remains. Can the efficiency of network analysis queries be improved by leveraging their semantics at the conceptual level?

– *Network dynamics* Network analysis applications are dynamic and evolving over time. Can network analysis be dynamically performed at different scales and over different time periods so as to predict trends and patterns?

The root of these questions stems from two different perspectives on networks - one is from the data management perspective (i.e., how to control data), and the other is from the data analysis perspective (i.e., how to use data). These two perspectives are closely related but have different concerns. We believe that conceptual modelling can play an important role in bridging these two perspectives, and contribute to answering the above questions. This paper aims to explore this, and in a broader sense, it also attempts to envision the role of conceptual modelling in the era of Big-data analytics since network analysis is at the core of Big-data analytics.

Example 1. Fig. 1.(a) depicts a simple network in which each vertex represents an author, and each edge represents that two authors have coauthored one or more articles. Suppose that we have two network analysis queries: (1) Q_c - find the collaborative communities of authors according to how closely they collaborate with each other to write articles together, and (2) Q_a - find the top-k influential researchers. With the results of Q_c and Q_a available (i.e., as shown in Fig. 1.(a) and (b)), we may further ask: (3) Q_{ca} - what are the collaborative communities of these top-k influential researchers? (4) Q_{ac} - are these top-k influential researchers the central ties in their collaborative communities? To answer Q_{ca} and Q_{ac}, we would like to know whether Q_c and Q_a are semantically consistent (i.e., use the same set of authors and articles). If they are, we can leverage the results of Q_c and Q_a to efficiently answer Q_{ca} and Q_{ac}. Ideally, we would also like to analyze the changes of collaborative communities and influential researchers over time to discover unknown interactions and trends.

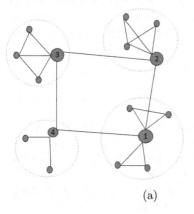

Influential Researchers	
AUTHOR-ID	INFLUENCE
8	2.4
6	2.2
2	1.8
4	1.5
10	1.3
3	1.3
. . .	. . .

(a)   (b)

Fig. 1. (a) a simple network with collaborative communities described by dashed circles; (b) a collection of influential researchers

Contributions. The first contribution of this paper is the development of a conceptual modelling method for network analysis applications. We propose the Network Analytics ER model (NAER) that extends the concepts of the traditional ER models in three aspects: (a) the *structural* aspect - analytical types are added; (b) the *manipulation* aspect - topological constructs are added; and (c) the *integrity* aspect - semantic constraints are extended.

Then we introduce an analytical framework for network analysis applications, which has three components: a collection of query topics, a number of small topology schemas, and a relatively large core schema. The *core schema* consists of base types, while topology schemas consists of analytical types that have support from base types in the core schema. A query topic is a tree representing a hierarchy of object classes with each level being built from lower levels, and the leaves of such a tree can be specified using topological constructs over one or more topology schemas, or using the core schema. Topology schemas are usually small and dynamic, which describe topological structures of interest based on query requirements. The reason for having small topology schemas is to support flexible abstraction on topological structures.

We further develop the design guidelines of establishing such an analytical framework for network analysis applications. The key idea is that, in addition to data requirements, query requirements should also be taken into account in the modelling process. This enables an integrated view on the semantics of analysis tasks, and can thus provide a conceptual platform for sharing the theories and algorithms behind different analytical models. In doing so, such a conceptual model can circumvent the design limitations of conventional modeling techniques which do not consider analysis queries. It thus brings us several significant advantages for managing analysis tasks in networks, such as managing the complexity of computational models, handling the semantic integration of different data analysis results, and enabling comparative network analysis.

Outline. The remainder of the paper is structured as follows. We start with a motivating example in Section 2. Then we introduce the NAER model in Section 3. After that, we present a high-level overview for the analytical framework of network analysis applications, and discuss the general design principles that underlie the development of such an analytical framework in Section 4. We discuss the related works in Section 5 and conclude the paper in Section 6.

2   Motivating Example

We start with a bibliographical network, i.e., each article is written by one or more authors, an article is published in a conference or a journal, and one article may cite a number of other articles. Using the traditional ER approaches [5,19], one can design a simple ER diagram as depicted in Fig. 2.

Based on this network, a variety of network analysis tasks can be performed. Typical examples include: community detection [8,10] that is to identify sets of entities that have certain common properties, cocitation analysis [4] that is to identify sets of articles that are frequently cited together, and link predication

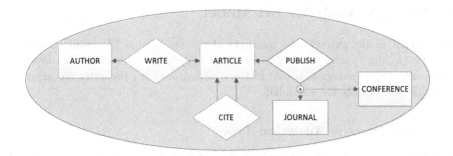

Fig. 2. An ER diagram

[14] that is to find out links among entities which will probably appear in the future. We exemplify some of such analysis tasks by the following queries.

Q1: (Collaborative communities) *Find the communities that consist of authors who collaborate with each other to publish articles together.*

Q2: (Most influential articles) *Find the most influential article of each VLDB conference, together with the authors of the article.*

Q3: (Top-k influential researchers) *Find the top 10 influential researchers in terms of the influence of articles (i.e., the citation counts) they have published.*

Q4: (Correlation citation) *Find the correlation groups of journals which publish articles that are often cited by each other.*

Conceptually, these network analysis queries either require or generate some entities and relationships that are not explicitly represented in Fig. 2. For instance, the query Q1 generates a set of author groups, each being referred as a *collaborative community*, and the detection of such collaborative communities is based on the *coauthorship* relationships between authors, i.e., two authors have written an article together.

Capturing implicit entities and relationships, and represent them explicitly in a conceptual model can bring several benefits for network analysis applications: (1) It enables semantic integrity checking across different analysis results. (2) It supports comparative analysis on different dimensions in order to predict trends and discover new insights. (3) It can improve query performance by reformulating queries in a way that can leverage existing results whenever possible. Nevertheless, how should we specify such entities and relationships? Take the query Q1 for example, the question is how to model the concept of *collaborative community* and the relationship of *coauthorship* among authors. In most cases, they are algorithmically defined, without a precise a priori definition. Motivated by these questions, we will discuss the NAER model in Section 3.

3   Network Analytics ER Model

Our NAER model extends the concepts of the traditional ER models in three aspects: (a) the *structural* aspect - analytical types are added; (b) the *manipulation* aspect - topological constructs are added; and (c) the *integrity* aspect - semantic constraints are extended.

3.1   Base Types vs Analytical Types

Two kinds of entities and relationships are distinguished in the NAER model: (1) *base entity and relationship types* contain entities and relationships, respectively, as defined in the traditional ER models; (2) *analytical entity and relationship types* contain analytical entities and relationships, respectively, such that

- an *analytical entity* is an object of being analyzed, which may be a concrete thing or an abstract concept;
- an *analytical relationship* is a link among two or more analytical entities.

Base and analytical types serve rather different purposes. Base types specify first-class entities and relationships from the data management perspective, and analytical types specify first-class entities and relationships from the data analysis perspective. These two perspectives may lead to different decisions about which entities and relationships to emphasise, and which to ignore. For example, COAUTHORSHIP and AUTHOR are often interesting analytical types to consider in network analysis queries like Q1, but the corresponding base types AUTHOR, WRITE and ARTICLE are more natural and informative for managing what entities involve and how they interact.

In the NAER model, base types are the root from which analytical types can be derived. Let $\mathcal{B}(\varUpsilon)$ be a set of base types that represent data in a network $\varUpsilon$. Then a set $\mathcal{A}(\varUpsilon)$ of analytical types in $\varUpsilon$ can be defined over $\mathcal{B}(\varUpsilon)$ such that each $A \in \mathcal{A}(\varUpsilon)$ is determined by a subset of base types in $\mathcal{B}(\varUpsilon)$, and these base types that define A are called the *support* of A, denoted as $supp(A)$. To ensure that analytical types are well-defined, the following criteria must be applied:

- $supp(A) \subseteq \mathcal{B}(\varUpsilon)$ for each analytical type A;
- $supp(A_E) \subseteq supp(A_R)$ for each analytical relationship type A_R, and every analytical entity type A_E that associates with A_R.

An analytical type A may have attributes, each of which must be derivable from the base types in its support $supp(A)$. To avoid redundant information, it is prohibited to have attributes in an analytical type as a copy of some attributes in base types. A *schema* S consists of a set of connected and well-defined types that are *complete*, i.e., if a relationship type $T_R \in S$, then for every type T that participates in T_R, we have $T \in S$.

Example 2. Suppose that all the entity and relationship types in Fig. 2 are base types in the network $\varUpsilon_{bib}$, then we can define several analytical types over these base types, as depicted in Fig. 3.(a)-(c), i.e.,

- $\mathcal{B}(\Upsilon_{bib})$={AUTHOR, ARTICLE, CONFERENCE, JOURNAL, WRITE, CITE, PUBLISH};
- $\mathcal{A}(\Upsilon_{bib})$={AUTHOR*, COAUTHORSHIP, ARTICLE*, CITATION, JOURNAL*, COCITATION}.

Both COAUTHORSHIP and COCITATION may have an attribute WEIGHT, which respectively indicate how many articles two authors have written together, and how many times two journals are cocited by articles. The analytical types in $\mathcal{A}(\Upsilon_{bib})$ have the following support:

(a) $supp$(AUTHOR*) = {AUTHOR} and
   $supp$(COAUTHORSHIP) = {AUTHOR, ARTICLE and WRITE};
(b) $supp$(ARTICLE*) = {ARTICLE} and $supp$(CITATION) = {ARTICLE and CITE};
(c) $supp$(JOURNAL*) = {JOURNAL} and
   $supp$(COCITATION) = {ARTICLE, CITE, JOURNAL and PUBLISH}.

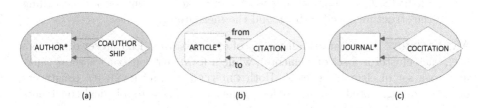

Fig. 3. (a) coauthorship schema S_{co}; (b) citation schema S_{ci}; (c) cocitation schema S_{jo}

3.2   Topological Constructs

A common scenario in network analysis is to analyze topological structures that are hidden underneath base entities and relationships. To explicitly represent a topological structure of interest, one can define analytical entities as vertices and analytical relationships as edges in a graph that may be directed or undirected, weighted or unweighted, etc. However, as illustrated by the following example, base and analytical types alone are still not sufficient to provide a clearly defined conceptual description for network analysis applications.

Example 3. To analyze collaborative communities as described in the query Q1, we may design the coauthorship schema S_{co}, i.e., Fig. 3.(a), consisting of the analytical entity type AUTHOR* and the analytical relationship type COAUTHORSHIP. Nevertheless, the problem of how to model the concept of *collaborative community* in terms of S_{co} still remains. Solving this problem requires us to take into account topological measures and operators, together with analytical types.

Topological measures play an important role in characterizing topology properties of a network [2,12]. Two of the most commonly used topological measures are centrality and similarity. Let A be an analytical type.

- CENT: $A \mapsto \mathbb{N}$ is a centrality measure that describes how central elements are in A, and return a rank CENT(v) for an element v. This measure can be implemented in different ways, such as degree, betweenness and closeness centrality [9].
- SIMI: $A \times A \mapsto \mathbb{N}$ is a similarity measure that describes the similarity between two elements in A, and generates a rank SIMI(v_1, v_2) for a pair (v_1, v_2) of elements. This measure can also be implemented in different ways, such as q-gram, adjacency-based and distance-based similarity [8].

Based on topological measures, we introduce two families of topological constructs in the NAER model - clustering and ranking. Let S be a schema, $T \in S$, and m be a topological measure. Then we have

(1) CLUSTER-BY(S, T, m) that contains a set of clusters over T, according to the structure specified by S and the measure m;
(2) RANK-BY(S, T, m) that contains to a set of ranked elements over T, according to the structure specified by S and the measure m.

A CLUSTER-BY construct classifies a set of elements over A into a set of clusters (i.e., each cluster is a set of elements), while a RANK-BY construct assigns rankings to a set of elements over A. Both CLUSTER-BY and RANK-BY constructs need to be augmented with a topological measure. These topological constructs provide us an ability to specify existing prominent techniques of network analysis into the conceptual modelling process without being exposed to low-level implementation details.

Example 4. Consider the following concepts relating to the queries Q1-Q4.

- *Collaborative community* in the query Q1 can be modelled using

$$\text{CLUSTER-BY}(S_{co}, \text{AUTHOR}^*, \text{CENT-CLOSENESS}).$$

That is, each collaborative community is a group of authors in a network specified by S_{co}, and the measure for determining community membership is closeness centrality.
- *Influence of article* in the queries Q1-Q2 can be modelled using

$$\text{RANK-BY}(S_{ci}, \text{ARTICLE}^*, \text{CENT-INDEGREE}).$$

That is, each article is associated with a ranking that indicates its influence in terms of a network specified by S_{ci}, and the measure for determining rankings is indegree centrality.
- *Correlation group* in the query Q4 can be modelled using

$$\text{CLUSTER-BY}(S_{jo}, \text{JOURNAL}^*, \text{CENT-BETWEENNESS}).$$

That is, each correlation group contains journals that are correlated in a network specified by S_{jo} and the measure for determining the correlation among journals is betweenness centrality.

3.3   Integrity Constraints

In the NAER model, integrity constraints that are allowed in the traditional ER models can be extended to analytical entity and relationship types in a similar manner. Moreover, we can also define integrity constraints over topological constructs. The following are some typical constraints:

- DISJOINT *(resp.* OVERLAPPING*) constraints on* CLUSTER-BY
  Clusters identified by a CLUSTER-BY construct must be disjoint, i.e., no element can be a member of more than one cluster, (resp. can be overlapping).
- CONNECTED *constraints on* CLUSTER-BY
  For each cluster identified by a CLUSTER-BY construct, there is a path between each pair of its members, running only through elements of the cluster.
- EDGE-DENSITY *constraints on* CLUSTER-BY
  For each cluster identified by a CLUSTER-BY construct, its members have more edges inside the cluster than edges with other members who are outside the cluster.
- TOTAL *(resp.* PARTIAL*) constraints on* RANK-BY
  Every element in a given set must be (resp. may not necessarily be) ranked by a RANK-BY construct.

4   Analytical Framework

In this section, we discuss how to use the NAER model to establish an analytical framework for network analysis applications at the conceptual level.

4.1   High-Level Overview

Fig. 4 illustrates an analytical framework of the bibliographical network described in our motivating example. In general, such an analytical framework has three components $\langle S_q, S_t, S_c \rangle$: (1) a collection of query topics S_q, (2) a number of small topology schemas S_t, and (3) a relatively large core schema S_c. The *core schema* S_c contains a set of base types. Each *topology schema* $S \in S_t$ contains a set of analytical types, and the support of each analytical type in S is a subset of base types in S_c. Each *query topic* in S_q is a tree representing a hierarchy of object classes with each level being built from lower levels, and the leaves of such a tree can be specified using topological constructs CLUSTER-BY or RANK-BY over one or more topology schemas, or using the core schema if the attributes of base types need to be processed.

In Fig. 4, three topology schemas $\{S_{co}, S_{ci}, S_{jo}\}$ are built upon the core schema, which represent three topological structures that are of interest for network analysis queries over Υ_{bib}: (1) the coauthorship schema S_{co} for the query Q1, (2) the citation schema S_{ci} for the queries Q2 and Q3, and (3) the cocitation schema S_{jo} for the query Q4. Consequently, the four queries Q1-Q4 lead to four query topics, in which the query topics of the queries Q2 and Q3 are overlapping and having the same leave INFLUENCE OF ARTICLE (will be discussed in detail in the next subsection).

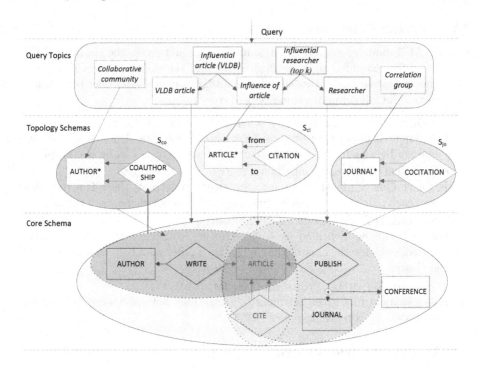

Fig. 4. An analytical framework

4.2 Design Principles

We now present the design guidelines that support the development of an analytical framework for network analysis applications. The central idea is to incorporate both data and queries into the conceptual modelling process. Generally, there are six steps involved:

(1) Identify data requirements (i.e., a set of business rules of interest);
(2) Design the core schema based on the data requirements;
(3) Identify query requirements (i.e., a set of analysis queries of interest);
(4) Design topology schemas based on the query requirements and query topics;
(5) Identify constraints on the query topics, and core and topology schemas.

The steps (1) and (2) are exactly the same as in the traditional ER models, the steps (3) and (4) are additional but critical for network analysis applications, and the step (5) extends integrity constraints of the traditional ER models to analytical types in topology schemas and topological constructs in query topics accordingly. In the rest of this section, we focus on discussing three key aspects: (i) what are data and query requirements; (ii) how are query requirements and query topics related; and (iii) how are the core and topology schemas designed.

Data and Query Requirements. Data and queries are two different kinds of requirements. Data requirements describe what information an application should manage, while query requirements describe how the information of an application should be used. Although our NAER model can conceptually represent both data and query requirements for network analysis applications, the questions to be clarified are: (a) Do we need to consider all queries? (b) If not, what are the query requirements of interest?

Queries in network analysis applications may exist in various forms. For example, *database queries* in the traditional sense, such as "find all journal articles published in 2013", often use a database language (e.g., SQL) to process data, and *analysis queries* from a topological perspective, such as the queries Q1, Q3 and Q4, often use certain data mining and machine learning techniques to process data. In a nutshell, database queries and analysis queries are fundamentally different in two respects:

- *Logical vs topological*: Database queries are concerned with the logical properties of entities and relationships, while analysis queries focus on the topological properties of entities and relationships. In most cases, analysis queries are formulated using software tools in a much more complicated way than database queries.

- *Indefinite vs definite*: Analysis queries often have indefinite answers, which depends on not only the underlying structure but also the choice of topological measures. It can be difficult to know which measure is better than the others, and which answer is optimal. In contrast, database queries have definite answers that are determined by the underlying database.

In many real-life applications, analysis and database queries are commonly combined in order to find useful information [17]. For example, the query Q2 can be viewed as the combination of an analysis query *"find the most influential articles"* and a database query *"find articles of each VLDB conference, together with the authors of the article"*.

When designing a conceptual model for network analysis applications, we are only interested in analysis queries. There are two reasons: (1) analysis queries are often computationally expensive so that modelling analysis queries can help improve performance; (2) analysis queries are often isolated so that modelling analysis queries can help maintain their semantic integrity. Therefore, given a set Q of queries for modelling a network analysis application, which may contain database queries, analysis queries or a combination of both, queries in Q are first transformed into Q' by removing any database queries in Q.

Query Topics. After identifying query requirements, i.e., queries of interest, we need to analyze these queries to understand their semantics and required computations. Analyzing queries is to unravel the structures of queries, which has at least two aspects to consider: (1) the structure of a query, and (2) the structure among a set of queries. Since queries may be described in various syntactical forms, here we focus on exploiting the semantic structures of queries.

For each query Q, we associate it with a query topic $t(Q)$, which is a tree with each node C corresponding to an object class, and an edge from a node

C_1 to a node C_2 expressing that C_1 depends on C_2. This dependence relation between object classes is closed under transitivity, i.e., if C_1 depends on C_2, and C_2 depends on C_3, then C_1 depends on C_3. The query topic $t(Q)$ of a query Q can be defined at *a flexible level of abstraction*. That is, the level of granularity for nodes in a query tree is a design choice depending on individual applications.

For each query Q, we thus have a set of object classes that are in one-to-one correspondence with the nodes of $t(Q)$. A node $C_1 \in t(Q_1)$ in one query topic may have certain relationships with a node $C_2 \in t(Q_2)$ in a different query topic. Such relationships include that: (1) C_1 depends on C_2; or (2) C_1 and C_2 are the same. Nevertheless, it is impossible that C_1 depends on C_2, and meanwhile C_2 depends on C_1 or any of its descendant nodes. If two different query topics $t(Q_1)$ and $t(Q_2)$ contain the same node C, then $t(Q_1)$ and $t(Q_2)$ are connected by the node C, and merged as one tree.

Example 5. Consider the queries Q1-Q4 in our motivating example. We have one query topic for each of the queries as depicted in Fig. 5.(a), and three trees corresponding to the whole set $\{Q_1, Q_2, Q_3, Q_4\}$ as depicted in Fig. 5.(b).

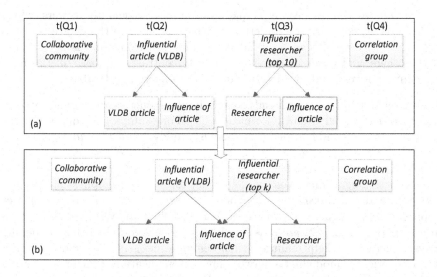

Fig. 5. Query topics (a). for individual queries; (b) for a set of queries

Core and Topology Schemas. For a network analysis application, the design of its core schema and topology schemas is carried out in two steps. First, the core schema is designed based on data requirements as in the traditional ER models. Second, the topology schemas are designed based on query requirements following a method of grouping the leaves of query topics that are associated with query requirements. All leaves that can be handled by database queries over the core schema are grouped together, while the other leaves are grouped in terms of what analytical types they need for analysis, and each of such groups correspond to one topology schema. It also implies that, each object class represented by a leave corresponding to some topology schema S_t can be specified by using a topological construct over S_t. In general, the central idea is that all data requirements should be captured by the core schema, and the analysis part of all query requirements should be captured by a collection of topology schemas.

Example 6. For the query topics of Q1-Q4, we can group their leaves as below, where C_i denotes the leave with the initials i. As a result, three topology schemas $\{S_{co}, S_{ci}, S_{jo}\}$ can be designed as described in Fig. 4.

Queries	Core schema	Topology schemas		
		S_{co}	S_{ci}	S_{jo}
Q1		C_{cc}		
Q2	C_{va}		C_{ioa}	
Q3	C_r		C_{ioa}	
Q4				C_{cg}

Example 4 showed that the object classes *collaborative community, influence of article* and *correlation group*, which are respectively represented by C_{cc}, C_{ioa} and C_{cg}, can be specified using topological constructs.

One distinguished feature of topology schemas is that, rather than taking objects in all their complexity, topology schemas only focus on specifying a simple but concise representation for objects. Therefore, topology schemas need to be designed in accordance with the following criteria:

1. *Topology schemas should be small.* Topology schemas are the basic building blocks of supporting analysis queries. The smaller topology schemas are, the easier they can be composed to support flexible modelling needs.
2. *Topology schemas should be dynamic.* Query requirements may be changing over time. Correspondingly, topology schemas need to be adaptive enough to reflect the dynamics of query requirements.

Two topology schemas in an analytical framework may be overlapping. In fact, certain degree of overlapping can facilitate comparative analysis over different topology schemas. Nevertheless, duplicate topology schemas should be avoided because this would cause redundant storage and inconsistence. The following example shows that our analytical framework supports an integrated and coherent view on core and topology schemas.

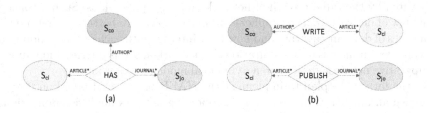

Fig. 6. Composing core and topology schemas

Example 7. The three topology schemas $\{S_{co}, S_{ci}, S_{jo}\}$ can be composed by leveraging base types in the core schema. Fig. 6 shows three possible compositions: (a) three topology schemas are composed by an analytical relationship type HAS that is determined by several base types; (b) two schemas are composed by a base relationship type (i.e., PUBLISH and WRITE) directly.

5   Related Works

Recently, a number of works have proposed to use database technologies for managing and analyzing network analysis [6,7,20]. However, they have mostly focused on designing logical data models and their corresponding query languages for supporting network analysis. So far, only very limited work has considered the design process of conceptual modeling [1]. In general, the previous works on modelling network analysis applications at the logical level fall into two lines of research:

(1) Extending traditional database technologies (i.e., the relational model and SQL) to support data mining algorithms, such as SiQL [20] and Oracle Data Miner.
(2) Extending object-oriented or graph database technologies to incorporate graph-theoretic and data mining algorithms, such as GOQL [18], and other works discussed in the survey paper [21].

Our work in this paper focused on the conceptual modelling of network analysis, and leaves the transformation to a logical model (e.g., the relational model, a graph model or a combination of several data models) as a decision of the user. For example, in [17], a hybrid memory and disk engine was developed for evaluating queries, which maintains topological structures in memory while the data is stored in a relational database. An analytical framework designed in our work can be well transformed into this data model and be implemented over the hybrid engine by separating topological structures specified by topology schemas from the database structure specified by the core schema.

6   Conclusions

In this paper, we proposed the NAER model and a conceptual modelling paradigm that incorporates both data and query requirements of network analysis. This was motivated by the rapid growth of network analysis applications. Such a conceptual view of network analysis applications can enable us to better understand the semantics of data and queries, and how they interact with each other. In doing so, we can avoid unnecessary computations in network analysis queries and support comparative network analysis in a dynamical modeling environment.

In the future, we plan to implement the NAER model, and based on that to establish an analytical framework for supporting network analysis applications, including the development of a concrete modelling language for network analysis and a query engine for processing topic-based queries.

References

1. Bao, Z., Tay, Y.C., Zhou, J.: sonSchema: A conceptual schema for social networks. In: Ng, W., Storey, V.C., Trujillo, J.C. (eds.) ER 2013. LNCS, vol. 8217, pp. 197–211. Springer, Heidelberg (2013)
2. Brandes, U., Erlebach, T.: Network Analysis. LNCS, vol. 3418. Springer, Heidelberg (2005)
3. Brughmans, T.: Connecting the dots: towards archaeological network analysis. Oxford Journal of Archaeology 29(3), 277–303 (2010)
4. Chen, C., Song, I.-Y., Zhu, W.: Trends in conceptual modeling: Citation analysis of the ER Conference papers (1979-2005)
5. Chen, P.: The entity-relationship model – toward a unified view of data. ACM TODS 1(1), 9–36 (1976)
6. Cohen, S., Ebel, L., Kimelfeld, B.: A social network database that learns how to answer queries. In: CIDR (2013)
7. Dries, A., Nijssen, S., De Raedt, L.: A query language for analyzing networks. In: CIKM, pp. 485–494 (2009)
8. Fortunato, S.: Community detection in graphs. Physics Reports 486(3), 75–174 (2010)
9. Freeman, L.C.: Centrality in social networks conceptual clarification. Social Networks 1(3), 215–239 (1979)
10. Girvan, M., Newman, M.E.: Community structure in social and biological networks. Proceedings of the National Academy of Sciences 99(12), 7821–7826 (2002)
11. Huisman, M., Van Duijn, M.A.: Software for social network analysis. Models and Methods in Social Network Analysis, 270–316 (2005)
12. Jamakovic, A., Uhlig, S.: On the relationships between topological measures in real-world networks. Networks and Heterogeneous Media 3(2), 345 (2008)
13. Kumar, R., Novak, J., Tomkins, A.: Structure and evolution of online social networks. In: Link Mining: Models, Algorithms, and Applications, pp. 337–357. Springer (2010)
14. Lü, L., Zhou, T.: Link prediction in complex networks: A survey. Physica A: Statistical Mechanics and its Applications 390(6), 1150–1170 (2011)
15. Newman, M.E.: Scientific collaboration networks. i. network construction and fundamental results. Physical Review E 64(1), 016131 (2001)
16. Pavlopoulos, G.A., Wegener, A.-L., Schneider, R.: A survey of visualization tools for biological network analysis. Biodata Mining 1(1), 1–11 (2008)
17. Sakr, S., Elnikety, S., He, Y.: G-SPARQL: A hybrid engine for querying large attributed graphs. In: CIKM, pp. 335–344 (2012)
18. Sheng, L., Ozsoyoglu, Z.M., Ozsoyoglu, G.: A graph query language and its query processing. In: ICDE, pp. 572–581 (1999)
19. Thalheim, B.: Entity-relationship modeling: foundations of database technology. Springer (2000)
20. Wicker, J., Richter, L., Kessler, K., Kramer, S.: SINDBAD and SiQL: An inductive database and query language in the relational model. In: Daelemans, W., Goethals, B., Morik, K. (eds.) ECML PKDD 2008, Part II. LNCS (LNAI), vol. 5212, pp. 690–694. Springer, Heidelberg (2008)
21. Wood, P.: Query languages for graph databases. ACM SIGMOD Record 41(1), 50–60 (2012)

Model-Driven Design of Graph Databases

Roberto De Virgilio, Antonio Maccioni, and Riccardo Torlone

Dipartimento di Ingegneria
Università Roma Tre, Rome, Italy
{dvr,maccioni,torlone}@dia.uniroma3.it

Abstract. Graph Database Management Systems (GDBMS) are rapidly emerging as an effective and efficient solution to the management of very large data sets in scenarios where data are naturally represented as a graph and data accesses mainly rely on traversing this graph. Currently, the design of graph databases is based on best practices, usually suited only for a specific GDBMS. In this paper, we propose a model-driven, system-independent methodology for the design of graph databases. Starting from a conceptual representation of the domain of interest expressed in the Entity-Relationship model, we propose a strategy for devising a graph database in which the data accesses for answering queries are minimized. Intuitively, this is achieved by aggregating in the same node data that are likely to occur together in query results. Our methodology relies a logical model for graph databases, which makes the approach suitable for different GDBMSs. We also show, with a number of experimental results over different GDBMSs, the effectiveness of the proposed methodology.

1 Introduction

Social networks, Semantic Web, geographic applications, and bioinformatics are examples of a significant class of application domains in which data have a natural representation in terms of graphs, and queries mainly require to traverse those graphs. It has been observed that relational database technology is usually unsuited to manage such kind of data since they hardly capture their inherent graph structure. In addition, graph traversals over highly connected data involve complex join operations, which can make typical operations inefficient and applications hard to scale. This problem has been recently addressed by a new brand category of data management systems in which data are natively stored as graphs, nodes and edges are first class citizens, and queries are expressed in terms of graph traversal operations. These systems are usually called GDBMSs (Graph Database Management Systems) and allow applications to scale to very large graph-based data sets. In addition, since GDBMSs do not rely on a rigid schema, they provide a more flexible solution in scenarios where the organization of data evolves rapidly.

GDBMSs are usually considered as part of the NoSQL landscape, which includes non-relational solutions to the management of data characterized by elementary data models, schema-free databases, basic data access operations,

E. Yu et al. (Eds.): ER 2014, LNCS 8824, pp. 172–185, 2014.

and eventually consistent transactions [8,13]. GDBMSs are considered however a world apart from the other NoSQL systems (e.g., key-value, document, and column stores) since their features are quite unique in both the data model they adopt and the data-access primitives they offer [18].

In this framework, it has been observed that, as it happens with traditional database systems [5], the availability of effective design methodologies would be very useful for database developers [3,8,13]. Indeed, also with NoSQL systems, design choices can have a significant impact on the performances and the scalability of the application under development [18]. Unfortunately however, database design for GDBMS is currently based only on best practices and guidelines, which are usually related to a specific system, and the adoption of traditional approaches is ineffective [4]. Moreover, design strategies for other NoSQL systems cannot be exploited for graph databases since the underlying data models and the systems used for their management are very different.

In this paper, we try to fill this gap by proposing a general, model-driven [19] methodology for the design of graph databases. The approach starts, as usual, with the construction of a conceptual representation of application data expressed in the ER model. This representation is translated into a special graph in which entities and relationships are suitably grouped according to the constraints defined on the ER schema. The aim is to try to minimize the number of access operations needed to retrieve related data of the application. This intermediate representation refers to an abstract, graph-based data model that captures the modeling features that are common to real GDBMSs. This makes the approach independent of the specific system that will be used to store and manage the final database. We also provides a number of experimental results showing the advantages of our proposal with respect to a naive approach in which a graph database is derived by simply mapping directly conceptual to physical objects.

The rest of the paper is organized as follows. In Section 2 we introduce an abstract model for graph database and discuss basic strategies for modeling data with a GDBMS. Section 3 illustrates in detail our design methodology whereas Section 4 illustrates the experimental results. In Section 5 we discuss related works and finally, in Section 6, we sketch conclusions and future work.

2   Modeling Graph Databases

2.1   Graph Databases

The spread of application domains involving graph-shaped data has arisen the interest on graph databases and GDBMSs. Unfortunately, due to diversity of the various systems and of the lack of theoretical studies on them, there is no widely accepted data model for GDBMSs and of the basic features they should provide. However, almost all the existing systems exhibit three main characteristics.

First of all, a GDBMS stores data by means of a multigraph[1], usually called *property graph* [17], where both nodes and edges are labelled with data in the form of key-value pairs.

---

[1] A multigraph is a graph where two nodes can be connected by more than one edge.

Definition 1 (Graph database). *A graph database, is a directed multigraph* $\mathbf{g} = (N, E)$ *where every node* $n \in N$ *and every edge* $e \in E$ *is associated with a set of pairs* ⟨*key, value*⟩ *called properties.*

A simple example of graph database is reported in Fig. 1: it represents a portion of a database storing information about blogs, having users as administrators and/or followers. Nodes n_1 and n_2 represent a user and a blog, respectively. They both have an id and a name as properties. The edges between n_1 and n_2 represent the relationships follower and admin, respectively (in our case, the user is both follower and admin of the blog), and are associated with properties that simply specify these relationships.

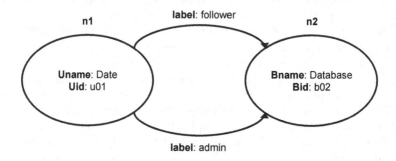

Fig. 1. An example of property graph

Note that this notion of graph database is very flexible since no further constraint is imposed on graphs and their topology. In particular, nodes representing objects of the same class (e.g., different users) can differ in the number of properties and in the data type of a specific property. This makes the data model very general and able to capture various graph-based data models, such as RDF and RDFS. Indeed, GDBMSs are often used in Semantic Web applications [1,14].

The second important feature of a GDBMS is the property of *index-free adjacency.*

Definition 2 (Index Free Adjacency). *We say that a graph database* g *satisfies the index-free adjacency if the existence of an edge between two nodes of* g *can be tested by visiting those nodes and does not require the existence of an external, global, index.*

In other words, each node carries the information about its neighbors and no global index of reachability between nodes exists. As a result, the traversal of an edge from a node is independent on the size of data and can be tested in constant time. This guarantees that local analysis can be performed very efficiently on GDBMS and this makes those systems suitable in scenarios where the size of data increases rapidly.

The third feature common to GDBMSs is the fact that data is queried using path traversal operations expressed in some graph-based query language, such as Gremlin[2]. We will not address specific query languages in this paper.

2.2 Modeling Strategies for Graph Databases

A main goal in the design of a graph database is the minimization of data access operations needed in graph traversals at query time. Intuitively, this can be achieved in two different ways: (i) by adding edges between nodes or (ii) by merging different nodes. We call these approaches *dense* and *compact* strategy, respectively.

Basically, the *dense* strategy heavily relies on adding as many edges as possible between nodes representing conceptual entities. This clearly reduces the length of paths between nodes and so the number of data access operations needed at run time. However, it requires to add edges that do not correspond to conceptual relationships in the application domain and such "semantic enrichment" demands an additional effort of the designer.

Conversely, the *compact* strategy relies on aggregating in the same node data that are related but are stored in different nodes. This clearly reduces the number of data accesses as well but, on the other hand, it asks the designer to deal with possible data inconsistencies. Consider for instance the case in which we decide to merge each user node with the blog nodes he follows in the database in Fig. 1 to make more efficient queries involving both users and blogs. If the users follow multiple blogs we have a conflict on the Bname property, which requires a suitable renaming of keys.

Actually, some modeling approaches for graph-shaped data (e.g., in the direct conversion of relational data into RDF graphs [20]) follow yet another strategy, which we call *sparse*. Basically, in the sparse strategy the properties of an object with n properties is decomposed into a set of n different nodes, with the goal of minimizing the number of edges incident to the nodes of the graph. This avoids potential conflicts between the properties of a node but it usually increases largely the number of nodes that need to be traversed during query execution. Moreover, it can make database updates inefficient since the simple insertion or deletion of an object requires multiple database accesses, one for each property of the object.

3 Graph Database Design

This section illustrates a design methodology for graph databases. Our solution supports the user in the design a graph database for the application on the basis of an automatic analysis of a conceptual representation of the domain of interest. In principle, any conceptual data model could be used and in this paper we will consider the Entity-Relationship (ER) model.

---

[2] https://github.com/thinkaurelius/titan/wiki/Gremlin-Query-Language

As in the compact strategy, our technique tries to reduce the number of data access required at runtime by aggregating objects occurring in the conceptual representation as much as possible. In addition, to preserve the semantics of the application domain, we also try to take advantage from the benefits of the sparse strategy discussed in Section 2.2. In fact, similarly to the sparse strategy, the aggregation technique avoids potential inconsistencies between properties of nodes. This is done by carefully analyzing the many-to-many relationships of the the ER diagram, which may introduce many connections between nodes and thus conflicting properties in their aggregation.

In our methodology human intervention is extremely reduced: in most cases the translation between the conceptual representation and the graph database is completely automatic and the designer does not need to introduce artificial concepts and relationships. Indeed, all the elements of the output database originate directly from concepts appearing in the input Entity-Relationship diagram. This is coherent with the NoSQL philosophy where the persistence layer is semantically close to the design layer.

In this paper, we refer to a basic version of the ER including entities, relationships, attributes and cardinalities. However such a choice does not introduce limitations on the generality of our approach.

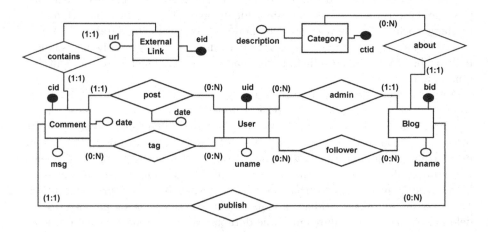

Fig. 2. An example of ER diagram

In the following, we will consider, as running example, an application domain of blogs represented in conceptual terms by the ER diagram in Fig. 2. Intuitively, our strategy aims at building a "template" of a graph database for this initial schema. This template describes how data have to be organized into nodes and how nodes have to be connected to each other. The design strategy is organized in three different phases: (i) generation of an oriented ER diagram, (ii) partitioning of the elements (entities and relationships) of the obtained diagram and (iii) definition of a template over the resulting partition.

3.1   Generation of an Oriented ER Diagram

In the first phase, we transform an ER diagram, which is an undirected and labelled graph, into a directed, labelled and weighted graph, called *Oriented ER* (O-ER) diagram. In O-ER diagrams, a special function w assigns a weight with each edge of the diagram.

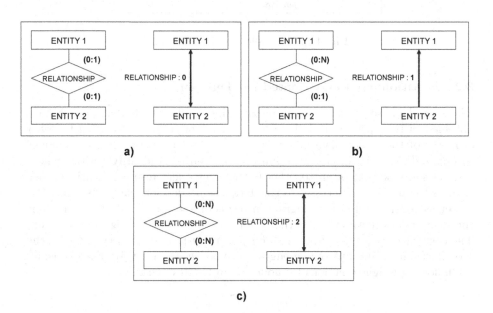

Fig. 3. Rules for generating an O-ER diagram

As illustrated in Fig. 3, the O-ER diagram is generated by applying to an ER diagram the following transformation rules.

a) A one-to-one relationship becomes a double directed edge e such that $w(e) = 0$;
b) A one-to-many relationship becomes a single-directed edge e such that $w(e) = 1$ going from the entity with lower multiplicity to the entity with higher multiplicity;
c) A many-to-many relationship becomes a double-directed edge e with $w(e) = 2$.

All entities and attributes (including those of relationships) are kept in the output O-ER diagram.

For instance, given the ER diagram of Fig. 2, by applying the rules discussed above we obtain the O-ER diagram shown in Fig. 4 (in the figure, we have omitted the attributes for the sake of readability).

Note that our methodology can refer to other data modeling formalisms, such as UML, by just adapting this phase.

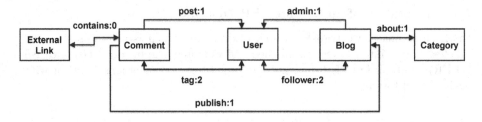

Fig. 4. An example of O-ER diagram

3.2   Partitioning of an Oriented ER Diagram

The second phase consists in the partitioning of the O-ER diagram we have
obtained in the first phase. It is based on a set of rules for grouping together
elements of the O-ER diagram so that every element of the diagram belongs
to one and only one group. The aim of this step is to identify entities whose
instances are likely to occur together in the same query results. Intuitively, this
reduces the number of accesses to the database needed for query answering.

Let us consider an O-ER diagram in terms of a graph $\langle N, E, w \rangle$, where N is
the set of nodes (entities), E is the set of edges, and w the weighting function.
Then let $\mathsf{in}(n) = \{(m, n) \mid (m, n) \in E\}$ and $\mathsf{out}(n)\{(n, m) \mid (n, m) \in E\}$ be the
sets of incoming and outcoming edges of a node n, respectively. Then consider
the following weight functions for nodes of an O-ER diagram:

$$w^+(n) = \sum_{e \in out(n)} w(e)$$

$$w^-(n) = \sum_{e \in in(n)} w(e)$$

The functions $w^-(n)$ and $w^+(n)$ compute the sum of the weights of the incoming
and outcoming edges of a node n, respectively. For instance, referring to Fig. 4,
the weights associated with the node Comment are the following

$$w^+(\mathsf{Comment}) = w(\mathsf{post}) + w(\mathsf{tag}) + w(\mathsf{publish}) + w(\mathsf{contains}) = 1 + 2 + 1 + 0 = 4$$

$$w^-(\mathsf{Comment}) = w(\mathsf{tag}) + w(\mathsf{contains}) = 2 + 0 = 2$$

The partitioning is then based on the following rules for grouping nodes of an
O-ER diagram.

- **Rule 1:** if a node n is disconnected then it forms a group by itself;
- **Rule 2:** if a node n has $w^-(n) > 1$ and $w^+(n) \geqslant 1$ then n forms a group
  by itself. Intuitively, in this case the node n represents an entity involved
  with high multiplicity in many-to-many relationships. Therefore we do not
  aggregate n with other nodes having a similar weight. This rule applies for
  example to the nodes User, Comment and Blog in the diagram of Fig. 4;

– **Rule 3:** if a node n has $w^-(n) \leqslant 1$ and $w^+(n) \leqslant 1$ then n is added to the group of a node m such that there exists the edge (m, n) in the O-ER diagram. In this case, the node n corresponds to an entity involved in a one-to-one relationship or in a one-to-many relationships in which n has the lower multiplicity. This rule applies for example to the nodes Category and External Link in the diagram of Fig. 4: Category is aggregated with Blog and External Link with Comment.

Note that these rules can be applied either recursively or iteratively. An iterative procedure would analyze once every node of the O-ER diagram. By applying these rules to the diagram in Fig. 4, we obtain the partition shown in Fig. 5.

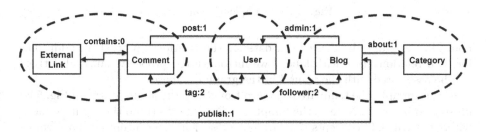

Fig. 5. An example of partitioning.

3.3   Definition of a Template over a Graph Database

Once the groups are formed, the third phase generates a *template* for the final graph database. While it is improper to speak of a schema for graph databases (as usually data do not strictly adhere to any schema), there are always similar nodes in a graph database, that is, nodes that share many attributes and are connected by the same kind of edges. Therefore we can say that homogeneous nodes identify a "data type". Basically, a *template* describes the data types occurring in a graph database and the ways they are connected. Thus, it represents a logical schema of the graph database that can be made transparent to the designer and to the user of the target database.

Indeed, the database instance is not forced to conform the template in a rigid way. Rather, it is the initial structure of the graph database that can be later extended or refined. In addition, it is a valid mean to address the impedance mismatch between the persistence layer and the application layer.

Then, a template works as a "schema" for a graph database where each node and each edge is equipped with the names (i.e., the keys) of the involved properties. The names of properties originate from the attributes of the entities occurring in the same group. Every attribute determines a property name of the instance of an entity. In a template, a property name is composed by the name of the entity concatenated to the name of the attribute it originates from (e.g., User.uname). In the same way, the attributes of the relationships between entities determine the names of the property of the edges connecting the corresponding

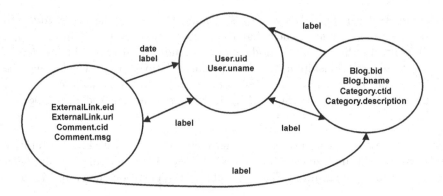

Fig. 6. An example of template.

nodes in the graph database (e.g., date for the relationship post). In addition, for each relationship r with label l we introduce the property name label that will be associated with the value l in the graph database.

As an example, the template produced from the partitioning shown in Fig. 5 is illustrated in Fig. 6. Note as the template adheres perfectly to the input domain without "artificial" concepts that are not present in the conceptual representation. Using the template, we can generate different instances. For example, Fig. 7 illustrates an instance of graph database conforming to the template in Fig. 6. In this case we have three instances of User, three instances of Blog (with the corresponding Category) and one instance of Comment (with the corresponding External Link).

4   Experimental Results

In order to evaluate the effectiveness of our methodology, we have implemented a tool that aggregates data using the technique illustrated in Section 3. In particular, we have extended a system, called R2G, that we have developed for migrating relational to graph databases [11].

With this tool, we have compared the query performances of graph databases obtained with our strategy with those obtained with the sparse strategy, which is adopted by the most common GDBMSs: Neo4J [22], ArangoDB[3], Infinite-Graph[4], Oracle NoSQL[5], OrientDB[6] and Titan[7]. Our system makes use of the Blueprints framework[8], a general, open-source API for graph databases adopted by all GDBMS. Blueprints, as JDBC, allows developers to plug-and-play their

---

[3] https://www.arangodb.org/

[4] http://www.objectivity.com/infinitegraph

[5] http://www.oracle.com/technetwork/database/database-technologies/ nosqldb/overview/index.html

[6] http://www.orientechnologies.com/orientdb/

[7] http://thinkaurelius.github.io/titan/

[8] https://github.com/tinkerpop/blueprints/wiki

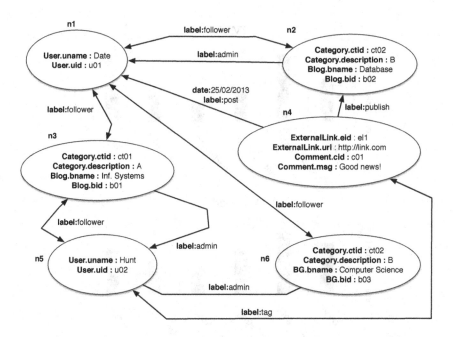

Fig. 7. The final graph database

graph database back-end. In this way, R2G is able to connect to each GDBMS and import data by using both the proprietary strategy (sparse-like) and our strategy.

Experiments were conducted on a dual core 2.66GHz Intel Xeon, running Linux RedHat, with 4 GB of memory and a 2-disk 1Tbyte striped RAID array.

Aggregate data sources. In a first experiment we considered, as in [11], aggregate datasets with different sizes. Such data sources present data highly correlated where the sparse strategy fits nicely (i.e. graph traversal operations are performed over quite short paths). We used a relational representation of MON-DIAL (17.115 tuples and 28 relations) and of two ideal counterpoints (due to the larger size): IMDB (1.673.074 tuples in 6 relations) and WIKIPEDIA (200.000 tuples in 6 relations), as described in [9]. The authors in [9] defined a benchmark of 50 keyword search queries for each dataset. We used the tool in [7] to generate SQL queries from the keyword-based queries defined in [9]. The SQL queries are then mapped to the Gremlin language supported by the Blueprints framework.

Then, we evaluated the performance of query execution. For each dataset, we ran the 50 queries ten times and measured the average response time. We performed *cold-cache* experiments (i.e. by dropping all file-system caches before restarting the various systems and running the queries) and *warm-cache* experiments (i.e. without dropping the caches). Fig. 8 shows the performance for cold-cache experiments. Due to space constraints, in the figure we report times only on IMDB and WIKIPEDIA, since their much larger size poses more

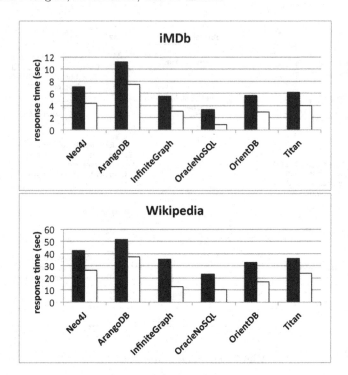

Fig. 8. Performance on aggregate data sources: black bars refer to the sparse strategy and white bars refer to our strategy

challenges. In the figure, for each GDBMS we consider the time to perform a query on the graph database generated by using the sparse strategy (i.e. black bar) and the time to perform the same query on the graph database generated by using our strategy (i.e. white bar).

Our methodology allows to each system to perform consistently better for most of the queries. This is due to our strategy reducing the space overhead and consequently the time complexity of the overall process w.r.t. the competitors strategy that spends much time traversing a large number of edges. Warm-cache experiments follow a similar trend.

A significant result is the *speed-up* between the two strategies. For each dataset D, we computed the speed-up for all systems P as the ratio between the average execution time over the graph database generated by the sparse strategy of P, and that of our strategy in R2G, or briefly $S_D = t_P/t_{R2G}$: $S_{\mathrm{IMDB}} = 2,03$, $S_{\mathrm{WIKIPEDIA}} = 1,97$, and $S_{\mathrm{MONDIAL}} = 2,01$.

Disaggregate data sources. In a second experiment we used a different benchmark for path-traversal queries. In particular, we have considered disaggregate datasets with a large number of nodes sparsely connected and long paths between nodes. To this aim, we used the *graphdb-benchmarks project*[9] that involves

---

[9] https://github.com/socialsensor/graphdb-benchmarks

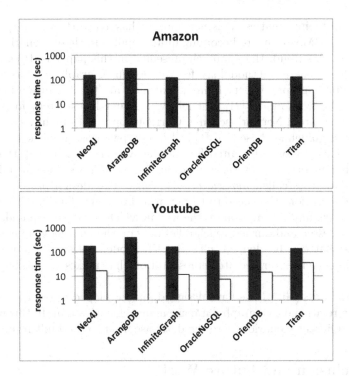

Fig. 9. Performance on disaggregate data sources: black bars refer to the sparse strategy and white bars refer to our strategy

social data from AMAZON, YOUTUBE and LIVEJOURNAL. This benchmark involves different path-traversal queries: (i) to find the neighbors of a node, (ii) to find the nodes of a edge and (iii) to find the shortest path between two nodes.

As in the first experiment, for each dataset we ran the queries ten times and measured the average response time. The final results are depicted in Fig. 9 (times are in seconds and the scale is logarithmic). Due to space constraints we omitted the results for LIVEJOURNAL since they are quite similar to the other datasets. In this case our strategy generates databases that perform significantly better in each system. In this context, the aggregation at the basis of our methodology reduces significantly the number of nodes to traverse, contrary to the sparse strategy, as shown by the following speed-up: $S_{\text{AMAZON}} = 9,97$, $S_{\text{YOUTUBE}} = 10,01$, $S_{\text{LIVEJOURNAL}} = 9,98$. In words, our strategy allows us to perform queries 10 times better than the proprietary strategy of each system.

5 Related Work

The idea of storing and managing graph-based data natively is quite old (see [2] for an extensive survey on this topic) and is recently re-born with the advent of the Semantic Web and other emerging application domains, such as social networks and bioinformatics. This new interest has led to the development of a number of GDBMSs that are becoming quite popular in these scenarios.

In spite of this trend, the approach presented in this paper is, to our knowledge, the first general methodology for the design of graph databases and so the related bibliography is very limited. Batini et al. [6] introduce a logical design for the Network model [21] that follows a sparse-like strategy for mapping an ER schema into a Network schema. Current approaches mainly rely on best practices and guidelines based on typical design patterns, published by practitioners in blogs [15] or only suited for specific systems [16]. In [12], the author gathers different design patterns for various NoSQL data stores, including one for graph databases called *application side joins*. This design pattern is based on the join operations that need to be performed over the database. Conversely, we do not make any assumption on the way in which the database under development is accessed and our approach relies only on the knowledge of conceptual constraints that can be defined with the ER model. Moreover, it provides a system-independent intermediate representation that makes it suitable for any GDBMS.

In earlier works [10,11], we have designed and developed a tool for migrating data from a relational to a graph database management system. In this work, we consider a different scenario where the database needs to be built from scratch.

6   Conclusion and Future Work

In this paper we have presented a design methodology for graph databases. Our approach involves a preliminary conceptual design phase followed by a strategy for translating the conceptual representation into a intermediate representation that is still independent of the specific target system. The goal is to try to keep together data that are likely to occur together in query results while keeping separate independent concepts. An evaluation study shows that our methodology provides considerable advantages in terms of query performance with respect to naive approaches.

In the future work we will consider more aspects for driving the design process such as transaction requirements and query operation loads for the application at hand. This information can improve the effectiveness of the methodology by helping to disambiguate between different, possible decisions. We also intend to verify if a similar approach is also possible for other NoSQL data stores, in particular to key-value and document stores.

References

1. Angles, R., Gutierrez, C.: Querying RDF data from a graph database perspective. In: Gómez-Pérez, A., Euzenat, J. (eds.) ESWC 2005. LNCS, vol. 3532, pp. 346–360. Springer, Heidelberg (2005)
2. Angles, R., Gutierrez, C.: Survey of graph database models. ACM Comput. Surv. 40(1), 1–39 (2008)

3. Atzeni, P., Jensen, C.S., Orsi, G., Ram, S., Tanca, L., Torlone, R.: The relational model is dead, SQL is dead, and i don't feel so good myself. SIGMOD Record 42(2), 64–68 (2013)
4. Badia, A., Lemire, D.: A call to arms: revisiting database design. SIGMOD Record 40(3), 61–69 (2011)
5. Batini, C., Ceri, S., Navathe, S.B.: Conceptual Database Design: An Entity-Relationship Approach. Benjamin/Cummings (1992)
6. Batini, C., Ceri, S., Navathe, S.B.: Conceptual Database Design: An Entity-Relationship Approach. Benjamin/Cummings (1992)
7. Bergamaschi, S., Domnori, E., Guerra, F., Lado, R.T., Velegrakis, Y.: Keyword search over relational databases: A metadata approach. In: SIGMOD Conference, pp. 565–576 (2011)
8. Cattell, R.: Scalable SQL and NoSQL data stores. SIGMOD Record 39(4), 12–27 (2010)
9. Coffman, J., Weaver, A.C.: An empirical performance evaluation of relational keyword search techniques. TKDE 26(1), 30–42 (2014)
10. De Virgilio, R., Maccioni, A., Torlone, R.: Converting relational to graph databases. In: SIGMOD Workshops - GRADES (2013)
11. De Virgilio, R., Maccioni, A., Torlone, R.: R2G: A tool for migrating relations to graphs. In: EDBT (2014)
12. Katsov, I.: NoSQL data modeling techniques (2012), http://highlyscalable. wordpress.com/2012/03/01/nosql-data-modeling-techniques
13. Mohan, C.: History repeats itself: sensible and NonsenSQL aspects of the NoSQL hoopla. In: EDBT, pp. 11–16 (2013)
14. Ovelgönne, M., Park, N., Subrahmanian, V.S., Bowman, E.K., Ogaard, K.A.: Personalized best answer computation in graph databases. In: Alani, H., et al. (eds.) ISWC 2013, Part I. LNCS, vol. 8218, pp. 478–493. Springer, Heidelberg (2013)
15. Parastatidis, S.: On graph data model design (2013), http://savas.me/2013/03/ on-graph-data-model-design-relationships/
16. Robinson, I.: Designing and building a graph database application with neo4j. In: Graph Connect (2013)
17. Rodriguez, M.A., Neubauer, P.: Constructions from dots and lines. CoRR abs/1006.2361 (2010)
18. Sadalage, R.J., Fowler, M.: NoSQL Distilled: A Brief Guide to the Emerging World of Polyglot Persistence. Addison-Wesley Professional (2012)
19. Schmidt, D.C.: Guest editor's introduction: Model-driven engineering. IEEE Computer 39(2), 25–31 (2006)
20. Sequeda, J., Arenas, M., Miranker, D.P.: On directly mapping relational databases to RDF and OWL. In: WWW, pp. 649–658 (2012)
21. Taylor, R.W., Frank, R.L.: Codasyl data-base management systems. ACM Comput. Surv. 8(1), 67–103 (1976)
22. Webber, J.: A programmatic introduction to neo4j. In: SPLASH, pp. 217–218 (2012)

Utility-Friendly Heterogenous Generalization in Privacy Preserving Data Publishing

Xianmang He[1], Dong Li[2,*], Yanni Hao[2], and Huahui Chen[1]

[1] School of Information Science and Engineering, NingBo University
NO 818, Fenghua Road, Ningbo, Zhejiang 315122, P.R. China
[2] Information Center, National Natural Science Foundation of China
NO.83, Shuangqing Road, Haidian District, Beijing 100085, P.R. China
lidong@nsfc.gov.cn

Abstract. K-anonymity is one of the most important anonymity models that have been widely investigated and various techniques have been proposed to achieve it. Among them generalization is a common technique. In a typical generalization approach, tuples in a table was first divided into many QI(quasi-identifier)-groups such that the size of each QI-group is larger than K. In general, utility of anonymized data can be enhanced if size of each QI-group is reduced. Motivated by this observation, we propose linking-based anonymity model, which achieves K-anonymity with QI-groups having size less than K. To implement linking-based anonymization model, we propose a simple yet efficient heuristic local recoding method. Extensive experiments on real data sets are also conducted to show that the utility has been significantly improved by our approach compared to the state-of-the-art methods.

Keywords: privacy preservation, K-anonymity, linking-based anonymization, Heterogenous Generalization.

1 Introduction

Privacy leakage is one of major concerns when publishing data for statistical process or data analysis. In general, organizations need to release data that may contain sensitive information for the purposes of facilitating useful data analysis or research. For example, patients' medical records may be released by a hospital to aid the medical study. Records in Table 1 (called the microdata) is an example of patients' records published by hospitals. Note that attribute *Disease* contains sensitive information of patients. Hence, data publishers must ensure that no adversaries can accurately infer the disease of any patient. One straightforward approach to achieve this goal is excluding unique identifier attributes, such as *Name* from the table, which however is not sufficient for protecting privacy leakage under *linking-attack* [1–3]. For example, the combination of *Age*, *Zipcode* and *Sex* can be potentially used to identify an individual in Table 1, and has been called a quasi-identifier (QI for short) [1] in literatures. If an adversary

---

* Correspondence author.

E. Yu et al. (Eds.): ER 2014, LNCS 8824, pp. 186–194, 2014.
© Springer International Publishing Switzerland 2014

Table 1. Microdata

	Age	Zip	Sex	Disease
Lily	19	12k	F	Bronchitis
Jane	21	13k	F	Pneumonia
Alex	19	14k	F	Emphysema
Lucy	21	12k	F	Dyspepsia
Sarah	21	20k	M	Flu
Bob	25	18k	M	Gastritis
Mary	25	24k	F	Pneumonia
Andy	34	20k	M	Bronchitis
Bill	37	16k	F	Flu
Linda	34	24k	F	Pneumonia

Table 2. 4-Anonymity

GID	Age	Zip	Sex	Disease
1	[19-25]	[12k-20k]	F/M	Bronchitis
1	[19-25]	[12k-20k]	F/M	Pneumonia
1	[19-25]	[12k-20k]	F/M	Emphysema
1	[19-25]	[12k-20k]	F/M	Dyspepsia
1	[19-25]	[12k-20k]	F/M	Flu
1	[19-25]	[12k-20k]	F/M	Gastritis
2	[25-37]	[16k-24k]	F/M	Pneumonia
2	[25-37]	[16k-24k]	F/M	Bronchitis
2	[25-37]	[16k-24k]	F/M	Flu
2	[25-37]	[16k-24k]	F/M	Pneumonia

Table 3. Linking-based 4-Anonymity

GID	Age	Zip	Sex	Disease
1	[19-25]	[12k-20k]	F/M	Emphysema
1	[19-25]	[12k-20k]	F/M	Dyspepsia
2	[19-21]	[12k-14k]	F	Flu
2	[19-21]	[12k-14k]	F	Gastritis
3	[19-25]	[12k-20k]	F/M	Bronchitis
3	[19-25]	[12k-20k]	F/M	Pneumonia
4	[25-37]	[16k-24k]	F/M	Flu
4	[25-37]	[16k-24k]	F/M	Pneumonia
5	[25-37]	[16k-24k]	F/M	Pneumonia
5	[25-37]	[16k-24k]	F/M	Bronchitis

Table 4. 2-anonymity

GID	Age	Zip	Sex	Disease
1	[19-21]	[12k-13k]	F	Bronchitis
1	[19-21]	[12k-13k]	F	Pneumonia
2	[19-21]	[12k-14k]	F	Emphysema
2	[19-21]	[12k-14k]	F	Dyspepsia
3	[21-25]	[18k-20k]	M	Flu
3	[21-25]	[18k-20k]	M	Gastritis
4	[25-34]	[20k-24k]	F/M	Pneumonia
4	[25-34]	[20k-24k]	F/M	Bronchitis
5	[34-37]	[16k-24k]	F	Flu
5	[34-37]	[16k-24k]	F	Pneumonia

Table 5. Candidate Set

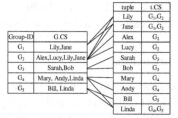

Group-ID	G.CS
G_1	Lily,Jane
G_2	Alex,Lucy,Lily,Jane
G_3	Sarah,Bob
G_4	Mary, Andy,Linda
G_5	Bill, Linda

tuple	t.CS
Lily	G_1,G_2
Jane	G_1,G_2
Alex	G_2
Lucy	G_2
Sarah	G_3
Bob	G_3
Mary	G_4
Andy	G_4
Bill	G_5
Linda	G_4,G_5

has the background knowledge about Lily, that is: Age=19, Zipcode=12k and Sex=F, then by joining the background knowledge to Table 1, he can accurately infer Lily's disease, that is bronchitis.

To effectively limit privacy disclosure, we need to measure the disclosure risk of an anonymized table. For this purpose, Samarati and Sweeney [2] proposed K-anonymity ($K \geq 2$), which requires that each record in a table is indistinguishable from at least $K-1$ other records with respect to certain quasi-identifiers. In general, the larger K is, the better the privacy is protected.

To achieve K-anonymity model, numerous approaches have been proposed. Many of them adopt generalization as their anonymization solutions [1–6]. Generalization is applied on the quasi-identifiers and replaces QI-values with the less-specific but semantically consistent values. As a result, more records will have the same set of QI-values, thus are indistinguishable from each other. Enough degree of generalization will hide a record in a crowd with at least K records having the same QI-values, thus K-anonymity is satisfied. As an example, Table 2 is 4-anonymized by generalizing QI-values in Table 1, e.g. Age 19, Zipcode 12k and Sex F of tuple Lily has been replaced with intervals [19-25], [12k-20k] and [F/M], respectively. As a result, even if an adversary has the exact QI-values of Lily, he can not infer exactly which tuple in the first QI-group is Lily. Clearly, above generalization procedure results in two equivalence classes as indicated by their group-IDs. Each equivalence class is referred to as a QI-group.

Contributions and Organization. In this paper, we propose an anonymity model: the linking-based anonymization and systematically investigate the property of the model. We provide a heuristic local recoding approach to achieve the model. We conduct extensive experiments on real data sets to show the performance and utility improvement of our model.

The rest of the paper is organized as follows. In Section 2, we give the Definitions of key concepts of K-anonymity. In Section 3, theory underlying linking-based anonymization is introduced. In Section 4, we present the details of our amonymization algorithm. We review the previously related research in Section 5. Limited by space, we have to omit all the experiments. Finally, the paper is concluded in Section 7.

2   Fundamental Definitions

In this section, we will first give the basic notations that will be used in the following texts. Then give the formal Definition of linking-based anonymity model. At last, the complexity of linking-based anonymization is analyzed.

2.1   Basic Notations

Let T be a microdata table that contains the private information of a set of individuals. T has n QI-attributes $A_1, ..., A_n$, and a sensitive attribute (SA). SA and every QI-attribute A_i $(1 \leq i \leq d)$ can be either numerical or categorical. All attributes have finite and positive domains. For each tuple $t \in T$, $t.A_i$ $(1 \leq i \leq d)$ denotes its value on A_i, and $t.SA$ represents its SA value.

A *quasi-identifier* $QI = \{A_1, A_2, \cdots, A_d\} \subseteq \{A_1, A_2, \cdots, A_n\}$ is a minimal set of attributes, which can be joined with external information in order to reveal the personal identity of individual records. A partition P consists of several subsets $G_i (1 \leq i \leq m)$ of T, such that each tuple in T belongs to exactly one subset and $T = \bigcup_i^m G_i$. We refer to each subset G_i as a QI-group. As an example, The group-IDs of Table 2 induce a partition on all records of Table 1, which is {{Lily, Alex, Jane, Bob, Lucy, Sarah},{Mary, Andy, Bill, Linda}}.

In this paper, generalization (see [1–3]) will be used as the major techniques to achieve anonymization. Formally, given a parameter K and the quasi-identifier, a table T satisfies the K-anonymity requirement if and only if each unique tuple in the projection of T on quasi-identifier occurs at least K times.

2.2   Problem Definition

In our anonymization framework, K-anonymity of T^* is achieved by QI-groups with size of k. In general, we use a divisor of K as k such that each tuple in T^* satisfies $\frac{K}{k}$ QI-groups through linking operation simultaneously. The number of QI-groups satisfying a tuple is called the *order* of our anonymization approach. It is better but not necessary that k is a divisor of K. Assume that a publisher plans to anonymize a table to be 1000-anonymity, which can be achieved by either 200-anonymity with *order* 5 or 334-anonymity with *order* 3.

Definition 1 (Linking-based K-anonymity). *A generalized table T^* is linking-based K-anonymity with order $\frac{K}{k}$ if each QI-group in the anonymized table T^* has a cardinality between k and $2k - 1$, and each tuple in the projection of T on quasi-identifier occurs at least K times.*

Our model is a generalized version of the basic K-anonymity model since the size of each QI-group is not K but a smaller value between k and $2k - 1$. When $order = 1$, our model degrades into the basic K-anonymity mode. Such an approach, to which we refer as homogeneous generalization. When $order = K$, our model degrades into the Non-homogeneous generalization technique presented in paper [7,8], which requires each QI-group contains only a single tuple, and each tuple in the projection of T^* has a cardinality no less than K. When $1 < order < K$, the size of each QI-group of our model is significantly reduced, which consequently reduces the information loss of anonymized data. In this paper, our approach is termed as *Heterogenous Generalization*.

Now, we are ready to give the formal definition about the problem that will be addressed in this paper. (We adopt the normalized certainty penalty [4] to measure the information loss).

Definition 2 (Problem Definition). *Given a table T and an integer K, anonymize it to be T^* such that T^* is linking-based K-anonymity and information loss is minimized.*

2.3 Complexity

The studies [5,9] show that the problem of optimal K-anonymity is NP-hard even a simple quality metric is employed. Paper [4] proved that under the metric of NCP, the K-anonymity is NP-hard for $K \geq 2$. We have the following results on the complexity for linking-based model proposed in this paper (due to space limitation, all proofs are omitted).

Theorem 1. *(Complexity) The problem of optimal linking-based anonymization is NP-hard.*

3   Linking-Based K-Anonymization

In this section, we will introduce key concepts that underly the linking-based anonymization.

3.1   Multi-attribute Domain

In a relational database, each attribute of a relation is associated with a domain, for which we can construct a more generalized domain in multiple possible ways. In Table 2, the age domain was generalized into ranges: [19-25] and [25-37]. We use $D_i \leq D_j$ to denote the fact that domain D_j is either identical to or one of its generalization of D_i. When $D_i \leq D_j$ and $D_i \neq D_j$, we denote it by $D_i < D_j$. For quasi-identifer consisting of multiple attributes $(A_1, A_2, \cdots, A_d)$, we can define corresponding d-dimension vector $V_A = \langle D_{A_1}, D_{A_2}, \cdots, D_{A_d} \rangle$ with each D_{A_i} being the domain of A_i. Such kind of d-dimension vector for the set of d attributes is referred to as *multi-attribute domain*. The multi-attribute domain of the G_1 in Table 2 is $\langle$[19-25], [12k-20k], $F/M\rangle$. Given two d-dimension attribute domains $V_A = \langle D_{A_1}, D_{A_2}, \cdots, D_{A_d} \rangle$ and $V_B = \langle D_{B_1}, D_{B_2}, \cdots, D_{B_d} \rangle$, V_B is a *multi-attribute domain generalization* of V_A (this relationship is also denoted by $\leq$) if for each j, $D_{A_j} \leq D_{B_j}$.

A tuple t is *covered* by a multi-attribute domain $V_A = \langle D_{A_1}, D_{A_2}, \cdots, D_{A_d} \rangle$, if for each i ($1 \leq i \leq d$), $t.A_i \in D_{A_i}(1 \leq i \leq d)$, that is $t.A_i$ lies in the ranges of corresponding attribute's domain. Continue our example, Jane's tuple $\langle 21, 13k, F \rangle$ is covered by G_1's domain since $19 \leq 21 \leq 25, 12k \leq 13k \leq 20k$, $F \in \{F, M\}$, while Linda's tuple $\langle 34, 24k, F \rangle$ is not covered by the domain since $34 \notin [19, 25]$.

3.2 Candidate Set

In this subsection we introduce a key concept in linking-based anonymization: candidate set.

Definition 3 (Tuple Candidate Set). *Given a table T and its anonymized table T^*, the candidate set $t.CS$ of tuple t ($t \in T$) is the set of QI-groups G_i ($G_i \in T^*$) whose multi-attribute domain covers t.*

The candidate set of tuple plays a key role in following anonymization algorithm. The candidate set of tuple represents the extent that anonymity has been achieved. The key issue about it is its computation. A straightforward way is to examine each QI-group for each tuple, which however costs $O(|T| \cdot |GS|)$ time(between $O(\frac{|T|^2}{2k-1})$ and $O(\frac{|T|^2}{k})$), where $|GS|$ is the number of QI-groups in the generalized table T^*. This is unacceptable when the microdata contains a large number of tuples. In following sections we will develop efficient algorithms to attack computation complexity.

Definition 4 (Group Candidate Set). *Given a table T and its anonymized table T^*, the group candidate set $G_i.CS$ of QI-group G_i ($G_i \in T^*$) is the set of tuples which are covered by the multi-attribute domain of G_i.*

Proposition 1. *Let G_1, G_2 be two QI-groups in the generalized table T^* such that $G_1 \leq G_2$, i.e., G_2 is the domain generalization of G_1, then $G_1.CS \subseteq G_2.CS$.*

3.3 Mapping between Candidate Set of Groups and That of Records

It is clear that candidate set of a tuple can be obtained from the candidate set of the group containing the tuple by a mapping. The mapping is established from the candidate set of the group to the candidate set of the tuple, as follows: $\forall t \in G.CS$, add G into $t.CS$.

Example 1. Table 5 illustrates the mapping between candidate set of the group and that of records for Table 4. Specifically, Lily with tuple $\langle 21, 12k, F \rangle$ appears in group G_1 and G_2, therefore Lily's candidate set is $\{G_1, G_2\}$. Simultaneously, we have $Jane.CS = \{G_1, G_2\}$. Hence, for Lily and Jane, 4-anonymity is achieved. However, $Alex.CS$ only contains G_3, which implies that for Alex 2-anonymity is achieved. At last the candidate sets of each tuple are obtained (see Table 5).

4   Generalization Algorithm

In this section, we will present the details of our linking-based anonymization approach. The key of our algorithm is finding candidate set of all tuples efficiently and correctly. In the nutshell, the algorithm consists of two major steps:

Step 1. anonymize the input table T into a k-anonymous table T^*, and meanwhile obtain each tuple's candidate set;

Step 2. regroup QI-groups generated by the previous step into larger K-anonymity.

4.1   Partitioning Algorithm

This section elaborates the details of the procedure to obtain the candidate sets for all tuples. In our approach, we use the partitioning algorithm in [4] to produce a partition of T.

The algorithm framework is shown in Figure 1. We first partition the microdata table T into two disjoint subsets T_1 and T_2 by certain off-the-shelf partitioning algorithms, such as the top-down partition algorithm used in [4]. We run the partitioning algorithm recursively until the size of the partition is $\leq 2k - 1$. At each iteration a list of groups is updated. The cardinality of the two subsets should $\geq k$, otherwise adjustment is needed (Step 3). Without loss of generality, assume that $T_1 < k$, we need to borrow $k - |T_1|$ tuples from T_2 to make sure that T_1 has a cardinality $\geq k$.

Next, we need to examine whether each tuple in T_1 is included in the candidate set of T_2 (Step 4). If so, we insert the tuple into $T_2.CS$. Similarly, add the tuples that belong to candidate set of T_1) into $T_1.CS$ (Step 5). Next, we need to examine whether each tuple in the candidate set of the set T is included in the candidate sets of T_1 and T_2. If so, add the tuple into the candidate sets separately (Step 6).

Finally, the data sets T_1 and T_2 will be divided recursively (Step 7 and 8). We have that the partitioning algorithm will terminate when the size of all groups is between k and $2k - 1$. With this algorithm, we can get a generalized table satisfying k-anonymity as well as the candidate sets of each QI-group from which we can easily get the candidate set of each tuple.

4.2   Regrouping

In general, we can only ensure the anonymized table produced by above partitioning algorithm is k-anonymity. Hence, we need to further use regrouping to accomplish large K-anonymity with QI-groups with small size(from k to $2k - 1$). Note that a complete binary tree is generated by the partitioning algorithm. Each leaf node in the tree corresponds to a QI-group. Hence, the information loss caused by generalizing two QI-groups can be measured by the *Hierarchical Distance* between these two QI-groups. Mathematically, let H be the height of the tree, the distance between two QI-groups G_1 and G_2 is defined as $\frac{level(G_1, G_2)}{H}$,

Procedure: Partition-Alg(T, k)
Input: A table T, Privacy Level k
Output: Group list L;
Method:
1. If $|T| \leq 2k - 1$, then add T into L, Return;
2. Partition T into two exclusive subsets T_1 and T_2, $T_1.CS = T_2.CS = \emptyset$;
3. Adjust the groups so that each group has at least k tuples;
4. For each tuple t in T_1
    If the multi-attribute domain of T_2 covers t, then $T_2.CS = \{t\} \cup T_2.CS$;
5. For each tuple t in T_2
    if the multi-attribute domain of T_1 covers t, then $T_1.CS = \{t\} \cup T_1.CS$;
6. For each tuple t in $T.CS$
    If the multi-attribute domain of T_1 covers t, then $T_1.CS = \{t\} \cup T_1.CS$;
    If the multi-attribute domain of T_2 covers t, then $T_2.CS = \{t\} \cup T_2.CS$;
7. Recursively Partition-Alg(T_1,k);
8. Recursively Partition-Alg(T_2,k);

Fig. 1. The framework of partitioning algorithm

where $level(G_1, G_2)$ is the height of the lowest common ancestor node of G_1 and G_2. Let $L = \{G_1, G_2, \cdots, G_{|GS|}\}$ be the set of all QI-groups produced by previous partitioning algorithm.

In general, the first step of anonymization can not ensure that the accumulated size of tuple's candidate QI-groups reaches to K. Hence, we may further need to find more QI-groups to be generalized so that after generalization these QI-groups will be tuple t's candidate QI-groups. This step is critical for the information loss of the resulting anonymized table, deserving careful design. Hierarchical distance is a good heuristic guiding us to find the candidate QI-groups for a tuple t: *for tuple $t \in G_i$, repeatedly select G_j that has minimal hierarchical distance to G_i and add G_j to $t.CS$ until the accumulated size of $t.CS$ reaches to K.* When G_j is added to $t.CS$, we also add t to $G_j.CS$ so that we just need to perform one generalization on each G_i whose candidate set has been updated.

We show that linking-based anonymization provides equal or better utility than basic K-anonymity. In the regrouping phase, if QI-groups are rolled back to the non-leaf node with cardinality no less than K in the partitioning tree, the linking-based K-anonymity will degenerates to the basic K-anonymity model. If QI-groups benefit from the tuple candidate set, better utility can be achieved.

Theorem 2. *Linking-based K-anonymization produces a K-anonymized table T^* that is of equal or better utility than that produced by a basic generalization under the same partition.*

5   Related Work

In this section, previous related work will be surveyed. Efficient greedy solutions following certain heuristics have been proposed [4, 8, 10, 11] to obtain a near optimal solution. Generally, these heuristics are general enough to be used in many anonymization models. Incognito [12] provides a practical framework for implementing full-domain generalization, borrowing ideas from frequent item set mining, while Mondrian [5] takes a partitioning approach reminiscent of KD-trees. To achieve K-anonymity, [6] presents a framework mapping the multi-dimensional quasi-identifiers to 1-Dimensional(1-D) space. For 1-D quasi-identifiers, an algorithm of $O(K \cdot N)$ time complexity for optimal solution is also developed. It is discovered that K-anonymizing a data set is strikingly similar to building a spatial index over the data set, so that classical spatial indexing techniques can be used for anonymization [13].

The idea of non-homogeneous generalization was first introduced in [7], which studies techniques with a guarantee that an adversary cannot associate a generalized tuple to less than K individuals, but suffering additional types of attack. Authors of paper [8] proposed a randomization method that prevents such type of attack and showed that k-anonymity is not compromised by it, but its partitioning algorithm is only a special of the top-down algorithm presented in [4]. The anonymity model of the paper [7,8] is different to us. In their model, the size of QI-groups is fixed as 1, while in our model it is varying from 1 to K. Benefitting from the concept of the candidate set, the utility of our approach can outperform the previous works.

6 Conclusion

In this paper, we propose linking-based anonymization as our anonymization model, which uses QI-groups with small size to achieve K-anonymity requirement. We systematically investigate the property of this model and implement the model by a heuristic local recoding method. Through extensive experiments on real data sets, we show that our method has an excellent performance and significantly improve the utility of the anonymized data compared to the existing state-of-the-art technique presented in [8].

Acknowledgement. This work was supported in part by the National Natural Science Foundation of China (NO.61202007), the Postdoctoral Science Foundation (NO.2013M540323), the Education Department of Zhejiang Province (NO.Y201224678), the Natural Science Foundation of NingBo (NO.2013A610110).

References

1. Sweeney, L.: k-anonymity: A model for protecting privacy. Int. J. Uncertain. Fuzziness Knowl.-Based Syst. 10(5), 557–570 (2002)
2. Samarati, P., Sweeney, L.: Generalizing data to provide anonymity when disclosing information (abstract). In: PODS 1998, New York, p. 188 (1998)
3. Samarati, P.: Protecting respondents' identities in microdata release. IEEE Trans. on Knowl. and Data Eng. 13(6), 1010–1027 (2001)
4. Xu, J., Wang, W., Pei, J., Wang, X., Shi, B., Fu, A.W.-C.: Utility-based anonymization using local recoding. In: KDD 2006, pp. 785–790. ACM (2006)

5. LeFevre, K., DeWitt, D.J., Ramakrishnan, R.: Mondrian multidimensional k-anonymity. In: ICDE 2006, Washington, DC, USA, p. 25 (2006)
6. Ghinita, G., Karras, P., Kalnis, P., Mamoulis, N.: Fast data anonymization with low information loss. In: VLDB 2007, pp. 758–769. VLDB Endowment (2007)
7. Gionis, A., Mazza, A., Tassa, T.: k-anonymization revisited. In: ICDE 2008, pp. 744–753. IEEE Computer Society, Washington, DC (2008)
8. Wong, W.K., Mamoulis, N., Cheung, D.W.L.: Non-homogeneous generalization in privacy preserving data publishing. In: SIGMOD 2010, pp. 747–758. ACM, New York (2010)
9. Bayardo, R.J., Agrawal, R.: Data privacy through optimal k-anonymization. In: ICDE 2005, pp. 217–228. IEEE Computer Society, Washington, DC (2005)
10. Fung, B.C.M., Wang, K., Yu, P.S.: Top-down specialization for information and privacy preservation. In: ICDE 2005, pp. 205–216 (2005)
11. LeFevre, K., DeWitt, D.J., Ramakrishnan, R.: Workload-aware anonymization. In: KDD 2006, pp. 277–286. ACM, New York (2006)
12. LeFevre, K., DeWitt, D.J., Ramakrishnan, R.: Incognito: efficient full-domain k-anonymity. In: SIGMOD 2005, pp. 49–60. ACM, New York (2005)
13. Iwuchukwu, T., Naughton, J.F.: K-anonymization as spatial indexing: toward scalable and incremental anonymization. In: VLDB 2007, pp. 746–757 (2007)

From Conceptual Models to Safety Assurance

Yaping Luo, Mark van den Brand, Luc Engelen, and Martijn Klabbers

Eindhoven University of Technology
P.O. Box 513, 5600 MB, Eindhoven, The Netherlands
{y.luo2,m.g.j.v.d.brand,l.j.p.engelen,m.d.klabbers}@tue.nl

Abstract. Safety assurance or certification is one of the most costly and time-consuming tasks in automotive, railway, avionics, and other safety-critical domains. Different transport sectors have developed their own specific sets of safety standards, which creates a big challenge to reuse pre-certified components and share expertise between different transport sectors. In this paper, we propose to use conceptual models in the form of metamodels to support certification data reuse and facilitate safety compliance. A metamodel transformation approach is outlined to derive domain or project specific metamodels using a generic metamodel as basis. Furthermore, we present a metamodel refinement language, which is a domain-specific language that facilitates simple refinement of metamodels. Finally, we use two case studies from the automotive domain to demonstrate our approach and its ability to reuse metamodels across companies.

Keywords: Conceptual Model, Metamodel, Safety Assurance, Safety-Critical Systems, Metamodel transformation.

1 Introduction

In safety-critical domains such as automotive, railway, and avionics, even a small failure of a system might cause injury or death to people. A number of international safety standards are introduced as guidelines for system suppliers to keep the risk of systems at an acceptable level. Compliance with safety standards is one of the key tasks of safety assurance, which is usually costly and time-consuming due to the amount of manual work involved. Moreover, when a system evolves, some of the existing safety-assurance data needs to be regathered or re-validated because of changes to the system. Most of those data is hard to reuse, which makes safety assurance even more costly.

Model-driven engineering has been introduced to increase the level of abstraction and reduce software development cost [5]. Recently, it is also used to reduce the high costs for safety assurance. Modeling safety standards facilitates compliance demonstration and safety assessment [11] [15]. Analyzing current safety standards and safety argumentation provides an efficient way of how to reuse current certification data [12]. Additionally, model-driven technology supports system suppliers to manage the system development process [7] as well as the evidence for safety assurance generated from that process [16].

E. Yu et al. (Eds.): ER 2014, LNCS 8824, pp. 195–208, 2014.

A metamodel used in safety-critical domains is a conceptual model with concept-mediated semantics [17]. The elements of aforementioned metamodels represent safety related concepts, which represent things ("the real world") in safety-critical domains. Different conceptual models are proposed or created based on different usages. In recent years, some companies have started investigating how to build their own conceptual models based on their domain knowledge, for example an IEC 61508 [15], and an ISO 26262 conceptual model [11]. Those conceptual models are called domain-specific conceptual models. Each company uses different concepts and relations to describe safety certification data. Therefore, the certification data or expertise reuse between different companies or domains tends to be a big challenge.

OPENCOSS (see Section 2.2), a European project aimed at cross-domain reuse of safety-assurance data, proposes two kinds of conceptual models: a compositional conceptual model and a generic conceptual model. The idea of a compositional conceptual model is to cover all the concepts from three safety-critical domains (automotive, railway, and avionics). However, even for the same concept, it has different interpretations and usages for different domains or companies. This makes the compositional conceptual model too big and complex to be useful. Therefore, a generic conceptual model becomes promising, because it contains the common concepts between those domains. A concrete example of this is a Generic Meta-Model (GMM) of safety standards, the benefits of which are: patterns of certification assessment can be shared, and cost-effective re-certification between different standards is supported [19] [2]. Consequently, when introducing this GMM to the companies in safety-critical domains, their current way of working must be changed to conform to the GMM, and extra cost will be required. In practice, those companies want to get the benefits of the GMM while minimizing the required changes to do so. Additionally, because the concepts in the GMM are limited and generic, some ambiguities will rise when interpreting and using those concepts.

In this paper, we propose a combined approach to reduce the loss of capacity and keep or even increase the benefits. The approach uses the GMM as starting point, and create a specific conceptual model in the form of Specific MetaModel (SMM) for specific usage. Model transformation technology can be used to bridge the gap between the conceptual models at different abstraction levels [14]. We present a metamodel transformation approach to facilitate the process of creating metamodels for a specific safety standard, domain or company. Also, our approach supports reuse by an automatic comparison between concepts in different domains using the traceable changes that are documented in the specific metamodel transformations. A Metamodel Refinement Language (MMRL) is defined to support system suppliers to build their own metamodels based on the GMM. The language allows system suppliers to introduce domain or project concepts to the GMM, and then to generate a specific model editor based on the resulting SMM. Moreover, the traceability information can be found in MMRL specifications and analyzed for conceptual mappings between different metamodels (derived from the same metamodel). Therefore, it facilitates the certification data reuse between different companies or domains.

The remaining paper is organized as follows: Section 2 introduces the relevant background information. Section 3 outlines our overall metamodel transformation approach. Section 4 presents a domain specific language for refining metamodels. Section 5 discusses the results of two case studies from the automotive domain. Section 6 introduces the related work of our approach. Finally, Section 7 summarizes our conclusions and future work.

2 Background Information

In this section, we describe the relevant background information. First, we introduce the applied metamodeling architecture, and then our contribution to the OPENCOSS project.

2.1 Metamodeling Architecture

Currently, there are two well-known architectures for multilevel metamodeling: the metamodeling architecture of the OMG and the Eclipse Modeling Framework (EMF). Both of these architectures introduce four levels (Figure 1) and use linguistic classification [4] to divide elements over these levels. Linguistic classification divides elements into two groups: groups of instances and groups of types. Each element of the first group is an instance of an element of the second group. The types of all of the instances on a given level reside on the nearest higher level and describe the properties of the instances.

Atkinson and Kühne identify a second, orthogonal dimension of metamodeling [4]. They state that the dimension of linguistic classification is concerned with language definition and makes use of linguistic instantiation. The other dimension is concerned with domain definition and uses ontological instantiation. Ontological instantiation does not cross the linguistic metalevels, but relates elements on the same level instead. In other words, ontological instantiation makes it possible to specify that an element on a given level is an instance of an element at the same level.

The approach described in this paper strictly focusses on linguistic instantiation. Although we appreciate the usefulness of the other dimension of metamodeling, our aim is to investigate the possibilities offered by the more traditional metamodeling approach first. An advantage of doing so is the fact that popular implementations of frameworks for metamodeling support linguistic instantiation.

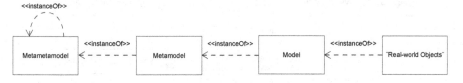

Fig. 1. Traditional multilevel metamodeling architectures introduce four levels: the metameta level, the meta level, the model level, and the object level

2.2 OPENCOSS Project

The OPENCOSS project [6] is an FP7 large-scale integrated project with a consortium of 17 European partners. The ultimate goal of the project is to reduce the high and non-measured costs for (re)certification and to increase product safety through the introduction of more systematic certification practices.

As one of the key challenges of the OPENCOSS project is to define a common conceptual framework for specifying certification assets [2], a generic metamodel for safety standards have been developed as a part of this framework [19]. It includes most of the common concepts and relations between different standards and domains for safety certification. Note that, the GMM used in this paper is mainly based on the published version with some changes according to our GMM implementation [2]. The work in this paper represents our own perspective inside OPENCOSS project.

3 Metamodel Transformation

As mentioned before, the current generic metamodel proposal oversimplifies the modeling needs of safety engineers and assessors. This can lead to overgeneralization, additional manual work, and less support for automatic consistency checks. To address this, extended metamodels are refined from the GMM; if new domain concepts are required for the system supplier's purpose, they will be added into the GMM. Extending the GMM into domain-specific metamodels provides the advantage of creating a language that is closer to the world of experience of the safety engineer in a certain domain and will ease the effort to produce the reference assurance. Besides, domain-specific metamodels can reduce the ambiguities in the GMM in order to prevent safety engineers from making interpretation mistakes while creating models. Additionally, domain-specific metamodels only need to be defined once by the best expert(s) available in a certain domain.

An overview of our approach is shown in Figure 2. We defined a metamodel refinement language to introduce domain concepts into the GMM. A metamodel transformation is executed, which takes the GMM along with those domain concepts described in MMRL as inputs, and produces a SMM as output. Finally, a graphical editor, based on the SMM, can be automatically generated, which

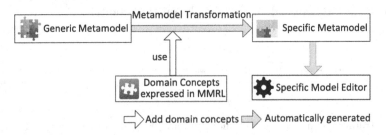

Fig. 2. Overview of our approach

Fig. 3. Generic use of our approach

facilitates safety engineers in building their models using concepts from their own domain.

Our approach can be divided into multiple specialization steps. Figure 3 shows a two-steps scenario. In the first step, the GMM could be updated by adding domain concepts. For example, by adding concepts from the ISO 26262 standard, an ISO 26262 metamodel can be obtained. Then, in the second step, the company-specific or project-specific metamodels can be generated from the updated GMM. For instance, for a company X, a project metamodel for fuel cars and a project metamodel for electrical cars are derived from the same ISO 26262 metamodel. Then by analyzing the corresponding MMRL specifications, a conceptual mapping between those two metamodels can be found through the ISO 26262 metamodel. Finally, reuse of safety-assurance data between these two projects can be supported based on the conceptual mapping. Therefore, the two key benefits of our approach are that the changes made to the GMM are documented and defined unambiguously in the form of refinement specifications, thus making traceability amenable for analysis, and the SMMs or the intermediate domain-specific metamodels can be reused in other domains or by other companies.

4   Metamodel Refinement Language

We defined and implemented a MetaModel Refinement Language (MMRL) that can be used to refine metamodels. It is a simple domain-specific language, which offers operations to rename elements of a metamodel, replace annotations of metamodel elements, make certain metaclasses of a metamodel abstract, and add elements to a metamodel. By applying these operations to an existing metamodel, a new, refined version of this metamodel is created. Each refinement specification defined using our MMRL clearly specifies the relation between the input and the output metamodel. The syntax of the language is defined with EMFText[1], and the language has been implemented using the Epsilon Transformation Language (ETL) [8].

The metamodel refinement language allows the system supplier to describe their domain concepts in terms of the existing GMM concepts using the provided operators.

The operations can be classified as follows:

---

[1] http://www.emftext.org/

- The structural feature operations *AddPackage*, *AddClass*, *AddAttribute*, *AddData-Type* and *AddReference* are defined for adding structural features of metamodels.
- The Annotation operations *ReplaceAnnotation* and *AddAnnotation* are defined to add annotations of metamodels, which can support generating graphical editors from metamodels.
- The enumeration operations: *AddEnum* and *AddEnumLiteral* are used to create a new enumeration class or a new literal for existing enumeration class.
- The modification operations: *Abstract* and *RenameElement* enable system suppliers to rename some element (package, class, attribute and reference etc) or make some class abstract. If a class become abstract, it means that class will not be visible in a graphical editor.

In our MMRL, there is no operation for deleting elements from the input metamodel. Note that, in our approach, the input is the GMM, but it is not GMM specific. All the concepts in the GMM have been selected and validated by domain experts. Therefore, we have an assumption that there are no redundant elements in the GMM. In the following two sections, we discuss structural feature operations and annotation operations, which are the two core parts in the definition of our MMRL. Structural feature operations are used to manipulate the main structure of refined metamodels, and annotation operations facilitate tool generation.

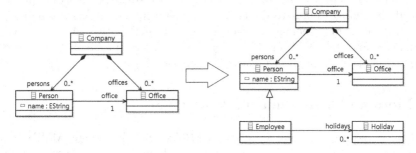

Fig. 4. The metamodel on the right is transformed into the metamodel on the left by applying the refinement specification in Listing 1.1

Figure 4 and Listing 1.1 present a small example to illustrate the process of refining metamodels. On the left of Figure 4, a small metamodel is shown, which consists of three classes (*Company*, *Person*, and *Office*) and three references (*persons*, *offices*, and *office*). After applying the refinement specification given in Listing 1.1, this metamodel is transformed into the metamodel shown on the right of Figure 4.

4.1 Structural Feature Operations

The structural feature operations in MMRL are designed in accordance with the Ecore metamodel. Figure 5 shows an extract of our MMRL on the structural feature operations, highlighting the key relationships between four operations:

Listing 1.1. This refinement specification performs five operations: it defines that the class named *Person* in package *company* should be abstract (line 2), it renames the class named *Office* in the same package to *Address* (line 3), it adds a class named *Employee* that inherits from *Person* (line 4) and a class named *Holiday* to this package (line 5), and it adds a reference named *holidays* with type *Holiday*, lower bound 0, and upper bound -1 to the class *Employee* (line 6-8).

```
1  operations
2    abstract company.Person
3    rename company.Office to Address
4    add class Employee {superTypes {company.Person}} to company
5    add class Holiday {} to company
6    add reference holidays {
7      lowerBound 0 upperBound -1 type company.Holiday
8    } to company.Employee
```

AddPackage, *AddClass*, *AddAttribute*, and *AddReference*. An *AddPackage* operation has a *PackageDefinition*. Each *PackageDefinition* has a number of *ClassifierDefinitions*, which are specialized into *ClassDefinition*. As each *AddClass* operation has a *ClassDefinition*, it specifies that a number of new classes could be added to a new package or an existing one. Similarly, a *ClassDefinition* has a number of *StructuralFeatureDefinition*. Then *StructuralFeatureDefinition* is specialized into *ReferenceDefinition* and *AttributeDefinition*, which are associated with *AddReference* and *AddAttribute* operation respectively. Therefore, it shows that a number of references or attributes can be added to a new class or an existing one.

After adding concrete syntax to our MMRL, system supplier can call those operations though some keywords. For example, in List 1.1, by using a keyword "add class", the *AddClass* operation has been performed. Eventually, two new classes (class *Employee* and class *Holiday*) have been added to the original model.

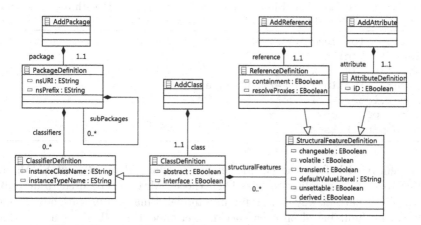

Fig. 5. Structural feature definition in our MMRL metamodel

4.2   Annotation Operations

In our MMRL, annotation operations are designed for annotating metamodels during metamodel transformation. Figure 6 shows a depiction of the annotation definition in our MMRL. The *ModelElementDefinition* element is the container of *AnnotationDefinition*, while *AnnotationDefinition* is a kind of *ModelElement-Definition*. Each *AnnotationDefinition* has a number of *KeyValuePairs*, where key and value attributes are defined. Two operators use the annotation definition: *ReplaceAnnotation* and *AddAnnotation*. Each of these two operators is associated with a concrete *AnnotationDefinition* and is used for modifying current annotations or adding a new one.

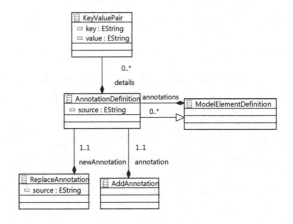

Fig. 6. Annotation definition in our MMRL metamodel

Listing 1.2. This refinement specification adds an annotation to the class *Person* in the package *company* that can be processed by EuGENia. Among other things, it specifies that this class should be represented as a node (line 1) with a certain label (line 2), size (line 3) and figure (line 4) in the graphical editor.

```
1  add annotation "gmf.node" {
2    "label" = "name",
3    "size" = "70,50",
4    "figure" = "figures.PersonFigure",
5    "label.icon" = "false",
6    "label.placement" = "external"
7  } to company.Person
```

As mentioned before, the GMM can be transformed to different SMMs according to system supplier's needs. Then those SMMs can be used to describe the supplier's current way of working in a model. Finally, a user friendly framework can be built based on each specific metamodel. EuGENia is a tool that can generate graphical editors from annotated metamodels [9]. It simplifies the complex graphical editor generating process of GMF and provides a number of annotations for users to annotate their metamodels. Because our metamodel refinement language can be used to add annotations to metamodels or replace existing annotations, it can also be used to create metamodels that can be processed by EuGENia directly. The refinement specification in Listing 1.2 provides an example of a specification that adds an annotation for EuGENia.

4.3   Sequence of Transformations

By repeatedly applying refinement specifications to metamodels, a family of metamodels can be created (Figure 7). By family of metamodels, we refer to a closely related set of metamodels, where each metamodel in the set (except the root metamodel) can be defined in terms of another metamodel from the same set. Each of the metamodels (except the root metamodel) is defined in terms of an existing metamodel and a set of changes. For example, an IEC 61508 metamodel can be refined into an ISO 26262 metamodel and an EN 50128 metamodel with some changes. Therefore, the elements in each of the metamodels can be traced back to a refinement specification (or the corresponding intermediate metamodel) or the metamodel that formed the starting point of the family. For instance, the element *ASIL* in a project-specific conceptual model A can be traced back to the *ASIL* in the company-specific conceptual model, the *ASIL* in the ISO 26262 metamodel, the *SIL* in IEC 61508 metamodel, or the *CriticalityLevel* in the generic conceptual model. As changes of metamodels are stored in metamodel refinement specifications, traceability information in the transformation sequence can be obtained and maintained by analyzing those specifications.

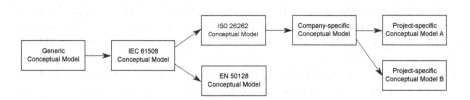

Fig. 7. By successively refining metamodels, a family of closely related metamodels is created. For clarity, the metamodel transformations and the domain concepts introduced by refinement specifications of Figure 2 are not shown in this figure.

Each metamodel in a family of metamodels could be used as a basis for a tool to edit models that conform to this metamodel. By taking the EuGENia annotations into account while creating a family of metamodels, a closely related set of graphical editors can be generated from this family. The concepts and relations in the models created with these editors can be related across models by tracing their relationships through the refinement specifications.

5   Results and Tool Support

We have implemented our approach using the Eclipse Modeling Framework with
the following plug-ins: EMFText is used to define the concrete syntax of MMRL,
ETL is used to build the model transformation between the GMM and SMM. Finally, a graphical editor can be automatically generated by GMF and EuGENia
based on a resulting SMM.

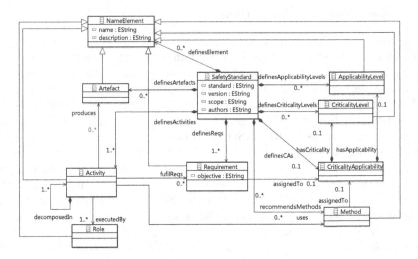

Fig. 8. The generic metamodel for safety standards

For our demonstration, we use two case studies from the automotive domain
related to ISO 26262[1]: company X and company Y. Figure 8 shows an extract of
the GMM. The definition of each element in the GMM is defined in [19]. Figure 9
shows the GMM refined by those two companies according to their needs. The
black, light grey, and dark grey elements result from the application of MMRL
operations. The black elements are only modified by company X. The light grey
elements are only modified by company Y. The dark grey elements are modified
by both companies. By comparing the GMM and the refined metamodel, we
could see that:

1. Two classes have been renamed by company X and company Y. *SafetyS-
   tandard* and *ArtefactType* have been renamed to *ISO26262Framework* and
   WorkProduct respectively.
2. A new class (*ExternalElement*) has been added by company X.
3. Two classes have been renamed only by company Y. *ApplicabilityLevel* and
   CriticalityLevel have been renamed to *Importance* and *ASIL* respectively.
4. Three new classes have been added by company Y: *SafetyGoal*, *Hazard*, and
   HazardEvent.

---

[1] Due to the confidential issue, we use company X and company Y to represent two
different automotive companies.

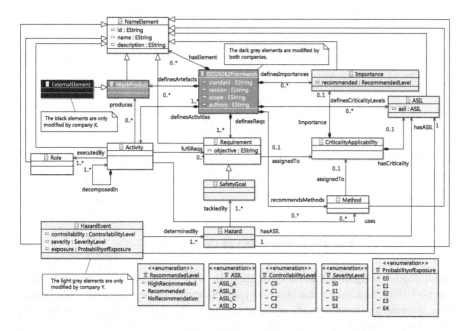

Fig. 9. Two company-specific metamodels derived from previous GMM

5. Seven new references have been added by company Y: one for *SafetyGoal*, three for *Hazard*, and three for *HazardEvent*.
6. Five new enumerations have been introduced by company Y: *Recommand-edLevel*, *ASIL*, *ProbabilityofExposure*, *ControllabilityLevel*, and *SeverityLevel*.
7. Five new attributes have been added by company Y: *recommended* for *Important*; *asil* for *ASIL*; and *controllability*, *severity* and *exposure* for *HazardEvent*.

Through the GMM and two refinement specifications, we could see that there are a number of common concepts between the conceptual models of company X and Y. Thus, a conceptual mapping between these two company-specific metamodels can be built. For example, the concept *ExternalElement* in the conceptual model of company X could be mapped to the concept *WorkProduct* in the conceptual model of company Y. The concept *Activity* in the conceptual model of company X is the same as the concept *Activity* in the conceptual model of company X. The conceptual mapping shows which concepts are related in those company-specific metamodels and indicates possible overlaps in safety assurance data. Therefore, this conceptual mapping can be used to support the certification data reuse between these two companies.

Moreover, in our refinement process, both company-specific metamodels have been annotated. A graphical framework based on each of those metamodels has been generated using EuGENia. Figure 10 shows the editor generated for company Y. Safety engineers of company Y can use the resulting editor to create their own models using ISO 26262 concepts, which helps them to show that their development process complies with the ISO 26262 standard. They can design their develop

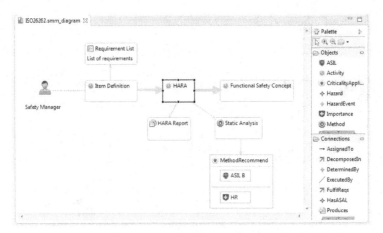

Fig. 10. A screen shot of company Y editor

process model using ISO 26262 as guideline. Besides, they could specify one or more person(s), such as a safety manager, to take charge of those activities. One benefit of our approach is that domain concepts or project-related concepts can be kept, and system suppliers do not need to change their current way of working to conform to the GMM. Besides, the traceability and its documentation from the GMM to the SMM is realized using our MMRL.

6   Related Work

Related research is found in modeling safety standards, metamodel refinement, and traceability management.

Modeling Safety Standards. Conceptual models of safety standards are widely used in different domains for different usages. As mentioned in Section 1, a conceptual model of IEC 61508 is proposed for characterizing the chain of evidence for safety certification in the petroleum industry [15]. A conceptual model of aeronautic standard DO 178B is provided in [21] to improve communication and collaboration among safety engineers in the avionic domain. Moreover, conceptual modeling in the context of ISO 26262 has been carried out in [1] [10].

Metamodel Refinement. Metamodel refinement is strongly related with metamodel evolution and metamodel adaptation. In [20], the use of transformation patterns in the form of QVT relations for metamodel refinement is introduced. By introducing new concepts, the target metamodel can be extended though model transformation. A model change language with a number of migration rules is presented in [13] for defining metamodel changes. It is a high-level visual language and is designed for describing metamodel evolution. Our approach presented in this paper is discussed in the context of safety-critical domains and focuses on metamodel refinement with metamodel transformation rather than metamodel evolution. The metamodel evolution is caused by external factors, whereas the metamodel refinement is a design process.

Traceability Management. In [18], a model-driven framework for traceability management, called iTrace, is developed, which enables the analysis of traceability information of the different models involved in the software development cycle. Also, in [3], traceability visualization in model transformations has been done to facilitate traceability analysis. In this paper, we focus on traceability management of metamodels rather than models, and we propose to use metamodel refinement specifications to support the traceability management and the analysis of traceability information.

7 Conclusions and Future Work

In this paper, we proposed a metamodel transformation approach to facilitate safety assurance. Based on previous research, we present a refinement process for a generic metamodel according to a system supplier's input. Then a graphical editor can be generated based on the resulting specific metamodel. Therefore, it not only enables the system supplier to reuse the existing certification data by means of a conceptual mapping, which is supported by the GMM, but also respects their current way of working by means of specific metamodels support. Besides, a metamodel refinement language is defined. With its help, the traceability information from the GMM to SMMs can be maintained. Refine specifications support the documentation of the traces between generic and more specific metamodels and vice versa. They can be used to automatically determine the similarity between concepts in different domains. Also, system suppliers can get their own metamodel and tool support easier and quicker. As future work, we could investigate the construction of mappings between specific metamodels based on MMRL transformations, and traceability management and analysis among those transformations. And we would like to improve the concrete syntax of our MMRL to make it more user-friendly for system suppliers. Moreover, more cross-domain case studies need to be worked on to evaluate our approach.

Acknowledgements. The research leading to these results has received funding from the FP7 programme under grant agreement n° 289011 (OPENCOSS).

References

1. Meta Modeling Approach to Safety Standard for Consumer Devices (2013), http://www.omg.org/news/meetings/tc/agendas/ut/SysA_Slides/taguchi.pdf
2. OPENCOSS: Deliverable D4.1 - Baseline for the common certification language (2013), http://www.opencoss-project.eu/node/7
3. van Amstel, M.F., van den Brand, M.G.J., Serebrenik, A.: Traceability Visualization in Model Transformations with TraceVis. In: Hu, Z., de Lara, J. (eds.) ICMT 2012. LNCS, vol. 7307, pp. 152–159. Springer, Heidelberg (2012)
4. Atkinson, C., Kühne, T.: Model-Driven Development: A Metamodeling Foundation. IEEE Software (2003)
5. van den Brand, M.G.J.: Model-Driven Engineering Meets Generic Language Technology. In: Gašević, D., Lämmel, R., Van Wyk, E. (eds.) SLE 2008. LNCS, vol. 5452, pp. 8–15. Springer, Heidelberg (2009)

6. Espinoza, H., Ruiz, A., Sabetzadeh, M., Panaroni, P.: Challenges for an Open and Evolutionary Approach to Safety Assurance and Certification of Safety-Critical Systems. In: 2011 First International Workshop Software Certification (WoSoCER), Hiroshima, Japan (2011)
7. Habli, I., Kelly, T.: A Model-Driven Approach to Assuring Process Reliability. In: Proceedings of ISSRE 2008, Washington, DC, USA, pp. 7–16 (2008)
8. Kolovos, D., Paige, R., Polack, F.: The Epsilon Transformation Language. In: Proceedings of ICMT 2008 (2008)
9. Kolovos, D.S., Rose, L.M., Abid, S.B., Paige, R.F., Polack, F.A.C., Botterweck, G.: Taming EMF and GMF Using Model Transformation. In: Petriu, D.C., Rouquette, N., Haugen, Ø. (eds.) MODELS 2010, Part I. LNCS, vol. 6394, pp. 211–225. Springer, Heidelberg (2010)
10. Krammer, M., Armengaud, E., Bourrouilh, Q.: Method Library Framework for Safety Standard Compliant Process Tailoring. In: 37th EUROMICRO Conference on Software Engineering and Advanced Applications, pp. 302 –305 (2011)
11. Luo, Y., van den Brand, M., Engelen, L., Favaro, J., Klabbers, M., Sartori, G.: Extracting Models from ISO 26262 for Reusable Safety Assurance. In: Favaro, J., Morisio, M. (eds.) ICSR 2013. LNCS, vol. 7925, pp. 192–207. Springer, Heidelberg (2013)
12. Luo, Y., Brand, M., Engelen, L., Klabbers, M.: A Modeling Approach to Support Safety Certification in the Automotive Domain. In: FISITA 2014, World Automotive Congress (2014) (submitted for publication)
13. Narayanan, A., Levendovszky, T., Balasubramanian, D., Karsai, G.: Automatic Domain Model Migration to Manage Metamodel Evolution. In: Schürr, A., Selic, B. (eds.) MODELS 2009. LNCS, vol. 5795, pp. 706–711. Springer, Heidelberg (2009)
14. Panach, J.I., España, S., Moreno, A.M., Pastor, Ó.: Dealing with Usability in Model Transformation Technologies. In: Li, Q., Spaccapietra, S., Yu, E., Olivé, A. (eds.) ER 2008. LNCS, vol. 5231, pp. 498–511. Springer, Heidelberg (2008)
15. Panesar-Walawege, R.K., Sabetzadeh, M., Briand, L.: Using UML Profiles for Sector-Specific Tailoring of Safety Evidence Information. In: Jeusfeld, M., Delcambre, L., Ling, T.-W. (eds.) ER 2011. LNCS, vol. 6998, pp. 362–378. Springer, Heidelberg (2011)
16. Panesar-Walawege, R., Sabetzadeh, M., Briand, L.: Using Model-Driven Engineering for Managing Safety Evidence: Challenges, Vision and Experience. In: 2011 First International Workshop on Software Certification (WoSoCER), pp. 7–12 (November 2011)
17. Partridge, C., Gonzalez-Perez, C., Henderson-Sellers, B.: Are Conceptual Models Concept Models? In: Ng, W., Storey, V.C., Trujillo, J.C. (eds.) ER 2013. LNCS, vol. 8217, pp. 96–105. Springer, Heidelberg (2013)
18. Santiago, I., Vara, J.M., de Castro, M.V., Marcos, E.: Towards the Effective Use of Traceability in Model-Driven Engineering Projects. In: Ng, W., Storey, V.C., Trujillo, J.C. (eds.) ER 2013. LNCS, vol. 8217, pp. 429–437. Springer, Heidelberg (2013)
19. de la Vara, J.L., Panesar-Walawege, R.K.: SafetyMet: A Metamodel for Safety Standards. In: Moreira, A., Schätz, B., Gray, J., Vallecillo, A., Clarke, P. (eds.) MODELS 2013. LNCS, vol. 8107, pp. 69–86. Springer, Heidelberg (2013)
20. Wachsmuth, G.: Metamodel Adaptation and Model Co-adaptation. In: Ernst, E. (ed.) ECOOP 2007. LNCS, vol. 4609, pp. 600–624. Springer, Heidelberg (2007)
21. Zoughbi, G., Briand, L., Labiche, Y.: Modeling Safety and Airworthiness (RTCA DO-178B) Information: Conceptual Model and UML Profile. Softw. Syst. Model. 10(3), 337–367 (2011)

A New Approach for N-ary Relationships in Object Databases[*]

Jie Hu[1], Liu Chen[2], Shuang Qiu[1], and Mengchi Liu[3]

[1] Faculty of Computer Science and Information Engineering, Hubei University, China
[2] School of Computer Science, Wuhan University, China
[3] School of Computer Science, Carleton University, Canada

Abstract. In an object-oriented or object-relational database, an n-ary relationship among objects is normally represented in a relation that is separated from other properties of objects at the logical level. In order to use such a database, the user needs to know the structure of the database, especially what kind of relations and classes there are, how they are organized and related in order to manipulate and query object data. To make the logical level closer to the conceptual level so that the database is easier to use, we propose a novel approach that allows the user to represent n-ary relationships among objects in their class definitions so that the user can directly manipulate and query objects based on the class definitions, rather than explicitly join relations at the logical level. Based on the class definitions, the system can automatically generate the modified class/object relation definitions and the corresponding regular relation definition for the n-ary relationship at the physical level to reduce redundancy and convert data manipulation and query statements based at the logical level to ones at the physical level.

Keywords: Object-oriented model, object-relational model, n-ary relationships, database design.

1 Introduction

One of the most important improvements of the new generation databases such as object-oriented databases (OODB) and object-relational databases (ORDB) with regard to the relational ones is their capacity to support complex objects and structures [1,2]. In order to achieve this, the corresponding data models are more expressive using powerful constructs so that they are much closer to the conceptual models than the relational model. However, some important conceptual constructs such as n-ary relationships are not still directly supported by such databases so that the semantics has to be dealt with by the applications.

A relationship is an association between two or more objects. When only two objects participate in the association, the relationship is called binary. In

---

[*] This work is supported by the National Natural Science Foundation of China under Grant No. 61202100 and China Scholarship Council under Grant No. [2013]3018.

E. Yu et al. (Eds.): ER 2014, LNCS 8824, pp. 209–222, 2014.

spite of several proposals extending the relationship semantics to support different meanings of the relationship concept, some object-oriented models such as ODMG just support binary relationships. In ODMG [3], a binary relationship and its inverse must be explicitly specified in pairs in the corresponding classes by providing the traversal paths. However, relationships that associate more than two objects are quite common in applications. In such cases they are called n-ary relationships. A ternary relationship is a special case of an n-ary relationship in which n is three.

All conceptual models such as ER [4], EER [5], and UML [6,7], etc. support n-ary relationships. However, relational, object-oriented, and object-relational databases such as SQL-Server, ORION [8], DB2, Oracle, etc. can not naturally and directly support them.

In a relational database, an n-ary relationship is mapped to $n+1$ relations in which the relationship relation contains attributes that refer to the primary key attributes of the n participating entity relations.

The object-relational model grew out of the research in 1990s. It extends the popular relational model by adding object-oriented features such as object identity, complex objects, user-defined types, methods, class hierarchy, structural and behavioural inheritance, etc. It distinguishes two kinds of relations: regular relations and object relations. In such kind of databases, an n-ary relationship is mapped to a regular relation and entities participating in the n-ary relationship to object relations. Unlike in traditional relational databases where key values are used to represent entities in n-ary relationships, references (oids) to objects are used instead in object-relational databases.

The main difference between the two kinds of mapping is that the logical level in OODB and ORDB is much closer to the conceptual level than RDB, because real-world entities are mapped to objects in OODB and ORDB instead of tuples in relations in RDB. However, they do not take the same approach for n-ary relationships [9,10].

The most effective way to represent an n-ary relationship is to use a flat regular relation as it reduces redundancy [11,12]. However, this is the most non-informative way from the user point of view. The reason mainly lies in that information about real-world entities in object-relational databases is scattered among two kinds of relations. In order to use such a system, the user needs to know the structure of the database, especially what kind of relations there are, how they are organized and related in order to query object data. The case for object-oriented databases is the same. Besides classes, the user still needs to use flat relations to deal with n-ary relationships so that two different mechanisms have to be used to represent data.

In our opinion, ideally the user should be able to access all the information of an object, including various relationships they participate in, directly from the object without any need to know the detail of what kind of and how many relations are used. This observation suggests that the relation for n-ary relationships should be at the physical level rather than at the logical level. To obtain the desired result, the user just needs to specify how the object is related to other objects in its class definition and use this definition to access, manipulate, and query the object data at the logical level. At the physical level, the system should automatically generate the modified class/object relation definitions and the corresponding relation definition for the n-ary relationships embedded in the class definitions at the logical level to reduce the redundancy.

In this paper, we propose such an approach. The paper is organized as follows. Section 2 provides the motivation of our approach. Section 3 shows how to define classes at the logical level and generate the class and n-ary relation definitions at the physical level. Sections 4 and 5 illustrate how to manipulate and query objects based on the class definitions at the logical level without explicitly joining objects with relations, and how to convert them to objects and relations at the physical level. In section 6, we conclude and comment on our future plans.

2   Motivation

Let us consider a typical ternary relationship *SPJ* which involves entities *Supplier*, *Part* and *Project*. Also, *Supplier* and *Address* have many to one binary relationship. The corresponding ER diagram is shown in Fig. 1.

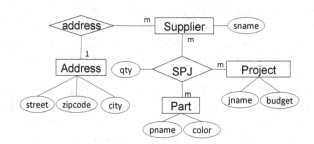

Fig. 1. Relationships in ER Diagram

In an object-relational database, entity types *Supplier*, *Part* and *Project* are represented as object relations, whereas ternary relationship type *SPJ* is represented as a regular relation. The objects and the ternary relationship SPJ(S, P, J, qty) are shown in Fig. 2.

If we want to find the address of suppliers who supply part *nut* to project *raid*, we can use SQL in Oracle as follows:

select deref(S.address) from supplier S, Part P, Project J, SPJ Q where ref(S)=Q.S and ref(P)= Q.P and ref(J)=Q.J and P.pname = 'nut' and J.jname='raid'

The results are as follows:

DEREF(S.ADDRESS)(CITY, STREET, ZIPCODE)

....

ADDRESS_T('BS', 'Morris Blvd', 5581)
ADDRESS_T('NY', '52nd Street', 7943)

Supplier

	sname	address
s_1	smith	a_1
s_2	jone	a_2

Part

	pname	color
p_1	bolt	black
p_2	nut	red

Address

	city	street	zipcode
a_1	BS	Morris Blvd	5581
a_2	NY	52nd Street	7943

Project

	jname	budget
j_1	raid	3
j_2	display	4
j_3	tape	5
j_4	eds	6
j_5	scorter	1

SPJ

S	P	J	qty
s_1	p_2	j_5	100
s_1	p_2	j_1	200
s_1	p_1	j_2	300
s_1	p_1	j_3	400
s_2	p_2	j_4	100
s_2	p_2	j_1	200

Fig. 2. Ternary relationship representation in Object-Relational Model

Here the user needs to explicitly join object relations *Supplier*, *Part*, *Project* to the regular relation *SPJ* based on how they are related. But for the binary relationship *address*, we can simply use the path expression. Also, the user needs to distinguish object properties such as *address*, *color* and *budget* from the property *qty* of the ternary relationship *SPJ* at the logical level. The main problem lies in two aspects: (1) it does not use an uniform way to represent binary relationships and higher degree relationships at the logical level; (2) it is not natural and flexible enough as the user needs to know the existence of the ternary relationship and use it properly in order to get information from it.

In our method, there is no difference between binary relationships and higher degree relationships at the logical level. They differ only at the physical level which is invisible to the user. Thus the user just needs to specify how an object is related to other objects in the schema then manipulate and query objects and their relationships in the instance. In this way, they can access any information of objects without any need to know the detail of what kind of and how many relations are used. So our approach makes the logical level closer to the conceptual level.

3   Schema

In the object-relational model, relationships are usually represented as regular relations. Objects participating in these relationships are linked through the relation. Such structures are similar to the modeling of relationships in the relational model, which uses key values instead of references(oids). In our method, an n-ary ($n > 2$) relationship is not explicitly defined as a relationship object type then the involved classes are linked through it. Instead, it is derived from the classes participating in the n-ary relationship.

Example 1. Consider the following example:

```
create class Supplier [
  address:Street(inverse supplier),
  supply *:[part:Part, project*:Project[@qty:int]]]
create class Part [
  @color:string,
  made *:[supplier:Supplier, project*:Project[@qty:int]]]
create class Project [
  @budget:int,
  used *:[supplier:Supplier, part*:Part[@qty:int]]]
```

The first definition specifies that *address* is a binary relationship and its inverse is *supplier*. Like ODMG, various inverse relationship can be defined here for any binary relationship. But unlike ODMG, there is no need to repeat the definition in both classes. The second and third ones define the attributes *color* and *budget* and their types are *string* and *int* respectively. Moreover, the definitions involve three classes *Supplier*, *Part* and *Project* which compose a ternary relationship. Here the star (*) in the first definition specifies that the cardinality on the number of projects that a supplier can supply is multiple. For the other two, the cases are similar.

Based on the class definitions above, the system automatically generates a new relation *SPJ* with the following schema that is used to store the ternary relationship.

```
SPJ[rid:int, supplier:Supplier, part:Part, project:Project, qty:int]
```

Using *SPJ*, the system generates the following class definitions at the physical level.

```
class Supplier [address:Street,supply *:SPJ]
class Part [@color:string, made *:SPJ]
class Project [@budget:int,used *:SPJ]
```

The relation and class definitions above are invisible to the user. Note that in our method the implied ternary or higher degree relationships are derived from all of the participating classes. If just partial classes are involved in definitions, it should not derive any n-ary relationship.

Consider the following example:

```
create class AnnualOscar [
  BestOriginalSongWinner *:[movie:Movie, orignalsong:Song, music:Composer,
    lyrics:Lyrics]]
create class Song[
  movie *:[in:Movie, music: Composer, lyrics:Lyrics, awards:AnnualOscar]]
create class Movie [song *:[orignalsong:Song, awards:AnnualOscar]]
create class Composer[song *:[asComposer:Song, awards:AnnualOscar]]
create class Lyrics [song *:[asLyrics:Song,awards:AnnualOscar]]
```

Here, the first two definitions involve five classes *AnnualOscar*, *Movie*, *Song*, *Composer* and *Lyrics*. However, the last three definitions just cover parts of them. Therefore, they do not derive any n-ary relationship. In our method, they are aggregation relationships instead.

4   Instance

In our method, a real-world entity is represented by exactly one object that is uniquely represented by an oid. All the information regarding a real-world object including their n-ary relationships is grouped in one instance instead of scattered in several objects and relations so that the user can directly access the relationship from the object without explicitly joining objects with relations at the logical level. A novel feature of our method is its built-in maintenance for multiple objects participating in the n-ary relationship. None of the existing models or languages support this feature and thus require tedious and manual operations to maintain the consistency.

4.1   Insertion

The user can create new objects and assign their relationship values using the insert command. Unlike other object-oriented languages such as ODMG OML and Oracle SQL, they have to first have the object and then establish the relationships with them. Also, they have to use *update* command to maintain the properties of objects which already exist in the database. In our method, the insert command is used to either generate new objects with various relationships with other objects or update properties of objects existing in the database. When we insert an object, all other objects participating in its various relationships will be also automatically generated if they are not in the database. Moreover, different properties regarding an object can be inserted into the database either once or several times. We believe that this way is more flexible and can significantly lessen the user's burden when they manipulate the objects as they do not need to know whether the objects connected by relationships are in the database or not.

Consider the classes and the ternary relationship defined in Example 1. In order to generate the data same as shown in Fig. 2, we demonstrate how to insert objects respectively from *Supplier*, *Part*, and *Project*. Firstly, we insert a supplier *smith* as follows:

```
insert Supplier smith [
    supply:{[part:nut, project:{scorter[@qty:100], raid[@qty:200]}],
            [part:bolt, project:{display[@qty:300], tape[@qty:400]}]}]
```

According to the relation for the derived ternary relationship in Example 1, it generates the relation *SPJ* as follows:

rid	Supplier	Part	Project	qty
1	smith	nut	scorter	100
2	smith	nut	raid	200
3	smith	bolt	display	300
4	smith	bolt	tape	400

According to the schema and the above relation, the objects including supplier *smith*, parts *nut* and *bolt*, and projects *scorter*, *raid*, *display*, and *tape* are also generated automatically as follows:

Supplier smith [supply:{1,2,3,4}]
Part nut[made:{1,2}]
Part bolt[made:{3,4}]
Project scorter[used:1]
Project raid[used:2]
Project display[used:3]
Project tape[used:4]

Then we insert a part *nut* as follows:

insert Part nut [made:[supplier:jone, project:{eds[@qty:100], raid[@qty:200]}]]

The relation will be extended as follows:

rid	Supplier	Part	Project	qty
1	smith	nut	scorter	100
2	smith	nut	raid	200
3	smith	bolt	display	300
4	smith	bolt	tape	400
5	*jone*	*nut*	*eds*	*100*
6	*jone*	*nut*	*raid*	*200*

The objects *jone* and *eds* are generated as follows:

Supplier jone [supply:{5,6}]
Project eds[used:5]

Moreover, the objects *nut* and *raid* are modified as follows:

Part nut[made:{1,2,*5,6*}]
Project raid[used:{2,*6*}]

Finally, we insert a project *display* as follows:

insert Project display [used:[supplier:blake,part:{nut[@qty:100],bolt[@qty:300]}]]

The relation will be extended as shown in Table 1.

Table 1. Relation for the ternary relationship after insertion

rid	Supplier	Part	Project	qty
1	smith	nut	scorter	100
2	smith	nut	raid	200
3	smith	bolt	display	300
4	smith	bolt	tape	400
5	jone	nut	eds	100
6	jone	nut	raid	200
7	*blake*	*nut*	*display*	*100*
8	*blake*	*bolt*	*display*	*300*

The object *blake* is generated as follows:

Supplier blake [supply:{7,8}]

Moreover, the objects *nut*, *bolt*, and *display* are modified as follows:

Algorithm: LogicalObject(c, o, r, ids)

Input: A class name **c**
        An object name **o** that belongs to class **c**
        An n-ary relationship name **r** of object **o**
        A rid list **ids** of relationship **r**
Output: An object representation **Result** at the logical level
        A boolean **Flag** that indicates whether the conversion is successful
1 **Sch** = NULL, **T**= NULL, **Flag** = FALSE, and **Result** = NULL
2 **Sch= GetDef(c,r)** get the definition of class **c** for relationship **r** in the schema
3 **IF Sch != NULL**
4   **FOR** each relationship in **r** of **Sch**
5   Let r_i be the relationship name
6   Let d_i be the cardinality
7   Let t_i be the target class name
8   **END FOR**
9 **ELSE**
10   RETURN
11 **END IF**
12 **T = GetTuple(ids)** get tuples from the relation where rid is in the list **ids**
13 V_1 = NULL and V_m = NULL
14 **IF T != NULL**
15   V_1 = **GetObjectIsOne(T, $\{d_i\}$)** get objects of target class list $\{t_i\}$ whose
                    cardinality is one
16   V_m = **GetObjectIsMultiple(T, $\{d_i\}$)** get objects of target class list $\{t_i\}$
                    whose cardinality is multiple
17   **A = Attribute(T)** get attributes in **T** and generate attribute assignments
18   **IF** V_1 != NULL and V_m != NULL
19   **R** = **c** o[r:[r_1:o_1,...,r_i:o_i,..., r_j:$\{o_j\}$, ..., r_n:$\{o_n\}$]] where o_1,..., $o_i \in V_1$
        and $\{o_j\}$,..., $\{o_n\} \subset V_m$, that is, group V_m by V_1
20   **END IF**
21   **IF** V_1 = NULL and V_m != NULL
22   **R** = **c** o[r:[r_1:$\{o_1\}$, ..., r_n:$\{o_n\}$]] where $\{o_1\}$,..., $\{o_n\} \subset V_m$
23   **END IF**
24   **IF** V_1 != NULL and V_m = NULL
25   **R** = **c** o[r:[r_1:o_1, ..., r_n:o_n]] where o_1,..., $o_n \in V_m$
26   **ENDIF**
27   nest attribute assignment in **A** into **R** and form **Result**
28   **Flag**=TRUE
29 **END IF**

Fig. 3. Algorithm of Object Conversion

Part nut[made:$\{1,2,5,6,7\}$]
Part bolt[made:$\{3,4,8\}$]
Project display[used:$\{3,7,8\}$]

Note that the above representation for objects is at the physical level instead of the logical level. An object viewed by the user is obtained from the class definition, the instance, and the tuples of the corresponding relation at the physical

Supplier smith [
   supply:{[part:nut, project:{scorter[@qty:100],raid[@qty:200]}],
        [part:bolt, project:{display[@qty:300],tape[@qty:400]}]}]
Supplier jone [
   supply:[part:nut, project:{eds[@qty:100],raid[@qty:200]}]]
Supplier blake [
   supply:{[part:nut, project:display[@qty:100]],
        [part:bolt, project:display[@qty:300]]}]
Part nut [
   made:{[supplier:smith, project:{scorter[@qty:100],raid[@qty:200]}],
        [supplier:jone, project:{eds[@qty:100],raid[@qty:200]}],
        [supplier:blake, project:display[@qty:100]]}]
Part bolt [
   made:{[supplier:smith, project:{display[@qty:300],tape[@qty:400]}],
        [supplier:blake, project:display[@qty:300]]}]
Project scorter[used:[supplier:smith,part:nut[@qty:100]]]
Project raid[
   used:{[supplier:smith,part:nut[@qty:200]],
        [supplier:jone,part:nut[@qty:200]]}]
Project display[
   used:{[supplier:smith,part:bolt[@qty:300]],
        [supplier:blake,part:{nut[@qty:100],bolt[@qty:300]}]}]
Project tape[used:[supplier:smith,part:bolt[@qty:400]]]
Project eds[used:[supplier:jone,part:nut[@qty:100]]]

Fig. 4. Objects at the logical level

level via the algorithm shown in Fig. 3. Objects at the logical level are shown in Fig. 4.

4.2 Update

The user can add, modify, and delete relationships of objects using the update command which is distinguished three kinds : update ··· add, update ··· modify, and update ··· delete.

Consider the object *tape* in Fig. 4, if we add a relationship *used* as follows:
   update tape add used:[supplier:jone, part:bolt/qty:500]
The tuple [9, jone, bolt, tape, 500] will be added into the relation in Table 1. Objects *tape*, *jone* and *bolt* are modified as follows:
   Project tape[used:{4,9}]
   Supplier jone[supply:{5,6,9}]
   Part bolt[made:{3,4,8,9}]
Their representation at the logical level is as follows:
   Project tape[
       used:{[supplier:smith,part:bolt[@qty:400]],
          [supplier:jone,part:bolt[@qty:500]]}]

Supplier jone [
    supply:{[part:nut, project:{eds[@qty:100],raid[@qty:200]}],
       [part:bolt, project:tape[@qty500]]}]
Part bolt [
    made:{[supplier:smith, project:{display[@qty:300],tape[@qty:400]}],
       [supplier:blake, project:display[@qty:300]],
       [supplier:jone, project:tape[@qty:500]]}]

For the object *bolt*, if we modify the supplier *smith* with *sue*, the corresponding projects *tape* and *display* with *raid* using the following command:
    update bolt/used:[supplier:smith, project:{tape,display}] modify [supplier:sue,
    project:raid/qty:600]
The tuples [3, smith, bolt, display, 300] and [4, smith, bolt, tape, 400] are deleted and the tuple [10, sue, bolt, raid, 600] will be added into the relation. Thus objects *bolt*, *smith*, *tape*, *display* and *raid* are modified as follows:
    Part bolt[made:{8,9,10}]
    Supplier smith [supply:{1,2}]
    Project tape[used:9]
    Project display[used:{7,8}]
    Project raid[used:{2,6,10}]
The object *sue* is generated as follows:
    Supplier sue [supply:10]
Their representation at the logical level is as follows:
    Part bolt [
      made:{[supplier:blake, project:display[@qty:300]],
         [supplier:jone, project:tape[@qty:500]],
         [supplier:sue, project:raid[@qty:600]]}]
    Supplier smith [
      supply:[part:nut, project:{scorter[@qty:100], raid[@qty:200]}]]]
    Project tape [used:[supplier:jone, part:bolt[@qty:500]]]
    Project display [
      used:[supplier:blake, part:{nut[@qty:100], bolt[@qty:300]}]]]
    Project raid [
      used:{[supplier:smith, part:nut[@qty:200]],
         [supplier:jone, part:nut[@qty:200]],
         [supplier:sue, part:bolt[@qty:600]]}]
    Supplier sue [supply:[part:bolt, project:raid[@qty:600]]]]

If we delete the part *nut* and all the projects of object *smith* as follows:
    update smith delete [part:nut, project]
The tuples [1, smith, nut, scorter, 100] and [2, smith, nut, raid, 200] are deleted from the relation. Also, objects *smith* and *scorter* are deleted because all of their relationship values have been deleted. Objects *nut* and *raid* are modified as follows:
    Part nut[made:{5, 6,7]
    Project raid[used:{6,10}]

Their representation at the logical level is as follows:

```
Part nut [
    made:{[supplier:jone, project:{eds[@qty:100],raid[@qty:200]}],
            [supplier:blake, project:display[@qty:100]]}]
Project raid [
    used:{[supplier:jone, part:nut[@qty:200]],
            [supplier:sue, part:bolt[@qty:600]]}]
```

Finally, the relation in Table 1 is modified as shown in Table 2.

Table 2. Relation for the ternay relationship after update

rid	Supplier	Part	Project	qty
5	jone	nut	eds	100
6	jone	nut	raid	200
7	blake	nut	display	100
8	blake	bolt	display	300
9	jone	bolt	tape	500
10	sue	bolt	raid	600

4.3 Deletion

The delete command is used to delete objects in the instance database instead of the relationships of objects. When we delete an object, its relationships will be recursively deleted.

If we delete the object *bolt* as follows:

```
delete bolt
```

The relationship *made* of object *bolt* is deleted. Therefore, the tuples with rids 8, 9, and 10 in Table 2 are deleted. Moreover, the objects *sue* and *tape* are recursively deleted as well. Also, the objects *blake, jone, display* and *raid* are modified as follows:

```
Supplier blake [supply:7]
Supplier jone [supply:{5,6}]
Project display [used:7]
Project raid [used:6]
```

The following are their representation at the logical level.

```
Supplier blake [supply:[part:nut, project:display[@qty:100]]]
Supplier jone [supply:[part:nut, project:{eds[@qty:100],raid[@qty:200]}]]
Project display [used: [supplier:blake, part:nut[@qty:100]]]
Project raid [used:[supplier:jone, part:nut[@qty:200]]]
```

5 Query

For a database with complex structure, a query normally has two parts: retrieval part and result construction part. Most well-known query languages for such kind of data, such as SQL, OQL, XQuery etc. intermix the retrieval part and the result part so that the query is no longer declarative anymore and it is cumbersome to express and difficult to read and comprehend. In our method, the query language is logic-based and takes a different approach. It strictly separates the retrieval part from the result part. In the retrieval part, we use logical variables which start with $ to get all the values based on their positions whereas in the result construction part, we specify how to construct the result using the variables bound to various values. Therefore, queries in our language are more concise and declarative and thus easier to use and understand.

There are two kinds of queries in our approach: schema query and instance query. Due to space limitation, we mainly focus on instance queries to retrieve information about objects and their binary and higher degree relationships in the instance database.

A query is an expression of the form:

$$\textbf{query } E_1, \ldots, E_n \textbf{ construct } C$$

where $E_1, \ldots, E_n$ are retrieval expressions with $n \geq 1$, C is a construction expression and *construct C* is optional.

At the logical level, information about objects and their n-ary relationships is organized into composition hierarchies. Thus we introduce path expressions in the query language. To go down one level at a time, we use a slash ($/$), and to go down multiple levels at a time, we can use double slash ($//$).

Now we use several examples to illustrate how to query objects and their ternary relationships based on the instance shown in Fig. 4.

query smith/supply:x construct x
It finds what *smith* supplies. The variable x in the retrieval part is bound to tuples [part:nut, project:{scorter[@qty:100],raid[@qty:200]}] and [part:bolt, project:{display[@qty:300],tape[@qty:400]}]. The construction part specifies that display the values bound to x. Thus the result is as follows:
    [part:nut, project:{scorter[@qty:100],raid[@qty:200]}]
    [part:bolt, project:{display[@qty:300],tape[@qty:400]}]

query Supplier x/[part:nut, project:y/qty:z] construct x/supply:[project:y/qty:z]
It finds the supplier using part *nut*, the projects and the corresponding quantity supplied by the supplier. The variable x is respectively bound to smith, jone and blake. When x is bound to smith, y is to scorter and z to 100, y to raid and z to 200. When x is bound to jone, y is to eds and z to 100, y to raid and z to 200. When x is bound to blake, y is to display and z to 100. The construction part specifies that display x, its project y and the corresponding quantity z in which y is grouped by x and z is grouped by y. To get the same information, we can also retrieval them started from the part or project. It can be equivalently represented as follows:
    query nut/[supplier:x, project:y/qty:z] construct x/supply:[project:y/qty:z]
    query Project y/[supplier:x, part:nut/qty:z]construct x/supply:[project:y/qty:z]
The query result is as follows:
    smith[supply:[project:{scorter[qty:100],raid[qty:200]}]]

jone[supply:[project:{eds[qty:100],raid[qty:200]}]]
blake[supply:[project:display[qty:100]]]

query smith/[part:x, project:y] construct [part:x,project:{y}]

It finds the part and the corresponding project supplied by *smith*. The variable x is respectively bound to nut and bolt. The variable y is bound to scorter[@qty:100] and raid[@qty:200] when x is to nut, display[@qty:300] and tape[@qty:400] when x is to bolt. The construction part specifies that display the tuple in which the project y is grouped by the part x. It can be equivalently represented as query Part x/[supplier:smith, project:y] construct [part:x,project:{y}] The query result is as follows:

[part:nut,project:{scorter[@qty:100], raid[@qty:200]}]
[part:bolt,project:{display[@qty:300],tape[@qty:400]}]

query jone//part:x/made:y construct x/made:y

It finds the part which is supplied by *jone* and what the part made. The variable x is bound to *nut* and y to three tuples [supplier:smith, project:{scorter[@qty:100], raid[@qty:200]}], [supplier:jone, project:{eds[@qty:100],raid[@qty:200]}] and [supplier: blake, project:display[@qty:100]]. The construction part specifies that display x and y that is made by x. The query result is as follows:

nut[made:{[supplier:smith, project:{scorter[@qty:100], raid[@qty:200]}],
[supplier:jone, project:{eds[@qty:100],raid[@qty:200]}],
[supplier: blake, project:display[@qty:100]]}]

In our query language, the user can directly explore the natural structure of an object and access any part of the object without knowing the existence of the relation and explicitly joining objects with relations to extract meaningful results at the logical level.

6 Conclusion

In this paper, we have proposed a new approach to eliminate the relations for n-ary relationships at the logical level in object databases.

In the schema, the representation for an n-ary relationship is more natural and close to the conceptual level as it is derived from the classes participating in the relationship instead of explicitly defined as a relation then the involved classes are linked through it. In the instance, a real-world entity is represented by exactly one object that is uniquely represented by an oid. All the information regarding a real-world object including their n-ary relationships is grouped in one instance instead of scattered in several objects and relations so that the user can directly access the relationship from the object without explicitly joining objects with relations at the logical level. Moreover, our approach supports built-in maintenance for multiple objects participating in the n-ary relationship. None of existing databases support this feature and thus require tedious and manual operations to maintain the consistency. Our logic-based query language separates the retrieval part from the result construction part. The retrieval part is used to get all the values based on their positions whereas the result construction part is used to construct the result. Queries in our method are more concise and declarative and thus easier to use and understand.

We have systematically implemented a new full-fledged client/server-based database management system called INM-DBMS using GLib 2.25.13 and Berkeley DB 4.7 on SUN M5000 server under Solaris 10. The server itself has over 190,000 line of C++ code. It is based on the Information Networking Model [13] and incorporate the n-ary relationship presented here.

Currently, we are investigating various query optimization techniques in order to enhance the performance of the system. We would also like to use INM-DBMS to build semantic search systems in academic social network and other areas.

References

1. Stonebraker, M., Moore, D., Brown, P. (eds.): Object Relational DBMSs: The Next Great Wave, 2nd edn. Morgan Kaufmann (1998)
2. Silberschatz, A., Korth, H.F., Sudarshan, S. (eds.): Database System Concepts, 6th edn. McGraw-Hill (2011)
3. Cattell, R., Barry, D., Berler, M., Eastman, J., Jordan, D., Russel, C., Schadow, O., Stanienda, T., Velez, F. (eds.): The Object Database Standard: ODMG 3.0. Morgan Kaufmann, Los Altos (2000)
4. Chen, P.P.: The entity-relationship model - toward a unified view of data. ACM Transaction On Database Systems (TODS) 1(1), 9–36 (1976)
5. Elmasri, R., Weeldreyer, J.A., Hevner, A.R.: The category concept: An extension to the entity-relationship model. Data & Knowledge Engineering 1(1), 75–116 (1985)
6. Halpin, T.A.: Comparing metamodels for er, orm and uml data models. In: Advanced Topics in Database Research, vol. 3, pp. 23–44 (2004)
7. Génova, G., Lloréns, J., Martínez, P.: The meaning of multiplicity of n-ary associations in uml. Software and System Modeling 1(2), 86–97 (2002)
8. Kim, W., Ballou, N., Chou, H.T., Garza, J.F., Woelk, D.: Features of the orion object-oriented database system. In: Object-Oriented Concepts, Databases, and Applications, pp. 251–282 (1989)
9. Dahchour, M., Pirotte, A.: The semantics of reifying n-ary relationships as classes. In: ICEIS, pp. 580–586 (2002)
10. Benchikha, F., Boufaïda, M., Seinturier, L.: Viewpoints: A framework for object oriented database modelling and distribution. Data Science Journal 4, 92–107 (2005)
11. Camps, R.: From ternary relationship to relational tables: A case against common beliefs. SIGMOD Record 31(2), 46–49 (2002)
12. Cuadra, D., Iglesias, A., Castro, E., Fernández, P.M.: Educational experiences detecting, using, and representing ternary relationships in database design. IEEE Transactions on Education 53(3), 358–364 (2010)
13. Liu, M., Hu, J.: Information networking model. In: Laender, A.H.F., Castano, S., Dayal, U., Casati, F., de Oliveira, J.P.M. (eds.) ER 2009. LNCS, vol. 5829, pp. 131–144. Springer, Heidelberg (2009)

Database Design for NoSQL Systems

Francesca Bugiotti[1,*], Luca Cabibbo[2], Paolo Atzeni[2], and Riccardo Torlone[2]

[1] Inria & Université Paris-Sud
[2] Università Roma Tre

Abstract. We propose a database design methodology for NoSQL systems. The approach is based on NoAM (NoSQL Abstract Model), a novel abstract data model for NoSQL databases, which exploits the commonalities of various No-SQL systems and is used to specify a system-independent representation of the application data. This intermediate representation can be then implemented in target NoSQL databases, taking into account their specific features. Overall, the methodology aims at supporting scalability, performance, and consistency, as needed by next-generation web applications.

1 Introduction

NoSQL database systems are today an effective solution to manage large data sets distributed over many servers. A primary driver of interest in NoSQL systems is their support for next-generation web applications, for which relational DBMSs are not well suited. These are OLTP applications for which (i) data have a structure that does not fit well in the rigid structure of relational tables, (ii) access to data is based on simple read-write operations, (iii) scalability and performance are important quality requirements, and (iv) a certain level of consistency is also desirable [7,20].

NoSQL technology is characterized by a high heterogeneity [7,21], which is problematic to application developers. Currently, database design for NoSQL systems is usually based on best practices and guidelines [12], which are specifically related to the selected system [19,10,17], with no systematic methodology. Several authors have observed that the development of high-level methodologies and tools supporting NoSQL database design are needed [2,3,13].

In this paper we aim at filling this gap, by presenting a design methodology for NoSQL databases that has initial activities that are independent of the specific target system. The approach is based on *NoAM* (*NoSQL Abstract Model*), a novel abstract data model for NoSQL databases, which exploits the observation that the various NoSQL systems share similar modeling features. Given the application data and the desired data access patterns, the methodology we propose uses NoAM to specify an intermediate, system-independent data representation. The implementation in target NoSQL systems is then a final step, with a translation that takes into account their peculiarities.

Specifically, our methodology has the goal of designing a "good" representation of these application data in a target NoSQL database, and is intended to support *scalability*, *performance*, and *consistency*, as needed by next-generation web applications. In general, different alternatives on the organization of data in a NoSQL database are possible,

---

* Part of this work was performed while this author was with Università Roma Tre.

E. Yu et al. (Eds.): ER 2014, LNCS 8824, pp. 223–231, 2014.

but they are not equivalent in supporting performance, scalability, and consistency. A "wrong" database representation can lead to the inability to guarantee atomicity of important operations and to performance that are worse by an order of magnitude.

The design methodology is based on the following main activities:

- *conceptual data modeling*, to identify the various entities and relationships thereof needed in an application;
- *aggregate design*, to group related entities into aggregates [9,11];
- *aggregate partitioning*, where aggregates are partitioned into smaller data elements;
- *high-level NoSQL database design*, where aggregates are mapped to the NoAM intermediate data model, according to the identified partitions;
- *implementation*, to map the intermediate data representation to the specific modeling elements of a target datastore; only this activity depends on the target system.

The remainder of this paper presents our methodology for NoSQL database design. As a running example, we consider an application for an on-line social game. This is a typical scenario in which the use of a NoSQL database is suitable. For space reasons, many details have been omitted; they can be found in the full version of the paper [6].

2   The NoAM Abstract Data Model

In this section we present the NoAM abstract data model for NoSQL databases. Preliminarily, we briefly sum up the data models used in NoSQL databases.

NoSQL database systems organize their data according to quite different data models. They usually provide simple read-write data-access operations, which also differ from system to system. Despite this heterogeneity, a few main categories of systems can be identified according to their modeling features [7,20]: key-value stores, extensible record stores, document stores, plus others that are beyond the scope of this paper.

In a *key-value store*, a database is a schemaless collection of key-value pairs, with data access operations on either individual key-value pairs or groups of related pairs (e.g., sharing part of the key). The key (or part of it, thereof) controls data distribution.

In an *extensible record store*, a database is a set of tables, each table is a set of rows, and each row contains a set of attributes (columns), each with a name and a value. Rows in a table are not required to have the same attributes. Data access operations are usually over individual rows, which are units of data distribution and atomic data manipulation.

In a *document store*, a database is a set of documents, each having a complex structure and value. Documents are organized in collections. Operations usually access individual documents, which are units of data distribution and atomic data manipulation.

NoAM (NoSQL Abstract Data Model) is a novel data model for NoSQL databases that exploits the commonalities of the data modeling elements available in the various NoSQL systems and introduces abstractions to balance their differences and variations.

The NoAM data model is defined as follows.

- A NoAM *database* is a set of *collections*. Each collection has a distinct name.
- A collection is a set of *blocks*. Each block in a collection is identified by a *block key*, which is unique within that collection.
- A block is a non-empty set of *entries*. Each entry is a pair $\langle ek, ev \rangle$, where ek is the *entry key* (which is unique within its block) and ev is its value (either complex or scalar), called the *entry value*.

Player

mary	username	"mary"
	firstName	"Mary"
	lastName	"Wilson"
	games[0]	⟨ game : **Game:2345**, opponent : **Player:rick** ⟩
	games[1]	⟨ game : **Game:2611**, opponent : **Player:ann** ⟩

Game

2345	id	2345
	firstPlayer	**Player:mary**
	secondPlayer	**Player:rick**
	rounds[0]	⟨ moves : ..., comments : ... ⟩
	rounds[1]	⟨ moves : ..., actions : ..., spell : ... ⟩

Fig. 1. A sample database in the abstract data model (abridged)

Figure 1 shows a sample NoAM database. In the figure, inner boxes show entries, while outer boxes denote blocks. Collections are shown as groups of blocks.

In NoAM, a *block* is a construct that models a data access and distribution unit, which is a data modeling element available in all NoSQL systems. By "data access unit" we mean that the NoSQL system offers operations to access and manipulate an individual unit at a time, in an atomic, efficient, and scalable way. By "distribution unit" we mean that each unit is entirely stored in a server of the cluster, whereas different units are distributed among the various servers. With reference to major NoSQL categories, a block corresponds to: (i) a record/row, in extensible record stores; (ii) a document, in document stores; or (iii) a group of related key-value pairs, in key-value stores.

Specifically, a block represents a *maximal* data unit for which atomic, efficient, and scalable access operations are provided. Indeed, in the various systems, the access to multiple blocks can be quite inefficient. For example, NoSQL systems do not provide an efficient "join" operation. Moreover, most NoSQL systems do not provide atomic operations over multiple blocks. For example, MongoDB [14] provides only atomic operations over individual documents.

In NoAM, an *entry* models the ability to access and manipulate just a component of a data access unit (i.e., of a block). An entry is a smaller data unit that corresponds to: (i) an attribute, in extensible record stores; (ii) a field, in document stores; or (iii) an individual key-value pair, in key-value stores. Note that entry values can be complex.

Finally, a NoAM *collection* models a collection of data access units. For example, a table in extensible record stores or a document collection in document stores.

In summary, NoAM describes in a uniform way the features of many NoSQL systems. We will use it for an intermediate representation in the design process.

3 Conceptual Modeling and Aggregate Design

The methodology starts, as it is usual in database design, by building a conceptual representation of the data of interest. See, for example, [5]. Following Domain-Driven Design (DDD [9]), which is a popular object-oriented methodology, we assume that the outcome of this activity is a conceptual UML class diagram, defining the entities, value objects, and relationships of the application. An *entity* is a persistent object that has independent existence and is distinguished by a unique *identifier*. A *value object* is a persistent object which is mainly characterized by its value, without an own identifier.

For example, our application should manage various types of objects, including players, games, and rounds. A few representative objects are shown in Fig. 2. (Consider, for now, only boxes and arrows, which denote objects and links between them.)

The methodology proceeds by identifying aggregates [9]. Intuitively, each *aggregate* is a "chunk" of related data, with a complex value and a unique identifier, intended

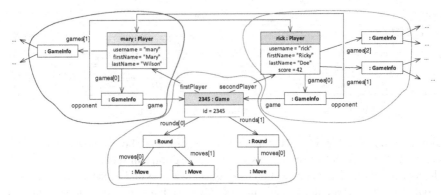

Fig. 2. Sample application objects

to represent a unit of data access and manipulation for an application. Aggregates are also important to support scalability and consistency, as they provide a natural unit for sharding and atomic manipulation of data in distributed environments [11,9]. An important intuition in our approach is that each aggregate can be conveniently mapped to a NoAM block (Sect. 2), which is also a unit of data access and distribution. Aggregates and blocks are however distinct concepts, since they belong, respectively, to the application level and the database level.

Various approaches to aggregate design are possible. For example, in DDD [9], entities and value objects are then grouped into aggregates. Each *aggregate* has an entity as its root, and optionally it contains many value objects. Intuitively, an entity and a group of value objects define an aggregate having a complex structure and value.

Aggregate design is mainly driven by data access operations. In our running example, when a player connects to the application, all data on the player should be retrieved, including an overview of the games she is currently playing. Then, the player can select to continue a game, and data on the selected game should be retrieved. When a player completes a round in a game she is playing, then the game should be updated. These operations suggest that the candidate aggregate classes are players and games. Figure 2 also shows how application objects can be grouped in aggregates. (There, a closed curve denotes the boundary of an aggregate.)

Aggregate design is also driven by consistency needs. Specifically, aggregates should be designed as the units on which atomicity must be guaranteed [11] (with eventual consistency for update operations spanning multiple aggregates [18]). Assume that the application should enforce a rule specifying that a round can be added to a game only if some condition that involves the other rounds of the game is satisfied. A game (comprising, as an aggregate, its rounds) can check the above condition, while an individual round cannot. Therefore, a round cannot be an aggregate by itself.

Let us now illustrate the terminology we use to describe data at the aggregate level. An *application dataset* includes a number of *aggregate classes*, each having a distinct name. The extent of an *aggregate class* is a set of *aggregate objects* (or, simply, *aggregates*). Each aggregate has a *complex value* [1] and a unique *identifier*. In conclusion, our application has aggregate classes **Player** and **Game**.

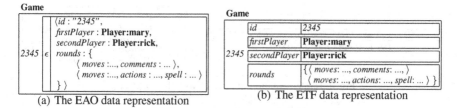

Fig. 3. Data representations (abridged)

4 Data Representation in NoAM and Aggregate Partitioning

In our approach, we use the NoAM data model as an intermediate model between application datasets of aggregates and NoSQL databases. Specifically, an application dataset can be represented by a NoAM database as follows. We represent each aggregate class by means of a distinct collection, and each aggregate object by means of a block. We use the class name to name the collection, and the identifier of the aggregate as block key. The complex value of each aggregate is represented by a set of entries in the corresponding block. For example, the application dataset of Fig. 2 can be represented by the NoAM database shown in Fig. 1. The representation of aggregates as blocks is motivated by the fact that both concepts represent a unit of data access and distribution, but at different abstraction levels. Indeed, NoSQL systems provide efficient, scalable, and consistent (i.e., atomic) operations on blocks and, in turn, this representational choice propagates such qualities to operations on aggregates.

In general, an application dataset can be represented by a NoAM database in several ways. The various data representations for a dataset differ in the choice of the entries used to represent the complex value of each aggregate.

A simple data representation strategy, called *Entry per Aggregate Object* (*EAO*), represents each individual aggregate using a single entry. The entry key is empty. The entry value is the whole complex value of the aggregate. The data representation of the aggregates of Fig. 2 according to the EAO strategy is shown in Fig. 3(a). (For the sake of space, we show only the data representation for the game aggregate object.)

Another strategy, called *Entry per Top-level Field* (*ETF*), represents each aggregate by means of multiple entries, using a distinct entry for each top-level field of the complex value of the aggregate. For each top-level field f of an aggregate o, it employs an entry having as value the value of field f in the complex value of o (with values that can be complex themselves), and as key the field name f. See Fig. 3(b).

The data representation strategies described above can be suited in some cases, but they are often too rigid and limiting. The main limitation of such general representations is that they refer only to the structure of aggregates, and do not take into account the required data access operations. Therefore, they do not usually support the performance of these operations. This motivates the introduction of aggregate partitioning.

In NoAM we represent each aggregate by means of a *partition* of its complex value v, that is, a set E of entries that fully cover v, without redundancy. Each entry represents a distinct portion of the complex value v, characterized by a location in its structure (specified by the entry key) and a value (the entry value). We have already applied this

key (/major/key/-) value
/Game/2345/- { id: "2345", firstPlayer: "Player:mary", ... }

(a) EAO in Oracle NoSQL

key (/major/key/-/minor/key)	value
/Game/2345/-/id	2345
/Game/2345/-/firstPlayer	Player:mary
/Game/2345/-/secondPlayer	Player:rick
/Game/2345/-/rounds	[{ ... }, { ... }]

(b) ETF in Oracle NoSQL

Fig. 4. Implementation in Oracle NoSQL (abridged)

key (/major/key/-/minor/key)	value
Game/2345/-/id	2345
Game/2345/-/firstPlayer	"Player:mary"
Game/2345/-/secondPlayer	"Player:rick"
Game/2345/-/rounds[0]	{moves: ..., comments: ...}
Game/2345/-/rounds[1]	{moves: ..., actions: ..., spell: ...}

Fig. 5. Implementation in Oracle NoSQL for the sample database of Fig. 1 (abridged)

intuition in the ETF data representation (shown in Fig. 3(b)), which uses field names as entry keys and field values as entry values.

Aggregate partitioning can be driven by the following guidelines (which are a variant of guidelines proposed in [5] in the context of logical database design):

- If an aggregate is small in size, or all or most of its data are accessed or modified together, then it should be represented by a single entry.
- Conversely, an aggregate should be partitioned in multiple entries if it is large in size and there are operations that frequently access or modify only specific portions of the aggregate.
- Two or more data elements should belong to the same entry if they are frequently accessed or modified together.
- Two or more data elements should belong to distinct entries if they are usually accessed or modified separately.

The application of the above guidelines suggests a partitioning of aggregates, which we will use to guide the representation in the target database. For example, the data representation for games shown in Fig. 1 is motivated by the following operation: when a player completes a round in a game she is playing, then the aggregate for the game should be updated. In order to update the underlying database, there would be two alternatives: (i) the addition of the round just completed to the aggregate representing the game; (ii) a complete rewrite of the whole game. The former is clearly more efficient. Therefore, each round is a candidate to be represented by an autonomous entry.

5 Implementation

In the last step, the selected data representation in NoAM is implemented using the specific data structures of a target datastore. For the sake of space, we discuss the implementation only with respect to a single system: Oracle NoSQL. We have also implementations for other systems [6].

Oracle NoSQL [16] is a key-value store, in which a database is a schemaless collection of key-value pairs, with a key-value index. *Keys* are structured; they are composed of a *major key* and a *minor key*. The major key is a non-empty sequence of strings. The minor key is a sequence of strings. On the other hand, each *value* is an uninterpreted binary string.

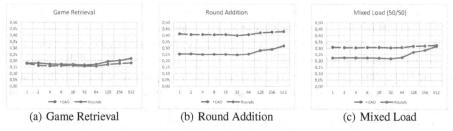

| (a) Game Retrieval | (b) Round Addition | (c) Mixed Load |

Fig. 6. Experimental results

A NoAM database D can be implemented in Oracle NoSQL as follows. We use a key-value pair for each entry $\langle ek, ev \rangle$ in D. The major key is composed of the collection name C and the block key id, while the minor key is a proper coding of the entry key ek. The value associated with this key is a representation of the entry value ev. The value can be either simple or a serialization of a complex value, e.g., in JSON.

For example, Fig. 4(a) and 4(b) show the implementation of the EAO and ETF data representations, respectively, in Oracle NoSQL. Moreover, Fig. 5 shows the implementation of the data representation of Fig. 1.

An implementation can be considered *effective* if aggregates are indeed turned into units of data access and distribution. The effectiveness of this implementation is based on the fact that in Oracle NoSQL the major key controls distribution (sharding is based on it) and consistency (an operation involving multiple key-value pairs can be executed atomically only if the various pairs are over a same major key).

6 Experiments

We now discuss a case study of NoSQL database design, with reference to our running example. For the sake of simplicity, we focus only on the representation of aggregates for games. Data for each game include a few scalar fields and a collection of rounds. The important operations over games are: (1) the retrieval of a game, which should read all the data concerning the game; and (2) the addition of a round to a game. To manage games, the candidate data representations are: (i) using a single entry for each game (as shown in Fig. 3(a), in the following called EAO); (ii) splitting the data for each game in a group of entries, one for each round, and including all the remaining scalar fields in a separate entry (a variant of the representation shown in Fig. 1, called ROUNDS).

We ran a number of experiments to compare the above data representations in situations of different application workloads and database sizes, and measured the running time required by the workloads. The target system was Oracle NoSQL, a key-value store, deployed over Amazon AWS on a cluster of four EC2 servers. (This work was supported by AWS in Education Grant award.)

The results are shown in Fig. 6. Database sizes are in gigabytes, timings are in milliseconds, and points denote the average running time of a single operation. The experiments show that the retrieval of a game (Fig. 6(a)) is always favored by the EAO data representation, for any database size. They also show that the addition of a round to an existing game (Fig. 6(b)) is always favored by the ROUNDS data representation. Finally, the experiments over the mixed workload (Fig. 6(c)) show a general advantage of

ROUNDS over EAO, which however decreases as the database size increases. Overall, it turns out that the ROUNDS data representation is preferable.

We also performed other experiments on a data representation that does not conform to the design guidelines proposed in this paper. Specifically, we divided the rounds of a game into independent key-value pairs, rather than keeping them together in a same block. In this case, the performance of the various operations worsened by an order of magnitude. Moreover, it was not possible to update a game in an atomic way.

Overall, these experiments show that: (i) the design of NoSQL databases should be done with care as it affects considerably the performance and consistency of data access operations, and (ii) our methodology provides an effective tool for choosing among different alternatives.

7   Related Work

Several authors have observed that the development of methodologies and tools supporting NoSQL database design is demanding [2,3,13]. However, this topic has been explored so far only in some on-line papers, published in blogs of practitioners, in terms of best practices and guidelines for modeling NoSQL databases (e.g., [12,15]), and usually with reference to specific systems (e.g., [19,10,17]). To the best of our knowledge, this is the first proposal of a system-independent approach to the design of NoSQL databases, which tackles the problem from a general perspective.

Domain-Driven Design [9] is a widely followed object-oriented approach that includes a notion of aggregate. Also [11] advocates the use of aggregates (there called entities) as units of distribution and consistency. We also propose, for efficiency purposes, to partition aggregates into smaller units of data access and manipulation.

In [4] the authors propose entity groups, a set of entities that, similarly to our aggregates, can be manipulated in an atomic way. They also describe a specific mapping of entity groups to Bigtable [8]. Our approach is based on a more abstract database model, NoAM, and is system independent, as it is targeted to a wide class of NoSQL systems.

References

1. Abiteboul, S., Hull, R., Vianu, V.: Foundations of Databases. Addison-Wesley (1995)
2. Atzeni, P., Jensen, C.S., Orsi, G., Ram, S., Tanca, L., Torlone, R.: The relational model is dead, SQL is dead, and I don't feel so good myself. SIGMOD Record 42(2), 64–68 (2013)
3. Badia, A., Lemire, D.: A call to arms: revisiting database design. SIGMOD Record 40(3), 61–69 (2011)
4. Baker, J., et al.: Megastore: Providing scalable, highly available storage for interactive services. In: CIDR 2011, pp. 223–234 (2011)
5. Batini, C., Ceri, S., Navathe, S.B.: Conceptual Database Design: An Entity-Relationship Approach. Benjamin/Cummings (1992)
6. Bugiotti, F., Cabibbo, L., Torlone, R., Atzeni, P.: Database design for NoSQL systems. Technical Report 210, Università Roma Tre (2014), Available from http://www.dia.uniroma3.it/Plone/ricerca/technical-reports/2014
7. Cattell, R.: Scalable SQL and NoSQL data stores. SIGMOD Record 39(4), 12–27 (2010)
8. Chang, F., et al.: Bigtable: A distributed storage system for structured data. ACM Trans. Comput. Syst. 26(2) (2008)
9. Evans, E.: Domain-Driven Design. Addison-Wesley (2003)
10. Hamrah, M.: Data modeling at scale (2011)

11. Helland, P.: Life beyond distributed transactions: an apostate's opinion. In: CIDR 2007, pp. 132–141 (2007)
12. Katsov, I.: NoSQL data modeling techniques. Highly Scalable Blog (2012)
13. Mohan, C.: History repeats itself: sensible and NonsenSQL aspects of the NoSQL hoopla. In: EDBT, pp. 11–16 (2013)
14. MongoDB Inc. MongoDB, http://www.mongodb.org (accessed 2014)
15. Olier, T.: Database design using key-value tables (2006)
16. Oracle. Oracle NoSQL Database, http://www.oracle.com/technetwork/products/nosqldb (accessed 2014)
17. Patel, J.: Cassandra data modeling best practices (2012)
18. Pritchett, D.: BASE: An ACID alternative. ACM Queue 6(3), 48–55 (2008)
19. Rathore, A.: HBase: On designing schemas for column-oriented data-stores (2009)
20. Sadalage, P.J., Fowler, M.J.: NoSQL Distilled. Addison-Wesley (2012)
21. Stonebraker, M.: Stonebraker on NoSQL and enterprises. Comm. ACM 54(8), 10–11 (2011)

Fixing Up Non-executable Operations in UML/OCL Conceptual Schemas

Xavier Oriol[1], Ernest Teniente[1], and Albert Tort[2]

[1] Department of Service and Information System Engineering
Universitat Politècnica de Catalunya – BarcelonaTech, Barcelona, Spain
{xoriol,teniente}@essi.upc.edu
[2] Sogeti España, Barcelona, Spain
albert.tort@sogeti.com

Abstract. An operation is executable if there is at least one information base in which its preconditions hold and such that the new information base obtained from applying its postconditions satisfies all the integrity constraints. A non-executable operation is useless since it may never be applied. Therefore, identifying non-executable operations and fixing up their definition is a relevant task that should be performed as early as possible in software development. We address this problem in the paper by proposing an algorithm to automatically compute the missing effects in postconditions that would ensure the executability of the operation.

Keywords: Conceptual schema, UML, operations.

1 Introduction

Pursuing the correctness of a conceptual schema is a key activity in software development since mistakes made during conceptual modeling are propagated throughout the whole development life cycle, thus affecting the quality of the final product. The high expressiveness of conceptual schemas requires adopting automated reasoning techniques to support the designer in this important task.

The conceptual schema includes both structural and behavioral knowledge. The structural part of the conceptual schema consists of a taxonomy of classes with their attributes, associations among classes, and integrity constraints which define conditions that the instances of the schema must satisfy [1].

The behavioral part of a conceptual schema contains all operations required by the system. Each operation is defined by means of a contract, which states the changes that occur on the Information Base (IB) when the operation is executed. In UML [2], an *operation contract* is specified by a set of *pre/postconditions*, which states conditions that must hold in the IB before/after the execution of the operation [3]. Such pre/postconditions are usually specified in OCL [4]. An operation is *executable* if there is at least one IB in which its preconditions are satisfied and such that the new IB obtained from applying its postconditions is consistent, i.e. satisfies all the integrity constraints. A non-executable operation is useless and the designer should avoid this situation by modifying its contract.

E. Yu et al. (Eds.): ER 2014, LNCS 8824, pp. 232–245, 2014.

1.1   Motivation

Consider the class diagram in Fig. 1 stating information about medical teams, their expertise, physicians being members or managers of a team and their medical specializations. The OCL constraints provide additional semantics. *SpecialistOfTeamsExpertise* ensures that a physician is not a member of a medical team if he does not have its expertise. *ManagerIsMember* states that all managers of a medical team must also be members of that team. Finally, *ExclusiveMembership* states that members of a critical team can not be members of other teams. We assume that the attributes are primary keys of their owner classes.

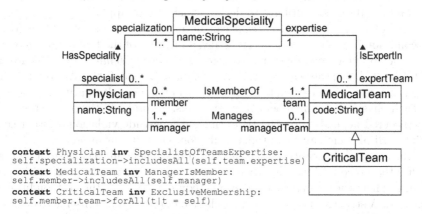

```
context Physician inv SpecialistOfTeamsExpertise:
self.specialization->includesAll(self.team.expertise)
context MedicalTeam inv ManagerIsMember:
self.member->includesAll(self.manager)
context CriticalTeam inv ExclusiveMembership:
self.member.team->forAll(t|t = self)
```

Fig. 1. A UML/OCL schema for the domain of medical teams

Consider now the following UML/OCL operation contracts aimed at inserting and deleting an instance of a *Critical Team*, respectively:

Operation: newCriticalTeam(p: Physician, s: MedicalSpeciality, cd: String)
pre: MedicalTeam.allInstances()->forAll(m|m.code<>cd) and p.specialization->includes(s) and p.managedTeam->isEmpty()
post: CriticalTeam.allInstances()->exists(c|c.oclIsNew() and c.code = cd and c.expertise = s and c.manager->includes(p))

Operation: deleteCriticalTeam(criticalTeam: CriticalTeam)
post: CriticalTeam.allInstances()->excludes(criticalTeam)
–we assume that deleting an instance of a class also deletes its links to other instances.

Both operations are non-executable. *newCriticalTeam* would always violate *ManagerIsMember* while *deleteCriticalTeam* would always violate the minimum cardinality 1 of the team role. This is because *ExclusiveMembership* forces all employees of a critical team to be members only of that team. So, those physicians will have no team when a critical team is deleted through this operation.

Several approaches have been proposed to identify non-executable operations [5,6,7,8,3,9] and most of them should be able to determine the non-executability of the previous operations. However, to our knowledge, none of them is able to provide the designer with additional information on how to modify the operation contracts to make them executable. Note that it is a very hard task to do it manually because of the huge expressive power of UML/OCL schemas.

1.2   Contribution

We propose a new method that allows identifying non-executable operations while providing information about how to fix up the problem. This information is given in terms of the missing effects on the operation postconditions that allow ensuring that all constraints are satisfied after executing the operation. In general, several different sets of missing effects for fixing up an operation may exist and the designer will have to decide which one to apply.

In our example, *newCriticalTeam* can be made executable by adding to its postcondition that the new manager is also a member of the team and removing all his/her previous memberships (to satisfy *ExclusiveMembership*). Regarding *deleteCriticalTeam*, there are several ways to make it executable. We could delete the physicians that were members of the critical team or, alternatively, we could add such physicians as members of other teams. Several additional effects might be considered depending on the IB to prevent a cascade violation of other constraints. All of them can be automatically computed in our approach.

Given an operation contract, our method starts generating a consistent IB that satisfies the precondition. This IB may optionally be manually modified by the designer. Then, the set of structural events required to satisfy the postcondition is computed. A structural event is a basic change in the IB, i.e. a insertion/deletion of an instance of a class or association. If the application of these structural events leads to the violation of an integrity constraint, our method applies a chase-like procedure to determine the additional structural events required to ensure the satisfaction of all the integrity constraints. This is achieved keeping the track of all the different minimal solutions that exist. We consider a solution to be minimal if no subset of the solution is itself a solution. From these results, the designer may know all the different alternatives (if any) that he/she can use to fix up the non-executability of the initial operation contract.

The contribution of this paper is threefold: (1) our method identifies non-executable operations while providing information to fix up this problem in the form of structural events that ensure operation executability when added in the postcondition, (2) our method can be used by current UML/OCL animation tools like USE [5] to find all the different ways to get a new consistent IB whenever a change applied to a previously consistent IB violates some integrity constraint, (3) we contribute to the conceptual-schema centric development grand challenge of *enforcement of integrity constraints in conceptual schemas* [10].

2   Basic Concepts and Notation

Information Base. An information system maintains a representation of the state of a domain in its *Information Base* (IB). The IB is the set of instances of the classes and associations defined in the conceptual schema. The integrity constraints of the conceptual schema define conditions that the IB must satisfy. We say that an IB is consistent if no constraint is violated on it.

Logic Formalization of the Schema. As proposed in [11] we formalize each class C in the schema with attributes $\{A_1, \ldots, A_n\}$ by means of a base atom $c(Oid, A_1, \ldots, A_n)$, and each association R between classes $\{C_1, \ldots, C_k\}$ by means of a base atom $r(C_1, \ldots, C_k)$. The set of instances of the IB is represented by the set of facts about the atoms obtained from such formalization. An atom $v(\overline{x})$ is derived (i.e., a view) if it is defined by a rule of the form: $v(\overline{x}) \leftarrow l_1(\overline{x_1}), \ldots, l_k(\overline{x_k})$ where the variables in $\overline{x}$ are taken from $\overline{x_1}, \ldots, \overline{x_k}$. Each literal l_i is an atom, either positive or negative. Every variable occurring in the head or in a negative atom of the body must also occur in a positive atom of the body.

Structural Events. A *structural event* is an elementary change in the population of a class or association [1]. I.e. a change in the IB. We consider four kinds of structural events: class instance insertion, class instance deletion, association instance insertion and association instance deletion. We denote insertions by ι and deletions by δ. Given a base atom $P(\overline{x})$, where $\overline{x}$ stands for the set of variables $x_1, \ldots, x_n$, insertion structural events are formally defined by the formula $\forall \overline{x}(\iota P(\overline{x}) \leftrightarrow P^n(\overline{x}) \wedge \neg P(\overline{x}))$, while deletion structural events by $\forall \overline{x}(\delta P(\overline{x}) \leftrightarrow P(\overline{x}) \wedge \neg P^n(\overline{x}))$, where P^n stands for predicate P evaluated in the new IB, i.e. the one obtained after applying the change.

Dependencies. A *Tuple-Generating Dependency (TGD)* is a formula of the form $\forall \overline{x}, \overline{z}(\varphi(\overline{x}, \overline{z}) \rightarrow \exists \overline{y} \psi(\overline{x}, \overline{y}))$, where $\varphi(\overline{x}, \overline{z})$ is a conjunction of base literals (i.e. positive or negative atoms) and built-in literals (i.e. arithmetic comparisons) and $\psi(\overline{x}, \overline{y})$ is a conjunction of base atoms. A *denial constraint* is a special type of TGD of the form $\forall \overline{x}(\varphi(\overline{x}) \rightarrow \perp)$, in which the conclusion only contains the $\perp$ atom, which cannot be made true.

A *Disjunctive Embedded Dependency (DED)* is a TGD where the conclusion, i.e. $\psi(\overline{x}, \overline{y})$, is a disjunction of base atoms. A *Repair-Generating Dependency (RGD)* is a DED where the premise, i.e. $\varphi(\overline{x}, \overline{z})$, contains necessarily at least one structural event and optionally a derived negative atom, whereas the conclusion is either a single structural event or a disjunction of several structural events, i.e. it has the form $Ev_1 \vee \ldots \vee Ev_k$, where each Ev_i is a structural event. An *Event-Dependency Constraint (EDC)* is an RGD in which the conclusion only contains the atom $\perp$.

3   Determining the Missing Effects of Postconditions

Given a UML/OCL structural schema and an operation Op to be analyzed, our goal is to determine whether Op is executable and to provide information to fix up the problem if this is not the case. Our method starts by automatically generating a consistent IB satisfying the operation precondition to test whether Op is executable in such IB. The designer could also define his preferred initial IB from scratch or by modifying the automatically generated one.

Then, our method translates the postcondition of such operation into a set of structural events $EV = (Ev_1, \ldots, Ev_k)$. If the IB resulting from applying EV to the initial state is consistent, then Op is executable. Otherwise, our method looks for additional *repairing* structural events, $RE = (Re_1 \ldots, Re_m)$, such that we get a consistent IB when applying $EV \cup RE$. We want to keep the set RE minimal in the sense that there is no $RE' \subsetneq RE$ such that $EV \cup RE'$ leads also to a consistent IB. Note that, in particular, Op is executable if RE is an empty set of structural events.

In general, several repairs RE_i may exist since there may be different ways of satisfying an integrity constraint. It may also happen that no RE is obtained. That means that EV cannot be applied to the IB without necessarily violating any constraint. I.e., there is no way to fix up the executability of the operation by just considering additional effects in the postcondition.

Our method computes the different repairing sets RE_i by means of the following steps: (1) encoding the UML/OCL conceptual schema into logic, (2) obtaining a set of rules, the repair-generating dependencies, that allows identifying when a constraint is violated and computing the structural events for repairing such violation, and (3) chasing the repair-generating dependencies to obtain the repairing sets RE_i.

3.1   Encoding the UML/OCL Conceptual Schema into Logic

We must encode first the UML/OCL conceptual schema into logic as proposed in [11]. Recall that each class C in the schema with attributes $\{A_1, \ldots, A_n\}$ is encoded as $c(Oid, A_1, \ldots, A_n)$, each association R between classes $\{C_1, \ldots, C_k\}$ is encoded as $r(C_1, \ldots, C_k)$ and each association class R between $\{C_1, \ldots, C_k\}$ and with the attributes $\{A_1, \ldots, A_n\}$ as $r(R, C_1, \ldots, C_k, A_1, \ldots, A_n)$. Without loss of generality, we will use the primary key attributes of classes as their *oid*.

As an example, the schema in Fig. 1 would be encoded as follows:

$physician(P), medicalSpeciality(MS), hasSpeciality(P, MS), medicalTeam(T)$

$isExpertIn(T, MS), isMemberOf(P, T), manages(P, T), criticalTeam(T)$

Each UML/OCL integrity constraint is encoded as a denial constraint as proposed in [11]. For example, the encoding of the first two OCL constraints in our running example is the following:

$$manages(P, T) \land \neg isMemberOf(P, T) \to \bot \tag{1}$$

$$isMemberOf(P, T) \land isExpertIn(T, MS) \land \neg hasSpeciality(P, MS) \to \bot \tag{2}$$

Rule 1 states that there may not be a medical team T managed by a physician P who is not a member of T, while rule 2 prevents a physician being a member of a medical team if his/her specializations do not include the expertise of the team.

To ensure that denial constraints are defined only in terms of base predicates, we assume that each OCL integrity constraint C has the form `context C inv:` `ExpBool`, where `ExpBool` is defined according to the following syntax rules (where `OpComp` is any OCL comparison operator):

```
ExpBool      ::= ExpBool ∧ ExpBool       | ExpBool ∨ ExpBool
             | ExpOp
ExpOp        ::= Path->excludesAll(Path) | Var.Member->includesAll(Path)
             | Path->excludes(Path)      | Var.Member->includes(Var)
             | Path->isEmpty()           | Path->forAll(Var| ExpBool)
             | Path OpComp Constant      | not Path.oclIsKindOf(Class)
             | Path OpComp Path          | Path.oclIsKindOf(Class)
Path         ::= Var.Navigation          | Class.allInstances().Navigation
Navigation ::= Member.Navigation         | oclAsType(Class).Navigation
             | Member                    | Attribute
             | oclAsType(Class)
```

We also encode into logic the graphical and structural constraints of the UML schema, i.e. primary key constraints, referential integrity constraints, identifiers of association classes, disjointness and completeness integrity constraints and maximum cardinality constraints (see [11] for the details of this encoding).

Assuming that denial constraints are defined only in terms of base predicates is not a restrictive assumption since the constraints we can handle are a superset of those constraints specified according to the patterns defined in [12], which have been shown to be useful for defining around the 60% of the integrity constraints found in real schemas. The only exception is the path inclusion constraint pattern for which we can only specify the situations that are compliant to our grammar.

3.2   Obtaining Repair-Generating Dependencies

The next step is to obtain the repair-generating dependencies (RGDs) that will allow us to identify the situations where an integrity constraint is violated by the current set of structural events under consideration and also to compute the sets of structural events RE_i which ensure that applying $EV \cup RE_i$ to the initial IB leads to a new consistent IB.

We start by describing the transformation required by general UML/OCL constraints, i.e. those that have been encoded into logic. Then, we show how to handle minimum cardinality constraints.

Dependencies for General UML/OCL Constraints. The RGDs for a general UML/OCL constraint ic are obtained in two steps. First, we generate the Event-Dependency Constraints (EDCs) for ic. Then, for each EDC we obtain a corresponding RGD whenever possible.

Generating Event-Dependency Constraints. Each denial constraint obtained as a result of the logic encoding of the UML/OCL constraint will be translated into several dependencies. Each such dependency will prevent a different situation in which the constraint would be violated in the new IB. This is achieved by replacing each literal in the denial by the expression that allows us to compute it in the new IB. Positive and negative literals must be handled differently according to the following formulas:

$$\forall \overline{x}(P^n(\overline{x}) \leftrightarrow (\iota P(\overline{x}) \wedge \neg P(\overline{x})) \vee (\neg \delta P(\overline{x}) \wedge P(\overline{x}))) \tag{3}$$

$$\forall \overline{x}(\neg P^n(\overline{x}) \leftrightarrow (\neg \iota P(\overline{x}) \wedge \neg P(\overline{x})) \vee (\delta P(\overline{x}) \wedge P(\overline{x}))) \tag{4}$$

Rule 3 states that an atom $P(\overline{x})$ (e.g. *medicalTeam(neurology)*) will be true in the new IB if it was false in the old IB but its insertion structural event has been applied (e.g. the medical team *neurology* did not exist in the previous IB but it has been inserted right now) or if it was already true in the old IB and its deletion structural event has not been applied (e.g. the medical team *neurology* existed in the previous IB and it has not been removed). In an analogous way, rule 4 states that $P(\overline{x})$ will be false in the new IB if it was already false and it has not been inserted or if it has been deleted.

Algorithm 1. getEventDependencies(*premise* → ⊥)

$EDC := \{\emptyset \rightarrow \bot\}$
for all Literal P in *premise* **do**
$\quad EDC_{Pre} := EDC$
$\quad EDC := \emptyset$
$\quad$**for all** Dependency $premise_{Pre} \rightarrow \bot$ in EDC_{Pre} **do**
$\quad\quad$**if** P is Built-in-literal **then**
$\quad\quad\quad EDC := EDC \cup \{premise_{Pre} \wedge P \rightarrow \bot \}$
$\quad\quad$**else**
$\quad\quad\quad$**if** P is positive **then**
$\quad\quad\quad\quad EDC := EDC \cup \{premise_{Pre} \wedge P \wedge \neg\delta P \rightarrow \bot\} \cup \{premise_{Pre} \wedge \iota P \wedge \neg P \rightarrow \bot\}$
$\quad\quad\quad$**else**
$\quad\quad\quad\quad EDC := EDC \cup \{premise_{Pre} \wedge P \wedge \delta P \rightarrow \bot\} \cup \{premise_{Pre} \wedge \neg\iota P \wedge \neg P \rightarrow \bot\}$
$\quad\quad\quad$**end if**
$\quad\quad$**end if**
$\quad$**end for**
end for
EDC.removeFirst()
return EDC

By applying the substitutions above, we get a set of EDCs that state all possible ways to violate a constraint by means of the structural events of the schema. EDCs are grounded on the idea of *insertion event rules* which were defined in [13] to perform integrity checking in deductive databases. In general, we will get $2^k - 1$ EDCs for each denial constraint dc, where k is the number of literals in dc. The pseudocode of the algorithm *getEventDependencies*, which performs this transformation, is shown in Algorithm 1.

Intuitively, the algorithm interprets each literal P as P^n and performs an unfolding according to the definition given by formulas 3 and 4. The first dependency generated corresponds to a dependency that would be activated just in case the constraint was violated in the previous IB. Taking advantage of the guaranteed consistency of the initial IB generated by our method, we can safely delete such dependency.

Applying Algorithm 1 to the constraint *ManagerIsMember*, which has been encoded into the denial constraint $manages(P, T) \wedge \neg isMemberOf(P, T) \rightarrow \bot$, we get the following event-dependency constraints:

$$manages(P,T) \wedge \neg\delta manages(P,T) \wedge isMemberOf(P,T) \wedge \delta isMemberOf(P,T) \rightarrow \bot \qquad (5)$$

$$\neg manages(P,T) \wedge \iota manages(P,T) \wedge \neg isMemberOf(P,T) \wedge \neg \iota isMemberOf(P,T) \rightarrow \bot \qquad (6)$$

$$\neg manages(P,T) \wedge \iota manages(P,T) \wedge isMemberOf(P,T) \wedge \delta isMemberOf(P,T) \rightarrow \bot \qquad (7)$$

Rule 5 is an EDC stating that the constraint will be violated for a physician p and a team t if we delete the fact that p is a member of t but we do not delete at the same time that p is a manager of t. EDC 6 identifies a violation to happen when a new manager p of t is inserted without inserting p as a member of t at the same time. EDC 7 states that *ManagerIsMember* will be violated if we delete the membership association among p and t while inserting the manage association.

Obtaining Repair-Generating Dependencies (RGDs). EDCs let us identifying the situations where an integrity constraint is violated as a consequence of the application of a set of structural events. However, they do not directly provide any information on how this violation could be repaired by considering additional structural events. We transform EDCs into RGDs for this purpose by means of the algorithm *getRepairDependencies*, reported in Algorithm 2.

Intuitively, each negated structural event in the premise of the dependency constraint represents a different way to repair the constraint. Therefore, the negated structural events of the constraint are removed from the premise and placed positively in the conclusion. If there is more than one negated structural event in the premise, the conclusion of the RGD will be a disjunction of structural events. Note that we will obtain exactly one RGD for each EDC.

Applying Algorithm 2 to the EDCs defined by the rules 5, 6, 7, we get the following RGDs:

$$manages(P,T) \land isMemberOf(P,T) \land \delta isMemberOf(P,T) \to \delta manages(P,T) \qquad (8)$$

$$\neg manages(P,T) \land \iota manages(P,T) \land \neg isMemberOf(P,T) \to \iota isMemberOf(P,T) \qquad (9)$$

$$\neg manages(P,T) \land \iota manages(P,T) \land isMemberOf(P,T) \land \delta isMemberOf(P,T) \to \bot \qquad (10)$$

Rule 8 is an RGD stating that when the structural event $\delta isMemberOf(p,t)$ occurs in an IB where p is a manager of t, then it is also required the structural event $\delta manages(p,t)$ to take place in order ensure that the constraint *ManagerIsMember* will not be violated. In a similar way, RGD 9 establishes that $\iota manages(p,t)$ requires $\iota isMemberOf(p,t)$ to take place as well. Rule 10 is exactly the EDC 7 meaning that no RGD can be obtained from it. That is, there is no possible way to repair the situation identified by EDC 7. In other words, structural events $\iota manages(p,t)$ and $\delta isMemberOf(p,t)$ cannot happen together.

Algorithm 2. getRepairDependencies($premise \to \bot$)

```
new_Conclusion := ⊥
new_Premise := ⊤
for all Literal P in premise do
    if P is negated structural event then
        new_Conclusion := new_Conclusion ∨ positive(P)
    else
        new_Premise := new_Premise ∧ P
    end if
end for
return  new_Premise → new_Conclusion
```

Dependencies for Minimum Cardinality Constraints. Repair-generating dependencies for min. cardinality constraints can be directly generated by taking advantage of the precise semantics of this constraint. The following rules summarize how to obtain such RGDs for a minimum cardinality constraint of 1 in a binary association R between members C_1, C_2:

$$c_1(Oid_1, ...) \land \neg someRelationAlife(Oid_1) \rightarrow \delta c_1(Oid_1, ...) \lor \iota r(Oid_1, Oid_2) \tag{11}$$
$$someRelationAlife(Oid_1) \leftarrow r(Oid_1, Oid_2) \land \neg \delta r(Oid_1, Oid_2)$$
$$\neg c_1(Oid_1, ...) \land \iota c_1(Oid_1, ...) \rightarrow \iota r(Oid_1, Oid_2) \tag{12}$$

Applying such patterns to the minimum cardinality constraint on the role *manager* in the example of Figure 1, we would get the following RGDs:

$$medicalTeam(T) \land \neg someManagerAlife(T) \rightarrow \delta medicalTeam(T) \lor \iota manages(P, T) \tag{13}$$
$$someManagerAlife(T) \leftarrow manages(P, T) \land \neg \delta manages(P, T)$$
$$\neg medicalTeam(T) \land \iota medicalTeam(T) \rightarrow \iota manages(P, T) \tag{14}$$

RGD 13 states that if the IB contains a medical team for which all its manages associations have been deleted, then either we delete the medical team or we insert a new manages association in order to satisfy the minimum cardinality constraint. We know whether it has at least one manage association which have not been deleted by means of the derived atom *someManagerAlife*. RGD 14 asserts that whenever a medical team is created a manage association for this team must be created as well.

3.3 Chasing Repair-Generating Dependencies

Once we have the *RGDs*, we need an initial information base *IB* and the initial structural events *EV* in order to compute which are the missing structural event sets RE_i such that $EV \cup RE_i$ leads the current *IB* to a new consistent IB. We first explain how to obtain such initial *IB* and *EV* and then, how do we chase the *RGDs* using *IB* and *EV* to compute the different RE_i.

Obtaining the Initial IB and Structural Events. We need a consistent IB compliant with the precondition of the operation to test. There exist several proposals that allow obtaining such IB automatically from an OCL precondition. Most of these methods are based on translating the schema in some logic formalism and check for a witness of the satisfiability of the precondition. We can use any of them for our purposes. In our example, by applying [8] to the precondition of *newCriticalTeam* we would get:

medicalTeam($t1$)	*medicalSpeciality*(*neurology*)
isExpertIn($t1$, *neurology*)	*manages*(*mary*, $t1$)
physician(*john*)	*physician*(*mary*)
isMemberOf(*john*, $t1$)	*isMemberOf*(*mary*, $t1$)
hasSpeciality(*john*, *neurology*)	*hasSpeciality*(*mary*, *neurology*)

Now, to obtain the structural events *EV* we use the mapping from OCL postcondition expressions to structural events that was initially proposed in [8], and which is briefly summarized in Table 1.

Table 1. Summarized mapping from OCL to structural events

OclExpression	Generated Structural Events
Class.allInstances()->exists(x|x.oclIsNew() ...)	$\iota Class(x,...)$ and superclasses
Class.allInstances()->excludes(x)	$\delta Class(x,...)$ and super/subclasses
x.oclIsTypeOf(Class)	$\iota Class(x,...)$ and superclasses
not(x.oclIsTypeOf(Class))	$\delta Class(x,...)$ and subclasses
x.memberEnd->includes(y)	$\iota Association(x,y)$
x.memberEnd->excludes(y)	$\delta Association(x,y)$

Where any $\delta Class(x,...)$ is followed by several $\delta Association(x,y)$ corresponding to the association links of x as a member of Class.

By applying this mapping to the postcondition of *newCriticalTeam* in the previously shown IB, we get the structural events:

$$EV = \{\iota criticalTeam(t2), \iota medicalTeam(t2), \iota isExpertIn(t2, neurology), \iota manages(john, t2)\}$$

Chasing RGDs to Compute Repairing Structural Events. We must now chase the RGDs to determine the additional repairing sets of structural events RE_i that make the application of $EV \cup RE_i$ to the initial IB leading to a consistent IB'. Intuitively, an RGD is chased by querying its premise on the initial IB and the set of structural events under consideration (i.e. EV and the subset of RE_i already determined). Then, for each set of constants satisfying this query, one of the structural events in the conclusion must belong to $EV \cup RE_i$ to ensure that the constraint from which we have obtained the RGD is not violated. Disjunctions in the conclusion correspond to alternative solutions that keep the IB consistent. Existential variables in the conclusion are handled either by considering an existing constant in $IB \cup EV \cup RE_i$ or by inventing a new one (VIPs approach [14]). They also define different possible ways of repairing the constraint. This chasing process is formalized in Algorithm 3.

Algorithm 3. chaseRGDs(*RGDs, IB, EV, RE, Result*)

$D := getViolatedDependency(RGDs, IB, EV, RE)$
if $D = null$ **then**
    $Result.add(RE)$
else
    for all Literal R in $(D.conclusion)$ **do**
        $\sigma_{rs} := getRepairingSubstitutions(R, IB, EV, RE)$
        for all σ_r in σ_{rs} **do**
            chaseRGDs($RGDs, IB, EV, RE \cup \{R\sigma_r\}, Result$)
        end for
    end for
end if

Initially, the algorithm is called with $RE = \emptyset$ and $Result = \emptyset$. The *getViolatedDependency* function looks for a dependency being violated and returns it substituting its variables for the constants that provoke the violation. If no dependency is violated, then $EV \cup RE$ is already executable.

To repair the dependency we try all the possible literals in its conclusion. Moreover, for each of these literals, we try all the suitable variable-to-constant substitutions for the existential variables of the literal. This is achieved by means of the *getRepairingSubstitutions* function which implements the VIPs approach, thus, returning as many different substitutions as different constants may take each variable according to the currently used constants in $IB \cup EV \cup RE$.

Once the dependency is repaired, we continue looking for other/new violated dependencies by means of a recursive call to the same algorithm.

We illustrate this execution by applying the operation *newCriticalTeam*, using the previously obtained *IB* and *EV*. The relevant RGDs to facilitate understanding of the example are the following:

$$\neg medicalTeam(T) \wedge \iota medicalTeam(T) \rightarrow \iota manages(P, T) \tag{15}$$

$$\neg manages(P, T) \wedge \iota manages(P, T) \wedge \neg isMemberOf(P, T) \rightarrow \iota isMemberOf(P, T) \tag{16}$$

$$\neg criticalTeam(C) \wedge \iota criticalTeam(C) \wedge \neg isMemberOf(P, C) \wedge \iota isMemberOf(P, C) \wedge$$
$$isMemberOf(P, T) \wedge T <> C \rightarrow \delta isMemberOf(P, T) \tag{17}$$

The algorithm starts looking for a violated RGD. Although the premise of 15 holds, this RGD is not violated because its conclusion is already included in *EV*. Thus, the algorithm picks 16. Indeed, the premise of 16 evaluates to true because of the literal $\iota manages(john, t2)$. Therefore, its conclusion $\iota isMemberOf(john, t2)$ must be included in *RE*. In this way, the method repairs a violation of the *ManagerIsMember* constraint.

Now, because of this new literal in *RE*, the premise of 17 holds. Indeed, the literals $\iota CriticalTeam(t2)$, $\iota isMemberOf(john, t2)$, $isMemberOf(john, t1)$ produce a violation. For repairing it, we add the conclusion $\delta isMemberOf(john, t1)$ to *RE*. In this case, we have repaired a violation of the *ExclusiveMembership* constraint that was produced when repairing *ManagerIsMember*.

Finally, no more RGDs are violated, so, the result consists of just one *RE*:

$$RE = \{\iota isMemberOf(john, t2), \delta isMemberOf(john, t1)\}$$

From this result, the designer may realize that the postcondition of *newCriticalTeam* is underspecified since it does not state that the new manager of the team must also be added as a member of the team and that the old membership of this manager must be deleted. These additional effects are required to satisfy the *ManagerIsMember* and the *ExclusiveMembership* constraints.

It is worth noting that this kind of feedback is very relevant for the designer to ensure that all the operations of the schema are executable since in general it is very hard to manually identify how to fix the non-executability of an operation.

4   Experiments

We have implemented a prototype tool of our approach to show the scalability of our method in real conceptual schemas. The analysis of an operation in our tool is performed as follows: (1) loading a conceptual schema from an XMI file, (2) selecting the operation to analyze, (3) optionally modifying the automatically generated initial IB in which to apply the operation, (4) determining the sets of minimal structural events RE_i that, when applied together with the postcondition, bring the current IB to a new consistent IB.

We have applied this tool to help us define correct operations in the DBLP case study [15], whose structural conceptual schema has 17 classes, 9 specialization hierarchies, 18 associations and 25 OCL integrity constraints. When translated to our logical formalization this schema amounts to 128 denial constraints.

We have defined 11 different operations aimed at adding or removing publications from the schema (like new journal paper, or new edited book) and we have checked whether they were executable. These experiments have been performed with a C# implementation of the reasoning method on an Intel Core i7-4700HQ 2.4GHz processor, 8GB of RAM with Windows 8.1 and the average execution time has been about 50-55 seconds.

We have repeated the experiments by removing randomly some statement in the postcondition of each operation and checked the time required to compute the missing structural events. We have found that our tool has been able to recompute exactly the events corresponding to the missing statements with a similar amount of time as before.

We summarize our results in Table 2 by showing the results for those operations having a larger number of structural events in the postcondition. The first column states the name of the operation. The second column gives the number of instances in the initial IB satisfying the precondition of each operation and used by the test. The third column shows the number of structural events in the postcondition. The last three columns show, respectively, the time (in seconds) required to check executability of the operation and to compute the missing structural events when 1 or 2 statements were removed from the postcondition.

Table 2. Execution time for some of the operations in DBLP

Operation	Initial IB	Struct. events	Time	1 Miss	2 Miss
newAuthoredBook	6	5	50.72s	50.86s	52.21s
newEditedBook	5	6	50.91s	85.21s	52,80s
newBookSeriesIssue	6	9	51.74s	59.87s	52.64s
newJournalPaper	14	5	51.23s	51.68s	52.61s
delAuthoredBook	11	5	52.31s	50.64s	51.39s
delBookchapter	10	4	52.96s	50.58s	50.97s
delBookSeriesIssue	16	8	52.23s	50.92s	51.11s
delEditedBook	11	6	50.92s	50.86s	51.11s
delJournalPaper	17	5	51.23s	51.47s	51.34s
		Average	51.58s	55.79s	51.80s

5 Related Work

Previous proposals can be classified according to the following approaches: (1) checking desirable properties of operations, (2) animating the operations to explore their behavior, and (3) automatically generating operations contracts.

Checking Desirable Properties of Operations. Several techniques have been proposed to check desirable properties of an OCL operation, such as executability [6,8,3,9]. These techniques are fully automatic and aimed at obtaining a consistent IB that proves the property being checked, i.e. an IB where the operation can be executed when checking for executability. However, if no such IB is obtained, no feedback is provided to the designer to help him/her fix up the operation definition. This is, in fact, its main drawback as compared to ours.

Operation Animation. Some proposals analyze the operation execution by means of animation [5,7,16]. Animation is achieved by simulating the execution of an operation in a specific IB and checking whether this execution violates some integrity constraint [5,7] or by reducing the satisfaction of the postcondition and class invariants to SAT [16]. Similarly to the previous approach, no feedback is provided to the designer to allow him/her to find the additional structural events required not to violate any constraint. As we have seen, having to do this manually is time consuming and error prone due to the difficulty of having to analyze by hand all the interactions among possible violations of the constraints.

Automatic Generation of Operation Contracts. [17] addresses the automatic generation of basic operation contracts from the structural part of the conceptual schema which are ensured to be executable regarding the constraints of the class diagram and some simple provided stereotypes. However, this proposal is not able to deal with general OCL constraints nor with user-defined domain events as we do in this paper.

Summarizing, we may conclude that the approach we present in this paper is the first one that, given an operation contract and an IB, is able to automatically compute all missing structural events that should be covered by the postcondition to make the operation executable.

6   Conclusions

Ensuring the quality of a conceptual schema is a critical challenge in software development, particularly in the context of Model-Driven Development where the software being developed is the result of an evolution of models. For this reason, several techniques have been proposed to check the correctness of the behavioral conceptual schema. Most of these techniques are just concerned with identifying non-executable operations from the schema.

In contrast, we have proposed an approach both for identifying non-executable operations and also for providing the designer with information for fixing up the problem. This information is given in terms of missing structural events not initially stated in the operation postcondition, that ensure operation executability when taken into account. Thus, we extend previous approaches by providing the designer with relevant feedback when a non-executable operation is detected.

We have also implemented a prototype tool of our approach to analyze the scalability of our method in practice. We have shown that our tool is able to perform several complex tests in the conceptual schema of the DBLP case study in an average time of about 50 to 55 seconds.

This work can be extended in several directions. First, we would like to adapt our method to other modeling languages by taking advantage of the fact that our underlying reasoning process is based on a logic formalization. Second, we would like to analyze the applicability of the dependencies proposed in this paper to other constraint-related problems such as integrity-constraint checking.

Acknowledgements. This work has been partly supported by the Ministerio de Ciencia e Innovación under project TIN2011-24747 and by the FI grant from the Secreteria d'Universitats i Recerca of the Generalitat de Catalunya.

References

1. Olivé, A.: Conceptual Modeling of Information Systems. Springer, Berlin (2007)
2. Object Management Group (OMG): Unified Modeling Language (UML) Superstructure Specification, version 2.4.1 (2011), http://www.omg.org/spec/UML/
3. Cabot, J., Clarisó, R., Riera, D.: Verifying UML/OCL operation contracts. In: Leuschel, M., Wehrheim, H. (eds.) IFM 2009. LNCS, vol. 5423, pp. 40–55. Springer, Heidelberg (2009)
4. Object Management Group (OMG): Object Constraint Language (UML), version 2.3.1 (2012), http://www.omg.org/spec/OCL/
5. Hamann, L., Hofrichter, O., Gogolla, M.: On integrating structure and behavior modeling with OCL. In: France, R.B., Kazmeier, J., Breu, R., Atkinson, C. (eds.) MODELS 2012. LNCS, vol. 7590, pp. 235–251. Springer, Heidelberg (2012)
6. Soeken, M., Wille, R., Drechsler, R.: Verifying dynamic aspects of UML models. In: Design, Automation Test in Europe Conference Exhibition (DATE), pp. 1–6 (2011)
7. Roldán, M., Durán, F.: Dynamic validation of OCL constraints with mOdCL. In: International Workshop on OCL and Textual Modelling (2011)
8. Queralt, A., Teniente, E.: Reasoning on UML conceptual schemas with operations. In: van Eck, P., Gordijn, J., Wieringa, R. (eds.) CAiSE 2009. LNCS, vol. 5565, pp. 47–62. Springer, Heidelberg (2009)
9. Brucker, A.D., Wolff, B.: HOL-OCL: A formal proof environment for UML/OCL. In: Fiadeiro, J.L., Inverardi, P. (eds.) FASE 2008. LNCS, vol. 4961, pp. 97–100. Springer, Heidelberg (2008)
10. Olivé, A.: Conceptual schema-centric development: A grand challenge for information systems research. In: Pastor, Ó., Falcão e Cunha, J. (eds.) CAiSE 2005. LNCS, vol. 3520, pp. 1–15. Springer, Heidelberg (2005)
11. Queralt, A., Teniente, E.: Verification and validation of UML conceptual schemas with OCL constraints. ACM TOSEM 21(2), 13 (2012)
12. Costal, D., Gómez, C., Queralt, A., Raventós, R., Teniente, E.: Improving the definition of general constraints in UML. Software & Systems Modeling 7(4), 469–486 (2008)
13. Olivé, A.: Integrity constraints checking in deductive databases. In: Proceedings of the 17th Int. Conference on Very Large Data Bases (VLDB), pp. 513–523 (1991)
14. Farré, C., Teniente, E., Urpí, T.: Checking query containment with the CQC method. Data & Knowledge Engineering 53(2), 163–223 (2005)
15. Planas, E., Olivé, A.: The DBLP case study (2006), http://guifre.lsi.upc.edu//DBLP.pdf
16. Krieger, M.P., Knapp, A., Wolff, B.: Automatic and efficient simulation of operation contracts. In: 9th International Conference on Generative Programming and Component Engineering, GPCE 2010, pp. 53–62. ACM, New York (2010)
17. Albert, M., Cabot, J., Gómez, C., Pelechano, V.: Generating operation specifications from UML class diagrams: A model transformation approach. Data & Knowledge Engineering 70(4), 365–389 (2011)

Generic Data Manipulation in a Mixed Global/Local Conceptual Model

Scott Britell[1], Lois M.L. Delcambre[1], and Paolo Atzeni[2]

[1] Department of Computer Science, Portland State University
Portland, OR 97207 USA
britell@cs.pdx.edu, lmd@pdx.edu
[2] Dipartimento di Ingegneria, Università Roma Tre
Via della Vasca Navale 79, 00146 Roma, Italy
atzeni@dia.uniroma3.it

Abstract. Modern content management systems allow end-user schema creation, which can result in schema heterogeneity within a system. Building functionality to create and modify data must keep pace with this heterogeneity, but the cost of constant development is high. In this paper, we present a novel approach that extends our previous integration system that uses domain structures—global schema fragments—and local type and integration operators by introducing new local record operators and global insert and update operators. We present two widgets that use the new operators: (i) a generic clone widget that allows users to selectively clone records shown in a global widget while creating new local records; (ii) a generic clone exploration widget that allows users to browse the *CloneOf* relationships and reason about how different cloned records and structures have evolved. We demonstrate our system with a running example of the clone and exploration widgets in a robotics educational repository.

1 Introduction

Using modern content management systems, it is easy for end-users to define schemas for their data, e.g., by defining new content types. In a course repository, different instructors might structure their courses in different ways as reflected in their schemas. In such a setting, we have been working to facilitate the construction of generic widgets (such as a structured navigation bar) that work for all relevant schemas in the site. Our approach uses global schema fragments (what we call *domain structures*) coupled with simple mappings from the domain structure to the various local schemas. Generic widgets can then be implemented against the domain structure [4]. One key feature of the work is that query results can include type information from the various local schemas (because users may wish to see local types/names), thus mixing the local conceptual model with the global one.

We consider how to enable generic widgets to insert and update local data—including local data that is not mapped to the global schema. As an example, a

E. Yu et al. (Eds.): ER 2014, LNCS 8824, pp. 246–259, 2014.

user might want to copy and modify existing content. The challenge then is how to generically modify data in the various local schemas using a domain structure that is (by design) not complete. That is, how can we access local schema and insert local data that sit outside the mappings.

In this paper, we extend our information integration system to support local insert and update from the global level, including local information not present in the global schema. We present a motivating example of a clone widget for an educational repository in Section 2. In Section 3, we review our approach to information integration that mixes the global and local schemas and define five new operators that support local insert and update through domain structures. We describe how we implement widgets that insert and update local data using these operators in Section 4. Section 5 presents related work and Section 6 concludes with suggestions for future work.

2   Motivating Example

We first describe a repository of educational materials to motivate this work. The repository contains schemas for different course structures as well as books and other educational materials. One course schema is shown in Figure 1 where a course has units and a unit has lessons. A book schema (shown in Figure 2) has chapters and a chapter has sections.

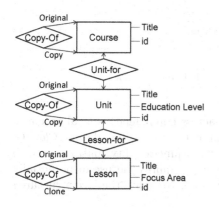

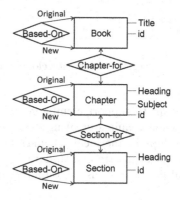

Fig. 1. The course local schema   **Fig. 2.** The book local schema

Our educational repository hosts master curricula that have been created to help teachers who are new to a subject. These curricula are often used alongside a professional development program where new teachers spend a week or two learning the materials in order to be ready to teach students. After using the materials as-is once or twice, teachers may find that they prefer to use the materials in a different order, add additional materials, or omit some materials.

It is useful for them to create their own copy of the course which they then modify to suit their specific needs. These same actions may also happen with a book. Our local schemas shown in Figures 1 and 2 include a *CopyOf* and *Based-On* relationship, respectively, to track these copy/modify actions.

As an example, in the STEMRobotics[1] repository, the "STEM Robotics 101" course has been taught in numerous professional development programs. It is used by teachers throughout the United States in middle and high school classrooms as well as after-school programs. In many cases, a teacher has decided to rearrange and augment the master curriculum. To facilitate this, we created the drag-and-drop cloning widget shown in Figure 3. The left side of the figure shows a clone of the "STEM Robotics 101" course being created. The user has selected the course guide, the classroom resources, all of unit 3, and lessons 1, 2, and 6 from unit 1. The user also moved unit 3 to come before unit 1. The right side of Figure 3 shows a similar process occurring for a book.

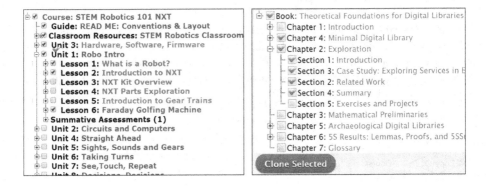

Fig. 3. Widgets for cloning a course (left) and a book (right)

We want to support cloning generically, across heterogeneous local schemas. But cloning requires creating new local content (such as populating *CloneOf* relationships in the local schema) so the global functionality must be able to perform local inserts and updates. And cloning requires the use of potentially all local fields—not just those integrated in order to create the tree structured widget.

Seeing how the master course has been cloned and modified is important to the original author because new materials added to clones can be valuable for other teachers using the original course. Additionally, since the master course is not static, it is useful for a teacher of the cloned course to see the differences between the master course and the clone. To facilitate this we have developed a clone exploration widget, shown in Figure 4 to show the structural differences between a clone and the original. In the figure, a unit and its clone are being compared. The squares on the right represent the original unit and its lessons, while the

---

[1] http://stemrobotics.cs.pdx.edu

squares on the left represent the cloned resources. Lines between the squares represent *PartOf* relationships (vertically oriented) and *CloneOf* relationships (horizontally oriented). Additionally the widget can show if resources in the clone have been reordered compared to the originals. Here, all but one of the lessons have been cloned and one lesson is used as it is in the original in the clone (the small square in the middle of the figure linked to both units).

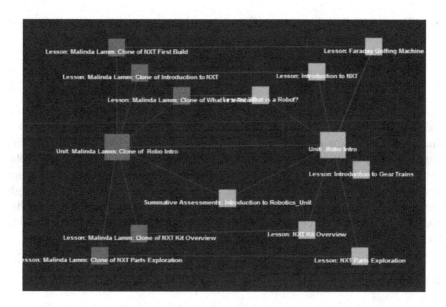

Fig. 4. Exploring a clone of a course

The generic clone exploration widget is written against a global schema. But in order to accurately compare the clones and the originals, we must know everything about the local records not just what is available through the mappings to the global schema.

3   Our System

We begin by introducing our system for information integration. The system has three main parts: 1) small global schema fragments called *domain structures*, 2) mappings from the domain structures to local schemas, and 3) a query language for the domain structures. We briefly describe the domain structures used for our example and their mappings to the local schemas. We then describe the new operators that enable global creation and manipulation of local data. We show how queries are written against the domain structures and transformed to local queries for each new local schema mapped to the domain structures.

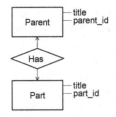

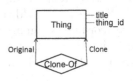

Fig. 5. The Parent-Part domain structure

Fig. 6. The clone domain structure

3.1   Domain Structures

To build the hierarchy used in the clone widget (Figure 3) we use the "Parent-Part" domain structure shown in Figure 5. The domain structure contains two domain entities (*Parent* and *Part*), and a domain relationship (*Has*); each domain entity has an *id* and a *title* domain attribute. To populate local clone relationships and to enable the clone exploration widget we use the clone domain structure shown in Figure 6. This structure consists of a single domain entity (*Thing*) with *title* and *id* domain attributes, and the *Clone-Of* domain relationship with labels *Original* and *Clone* for the two ends of the domain relationship.

3.2   Mappings

Domain structures are mapped to local schemas where a mapping consists of a set of correspondences between domain structure parts and local schema parts. Mappings are only loosely constrained—i.e., domain entities must be mapped to local entities and domain attributes must be mapped to local attributes. Domain relationships may be mapped to local relationships or join paths—discussion of the use of join paths is beyond the scope of this paper. We do not require a mapping to be complete but rather take a pay-as-you-go approach where queries work with as much of the local schema as has been mapped.

Figure 7 shows one mapping of the "Parent-Part" domain structure to the course schema, where the mapping consists of the entire set of correspondences shown in the figure. Here, correspondences have been drawn between the *Parent* domain entity and the *Course* local entity, as well as their respective *title* attributes. The *Has* domain relationship corresponds to the *Unit-for* local relationship. Correspondences have been drawn from the *Part* domain entity and its *title* domain attribute to the *Unit* local entity and its *title* attribute.

Figure 8 shows a similar mapping of the "Parent-Part" domain structure to the book local schema. Correspondences have been drawn from the *Parent* domain entity to the *Chapter* local entity, from the *Has* domain relationship to the *Section-For* local entity, and from the *Part* domain entity to the *Section* local entity.

To build the entire hierarchy shown in the clone widget, the "Parent-Part" domain structure is mapped to all levels of the course and book schemas. Figures showing these mappings have been omitted for the sake of brevity.

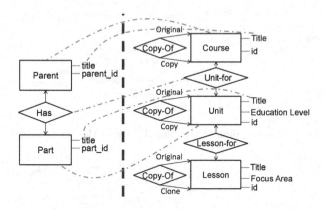

Fig. 7. One mapping of the Parent-Part DS to the course schema

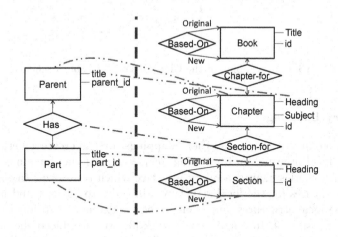

Fig. 8. One mapping of the Parent-Part DS to the book schema

Figures 9 and 10 show mappings of the "CloneOf" domain structure to the course and book local schemas: the *Thing* domain entity is mapped to a local entity and the *CloneOf* relationship is mapped to the local relationship attached to the mapped local entity.

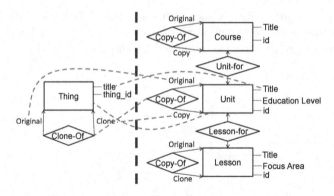

Fig. 9. One mapping of the CloneOf DS to the course schema

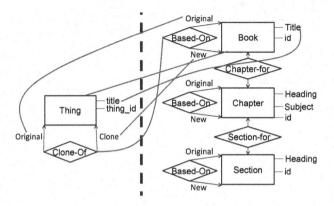

Fig. 10. One mapping of the CloneOf DS to the book schema

3.3   Query Language

Given the domain structures and their mappings, we can create generic widgets that access local information by writing queries against the domain structures. Widgets pose queries against a query interface which transforms them into the appropriate queries for the local structures. In order to interact and interoperate with the local structures, our query interface extends traditional relational algebra (σ, π, $\bowtie$, ...). In our previous work [3], we introduced the apply and local type operators (shown in Table 1). The Apply operator ($\alpha(DS)$) is the basis of each query in our system. Given a domain structure DS, Apply will generate table scan queries for all local structures that the domain structure has been mapped to and take the union of the results. The Apply operator transforms queries from our ER-based conceptual model into queries on the relational model. The result of the apply operator is a set of relational tuples; this allows the Apply operator to be combined with other relational algebra operators in more complex queries. The returned tuples also include the identifiers of the mappings to the local schema that were used to create the result. The local type operator (τ), given a domain structure part (DS) and a query (χ), introduces an attribute into the query result containing the local structure name to which the domain structure has been mapped. In order to get the local semantics (i.e., the local structure names), our system accesses the data dictionary of each local system.

The software needed to build the interface is composed of two parts, one common to all implementations (that supports the genericity of the operations and the query interface) and, one specific to each local system, a "driver" which maps the generic operations to the local system.

Table 1. Extended query operators

Operator	Name
$\alpha(DS)$	Apply
$\tau_{DS}(\chi)$	Local Type
$\beta_{DS}(\chi)$	Local Record
$\mu_{DS,P}(\chi)$	Mapping Operator
$\epsilon_{DS,mid}(\chi)$	Empty Document Operator
$I(DS, Doc)$	Insert
$U(DS, Doc, P)$	Update

In this paper we introduce five operators that enable global manipulation of local data. The local record operator (β) and empty document operator (ϵ). Each of the operators, given a query (χ) and a domain structure part (DS), will add an attribute to the query result containing a self-describing document that represents the full local schema of elements to which the domain structure part has been mapped, as well as the domain structure parts and mappings used. The difference between the two operators is that β will generate a document populated with data from the local database whereas ϵ will generate an empty document with the full local schema structure but no data. Examples of the operators are described in more detail in Section 4; Figures 11 and 13 show examples of the documents respectively.

The mapping operator (μ) is used to query the mappings between a domain structure and a local schema. Given a domain structure (DS), a predicate (P) and a query (χ), the mapping operator will query the mappings for the given domain structure and return all mapping identifiers where predicate P is true for the given query χ. A detailed example is presented below.

The insert and update operators allow local data creation and modification from the global level. Given a self-describing document (Doc)—such as those created by the β and ϵ operators—and a domain structure (DS), the insert operator ($I(DS, Doc)$) translates the document into the appropriate insert statements for the local database. The update operator ($U(DS, Doc, P)$) takes an additional parameter, a predicate P that must be satisfied for the update to succeed. The update operator then translates the given document into the appropriate local update statements. Since the documents contain the full local schemas, not just the parts mapped to domain structures, we need not worry about the view update problem. Although, inserts or updates may still fail if local schema constraints (e.g., not null or cardinality constraints) are not met. Examples of each operator are provided in the next section.

4   Implementing Domain Widgets

We have implemented our system using the Drupal[2] content management system. Widgets are added to Drupal by writing modules that can be enabled in a given site. We have built a query interface for our language and mappings that, once installed, can be used by other widgets. Queries are written in our extended algebra and when posed to the query interface return a database result object identical in structure to the original database query objects defined in the base Drupal system. Using this, developers can then write widgets as they would normally in Drupal but gain the benefit of our integrated queries. In the rest of this section we show the queries that are used to build the widgets shown in Section 2.

4.1   Clone and Structural Edit

The cloning widget shown in Figure 3 uses both the "Parent-Part" and "CloneOf" domain structures. To build the hierarchical structure we first define a query to get all children of a resource with a given id *id* as follows.

$$Children = \pi_{Part,Part\_type,Part\_mid}(\tau_{Part}(\sigma_{Parent=id}(\alpha(Has))))$$

We use the apply operator on the *Has* domain relationship. This returns a relation with the tuples for all local relationships to which the *Has* domain relationship has been mapped with a relational schema Has(Parent, Parent_mid, Part, Part_mid). We select the tuples where the parent is the given id. We then use the type operator to get the local type of the parts. This is what supplies the local type information shown in the widget such as "Unit" or "Section". The id, type, and mapping id of the part are then projected. The hierarchical structure (e.g., for a course or book) is built by running this query recursively.

Once the hierarchy is built, as the user selects items within the tree to include in the clone, the document for each item and its children is retrieved using its id with the following query:

$$Doc = \beta_{\{Parent,Has\}}(\sigma_{parent\_id=id}(\alpha(Parent) \bowtie_{parent\_id=parent\_id} \alpha(Has)))$$

An example of the document created before anything has been moved by the user as seen in the left side of Figure 3 is shown in Figure 11. The document begins with the local identifier, the first field is the local schema id, and the second field of each record is the mapping id that was used to create the document. Next

---

[2] http://drupal.org

all local schema attributes appear. Then since we joined *Parent* with the *Has* domain relationship we also get the parts, in this case units.

As the user rearranges the hierarchy in the interface, the widget updates the document accordingly. Figure 12 shows that the "Robot Intro" unit (id 241) has been moved below the "Hardware..." unit (id 387). Once the user is finished with their modification, the widget performs the clone operation by setting the document id to "NULL" and removing all unselected items. Then the document is inserted in the local schema. The "NULL" id tells the system to create an id for the record.

Once the inserts succeed, the local id is returned to the widget that then also executes an insert into the *CloneOf* domain structure, with the old and new ids, to create local *CloneOf* records. To perform the insert we retrieve an empty document for the *CloneOf* domain structure with a mapping in the same local schema as the cloned resource. To do this, we use the mapping operator (μ) to get the mapping ids of all mappings of the *CloneOf* domain structure to the local schema that the parent document came from where the *Thing* domain entity is mapped to the same type as the *Parent* domain entity (note, there may be more than one such mapping):

$$Mids = \mu_{\substack{CloneOf,CloneOf\_sid=Has\_sid\vee \\ Thing\_type=Parent\_type}}(\sigma_{Parent\_id=id}(\tau_{Parent}(\alpha(Has))))$$

We retrieve an empty document(s) for the *CloneOf* domain structure using the following ϵ query. If more than one mapping id was retrieved multiple empty documents will be retrieved and the widget will have to decide how to handle that case. In the current implementation, all retrieved empty documents are populated and inserted but other widget writers may make different decisions.

$$empty\_clone = \epsilon_{CloneOf}(Mids)$$

Figure 13 shows the empty document retrieved for the *CloneOf* domain relationship based on the local schema id and type of the *Course* document shown in Figure 11. The document contains the mapping id and schema id from which it was retrieved as well as the local names (*CopyOf*, *Original*, and *Copy*) and their domain counterparts (*CloneOf*, *Original*, and *Clone*). All local values are set to null. Figure 14 shows the document populated with the ids of the original course and the new clone created, ready to be inserted back into the local database.

We have also used the cloning interface (Figure 3) as a structural editing interface to allow users to rearrange their existing content. The only difference between the editing and cloning widgets is that the editing interface keeps the original identifier in the document and then updates the local records instead of inserting new items.

4.2   Exploration and Comparison

The clone exploration widget shown in Figure 4 is built using two domain queries. First in order to get the clones of a given item with id *id*, the following query is

```
291:                                      NULL:
    sid: 2                                    sid: 2
    mid: 3                                    mid: 3
    ds: Parent                               ds: Parent
    type: Course                             type: Course
    title: STEM Robotics 101 NXT             title: Clone of: STEM ...
    field_guide: 706                         field_guide: 706
    field_classroom_resources: 1010         field_classroom_resources:
    field_unit:                              field_unit:
        - 241:                                   - 387:
            ds: Part                                 ds: Part
        - 301                                    - 241:
            ds: Part                                 ds: Part
        - 387:
            ds: Part
    . . .
```

Fig. 11. Local document of the *Parent* and *Has* domain structures

Fig. 12. Rearranged document with id set to "NULL" for insert into local

executed.

$$Clones(id) = \pi_{clone\_id}(\sigma_{original\_id=id}(\alpha(CloneOf)))$$

The apply operator is used to get a relation with data from all the local relationships to which the *CloneOf* relationship is mapped. We select only those tuples where the original id is the given id and then project the ids of the clones. To compare the clones with the original, we get the local records of the original and the clones with the following query.

$$Docs = \beta_{clone\_id}(\sigma_{thing\_id=id\vee \atop thing\_id\in clone\_ids}(\alpha(Thing)))$$

We begin by retrieving the tuples of everything mapped and then select only the tuples we want and then retrieve the local records for those ids, where *clone_ids* is the set of ids of all clones of the given id.

Using the documents of the original and the clones we then populate the clone exploration widget using a utility similar to the diff Unix command that shows how the two given documents differ.

5   Related Work

Our basic integration system uses a global-as-view model similar to traditional integration [10] but where traditional integration uses a single global schema, we use many, small, global schema fragments (domain structures). Our domain

```
NULL:                          NULL:
    sid: 2                         sid: 2
    mid: 7                         mid: 7
    ds: CloneOf                    ds: CloneOf
    type: CopyOf                   type: CopyOf
    Original:                      Original:
        NULL:                          291:
            ds: Original                   ds: Original
    Copy:                          Copy:
        NULL:                          1123:
            ds: Clone                      ds: Clone
```

Fig. 13. Empty *CopyOf* document with *CloneOf* domain structure types

Fig. 14. Document to create local CopyOf records

structures can be seen as abstract superclasses of the various local schema types to which the domain structures have been mapped, much like view integration and cooperation [15]. We extend these existing approaches by bringing the local semantics through to the integrated functionality using our local type and records operators and by leveraging these operators to allow local insert and update via the global schema. By retaining all mapping information and therefore the ability to retrieve the full local record no matter the global view, we avoid the traditional view update problem [6] and we don't need complicated schema translation operations such as channels [14] or relational lenses [2].

Our work is inspired by the work on data modeling patterns such as those presented by Blaha [1] and the Co-design and metastructure approach [11,16]. We see our domain structures as similar to patterns. But instead of using patterns to develop schemas and systems as in prior work, we use them to integrate heterogeneous schemata flexibly.

Bringing local schema metadata to the global level during integration has been studied and developed in systems like SchemaSQL [9] and the Federated Interoperable Relational Algebra (FIRA) [18] and has been added to systems like Clio [7]. These systems use pivot/unpivot operations [17,14] to address the problem where data in one schema may exist as metadata in another schema (e.g., one schema may have city as an attribute of a company table whereas another schema may have one table for every city of interest thus placing the city name in the schema). In contrast, we bring local schema metadata to our domain structures in order to use it at the global level. Our approach is less complex; we allow users to apply local type and record operators to any domain structure type at any point in a query.

Building widgets with documents built from local schemas is somewhat analogous to object-relational mapping (ORM) systems [8,13] where application objects are defined and created through mappings to relational databases and object manipulations are translated to database inserts and updates. Unlike

ORMs, we do not transform the local schema other than to add mapping identifiers and domain structure types when we create documents. Additionally we use our mappings to access multiple heterogeneous local documents globally as opposed to defining mappings to specific global objects.

Our self-describing local documents are inspired by the many standards and systems for self-describing documents and their datastores—from XML[3] to modern NoSQL document stores [5]. Since we use our documents as a generic serialization of local data in a local schema and represent them as additional data in a relational tuple we avoid complex formalisms that combine NoSQL and relational models such as the correlational model [12].

6   Conclusion

In this paper, we have shown how we extend our information integration system that uses simple correspondences and global schema fragments to support global inserts and updates of local data. We plan to extend this work to support local schema manipulation from a global level, as well. For example, we want our cloning widget to create new local subtypes of the original local schema whenever a user rearranges parts of an existing course into a new schema.

We plan to implement widgets that use more complex reasoning techniques to better explore local data relationships through domain structures. For example, we may reason about courses and their clones, or prerequisite/corequisite relationships among educational materials.

By creating generic widgets that exploit common domain knowledge, we believe we can make simple interfaces that help users understand their data. Additionally, we believe that we can incentivize non-expert users to integrate their own local schemas by providing useful functionality through simple mappings.

Acknowledgments. This work was supported in part by National Science Foundation grants 0840668 and 1250340. Any opinions, findings, and conclusions or recommendations expressed in this material are those of the author(s) and do not necessarily reflect the views of the National Science Foundation.

References

1. Blaha, M.: Patterns of Data Modeling. CRC Press (June 2010)
2. Bohannon, A., Pierce, B.C., Vaughan, J.A.: Relational lenses: a language for updatable views. In: PODS 2006, p. 338. ACM Press, New York (2006)
3. Britell, S., Delcambre, L.M.L., Atzeni, P.: Flexible Information Integration with Local Dominance. In: International Conference on Information Modelling and Knowledge Bases. Kiel, Germany (2014)
4. Britell, S., Delcambre, L.M.L.: Mapping Semantic Widgets to Web-based, Domain-specific Collections. In: Atzeni, P., Cheung, D., Ram, S. (eds.) ER 2012. LNCS, vol. 7532, pp. 204–213. Springer, Heidelberg (2012)

---

[3] http://www.w3.org/XML/

5. Cattell, R.: Scalable SQL and NoSQL data stores. ACM SIGMOD Record 39(4), 12 (2011)
6. Dayal, U., Bernstein, P.A.: On the correct translation of update operations on relational views. ACM Transactions on Database Systems 7(3), 381–416 (1982)
7. Hernández, M.A., Papotti, P., Tan, W.C.: Data exchange with data-metadata translations. Proceedings of the VLDB Endowment 1(1), 260–273 (2008)
8. Keller, A.M., Jensen, R., Agarwal, S.: Persistence software: bridging object-oriented programming and relational databases. ACM SIGMOD Record 22(2), 523–528 (1993)
9. Lakshmanan, L.V.S., Sadri, F., Subramanian, S.N.: SchemaSQL: An extension to SQL for multidatabase interoperability. ACM Transactions on Database Systems 26(4), 476–519 (2001)
10. Lenzerini, M.: Data integration: a theoretical perspective. In: PODS 2002: Proceedings of the Twenty-First ACM SIGMOD-SIGACT-SIGART Symposium on Principles of Database Systems, pp. 233–246. ACM, New York (2002)
11. Ma, H., Noack, R., Schewe, K.D., Thalheim, B.: Using Meta-Structures in Database Design. Informatica 34, 387–403 (2010)
12. Meijer, E., Bierman, G.: A co-relational model of data for large shared data banks. Communications of the ACM 54(4), 49 (2011)
13. Melnik, S., Adya, A., Bernstein, P.A.: Compiling mappings to bridge applications and databases. ACM Transactions on Database Systems 33(4), 1–50 (2008)
14. Terwilliger, J.F., Delcambre, L.M.L., Maier, D., Steinhauer, J., Britell, S.: Updatable and evolvable transforms for virtual databases. Proceedings of the VLDB Endowment 3(1-2), 309–319 (2010)
15. Thalheim, B.: Entity-relationship modeling: foundations of database technology, 1st edn. Springer, New York (2000)
16. Thalheim, B., Schewe, K.D., Ma, H.: Conceptual Application Domain Modelling. In: Link, S., Kirchberg, M. (eds.) Sixth Asia-Pacific Conference on Conceptual Modelling (APCCM 2009). CRPIT, vol. 96, pp. 49–57. ACS, Wellington (2009)
17. Wyss, C.M., Robertson, E.L.: A formal characterization of PIVOT/UNPIVOT. In: Proceedings of the 14th ACM International Conference on Information and knowledge Management CIKM 2005, p. 602. ACM Press, New York (2005)
18. Wyss, C.M., Robertson, E.L.: Relational languages for metadata integration. ACM Transactions on Database Systems 30(2), 624–660 (2005)

Evaluating Modeling Languages:
An Example from the Requirements Domain

Jennifer Horkoff, Fatma Başak Aydemir, Feng-Lin Li,
Tong Li, and John Mylopoulos

University of Trento, Italy
{horkoff,aydemir,fenglin.li,tong.li,jm}@disi.unitn.it

Abstract. Modeling languages have been evaluated through empirical studies, comparisons of language grammars, and ontological analyses. In this paper we take the first approach, evaluating the expressiveness and effectiveness of *Techne*, a requirements modeling language, by applying it to three requirements problems from the literature. We use our experiences to propose a number of language improvements for *Techne*, addressing challenges discovered during the studies. This work presents an example evaluation of modeling language expressiveness and effectiveness through realistic case studies.

Keywords: Requirements Modeling, Empirical Evaluation, Goal Modeling, Model Reasoning, Trade-off Analysis.

1 Introduction

Once a conceptual modeling language has been proposed, it must be evaluated. There are several approaches for doing so in the literature. For instance, [10] conducts a comparative evaluation of languages focusing on their underlying grammars, while, in the requirements domain, [20] evaluates language quality through empirical studies, and [12] adopts an ontological perspective by comparing the primitive concepts of the language to those of foundational or domain ontologies. Along a different path, language utility has been evaluated via experiments, often using student subjects, focusing on language comprehension (e.g., [22]) and/or the users' ability to carry out meaningful tasks (e.g., [15]). Other evaluations have focused on the effectiveness of a language's graphical syntax by comparison to standard principles (e.g., [21]), or through applications of the language to realistic examples or case studies (e.g, [9]).

In this study, we adopt the last type of language evaluation, studying the expressiveness and effectiveness of a language in capturing phenomena in three realistic case studies. Although existing work has advocated for an evaluation of language expressiveness (e.g., [10, 12]), evaluation has focused on theoretical expressiveness via comparison to grammars or ontologies. Here we focus on evaluating both expressiveness and effectiveness through realistic examples. Expressiveness measures the degree to which a language allows its users to capture phenomena in the domain. For our purposes, effectiveness measures the degree to which a language supports typical modeling tasks, in our case domain conceptualization and model reasoning for decision making. Although

E. Yu et al. (Eds.): ER 2014, LNCS 8824, pp. 260–274, 2014.

similar, our notion of effectiveness is broader than typical definitions of usability, including the ease of eliciting domain information needed to use language constructs. Our study constitutes an empirical evaluation – we argue that this type of evaluation is critical for evaluating a modeling language. As such, we provide an example of how to conduct such a study.

The subject of our study is the *Techne* Requirements Modeling Language (RML), an RML intended for modeling, stakeholder communication, and reasoning, first proposed in 2010 [16]. Since the 1990s, RMLs have modeled stakeholder requirements as goals, supporting an analysis that compares alternative solutions and trade-offs, especially among non-functional requirements captured as softgoals [4]. Existing analysis procedures for goal-oriented models, e.g. [4, 15], allow analysts to evaluate alternatives, discover conflicts and determine the viability of particular alternative solutions. Despite the impact of such techniques, it has been argued that languages and approaches for qualitative goal model reasoning have several limitations [16], including a limited vocabulary of concepts and relationships (goal, softgoal, goal decomposition, etc.) and limited analysis power, often founded on coarse-grained qualitative reasoning. In their RE'10 paper, Jureta et al. [16] introduce the *Techne* goal-oriented RML, with the stated intention of addressing some of these limitations. The proposal offers an abstract RML, enriching goal model primitives with concepts from the core requirements ontology [17], including mandatory and preferred (nice-to-have) goals, domain assumptions, quality constraints, and priorities.

Although the concepts and reasoning techniques proposed by *Techne* have theoretical advantages over existing RMLs for expressing and analyzing a requirements problem, these advantages have not been fleshed out through case studies and applications of the *Techne* proposal. In contrast, goal-oriented languages such as *i** [23] have benefited from a body of evaluation work using a variety of evaluation strategies (e.g., [9, 12, 20–22]). Example *Techne* or *Techne*-style models have been provided as part of successive work on *Techne* [7, 11]; however, these examples were created to illustrate particular uses of or extensions to the language, rather than for evaluation purposes.

In this paper we provide such an evaluation, testing the expressiveness and effectiveness of concepts and relationships (the grammar) provided by *Techne*, evaluating their ability to capture requirements phenomena in real domains. We focus on two particular tasks: model creation and reasoning in support of alternative selection trade-off analysis.

We measure expressiveness (*Ex*) of the *Techne* grammar by noting: how well the language grammar covers domain phenomena. In this study, we test the expressiveness (*Ex*) of *Techne* by going through three requirements analysis cases, noting when the language is not able to capture information or concepts deemed important for requirements analysis. We measure language effectiveness (*Ef*) by making note of: (*Efa*) how easy is it to use the grammar to capture domain phenomena, and (*Efb*) how easy is it to elicit and find information from domain sources corresponding to language concepts. In this work, we test the effectiveness of *Techne* by noting how easy or difficult it is to use the language to model the three selected requirements case studies, and to what degree the information needed for the models is readily available from the example sources. We further evaluate the effectiveness of *Techne* reasoning by determining to what degree it supports the selection amongst alternatives arising in the three case studies, particularly as compared to *i**-style analysis [15].

Each of the three studies applying *Techne* to realistic requirements analysis examples brought to light challenges with the *Techne* grammar. As such, before applying *Techne* again, we propose solutions to some of these challenges, and use these in subsequent studies. Thus, the paper presents a series of applications, challenges, and proposed solutions.

The contributions of this work include: (1) Evaluation of the expressiveness and effectiveness of *Techne* concepts and relationships; (2) Proposal of patterns that aid the transformation of *i** contribution links to *Techne* concepts; (3) Proposal of a systematic process for requirements elicitation by pinpointing information needed to facilitate *Techne* modeling and analysis; (4) An example study showing how to assess practical language expressiveness and effectiveness.

The rest of the paper is organized as follows. Sec. 2 provides background on goal modeling and *Techne*.Sec. 3 presents an overview of our three studies, while details, challenges, and solutions for the three studies are found in Sections 4, 5, and 6, respectively. We conduct a comparison of *i** and *Techne* analysis in Sec. 7. Related work is described in Sec. 8, while conclusions, threats to validity, and future work are discussed in Sec. 9.

2   Background

Goal Modeling. Goal modeling frameworks, such as the *NFR* (Non-Functional Requirements) and *i** (distributed intentionality) Frameworks [4, 23], include concepts such as *goals*, *softgoals* (objectives without clear-cut criteria for fulfillment), and *tasks*. Relationships include *dependencies* between actors, AND and OR (means-ends) *decomposition* of (soft)goals and tasks, and *contribution* links (*Make*(++), *Help*(+), *Hurt*(-), *Break*(−)) to capture qualitative trade-offs between non-functional requirements captured as *softgoals*. For example, Fig. 1 captures an example trade-off in the eTourism domain, where a Hotel can either rent or build a Computer Reservation System (CRS) in house, making a trade-off between Maximize profit and Facilitate control.

Several qualitative reasoning techniques have been introduced for goal models, e.g., [4, 15]. We can apply such techniques to our example model, evaluating alternatives, e.g., renting the CRS or developing it in house. Renting partially satisfies Maximize profit, but partially denies (provide negative evidence for) Facilitate control. The in house option produces the opposite effects. On the left side of the model, both the Quick-fix and Long-term web strategies alternatives have the same effect (*Help*, partial satisfaction) on Website usability/friendliness, as such it is impossible to choose between them. Our example illustrates a limitation of qualitative analysis. The model, as is, does not contain enough information to allow us to choose amongst alternatives. We must use our implicit domain knowledge to make decisions or enrich the model with more detail, i.e. further trade-offs to differentiate amongst alternatives.

***Techne* Abstract RML.** The *Techne* RML, as introduced in [16], consists of several concepts: *goals* (g), *softgoals* (s), *tasks* (t), *domain assumptions* (k), and *quality constraints* (q). Together these concepts are called requirements. Requirements can be

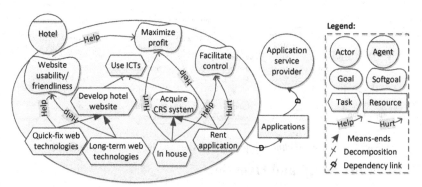

Fig. 1. Subset of an *i** model for eTourism

mandatory (*M*) or *preferred* (nice-to-have) (*Pf*). The framework provides three re-lations between elements: *inference* (*I*), *conflict* (*C*), and *priority* (*P*). If a premise element (*g*, *s*, *q*, or *t*), e.g., e_1, infers a conclusion element, *e*, this means that the achievement of *e* can be inferred from the achievement of e_1. Multiple premise ele-ments, e.g., e_1 ... e_n, can infer the same conclusion element, *e*, and this is treated as a (non-exclusive) OR, where achievement of any e_1 ... e_n means *e* is achieved. Multiple premise elements can also be aggregated together to infer a conclusion element, *e*. The aggregation is described using functions of arbitrary complexity captured by associated domain assumptions (*k*). The most common aggregation is AND, meaning e_1 ... e_n must all be achieved for the *e* to be achieved. For simplicity, [16] suggests that a con-crete syntax may be used to represent OR and aggregation via AND. As a shorthand we refer to OR and AND inferences throughout the paper.

Conflict (*C*) and priority (*P*) relations map a single element to a single element. Relating elements via conflict means that these elements cannot be satisfied simulta-neously. Priorities between elements mean that one element has a higher priority than another. Note that we use preference and priority differently than in the original *Techne* proposal [16], which used optional and preference, respectively. Our terminology is more consistent with AI planning and later related work [19].

Reasoning with *Techne*. The *Techne* proposal outlines the discovery of candidate solutions, sets of tasks and domain assumptions which satisfy at least all mandatory requirements. Selection between these solutions can then be made using modeled pri-orities, although a detailed algorithm is not provided. Further work by Ernst et al. [8] suggests that solutions for a goal (*Techne*) model should first be ranked using priorities, and then should be ranked by the number of implemented preferred goals.

In theory, the richness of the *Techne* language should allow modelers to address the challenges illustrated with Fig. 1. In this case, a modeler could use priorities (*Ps*) between softgoals (**Maximize profit** and **Facilitate control**) to differentiate between options in the first alternative, and use quality constraints (*qs*) to distinguish the effects of each option in the second alternative (Fig. 2). [1] In this simple example, the optimal solution is now clear (**Rent application** and **Long-term web strategies**).

---

[1] In order to draw *Techne* models, we introduce a concrete visual syntax based on *i** syntax (see legend in Fig. 2 and Fig. 6).

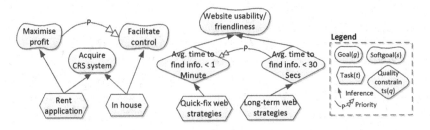

Fig. 2. Example *Techne* snippets addressing challenges shown in Fig. 1

3   Case Study Setup and Overview

The studies were conducted in several interactive modeling sessions with three to four of the authors. All participants had experience in goal modeling, particularly with *i*/NFR* modeling. In each study, sources were used to collaboratively construct a goal model. Models for each study took a total of 6 - 12 hours to create. An overview of our process, including derived solutions and subsequent solution applications is shown in Fig. 3.

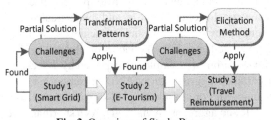

Fig. 3. Overview of Study Process

The first study evaluated the effectiveness of the *Techne* grammar via application to a Smart Grid example. This study revealed several challenges with *Techne* in practice (more details in Sec. 4). To address some of these challenges we proposed to start modeling using high-level concepts from *i*/NFR*, transforming these concepts to the richer ontology of *Techne* using developed patterns. The second study in the eTourism domain applied this proposal, testing the usability of our proposed patterns (Sec. 5). Here we uncovered challenges including difficulties in eliciting information needed for *Techne* modeling. We addressed this challenge by coming up with a method for systematically determining the information needed in order to choose between model alternatives. In the third study, focusing on a university travel reimbursement system, we applied this elicitation method, as well as the transformation patterns, recording our experiences (Sec. 6). Finally, we applied both *Techne* and *i** reasoning to our models, recording and comparing results (Sec. 7).

4   Study 1: Applying *Techne* to a Smart Grid Domain

The study focused on collaborative modeling of the Smart Grid domain, an information technology enhanced power grid, designed to optimize the transmission and distribution of electricity from suppliers to consumers [5].

Results. Statistics for the resulting model can be found in the first row of Table 1[2]. When modeling, we tried to capture the information provided in the source document

---

[2] Full versions of all models available: www.cs.utoronto.ca/~jenhork/ TechneEval/

Table 1. Model statistics for Study 1 to 3

Model		a	g	s	t	r	k	q	I	C	P	M	Pf	Dec	Dep	ME	Hp	Ht	Mk	Bk	Un
Study 1	Techne	25	45	41	20	15	0	0	107	1	0	0	0	-	-	-	-	-	-	-	-
Study 2	i*	31	22	65	52	7	19	-	-	-	-	-	-	52	23	12	35	9	22	7	1
	Techne	-	22	83	52	7	19	58	226	15	13	1	0	-	-	-	-	-	-	-	-
Study 3	i*	6	42	8	30	1	0	-	-	-	-	-	-	36	7	30	5	4	0	0	0
	Techne	-	2	18	19	0	0	28	72	0	23	0	14	-	-	-	-	-	-	-	-

a: actor, r: resource, Dec: decomposition, Dep: dependency, ME: means-ends, Hp: help, Ht: hurt, Mk: make, Bk: break, Un: unknown

without extensive extrapolation. As such, we drew no quality constraints (q) or domain assumptions (k), did not mark any goals as mandatory/preferred (M/Pf), and did not include any priority (P) links. In these cases, when information corresponding to a particular language concept was not readily available in our sources, a count of 0 was added to the table. The '-' symbol is used when a concept in the table was not part of an applied language (e.g., i* has no quality constraints (q), Techne has no decompositions (Dec)).

Challenges. *Availability of Information.* In this case, as shown in Table 1, our source document did not include information for identifying some *Techne*-specific concepts (q, k, P, M, Pf). This observation may change depending on available sources, or may be acquirable when interacting directly with stakeholders. We describe a proposed solution to this challenge in subsequent sections.

Representing Trade-offs. In drawing this initial *Techne* model, we had difficulty representing the notion of a trade-off between softgoals, finding the *Techne* concepts too absolute for modeling informal domains, which requirements problems usually are. In other words, it was difficult to capture weaker trade-offs between requirements using the binary, yes/no concepts offered by *Techne*. For example, the task Encrypt data had a positive effect on Communication Security but had a negative effect on Low cost technology. These effects could be best represented by the *Techne* inference (I) and conflict (C) relationships, respectively.

We found multiple possible placements for the conflict link representing the negative effect (see Fig. 4). However, unless Low cost is inferred by a further element, the three conflict possibilities have equal effect: in each case Low cost and Security cannot be simultaneously achieved when Encrypt data is implemented.

Using the *Techne* concept of priority, this model could have a solution. Either the users give higher priority to Low cost than they do to Security or vice versa, meaning that Encrypt data is not or is part of the solution, respectively. But asking users to express their priorities over such high-level goals may be problematic, most

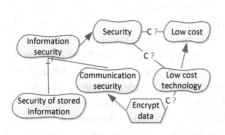

Fig. 4. Representing trade-offs in *Techne*

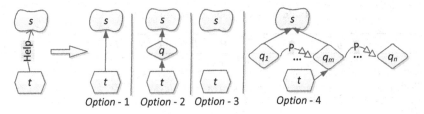

Fig. 5. *i**-to-*Techne* transformation pattern for *Help*

users would like to maximize both softgoals, instead of making a clear choice between them.

Solution: *i**-to-*Techne* Transformation Patterns. This study has pointed out the following challenges with the effectiveness of the *Techne* grammar: (*Efa*) difficulty in expressing tradeoffs, particularly between softgoals, difficulty in selecting the most appropriate placement of conflict relations, and (*Efb*) several concepts are not easily determined on the basis of information available in our source. We address the *Efa* issue by developing a method which combines the expressiveness of *Techne* with the expressiveness of *i**/*NFR*-style languages. The method starts with high-level *i**/*NFR* style models with contribution links expressing trade-offs, and moves towards more precise *Techne* models, allowing for an eventual ranking of possible solutions. A solution to the *Efb* challenge is presented in Sec. 5.

We developed a series of patterns guiding users in transforming *i** contribution links to *Techne* concepts, mainly quality constraints and priorities. We show the transformation pattern for *Help* in Fig. 5. Patterns for other contribution links, *Make*, *Break* and *Hurt*, can be derived from this pattern, as follows. When transforming a *Make* contribution link, users can choose between the first two options: (1) replacing the link with an inference link, having the same semantics in both *i** and *Techne*, or (2) adding an inference link and a quality constraint, describing how the softgoal is approximated by a measure which is achieved by the contributing task/goal. The case for a *Break* link is similar, using a conflict link instead of an inference. As *Help*/*Hurt* represents the presence of partial positive/negative evidence, when transforming a *Help* or *Hurt* link, the user has two additional options (option 3 and 4): (3) ignore this evidence, indicating that it is not significant enough to retain in the model, or (4) capture this evidence as partial, meaning the contributing element infers a certain quality constraint (e.g., q_m, $m > 1$), but there are one or more quality constraints (e.g., q_1) with higher priorities which are not inferred by this element. In this case, *Hurt* may be distinguished from *Help* by the presence of quality constraints (e.g., q_n, $n > m$) with lower priorities. Although this process can be tool-supported, user judgment is required to select amongst transformation options and enhance the initial *i** model with additional required information.

Transformation from *i** to *Techne* may also involve refining softgoals into more detailed softgoals. If, for example, a softgoal has applicable quality constraints in multiple quality dimensions (time, cost, number of clicks, etc.) then the softgoal should be decomposed into more detailed softgoals expressing desires over each of these dimensions. We recommend that all quality constraints for a softgoal be in the same dimension. If this holds, then priorities between quality constraints can be derived auto-

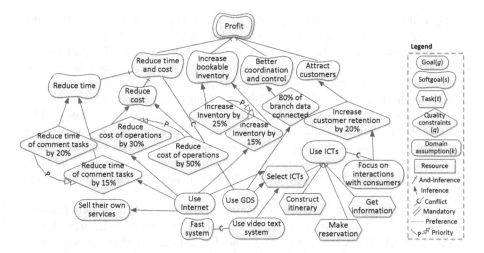

Fig. 6. Excerpt of the transformed *Techne* model for the Travel Agency actor in the eTourism domain

matically. E.g., if the softgoal is **save time** then the constraint q_1: **time < 20 seconds** is given higher priority than q_2: **time < 1 minute** automatically.

Other *Techne* specific information such as priorities not between quality constraints of the same dimension, domain assumptions or mandatory/preferred goals must be gathered using domain knowledge or further elicitation, i.e., this information cannot be derived from the *i** model.

5   Study 2: Applying Transformation Patterns to an eTourism Domain

Our second study focused on the eTourism domain, as described in [3]. We started by drawing a large *i** model covering the major sections of the document. Although we focused on *i** modeling, if we found any information corresponding to *Techne*-specific concepts (e.g., P, q, k), we included them in the *i** model, using our visual syntax. We then performed *i**-style qualitative analysis on this model, using the OpenOME tool [15], in order to evaluate the various alternatives in the model. Next, we applied our patterns in order to transform the model to *Techne*, creating models for each actor in the *i** model, noting challenges which arose. Finally, we conducted *Techne*–style analysis finding and ranking candidate solutions. Analysis results are discussed in Sec. 7.

Results. See Table 1 for statistics concerning the resulting models. In this case, we were able to come up with more *Techne*-specific concepts, including priorities, conflicts, and quality constraints, due to the application of our transformation patterns. We were also able to come up with several domain assumptions. We show a partial view of a model for the Travel Agency actor in Fig. 6.

Challenges. *Availability of Information.* When performing the transformation, we were generally able to come up with quality constraints for all softgoals; however, as this information was not available in our sources, our constraints were fairly arbitrary, making educated guesses concerning relevant measures and cut-off points. Priorities were also difficult to add using our own knowledge of the domain, unless they were over quality constraints in the same dimension. We made the same observations with designating goals as mandatory/preferred, although here we could assume the top-level goals of each actor, e.g. Profit in Fig. 6, were mandatory. Our experiences indicate that most of this information must be elicited directly from stakeholders.

Contributions between Softgoals. While our transformation patterns worked well for contributions between tasks and softgoals, they were difficult to apply to contributions between softgoals, occurring frequently in our *i** model. Such situations may result in inference links between softgoals or softgoals inferring quality constraints inferring softgoals. Although the latter is possible in *Techne*, it seemed peculiar to refine from soft to hard (quality constraint) to soft.

Contribution Aggregation. When combining together the effects of softgoals on a higher-level softgoal, even using our transformation patterns, we were left with choices between either AND or OR aggregated inference links, neither of which seem appropriate. For example, in Fig. 6, the top mandatory softgoal Profit is refined to several other softgoals including Increase bookable inventory and Reduce time and cost. Aggregating these softgoals together with OR was too weak, while using AND (as shown in Fig. 6) was too strong.

Techne provides a solution to this problem by allowing us to express an aggregation function of arbitrary complexity as part of the domain assumption associated with the aggregation of inference links. However, stakeholders must come up with a reasonable function that aggregates all inferring or contributing elements. How can Increase bookable inventory, Reduce time and cost and other softgoals be combined to determine the satisfaction of Profit? Such functions may be difficult for stakeholders to formulate.

Solution: Elicitation Method. The results of our second study helped us to identify challenges with the expressiveness and effectiveness of the *Techne* grammar: (*Ex*) it was difficult to capture contributions between softgoals, (*Efa*) it was difficult to capture and elicit complex aggregation of contributions, and (*Efb*) it was difficult to add accurate *Techne*-specific information to the models using information provided in our source. We propose a solution to address the *Efb* challenge, encountered in both the first and second studies, leaving the *Ex* and *Efa* challenges for future work. Specifically, we provide a list of suggested questions which can be asked to elicit *Techne*-specific elements:

1. Priority (P): For each pair of softgoals at the same level of decomposition, ask, "Which one do you prefer?" The answer results in a *priority* relationship.
2. Quality Constraint (q): For each softgoal, ask, "how can it be measured?" The answer results one or more quality constraints. If there is no answer, ask, "What do you mean by this softgoal?" The result is the refinement of the softgoal into more detailed softgoals.
3. Inference (I): For each new quality constraint or softgoal resulting from question 2, ask for each task, "Will this task satisfy the quality constraint or softgoal"? The answer introduces an inference link from the task to the quality constraint or softgoal.
4. Mandatory/Preferred (M/Pf): For each (soft)goal, ask if it is mandatory.

Asking such questions for all elements in a model would be laborious. Even for our simple Fig. 1 *i** model, we would have to ask 1, 3, at least 6, and 3 questions to elicit priorities, quality constraints, inferences, and mandatory/optional, respectively, a total of at least 13 questions. Thus we focus on eliciting only the information necessary to select between candidate solutions.[3] Starting with the high-level *i** model, we suggest the following method for targeted elicitation:

1. Apply *i** analysis (e.g., [15]) to evaluate possible alternatives (identified with OR inference links).
2. Use results of the analysis to determine if decisions can be made clearly for each OR alternative. Example cases where decisions cannot be made have been described in Sec. 2.
3. For each decision which cannot be made using *i** analysis, take a slice of the model starting with the OR alternative and moving up to all connected softgoals.
4. Convert each slice to *Techne*, combine slices together, if applicable. Conversion will apply transformation patterns as introduced in Sec. 4.
5. Apply questions as above to each element within this slice. The results of the patterns will determine whether which questions to ask stakeholders. For example, if *Option-2* or *4* in Fig. 5 are chosen, quality constraint questions should be asked.
6. Apply *Techne* reasoning to converted slices to determine the optimal model solution(s).

Step 5 may be further optimized by determining precisely which priorities and quality constraints are needed within a slice to choose between alternatives. We leave the specifics of such an algorithm to future work. We test our proposed solution via application to the third study.

6 Study 3: Targeted Elicitation in a University Travel Domain

Our third study captured the travel approval and reimbursement system of the University of Trento. For this case study, we interviewed four stakeholders, a Ph.D. student, a research project assistant, a secretary, and a research project leader who is also a professor. The first and last participants had knowledge of goal models. We first created an *i** model for three of the different interviewees, merged the model into a single model, then applied the elicitation method introduced in Sec. 5, returning to our stakeholders to ask follow-up questions targeting specific *Techne* constructs needed to support decision-making.

Results. See Table 1 for statistics describing resulting models. As the resulting *Techne* model focuses only on the slices needed to select among alternatives, the number of elements is relatively small. The initial *i** model had 116 elements and 102 links, while the slice resulting from our elicitation method had 70 elements and 95 links, reductions of 39.7% and 6.9%, respectively.

Our method resulted in a list of 52 questions for our stakeholders (10 P, 14 q, 14 I, and 14 M/Pf questions, respectively). Stakeholders were able to answer 7/10 of the P questions and all of the I and M/Pf questions. Of the 14 q questions asked, 2

---

[3] When creating a complete requirements specification, further questions may be asked to elicit quality constraints for all softgoals, ensuring they are eventually measurable.

questions elicited a softgoal decomposition, 1 question elicited a softgoal and a quality constraint, 8 questions elicited 16 quality constraints, while 3 questions could not be answered.

Challenges. Generally, stakeholders had some difficulty in quantifying softgoals into quality constraints, and were sometimes not able to provide priorities between softgoals. Often stakeholders responded with "it depends", meaning that there was some domain context not well-captured by the models. Our experiences emphasize the importance of perspective when drawing goal models, expressible using actors in *i**. The elicitation of quality constraints can differ greatly depending on the actor who desires the goal, e.g., Fast reimbursement time is evaluated very differently from the perspective of travelers and administrators.

The results of our third study helped us to identify challenges with the expressiveness and effectiveness of the *Techne* grammar: (*Ex*) the language did cover the actor concept well, important in capturing perspective; the language may require a richer means of capturing context; and (*Efb*) stakeholders sometimes had difficulty providing quality constraints and priorities.

7 Qualitative *i**/*NFR* and *Techne* Reasoning Applied

As a point of comparison, we applied qualitative forward "what if?" *i** reasoning [15] to our *i** model in the second and third studies (we found no alternatives in the first study). That is, we placed initial qualitative values on model elements reflecting a particular decision over alternatives, then used *i** semantics to propagated these labels through the links, using human judgment to resolve conflicting or partial labels. The applied procedure is similar to other 'typical' qualitative goal model reasoning procedures, see [14] for a comparison.

In each model, we focused analysis on areas of the model connected to means-ends (OR) alternatives. We found three such decision-points in the eTourism Study and seven points in the University Travel Study. In some cases *i** analysis led to the clear selection of an alternative, while in other cases (see simple examples in Sec. 2) it was unable to clearly distinguish between available choices. We summarize these results in the third column of Table 2.

We also applied *Techne* reasoning as described in Sec. 2 to the models produced as a result of our transformations. In most cases, *Techne* analysis could find one or more clearly ranked solutions, making selections amongst alternatives. For example, in Fig. 2, a snippet from an eTourism study *Techne* model, there were a total of four possible solutions. The priorities added between quality constraints and softgoals allowed us to choose an optimal solution which includes both In house and Long-term web strategies. In other cases, solutions could not be ranked. For example, in Fig. 6, it was impossible to find a solution which satisfied the mandatory goal Profit, due to the AND-aggregated inference links between Profit and its refinements, and the inference and conflict links attached to Use GDS (i.e. Use GDS conflicts with Reduce time and cost while inferring Better coordination and control). *Techne* analysis results are listed in the fourth column of Table 2.

Table 2. Summary of *i** and *Techne* reasoning results

Decision-point	Actor	*i**	*Techne*
Quick-fix vs. Long-term	Hotel	CD	Long-term
Rent application vs. In house	Hotel	In house	In house
Internet vs. GDS vs. Videotext	Travel Agency	CD	Conflict: No solution
Ticket bought by agent vs. yourself	Student	CD	buy yourself
Hotel booked by agent vs. yourself	Student	CD	buy yourself
Book hotel vs. university acc.	Assistant	CD	Missing P: no solution
Cheap ticket vs. Ticket with short duration	Assistant	CD	short duration
Hotel close to the city center vs. conference center	Assistant	CD	close to conference center
Cheap ticket vs. Ticket with short duration	Professor	CD	short duration
Hotel close to city center vs. conference center	Professor	CD	close to conference center

CD: cannot distinguish

Our results show that the additional expressiveness provided by *Techne* allows the reasoning procedures to select amongst alternatives in more cases, when compared to the *i** procedure.

8   Related Work

As mentioned in the introduction, much work has been devoted to evaluating goal–oriented RMLs, notably the *i** Framework. The most relevant studies are those that focused on evaluation through case studies. For instance, Estrada et al. [9] conducted an empirical evaluation of the *i** modeling framework by using three industrial case studies. Their evaluation was based on a set of features that fall into two categories: modeling language (e.g modularity, expressiveness, and traceability) and pragmatics of the modeling method (e.g. scalability and domain applicability). The study reported good expressiveness and domain applicability, but poor modularity and scalability of *i**. In contrast, we have focused only on the expressiveness and effectiveness of the *Techne* grammar, including reasoning and decision-making, without focusing on scalability. Further case studies applying *i** in industrial contexts can be found as part of the iStar Showcase [1]. These studies typically focus on benefits and drawbacks of applying goal modeling in practice, without focusing on evaluating language expressiveness and effectiveness.

The *Techne* language has been applied and expanded in successive work, focusing, for example, on reasoning or product portfolio optimization [7, 11]. Some of these applications have introduced their own concrete syntax for *Techne*. Although their syntax was applied to illustrative examples in the paper, the focus was not on evaluating the usability of the syntax or the language, but on illustrating language expansion or reasoning for some further purpose. In [8], the authors provide intuitive guidelines for identifying preferred goals. For example, non-functional goals are ideal candidates for preferred goals, while top-level goals are typically mandatory goals. These guidelines can be useful to incorporate in our *i**-to-*Techne* patterns.

We have focused on assessing the reasoning powers of *Techne* compared to qualitative *i** reasoning. Other techniques for qualitative goal model reasoning exist, see [14] and [13] for relevant surveys. *Techne*'s use of priorities make it's reasoning capabilities unique when compared to other qualitative techniques, allowing for a final ordering of possible solutions. Yet other approaches have applied quantitative analysis procedures to such models, see [13] for examples. Although the analysis results produced by such procedures are more fine-grained, allowing users to better choose amongst alternatives, the accuracy of quantitative values propagated through goal models is suspect; furthermore, this information is difficult to acquire as part of early requirements analysis [6, 15].

Liaskos et al. [19] have proposed a concrete goal modeling language that uses preferences and priorities to choose between alternative solutions, bearing similarity to *Techne*. In their proposal, preference goals are prioritized using numerical weights obtained through *AHP* (Analytical Hierarchy Process). In this way, the challenge of eliciting numbers during early requirements is at least partially addressed. Accordingly, a solution that satisfies preference goals to a higher degree (i.e. the sum of the weights of satisfied preference goals) will be optimal. Further studies should evaluate whether this approach suffers from the challenges we have found for *Techne*, or whether numerical analysis with *AHP* is a feasible approach to find the aggregation function needed to evaluate high-level softgoals.

9   Discussion and Conclusions

We have provided an example study testing the expressiveness and effectiveness of the grammar of a conceptual modeling language using realistic cases. Specifically, we have conducted three studies evaluating the expressiveness and effectiveness of the *Techne* grammar. We have found several challenges relating to language expressiveness and effectiveness, including: (*Ex*) phenomena in the examples which are difficult to capture, including contributions between softgoals, actors, and context; (*Efa*) difficulty in expressing tradeoffs, placing conflict relations, and capturing complex aggregation of contributions; and (*Efb*) difficulty in finding or eliciting priorities, quality constraints, domain assumptions, and mandatory/optional goals. Overall, we find that *Techne*, as proposed, has reasonable expressiveness, but has significant challenges in regards to effectiveness.

We have addressed challenges related to language effectiveness by presenting two solutions: transformation patterns from *i** to *Techne*, allowing for easier capture of tradeoffs and prompting users to add *Techne*-specific constructs to their models; and elicitation methods focusing on targeted elicitation of *Techne*–specific constructs needed for decision-making.

This work has compared qualitative *i** to *Techne* reasoning, finding that *Techne* reasoning is able to choose between alternatives in more cases, providing enhanced reasoning power, given the availability of *Techne*–specific concepts.

Threats to Validity. *Internal.* In order to apply Techne, we have created a concrete syntax based on *i**. However, our purpose in this work was to evaluate the language grammar, not the visual syntax, thus we believe these choices did not impact our results. Our first two studies are limited by the nature of the sources, with information coming from a single document, without the opportunity to interact with stakeholders. Our third study is limited by its size, only interacting with four stakeholders, two of which were familiar with goal modeling. Challenges initially result from only a single study, although subsequent studies confirm discovered challenges in some cases.

External. We have selected domains representing complex socio-technical systems in order to evaluate the effectiveness of *Techne*. Although the choices of these domains may affect the ability to reproduce our results, we mitigate this threat via our use of three different domains. The studies were executed by researchers with goal model experience, hindering study repeatability. However, as this is (to our knowledge) the first study evaluating the effectiveness of *Techne* concepts, it is sensible to start with simpler domains and experienced users. The researchers applying the studies were also biased by their past experience using *i*/NFR*-style frameworks. However, as these frameworks have received much attention in research, it is reasonable to expect that many new *Techne* users would have a similar bias.

Future Work. We propose to look at techniques for expressing and eliciting complex aggregations for softgoals through an interactive, qualitative analysis in the spirit of [15]. We also plan to develop a tool–supported process that applies the transformation patterns proposed here into areas of the model critical for reasoning, automatically generating a list of questions for stakeholders covering missing information. Challenges in language expressiveness can be addressed by integrating *Techne* with existing goal–oriented approaches using actors [23] or context [2]. Combining the proposed *Techne* solutions with methods aimed at easing model elicitation, as in [18] and [6], may be another promising direction.

Acknowledgments. This work has been supported by the ERC advanced grant 267856, "Lucretius: Foundations for Software Evolution" (April 2011 - March 2016).

References

1. iStar Showcase 2011: Exploring the goals of your systems and businesses, practical experiences with i* modeling (2011), http://istar.rwth-aachen.de/tiki-index.php?page=iStar+Showcase
2. Ali, R., Dalpiaz, F., Giorgini, P.: A goal-based framework for contextual requirements modeling and analysis. Requir. Eng. 15(4), 439–458 (2010)
3. Buhalis, D., Jun, S.H.: E-tourism. Information Technology for Strategic Tourism Management (2003)
4. Chung, L., Nixon, B.A., Yu, E., Mylopoulos, J.: Non-Functional Requirements in Software Engineering, vol. 5. Kluwer Academic Pub. (2000)
5. Cuellar, J., Suppan, S.: A smart metering scenario, Network of Excellence on Engineering Secure Future Internet Software Services and Systems, eRISE (2013)
6. Elahi, G., Yu, E.: Requirements trade-offs analysis in the absence of quantitative measures: A heuristic method. In: Proceedings of the 2011 ACM Symposium on Applied Computing, pp. 651–658. ACM (2011)
7. Ernst, N.A., Borgida, A., Mylopoulos, J., Jureta, I.J.: Agile requirements evolution via paraconsistent reasoning. In: Ralyté, J., Franch, X., Brinkkemper, S., Wrycza, S. (eds.) CAiSE 2012. LNCS, vol. 7328, pp. 382–397. Springer, Heidelberg (2012)
8. Ernst, N.A., Mylopoulos, J., Borgida, A., Jureta, I.J.: Reasoning with optional and preferred requirements. In: Parsons, J., Saeki, M., Shoval, P., Woo, C., Wand, Y. (eds.) ER 2010. LNCS, vol. 6412, pp. 118–131. Springer, Heidelberg (2010)
9. Estrada, H., Rebollar, A.M., Pastor, Ó., Mylopoulos, J.: An empirical evaluation of the i* framework in a model-based software generation environment. In: Martinez, F.H., Pohl, K. (eds.) CAiSE 2006. LNCS, vol. 4001, pp. 513–527. Springer, Heidelberg (2006)

10. Gemino, A., Wand, Y.: A framework for empirical evaluation of conceptual modeling techniques. Requirements Engineering 9(4), 248–260 (2004)
11. Gillain, J., Faulkner, S., Heymans, P., Jureta, I., Snoeck, M.: Product portfolio scope optimization based on features and goals. SPLC, pp. 161–170 (2012)
12. Guizzardi, R.S.S., Franch, X., Guizzardi, G., Wieringa, R.: Ontological distinctions between means-end and contribution links in the i* framework. In: Ng, W., Storey, V.C., Trujillo, J.C. (eds.) ER 2013. LNCS, vol. 8217, pp. 463–470. Springer, Heidelberg (2013)
13. Horkoff, J., Yu, E.: Analyzing goal models: Different approaches and how to choose among them. In: Proceedings of the 2011 ACM Symposium on Applied Computing, SAC 2011, pp. 675–682. ACM (2011)
14. Horkoff, J., Yu, E.: Comparison and evaluation of goal-oriented satisfaction analysis techniques. Requirements Engineering 18(3), 199–222 (2013)
15. Horkoff, J., Yu, E., Ghose, A.: Interactive goal model analysis Applied-Systematic procedures versus ad hoc analysis. In: van Bommel, P., Hoppenbrouwers, S., Overbeek, S., Proper, E., Barjis, J. (eds.) PoEM 2010. LNBIP, vol. 68, pp. 130–144. Springer, Heidelberg (2010)
16. Jureta, I., Borgida, A., Ernst, N.A., Mylopoulos, J.: Techne: Towards a New Generation of Requirements Modeling Languages with Goals, Preferences, and Inconsistency Handling. In: RE 2010 (2010)
17. Jureta, I., Mylopoulos, J., Faulkner, S.: Revisiting the Core Ontology and Problem in Requirements Engineering. In: RE 2008. IEEE (2008)
18. Liaskos, S., Jalman, R., Aranda, J.: On eliciting contribution measures in goal models. In: RE 2012, pp. 221–230. IEEE (2012)
19. Liaskos, S., McIlraith, S.A., Sohrabi, S., Mylopoulos, J.: Representing and reasoning about preferences in requirements engineering. Requirements Engineering, 227–249 (2011)
20. Matulevičius, R., Heymans, P.: Comparing goal modelling languages: An experiment. In: Sawyer, P., Heymans, P. (eds.) REFSQ 2007. LNCS, vol. 4542, pp. 18–32. Springer, Heidelberg (2007)
21. Moody, D.L., Heymans, P., Matulevicius, R.: Improving the effectiveness of visual representations in requirements engineering: An evaluation of i* visual syntax. In: RE 2009, pp. 171–180. IEEE (2009)
22. Teruel, M.A., Navarro, E., López-Jaquero, V., Montero, F., Jaen, J., González, P.: Analyzing the understandability of requirements engineering languages for CSCW systems: A family of experiments. Information and Software Technology 54(11), 1215–1228 (2012)
23. Yu, E.: Towards modelling and reasoning support for early-phase requirements engineering. In: RE 1997, pp. 226–235. IEEE (1997)

Nòmos 3: Legal Compliance of Roles and Requirements

Silvia Ingolfo[1], Ivan Jureta[2], Alberto Siena[3], Anna Perini[3], and Angelo Susi[3]

[1] University of Trento, via Sommarive 7, Trento, Italy
[2] University of Namur, 8, rempart de la vierge, 5000 Namur, Belgium
[3] FBK-Irst, via Sommarive 18, Trento, Italy
ingolfo@unitn.it, ivan.jureta@unamur.be, {siena,susi,perini}@fbk.eu

Abstract. The problem of regulatory compliance for a software system consists of ensuring through a systematic, tool-supported process that the system complies with all elements of a relevant law. To deal with the problem, we build a model of the law and contrast it with a model of the requirements of the system. In earlier work, we proposed a modelling language for law (Nòmos 2) along with a reasoning mechanism that answers questions about compliance. In this paper we extend Nòmos 2 to include the concepts of role and requirement so that we can reason about compliance in specific domains. Also, Nòmos 3 represents the distribution of responsibilities to roles, distinguishing social from legal roles. Nòmos 3 models allow us to reason about compliance of requirements and roles with the norms that constitute a law. A small case study is used to illustrate the elements of Nòmos 3 and the kinds of reasoning it supports.

Keywords: requirement engineering, regulatory compliance, roles.

1 Introduction

Government has become increasingly interested in how to regulate software systems, given numerous mishaps with significant and expensive consequences to the public. When designing a new system, it is becoming necessary to demonstrate that the system complies with applicable legislation. Similarly, given an existing running system and a new law coming into force, it is important to evaluate its compliance and adapt the system design accordingly. The new challenge for software engineers is to understand the various ways a system can achieve its purpose, while complying with applicable laws.

In previous work we have introduced Nòmos 2 [13], a modeling language, tailored to represent norms and support formal reasoning about alternative ways to comply with them. It relies on the intuition that laws generally establish *norms* (i.e., duties and rights), but also the *context* in which these norms apply, their pre-conditions, exceptions and relationships. Nòmos 2 takes into account this complex structure of a law and allows the analyst to answer questions regarding the *applicability* and *satisfaction* of norms in different situations. In Nòmos 2 *compliance* to a norm is analyzed with respect to those two factors.

E. Yu et al. (Eds.): ER 2014, LNCS 8824, pp. 275–288, 2014.

However, an important factor in evaluating the compliance of requirements to a norm comes from the analysis of *who* must comply with it, which is just as important as *what* compliance entail. One of the contributions of this paper rests in the intuition that if the right requirement is assigned to the wrong actor in the domain, we have non-compliance. This is particularly critical when designing the system-to-be. Software systems are typically complex systems comprised by many software and hardware components and integrated into social systems, such as business processes and other organizational structures. Requirements analysts assign responsibilities to these technical and social parts of the systems, and the responsibilities must meet those that are given by law. For example, The Italian Privacy Law addresses *Data Subject* and *Data Processor* in its norms, but in a set of requirements describing a software system for phone companies, relevant roles might include *SIM-user* or *Phone Operator*. When the analyst specifies that the *SIM-user* provides its data, it is binding this role of the domain to that of the *Data Subject*, making the *SIM-user* responsible for the norms addressing this legal role. In other words, by designing system roles and deciding which requirements they are responsible for, the analyst implicitly defines to which legal roles are involved. These two aspects — identifying which norms a role is responsible for, and *who* is the responsible for the norms in the domain — are crucial aspects for the evaluation of compliance of a set of requirements, and we need to be able to represent these aspects in our modeling language.

In this paper we extend our previous work in order to represent roles and requirements, and reason about roles and their responsibilities in the evaluation of compliance for a set of requirements. The main contribution of this paper is to introduce Nòmos 3, a modelling language for evaluating compliance of roles and requirements in the domain of Requirement Engineering (RE). This modeling language is supposed to be used by requirement analysts who use requirements models and existing models of the law to perform the analysis. One important feature of Nòmos 3 is the ability to represent and clarify: when a role is responsible for bringing about a situation, and what it means for a role to have 'fulfilled' its responsibilities. Nòmos 3 extends the reasoning capabilities of Nòmos 2 by offering answers to the following important questions: **Q1**: Which roles in the requirements are subject to norms?; **Q2**: To which norms these roles must comply?; **Q3**: Which roles in the requirements have fulfilled their responsibilities/which roles comply?; **Q4**: If a role in the domain fulfills its requirements, has it fulfilled its legal responsibilities?

The paper is organized as follows. We first introduce Nòmos 2 as our baseline (section 2). Section 3 describes the core language of Nòmos 3, some basic relationships, and section 4 how Nòmos 3 supports reasoning for compliance evaluation. We describe in section 5 the validity of our proposal through an illustrative case study. In section 6 we discuss related work, and we conclude in section 7.

2   Baseline

Regulatory documents, such as laws, regulations and policies, are complex artefacts: they contain elements such as conditions, exceptions or derogations defining the applicability or satisfaction conditions for the norms (rights and obligations) that constitute a law. Nòmos 2 is a modelling language proposed in [13] that aims at capturing the complexity of regulatory documents by means of conceptual models. The language is founded on the premise that conceptual models may help the communication with the stakeholders, and is based on the concepts of Norm and Situation. A *Norm* is the most atomic fragment of law with a deontic status, and in combination with Situations it is used to make inferences about compliance. A Norm can be *applicable*, if its pre-conditions hold; *satisfied* if its post-conditions hold; *complied* if it is applicable and satisfied. The applicability and satisfaction of a norm depends on the situations (partial states of the world, or states-of-affairs) holding, the idea being that if some situations hold, the norm will apply/be satisfied.

Relationships in Nòmos 2 act as label-propagation channels from their source (for example, a situation or norm) to their target. Forward and backward reasoning algorithms are used to support useful analysis of norm models, such as *applicability analysis*, intended to find the (sub)set of norms applicable to a given (sub)set of situations; *compliance analysis*, which aims at providing evidence of compliance (or violation) of a norm model; *compliance search*, which aims at finding a solution described in terms of a set of situations holding that will make some given norms complied with.

Nòmos 2 effectively explores compliance alternatives, however it fails in capturing the implications that follow from the existence of different roles, which can charged with the duty of complying.

3   Concepts, Relations, and Value Types in Nòmos 3

A Nòmos 3 model consists of a set of propositions, which can be either instances of concepts or relationships between concepts. All concepts and relationships have two purposes. One is *representation*, for the sake of documentation of a domain for model users; after all, this is what "making models" or "modelling" usually refer to. The other is *reasoning*, which here means making inferences from the elements of a model. This is accomplished by allowing propositions to obtain values. Values in Nòmos 3 reflect concerns that we believe are useful for evaluating compliance, and value types constitute a generalization of the notion of truth value in logic. We introduce the following notational conventions: if the name of a concept is "norm", we write C-Norm, and Norm for its generic instance; if the name of a relation is "satisfaction", then we write R-Satisfaction; if the name of a value type is "assignment", we write V-Assignment.

3.1   Primitives

Concepts, relations, and value types presented below are primitive, that is, not defined in terms of others, or of one another. All other concepts, relations, and value types in Nòmos 3 are defined from this language core.

Situations. Instances of C-Situation are propositions used to represent states of the world. Situations are used to represent pre- and post-conditions of norms (Nòmos 2), and will be used similarly to represent requirements in Nòmos 3. It is the concept of Situation that makes Nòmos 3 versatile, in the sense that its models can be combined with requirements models made with various requirements modelling languages. For example, a requirements model may include a goal that "User should be able to ask for reimbursement, if dissatisfied with a product". The resulting system may generate two Situations "User is dissatisfied with a product" and "System allows the user to ask for reimbursement"; if we want to look at the consequences on compliance of the goal being satisfied, we can set the values of both Situations to be satisfied, and compute how this influences the compliance with Norms.

C-Situation is associated with a single value type, called V-Satisfaction. This value type allows an instance to take one of three values:
- Satisfied (abbreviated ST), if the Situation corresponds to the world,
- Failed (SF), if the Situation does not correspond to the world,
- Unknown (SU), if it is unknown if the Situation is satisfied. We use the third value (unknown), because our assignments of labels may be incomplete, yet we may want to do reasoning over models where we do not know, or do not want to assign a value before we start reasoning. With the third value, we avoid assuming that such leaf nodes without values are, by default, satisfied or failed (the use of three values is somewhat non-standard, but is not new [12]).

The satisfaction value that a Situation gets in a Nòmos 3 model depend on the values assigned to relationships that it is in. Rules for computing values are defined later.

Roles. We use Roles to represent the distribution of responsibility, and to evaluate the effects of fulfilling or failing these responsibilities. *Responsibilities are allocations of Situations to Roles*, such that if the Situations are satisfied, the responsibilities are fulfilled, and if all responsibilities are, then we can say that the Role is fulfilled.

There are two kinds of Roles. C-Role.Legal is responsible for Situations that appear in Norms, while C-Role.Social is responsible for Situations that appear in Goals. The intuition is that there are Roles which are not defined by laws and regulations, but rather in the domain where the requirements are defined: these are Social Roles. The Goals assigned to a Social Role represent requirements the role has, or goals assigned to a role for fulfillment. Legal Roles are defined by laws and regulations, and they exist only because laws and regulations dictate that some situations become true (obligations) and others can become true (rights), and in both cases somebody has the obligation/right to make this happen.

Since we allocate Situations to Roles — and call these allocations responsibilities — we will talk about the fulfilment of responsibilities, and thereby of Roles. We use the value type V-Fulfilment, with the following values:
- Fulfilled (FT), if the Role fulfilled all its responsibilities,
- Unfulfilled (FF), if the Role has not fulfilled all its responsibilities,
- Unknown (FU), if it is unknown if the Role is fulfilled.

The satisfaction values of Situations, which the Role is responsible for, determine the fulfilment value of the Role. Asserting that a Role is fulfilled, in turn, equates to asserting that all the Situations it is responsible for, are satisfied.

Primitive Relationships. In Nòmos 3 a relationship instance between two proposition p_1 and p_2 is also a proposition that has the format "if p_1 is satisfied, then p_2 is/is-not satisfied".

Since the value of p_2 depends on (a) the value of p_1 and (b) the type of relationship between the two, we consider relationship as propagating a value to their target when the relationship holds. In table 1 we summarize how V-Satisfaction and V-Fulfillment value are propagated over the three primitive relationships (see the complementary technical report [6] for more details).

Table 1. Propagation of values across the three basic relations

$p_1 \xrightarrow{\text{make}} p_2$		$p_1 \xrightarrow{\text{break}} p_2$		$p_1 \xrightarrow{\text{take}} p_2$	
p_1	p_2	p_1	p_2	p_1	p_2
ST	ST	ST	SF	ST	FT
SF	SU	SF	SU	SF	FF
SU	SU	SU	SU	SU	FU

Make. The R-Make relationship instance is a proposition that has the format "if Situation s_i is satisfied, then Situation s_j is". R-Make is a relationship between Situations s_i and s_j — R-Make(s_i, s_j) — and the V-Satisfaction value propagated depends on the V-Satisfaction value of s_i (see table 1).

Break. A R-Break relationship instance is a proposition that has the format "if Situation s_i is satisfied, then Situation s_j is not". R-Break is, roughly speaking, the opposite of R-Make. R-Break is also a relationship between Situations s_i and s_j — R-Break(s_i, s_j) — and the V-Satisfaction value propagated depends on the V-Satisfaction value of s_i (see table 1).

Take. R-Take relationship instance is a proposition with the format "Role r is responsible for Situation s", used to indicate that the Role is responsible for satisfying the Situation, and that the V-Fulfilment value of the Role depends on the V-Satisfaction value of the Situation. R-Take is a relationship between Situations and Roles s and r — R-Take(s, r) — and it is read as "if Situation s is satisfied, then Role r is fulfilled". We the say that a Role r fulfills its responsibility if Situation s has value ST, when it has value SF, r is not fulfilling its responsibility (see table 1).

AND/OR. R-AND/R-OR are meta-relationships. An instance of R-AND or R-OR is a relationship over a set of Make, Break, or Take relationships of the same type (so the set cannot include, for example, both Make and Break relationships). The value of a meta-relationship instance depends on the values of the relationships it is over. These values are assigned as in Nòmos 2: for example, R-AND will have the value ST iff all the sources of the relationships have the value ST, and when the target concept of the relationship is a Situation, it will therefore be assigned ST (FT if the target is a Role). An R-OR will be ST if at least one of the sources of the relationships in it is ST, and when the target concept of the relationship is a Role, it will be assigned FT. All rules for computing R-AND and R-OR values are defined in the technical report [6]. For example when two situations s_i, s_j in conjunction target a Role instance r, then the fulfillment value of r is FT only when the when both situations are ST.

Similarly, when two situations s_i, s_j in disjunction target another Situation instance s, then the satisfaction value of s is ST when s_i or s_j is ST. Nòmos 3 has its own rules for aggregating values that a situation or another node accumulates (see [6]). These aggregation rules apply whenever a situation has at least two or more incoming edges. For example, suppose that a Situation X has two incoming edges, one saying that X should have the value ST, the other SF. So we say that this Situation X accumulates ST and SF, and the aggregation rule should say which single value X should have, given those that it accumulates.

3.2   Language Parts for Compliance Evaluation

We evaluate *the compliance of a set of Requirements to Norms*. Requirements are represented in terms of Goals and Social Roles desiring them, and are described in a model in some modelling language (e.g. i*). We will call *domain model* this representation of the requirements. The model may describe actual elements (e.g., Goals) and conditions that will always hold in the domain (e.g. Domain Assumptions), and these can be represented by Situations. The model would also describe desirable actions and conditions whereby we still can identify Situations, but now both desirable ones, and undesirable ones, and evaluate the consequences of these alternatives on compliance. Moreover, by defining responsibilities for a Role, we are representing that some sets of Situations should be satisfied by that Role. We do not require all Situations to be responsibility of a Role: for example a Situation like "It is Christmas season" is not responsibility of any Role, and we refer to these as accidental Situations. We refer to intentional Situations those who are responsibility of a Role, like "Expressed shipping is requested".

To evaluate the compliance of the requirements to Norms, we need to represent actions and conditions imposed by law and regulations, that is define instances of the C-Norm.

A central idea in Nòmos 3 is that *to evaluate the compliance of a domain model to Norms, we need to determine (i) which Norms are applicable, and therefore need to be complied with, and (ii) which Social Roles, because of their responsibilities in the domain model, also are subject to Norms, and therefore accumulate the responsibilities of Legal Roles.* These two are closely tied: it is because of the accidental or intentional satisfaction of Situations, that some specific Norms become applicable; once they do, we have to worry about new Legal Roles and their responsibilities. The Social Roles in the domain model have to accumulate the responsibilities of these Legal Roles, so as to ensure compliance.

Norms. Instances of C-Norm are representations of conditions, which are given by laws or other regulations that the system-to-be should comply with, or are otherwise relevant in evaluating compliance. Like in Nòmos 2, a Norm is a written a the five-tuple $(n.type, n.holder, n.counterpart, n.antecedent, n.consequent)$ where n is the identifier for the Norm instance; $n.type$ categorizes the Norm as either duty or right;[1] $n.holder$ is the C-Role.Legal instance which takes the

---

[1] Obligations and prohibition in Deontic Logic can be captured by our concept of duty, and permission by the concept of right.

responsibility for satisfying the *n.consequent*; *n.counterpart* is the optional C-Role.Legal instance which benefits when the *n.consequent* is satisfied (if specified); *n.antecedent* are the C-Situation instances, which if satisfied, make the Norm applicable, that is *n.holder* should satisfy *n.consequent*; *n.consequent* are the C-Situation instances, such that the Norm is complied with if and only if these Situations are satisfied.

A Norm is evaluated with a V-Compliance value type. Each allowed value of V-Compliance corresponds to a composite predicate on the values of a Norm's holder, counterpart, antecedent, and consequent — this is a departure from Nòmos 2, where this value only depends on the antecedent and consequent Situations. The following rules introduce the compliance values:

- Compliant (CT) if the norm applies, is satisfied, the holder is fulfilled, and the counterpart is fulfilled (*when that counterpart Role exists*). In values we write compliance iff V-Fulfilment(*n.holder*)=FT and V-Fulfilment(*n.counterpart*)=FT and V-Satisfaction(*n.antecedent*)=ST and V-Satisfaction(*n.consequent*)=ST.
- Incidental Compliant if the norm applies, is satisfied, but the holder/counterpart is either not fulfilled, or its fulfilment is unknown. The interesting idea is that it allows to identify cases in which the correct Situations are brought about, but the Legal Roles have not actually fulfilled their responsibilities.
- Tolerance (CT) if the norm *does not* apply, it is satisfied and the holder/counterpart is fulfilled. The idea is that the role is correctly complying with a norm even if it does not have to.

The other two compliance values are the same as in Nòmos 2, and do not depend on the values on the holder/counterpart:
- Non-Compliant (CF) if the norm of type duty applies but it is not satisfied.
- Inconclusive (CU) if it is unknown if the norm applies.

Goals. Goals are state of affairs desired by a Social Role,[2] and are used to represent Requirements. For example "Apply for a reimbursement" represents a Goal desired by the Social Role *SIM-user*. Nòmos 3 evaluates the compliance of a given goal by taking into account: (i) the Role and its associated Goals, and (ii) the Situations describing the Goal. A set of Situations, in conjunction or disjunction, can represent the achievement of the Goal as well as the Situations that can be satisfied to achieve the Goal. For example the situation "Reimbursement claim is filed" is the situation associated to the achievement of the Goal "Apply for a reimbursement", and it can also be read as the situation that is satisfied when the goal is achieved. This former reading allows us to read the *SIM-user* as the holder of the Goal, and therefore being assigned/allocated the situations satisfying the Goal.

Domain Assumptions. A domain assumption is a state of affairs that is known to hold in a given scenario. For example the situation "The company is non-profit organization" can be included as an assumption where in the reasoning it is always considered with satisfaction value ST.

---

[2] In Nòmos 3 we are not interested in specific agents, so we relate a social role to the goal. The agent who ends up occupying it is the one who is assumed to desire the goal.

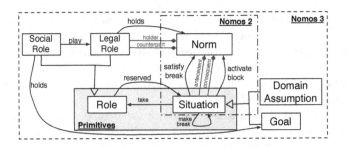

Fig. 1. Metamodel of Nòmos 3

Representing Responsibility and Compliance in Nòmos 3 Models.

In Nòmos 2 four basic relations are identified to propagate applicability and satisfiability values from Situations to Norms. The same is achieved and expanded in Nòmos 3 (figure 1), where we summarize the relations derived from the core-relations used in Nòmos 3 models:

• "activate/block" are Nòmos 2 relations which can be written as a R-Make/R-Break relations from Situations to Norms: when a Situation is satisfied, then the *antecedent* of the Norm is satisfied/not-satisfied.

• "satisfy/break" are Nòmos 2 relations which can be written as R-Make/R-Break relations from Situations to a Norm: when a Situation is satisfied, then the *consequent* of the target concept is satisfied/not-satisfied. In Nòmos 3 we use the same relation to also relate Situations with Goals. For example in figure 2, when either of the situations s_1 or s_2 is satisfied, then the goal G_1 is satisfied.

• "hold" is a relation from a Legal-Role to a Norms — and from a Social-Role to a Goal — representing the fact that the Role is responsible (R-Take) for bringing about the Situations in the consequent of that Norms/Goal. In figure 2, 'SR_3 holds G_3' represents that the *SIM User* is responsible for the Situations satisfying G_3 (i.e., s_{11}).

• "play" is a relation from a Social-Role to a Legal Role representing the fact that the Social Role plays the Legal Role and becomes responsible for bringing about the Situations for whom the Legal Role is responsible. In figure 2, 'SR_3 plays LR_3' represents that the Social Role SR_3 is responsible for the Situations consequent of the Norms that LR_3 holds.

• "reserved" is a R-Take from a Situation to a Role, identifying that the Role is *the only* responsible for that Situation. In figure 2 for example, the *Data Subject* is the only Legal Role who can give a consent ($s_{14} \xrightarrow{\text{reserved}} LR_4$); similarly, the association of a phone number to a user is only responsibility of the *Company Operator* ($s_{10} \xrightarrow{\text{reserved}} SR_2$).

• "imply/derogate/endorse" are relations between Norms introduced in Nòmos 2 to represent legal variability: an *imply* relation from N_1 to N_2 represents that when N_1 is complied, then also N_2 is; a *derogate* relation is used to represents that when N_1 is applicable, then N_2 is not; an *endorse* relation represents that when N_1 is applicable, also N_2 is. For example in figure 2, the Right R_3 for the customer to obtain a reimbursement is complied when the Seller complies with its duty D_3 to reimburse the money $(D_3 \xrightarrow{\text{imply}} R_3)$.

Responsibility for a Role is represented through two relations in Nòmos 3: the *reserved* relation for situations which can *only* be brought about by a specific Role, and through the *hold* relation for Situations that are assigned to a given Role in order to fulfill its Social/Legal responsibilities.

Visual notation. In a Nòmos 3 model (see figure 2) we represent Situations with rectangles, Norms with triangles, Goals with ovals and Roles with circles.

4 Reasoning in Nòmos 3

Adding Norms and Goals to the primitive language lets us make Nòmos 3 models that can answer interesting questions about compliance. Reasoning in Nòmos 3 amounts to different type of if-then analysis. By assigning values to a selected set of Situations, we can compute the values of other Situations and Roles, which are related via Make, Break, and Take relations. The compliance analysis provided by Nòmos 2 and still supported in Nòmos 3 was related to the following question:

SituationsToNorms: *Which Norms obtain the compliance value w, if we assign the satisfaction value v_1 to Situation s_1, v_2 to s_2, ..., v_n to s_n?*

The question summarizes a type of if-then analysis, where we are assuming some Situations are satisfied, failed, or whose satisfaction is unknown, and we want to understand the effects of this on compliance (which is now defined in terms of both Roles fulfillment and Situation satisfactions).

A new kind of analysis in Nòmos 3 involves Roles, which we use to evaluate the consequences on compliance, of fulfilling or failing responsibilities. If we assert that some specific Legal Roles are fulfilled, we can determine how that relates to compliance, which amounts to asking this question for a given Nòmos 3 model:

RolesToNorms: *Which Norms obtain the compliance value w, if we assign the fulfilment value v_1 to Legal Role r_1, v_2 to r_2, ..., v_n to r_n?*

We can also assert the fulfilment of Social Roles, to see the consequences on Legal Roles. This is summarized in the following question.

SocialRolesToLegalRoles: *Which Legal Roles obtain the fulfilment value w, if we assign the fulfilment value v_1 to Social Role r_1, v_2 to r_2, ..., v_n to r_n?*

It is an interesting question, because if the Social Role is fulfilled, it will satisfy Situations which may make Norms applicable. The Norms in turn introduce Legal Roles, and we want to know which of these Legal Roles are fulfilled as well.

Another issue is to look at the consequences on responsibility fulfilment, of having specific satisfaction values assigned to Situations:

SituationsToRoles: *Which Roles obtain the fulfilment value w, if we assign the satisfaction value v_1 to Situation s_1, v_2 to s_2, ..., v_n to s_n?*

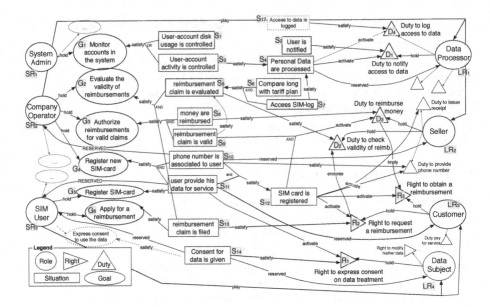

Fig. 2. Nòmos 3 model of the scenario

Adding Goals to Nòmos 3 does not change the questions we can ask, but simply how we read these questions and their answers. For example, if we want to evaluate the compliance of some Goals, then we are asking the same question as SituationsToNorms, except that now, we know that these Situations originate in instances of concepts from the goal model, and reflect the responsibilities of some Social Roles. In a goal model, then that question can read "Which Norms obtain the compliance value w, if goals $g_1, \ldots, g_n$ are achieved (that is, the situations $s_1, \ldots, s_n$ get the value ST?"

5 Nòmos 3 at Work

In this section we illustrate the Nòmos 3 language and its reasoning capabilities using as example a set of requirements for a software managing the reimbursement requests of the customers of a phone company. In figure 2 we provide the Nòmos 3 model of the example. On the left side of figure 2 we have represented some goals of the social roles involved (*System Admin, Company Operator*, and *SIM-user*). On the right side we have represented some norms regulating phone contracts and some norms from the Privacy Law regulating data processing.

Q1 *Which roles in the domain are subject to norms?* To answer this question, we start with a given set of goals (G_1–G_6) represented by: a set of situations holding, and social roles responsible for bringing about these situations. These situations make applicable norms in the legal model for which some legal roles are responsible. We identify and link a social role with the norms it has to comply with through the $\xrightarrow{\text{play}}$ relation. The *Company Operator* is therefore subject to the norms addressing the *Seller*. Moreover the *Company Operator* has to evaluate the reimbursement claim (G_2) and this requirement is satisfied also by accessing the SIM-log of the user (s_7). However when the log of the phone is accessed, the law considers this operation as type of processing of personal data ($s_7 \xrightarrow{\text{satisfy}} s_4$). Since s_7 is responsibility of the legal role *Data Processor*, the *Company Operator* is also subject to the norms addressing this legal role ($SR_2 \xrightarrow{\text{play}} LR_1$). Interestingly, the social role *System Admin* may/may not be subject to norms depending on the different situations involved: its requirement of monitoring the accounts (G_1) can involve a simple monitoring of disk usage (s_1), *or* monitoring the activity of the accounts (s_3). In the latter case the *System Admin* is also subject to the norms of the *Data Processor* because the control of user activity involves processing of personal data ($s_7 \xrightarrow{\text{satisfy}} s_4$). So unless the requirements for the *System Admin* differently specify or avoid accessing user accounts, this social role will be also subject to the norms of the *Data Processor*.

Q2 *To which norms these roles must comply?* The situations representing the set of goals (G_1–G_6) make norms applicable. For example, the *Company Operator* must comply with the norms addressing the *Seller*: some norms become directly applicable when "a SIM-card is registered" (e.g., duty to issue a receipt or the duty to provide a phone number), some other norms are applicable when also some other conditions happen. For example, the duty to check the validity of a reimbursement (D_2) applies because the *Customer* has the right to request a reimbursement ($R_2 \xrightarrow{\text{endorse}} D_2$). The *Company Operator* must be able to include in its goals ways to comply with this norm. Similarly, the *Seller* must comply with the duty to actually reimburse the money to the *Customer* (D_3), when the reimbursement claim is valid. The *Company Operator* must comply with the norms addressing the legal role it plays. Evaluating to which norms the roles must comply with, amounts to identifying the applicable norms and in a second step making sure that the norms are not violated — which amounts to identifying the situation that the legal role (through the goals of a social role) should bring about.

Q3 *Which roles in the domain have fulfilled their responsibilities?* Evaluating whether a social role has fulfilled its responsibilities amounts to identifying and evaluating *how a role fulfills its responsibilities*. A social role is responsible for the situations describing the goals it holds, however it also accumulates the responsibilities of the legal role(s) it plays: once the consequent of the norms of the legal role it plays are brought about, the social role has fulfilled its responsibilities. The *SIM-user* for example must comply with the norms applying to the legal role of *Customer* and *Data Subject*. So given the initial set of goals, we know that the situations holding make several norms applicable, like the right for the *Data Subject* to express consent on data treatment (R_1). The social role has therefore fulfilled its responsibilities when this applicable norm is complied with. This right is complied with when the *Data Subject* expresses a consent (s_{14}), and this situation should be brought about by the *SIM-user* in the domain. Until it is included in the requirements that the *SIM-user* should express the consent ($s_{14} \xrightarrow{\text{satisfy}} G_x$, G_x being a new goal "Express consent for data", dotted element in figure 2), the social role will have not fulfilled its responsibilities. The explicit indication that s_{14} is responsibility of the *SIM-user* identifies exactly which social role should include this responsibility in form of requirements. Moreover, the social role *Company Operator* is the one who must comply with the norms applying to the *Data Processor*, like the duty to log access to data is complied with when the access to the data is logged (s_{17}). However in this case it is not relevant for compliance *who* brings about *that* situation: s_{17} is not 'reserved' by any social role. So, as long as a social role includes it in its responsibility (e.g., by adding a new goal to the *System Admin*), the norm can be satisfied: both the legal role and the social role of *Company Operator* will have fulfilled their responsibilities. Should however the *System Admin* fail to bring about this situation, the responsibility of the violation of the norm would be still traced to its holder (the *Data Processor*, the *Company Operator*).

Q4 *If a role in the domain fulfills its responsibilities, what is the fulfillment value of the legal role it is playing?* When a social role fulfills its responsibility in the domain, it satisfies the situations it is responsible for — i.e., the situations describing the requirements it holds. For example, when the *SIM-user* fulfills its responsibilities in the model of figure 2, we can assert that the situations describing the goals G_5, G_6 are satisfied (s_{11}, s_{12}, s_{13}). These situations make applicable 3 norms for two legal roles (the *Data Subject* and *Customer*): R_1, R_2, R_3. These legal roles played by the *SIM-user* are fulfilled when the applicable norms are respected. R_1 and R_2 norms are complied with when the respective consequent is satisfied (s_{14}, s_{13}), while the compliance of R_3 depends on whether the *Seller* complies with his duty to reimburse money of a valid reimbursement claim ($D_3 \xrightarrow{\text{imply}} R_3$). By 'only' fulfilling its responsibility in the domain, the *SIM-user* does not also fulfill the responsibility of its legal counterpart as 1) some situations are not brought about 2) the compliance of a norm depends on the compliance of a norm of another role.

Compliance Discussion. Compliance of a set of requirements — expressed in terms of Goals — can be evaluated and explored using the Nòmos 3 modeling language and its reasoning capabilities. The identification of applicable norms and legal roles allows for example to identify requirements that should be revised in order not to make too many roles in the domain have to comply with norms: this is the case of the *System Admin* and whether it access the user account (aka, becomes a *Data Processor* or not). Secondly, our language allows to evaluate requirements compliance given the applicable norms, the situations that should be brought about to satisfy the norm, and the role — if a particular one is needed — that should bring about the situation. For example, in order for the *Data Processor* to comply with the duty to log the access to user's data, it is sufficient that the situation is brought about in the requirements. However, to comply with the *Data Subject* right to include its data, a consent should be given *only* from the *SIM-User* (s_{14}). In this way, by evaluating the satisfaction of the consequent of the applicable norms and the roles responsible for them, it is possible to identify the requirements compliance with a set of norms.

6   Related Work

Nòmos 3 is related to three research areas: role ontologies, normative multi-agent systems, and compliance of requirements. First, in the research area of ontology for roles, the work by Masolo et al. [9] and by F. Loebe [8] provide an important ontological characterization of the concept of Social Role. In the first work Masolo provides an extension of the DOLCE foundational ontology to deal with social concepts. In the second work, Loebe also provides a distinction between social and abstract roles. None of these works explicitly considers legal roles, which are instead characterized by Gangemi et al. [4]. Our characterization of the concepts of Legal and Social Roles is aligned with the principles laid down in these works.

In the AI field of Normative MultiAgent System (MAS) norms act as behavioural constraints that regulate and structure social order within a MAS. Typical problems addressed include the definition and derivation of those rules, also monitoring an agent's behaviour to determine compliance. For example, Bench Capon et al. [3] describes a method to dynamically assign norms to agents and, in line with our work they, also treat Norms as conditional elements. [11] proposes a normative extension to their framework for MAS based on Event Calculus which allows to model the responsibility of an agent depending on the role he plays. [15] takes a social perspective of MAS and proposes formal model for governance that provides similar type of compliance analysis similar to ours, in the domain of Socio Technical System with autonomous agents. [10] clarifies the concepts used in Normative MAS and illustrates how the so called *normative context* influences the actions that the autonomous agents can perform. The heavy-weight formal approach involved in most of these approaches makes it difficult to apply them to Requirement Engineering (RE).

In RE different solutions have been proposed for evaluating compliance. For example, Breaux et al. [1] use a text-based approach to extract and prioritize rights and obligations from legal texts and align them with a set of requirements. Darimont et al. [2] have used KAOS for the representation of elements extracted from legal texts. [5] also adopt a goal-based approach and provide an extension to the Goal-oriented Requirement Language to manage law and identify which requirements are not aligned. Siena et al. [14] also adopt a goal-modeling approach and introduce a 'dedicated' modeling language to provide a legal extension for the i* framework. [7] extended this framework by Siena et al. to represent non-compliance and used an argumentation-base approach to revise a set of requirements and achieve their compliance. Most of these approaches however tend to provide ad-hoc solutions for a specific requirement language or for a specific type of law and do not explicitly consider the attribution of responsibilities of roles or what happens when the wrong roles satisfy a norm.

7   Conclusions

In this paper we have presented Nòmos 3, a modeling language for evaluating compliance of roles in the domain of Requirement Engineering. Our propositional approach allows our modeling language to be an adequate lightweight solution for requirement engineering as opposed to other modeling language for law. The readability and complexity of our models is an important limitation that we plan to investigate and improve in future work. Work in progress is dedicated to a methodology to support the analyst in revising a set of requirements, as well as implementing our primitives in a reasoning tool like DLV in order to support the methodology with a reasoning tool (like for Nòmos 2). Current work in progress is also dedicated to a tool-supported methodology for the semi-automatic generation of Nòmos 3 model. Further work will also be dedicated in investigating and expanding our language to answer questions regarding delegations (of responsibilities, requirements, ...).

Acknowledgments. This work has been supported by the ERC advanced grant 267856 "Lucretius: Foundations for Software Evolution" (April 2011 – March 2016).

References

1. Breaux, T.D., Vail, M.W., Antón, A.I.: Towards Regulatory Compliance: Extracting Rights and Obligations to Align Requirements with Regulations. In: RE 2006 (2006)
2. Darimont, R., Lemoine, M.: Goal-oriented analysis of regulations. In: ReMo2V, held at CAiSE 2006 (2006)
3. Derakhshan, F., Bench-Capon, T., McBurney, P.: Dynamic assignment of roles, rights and responsibilities in normative multi-agent systems. Journal of Logic and Computation 23(2), 355–372 (2013)
4. Gangemi, A., Sagri, M.-T., Tiscornia, D.: A constructive framework for legal ontologies. In: Benjamins, V.R., Casanovas, P., Breuker, J., Gangemi, A. (eds.) Law and the Semantic Web. LNCS (LNAI), vol. 3369, pp. 97–124. Springer, Heidelberg (2005)
5. Ghanavati, S., Amyot, D., Peyton, L.: Towards a framework for tracking legal compliance in healthcare. In: Krogstie, J., Opdahl, A.L., Sindre, G. (eds.) CAiSE 2007 and WES 2007. LNCS, vol. 4495, pp. 218–232. Springer, Heidelberg (2007)
6. Ingolfo, S., Jureta, I., Siena, A., Susi, A., Perini, A., Mylopoulos, J.: Legal compliance of roles and requirements. Tech. rep., University of Trento, Italy, tR14-03-001 (2012), http://selab.fbk.eu/lawvariability/
7. Ingolfo, S., Siena, A., Mylopoulos, J., Susi, A., Perini, A.: Arguing regulatory compliance of software requirements. Data & Knowledge Engineering 87 (2013)
8. Loebe, F.: Abstract vs. social roles-a refined top-level ontological analysis. In: Procs. of AAAI Fall Symposium Roles 2005 (2005)
9. Masolo, C., Vieu, L., Bottazzi, E., Catenacci, C., Ferrario, R., Gangemi, A., Guarino, N.: Social roles and their descriptions. In: Procs. of KR 2004, pp. 267–277 (2004)
10. Okuyama, F.Y., Bordini, R.H., da Rocha Costa, A.C.: Situated normative infrastructures: the normative object approach. J. Logic Comput. 23, 397–424 (2013)
11. Sadri, F., Stathis, K., Toni, F.: Normative kgp agents. Comput. Math. Org. Theor. 2006, 101–126 (2006)
12. Seipel, D., Minker, J., Ruiz, C.: A characterization of the partial stable models for disjunctive databases. In: ILPS, pp. 245–259 (1997)
13. Siena, A., Jureta, I., Ingolfo, S., Susi, A., Perini, A., Mylopoulos, J.: Capturing variability of law with Nòmos 2. In: ER 2012 (2012)
14. Siena, A., Mylopoulos, J., Perini, A., Susi, A.: Designing law-compliant software requirements. In: ER 2009, pp. 472–486 (2009)
15. Singh, M.P.: Norms as a basis for governing sociotechnical systems. ACM Trans. Intell. Syst. Technol. 5(1), 21:1–21:23 (2014)

Towards an XBRL Ontology Extension
for Management Accounting

Barbara Livieri[1], Marco Zappatore[2], and Mario Bochicchio[2]

[1] Department of Economic Sciences
[2] Department of Engineering
University of Salento, Lecce, Italy
{barbara.livieri,marcozappatore,mario.bochicchio}@unisalento.it

Abstract. The Extensible Business Reporting Language (XBRL) is used in several countries to share business data and it is largely diffused, for example, for balance sheets exchange and archival. On the other side, the analysis of management accounting data poses more interoperability issues. In particular, it requires more sophisticate information models in order to integrate data generated by different parties (both internal and external to the enterprise) in different formats and for different purposes. For the same reason, the "flat" mapping, performed by automatic mechanisms often used to import XBRL streams into Web Ontology Language (OWL) for further processing, is inadequate and more sophisticate options are required. In this perspective, we propose a modification and extension of an existing XBRL ontology, with the aim of better supporting the concepts and the operations needed for management accounting.

Keywords: Ontologies, XBRL, Interoperability, Collaborative Enterprises.

1 Introduction and Motivation

The transition from intra-organizational to inter-organizational relationships characterized the last twenty years of evolution of enterprises. More recently the increasing importance of Collaborative Enterprises (CEs) and the growing impact of technologies on businesses drove the transition towards a new phase of trans-organizational relationship, characterized by an increased speed to create value [1]. In this perspective, the research interest on the exchange of business information is rapidly growing, tightly coupled with the interest for new techniques (e.g. Open Book Accounting) and new systems (e.g. cross-organizational ERP) whose same nature is established on the concept of business information exchange. An important step to effectively support this integration of business information has been done with Extensible Business Reporting Language (XBRL), a standard for the exchange of financial reports and accounting information. However, the business domain is complex and if some doubts have been risen on the effectiveness of XBRL for the interoperability at the financial statement level, due to the lack of a formal semantic, whereas only the grammar structure is analyzed [2], these doubts are even stronger when XBRL is applied to management accounting, which is a broader domain. Accounting information is structurally and semantically different in

E. Yu et al. (Eds.): ER 2014, LNCS 8824, pp. 289–296, 2014.

different firms, and this generates interoperability issues. While financial statements respect general accepted standards, no such standard exists for management accounting, making it more important to use formal semantics based on explicit and shared information models purposely designed to ease the gathering and integration of information from heterogeneous sources [3].

For this reason, several authors propose to use ontologies as means to offer a shared conceptualization of the domain of accounting. Ontologies, indeed, can be defined as *"an explicit, [formal,] partial specification of a conceptualization"* [4] that *"enables knowledge sharing and reuse across systems and human users"* [5]. Ontologies offer a broad range of appealing features to produce reusable descriptions of knowledge domains and to support enterprise engineers and business experts to design and build a new generation of Information Systems. However, an ontology to share business information need to be built on more basic (core) ontologies defining the key concepts underlying the world of enterprises. In particular, it is not enough to offer only a management accounting ontology, since XBRL is a widespread standard and the books keeping is often integrated for financial statements and management accounting. The XBRL ontology needs to be linked to other ontologies defining a broader sets of aspects which are central for the business domain, such as performance measurement and Key Performance Indicators (KPIs). For these reasons, in this work we build a more flexible semantic model starting from the XBRL Ontology [6], that we modified in order to make it more compliant with Web Ontology Language (OWL) [7] and descriptive logic, and extended through a modular structure. The extension is performed by exploiting KPI Ontology (KPIO), a modular library of ontologies developed by the authors to describe performance measurement and firms concepts. The aim is to: a) facilitate the information exchange of management accounting; b) facilitate the creation of KPIs; c) facilitate the creation of different management accounting frameworks.

The work is structured as follows. Section 2 is for related works, in Section 3 we describe the research method and Section 4 for the motivation and the requirements. In Section 5, we describe the modeling method and in Section 6 we sketched the mapping method, the resulting ontology and the integration with KPIO. In section 7 we validate the ontology and discuss the results. Finally, Section 8 is for conclusions.

2   Related Works

The effort to standardize financial reporting has resulted in XBRL, which is an XML-based language. It aims at facilitating the preparation, publication, exchange, and analysis of financial statements and of the information they contain [8]. However, XBRL and XML have some limitations, due to the lack of inference mechanisms and of formal semantics [9], which is particularly useful to solve interoperability issues in the business domain [2]. As stated in [10], there are still relevant limitation in the XBRL structure of financial statements, which could prevent an automatic retrieval of financial data and temporal attributes. One of the most significant limitation is the "flat" structure, i.e., with no hierarchical representation of items. To solve this issue, in [10] the authors propose the use of a taxonomy. In this sense, ontologies provide support in the description of the content and semantic embedded in financial documents [8, 11]. To this aim, many researchers and practitioners have studied the underlying ontological representation of business reporting data and have proposed mapping methods able to translate the XBRL file structure into OWL, in order to create and use ontology based representation of XBRL financial reporting data. More in detail, Lara et al. [3], after describing the information model of an investment fund by means of XBRL, propose an automatic translation of XBRL taxonomies in OWL ontologies, using JDOM and Jena software. In the mapping process tuples and items are considered as subclasses of the `Element` class, while `ContextEntity`, `ContextPeriod` and `ContextScenario` are subclasses of `Context`. Other schema transferring models have been proposed in [2] and [12]. Furthermore, Spies [13] offer an UML-based representation of XBRL through a meta-modeling approach. The author distinguishes between meta-data level, where concepts such as reporting taxonomy, legal reference, calculation rules and label are represented, and a data level, where facts such as reporting items, context and currency are shown. The author also states that an ontological representation of XBRL structures, strictly associated with its UML representation, should enable a *"semantically rich processing model of reporting data in innovative business intelligence applications* [and the use of] *inference mechanisms on reporting data"*. A methodology, called Net technique, for the development of accounting ontologies is proposed in [14]. In particular, the method consists of five phases, namely, the retrieval of accounting information (1), the analysis of its contents (2), the development of a taxonomy for financial items (3) and the import of accounting items in the database in order to store the information on the relationships among accounting items (4), and, finally, the automatic generation of an accounting ontology (5). However, to the best of our knowledge, there have been no attempts to integrate an ontology expressively designed for management accounting purposes, with ontologies able to support XBRL.

3   Research Method

The research method follows the Design Science Research methodology proposed by [15]. This approach implies the identification and motivation of the problem, with the definition of the possible solution (Relevance cycle), the design of the artefact and its evaluation (Design cycle). As a first step, we outline the general problem in order to motivate our proposal. The definition of the problem is also used for the requirements elicitation and for the development of the corresponding Competency Questions (CQs) to which the model should answer. Indeed, according to a widely-adopted approach [16], rooted in ontology engineering best practices, a set of informal CQs, written in natural language, was set up on the bases of the description of several motivating scenarios. CQs have been further categorized into basic (BCQs) and complex competency questions (CCQs). The former ones refer to the asserted ontology structure, whilst the latter ones mostly address inferred contents, since an ontology whose CQs do not look like simple lookup queries (as in the case of SCQs) cannot be considered a well-modeled one [17]. Finally, we present the ontology, the CQsand their renderings in SPARQL, for validation purposes.

Basic (BCQs) and complex competency questions (CCQs) were elicited to properly model the knowledge domain (see Section 3), as the ones exemplified in the following:

BCQ.1: What is a context entity type?

BCQ.2: Which context types are possible?

CCQ.1: Given a context entity type, what is the value of its "total cost of employee"?

CCQ.2: What is the context scenario type for the KPI "total cost of employee"?

4   Modeling Method

The ontology library KPIO was developed with a modular architecture (as a collection of axioms defining classes, instances and properties) in order to favor portability and reuse, domain decomposition and content categorization [18]. The widely-known OWL 2 DL [7] was chosen as modeling language since it is fully decidable (i.e., allow finite reasoning mechanisms) and adds many appealing features to its previous versions, such as semantic property composition and simple meta-modeling.

We modeled a core ontology (ontoPM) and a set of domain-dependent modules, namely ontoKPI for KPIs, ontoFirm and ontoCE, which gather concepts describing firms and collaborative enterprises respectively. The adoption of core and domain ontologies is a well-established custom in ontological engineering [19, 20]. A class-based approach was used to model knowledge resources, thus describing relevant entities as classes characterized by class expressions and property restrictions, so that end-users can easily populate the ontology by adding instances to those entities.

The mandatory requirement of importing already existing and widely accepted ontologies was followed as well. For instance, the Time ontology [21], proposed by W3C to describe temporal concepts and largely used for its simplicity, has been adopted to model KPI measurement periods. Similarly, the XBRL ontology [22] was added, which is the result of a translation of XBRL structures into OWL. However, we modified this ontology in order to make it more compliant with OWL structure.

KPIO was developed by using Protégé Desktop (v.4.3) [23], a freeware, java-based, open-source ontology editor. Ontology consistency, class expression satisfiability and finite reasoning time complexity were checked by using Pellet reasoner 2.2.0 [24]. The DL expressivity of the ontology is SHROIQ(D).

5   XBRL and KPI Ontologies for Management Accounting

In this section, we outline the mapping method used for modifying an already existing XBRL Ontology [22] in order to make it more compliant with OWL semantic and logic, since the existing ontology was created with an automatic system and has several issues, previously described in Section 2. After the enhancement of the existing ontology we show the integration process between the modified XBRL ontology and KPIO, providing some insight in how the combination of these two ontologies can enable an automatic representation of financial statements information and management accounting ones, solving the interoperability issues previously outlined.

5.1   Mapping of XBRL into OWL

The XBRL ontology [22], used as starting point, was originally composed by 58 classes, 19 object properties and 16 data properties, with DL expressivity: ALCN(D). Mapping process concerned three aspects: firstly, we improve the ontology by adopting a hierarchical structure of classes; also, we avoid the redundancy in classes and restrictions, by deleting or modifying the ones that have no usage in OWL.

Therefore, as a first step of the mapping process, we provided a hierarchical structure for the existing XBRL ontology [22] and we dealt with class redundancy. In particular (see **Fig. 1**), we considered the classes contextEntityType, context-PeriodType, contextScenarioType and contextType, which represents respectively the firm which a business fact is referred to, the time period of the fact, the report types and the possible types of context. Due to the conceptual meaning of these classes, we have considered the three former classes as children of the class contextEntityType, since each class is a type of context associated with a business fact.

As required from XBRL, business facts in XBRL ontology can be items or tuples. However, when we move from XML-based languages to Description Logic, tuples are multiple instances of a class; so there is no need to declare tuples as classes. Therefore, the class factsAttrs is no longer needed, since it should have only a child, itemAttrs, with the same conceptual meaning as factsAttrs. In our model, the class itemAttrs is connected to its context by means of the object property hasContextType. Moreover, as explained by the XBRL glossary, business facts (thus items as well), can refer to financial or temporal facts. In order to explicit this notion, we created two children for itemAttrs (i.e., financialItem and timeItem).

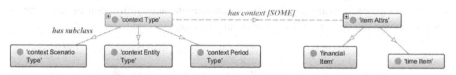

Fig. 1. Ontology fragment describing financial quantities

Each item can have assigned a financial/temporal value or other information. In the XBRL ontology, this was achieved with three classes, namely, essentialNumericItemAttrs, nonNumericItemAttrs and numericItemAttrs. However, in OWL it's possible to explicit the datatype of the information added through data properties. For this reason, we removed those three classes. As a result, itemAttrs has a data property hasNumericValue or hasInfo that declare its value or other information and the data type. Finally, we modified some of the existing restrictions. Restrictions of type (Class max 1 Thing) and (Class min 1 Thing) were changed into Class exactly 1 Thing. Restrictions of type Class min 0 Thing (e.g., any min 0 Thing) were deleted since in OWL this restriction is implicit. Furthermore, we deleted restrictions such as identifier min 1 Thing, since this can be properly expressed via data properties (instead of object properties) and data restrictions, such has hasId exactly 1 integer. We also simplified restrictions with 3 or more Boolean operators, that may mislead reasoners. The resulting ontology has 13 classes, 4 object and 6 data properties (DL expressivity: ALCHQ(D)).

5.2   Overview of the KPIO and Integration with the XBRL Ontology

To exemplify the proposed modeling approach (sSection 4), **Fig. 2** illustrates Financial Quantities (FQs) as subclasses of NumericalQuantity. Each FQ is part of a ReportType, which can be an actualReport, a budgetedReport or a projectedReport. Each FQ also has, as subclasses, Cost, Asset, Liability, Revenue and Return. Finally, each FinancialKPI, a subclass of KPI, is calculated with respect to a FinancialQuantity. KPIs are subclasses of PerformanceMeasure.

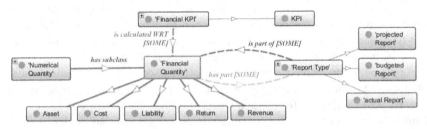

Fig. 2. Ontology fragment describing financial quantities

Furthermore, we integrated the KPIO and the modified XBRL ontology (**Fig. 3**). We applied the OWL property owl:equivalentClass to the class contextScenarioType (XBRL ontology), which refers to the type of report (i.e., actual, budgeted, projected), and to its class in OntoPM. Therefore, each instance or subclass of ReportType is, respectively, an instance or a subclass of contextScenarioType and vice versa: each instance added for management accounting can be used for financial statements, with an XBRL-compliant structure.

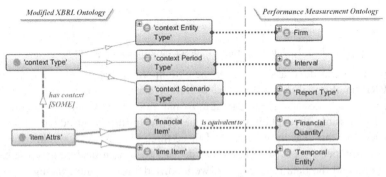

Fig. 3. Ontology fragment describing the equivalences between KPIO and XBRL ontology

We also applied equivalence to: a) contextEntityType, equivalent to Firm; b) contextPeriodType, equivalent to Interval; c) financialItem, equivalent to FinancialQuantity; d) timeItem, equivalent to TemporalEntity.

6   Validation and Discussion

Competency questions (CQs) (see Section 4) have been formalized into queries [25] to be run against the ontologies in order to evaluate their accuracy and quality by checking whether they contain enough information to answer CQs. Since CQ formalization into queries is a quite complex task, due to the presence of several issues (e.g., rules, inference mechanisms, etc.) a suitable query language must be adopted. We selected SPARQL 1.1 (Simple Protocol and RDF Query Language) [26] as it exhibits high expressivity, it allows to query any RDF graph and it is a good compromise when considering inferences. As an example, two SPARQL queries are now reported. The BCQ.2 dealt with context types, so we can search for any subclass of the type:

```
SELECT ?s WHERE { ?s rdfs:subClassOf xbrl_mod:ContextType . }
```

In the same way, CCQ.2 required to identify the context scenario type for the KPI "total cost of employee". It can be rendered in SPARQL as in the following:

```
SELECT ?x WHERE { p0:ContextScenarioType owl:equivalentClass
?x. ?x ?p1 ?o. ?o ?someValuesFrom ?s. ?s rdfs:subClassOf ?o2.
?s2 owl:someValuesFrom ?s. ?sc2 rdfs:subClassOf ?s2.
p0:TotalCostOfEmployee rdfs:subClassOf ?sc2 }
```

Where the equivalent class of `ContextScenarioType` is searched for amongst the ones semantically related to `TotalCostOfEmployee` class.

7   Conclusions

In this work, we propose an improvement of the existing XBRL to OWL mapping methods and we integrate the resulting ontology with a Key Performance Indicator ontology (KPIO), created in order to support management accounting exploitation. In particular we improved the XBRL ontology making it more compliant with OWL and more suitable for inference. This ontology has been used to semantically model and link financial statements with management accounting information. Indeed, books keeping and management accounting are often integrated in a general accounting systems, therefore so should be the semantic models. Our proposal solve the issue of lack of semantics of XBRL, without forcing firms to give up a universally accepted standard which is, anyway, useful for information retrieval purposes. More in detail, the use of equivalence properties enabled us to infer new knowledge on financial statements starting from information on management accounting. Future works will include the online publication of the ontology in order to make the collection generally accessible. For the purpose of our research, the ontology will be completed with a set of suitable software components with the aim of supporting users to effectively build, analyze and manage financial data.

References

1. Bititci, U., et al.: Performance Measurement: Challenges for Tomorrow. Int. J. Manag. Rev. 14, 305–327 (2012)
2. García, R., Gil, R.: Facilitating Business Interoperability from the Semantic Web State of the Art

3. Lara, R., Cantador, I., Castells, P.: XBRL taxonomies and OWL ontologies for investment funds. In: Roddick, J., et al. (eds.) ER Workshops 2006. LNCS, vol. 4231, pp. 271–280. Springer, Heidelberg (2006)
4. Schreiber, G., et al.: The CommonKADS Conceptual Modelling Language. A Futur. Knowl. Acquis. 867, 1–25 (1994)
5. Grüninger, M.U., Ontologies, M.: principles, methods, and applications. Knowl. Eng. Rev. 11, 93–155 (1996)
6. BizOntos - Business Ontologies,
   `http://rhizomik.net/html/ontologies/bizontos/`
7. Hitzler, P., et al.: M.K.: OWL 2 Web Ontology Language Primer, 2nd edn. (2012)
8. Guan, J., et al.: How AIS can progress along with ontology research in IS. Int. J. Account. Inf. Syst. 14, 21–38 (2013)
9. Erdmann, M., Studer, R.: How to Structure and Access XML Documents With Ontologies. Data Knowl. Eng. 36, 317–335 (2001)
10. Fisher, I.E.: On the structure of financial accounting standards to support digital representation, storage, and retrieval. J. Emerg. Technol. Account. 1, 23–40 (2004)
11. Pulido, J.R.G., et al.: Ontology languages for the semantic web: A never completely updated review. Knowledge-Based Syst. 19, 489–497 (2006)
12. Bao, J., Rong, G., Li, X., Ding, L.: Representing financial reports on the semantic web: In: Dean, M., Hall, J., Rotolo, A., Tabet, S. (eds.) RuleML 2010. LNCS, vol. 6403, pp. 144–152. Springer, Heidelberg (2010)
13. Spies, M.: An ontology modelling perspective on business reporting. Inf. Syst. 35, 404–416 (2010)
14. Chou, T.-H., et al.: Knowledge management via ontology development in accounting. Kybernetes 37, 36–48 (2008)
15. Hevner, A.R.: A Three Cycle View of Design Science Research. Scand. J. Inf. Syst. 19 (2007)
16. Grüninger, M., Fox, M.S.: Methodology for the Design and Evaluation of Ontologies (1995)
17. Uschold, M., et al.: The enterprise ontology. Knowl. Eng. Rev. 13, 31–89 (1998)
18. van Heijst, G., et al.: Using Explicit Ontologies for KBS Development. Int. J. Hum. Comput. Stud. 46, 183–292 (1997)
19. Breuker, J., et al.: Developing Content for LKIF: Ontologies and Frameworks for Legal Reasoning. In: JURIX 2006 19th Annu. Conf., vol. 152 (2006)
20. Pedrinaci, C., Domingue, J., Alves de Medeiros, A.K.: A Core Ontology for Business Process Analysis. In: Bechhofer, S., Hauswirth, M., Hoffmann, J., Koubarakis, M. (eds.) ESWC 2008. LNCS, vol. 5021, pp. 49–64. Springer, Heidelberg (2008)
21. Time Ontology, `http://www.w3.org/TR/owl-time/`
22. XBRL Instance Ontology, `http://rhizomik.net/ontologies/2007/11/xbrl-instance-2003-12-31.owl`
23. Protégé Ontology (ed.), `http://protege.stanford.edu`
24. Sirin, E., et al.: Pellet: A Practical OWL-DL Reasoner. Web Semant. Sci. Serv. Agents World Wide Web. Softw. Eng. Semant. Web. 5, 51–53 (2007)
25. Presutti, V., et al.: eXtreme design with content ontology design patterns. In: Proc. Workshop on Ontology Patterns, Washington, DC, USA (2009)
26. SPARQL 1.1 Query Language. W3C Recommendation,
    `http://www.w3.org/TR/sparql11-query/`

Representing Hierarchical Relationships in INM*

Mengchi Liu[1], Jie Hu[2,1], Liu Chen[3], and Xuhui Li[3]

[1] School of Computer Science, Carleton University, Canada
[2] School of Computer Science and Information Engineering, Hubei University, China
[3] School of Computer Science, Wuhan University, China

Abstract. Real-world organizations has various natural and complex relationships with all kinds of people and other organizations. Such relationships may form complex hierarchical or composite structures. Existing data models such as relational, object-oriented, or object-relational models oversimplify even ignore these relationships and their semantics so that the semantics has to be dealt with by the applications. To solve this problem, we present a concise but expressive language to naturally and directly represent the semantics of complex relationships in the real-world entities.

Keywords: Conceptual modeling, modeling language, hierarchical relationship.

1 Introduction

Real-world organizations have natural structures and entities in these organizations have various complex relationships with each other and via these relationships, they play various roles in time, and have the corresponding context-dependent properties. For instance, a university may have various institutions such as offices and faculties and people such as president and vice presidents which may be specialized into vice president research and vice president academic. Faculties may contain schools and departments and also have relationships with people such as dean and administrators. Similarly, a school or department may also have all kinds of people including director, students, and researchers which can be specialized into professors, associate professors, etc. Here, organizations and people in it should be modeled as objects. The titles of various people are both relationships between organizations and people, and roles people play in the corresponding organizations. Moreover, the semantics of relationships between organizations, organizations and people should be naturally represented by hierarchical relationships.

Since the early 1980s, object-oriented and object-relational databases have emerged to support complex objects and structure. Some important concepts and constructors such as object identity, complex objects, classes, classification,

---

* This work is supported by the National Natural Science Foundation of China under Grant No. 61202100, 61272110 and China Scholarship Council under Grant No. [2013]3018.

E. Yu et al. (Eds.): ER 2014, LNCS 8824, pp. 297–304, 2014.

inheritance, etc [1] have been introduced to directly model the real-world entities. Most research mainly focuses on the class membership of objects and inheritance, etc. For instance, the best known object-oriented database systems and languages such as Orion [2], O_2 [3] and ODMG [4] are mainly concerned with the static aspects of the real-world objects and lack of adequate object evolution mechanisms as every real-world entity is represented as a direct instance of the most specific class in a class hierarchy and cannot change its class membership during its lifetime [5,6]. To solve this problem, multiple inheritance with intersection subclasses may be allowed. However, multiple inheritance may lead to a combinatorial explosion in the number of subclasses [7]. To avoid such a combinatorial explosion, multiple classification with a single preferred class has been proposed in [8]. In order to deal with evolving objects, various role models and languages have been proposed [9,10]. Their main characteristics is the separation of object classes and role classes. Object classes concern static aspects whereas role classes concern dynamic and many-faceted aspects of entities and role classes are also organized hierarchically. A real-world entity is normally represented by an object instance and several role instances organized into an instance hierarchy. The problem with this approach is that object information is spread into several instances thus when users query an entity in the real world, they have to reorganize the information from several instances. However, existing research results seldom concern the semantics and structure of relationships between objects, between objects and relationships, and between relationships. In [11], we have proposed a novel model called Information Networking Model which can provide a one-to-one correspondence way to model the complex relationships of entities in the real-world organizations. In this paper, we present a concise but expressive language to directly represent hierarchical relationships in Information Networking Model. It provides powerful constructs to express the rich semantics associated with various relationships.

This rest of the paper is organized as follows. Section 2 presents the schema language and its semantics. Section 3 illustrates the instance language to show how to manipulate the relationships of inter-networked objects. Section 4 concludes and comments on our future plans.

2   Schema Language

In this section, we describe the relationship definitions. In our model, classes denote collections of objects that share common properties. Two kinds of classes are distinguished: object classes and role relationship classes. An *object class* is used to describe the static aspects of real-world entities. A *role relationship class* is used to describe the dynamic, many-faceted, and evolutional aspects of real-world entities which is induced by a role relationship. The following are examples of classes:

Object classes	Person	Univ	Faculty	School
Role relationship classes	VP	Secretary	Prof	Student

From the semantic point of view, there are five kinds of binary relationships in our language: role, context, role-based, contain, and normal relationship. Any relationship can have inverse as in ODMG [4]. But unlike ODMG in which a binary relationship and its inverse must be explicitly specified in pairs in the corresponding classes by providing the traversal paths, the inverse in our language is declared in its positive relationship definition. It is more concise and compact. Moreover, any relationship can form the hierarchy to directly represent the relationships between organizations, organizations and people in them.

The novel feature of our language is the introduction of role relationships and novel mechanisms to represent hierarchical and composite relationships between objects and the context-dependent information to reflect the temporal, dynamic, many-faceted, and evolutional aspects of real-world entities in a natural and direct way. A *role relationship* has two functions: (1) as a relationship to connect objects in the source class to objects in the target class. (2) as a role that the objects in the target class play in the relationship with objects in the source class. A role relationship can have role sub-relationships and thus it can form hierarchy that supports inheritance at the class level. We use *context relationship* to represent this kind of inverse relationship for the first function and *role label* to denote the description for further context of the role relationship under the corresponding context relationship for the second function. Also, any role relationship in the hierarchy can have *role-based relationships* to describe their properties.

Besides role relationships, their inverse (context relationships), and role-based relationships, we need additional notions to deal with other kinds of relationships. Instances of an object class may have relationships with other instances of either an object class or a role relationship class and the relationships may have inverse, we use *normal relationship* to represent this kind of relationships. Moreover, we use *contain relationship* to represent the part-of semantics between objects. Its inverse is a normal relationship.

Example 1. The following is a schema for universities, their institutions, and all kinds of people in them.

```
create class Univ [
    role VP [subordinate(inv superior):Univ.Secretary] →
        {VPResearch, VPAcademic}(position): Person(inv worksIn),
    role Administrator →  Secretary(position):Person(inv worksIn),
    contain institution → faculties(inv belongsTo):Faculty]
create class Faculty [
    contain Schools(inv belongsTo):School,
    role Dean(position):Person(inv worksIn)]
create class School [
    role Researcher [supervise(inv supervisor):School.GradStudent] → {
        Prof, AssoProf }(title):Person(inv worksIn),
    role Student [takes(inv takenBy):Course] → {
        GradStudent[takes(inv takenBy):GradCourse] → {MSc, PhD},
        UnderGrad[takes(inv takenBy):UnderCourse]
        } (status): Person (inverse studiesIn)]
```

```
create abstract class Course subsume {UnderCourse, GradCourse} [
    prerequisites (inv followedBy): Course]
create class Person [
    direct-relatives → {
        spouse (inv direct-relatives/spouse),
        parents (inv direct-relatives/children) }: Person]
```

In the first three definitions, object classes Univ, Faculty, and School model the real-world organizations universitities, faculties, and schools. The first definition specifies that object class Univ has two hierarchical role relationships with Person and inversely Person has context relationships worksIn. The root of the first hierarchy is VP which has a role-based relationship subordinate with Secretary of Univ and inversely Secretary has role-based relationship superior with VP. Also, VP is further specialized into role sub-relationships VPResearch and VPAcademic with the role label position. The root of the second hierarchy is Administrator which is further specialized into role sub-relationship Secretary with the role label position. Also, Univ has a hierarchical contain relationship with Faculty and inversely Faculty has normal relationship belongsTo. The root of the hierarchy is institution which further contains faculties. The second definition specifies that object class Faculty has a contain relationship Schools and a role relationship Dean respectively with School and Person. Inversely, School has normal relationship belongsTo and Person has context relationship worksIn with the role label position. The third one defines that object class School has two hierarchical role relationships with Person and inversely Person has context relationships worksIn and studiesIn respectively. The root of the first hierarchy is Researcher which has a role-based relationship supervise with GradStudent of School and inversely GradStudent has role-based relationship superior with Researcher. Also, Researcher is further specialized into role sub-relationships Prof and AssoProf with role label title. The root of the second hierarchy is Student which has role-based relationship takes with Course and inversely Course has normal relationship takenBy with Student. Also, Student is further specialized into role sub-relationships GradStudent and UnderGrad. GradStudent has role-based relationship takes with GradCourse and inversely GradCourse has normal relationship takenBy with GradStudent. Also, GradStudent is specialized into MSc and PhD with role label status. UnderGrad has role label status, role-based relationship takes with UnderCourse and inversely UnderCourse has normal relationship takenBy with UnderGrad. The fourth definition specifies that abstract object class Course has normal relationship prerequisites with Course . The inverse of prerequisites is followedBy. Also, it has subclasses UnderCourse and GradCourse. The fifth definition specifies that object class Person has a normal relationship hierarchy with Person. The root of the hierarchy is direct-relatives which is specialized into spouse and parents. The inverse of spouse and parents are spouse and children under direct-relatives respectively.

In semantics, a role relationship declaration generates directed relationship hierarchies from the source class to the target class. The definition of class *School* in Example 1 generates the corresponding role relationship hierarchies as follows:

School [
    role Researcher → {Prof, AssoProf } :Person,
    role Student → { GradStudent → {MSc, PhD},UnderGrad }: Person]

Like an object class that denotes a set of instances with common properties, a role relationship hierarchy also induces a set of instances that participate in the role relationship hierarchy in the context of the source class. Thus we use *role relationship classes* to represent the class hierarchy for this set of instances, which has the same structure as role relationship. Also, the superclass of the root in the role relationship class hierarchy is the target of the corresponding role relationship hierarchy.

Example 2. The definition of class *School* in Example 1 generates the corresponding role relationship class hierarchies as follows:

Research isa Person   Prof isa Research   AssoProf isa Research
Student isa Person   GradStudent isa Student   UnderGrad isa Student
MSc isa GradStudent PhD isa GradStudent

A role relationship hierarchy may have inverse relationship and each role relationship in the hierarchy can have role label. The role relationship class induced from the corresponding role relationship generates the context based on them. Also, as role-based relationships are used to describe properties of instances of induced role relationship, they are also under the corresponding role relationship class.

Role relationship classes in Example 2 generate the context and role-based relationships as follows:

Researcher [context worksIn:School[title:Researcher],
          role-based supervise:School.GradStudent]
Prof [context worksIn:School[title:Prof]]
AssociateProf [context worksIn:School[title:AssociateProf]]
Student[context studiesIn:School[status:Student], role-based takes:Course]
GradStudent [context studiesIn:School[status:GradStudent],
         role-based (takes:GradCourse, supervisor:School.Researcher)]
UnderGrad [context studiesIn:School[status:UnderGrad], role-based takes:UnderCourse]
MSc [context studiesIn:School[status:MSc]]
PhD [context studiesIn:School[status:PhD]]

The inverse of a normal or contain relationship is a normal relationship. They may also form hierarchy. The definitions of classes Course and Person in Example 1 respectively generate the normal relationships as follows.

Course [prerequisites:Course, followedBy:Course]
Person [direct-relatives → {spouse, parents, children }: Person]

Note that spouse is a reflexive relationship, relationships prerequisites and followedBy, parents and children are inverse of each other respectively.

Class Hierarchy and Inheritance. In our language, both object classes and role relationship classes can form disjoint hierarchies. They support inheritance with overriding at the schema level. The object class inheritance is same as in object-oriented languages but role relationship class inheritance is different. For example, object classes PriUniv and PubUniv are subclasses of Univ. It is defined as follows:

Univ subsume {PriUniv, PubUniv}

They inherit properties from Univ thus have declarations as follows:

PriUniv [

    role VP →{VPResearch, VPAcademic}: Person,

    role Administrator → Secretary:Person,

    contain institution → faculties:Faculty]

PubUniv [

    role VP →{VPResearch, VPAcademic}: Person,

    role Administrator → Secretary:Person,

    contain institution → faculties:Faculty]

The role relationship class hierarchy is induced from the corresponding role relationship hierarchy. The role relationship subclasses inherit or override normal, contain, role, role-based relationships from their superclass and then form their context-dependent information. The key novel feature of our language is the natural and direct support of context-dependent representation and access to object properties. The mechanism is to add context in front of role-based relationships to represent the context-dependent information of a role relationship class.

Every role relationship class in the hierarchy with the superclass Student of Example 2 inherits hierarchial normal relationship with the root direct-relatives from their superclass Person. Moreover, role-based relationships takes on GradStudent and UnderGrad are overridden respectively as they are redefined to GradCourse and UnderCourse. Also, MSc and PhD inherit role-based relationships takes and supervisor from GradStudent. Their context-dependent information can be represented as:

Student [context studiesIn:School[status:Student[role-based takes:Course]]]

GradStudent [context studiesIn:School[status:GradStudent[

               role-based(takes:GradCourse, supervisor:School.Researcher)]]]

UnderGrad [context studiesIn:School[status:UnderGrad [role-based takes:UnderCourse]]]

MSc [context studiesIn:School[status:MSc [

      role-based (takes:GradCourse, supervisor:School.Researcher)]]]

PhD [context studiesIn:School[status:PhD[

      role-based (takes:GradCourse, supervisor:School.Researcher)]]]

3   Instance Language

In information networking model, a real-world entity is represented by exactly one object that is uniquely represented by an oid and can belong to several role relationship classes to reflect the dynamic and many-faceted aspects of the entity. Objects may participate in various relationships and have the corresponding context-dependent properties nested within objects with proper context information to represent them. Moreover, objects can directly represent real-world organizational structures so that it is straightforward to build a reflection of the real-world.

As mentioned in Section 2, a relationship may have the corresponding inverse relationship. The inverse of a role relationship is a context relationship with nested role label, the inverse of a role-based relationship is either a normal relationship or a role-based relationship, the inverse of a contain relationship is a normal relationship.

The user can create new objects and assign their relationship values using *insert* commands. A novel feature of our language is its built-in maintenance for two objects participating in a relationship and its inverse. For any relationship, users just need to manipulate one side and the inverse will be automatically maintained by the system.

For example, we can insert a school CS and its role relationship hierarchies with roots Researcher and Student as follows:

insert School CS[
    role Researcher →Prof: Ann[supervise:{Ben,Bev}],
    role Student →GradStudent →{PhD:Ben[takes:{DB,AI}], MSc:Bev[takes:{DB,AI}]}]

It generates objects as follows:

    School CS[
        role Researcher →Prof:Ann,
        role Student →GradStudent →{PhD:Ben,MSc:Bev}]
    Prof Ann[context worksIn:CS[title:Prof[role-based supervise:{Ben, Bev}]]]
    PhD Ben[context studiesIn:CS[status:PhD[role-based(supervisor:Ann, takes:{DB, AI})]]]
    MSc Bev[context studiesIn:CS[status:MSc[role-based(supervisor:Ann, takes:{DB, AI})]]]
    GradCourse DB[takenBy:{Ben,Bev}]
    GradCourse AI[takenBy:{Ben,Bev}]

We can also insert the above objects from the inverse of the two role relationship hierarchichies as follows.

    insert Prof Ann[context worksIn:CS[title:Prof]]
    insert PhD Ben[
        context studiesIn:CS[status:PhD[role-based(supervisor:Ann, takes:{DB, AI})]]]
    insert MSc Jim[context studiesIn:CS[status:MSc[role-based(supervisor:Jim, takes:AI)]]]

Consider another normal relationship example, we can insert a person and its normal relationship hierarchies with the root direct-relatives as follows:

    insert Person Tom [direct-relatives →{spouse: Ann, children:{Ben, Bev}}]

It will generate an object Tom with the normal relationship hierarchy direct-relatives as follows.

    Person Tom[direct-relatives →{spouse: Ann, children:{Ben, Bev}}]

Also its inverse will be added in objects Ann, Ben, and Bev respectively. They are modified as follows.

    Prof Ann[
        context worksIn:CS[title:Prof[role-based supervise:{Ben, Bev}]],
        direct-relatives →spouse: Tom]
    PhD Ben[
        context studiesIn:CS[status:PhD[role-based (supervisor:Ann, takes:{DB, AI})]],
        direct-relatives →parents: Tom]
    MSc Bev[context studiesIn:CS[status:MSc[role-based(supervisor:Ann, takes:{DB, AI})]],
        direct-relatives →parents: Tom]

4 Conclusion

In this paper, we have presented a concise but expressive language for hierarchical relationships in Information Networking Model proposed before. It can represent real-world organizational structures and various complex relationships between objects as well as their context-dependent properties in a natural and concise way. In the schema, any kind of binary relationship and its inverse can be specified in its positive relationship definition instead of being defined in pairs in the corresponding classes by providing the traversal paths. It more concise and compact. In the instance, all the information regarding a real-world object is grouped in one instance instead of scattered in several objects and roles so that users can directly access the relationship from the object. For any relationship, users just need to manipulate one side and the inverse will be automatically maintained by the system, which greatly reduces the manual operations to maintain the consistency. We have systematically implemented a full- edged database management system that supports the language presented here. The system is available for downloading from the svn address: *mars.whu.edu.cn/inmproject*.

Currently, we are investigating various NoSQL databases. We plan to extend Information Networking Model to support schema-less and schema-mixed applications. It will be more flexible and fit more application requirements. We also attempt to extend the system to parallel distributed environment.

References

1. Benabbou, A., Bahloul, S.N., Amghar, Y.: An algorithmic structuration of a type system for an orthogonal object/relational model. CoRR abs/1007.3275 (2010)
2. Kim, W.: Introduction to Object-Oriented Databases. The MIT Press, Cambridge (1990)
3. Lecluse, C., Richard, P.: The O_2 Database Programming Language. In: Proceedings of VLDB, pp. 411–422. Morgan Kaufmann, Amsterdam (1989)
4. Cattell, R., Barry, D., Berler, M., Eastman, J., Jordan, D., Russel, C., Schadow, O., Stanienda, T., Velez, F. (eds.): The Object Database Standard: ODMG 3.0. Morgan Kaufmann, Los Altos (2000)
5. Gottlob, G., Schrefl, M., Röck, B.: Extending object-oriented systems with roles. TOIS 14(3), 268–296 (1996)
6. Wang, S., Yao, X.: Relationships between diversity of classification ensembles and single-class performance measures. IEEE Trans. Knowl. Data Eng. 25(1), 206–219 (2013)
7. Wong, R.K., Chau, H.L.: A data model and semantics of objects with dynamic roles. In: ICDE, Birmingham, U.K, pp. 402–411 (April 1997)
8. Bertino, E., Guerrini, G.: Objects with multiple most specific classes. In: Olthoff, W. (ed.) ECOOP 1995. LNCS, vol. 952, pp. 102–126. Springer, Heidelberg (1995)
9. Steimann, F.: On the representation of roles in object-oriented and conceptual modelling. Data & Knowledge Engineering 35(1), 83–106 (2000)
10. Dahchour, M., Pirotte, A., Zimányi, E.: A role model and its metaclass implementation. Information Systems 29(3), 235–270 (2004)
11. Liu, M., Hu, J.: Information networking model. In: Laender, A.H.F., Castano, S., Dayal, U., Casati, F., de Oliveira, J.P.M. (eds.) ER 2009. LNCS, vol. 5829, pp. 131–144. Springer, Heidelberg (2009)

Providing Foundation for User Feedback Concepts by Extending a Communication Ontology

Itzel Morales-Ramirez[1,2], Anna Perini[1], and Renata Guizzardi[3]

[1] Software Engineering Research Unit. Fondazione Bruno Kessler - IRST
imramirez,perini@fbk.eu
[2] International Doctoral School ICT- University of Trento, Italy
[3] Ontology and Conceptual Modeling Research Group, UFES, Brazil
rguizzardi@inf.ufes.br

Abstract. The term user feedback is becoming widely used in requirements engineering (RE) research to refer to the comments and evaluations that users express upon having experienced the use of a software application or service. This explicit feedback takes place in virtual spaces (e.g., issue tracking systems, app stores), aiming, for instance, at reporting on discovered bugs or requesting new features. Founding the notion of explicit user feedback with the use of an ontology may support a deep understanding of the feedback nature, as well as contribute to the development of tool-components for its analysis at use of requirements analysts. In this paper, we present a user feedback ontology as an extension of an existing communication ontology. We describe how we built it, along with a set of competency questions, and illustrate its applicability on an example taken from a collaborative communication related to RE for software evolution.

Keywords: User Feedback, Communication Ontology, Requirements Engineering.

1 Introduction

More and more, software users make use of social media to express their comments about a software service or to rate applications they often use. This information, which is easily accessible via the Internet, is considered an invaluable asset for software developers and service providers, to help them understand how to improve their software application or service, and get inspiration for new functionalities and products [1,2]. This information deliberately provided by the users is generally called *explicit user feedback* and can be used as a complement to *implicit user feedback*, i.e. information collected by means of observing the user behaviour through logs.

In [3] it is stated, "Feedback is one of the primary results of introducing the implemented software system into the real world. There is an immediate response to the system from those affected by it". This definition leads us to recognise user feedback both as an artefact and as a process. Taking the perspective of user feedback as an artefact, we revise the previous definition and propose the following one: "User feedback is a reaction of the user upon her experience in using a software service or application. Explicit user feedback could be based on multi-modal communication, such as natural language text, images, emoticons, etc.". Taking the perspective of the communication process, we claim that the roles of sender and receiver are essential to make clear the purpose of explicit feedback.

E. Yu et al. (Eds.): ER 2014, LNCS 8824, pp. 305–312, 2014.
© Springer International Publishing Switzerland 2014

In our research, we focus on explicit user feedback, with the ultimate goal of defining methods and techniques to support software system maintenance, as well as collaborative RE tasks as described in a recent paper [4]. We consider issues related to collecting and analysing user feedback. Indeed, different techniques may be needed for collection and for analysis, depending on the feedback type, and on the volume of the corresponding data. On one hand, structured feedback is collected according to a predefined input template. Consequently, in this case the analysis is driven by the schema underlying the template itself. On the other hand, unstructured user feedback is collected freely, without the aid of any predefined structure. Thus, the analysis in this case may require data mining and natural language processing (NLP) techniques to discover, retrieve, and extract information and opinions from huge textual information [5].

In this paper we present an ontology of user feedback, key for a deep understanding of the explicit user feedback and its further exploitation. To build the *user feedback* ontology we adopt a goal-oriented methodology that guide us in specifying the main stakeholders, including the users of our ontology (e.g. designers of feedback collector tools and analysts), and a set of competency questions (CQs) that the resulting ontology will answer [6]. For example, the following CQs emerged from the analysis of the goals of feedback analysts: (a) what are the types of user feedback presentation formats?; (b) how can user feedback be classified?; (c) and what are the speech acts commonly expressed by users in their explicit feedback?

Since feedback collection is seen as a communication process, we develop our ontology as an extension of a well-founded existing communication ontology [7]. Besides this, we consider users' feedback expressed in natural language (NL), therefore we take into account the speech act theory (SAT) of Searle [8,9].

The rest of the paper is organised as follows. Section 2 presents the concepts we borrow from pre-existing ontologies and SAT theory. Section 3 describes the user feedback ontology and the concepts that it involves. Related work is recalled in Section 4. Finally we draw some conclusions and point out future work in Section 5.

2   Baseline

Collecting *user feedback* basically consists in a process of communication between the developers and the users of existing software systems. We build on an existing Communication ontology [7] and extend it including *user feedback* concepts. This Communication ontology is especially attractive because it is grounded on a foundational ontology, namely the Unified Foundational Ontology (UFO) [10], which has been successfully applied to provide real-world semantics for ontologies in different fields. In the following we briefly recall the concepts that we reuse from UFO and from the Communication ontology.

UFO distinguishes between endurants and perdurants. Endurants do not have temporal parts, and persist in time while keeping their identity (e.g. a person and the colour of an apple). A Perdurant (also referred to as event), conversely, is composed of temporal parts (e.g. storm, heart attack, trip). Substantials are existentially independent endurants (e.g. a person or a car). Moments, in contrast, are endurants that are existentially dependent on other endurants or events, inhering in these individuals (e.g. someone's headache and the cost of a trip). Moments can be intrinsic or relational. Intrinsic

Moments are those that depend on one single individual in which they inhere. A Relator is a relational moment, i.e. a moment that inheres simultaneously in multiple individuals. Agents are substantials that can perceive events, perform action contributions and bear special kinds of intrinsic moments, named Intentional Moments (examples of agents are person, student and software developer). Action contributions are intentional participations of agents within an event (e.g. saying something to someone, writing a letter). An Intention is a type of intentional moment (other examples of intentional moments are belief and desire) that represents an internal commitment of the agent to act towards that goal and, therefore, causes the agent to perform action contributions.

The communication ontology considers sender and receiver as the central agents in the communication process. The Sender is an agent that sends a message through a communicative act. A Communicative Act is an action contribution that carries out the information exchanged in the communication process. This communicative act corresponds to what Searle names illocutionary act [8]. The exchanged information is here captured as a Message, which is the propositional content of the communicative act. A Receiver is an agent that perceives the communicated message. As the communicative act, a Perception is an action contribution that consists in the reception of the exchanged information (thus, also having a message as propositional content). A Communicative Interaction is a complex action composed of exactly one communicative act and one or more perceptions. In other words, in a communicative interaction, there is one sender agent and at least one receiver agent. Moreover, the communicative act and the perceptions involved in a communicative interaction have the same message as propositional content. Thus, this message is also said to be the propositional content of the communicative interaction.

In addition, due to the gathering of feedback is seen as a communication process, we extend the communication ontology with concepts coming from the literature about the characterisation, elaboration and use of user feedback. Specifically, we look at the feedback expressed in NL, hence, we rely on the linguistic theory of SAT [8,9].

3   User Feedback Ontology

In this section we explain the concepts of our ontology. Let's start with the concepts of the baseline, which are illustrated with a dark grey colour in Fig. 1. We have distinguished three key concepts of the communication ontology to be extended. These concepts are intention, message and communicative act.

We extend the concept of Intention into communicative intention and reflexive intention. The Communicative Intention refers to the internal commitment of a sender of conveying an information to a receiver or an audience, regardless of having this information understood. While a Reflexive Intention, according to H.P. Grice, as quoted in [9], refers to the sender's intention that is formulated and transmitted with the purpose of being recognised or understood by a receiver.

A message *bears* a given Topic, in UFO a topic is an intrinsic moment (i.e. a property of the message), that becomes the subject of conversation between agents. The last concept that is added and central in our ontology is the concept Speech Act that is per-se an action, i.e. an action contribution, and is the basic unit in a linguistic communication.

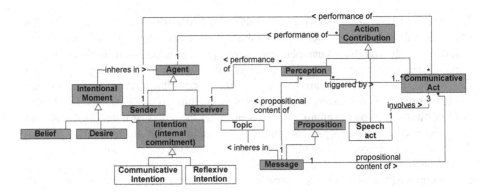

Fig. 1. Concepts extending the communication ontology. Baseline concepts in dark grey, new concepts extending the ontology in white.

Communication Ontology and SAT Concepts. A speech act *involves* three communicative acts, namely, locutionary, illocutionary and perlocutionary act that we consider specialisations of a communicative act. These acts are visualised in Fig. 2, in which we refine the relation between speech act and communicative act and connect the speech act directly to each one of the acts. A Locutionary Act is the act of "saying something" (production of words), an Illocutionary Act makes reference to the way in which the locutions are used and in which sense (intention to motivate the production of words), and a Perlocutionary Act is the effect the sender wants to accomplish on the receiver or audience. Let's consider the utterance *"Is there any example code I could look at?"*, the locutionary act corresponds to the utterance of this sentence, the illocutionary act corresponds to the speaker's intention to make the audience aware that she has a request, and the effect, i.e. the perlocutionary act, is that the speaker got the audience to handle her request. A speech act involves at least one act, what we mean is that someone could utter a senseless phrase (e.g.,"one the snow"), accomplishing the locutionary act, but the illocutionary and perlocutionary acts are not present. The Performative verb refers to the verb that *classifies* the illocutionary act into five categories that were introduced by Searle, and later revised by Bach and Harnish [9].

An intention *inheres in* the sender, in this case the reflexive intention that *causes* the illocutionary act. Then, this illocutionary act *triggers* the execution of a locutionary act through the utterance of specific words that will reify such a reflexive intention. The *consequence of* the illocutionary act is the sender's perlocutionary act that the receiver will *perceive* as the overall *effect of* a speech act. We need to clarify that the relation *consequence of* between the illocutionary and perlocutionary act is a type of indirect causation, i.e. if the communication is successful, the receiver will perform the action intended by the sender. Finally, a speech act is successful if the intention that the sender expresses is *identified* by the receiver by means of recognising such a sender's intention.

SAT Concepts. Our *user feedback* ontology builds on a revised taxonomy of speech acts proposed in a previous work [11], which considers speech acts commonly used in online discussions of an open source project. We grouped the selected speech acts in three main categories: constantive, directive, and expressive. We are currently consolidating

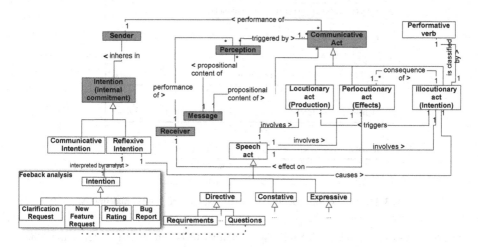

Fig. 2. Communicative acts involved in each speech act

the part of the ontology that considers concepts that are specific to feedback collection and analysis. An excerpt may be found in [6]. For reasons of space we only show the connection of the reflexive intention to the intention interpreted by a software requirements analyst. Once the analysis of the speech acts is performed, different results can be presented. For example, the categorisation of the feedback according to the user's reflexive intention. As can be found in the recent literature on feedback from software users, possible intentions for a user to send a feedback are Clarification Request, New Feature Request, Bug Report and Provide Rating. For instance, Bug Report is inspired on corrective or negative feedback [12,13] as in this case, the user feedback refers to information that should be used to correct the software, which means that this information has a negative connotation. The encouraging [14] and positive [13] feedback have been turned into Rating (e.g, stars in the AppStore) [2]. Strategic behaviour [14] in our ontology refers to a New Feature Request while Clarification means that the feedback contains questions or extra information (such as critical details), to make something clearer. These terms are indeed used in different works and our feedback ontology attempts at unifying all the different concepts in a single classification.

3.1 Illustrative Example

The following example, see Fig. 3, illustrates how the ontology may support the analysis of user feedback. We take an excerpt of an e-mail[1] sent by a user of a software application called XWiki[2]. Note that the ontological concepts are highlighted with a different font type to facilitate the understanding. This e-mail represents an instance of unstructured user feedback. The fields *Subject:* and *From:* are the concepts Topic and Sender, respectively, of our ontology. In the body of the e-mail we can distinguish different types of speech acts. In this example we find that the first speech act expresses

---

[1] Source: http://lists.xwiki.org/pipermail/users/attachments/
20080220/748039cc/attachment.html

[2] http://www.xwiki.org/xwiki/bin/view/Main/WebHome

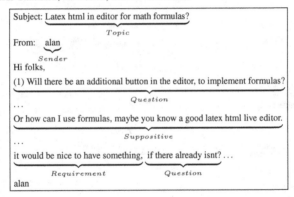

Fig. 3. Example of unstructured user feedback in the XWiki mailing list

the user's reflexive intention of making questions to be answered. After some other messages, we find the intention *suppose*, referring to the speech acts suppositives. The followed two speech acts requirement and question are also expressed.

Now let's see a detailed explanation of the analysis performed. Taking the previous example we first see the Message (1) is the *propositional content of* a Communicative Act. As highlighted before, this message *bears* the Topic *"Latex html in editor for math formulas?"* and the Sender is *alan*. The Reflexive Intention –*Make a question–* inheres in alan that *causes* the Illocutionary act *Quest*. This act produces an effect, i.e. Perlocutionary act that is a *consequence of* the Illocutionary act, which together with the Locutionary act *Elaborate a question* are the three acts involved in the Speech Act –*Question*. The ontology supports the understanding of such an intention expressed by a sender that must be recognised by a receiver. In this example the understanding that the sender is expressing a question is that of producing the Perlocutionary act – *Answer* –that will have the effect on the receiver, i.e. *XWiki community*, who through the Perception –*Reading–*, which is *triggered by* the communicative act, will eventually answer the posed question. However, the other speech acts (i.e. Suppositives, Requirements, and Questions) may provide to the analyst indicators for identifying a Feature Request in this feedback.

3.2 Discussion

At this stage of development the ontology is intended to clarify concepts useful to understand the nature of explicit feedback elaborated by software's users and to support requirements analysts when performing feedback analysis. Due to space limits, we only discuss one of the proposed CQs, namely (c) what are the speech acts commonly expressed by users in their explicit feedback? This CQ is answered by querying the part of the ontology where the concept speech act is specialised into the different sub-kinds (see Fig. 2, bottom-centre). Answers to this question are taken into account in tool-supported analysis technique for explicit unstructured *user feedback*, which exploits NLP tools. This tool supports the classification of phrases as instances of concepts representing speech acts that commonly appear in user feedback [11]. The ontology allows us to identify the relation between the types of speech acts (or their combination) to the type of user feedback (see Fig. 2, left-corner at the bottom). For example if the speech acts used in the feedback under analysis are classified as Suppositive, Requirement, and Questions, this may be interpreted as indicators for the analyst towards identifying a Feature Request.

Other capabilities of the proposed ontology, which can not be illustrated here due to space limits, concern the support for the identification of analysis techniques, based on the presentation format of the feedback, i.e. visual, audio and textual, or as a composition of linguistic and non-linguistic act (e.g. attachment, emoticons).

Concerning the scope of application of the proposed ontology, by construction we consider software requirements analysis and design of feedback collection techniques as application areas. Since we are building the *user feedback* ontology extending a foundational ontology we believe that it can help understand the nature of user feedback.

Regarding the current status and known limitations of the work, we are consolidating the ontology and a proper validation along all the CQs considered so far, is to be performed.

4   Related Work

We briefly recall work addressing the problem that motivates our research, namely how to collect and analyse explicit user feedback for the purpose of collaborative RE in software evolution and maintenance. Worth mentioning are tools, which enable users to give feedback in situ, based on semi-structured collection, e.g. [15,16]. Focusing on works that investigate how explicit, indirect user feedback analysis can support software maintenance and evolution tasks, the following approaches are worth to be mentioned: [17] presents an approach based on statistical analysis, to exploit explicit, indirect feedback by power users, reporting about software defects through the open bug reporting in the Mozilla project. Statistical analysis is applied by [2] to answer questions about how and when users provide feedback in the AppStore.

There is a vast literature about the application of ontologies in RE, but it is out of the scope of this paper to mention all that work. As examples in the case of requirements elicitation, we can mention [18] that presents an approach to build a domain ontology used to guide the analyst on domain concepts used for the elicitation of requirements. Our work differs from it because our ontology aims at supporting designers of feedback collector tools and requirements analysts to understand why and how *user feedback* is provided, as a previous step before determining the requirements.

5   Conclusion

In this paper we introduced a user feedback ontology that we are developing, which considers feedback as an artefact and as a special type of communication process. We described how we are building it by extending and integrating existing ontologies, borrowing concepts from different theories, including SAT. As future work, we intend to validate it systematically against the whole set of competency questions that it is built for. The ontology will provide foundation to our ongoing work on conversation analysis based on the automatic extraction of speech acts [11].

References

1. Kienle, H., Distante, D.: Evolution of Web Systems. In: Mens, T., Serebrenik, A., Cleve, A. (eds.) Evolving Software Systems, pp. 201–228. Springer (2014)
2. Pagano, D., Maalej, W.: User Feedback in the Appstore: An Empirical Study. In: RE, pp. 125–134. IEEE (2013)
3. Madhavji, N.H., Fernández-Ramil, J.C., Perry, D.E. (eds.): Software Evolution and Feedback: Theory and Practice. John Wiley and Sons Ltd (2006)
4. Morales-Ramirez, I., Vergne, M., Morandini, M., Siena, A., Perini, A., Susi, A.: Who is the Expert? Combining Intention and Knowledge of Online Discussants in Collaborative RE Tasks. In: ICSE Companion, pp. 452–455. ACM (2014)
5. Cambria, E., Schuller, B., Xia, Y., Havasi, C.: New Avenues in Opinion Mining and Sentiment Analysis. IEEE Intelligent Systems 28(2), 15–21 (2013)
6. Guizzardi, R.S.S., Morales-Ramirez, I., Perini, A.: A Goal-oriented Analysis to Guide the Development of a User Feedback Ontology. In: iStar. CEUR Workshop Proceedings (2014)
7. Oliveira, F.F., Antunes, J.C., Guizzardi, R.S.: Towards a Collaboration Ontology. In: Proc. of the Workshop on Ontologies and Metamodels for Software and Data Engineering (2007)
8. Searle, J.R.: Intentionality: An Essay in the Philosophy of Mind, vol. 143. Cambridge University Press (1983)
9. Bach, K., Harnish, R.M.: Linguistic Communication and Speech Acts. MIT Press, Cambridge, MA (1979)
10. Guizzardi, G., de Almeida Falbo, R., Guizzardi, R.S.S.: Grounding Software Domain Ontologies in the Unified Foundational Ontology (UFO): The case of the ODE Software Process Ontology. In: CIbSE, pp. 127–140 (2008)
11. Morales-Ramirez, I., Perini, A.: Discovering Speech Acts in Online Discussions: A Tool-supported method. In: CAiSE Forum. CEUR Workshop Proceedings, pp. 137–144 (2014)
12. Hattie, J., Timperley, H.: The Power of Feedback. Review of Educational Research 77(1), 81–112 (2007)
13. Brun, Y., et al.: Engineering Self-Adaptive Systems through Feedback Loops. In: Cheng, B.H.C., de Lemos, R., Giese, H., Inverardi, P., Magee, J. (eds.) Self-Adaptive Systems. LNCS, vol. 5525, pp. 48–70. Springer, Heidelberg (2009)
14. Mory, E.H.: Feedback Research Revisited. Handbook of Research on Educational Communications and Technology 45(1), 745–784 (2004)
15. Seyff, N., Ollmann, G., Bortenschlager, M.: AppEcho: a User-Driven, In Situ Feedback Approach for Mobile Platforms and Applications. In: MOBILESoft, pp. 99–108. ACM (2014)
16. Schneider, K.: Focusing Spontaneous Feedback to Support System Evolution. In: RE, pp. 165–174. IEEE (2011)
17. Ko, A.J., Chilana, P.K.: How Power Users Help and Hinder Open Bug Reporting. In: Proc. of the Conference on Human Factors in Computing Systems, CHI 2010, pp. 1665–1674. ACM (2010)
18. Omoronyia, I., Sindre, G., Stålhane, T., Biffl, S., Moser, T., Sunindyo, W.: A Domain Ontology Building Process for Guiding Requirements Elicitation. In: Wieringa, R., Persson, A. (eds.) REFSQ 2010. LNCS, vol. 6182, pp. 188–202. Springer, Heidelberg (2010)

Towards a Conceptual Framework and Metamodel for Context-Aware Personal Cross-Media Information Management Systems

Sandra Trullemans and Beat Signer

Web & Information Systems Engineering Lab
Vrije Universiteit Brussel
Pleinlaan 2, 1050 Brussels, Belgium
{strullem,bsigner}@vub.ac.be

Abstract. Information fragmentation is a well-known issue in personal information management (PIM). In order to overcome this problem, various PIM solutions have focussed on linking documents via semantic relationships. More recently, task-centered information management (TIM) has been introduced as an alternative PIM paradigm. While these two paradigms have their strengths and weaknesses, we aim for a new PIM system design approach to achieve better synergies with human memory. We further envision a cross-media solution where physical information is integrated with a user's digital personal information space. We present the Object-Concept-Context (OC2) conceptual framework for context-aware personal cross-media information management combining the best of the two existing PIM paradigms and integrating the most relevant features of the human memory. Further, we outline how the OC2 framework has been implemented based on a domain-specific application of the Resource-Selector-Link (RSL) hypermedia metamodel.

1 Introduction

The research field of Personal Information Management (PIM) investigates complex interactions with personal information. An emphasis is on the organisation and maintenance of personal information in file hierarchies, emails, on desks or in bookshelves. This personal information is spread over devices, tools and Web Services or managed in physical archives and piles. Several researchers investigated the effects that information fragmentation has on the organisation and re-finding of personal information. Bergman [1] observed that users experience a cognitive overload when re-finding information to fulfil their tasks since the information is stored in different tools (e.g. email client) as well as at different places in the hierarchical file system.

In order to overcome the information fragmentation problem, two main PIM paradigms have been introduced. Bush [2] described the Memex as a potential future PIM system and criticised the bad practice of information organisation in hierarchical storage systems. He proposed a new *unified view* paradigm where information items are linked with each other to form an interlinked personal

E. Yu et al. (Eds.): ER 2014, LNCS 8824, pp. 313–320, 2014.

information space. With the rise of semantic web technologies, a number of promising unified view-based PIM systems have been realised. The more recent *task-centered information management (TIM)* [3] paradigm focusses on providing task-related personal information.

We introduce a new PIM approach addressing the problem of information fragmentation. While the unified view and TIM paradigms are based on some human memory features, we aim for better synergies between PIM systems and the human memory where the PIM system acts as a memory prosthesis and supports intuitive and natural interaction [4]. We introduce the Object-Concept-Context (OC2) framework which combines the advantages of both, the unified view and TIM paradigms, and conforms to human memory in organising and re-finding activities. We further discuss an implementation of the OC2 framework based on a domain-specific application of the Resource-Selector-Link (RSL) hypermedia metamodel [5].

2   Background

The long-term information storage in human memory involves two memory systems [6]. The *episodic memory* includes the process of receiving and storing spatio-temporal information about events and their autobiographical references to previous events as well as perceptible properties (i.e. contextual factors). In contrast to the episodic memory, the *semantic memory* consists of semantic relationships between concepts. Each of these relationships has a weight which indicates how relevant the relationship is in a given context and might differ for the two directions of a bidirectional relationship between two concepts [7]. Note that the semantic memory does not store perceptible properties but rather references to the episodic memory [6]. Concepts instantiated in the semantic memory are general ideas formed in our mind to abstract the complexity of the real world. On the other hand, objects are observable artefacts which are categorised in concepts in order to give them semantics [8]. Barsalou [9] states that this classification depends on the goal or purpose people have in mind. Therefore, an information item which is present in the real world can be classified in more than one concept (cross-classification) and with a certain context relevance [10]. In order to retrieve information from semantic memory, the spreading activation theory where external stimuli activate various concepts based on their perceptible properties in the episodic memory is applied [11]. We can identify four main features of the human memory including the storage of contextual factors for each concept, context-dependent relationships between concepts, the context-dependent categorisation of objects and the use of spreading activation to retrieve the right information for a given context.

In order to provide a unified view of a user's personal information space, two approaches have been introduced. First, systems such as MyLifeBits [12] follow the idea of episodic memory by organising personal information on a timeline, but these systems lack the functionality to create associative relationships. A second category of PIM systems focusses on semantic memory based on Bush's

vision of associative trails between documents [2]. HayStack [13] enables the
linking of documents and supports the categorisation of objects into concepts.
In order to provide machine-readable semantic relationships, semantic desktops
such as Gnowsis [14] specify these relations through a personal ontology. TIM-
based solutions step away from focussing on information organisation [3]. Similar
to the unified view paradigm, they define a personal ontology for the modelling
of semantic relationships [15]. In OntoPIM, users can allocate objects to ontology
classes and extend the personal ontology through inheritance. In order to provide
task-centered information, Katifori et al. [16] implemented a spreading activation
algorithm for OntoPIM. By allocating a weight for a given task to the personal
ontology's entities, the most relevant concepts can be activated.

3   The OC2 Conceptual Framework for PIM Systems

In order to achieve a better synergy between PIM systems and the human memory, we extended the unified view and TIM paradigms to address the previously
mentioned four main features of the human memory as well as to support more
natural interactions. Our *Object-Concept-Context (OC2)* conceptual framework
for context-aware personal cross-media information management systems consists of the three *object*, *concept* and *context* layers outlined in Fig. 1.

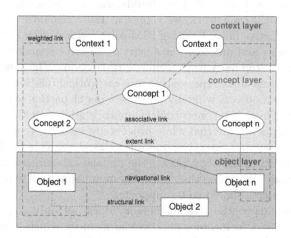

Fig. 1. Object-Concept-Context (OC2) conceptual framework

The object layer contains objects representing real-world elements which can
be observed in physical or digital space. An object might, for example, stand
for a physical paper document or a post-it note but also an email or a website.
Since objects are proxies for real-world elements, they need to be uniquely identifiable via a uniform resource identifier. Note that objects are not restricted to
single documents but can represent complex structures composed of individual
objects. For instance, an object representing a document can also be treated as

a composition of objects representing the paragraphs, allowing us to organise and retrieve information at a finer granularity level than the commonly used information units such as documents.

Elements of the OC2 object layer may have relationships with other objects via *navigational* or *structural links* as illustrated by the dotted red lines in Fig. 1. While currently most users navigate between files via file hierarchies, we would rather like to have the possibility to associate different objects across tools and devices in order to retrieve information in a more natural way. Since an object can be composed out of other objects, we also need structural links to represent these compositional relationships. Furthermore, structural links can be used to express organisational structures within a personal information space. The unified view paradigm is criticised since users often prefer their own organisational behaviour [17]. We should therefore offer the possibility to integrate a user's current organisational structures across the physical and digital space. Our conceptual model goes beyond mimicking the human memory and enables the description of a user's organisational behaviour.

The concept layer consists of conceptual elements (e.g. words or sentences) representing a user's conceptualisation and abstraction of observed objects similar to the definition of concepts in psychology [8]. On the concept layer, concepts may have *associative links* to other concepts as well as *extent links* to objects of the underlying object layer as indicated by the solid green lines in Fig. 1. As mentioned earlier, the human memory builds semantic associations between its elements. In our OC2 framework, we represent these semantic associations via bidirectional associative links. Existing PIM solutions are often based on semantic web technologies and ontologies are used to describe semantic associations, whereas in OC2 we step away from technical restrictions. The concept level further introduces extent links representing any categorical relationship between a concept and various objects whereby an object might participate in more than one extent link. Thus, our conceptual framework addresses the psychological theory that concepts are internal while objects are external to our mind [8]. In HayStack [13], automated extraction modules allocate objects to their semantic concept, whereas OntoPim [15] supports the manual categorisation of objects in a personal ontology. We argue that both, the manual as well as the automatic classification of objects should to be supported.

As elaborated earlier, the human memory does not only consist of the semantic memory but also includes an episodic memory which is responsible to store contextual factors about events. By preserving these contextual factors, users may search in their semantic memory based on contextual cues. Previous descriptive PIM research has observed the importance of contextual cues in refinding activities. For example, during retrieval users often use the contextual information squeezed into folder labels [18]. While the TIM paradigm mentions the exclusive use of personal information in executive tasks [3], we do not agree that personal information is only used in specific tasks such as managing a photo album. The OC2 contextual layer contains *context* elements for managing contextual factors about the semantic graph induced by elements of the concept and object layers. A context element describes a composition of contextual factors and a contextual factor can be any condition or observation. While most context-aware systems apply technology-driven contextual factors such as time and place, our context elements can be freely defined by a user [19].

Due to the fact that the human memory retrieves information by spreading activation [11], we should offer the basic building blocks to enable the application of a spreading activation algorithm. In the spreading activation theory, concepts are activated by external stimuli. We interpret these external stimuli as an activation of a context element representing a user's current context similar to the approach by Katifori et al. [16]. While Katifori et al. use a task as stimuli, we present a broader solution by using context as stimuli. In order to conform to human memory, a concept and its semantic relationships have to be relevant in a given context. Therefore, the OC2 framework specifies that concepts and their associative links can have a relevance (weight) for a given context element which is illustrated by the blue dashed lines in Fig. 1. Furthermore, as mentioned previously, objects are assigned to their semantic concepts in a context-relevant manner in human memory [10] and therefore our extent links can also have a weighted link to a context element. In contrast to existing work, we provide a context-sensitive categorisation of objects in their semantic concept and further support context-dependent structural links. Finally, navigational links have a relevance factor for given context elements in order to provide users with shortcuts to the most relevant digital or physical artefacts for a user's current context.

4   A Generic Context-Aware PIM Metamodel

The implementation of the OC2 framework is based on a domain-specific application and extension of the Resource-Selector-Link (RSL) metamodel for hypermedia systems by Signer and Norrie [5]. The main components of the RSL metamodel are illustrated in light grey in Fig. 2 whereas the necessary extensions are highlighted in blue. Note that the metamodel has been defined by using the OM data model [20] offering the concept of collections of objects as well as associations between objects. A collection is represented as a rectangle with the type of the included objects indicated in the shaded part. Associations and their cardinality constraints are visualised via oval shapes between collections.

The core elements of the RSL model are the **Resources**, **Selectors**, and **Links** collections which are all subcollections of the **Entities** collection. For each information item to be managed, a resource is instantiated and added to the **Resources** collection. We can not only link entire resources but also specific parts of a resource by using **Selectors**. Furthermore, RSL offers a plug-in mechanism to subtype the resource and selector concept for a particular type of media such as web resources, movies or even physical paper. Links in RSL are directed bidirectional many-to-many links between entities. Since both the **HasSource** and **HasTarget** associations have an entity as domain, we can define links between any of the three **Entities** subcollections. Note that the RSL metamodel also provides some user management on instantiated entities. A complete description of the RSL model can be found in [5].

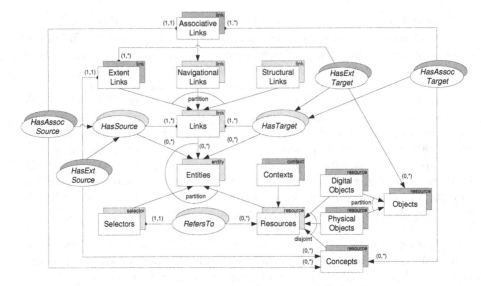

Fig. 2. OC2 framework as domain-specific RSL application

The domain-specific application of the RSL metamodel consists of three main extensions. Our OC2 conceptual framework distinguishes between concepts which are internal to the memory and objects external to the memory. Additionally, objects can be physical or digital objects. Due to the fact that our memory uses the extra information whether an object is physical or digital as a re-finding cue, this has to be taken into account in the modelling process. We therefore extended the `Resources` collection with the `Concepts`, `Physical Objects` and `Digital Objects` subcollections as shown in Fig. 2. A disjoint constraint between these three subcollections indicates that an information item (resource) can only be in one of these subcollections. Since `Physical Objects` and `Digital Objects` are objects external to the memory, we have introduced a more generic `Objects` collection. By modelling `Context` as a subcollection of `Resources`, a context can be linked to other entities and in particular to other contexts. Furthermore, the OC2 framework imposes a distinction between extent and associative links. `Extent Links` are a subcollection of `Links` since they link `Objects` to their semantic concept. The `HasExtSource` and `HasExtTarget` define the objects and the concept of a given OC2 extent link. `Associative Links` are a specific type of navigational links since they represent the navigation functionality between `Concepts`. Similarly to the extent links, an associative link has to participate in the `HasAssocSource` and `HasAssocTarget` associations since an associative link can only have one concept element as source and one or multiple concept elements as target.

In line with our OC2 conceptual framework, we have to define a weight for a specific context on concepts and objects as well as on the four different types of links. Since these elements are in fact subcollections of the `Entities` collection, we model the context relevancy via the `InContext` association as shown in Fig. 3. Furthermore, the weight is given through the participation of the `InContext`

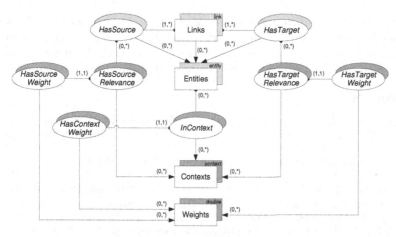

Fig. 3. Integration of context elements in the RSL metamodel

association and the `Weights` collection in the `HasContextWeight` association. Since the RSL metamodel defines links as many-to-many links, this implies that only the link itself can have a contextual relevancy. We aim for a finer granularity by supporting contextual relevancy at the level of the `HasSource` and `HasTarget` associations. The `HasSourceRelevance` and `HasTargetRelevance` associations together with the corresponding `HasSourceWeight` and `HasTargetWeight` associations are used to the define this relevancy. In this way, each source and target of a link may have their own relevance for a given context.

5   Discussion and Future Work

We have introduced the OC2 conceptual framework and its implementation integrating the strengths of both the unified view and TIM paradigms. While these two paradigms are based on principles of the human memory, they do not provide navigational and structural relationships on the object level. Additionally, they do not support the context-sensitive categorising of objects in their semantic concepts and no context relevancy can be defined on object elements.

Our current implementation focusses on the user-centric aspect to create a conceptual model. Nevertheless, machine-readable conceptual models do have advantages in PIM settings and we investigate the integration of conceptual models created by individual users with a more generic PIM ontology. While Katifori et al. [16] provide a spreading activation algorithm for TIM applications, we plan to extend this algorithm to include the full functionality offered by the OC2 framework and use context as activation element.

We have presented a new approach to PIM system design addressing the problem of information fragmentation and combining the strengths of the unified view and TIM paradigms with the most relevant aspects of the human memory. The OC2 framework has been implemented as a domain-specific application of the RSL hypermedia metamodel. Furthermore, he have developed a proof of concept semantic desktop application based on the OC2 framework. Last but not least, the presented OC2 framework for context-aware personal cross-media information management systems represents a research platform for innovative ideas in managing information across digital and physical information spaces.

References

1. Bergman, O., Beyth-Marom, R., Nachmias, R.: The Project Fragmentation Problem in Personal Information Management. In: Proc. of CHI 2006, Montreal, Canada (2006)
2. Bush, V.: As We May Think. Atlantic Monthly 176(1) (1945)
3. Catarci, T., Dix, A., Katifori, A., Lepouras, G., Poggi, A.: Task-Centered Information Management. In: Proc. of the 1st DELOS Conference, Pisa, Italy (2007)
4. Whittaker, S., Kalnikaite, V., Petrelli, D., Sellen, A., Villar, N., Bergman, O., Clough, P., Brockmeier, J.: Socio-Technical Lifelogging: Deriving Design Principles for a Future Proof Digital Past. Human-Computer Interaction 27 (2012)
5. Signer, B., Norrie, M.C.: As We May Link: A General Metamodel for Hypermedia Systems. In: Parent, C., Schewe, K.-D., Storey, V.C., Thalheim, B. (eds.) ER 2007. LNCS, vol. 4801, pp. 359–374. Springer, Heidelberg (2007)
6. Tulving, E.T., Donaldson, W.: Organization of Memory. Academic Press (1972)
7. Collins, A., Loftus, E.: A Spreading Activation Theory of Semantic Processing. Psychological Review 82(6) (1975)
8. Braisby, N., Gellatly, A.: Cognitive Psychology. Oxford University Press (2012)
9. Barsalou, L.: Ad-hoc Categories. Memory and Cognition 11(3) (1983)
10. Roth, E., Shoben, E.: The Effect of Context on the Structure of Categories. Cognitive Psychology 15(1) (1983)
11. Anderson, J.: A Spreading Activation Theory of Memory. Journal of Verbal Learning and Verbal Behavior 22(3) (1983)
12. Gemmell, J., Bell, G., Lueder, R., Drucker, S., Wong, C.: MyLifeBits: Fulfilling the Memex Vision. In: Proc. of Multimedia 2002, Juan-les-Pins, France (2002)
13. Karger, D., Bakshi, K., Huynh, D., Quan, D., Sinha, V.: Haystack: A Customizable General-Purpose Information Management Tool for End Users of Semistructured Data. In: Proc. of CIDR 2003, Asilomar, USA (January 2003)
14. Sauermann, L.: The Gnowsis Semantic Desktop for Information Integration. In: Proc. of IOA 2005, Tuscon, USA (February 2005)
15. Katifori, V., Poggi, A., Scannapieco, M., Catarci, T., Ioannidis, Y.: OntoPIM: How to Rely on a Personal Ontology for Personal Information Management. In: Proc. of ISWC 2005, Galway, Ireland (November 2005)
16. Katifori, A., Vassilakis, C., Dix, A.: Ontologies and Brain: Using Spreading Activation Through Ontologies to Support Personal Interaction. Cognitive Systems Research 11 (2010)
17. Bergman, O., Beyth-Marom, R., Nachmias, R., Gradovitch, N., Whittaker, S.: Improved Search Engines and Navigation Preference in Personal Information Management. Transactions on Information Systems 26(4) (2008)
18. Jones, W., Phuwanartnurak, A., Gill, R., Bruce, H.: Don't Take My Folders Away!: Organizing Personal Information to Get Things Done. In: Proc. of CHI 2005, Portland, USA (April 2005)
19. Bellotti, V., Edwards, K.W.: Intelligibility and Accountability: Human Considerations in Context-Aware Systems. Human-Computer Interaction 16 (2001)
20. Norrie, M.C.: An Extended Entity-Relationship Approach to Data Management in Object-Oriented Systems. In: Elmasri, R.A., Kouramajian, V., Thalheim, B. (eds.) ER 1993. LNCS, vol. 823, pp. 390–401. Springer, Heidelberg (1994)

Software as a Social Artifact:
A Management and Evolution Perspective

Xiaowei Wang[1], Nicola Guarino[2], Giancarlo Guizzardi[3], and John Mylopoulos[1]

[1] Department of Information Engineering and Computer Science, University of Trento, Italy
{xwang,jm}@disi.unitn.it
[2] ISTC-CNR, Trento, Italy
guarino@loa.istc.cnr.it
[3] Ontology and Conceptual Modeling Research Group (NEMO),
Federal University of Espírito Santo (UFES), Brazil
gguizzardi@inf.ufes.br

Abstract. For many, software is just code, something intangible best defined in contrast with hardware, but it is not particularly illuminating. Microsoft Word turned 30 last year. During its lifetime it has been the subject of numerous changes, as its requirements, code and documentation have continuously evolved. Still a community of users recognizes it as "the same software product", a persistent object undergoing several changes through a social process involving owners, developers, salespeople and users, and it is still producing recognizable effects that meet the same core requirements. It is this process that makes software something different than just a piece of code, and justifies its intrinsic nature as a social artifact. Building on Jackson's and Zave's seminal work on foundations of requirements engineering, we propose in this paper an ontology of software and related notions that accounts for such intuitions, and adopt it in software configuration management to provide a better understanding and control of software changes.

Keywords: Software, software evolution, software configuration management, software versioning, artifact, ontology, software requirements.

1 Introduction

Software has become an indispensable element of our culture, as it continues its relentless invasion of every facet of personal, business and social life. Despite this, building software applications is still an art more than science or engineering. Failure and partial failure rates for software projects still are stubbornly high and Software Engineering (SE) practice is often ahead of SE research, in virgin territory, where practitioners have few engineering principles, tools and techniques to turn to.

We believe that one of the reasons for this unhappy situation is a lack of consensus on what exactly is software, what are its defining traits, its fundamental properties and constituent concepts and how do these relate to each other. For many, both within and without the SE community, software is just code, something intangible best defined as

E. Yu et al. (Eds.): ER 2014, LNCS 8824, pp. 321–334, 2014.

the other side of hardware. For example, the Oxford English Dictionary defines software as "the programs and other information used by a computer" and other dictionaries adopt paraphrases. In a similar spirit, software maintenance tools such as Concurrent Versions System (CVS) and Apache Subversion (SVN), the version control systems of choice for almost 30 years, are used primarily for code management and evolution, while requirements, architectural specifications etc. are left out in the cold.

Unfortunately, treating software as simply code is not very illuminating. Microsoft (MS) Word turned 30 last year (2013). During its lifetime it has seen numerous changes, as its requirements, code and documentation have continuously evolved. If software is just code, then MS Word of today is not the same software as the original MS Word of 1983. But this defies the common sense that views software as a persistent object intended to produce effects in the real world, which evolves through complex social processes involving owners, developers, salespeople and users, having to deal with multiple revisions, different variants and customizations, and different maintenance policies. Indeed, software management systems were exactly intended to support such complex processes, but most of them consider software just as code, dealing with software versioning in a way not much different than ordinary documents: the criteria underlying the versioning scheme are largely heuristic, and the *change rationale* remains obscure.

Yet, differently from ordinary documents, software changes are deeply bound to the nature of the whole software development process, which includes both a requirements engineering phase and subsequent design and implementation phases. This means that, making a change to a software system may be motivated by the need to fix a bug (code), to adopt a more efficient algorithm or improve its functionality (program specification), adapt it to a new regulation (requirements) and so on. As we shall see, each of these changes affects a different *artifact* created within the software development process. In this paper we shall present an ontology that describes what these different artifacts are, and how they are inter-related.

The main contribution of this work consists of an argument, supported by ontological analysis, that software has a complex artifactual nature, as many artifacts result from a design process, each having an intended purpose that characterizes its identity. This is what distinguishes software artifacts from arbitrary code: they are recognizable as having a purpose, they are the result of an intentional act. A further characteristic of software is its social nature. In order to exist, software[1] presupposes the existence of a community of individuals who recognize its intended purpose. The members of such community may change in time, and, as already noted, may include developers, users, salespeople and stakeholders. In addition, certain software artifacts (*licensed software products*) have a further social character: they presuppose a pattern of mutual *commitments* between owners and users.

The rest of this paper is organized as follows: Firstly, we provide an ontological analysis of a number of concepts related to software and software engineering, underlining their artifactual and social nature in Section 2 and 3. The result of such analysis

---

[1] In our analysis here, we eschew the limit case of software that is privately produced and used.

is a layered ontology of software artifacts, presented in Section 4. Section 5 discusses the practical impact of our proposed ontology on software management and software modeling. Section 6 summarizes our contributions and sketches future work.

2   The Artifactual Nature of Software

2.1   State of the Art: Approaches to the Ontology of Software

In the literature, the term "software" is sometimes understood in a very general sense, independently of computers. For example, Osterweil [1] proposes that, in addition to computer software, there are other kinds of software, such as laws or recipes. Focusing on computational aspects, several scholars (e.g. Eden and Turner [2], Oberle [3]) have addressed the complex relationships among i) software *code*, consisting of a set of computer instructions; ii) a software *copy*, which is the embodiment of a set of instructions through a hard medium; iii) a *medium*, the hardware on which a software copy runs;   iv) a *process*, which is the result of executing the software copy.

A different approach to account for the artifactual nature of software is taken by Irmak [4]. According to Irmak, software is synonymous to program and can be understood in terms of the concepts of algorithm, code, copy and process, but none of these notions can be identified with software, because due to its artifactual nature, software has different identity criteria than these concepts. Therefore, a program is different from a code. We share many of Irmak's intuitions, as well as the methodology he adopts to motivate his conclusions, based on an analysis of the condition under which software maintains its identity despite change. However, he leaves the question of "what is the identity of software" open, and we answer this question here.

2.2   Code and Programs

Consider a *computer code base*, defined as a well-formed sequence of instructions in a Turing-complete language [2]. Two bases are identical iff they consist of exactly the same sequences of instructions. Accordingly, any syntactic change in a code base $c1$ results in a different code base $c2$. These changes may include variable renaming, order changes in declarative definitions, inclusion and deletion of comments, etc.

A code *implements* an algorithm. Following Irmak [4], we treat an algorithm as a language-independent *pattern of instructions*, i.e. an abstract entity correlated to a class of possible executions. So, two different code bases $c1$ and $c2$ are *semantically equivalent* if they implement the same algorithm. For instance, if $c2$ is produced from $c1$ by variable renaming, $c2$ will be semantically equivalent to $c1$, and still possess a number of properties (e.g., in terms of understandability, maintainability) that are lacking in $c1$.

Some authors, e.g. Lando et al. [5], who identify the notion of program with that of computer code, while others, such as Eden [2] and Oberle [3] distinguish program-script (program code) from program-process (whose abstraction is an algorithm). However, we agree with Irmak that we cannot identify a program neither with a code, a process, or an algorithm. The reason is that such identification conflicts with common sense, since the same program may have different code bases at different times, as a result of updates[2]. What these different code bases have in common is that, at a certain time, they are selected as *constituents* of a program that is intended to implement the very same algorithm.

To account for this intuition, we need a notion of (technical) artifact. Among alternatives in the literature works, Baker's proposal [6] works best for us: *"Artifacts are objects intentionally made to serve a given purpose"; "Artifacts have proper functions they are (intentionally) designed and produced to perform (whether they perform their proper functions or not)"; "What distinguishes artifactual [kinds] from other [kinds] is that an artifactual [kind] entails a proper function, where a proper function is a purpose or use intended by a producer. Thus, an artifact has its proper function essentially"*. These passages are illuminating in several respects. Firstly, Baker makes clear that artifacts are the results of intentional processes. Moreover, she connects the identity of an artifact to its proper function, i.e., one that fulfills its intended purpose. Finally, she recognizes that the relation between an artifact and its proper function exists even if the artifact does not perform its proper function. In other words, the connection is established by means of an intentional act.

In light of these observations, code is not necessarily an artifact. If we accidentally delete a line of code, the result might still be a computer code. It will not, however, be "intentionally made to serve a given purpose". In contrast, a program is *necessarily* an artifact, since it is created with a particular *purpose*. What kind of purpose? Well, of course the *ultimate* purpose of a program is –typically– that of producing useful effects for the prospective users of a computer system or a computer-driven machine, but there is an *immediate* purpose which belongs to the very essence of a program: producing a certain result *through execution on* a computer, *in a particular way*. We insist on the fact that the desired result and the relative behavior must come about *through* a computer, as they concern desired phenomena arising within the memory segment allocated to the program while the program runs. As usual, an abstract description of such phenomena is given by specifying a data structure and an algorithm that manipulates it [7]. Note that an algorithm, in turn, is defined as a procedure that implements a certain *function*, intended to bring about a desired change within the data structure. In summary, the immediate purpose of a program is described by a data structure, a desired change within such data structure, and a procedure to produce such change by manipulating the data structure. Altogether, such information is called a *program specification*. In contrast with code, every program has, necessarily, a purpose: satisfying its specification, namely implementing the desired function in the desired way. In order for a program to exist, its specification must exist, even if only in the programmer's mind.

According to the discussion above, we have to conclude that a program is not identical to code. This begs the question: what is the relation between the two, then? In general, the relation between an artifact and its material substratum is one of *constitution*.

---

[2] Irmak also admits that the same program may have different algorithms at different times, but we shall exclude this, distinguishing a program from a software system (see below).

As put by [6], the basic idea of constitution is that whenever a certain aggregate of things of a given kind is in certain circumstances, a new entity of a different kind comes into being. So, when code is in the circumstances that somebody intends to produce certain effects on a computer, then a new entity emerges, constituted by the code: a *computer program*. If the code does not actually produce such effects, it is the program that is faulty, not the code. In conclusion, a program is *constituted* by code, but it is not identical to code. Code can be changed without altering the identity of its program, which is anchored to the program's essential property: its intended specification.

2.3   Programs and Software Systems

We have seen that, since the identity of a program depends on its intended specification, and the specification includes both the desired function and the algorithm through which such function is supposed to be implemented, we cannot change the algorithm without changing the program, even if the function is the same. Yet, in the course of software development, it is often the case that software keeps its identity after a change in the algorithm: typically we say that *the software* is now more efficient after such a change. The strategy we shall adopt to account for such phenomena will be the same as before: we add a new entity to our layered ontology, a *software system*, which is constituted by a *software program*, which in turn is constituted by code. The essential property of a software system is being intended to satisfy a *functional specification (internal specification)*, concerning a desired change in a data structure inside a computer[3], abstracting away from the behavior. Note that, in the way we defined it, a program specification already includes a functional specification, so specifying a software system is just specifying a program in an abstract way, without constraining its behavior. This means that program specification and a software system specification overlap in the functional specification.

To give a concrete idea of our approach, let us introduce the example we shall use in the rest of the paper. Consider the following *functional specification (S)*, expressed here in natural language: *the system receives as input a connected, undirected graph G such that to each arc connecting vertices in G a positive numeric weight is assigned. The system returns a subgraph of G that is a tree and connects all vertices together. Moreover, the sum of weights in the returned tree must be equal or less than the sum of the weights in all possible trees of the same nature that are subgraphs of G.* This specification defines the desired function of finding a Minimum Spanning Tree (MST). Now, suppose that we start working on implementing this specification. First we decide the algorithm to implement, say Prim's Algorithm, and then we start writing the code. At a certain point, when this code sufficiently characterizes the program (i.e., we believe it may be correct, and it is ready to be tested), then, by an act of creation, we decide that this code now constitutes our program (let us call it *MST-Finder*). From that point on, we can keep changing the constituting code in order, for example, to fix bugs, improve readability and maintainability, etc. We can also

---

[3] We exclude from this discussion any function concerning events in the outside world, such as a robotic arm moving an object from position A to B.

improve its memory and time efficiency, while keeping the same algorithm. We can even change the programming language the initial and subsequent code bases are implemented in. Each of these changes creates a different code base but we still have the same program as long as we maintain the intention to implement the very same algorithm. On the contrary, if we replace the code by implementing Kruskal's instead of Prim's Algorithm, then what we get is a different program, although this new program, which however still constitutes the same software system.

2.4   Software Systems and Software Applications

As we have seen, programs and software systems, as defined, are software artifacts intended to produce effects inside a computer, i.e., changes concerning symbolic data structures, which reside in computer memory. Yet, as Eden and Turner observe [2], a peculiar aspect of software, with respect to other information artifacts such as books or pictures, is its *bridging role* between the abstract and the concrete: despite the fact that software has an abstract nature, it is designed to be *applied* to the real world. Therefore, it seems natural to us to take a requirements engineering perspective while analyzing the essence of software, instead of focusing on computational aspects only. So, we shall base our further analysis on a revisitation of the seminal works by Jackson and Zave (hereafter J&Z) on the foundations of requirements engineering [8], [9], [10] which clearly distinguishes the *external environment* (where the software *requirements* are typically defined), the *system-to-be* (a computer-driven machine intended to fulfill such requirements), and the interface between the two.

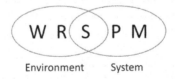

Environment   System

Fig. 1. A reference model for requirements and specifications (from [10])

Figure 1 presents the J&Z's reference model [10].The model consists of two overlapping sets of phenomena: environment phenomena, usually happenings in the world, and system phenomena that happen inside the computer. Importantly, the two sets overlap. This means that some phenomena happen at the interface between the computer and the environment and are visible both from within and without the computer.

The letters mark different kinds of phenomena, world assumptions (W), requirements (R), *specification* that describes desired behavior at the interface with the environment (S), program specification (P) that determines desired machine behavior, and assumptions on the machine behavior (M). Specifically, such assumptions concern a *programmable platform*[4] *properly connected with the external environment by means of I/O devices.*

---

[4] J&Z use the term *programming* platform. We believe that *programmable* platform is more perspicuous.

If the environment and system interact in the desired way, then the following condition needs to be satisfied: if world assumptions holds, and specification phenomena occur, then the requirements are satisfied [10]. In a compact form, J&Z describe this condition as: $W \wedge S \vDash R$. We say in this case that S *satisfies* R under the assumptions W.

This view constitutes a reference model for *requirements* engineering, emphasizing the role of the specification of machine behavior at its interface with the environment. From a *software* engineering perspective, however, we are interested not in the machine as such, but in the *program* which drives it, and ultimately in the relationship between the program and its requirements. As observed in [10], such relationship is in turn the composition of two relationships: *If (i) S properly takes W into account in saying what is needed to obtain R, and (ii) P is an implementation of S for M, then (iii) P implements R as desired.*

To properly account for this picture, it is important to make explicit the relationship between a program and its internal computer environment, which is only implicitly accounted by J&Z's approach. So we propose a revised model described in Fig. 2.

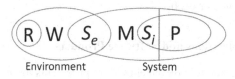

Environment   System

Fig. 2. Our revised reference model

In Figure 2, the difference is that now the programmable platform is isolated as a proper part of the system-to-be, and its interface with the program is made explicit. Reflecting the standard computer architecture, we shall assume that such platform includes operating system and I/O device phenomena. So the platform has *two* interfaces: an *external* interface (whose specification describes phenomena in the external world, such as light being emitted by the monitor or keys being pressed), and an *internal* interface, whose specification describes phenomena within the program and the operating system. A software system specification (S_i) then just concerns this internal interface, while a program specification (P) also concerns phenomena that are not visible to the platform.

Now, let us go back to our software system intended to solve the MST problem. In order for it to accept input from the user and display the results, it has to generate a sequence of machine-based phenomena, using the functionality of its programming platform. In addition, of course we want our system to interact with the user in a proper way. Such expected behavior is described by the *external* specification S_e. In order for the program to behave properly, a condition very similar to the one described above must hold: $M \wedge S_i \vDash S_e$. This means that our MST program has to interact with the particular machine at hand (say, running a Windows operating system) to produce the desired I/O behavior.

Again, we can apply in this case the same line of reasoning which motivated the distinctions between code, program, and software system: when a software system is explicitly *intended* to implement an external specification for a certain machine, then a new software artifact emerges: we shall call it a *software application*. A software application is constituted by a software system intended to determine a specific external behavior for a specific machine. Such intention is an essential property of a software application, which distinguishes it from a software system. Note that we follow here the popular terminology according to which a software application "causes a computer to perform useful tasks beyond of the running of the computer itself" [11], but, for the reasons explained below, we restrict its range to the "useful tasks" concerning the external interface only, not the outside environment.

As a final note, consider that S_e in the formula above plays the role of R in the original J&Z's formula, $W \wedge S \vDash R$. This shows the power and the generality of J&Z's model. Depending on where we place stakeholder requirements, in the scheme of Fig. 2, we can apply this general model to express the relationship between the requirements and the specification of what we have to realize in order to satisfy them. This paper, for reasons of brevity, we assume that stakeholder requirements concern the external environment, as shown in Fig. 2. This is the standard case of so-called *application* software, as distinct from *system* software, whose requirements concern phenomena inside the computer itself.

2.5   Software Applications and Software Products

Finally, let us consider the role of stakeholder requirements in the framework we have described so far. Going back to our MST example, a plausible description of such requirements could be *"We want to minimize the amount of cable necessary to connect all our network routers"*. So there is a desired state, obtained by manual intervention supported by computer assistance, such that the amount of cable used is the minimal. Obtaining this result by means of a certain software not only presupposes the solution of the abstract MST problem, but of course a lot of assumptions concerning the world and the people's skills and behaviors. Moreover, during the evolution of such software, assuming world and machine assumptions remain the same, different external specifications may be designed, corresponding to different user interfaces. In this case people may say that *the same software* is evolving. According to the methodology followed so far, this means that a new artifact emerges, constituted by a software application, which we shall call a *software product*. A software product is constituted by a software application intended to determine specific effects in the environment as a result of the machine behavior, under given world assumptions. Such intention is an essential property of a software product, which distinguishes it from a software application.

In conclusion, the notion of software product captures perhaps the most common use of the word "software" in the daily life. It is important to remark that a software product is intended to achieve some effects in the external environment *by means of a given machine*, and *under given environment assumptions*. So, assuming they have exactly the same high-level requirements, MS Word for Mac and MS Word for PC are different software products, since they are intended for different machines. Similarly, country-oriented customizations of Word for Mac may be understood as different products, since they presuppose different language skills, unless the requirements already explicitly include the possibility to interact with the system in multiple different languages.

3   The Social Nature of Software

In addition to its artifactual nature, discussed in detail above, software –at least software used every day in our society– has also a strong social nature, which impacts on the way it is produced, sold, used and maintained. There are two main social aspects of software we shall consider under our evolution perspective: *social recognition* and *social commitment*.

3.1   Social Recognition and Software Identity

We have seen the key role the constitution relation plays in accounting for the artifactual nature of software. But how is this constitution relation represented and recognized? In the simplest of cases, we can think of a program produced by a single programmer for personal use. In this case, we can imagine that the constitution relationship binding a program with its constituting code exists solely in the mind of this programmer. Likewise, if this program comes to constitute a software system, then this constitution relation, again, exists only in the mind of the programmer. Yet, in order for a software artifact to exist in a social context, we shall assume that the constitution relation between the artifact at hand and its constituent needs to be explicitly communicated by the software author, and recognizable by a community of people. As a minimal situation, we consider these communications about constitution and intentions to satisfy specifications as true communicative acts that create expectations, beliefs and contribute to the creation of commitments, claims and a minimal social structure (possibly reflecting division of labor) between the software creator(s) and the potential users or stakeholders. Once this social structure exists, the creators' actions become social actions and are subject to social and legal norms that support expectations and rights. To cite one example, we use the motion picture "The Social Network" based on the book "Accidental Billionaires" [12] reporting on the creation of Facebook. As shown there, the legal battle involving the authorship rights in Facebook was at moments based on the discussion of shared authorship between M. Zuckerberg and E. Saverin regarding an initial program (Saverin was allegedly a prominent proposer of the algorithm) and software system, much before the product Facebook existed. At other times, the legal battle between Zuckerberg and the Winklevoss brothers was based on a shared system specification of another program even if, as argued by Zuckerberg, no lines of the original code had been used by Facebook.

In more disciplined software engineering settings, anyway, the constitution relationships and the intended specifications are documented by program headers and possibly user manuals or separate product documentation. Notice that, without the explicit documentation of these relationships, the software artifacts will depend on their creators in order to exist, since the constitution relationships are sustained by their intentional states. Once these relationships are documented, these artifacts can outlive their creators, as long as this documentation can be properly recognized and understood. So, for instance, although Joseph Weizenbaum is no longer alive, by looking to a copy of the ELIZA [13] code, one can still reconstruct the chain of intentions from the informal requirements specification all the way down to the code. In formal ontological terms, this means that software artifacts are just historically (but not constantly) depending on their authors, and in addition they are generically constantly depending on a community of people who recognize their essential properties. If such community of people ceases to exist, the artifact ceases to exist.

3.2   Social Commitment and Software Licensing

As we have seen, the different kinds of software artifacts we have discussed are based on a requirements engineering perspective. We cannot ignore however another perspective that deeply affects the current practice of software engineering, namely the *marketing perspective*. In the present software market, software products do not come alone, since what companies sell are not just software products: in the vast majority of cases, a purchase contract for a software product includes a number of rights and duties on both parties, including the right to download updates for a certain period of time, the prohibition to give copies away, the right to hold the clients' personal data and to automatically charge them for specific financial transactions, and so on. Indeed, the very same software product can be sold at different prices by different companies, under different *licensing policies*. The result is that software products come to the market in the form of *service offerings*, which concern *product-service bundles*. According to [14], a *service offering* is in turn based on the notion of *service*, which is a social commitment concerning in our case maintenance actions. Service offerings are therefore meta-commitments, i.e., they are commitments to engage in specific commitments (namely, the delivery of certain services) once a contract is signed. So, before the contract is signed we have another software entity emerging: a *Licensable Software Product*. After the contract is signed, we have a *Licensed Software Product*. Notice that the services regulated by the contract may not only concern the proper functioning of software (involving the right to updates), but also the availability of certain resources in the environment where the software is supposed to operate, such as remote servers (used, e.g., for Web searching, VOIP communication, cloud syncing...). So, when Skype Inc. releases Skype, it publicly commits to engage in such kind of commitments. By the way, this means that, when buying Skype from Skype Inc., Microsoft is not only buying the software product, but it is also buying all the rights Skype Inc. has regarding its clients.

Note that, even in absence of a purchasing contract, when releasing a product as licensable product, the owner creates already social commitments and expectations towards a community of users and re-users of the product. For example, take the Protégé Ontology editor, which is a free open-source product released under the Mozilla Public License (MPL) [15]. This grants the members of the user community the right to change Protégé's code and to incorporate it even in commercial products.

4   A Layered Ontology of Software

The discussion so far induces a layered structure for our ontology of software arti-facts, based on their different identity criteria and on the constitution relationship that links them to each other. Such layered structure is shown in Figure 3. As usual, the subsumption relation is represented by an open-headed arrow. The closed-headed arrows represent some of the basic relations discussed in the paper. Starting from code, several kinds of software artifacts have been proposed, all eventually consti-tuted by code. The different essential properties characterizing their identity are shown to the right, linked by a relation of specific constant dependence. As the con-cepts have already been introduced, we give here only a brief account of the relations appearing in the picture. For some of them (constitution and specific constant depen-dence), the intended semantics is rather standard, while for others we just sketch their intended meaning, postponing a formal characterization to a future paper.

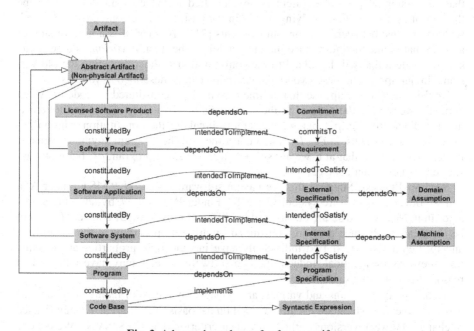

Fig. 3. A layered ontology of software artifacts

ConstitutedBy: We mean here the relation described extensively by Baker [6]. We just assume it being a kind of generic dependence relation that is both asymmetric and non-reflexive, and that does not imply parthood. We can assume here for this relation, the minimal axiomatization present in the DOLCE ontology [16].

DependsOn: Among the different kinds of dependence relations (described e.g. in the DOLCE ontology), *dependsOn* denotes in this paper a specific constant depen-dence relation: if *x* is specifically constantly depending on *y*, then, necessarily, at each time *x* is present also *y* must be present. Again, we can borrow the DOLCE axi-omatization for this relation. When this relation holds, being dependent on *y* is for *x* an essential property.

IntendedToImplement: This relation links an artifact to its specification, as a result of an intentional act. Note that the intention to implement does not imply that the implementation will be the correct one (e.g., bugs may exist).

IntendedToSatisfy: This relation is proposed to capture the intended role of a specification   in the general formula $S \wedge W \vDash R$. That is, S is intended to satify R, once the assumptions W holds.

5   Ontology-Driven Software Configuration Management

According to [17], Software Configuration Management (SCM) is "a discipline for controlling the evolution of software systems", and is considered as a core supporting process for software development [18]. A basic notion of any SCM system is the concept of version [19]. The IEEE *Software Engineering Body of Knowledge* states [20] that "a version of a software item is an identified instance of an item. It can be thought of as a state of an evolving item". In the past, the same source distinguished, within versions, between revisions and variants [21]: "A *revision* is a new version of an item that is intended to replace the old version of the item. A *variant* is a new version of an item that will be added to the configuration without replacing the old version". In our approach, these two kinds of version can be described as follows:

Revision Process. Suppose that at time t we have $p1$ constituted by code $c1$; when at time t' we replace the code $c1$ as the constituent of $p1$ by code $c2$, we are not creating a distinct program $p2$, but we are simply breaking the constitution relation between $p1$ and $c1$. Thus, at t', $c1$ is not a constituent of the program anymore; rather it is merely a code, so that at t' we are still left with the same program $p1$, but now constituted by a different code $c2$.

Variant Process. Suppose that we have a software system $s1$ ("MST-Finder A"), and we develop a software system $s2$ ("MST-Finder B") from $s1$ by adopting a new algorithm. Now $s1$ and $s2$ are constituted by different programs. Of course, $s1$ will not be identical to $s2$, since they are constituted by different programs at the same time, and by Leibniz's Law if two individuals have incompatible properties at the same time they are not identical. Indeed, the two software systems may have independent reasons to exist at the same time.

Traditionally, revisions and variants are managed by means of naming conventions and version codes which are usually decided on the basis of the *perceived* significance of changes between versions without any clear criterion (e.g. CVS, SVN). We believe that the layered ontology introduced in this paper can make an important contribution to make this process more disciplined by providing a general mechanism to explicitly express what is changed when a new version is created. This can be simply done by pointing to the software artifact that is affected by the change, and can be reflected by a simple versioning scheme (e.g. v 1.5.3.2: 1 - software application release number; 5 – software system release number, 3 – program release number; 2 – code release number). In addition to this scheme, we can document the *rationale* why a certain software artifact has been changed, by applying the revised reference model of Figure 2 and pointing to the specific source of change.

We believe that this ability to account both for what and why software is changed is essential for software engineering, because managing software and software evolution requires much more than managing code. For example, as Licensed Software Products are based on a chain of dependent artifacts culminating with a computer code, a software management system must be able to manage the impact that changes in the code ultimately have in terms of legal and financial consequences at the level of licensed products.

6   Conclusions and Future Work

Based on the work of J&Z and Irmak, we analyzed in this paper the identity criterion of software from the artifectual perspective, extending the analysis to the social nature of software as well. Several kinds of software artifacts have been identified, resulting in a layered ontological structure based on the constitution relation.

Besides clarifying core concepts in the domain of software engineering, our work can also serve as a foundation for software management and evolution. By checking the identity criteria of the software artifacts in different abstraction layers, we can judge the conditions when they keep their identities under changes, or new entities are created. Based on that, a refined versioning methodology and better software versioning control tools dealing with revisions and variants could be developed. As noted several times, traditional tools only focus on code changes. According to our work, software should be consistently expressed and tracked in multiple abstraction layers.

This work is part of a general project on the ontology of software evolution and software change. We hope our work could be used as a foundation for researchers and practitioners working on software maintenance, software project management, software measurements and metrics.

Acknowledgements. Support for this work was provided by the ERC advanced grant 267856 for the project entitled "Lucretius: Foundations for Software Evolution" (http://www.lucretius.eu), as well as the "Science Without Borders" project on "Ontological Foundations of Service Systems" funded by the Brazilian government.

References

1. Osterweil, L.J.: What is software? Autom. Softw. Eng. 15, 261–273 (2008).
2. Eden, A.H., Turner, R.: Problems in the ontology of computer programs. Appl. Ontol. 2, 13–36 (2007)
3. Oberle, D.: Semantic Management of Middleware. Springer, New York (2006)
4. Irmak, N.: Software is an Abstract Artifact. Grazer Philos. Stud. 86, 55–72 (2013)
5. Lando, P., Lapujade, A., Kassel, G., Fürst, F.: An Ontological Investigation in the Field of Computer Programs. In: Filipe, J., Shishkov, B., Helfert, M., Maciaszek, L. (eds.) Software and Data Technologies. CCIS, vol. 22, pp. 371–383. Springer, Heidelberg (2009)
6. Baker, L.R.: The ontology of artifacts. Philos. Explor. 7, 99–111 (2004)
7. Wirth, N.: Algorithms+ data structures= programs. Ser. Autom. Comput. (1976)
8. Jackson, M., Zave, P.: Deriving specifications from requirements: an example. In: Proceedings of the 17th International Conference on Software Engineering, pp. 15–24. ACM, New York (1995)
9. Zave, P., Jackson, M.: Four dark corners of requirements engineering. ACM Trans. Softw. Eng. Methodol. 6, 1–30 (1997)

10. Gunter, C.A., Jackson, M., Zave, P.: A reference model for requirements and specifications. IEEE Software 17, 37–43 (2000)
11. Wikipedia: Application software,
    http://en.wikipedia.org/wiki/Application_software
12. Mezrich, B.: The Accidental Billionaires: The Founding of Facebook: a Tale of Sex, Money, Genius and Betrayal. Anchor Books (2010)
13. Wikipedia: ELIZA, http://en.wikipedia.org/wiki/ELIZA
14. Nardi, J.C., De Almeida Falbo, R., Almeida, J.P.A., Guizzardi, G., Ferreira Pires, L., van Sinderen, M.J., Guarino, N.: Towards a Commitment-Based Reference Ontology for Services. In: 2013 17th IEEE International on Enterprise Distributed Object Computing Conference (EDOC), pp. 175–184 (2013)
15. Mozilla: Mozilla Public License, http://www.mozilla.org/MPL/
16. Masolo, C., Borgo, S., Gangemi, A., Guarino, N., Oltramari, A., Horrocks, I.: WonderWeb-D18: Ontology Library, Trento (2003)
17. Dart, S.: Concepts in Configuration Management Systems. In: Proceedings of the 3rd International Workshop on Software Configuration Management, pp. 1–18. ACM, New York (1991)
18. Chrissis, M.B., Konrad, M., Shrum, S.: CMMI for Development: Guidelines for Process Integration and Product Improvement. Pearson Education (2011)
19. Estublier, J., Leblang, D.B., van der Hoek, A., Conradi, R., Clemm, G., Tichy, W.F., Weber, D.W.: Impact of software engineering research on the practice of software configuration management. ACM Trans. Softw. Eng. Methodol. 14, 383–430 (2005)
20. Bourque, P., Fairley, R.E. (eds.): Guide to the Software Engineering Body of Knowledge Version 3.0. IEEE Computer Society Press (2014)
21. Abran, A., Moore, J.W.: Guide to the software engineering body of knowledge. IEEE Computer Society (2004)

Modelling Risks
in Open Source Software Component Selection

Alberto Siena, Mirko Morandini, and Angelo Susi

Fondazione Bruno Kessler
I-38123, Trento – Italy
{siena,morandini,susi}@fbk.eu

Abstract. Adopting Open Source Software (OSS) components is a decision that offers many potential advantages – such as cost effectiveness and reputation – but even introduces a potentially high number of risks, which span from the inability of the OSS community to continue the development over time, to a poor quality of code. Differently from commercial off-the-shelf components, to assess risk in OSS component adoption, we can rely on the public availability of measurable information about the component code and the developing communities. In the present paper, we present a risk evaluation technique that uses conceptual modelling to assess OSS component adoption risks. We root it in the existing literature on OSS risk assessment and validate it by means of our industrial partners.

Keywords: Risk assessment, Open Source Software, Automated reasoning.

1 Introduction

Developing complex software systems requires to make a high number of critical decisions, which could contribute to the success of the development project or ratify its failure. Choosing the right software components is one among the most critical decisions, as it concerns the evaluation of both, the technical aspects of the components, and their possible impact on higher level strategic objectives.

More and more, companies are interested in adopting Open Source Software (OSS) components, which promise to ease the achievement of internal objectives, such as a reduction of cost and time to market, quality improvements or independence from producers. However, OSS software components also introduce various risks that are not visible at the time of the adoption, but can manifest in later development and maintenance phases, causing unexpected failures.

Inadequate risk management was identified among the top mistakes when implementing OSS-based solutions. Understanding, managing and mitigating OSS adoption risks is therefore crucial to avoid a potential adverse impact on the business, in terms of time to market, customer satisfaction, revenue, and reputation. In OSS, the available data and meta-data, in code repositories, bug trackers, and discussion forums, can be an important source to discover correlations with prospective failure, thus indicating the presence of risks. The need to properly analyse such data calls for a (semi-)automated risk analysis.

E. Yu et al. (Eds.): ER 2014, LNCS 8824, pp. 335–348, 2014.

In this paper we present a framework for risk modelling and risk evaluation, which is tailored to assess OSS adoption risks. The framework is comprised by a conceptual modelling language and a quantitative reasoning algorithm that analyses models. It relies on the capability to exploit OSS measures as possible indicators of risk, and to relate them to higher level organisational elements. Several model-based approaches to risk analysis have been presented in literature, e.g. [1,3]. In contrast to defensive risk analysis approaches such as [8], which are appropriate e.g. for security risks, our approach considers also an offensive analysis, including the assessment of alternatives.

The paper is structured as follows. In Section 2 we define the problem and introduce the concepts used in the modelling language. In Section 3, the modelling language and its semantics are defined, while Section 4 explains how risk analysis is applied upon these models. Section 5 shows an application of a tool that implements the semantics, to a small scenario. Relevant related work is given in Section 6, while Section 7 concludes the work.

2   Context and Problem

Adopting OSS components exposes the adopter to various risks, some are general, but some also specific to OSS. Although OSS components have often technical qualities comparable to those of Commercial Off-The-Shelf (COTS) components, OSS is typically provided without legal contracts and certifications that guarantee the adopter over time about the component functionalities and qualities. Part of the risks is intrinsic to the openness and distribution of the OSS communities developing the component. Such factors are often not fully perceivable at the time of the choice, but could appear in the future, causing unpredicted costs. For example, *an OSS project in which people don't participate actively, contributing with frequent code commits and online discussions, may progressively by abandoned by contributors, thus letting the component development to die and the adopters without necessary new releases.* These uncertainties represent the risks for the adopter's business objectives.

The present work starts from the intuition that the possible future evolution of the OSS project (and of the OSS component thereof) is estimable from the analysis of some characteristics of the project itself. In particular, and differently from COTS, OSS projects make freely available their data, from the source code and its metadata in repositories, to bug trackers, forums and other communication channels. If we are able to get measures of such data, we can use them to estimate not only the quality of the software but also the dynamics in the community, and consequently the various risks to which an adopter is exposed when integrating a particular OSS component. The challenge is to identify a conceptual formalism, capable to provide at the same time (i) a good representation of the OSS domain under analysis, (ii) a representation of business goals of the adopter, and (iii) the available knowledge on how measures can propagate risk quantification on business goals.

We may think to the problem of inferring knowledge from OSS component measures as a Business Intelligence (BI) problem. In our case, we need to relate something, which is *external* to a company (the OSS component), to something *internal* (the business objectives), modulo a certain amount of *uncertainty* about the relation itself (the risk).

In BI, *indicators* (or *risk indicators*) provide a means to measure the state of things [2,7]. For example, "Number of commits per month" is a possible measure about an OSS, captured by an indicator. States of affairs can be represented by means of *situations* [2,4]. A situation is expressed by means of a proposition that describes the facts that are true or false in that situation. Consequently, it can have associated a certain evidence to be true. For example, "There have been no commits since the last 30 days" and "There are bugs that need to be fixed" are propositions expressing situations. Risk indicators combine available measures (in our context, OSS code and community measures), to contribute evidence for being in a certain situation. This evidence can be obtained e.g. through an empirical data analysis, or from experts' experience.

Situations are inherently linked to the concept of *event*. An event is a happening at a given place and time, and changes the state-of-affairs, thus it can modify a situation. Events describe a state change, also expressed through propositions. For example, "A new version is committed" and "A members leaves the community" are propositions describing an event, while "There is a lack of support in the community" describes a situation.

Such concepts help in providing primitives to model risk. The concept of *risk* is defined in several ways in literature. The ISO 31000:2009 standard defined risk as *an effect of uncertainty on objectives*, using the concepts of *likelihood* of occurrence of risky events and *severity* of their *impact* on business objectives. In this paper, for reasons of clarity, we limit to adverse, i.e. negative impacts, in line with other definitions such as NIST SP 800-30. Based on this definition of *risk* as a combined concept [11], the severity of the impact, together with the likelihood of the event, are the parameters that define *risk exposure*, which can be expressed in terms of a discrete (e.g. *low-risk, high-risk*) or a continuous value. We call an event for which a risk analysis is performed *risk event*. Certainly, not necessarily a consequence is severe enough and each event non-deterministic enough for the stakeholders to deserve a detailed risk analysis.

Situations may describe *possible causes* or preconditions for risk events. Examples in the security domain are the presence of a vulnerability or of an attacker. The *consequences* of an event can have a negative effect to the stakeholders' *goals*, which express a desire to maintain some asset or to achieve some situation.

3   Modelling OSS Component Risks with RiskML

In this section we propose a modelling language for risk modelling, called *RiskML*, defining its concepts, the underlying metamodel, its syntax and the ascribed semantics for performing risk assessment.

3.1   Concepts and Relations

Indicator. An Indicator is an abstract representation of a measure about a certain property of the OSS [2]. The *value* of an indicator by definition ranges between 0 and 1. An indicator determines the evidence of being in a certain situation. It is ideally retrieved with tool support.

Situation. We use the concept of situation to model the state of affairs under which a certain risk is possible. A situation is *satisfied* if the state of affairs (i.e. a partial state of the world) that it represents, holds [2,14]. If ϕ is a proposition describing a situation, $sat(\phi)$ defines the satisfaction of the situation. However, we do not aim at a complete, formal description of the world. Rather, situations capture circumstances relevant for modelling risk.

Event. We use the concept of event to model a change in the state of affairs, with a potential negative impact on goals. Events may have a certain quantitative *significance* and their occurrence may happen with a certain *likelihood*. If ϕ is a proposition describing an event, $lik(\phi)$ describes the *likelihood* of the event. $sig(\phi)$ describes the *significance* of the event for a stakeholder's goals.

Goal. We use the concept of goal to model the desire of a stakeholder in obtaining or maintaining some business value, i.e. some state of affairs. Goals are *satisfied* if the corresponding state of affairs is achieved. If ϕ is a proposition describing a goal, $sat(\phi)$ describes the satisfaction of the goal.

Risk. A *Risk* is a composed concept which expresses a lack of knowledge about some happening and what could be the (negative) consequences. Accordingly, we define a risk as a tuple $\langle$ S, E, G $\rangle$, where:
   - S are the situations, in which risk events potentially occur,
   - E is the event whose occurrence impacts on stakeholder goals,
   - G is the goal, which suffers a negative impact if the event occurs.

Relations. The defined relations link indicators, situations, events, and goals, and thus define implicitly the occurrence of a risk. We define six types of relations.

   – *Expose*, from a situation to an event: the higher the evidence that the situation is satisfied, the more likely the event is to happen (*evidence* represents the degree of confidence that a fact is true). For example, if the activeness of an OSS community appears to be too low, this may mean that in the future the community's activeness will fall completely, and the community will die. This is modelled through the *Expose* relation by saying that the situation of low community activeness exposes to the event of community death.
   – *Protect*, from a situation to an event: the higher the evidence that the situation is satisfied, the less likely the event is to happen. For example, if there seems to be large number of downloads of a given OSS software project, this may mean that the interest towards the OSS project is high, and this may mean that hardly the OSS community will be left die. This is modelled through the *Protect* relation by saying that the a high interest towards the OSS project protects from the event of community death.
   – *Increase*, from a situation to an event: the higher the evidence that the situation is satisfied, the bigger is the significance of the event consequence. For example, if a company, who wants to adopt a certain OSS software and needs to maintain its final product for a medium-long period of time, the presence of an active community behind the OSS project is considered important for the choice of adopting the OSS software. This is modelled through the *Increase* relation: if there is evidence that

the adopter is in the situation to need to maintain the product for a longer time, the significance of the consequence of a community death increases.

- **Reduce**, from a situation to an event: the higher the evidence that the situation is satisfied, the smaller is the significance of the event consequence. For example, if a company wants to decrease its risk exposure to the possibility of community death, it may decide to implement a plugin architecture; so in its vision, if the OSS community will die, the plugin-based architecture will allow to quickly switch to a different component, thus reducing the significance of the event consequence. This is modelled through the *Reduce* relation by saying that a plugin-based architecture reduces the significance of the consequence of a community death.
- **Impact**, from an event to a goal: the higher the impact, the higher is the *severity* of an event for the satisfaction of a stakeholder's goals. The impact thus defines the propagation the of risk exposure to goal satisfaction. For example, if a company has to provide support to its customers on its final product, if the event of community death will manifest, the company will be unable to provide further support. This is modelled through the *Impact* relation by saying that a community death impacts the goal of providing support to the final product.
- **Indicate**, from an indicator to a situation: the higher the value of an indicator, the higher the evidence that the situation is satisfied. For example, the more recent the posts in a forum are, the more evidence we have for an active community. This is modelled through the *Indicate* relation by saying that the number of recent posts in a forum (possibly among others) indicates an active community.

Additionally, the **Expose** and **Protect** relationships can be defined from one event to another, propagating likelihood: this is a shortcut to say that the situations, resulting from event happening, expose other events or protect against them.

3.2   Meta-model

Figure 1 depicts the overall meta-model of the RiskML modelling language. The meta-model defines the modelling primitives of risk and the interplay between risk, goals and the ecosystem. Situations and events are the core of the meta-model. The evidence to be in a certain situation can be quantified (especially in an OSS context) by means of indicators, which were empirically evaluated or approved by experts and base on measurements of available data. Situations represent the causes for risks to appear, while events represent the manifestation of a risk. Expose, increase, protect and reduce relations from situations (and events) to events quantify the likelihood for an event to occur and the significance of its consequences. Events impact the satisfaction of goals that actors desire to be achieved. This impact may be propagated to other goals, e.g. through *i** contribution and decomposition relationships [16].

As a means to achieve their goals, actors perform activities, which modify the state of the world – they are the means by which actors intentionally or unintentionally modify situations. Through the convergence of goals and tasks actors can also set up strategies to mitigate risk exposure. Actors live in an ecosystem comprised by other actors [9], and depend on them to achieve some of their goals. On the other hand, actors provide to other actors the capability to achieve their goals. Thus, an impact on one actor may also propagate its effects on the rest of the ecosystem.

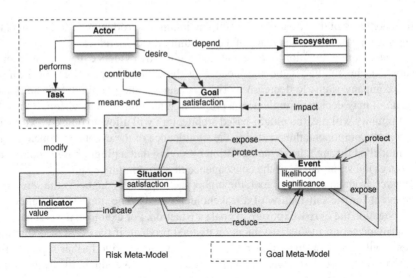

Fig. 1. Meta-model of the risk modelling language RiskML

3.3 Syntax and Semantics

Symbolic Syntax. Expressions of the language are generated via the BNF rules in Table 1. We use s for an atomic situation, e for a single event, g for an atomic goal, and i for an indicator. Expressions in the language are denoted by Greek letters. Symbols for relations are: $\wedge$ for conjunction, $\vee$ for disjunction, $\phi \xrightarrow{expose} \psi$ for Expose, $\phi \xrightarrow{protect} \psi$ for Protect, $\phi \xrightarrow{increase} \psi$ for Increase, $\phi \xrightarrow{reduce} \psi$ for Reduce, $\phi \xrightarrow{impact} \psi$ for Impact, and $\phi \xrightarrow{indicate} \psi$ for Indicate.

Semantics. A RiskML model is defined as a pair $\{\mathcal{C}; \mathcal{R}\}$, where $\mathcal{C}$ is a set of concept instances and $\mathcal{R}$ is a set of relation instances over $\mathcal{C}$. We call ϕ and ψ *proposition*s describing a concept instance. If $(\phi_1, \ldots, \phi_n; op) \xrightarrow{r} \psi$ is a relation $r \in \mathcal{R}$, we call $\phi_1 \ldots \phi_n$ the *source concepts* or source propositions, op the logical connector of the propositions $\phi_1, \ldots, \phi_n$ and ψ the *target concept* or target proposition. We call $\alpha \in \mathcal{A}$ an attribute of a concept instance, defined on a set $\mathcal{A}$ of attributes. Each relation r

Table 1. Syntax of RiskML models

(1) $S := s \mid S \wedge s \mid S \vee s$
(2) $E := e \mid E \wedge e \mid E \vee e$
(3) $G := g \mid G \wedge g \mid G \vee g$
(4) $I := i$
(5) $R := (S, E, G)$
(6) $\phi := S \mid E \mid G, \; \psi := S \mid E \mid G$
(7) $\alpha(\phi) := sat(\phi) \mid lik(\phi) \mid sig(\phi)$
(8) $Rel := \phi \xrightarrow{expose} \psi \mid \phi \xrightarrow{protect} \psi \mid \phi \xrightarrow{increase} \psi \mid \phi \xrightarrow{reduce} \psi \mid \phi \xrightarrow{impact} \psi \mid \phi \xrightarrow{indicate} \psi$

modifies the attribute value $\alpha(\psi)$ of the target concept, according to the attribute values of the source concepts and the function f which defines a type of relation.

If S is a proposition describing a situation, $sat(S)$ is an attribute of S describing the fact that the situation is satisfied or not satisfied. If E describes an event, $lik(E)$ describes its *likelihood* and $sig(E)$ describes its *significance*. If G is a proposition describing a goal, $sat(G)$ describes the *satisfaction* of this goal.

Table 2 summarises the semantics of a RiskML model. To evaluate how risky an event is, we calculate the exposure $exp(E)$ to its occurrence through a function f – the *risk aversion* function – of its likelihood to occur and the significance of its occurrence (A1). For sake of simplicity, the function is currently implemented as the average of the two values. The relations A2 to A7 propagate values across a risk model with the following meaning:

- Expose: evidence of satisfaction of the source Situation (S) is positively propagated to the target Event's (E) likelihood.
- Protect: evidence of satisfaction of the source Situation (S) is negatively propagated to the target Event's (E) likelihood.
- Increase: evidence of satisfaction of the source Situation (S) is positively propagated to the target Event's (E) significance.
- Reduce: evidence of satisfaction of the source Situation (S) is negatively propagated to the target Event's (E) significance.
- Impact: exposure (combining likelihood and significance) of the source risk event (E) is negatively propagated to the target Goal's (G) satisfaction.
- Indicate: the source Indicator (I) value $\mu(I)$, defined as an assignment of values (coming from a set of available data M, obtained, for example, from measurements, or expert opinions) is propagated to the evidence of being satisfied for the target situation S.

A8 states the general propagation rule in a risk model: given a node of the model ψ and a set of relations entering into the node $\alpha_1(\Phi_1) \xrightarrow{w_1} \beta(\psi), ..., \alpha_n(\Phi_n) \xrightarrow{w_n} \beta(\psi)$, the value propagated to $\beta(\psi)$ is the maximum among the values propagated by the single relations. Each relation can have multiple source nodes and one target node (A9). Source nodes can be put in AND- or OR- connection. In the first case, what is propagated is the product of the source values (attenuation), since propagation takes place only if both are present; in the second case, the difference between sum and product of source nodes (reinforcement), resembling a propagation of probabilities as used in [5].

3.4 Example

Figure 2 depicts a sample RiskML model. In this model, two indicators, [commit frequency] and [current/past commit frequency ratio], are used to capture available measures of the OSS project. The indicators are used to detect the condition of a low activeness in the community, represented by means of the [Low activeness] situation. Situations are the highest level representation of what is observed to be true or false at time t_0. At any time t_x, with $x > 0$ (i.e., at any time in the future), some events are possible to happen, such as [the community will die]. The *expose* relations inform that the more

Table 2. Axioms and propagation rules for RiskML models

Axioms

A1	$exp(E) = f(lik(E), sig(E))$	

Relations

	Relation	Definition
A2	$S \xrightarrow{expose} E$	$sat(S) \xrightarrow{+} lik(E)$
A3	$S \xrightarrow{protect} E$	$sat(S) \xrightarrow{-} lik(E)$
A4	$S \xrightarrow{increase} E$	$sat(S) \xrightarrow{+} sig(E)$
A5	$S \xrightarrow{reduce} E$	$sat(S) \xrightarrow{-} sig(E)$
A6	$E \xrightarrow{impact} G$	$exp(E) \xrightarrow{-} sat(G)$
A7	$I \xrightarrow{indicate} S$	$\mu(I) \xrightarrow{+} sat(S)$

Rules

	Rule	Definition
A8	$\alpha_1(\Phi_1) \xrightarrow{w1} \beta(\psi), ..., \alpha_n(\Phi_n) \xrightarrow{wn} \beta(\psi)$	$\beta(\psi) = max(w_1 * \alpha(\Phi_1), ..., w_n * \alpha(\Phi_n))$
A9	$\alpha(\Phi) \xrightarrow{w} \beta(\psi)$	$\alpha(op(\phi_1, ..., \phi_n)) \xrightarrow{w} \beta(\psi)$
A10	$(and) \ op = \wedge$	$\alpha(\Phi) = \alpha(\phi_1) + ... + \alpha(\phi_n)/n$
A11	$(or) \ op = \vee$	$\alpha(\Phi) = 1 - (\alpha(\phi_1) + ... + \alpha(\phi_n))/n$

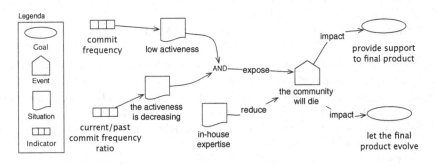

Fig. 2. Example of RiskML Risk Exposure Model

there is evidence that the community is low active, the higher is the likelihood of a future community death. Notice that in this paper we omit reasoning on the quantification of weights and assume a default weight of 0.5, if not differently specified. Also, if not differently specified, events have by default a significance of 0.5. In the example, the [In-house expertise] situation models the organisational fact that skilled programmers are available to the adopter, and this lowers the significance of a possible community death. If the events occurs, the *impact* relations show the affected business goals.

4   Reasoning with Risk Models

RiskML models are meant to be used to support automated reasoning for risk assessment. To do this we assign *evidence* values to known elements of the models (typically the indicators) and apply a label propagation algorithm to infer knowledge about unknown elements (typically the goals). An *evidence* is a numerical quantification of a certain truth value, expressed as a real number in the range [0..1]. An evidence represents the degree of confidence that the truth value holds, or does not hold. For example,

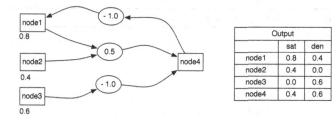

Fig. 3. The label propagation technique

with reference to "timeliness" (defined as the capability of a certain OSS community to deliver new releases according to its roadmap timetable), we may express as having evidence 1 is that the releases are always delivered on the announced day.

Positive vs. Negative Evidence. To each node two evidence values are associated: a value for satisfaction evidence, and a value for denial evidence. For example, for a node "The door is locked", a satisfaction evidence indicates that there is evidence that the door is locked; a denial evidence indicates that there is evidence that the door is not locked. Both values can hold at the same time, indicating that there is some positive evidence but also some negative evidence about the node. For example, a closed door with a key inserted into the keyhole may highlight that the door is locked (because the door is actually closed) but at the same time there is a possibility that the door is not locked (because of the presence of the key).

Model Stability. Separating satisfaction from denial evidence allows us to ensure monotonicity of label propagation algorithms. In turn, this allows us to manage cycles by calculating only stable models. Figure 3 illustrates how this technique works. node1 has an input value of +0.8; node2 has an input value of +0.4; node3 has an input value of +0.6; node1 and node2 propagate positively to (reinforce) node4 with a weight of 0.5. node3 propagates negatively to (inhibits) node4 by -1.0. node4 results in a satisfaction evidence of 0.4 (= max(0.8 * 0.5, 0.4 * 0.5)). Additionally, it has a denial evidence of 0.6 due to node3. node4, in turn, inhibits node1, which also assumes a denial evidence of 0.4. This value is not further propagated because, although it is in relation with node4, the denial evidence of node4 is 0.6, which is greater than 0.4. This example explains how the monotonicity achieved by means of decoupling the satisfaction from the denial evidence allows us to solve cycles.

Propagation Algorithm. Label propagation [12] is a forward reasoning techniques applied to graph analysis. Starting from the knowledge about some known nodes of the graph, it has the objective of inferring knowledge about unknown nodes. Label propagation has been successfully applied in [6] to support forward reasoning in goal analysis. We adapt their approach to our purposes, generalising it and supporting risk assessment. Label propagation is implemented using a forward quantitative reasoning algorithm, listed in Algorithm 1. The algorithm iterates over every node of the label graph, and evaluates the incoming propagation arcs. If the value(s) of the node is lower that the values of the source nodes, weighted by the arc's weight, the value(s) of the node is

---

Algorithm 1: Label propagation algorithm.

Data: Graph $G(C, R)$
Result: Labels propagated in G
begin
    boolean $graph\_changed = false$;
    repeat
        for *(c in C)* **do**
            double $max\_positive = 0$;
            double $max\_negative = 0$;
            for *(r in R)* **do**
                double $positive\_val = r.evalPositivePropagation()$;
                double $negative\_val = r.evalNegativePropagation()$;
                if *(positive_val > max_positive)* **then**
                    $c.setPositiveVal(r.attribute, positive\_val)$;
                    $max\_positive = positive\_val$;
                    $graph\_changed = true$;
                if *(negative_val > max_negative)* **then**
                    $c.setNegativeVal(r.attribute, negative\_val)$;
                    $max\_negative = negative\_val$;
                    $graph\_changed = true$;
    until *(graph_changed == false)*;

---

updated. When a complete iteration over the graph nodes is completed, without having done any propagation, the algorithm terminates. Because of the monotonicity property, the algorithm always terminates.

5   Application

We validated our approach by taking advantage from the experience of the industrial partners of the RISCOSS project (www.riscoss.eu), in which the present work is performed.

Scenario. A typical software company addressed in our project (referred to as "the adopter", from now on) produces software ("the final product") for end users, by using third party OSS components. While choosing a component to adopt, it seeks to fulfil requirements, which may come from both itself and its clients, and concern the business as well as the technical needs. For example, an adopter produces an end-user accounting software, which allows accountants and other employees together to edit online reports and publish them to the public audience. Once deployed, it is planned to run for a long time without being replaced. Thus, it needs to be possible to maintain it and to let it continuously evolve without having to replace it. Moreover, the effort of integration with the adopter's accounting software should be minimised. So the adopter is searching for a Wiki OSS component with the required characteristics. In such a setting, technical qualities of available OSS components are easily evaluable by using existing tools. Having done this for our validation scenario, three candidate Wikis have been identified as having the desired technical properties, namely: (i) Mediawiki; (ii) Dokuwiki; and (iii) XWiki. To choose the right one, we need to analyse their risks.

Risk Model. Figure 4 depicts an excerpt of a RiskML model for the Wiki case. The model represents the structural knowledge available to the adopter about possible events,

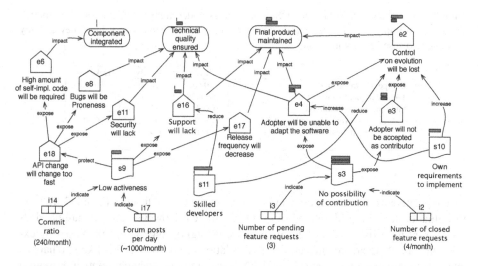

Fig. 4. A graphical representation of a RiskML model for the XWiki component, annotated with the analysis results

the conditions of their occurrence, and their possible impact on the business goals. It is worth noticing that the topology of the model is not fixed. Part of the ongoing project consists in gathering the information to build the most correct model, but in any case the model or some of its parts can be customised but the adopter. The depicted **goals** have been identified by means of an overview on large corporates and small enterprises. The model depicts in particular the goals that have been selected for the described scenario: [Component integrated], [Technical quality ensured], and [Final product maintained]. To goals are associated the risk **events** that impact on them. Events have been selected after a systematic literature review and an analysis of several industrial case studies; e.g. for the goal [Final product maintained] the risk events [Release frequency will decrease], [Adopter will be unable to adapt the software], and [Control on evolution will be lost] and [Support will lack] are modelled. The defined **situations** influence event likelihood ([Low activeness]) or significance ([Skilled developers]). Identified **indicators** mainly refer to code metrics and mailing lists statistics; e.g. the two indicators [Commit ratio] and [Forum posts per day] give evidence to the situation [Low activeness]. The measures defined by the indicators can be fed manually by the user or automatically from existing repositories. The indicator numbers are translated into evidence degrees by means of a normalising function. It is worth noticing that the topology of the model is not fixed. Part of the ongoing project consists in gathering the information to build the most correct model, but in any case the model or some of its parts can be customised but the adopter.

Results. On the models we applied the described label propagation algorithm, which has been implemented in a reasoning tool developed in Java. The tool takes as input a risk model, the functions and weights, and the input evidences, and produces as output the risk evidences. The results of the analysis on a single component, XWiki, are illustrated in Fig. 4. In the model, we see for example that the situation s3 receives

Table 3. Risk evidence for the three OSS components under analysis; notice that the reported values do not imply probabilities and do not have a meaning as standalone values: they are only intended to be used for comparison.

	Xwiki	MediaWiki	DokuWiki
Component integrated	0 / 0	0 / 0	0 / 0.2
Technical quality ensured	0 / 0.28	0 / 0.4	0 / 0.2
Final product maintained	0.38 / 0.5	0.3 / 0.4	0.1 / 0.6
Control on evolution will be lost	0.5 / 0.38	0.4 / 0.25	0.6 / 0.2
Adopter will be unable to adapt the software	0.5 / 0.38	0.4 / 0.3	0.6 / 0.1
...			

strong positive as well as negative evidence from the two indicators i2 and i3. In turn, the situation raises the likelihood of events e3 and e4. However, e3 for example does not present high risk exposure levels because its significance is not increased by explicit factors (there are no entering *increase* relations). Viceversa, e2 is likely to happen and, due to the need represented by s10, [Own requirements to implement], it presents a rather high risk exposure level. Finally, this exposure level impact on the [Final product maintained] goal, which is at danger of not being satisfied (red bar).

Table 3 shows how to use analysis results, by reporting a comparison among the results of the three components. On the first column are reported the goals and the impacting events. On the right part of the table, the impact values on goals are reported for the three candidate OSS components. Worth noticing that the values are intended to be used only for comparing the components with each other, so they can not be interpreted, for example, as probabilities. For each component, and for each element (goal/event), both the positive and negative values for satisfaction (or exposure) are reported. This allows us to make finer-grained comparisons among the components, in both their strength and weakness points. For example, we see that, with respect to the [Final product maintained] goal, MediaWiki seems to have less evidence of satisfaction than XWiki (0.3 vs. 0.38) but at the same time less evidence of not satisfaction (0.4 vs 0.5). Going in the details of each associated event allows to have an idea of *why* these numbers are produced, and consequently to make a better decision.

6   Related Work

The Goal-Risk framework [1] is a goal-oriented method based on *i** [16] that aims at capturing, analysing and assessing risk at an early stage of the requirements engineering process. A Goal-Risk model consists of nodes, relations and a set of impact relations. The nodes can be characterised by two properties: *Sat* and *Den*, indicating the evidence that the node is satisfied/fulfilled/present or denied/failed/absent, respectively. The model is comprised by an *asset layer*, modelling anything that has value to an organization (such as goals); an *event layer*, used to model phenomena likelihood through satisfiability/deniability evidences and severity, which indicates their capability to prevent goal achievement; a *treatment layer*, containing the countermeasures set up to mitigate the risks. KAOS [15] goal-oriented analysis methodology deals with risk management by complementing goal modelling and analysis with obstacle analysis that consists in identifying and modelling the adverse conditions that may prevent a goal to be achieved [3]. KAOS has a formal representation of the goal model, relies on strictly measurable variables and takes into account partial or probabilistic values for goal satisfaction, but does not integrate concrete measures and indicators. Adverse conditions are identified and modelled; then risk assessment is performed to reduce the likelihood or the severity of each obstacle, and mitigation is performed by applying countermeasure patterns in the goal model. EKD [13] is a methodology for mapping organizational processes that can serve as a basis for identification risk management tasks. It provides a controlled way of analysing and documenting an enterprise, its objectives and support systems and allow for the specification of enterprise knowledge models. During the model developing, the participant parties engage in tasks that involve deliberation and reasoning. The objective is to provide a clear, unambiguous picture of how enterprise processes function currently in an "as is" model or in a modified "should be" model. EKD proposes to exploit the concept of patterns in order to recognise risks and revise the practices in order to mitigate them. Finally, CORAS [8] is a model-based approach based on UML for performing security risk analysis and assessment based on security analysis techniques, CORAS is comprised by three different components: a risk modelling language; a method, for the security analysis process; and a tool for documenting, maintaining and reporting risk analysis results. It limits to a defensive risk analysis to protect company assets. The method does not rely on a particular reasoning technique but is flexible to be supported by several techniques such as graph label propagation and logic based techniques. The problem of evaluating the qualities and characteristics of OSS software components and development processes via metrics and statistical analysis for decision-making purposes has been considered in several projects. For example, the QualOSS project[1] had the purpose of defining a method to assess the quality of OSS projects, via a quality model composed of three types of interrelated elements: *quality characteristics* of a product or community, *metrics*, concrete aspects that can be measured, and *indicators* that define how to aggregate and evaluate the measurement values to obtain consolidated information. The recently started OSSMETER[2] project aims to develop a platform that will support decision makers in the process of discovering, assessing and monitoring the health, quality and activity of OSS.

7 Conclusion

In this paper we presented a modelling framework for assessing risk in open source software (OSS) components adoption. The framework relies on a language, tailored to describe available risk indicators, risk events, and their impact on business goals. A label propagation algorithm has been used to infer risk exposure values, starting form available indicators. Also, working risk models have been produced to asses risk in a controlled scenario. We acknowledge that the reliability of the framework in a production environment ultimately depends on the quality of the risk models. Currently, the model is instantiated with risks and indicators retrieved from a systematic literature

---

[1] http://www.qualoss.eu/
[2] http://www.ossmeter.eu

review and an analysis of several industrial case studies [10]. More work is ongoing in this direction.

Acknowledgement. This work is a result of the RISCOSS project, funded by the EC 7th Framework Programme FP7/2007-2013, agreement number 318249.

References

1. Asnar, Y., Giorgini, P., Mylopoulos, J.: Goal-driven risk assessment in requirements engineering. Requir. Eng. 16(2), 101–116 (2011)
2. Barone, D., Jiang, L., Amyot, D., Mylopoulos, J.: Reasoning with key performance indicators. In: Johannesson, P., Krogstie, J., Opdahl, A.L. (eds.) A Calculus of Communication Systems. LNBIP, vol. 92, pp. 82–96. Springer, Heidelberg (1980)
3. Cailliau, A., van Lamsweerde, A.: Assessing requirements-related risks through probabilistic goals and obstacles. Requir. Eng. 18(2), 129–146 (2013)
4. Gangemi, A., Guarino, N., Masolo, C., Oltramari, A.: Sweetening wordnet with dolce. AI Magazine 24(3), 13–24 (2003)
5. Giorgini, P., Mylopoulos, J., Nicchiarelli, E., Sebastiani, R.: Reasoning with goal models. In: Spaccapietra, S., March, S.T., Kambayashi, Y. (eds.) ER 2002. LNCS, vol. 2503, pp. 167–181. Springer, Heidelberg (2002)
6. Giorgini, P., Mylopoulos, J., Nicchiarelli, E., Sebastiani, R.: Formal reasoning techniques for goal models. J. Data Semantics 1, 1–20 (2003)
7. Kenett, R.S., Zacks, S.: Modern Industrial Statistics: with applications in R, MINITAB and JMP, 2nd edn. John Wiley and Sons (2014) With contributions by D. Amberti
8. Lund, M.S., Solhaug, B., Stølen, K.: Model-Driven Risk Analysis - The CORAS Approach. Springer (2011)
9. Messerschmitt, D.G., Szyperski, C.: Software Ecosystem: Understanding an Indispensable Technology and Industry. The MIT Press (2003)
10. Morandini, M., Siena, A., Susi, A.: Systematic literature review: Risks in oss adoption. Technical report, FBK, Trento (2013),
    http://selab.fbk.eu/riscoss_ontology/riskSLR.html
11. Morandini, M., Siena, A., Susi, A.: A context-specific definition of risk for enterprise-level decision making. In: The 8th International Workshop on Value Modeling and Business Ontology (2014)
12. Nilsson, N.J.: Problem-solving Methods in Artificial Intelligence. McGraw-Hill, New York (1971)
13. Rolland, C., Nurcan, S., Grosz, G.: Enterprise knowledge development: the process view. Information & Management 36(3), 165–184 (1999)
14. Siena, A., Jureta, I., Ingolfo, S., Susi, A., Perini, A., Mylopoulos, J.: Capturing Variability of Law with Nómos 2. In: Atzeni, P., Cheung, D., Ram, S. (eds.) ER 2012 Main Conference 2012. LNCS, vol. 7532, pp. 383–396. Springer, Heidelberg (2012)
15. van Lamsweerde, A., Letier, E.: Handling obstacles in goal-oriented requirements engineering. IEEE Trans. Software Eng. 26(10), 978–1005 (2000)
16. Yu, E.S.-K.: Modelling strategic relationships for process reengineering. PhD thesis, University of Toronto, Toronto, Ont., Canada, Canada (1996)

Modelling and Applying OSS Adoption Strategies

Lidia López[1], Dolors Costal[1], Claudia P. Ayala[1], Xavier Franch[1],
Ruediger Glott[2], and Kirsten Haaland[2]

[1] Universitat Politècnica de Catalunya, Barcelona, Spain
[2] UNU-MERIT, Maastricht, The Netherlands

Abstract. Increasing adoption of Open Source Software (OSS) in information system engineering has led to the emergence of different OSS business strategies that affect and shape organizations' business models. In this context, organizational modeling needs to reconcile efficiently OSS adoption strategies with business strategies and models. In this paper, we propose to embed all the knowledge about each OSS adoption strategy into an *i** model that can be used in the intentional modeling of the organization. These models describe the consequences of adopting one such strategy or another: which are the business goals that are supported, which are the resources that emerge, etc. To this aim, we first enumerate the main existing OSS adoption strategies, next we formulate an ontology that comprises the activities and resources that characterise these strategies, then based on the experience of 5 industrial partners of the RISCOSS EU-funded project, we explore how these elements are managed in each strategy and formulate the corresponding model using the *i** framework.

Keywords: OSS; Open Source Software; OSS adoption strategy; OSS ontology; *i** framework; i-star.

1   Introduction

The key purpose of any business is to create value and to achieve revenues. The business model of an organization holistically captures the ways and means how these goals can be achieved. Therefore, there is no organization without a business model, regardless of whether or not a company explicitly describes it [1][2].

A business strategy describes the approach of a business to successfully compete with other businesses in a given market. A business model can be seen as the translation of a company's business strategy into a blueprint of the company's logic of earning money [3]. Business strategies are dependent on many factors, and information technology (IT) approaches are one of them. At this respect, Open Source Software (OSS) has become a driver for business in various sectors, namely the primary and secondary IT sector. Estimates exist that in 2016, a 95% of all commercial software packages will include OSS components [4]. OSS adoption impacts in fact far beyond technology, because it requires a change in the organizational culture and reshaping IT decision-makers mindset. The way in which OSS affects and shapes business models is becoming object of increasing attention, and as a result, several OSS business strategies have been identified so far [5][6][7].

E. Yu et al. (Eds.): ER 2014, LNCS 8824, pp. 349–362, 2014.

Leveraging business strategies with the organization business model is a challenging task per se, and it implies reconciling them from very different perspectives [3]. Organizational modelling can provide a way to define the organization's goals and to serve as the context in which processes operate and business is done. In this context, in order to support organizations that would like to adopt OSS (hereafter OSS adopter) and analyze the implications of such adoption; we describe seven different OSS adoption strategies in terms of models that relate business goals and resources. These models can be used as a reference for understanding and assessing the impact of the OSS adoption strategies on the OSS adopter organization; as well as complementing the OSS adopter organizational model.

The remainder of the paper is organized as follows. Section 2 introduces the basic concepts needed in the paper. Section 3 presents the research method followed. Sections 4 to 6 develop the main contributions of the paper: the OSS ontology used, the arrangement of its elements into models for the OSS adoption strategies and the application of such models. Last, Section 7 provides conclusions and future work.

2   Background: OSS Adoption Strategies

OSS can play a role at any place of the business model of an organization. The most usual roles are: it can be received as a supply from an OSS community or another organization; it can be produced in-house; it can be part of the organization's value proposition (e.g. by lowering costs or by improving compatibility); it can be used as infrastructure for the development of software or for the execution of business processes; it can be sold in order to allow for revenues (e.g. based on a dual license); it can determine customer segments (e.g. other organizations that produce OSS); or it can be used in order to lower costs (e.g. by using a license free operating system for IT systems that are sold to customers).

Depending on from where OSS is received or how it is produced, and where in the business model and for which purposes OSS is used we may distinguish several types of OSS adoption strategies, which are not necessarily mutually exclusive. In the context of the FP7 RISCOSS project (www.riscoss.eu), we have identified the strategies below, and are the ones considered in the rest of the paper:

- *OSS Integration* means the integration of an organization in an OSS community with the purpose to share and co-create OSS. In this case, being part of the community in order to benefit from the commonly created OSS components is the key goal of the OSS strategy; it is not necessary for the adopter organization to play a leading role within the community.
- *OSS Initiative* means to initiate an OSS project and to establish a community around it. Usually, the key goal of this strategy is to create community support, but in contrast to the OSS Integration strategy, the adopter establishes the community as a resource that directly serves the company's business strategy and model. As a consequence, exercising control over the OSS community is typical for this strategy.
- *OSS Takeover* means to take over an existing OSS project/community and to control it. The main difference from the OSS Initiative strategy is that the OSS community already exists.

- *OSS Fork* means to create an own independent version of the software that is available from an existing OSS project or community. This strategy is usually followed when an OSS community on which the adopter organization depends develops in directions that contradict or hamper the organization's business goals. Exercising control over the forked community is typical but not necessary, as the fork community should consist of developers that share the adopter organization's view on how the community and the software should evolve.
- *OSS Acquisition* means to use existing OSS code without contributing to the underlying OSS project/community.
- *OSS Release* implies that the organization releases own software as OSS but does not care whether an OSS community takes it up or forms around it. This strategy can, for instance, be observed in the public sector, when software owned by public bodies is released under an OSS license and made available to other public bodies via a repository.

3   Research Approach

This research is performed in the context of the European FP7 RISCOSS project, which aims to support the OSS adopter organizations to understand, manage and mitigate the risks associated to OSS adoption. The consortium includes 5 industrial partners from public and private sectors, with diverse OSS adoption contexts, which have served to formulate the results presented here (as described below). In line with this objective, this paper focuses on supporting organizations in analyzing the implications of adopting a particular OSS business strategy. With this aim, our research approach was based on 3 complementary stages corresponding to 3 research questions:

RQ1: Which activities and resources characterize OSS projects?
This is aimed to understand the relevant activities and resources taking place in the context of OSS projects, especially related to software development and community management. To do so, we conducted a Systematic Literature Review (SLR) using the well-known guidelines defined in [8] in order to identify existing ontologies on the field. We analysed them with respect to our objectives and complemented the results with knowledge coming from RISCOSS industrial partners. The ontology is described in Section 4.

RQ2: How do OSS activities and resources map to OSS business strategies?
In this question, we wanted to inquiry about how the activities and resources emerging from RQ1 map into the different OSS business strategies enumerated in Section 2.1. Our aim was mainly to emphasize and represent the different effects that each OSS business strategy has over the OSS adopter organization. As a result, the detailed definition of the different models, one for strategy, was obtained. See Section 5 for details.

RQ3: How OSS strategies relate to organizational goals?
OSS business strategies' models resulting from RQ2 were mostly focused, as mentioned in the context of RQ1, on software development and community management activities and resources. However, in order to understand the impact of the activities

and resources enclosed in each strategy model, we needed to understand their relationship to the OSS adopter's organizational goals. Therefore, we held some off-line workshops with the five RISCOSS industrial partners, and ended up with a set of related goals that were integrated into the models. Furthermore, we devised a matching process to integrate the strategies' models with the OSS adopter organization. Thus, the use of the OSS business strategies models provides an efficient way to complete the OSS adopter organizational model.

It is important to highlight that these three RQs and their corresponding stages have a formative character as they are aimed to conceive the OSS business strategies models. In all the stages, the industrial partners of the RISCOSS project have been involved to shape and endorse our approach in their respective contexts. In addition, a proof of concept software prototype has been built in order to operationalize the resulting approach and help as a tool for the summative evaluation of the approach in the context of other industrial organizations besides the RISCOSS partners, which would become the last stage of our method (see Figure 1).

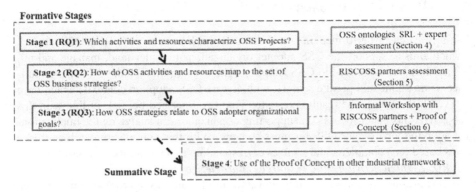

Fig. 1. Research method followed in the paper

4   An Ontology for OSS Adoption Strategies

In order to state the basis for defining OSS adoption strategies models, we have developed an ontology that embraces terms related to OSS projects and the business strategies involved in them. To do so, as a first step, we conducted a Systematic Literature Review (SLR) using the guidelines defined in [8] with the purpose of identifying existing OSS ontologies. The details of the SLR and the subsequent analysis can be found in [9].

Although the SLR was conducted in order to find ontologies related to OSS field, the search string included some terms besides the term ontology (metamodel, glossary, taxonomy and reference model) in order to avoid missing papers with a kind of implicit ontology. This also resulted in a large set of initial papers that was considerably pruned: from an initial set of 1214 primary studies, we selected 9 papers to be analysed as papers that contain an ontology (explicit or not), as a result of this analysis, we ended up with 4 of them that stated 3 relevant ontologies: Dhruv's ontology [10], OSDO [11][12], and OFLOSSC [13].

We finally chose OFLOSSC as departing point because: (1) it was the most complete amongst the ontologies reviewed (it actually includes parts of the other 2 OSS ontologies also covered in the SLR), and (2) it is an ontology for supporting OSS development communities and covers concepts related to community interactions for developing software. However, it lacks of adoption concepts related to OSS adopter organizations, therefore, we have extended the ontology with these missing (with respect to our purposes) concepts. To do so, we performed a thorough analysis of the activities and resources that an adopter organization should consider when participating in an OSS project by running off-line workshops (i.e., discussion that were centralized in a wiki tool) with partners of the RISCOSS project.

The results from such analysis in terms of the identified activities and resources are listed in Table 1. For each element, the table includes its identifier and a brief description. The elements identified have been classified into five groups: software development activities, community-oriented activities, communication activities, personnel activities and resources, as can be seen in Table 1.

The ontology concepts exhibit some relationships that are themselves part of the ontology. Some of these relationships can be expressed with plain logic, e.g. the responsible of developing an OSS component (Act-DEP) is also responsible of testing it (Act-TEST-Comp). Others may require introducing additional concepts, for instance the activity of reporting a bug (Act-RepBUG) *produces* a bug report resource (Res-BUG) and not other types of resources (such as patch, roadmap, etc.).

Table 1. Activities and resources for OSS business strategies

Identifier	Description
Software Development Activities	
Act-SEL	Selection of an OSS component for its deployment or integration in an organization
Act-DEP	Deployment of an OSS component for its actual use in the organization
Act-DEV	Development of an OSS component (specification, design, code)
Act-INT	Integration of an OSS component into another software artifact
Act-TEST-Comp	Testing of an OSS component
Act-TEST-Prod	Testing of a software artifact that integrates an OSS component
Act-MAINT-Comp	Maintenance of an OSS component
Act-MAINT-Prod	Maintenance of a software artifact that integrates an OSS component
Act-PATCH	Development of a patch to correct some bug or add some new feature for an OSS component
Community-Oriented Activities	
Act-NewCOMM	Creation of an OSS community
Act-DECIDE-Roadmap	Decision of the roadmap of an OSS component. It includes planning of releases and which features are included
Act-DECIDE-Acc	Acceptance of a contributor in an OSS community
Act-DECIDE-Wishlist	Decision of the desired features for the next releases of an OSS component (but without a concrete planning)
Act-RELEASE	Making available a software component under OSS license (either first time or an evolution)

Table 1. (*Continued*)

Communication Activities	
Act-RepPATCH	Communication of a patch for an OSS component
Act-RepBUG	Report of a bug
Act-SUPP	Any kind of support given to the OSS community (except bug reports and patches; e.g. organising or endorsing sponsoring events)
Personnel Activities	
Act-ACQ-Tech	Acquisition of the necessary knowledge about an OSS component to be able to master its technology
Act-ACQ-Man	Acquisition of the necessary knowledge about managing an OSS community
Act-LEARN	Acquisition of the necessary knowledge about an OSS component to be able to operate it (as end user)
Resources	
Res-OSS-Comp	An OSS component as a software artifact
Res-Tech-DOCUM	Technical documentation of an OSS component
Res-User-DOCUM	User documentation (e.g., tutorials) of an OSS component
Res-PATCH	Patch provided for an OSS component
Res-BUG	Report of a bug or post, etc., referred to an OSS component
Res-NEWFEATURE	Report of desired feature(s) for an OSS component
Res-ROADMAP	Strategy for new features and releases of an OSS component

5   Building OSS Adoption Strategy Models

We present next a catalogue of OSS adoption strategy models for each of the strategies described in Section 2. These models are built on top of the ontology presented in Section 4 and each of them combines the ontology elements as required by its corresponding strategy. Models focus on the adopter organization and refer to the particular OSS component under adoption. We have used the *i** framework [14] as modeling approach. *i** is an intentional actor-oriented modelling and analysis framework, which supports representing and analyzing synergistic and conflicting stakeholder interests and decision-making within and across organizational settings. In *i**, we find: the Strategic Dependency (SD) model, declaring the actors and their dependencies; and the Strategic Rationale (SR) model, declaring the goals and intentions of the actors.

The main actors involved in the OSS adoption strategies are: (1) the organization that adopts the OSS component and (2) the OSS community that produces it. The activities performed and the resources produced by each of these actors vary significantly depending on the business strategy, and this is the basis of the model construction: first, for each adoption strategy, we have allocated the activities and resources, presented in Section 4, to the two actors, depending on which one is responsible. Table 2 provides the allocation of activities and resources to the adopter organization actor depending on the adoption strategy followed. The expertise obtained from the RISCOSS partners has provided us the rationale to choose the most adequate allocation according to the main features of each identified OSS business strategy.

Table 2. Adopter Activities and resources (rows) per OSS strategies (columns)

	Integration	Initiative	Takeover	Fork	Acquisition	Release
Software Development Activities						
Act-SEL	X		X	X	X	
Act-DEP	X	X	X	X	X	X
Act-DEV		X				X
Act-INT	X	X	X	X	X	X
Act-TEST-Comp						
Act-TEST-Prod	X	X	X	X	X	
Act-MAINT-Comp						
Act-MAINT-Prod	X	X	X	X	X	X
Act-PATCH	X	X	X	X		
Community-oriented Activities						
Act-NewCOMM		X		X		
Act-DECIDE-Roadmap		X	X			
Act-DECIDE-Acc		X	X			
Act-DECIDE-Wishlist	X			X		
Act-RELEASE		X				X
Communication Activities						
Act-RepPATCH	X	X	X	X		
Act-RepBUG	X	X	X	X		
Act-SUPP	X	X	X	X		
Personnel Activities						
Act-ACQ-Tech	X	X	X	X	X	X
Act-ACQ-Man	X	X	X	X		
Act-LEARN	X		X	X	X	
Resources						
Res-OSS-Comp		X				X
Res-Tech-DOCUM		X				X
Res-User-DOCUM		X				X
Res-PATCH	X	X	X	X		
Res-BUG	X	X	X	X		
Res-NEWFEATURE	X			X		
Res-ROADMAP		X	X			

Some general observations on Table 2 are the following:

1. There are two strategies that do not require community involvement or contribution of the organization: acquisition and release. Therefore, the activities allocated to these strategies are mainly internal-oriented software development activities and not community-oriented or communication activities (except for *Act-RELEASE* in the release strategy case).

2. For the rest of strategies: the organization participates in communication activities (e.g. *Act-RepBUG*) and contributes with their corresponding resources (e.g. *Res-BUG*). Additionally, the organization develops different community-oriented activities depending, mainly, on whether it is exercising control over the community or not. Remarkably, in the initiative and takeo-

ver case, the organization decides the community roadmap (*Act-DECIDE-Roadmap, Res-ROADMAP*).

3.   Two of the strategies, namely, initiative and fork, require that the organization sets up an OSS community (*Act-NewCOMM*).

The activities of maintaining and testing the OSS component (*Act-MAINT-Comp* and *Act-TEST-Comp*) are not allocated to the organization in any strategy meaning that they are basically developed by the OSS community. Taking as a basis the allocation described in Table 2, we have built an *i** model for each strategy. These models have been complemented with two kind of goals: some goals used to structure the model (e.g. *Technical Quality* to embrace the tasks related to acquire skills for using the component Act-ACQ-Tech and Act-Learn) and some high-level goals and softgoals more related to the business strategy goals (e.g. *Take benefit from OSS community*) .

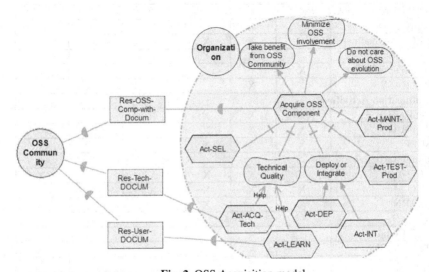

Fig. 2. OSS Acquisition model

Figure 2 and Figure 3 show the models corresponding to the Acquisition and Takeover strategies, respectively. They represent in detail the adoption strategy SR model that will be incorporated into the model of the adopter organization, and the dependencies that exist between the organization and the OSS community. The organization SR model permits to understand the relation of the allocated activities with the goals and softgoals they attain or they require. The dependencies permit to understand the vulnerabilities that the organization has with respect to the OSS community when adopting the strategy.

The model for the OSS acquisition strategy (see Figure 2) shows how the adopting organization only needs the component from the OSS community and does not give any return to it, therefore only outgoing dependencies stem from the organization actor. Meanwhile the OSS takeover model (see Figure 3) shows dependencies in both directions, because the OSS community receives some payback from the adopter (bug reports, patches…). Goals and activities such as *Community Managed*, *Act-DECIDE-Roadmap* and *Act-DECIDE-Acc* appear inside the organization actor in the takeover model because the organization controls the OSS community in this case. Also, some goals and tasks appear in order to contribute the OSS community (*OSS Community Contributed* and the tasks and softgoals that decompose it).

Taking as a central element the task representing the type of OSS strategy (*Acquire OSS Component* and *Takeover OSS Component*), the models include a set of high-level *business-related goals* directly attained by the strategy (goals above the task, e.g *Minimize OSS involvement* in Figure 2) and the low-level goals or tasks which are *requirements* for an adequate application of the OSS business strategy (below the task, e.g. *Act-SEL* and *Manage OSS Community* in Figure 3).

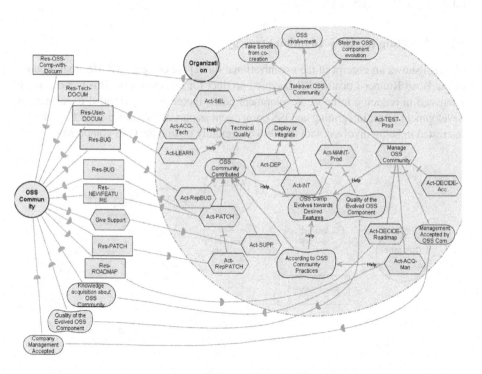

Fig. 3. OSS Takeover model

Models focus on the portion of the organization SR model that is influenced by its corresponding OSS adoption strategy and does not include the general set of (higher-level) business goals pursued by the organization. Nevertheless, the intentional elements shown in the models are certainly related to the more general business goals of the organization since they may contribute to their attainment. Section 6 provides the details about this issue.

6   Applying OSS Adoption Strategy Models in an Organization

OSS adoption strategy models have been developed as general models; therefore, a question to be answered is how to apply them in a specific situation (in our case, an OSS adopter organization). The question is twofold: first, when to apply an OSS adoption strategy model; and second, how to couple the organizational model with the strategy model. To answer the first question, we start by assuming the existence of an organizational model that declares the higher-level goals pursued by the organization and using this existing organizational model we select the most suitable OSS adoption strategy to the organization needs. To answer the second question, we describe the process of instantiation of the organizational model, i.e. extending the model with the elements from the selected OSS adoption strategy model and making the necessary retouches to these new elements.

6.1   Selecting the OSS Adoption Strategy

Figure 4 shows an excerpt of the organizational model for company *ACME*, that produces the Road Runner Locator (*RR Locator*) product for its customers. This is a company interested in reducing in-house development costs, therefore they decided to reduce the development effort integrating an OSS component as part of its software, but they are not interested in being involved with the OSS community behind the OSS component.

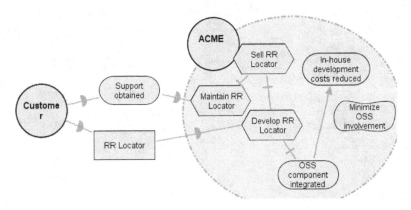

Fig. 4. Organizational model

In order to facilitate the process to find the more suitable OSS adoption strategy, we adopt the model matching approach presented in [15]. In this paper, *i** models are used to describe market segments and software packages in order to evaluate the matching between both models with an *i** organizational model, in order to select the best software package for the organization needs. In this paper, we may use the same idea and then evaluate the matching between an organizational model and the set of OSS business strategies models in order to identify the strategies that better match the organizational goals and eliminate those that clearly do not apply to the specific organization. [15] uses a concept called coverage for classifying the matching results, that is adapted in this paper as follows:

- Coverage of the Organizational model: a matching is org-complete if every intentional element from the Organization actor in the organizational SR model is matched at least with one intentional element in the OSS business strategy SR model, otherwise it is org-incomplete. In other words, in an org-complete matching, an adoption strategy supports all the business goals of the organization.

- Coverage of the OSS adoption strategy model requirements: a matching is str-complete if every intentional element, representing *requirements*, from the Organization actor in the OSS adoption strategy SR model is matched at least with one intentional element in the Organization actor in the organizational SR model, otherwise it is str-incomplete. In other words, in a str-complete matching, an adoption strategy can effectively be adopted by an organization since this organization fulfills all the needs of the strategy.

The aim of the matching is finding the OSS adoption strategies that cover as much as possible the organization business goals, taking into account that the company has or is willing to have the resources required by the strategy. Therefore, any combination where the coverage of the OSS adoption strategy model is incomplete due to some OSS adoption strategy requirements are missing, excludes the strategy from being used by the organization. Before discarding the strategy, the organizational model can be extended in order to have a str-complete requirements coverage.

As an example, Table 3 shows the matching between the ACME organizational model (Figure 4) and the OSS Acquisition strategy model (Figure 2) for the organizational model coverage. The coverage of the ACME organizational model by the strategy is almost complete, since the only element not covered is the task *Sell RR locator* which, nevertheless, represents a kind of activity not addressed by the OSS adoption strategies. Therefore, the Acquisition OSS adoption strategy is a good choice to be applied to the organization.

Table 3. Matching for organizational model coverage

OSS Organizational model	Matching with OSS business strategy model
Sell RR Locator	Missing
Maintain RR Locator	*Act-Maintain-Prod*
Develop RR Locator	*Act-INT* and *Act-TEST-Prod* are subtasks of task *Develop RR Locator*
OSS component integrated	*Acquire OSS component* is the means to achieve this goal
In-house development cost reduced	*Take benefit from OSS Community* is the means to achieve this goal
Minimize OSS involvement	The same as *Minimize OSS involvement*

Table 4 shows the matching for the OSS adoption strategy coverage. In this case, the coverage is incomplete. The requirements related to achieve the technical skills in order to use the component (*Technical Quality*, *Act-ACQ-Tech* and *Act-LEARN*) are missing, but in this case if an organization wants to use an external component

(OSS or not) has to be willing to acquire the necessary knowledge to use it. Therefore, the organizational model should be extended including them in order to have a complete OSS strategy requirements coverage.

Table 4. Matching for OSS acquisition strategy model coverage

OSS Acquisition strategy Requirements	Matching with Organizational Model
Acquire OSS Component	Means to achieve the goal *OSS component integrated*
Act-SEL	Considered part of the tasks defining the process related to the goal *OSS component integrated*
Technical Quality	Missing
Act-ACQ-Tech	Missing
Act-LEARN	Missing
Use or Deploy	This is an intermediate node, it does not need matching
Act-DEP	The component has to be "integrated", so this element has to deleted from the OSS business strategy model
Act-INT	This is the element kept in the OSS business model as a means to achieve the goal *OSS component integrated*
Act-TEST-Prod	Considered a subtask of *Develop RR Locator*
Act-MAINT-Prod	The same task as *Maintain RR Locator*

6.2   Instantiating the Organizational Model

Once the organization has decided the OSS adoption strategy is going to adopt, the instantiation process consists on the following steps:

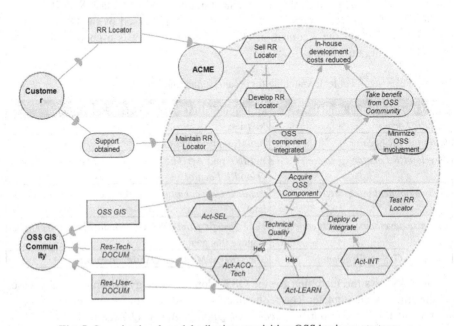

Fig. 5. Organizational model adhering acquisition OSS business strategy

1. Applying the matching, including the intentional elements from the selected OSS adoption strategy model into the organizational model. Only the matched elements are included (Table 3 and Table 4).

2. Making the needed retouches to the resulting model in order to adapt the general OSS adoption strategy model to the specific case.

In the case that we are using as example in this paper, the organization *ACME* is acquiring the component *OSS GIS* to be integrated in its product *RR Locator*, in order to know where the RR is as shown in Figure 5. The new elements that come from the OSS acquisition strategy model (Figure 2) are shown in italics. Task *Acquire OSS Component* and its decomposition is included as the means to achieve the goal *OSS component integrated*, except for the task *Act-DEP*, it does not appear in the model because the organization uses the OSS component integrating (*Act-INT*) it in its own software (*RR Locator*). The task *Maintain RR Locator* replaces the *Act-MAINT-Prod* and the task *Act-TEST-Prod* is renamed as *Test RR Locator*. *ACME* organization adheres to the business-related goal *Minimize the OSS involvement*, but does not agree with *Do not care about OSS component evolution*.

7   Conclusions and Future Work

In this paper, we have proposed the use of generic models as a way to model OSS adoption strategies. The main contributions of our work are:

- *An ontology for OSS adoption*. We have defined an ontology for activities and resources implied in OSS adoption strategies. As result of the SLR we undertook, we observed that there are several ontologies for OSS but they focus on the perspective of the community, with special attention to: roles of developers (committers, contributors, …), licenses, etc. In the context of business strategies for organizations, this perspective is not the right one, since the needs are different. Therefore, our ontology goes beyond the state of the art and possibilitates its use in other works that may be interested in the adopting organization perspective.

- *Characterisation of OSS adoption strategies*. For each identified OSS adoption strategy, we have assigned these activities and resources to the actor that is in charge: the adopting organization or the OSS community. As a result, we have provided a characterisation of each strategy in terms of activities undertaken, resources provided, and dependencies of these two actors on each other. Again this is a result that goes beyond the goal of our paper and maybe of interest for researchers that want an overall comparison of OSS adoption strategies.

- *Set of OSS adoption strategy models*. As ultimate result of the paper, we have designed a set of models for the different strategies expressed in the *i** language. The proposal relies upon expert assessment, is operational (has tool support, not presented here) and from a methodological point of view, it is integrated with the organizational model that can be expressed also in *i**. The use of these models provides an efficient way to build organizational models in those organizations that adopt OSS solutions.

Future work goes along several directions. First, we need to work further in the link among business models and OSS adoption strategies, so that the process that has been depicted in Section 6 becomes more prescriptive. Second, concerning the models for the patterns, we want to use i^* roles as a way to organize the ontology elements: roles like Contributor, Governance Body, OSS User, etc., may arrange the different activities and resources, and then the adoption strategies will simply put together the indicated roles in each case. Third, we need to be able to combine OSS adoption strategy models, either because more than one strategy applies at the same time for the same OSS component, or because more than one OSS component is being integrated in a project. Last, a validation plan based in case studies in the context of our RISCOSS project needs to be executed.

Acknowledgements. This work is a result of the RISCOSS project, funded by the EC 7th Framework Programme FP7/2007-2013, agreement number 318249.

References

[1] Chesbrough, H.: Open Business Models: How to thrive in the new Innovation Landscape. Harvard Business School Press (2006)

[2] Teece, D.J.: Business Models, Business Strategy and Innovation. Long Range Planning Journal 43(2-3) (2010)

[3] Osterwalder, A.: The business model ontology- a proposition in a design science approach. Lausanne, Switzerland: University of Lausanne. PhD Dissertation (2004)

[4] Driver, M.: Hype Cycle for Open-Source Software. Technical Report, Gartner (2013)

[5] Kudorfer, F., Laisne, J.P., Lauriere, S., Lichtenthaler, J., Lopez, G., Pezuela, C.: State of the art concerning business models for systems comprising open source software (2007)

[6] Daffara, C.: Business models in FLOSS-based companies (2008)

[7] Lakka, S., Stamati, T., Michalakelis, C., Martakos, D.: The Ontology of the OSS Business Model: An Exploratory Study. Open Source Software and Processes J. 3(1) (2011)

[8] Kitchenham, B.: Guidelines for performing Systematic Literature Reviews in Software Engineering v2.3. EBSE Technical Report EBSE-2007-01

[9] Ayala, C., López, L.: D1.1 Modeling Support (initial version). Technical Report, RISCOSS FP7 project

[10] Ankolekar, A., Sycara, K., Herbsleb, J., Kraut, R., Welty, C.: Supporting online problem-solving communities with the semantic web. In: Proceedings of WWW 2006, pp. 575–584 (2006)

[11] Simmons, G., Dillon, T.: Towards an Ontology for Open Source Software Development. In: Damiani, E., Fitzgerald, B., Scacchi, W., Scotto, M., Succi, G. (eds.) Open Source Systems. IFIP, vol. 203, pp. 65–75. Springer, Heidelberg (2006)

[12] Dillon, T.S., Simmonsg, G.: Semantic web support for open-source software development. In: Proceeding of SITIS 2008, pp. 606–613 (2008)

[13] Mirbel, I.: OFLOSSC, an ontology for supporting open source development communities. In: Proceedings of ICEIS 2009. SAIC, pp. 47–52 (2009)

[14] Yu, E.: Modelling Strategic Relationships for Process Reengineering. PhD. thesis, Toronto (1995)

[15] Franch, X.: On the Lightweight Use of Goal-Oriented Models for Software Package Selection. In: Pastor, Ó., Falcão e Cunha, J. (eds.) CAiSE 2005. LNCS, vol. 3520, pp. 551–566. Springer, Heidelberg (2005)

Detection, Simulation and Elimination of Semantic Anti-patterns in Ontology-Driven Conceptual Models

Giancarlo Guizzardi and Tiago Prince Sales

Ontology and Conceptual Modeling Research Group (NEMO), Computer Science Department,
Federal University of Espírito Santo (UFES), Vitória - ES, Brazil
gguizzardi@inf.ufes.br, tiago@semanticworks.org

Abstract. The construction of large-scale reference conceptual models is a complex engineering activity. To develop high-quality models, a modeler must have the support of expressive engineering tools such as theoretically well-founded modeling languages and methodologies, patterns and anti-patterns and automated support environments. This paper proposes Semantic Anti-Patterns for ontology-driven conceptual modeling. These anti-patterns capture error prone modeling decisions that can result in the creation of models that allow for unintended model instances (representing undesired state of affairs). The anti-patterns presented here have been empirically elicited through an approach of conceptual models validation via visual simulation. The paper also presents a tool that is able to: automatically identify these anti-patterns in user's models, provide visualization for its consequences, and generate corrections to these models by the automatic inclusion of OCL constraints.

Keywords: Ontology-Driven Conceptual Modeling, Semantic Anti-Patterns.

1 Introduction

Conceptual modeling is a complex activity. In [1], an analogy is made between the construction of large reference conceptual models (or reference ontologies) and the programming of large computer systems, referencing the famous E. W. Dijkstra's ACM Turing lecture entitled "The Humble Programmer". In both cases, we have an acknowledgement of the limitations of the human mind to address the large and fast increasingly intrinsic complexity of these types of activities. For this reason, human conceptual modelers and ontologists should make use of a number of suitable complexity management engineering tools to maximize the chances of a successful outcome in this enterprise. As discussed in [1], among these tools, we have modeling languages and methodologies, patterns and anti-patterns, as well as automated supporting environments for model construction, verification and validation.

In recent years, there has been a growing interest in the use of Ontologically Well-Founded Conceptual Modeling languages to support the construction and management of these complex artifacts. OntoUML is an example of a conceptual modeling language whose meta-model has been designed to comply with the ontological distinctions and axiomatization of a theoretically well-grounded foundational ontology

E. Yu et al. (Eds.): ER 2014, LNCS 8824, pp. 363–376, 2014.

named UFO (Unified Foundational Ontology) [2]. This language has been successfully employed in a number of industrial projects in several different domains, such as Petroleum and Gas, Digital Journalism, Complex Digital Media Management, Off-Shore Software Engineering, Telecommunications, Retail Product Recommendation, and Government. Besides the modeling language itself, the OntoUML approach also offers a model-based environment for model construction, verbalization, code generation, formal verification and validation [3]. In particular, the validation strategy employed there makes use of an approach based on visual model simulation [4]. In this paper, we make use of this approach for eliciting *anti-patterns*.

An anti-pattern is a recurrent error-prone modeling decision [5]. In this paper, we are interested in one specific sort of anti-patterns, namely, model structures that, albeit producing syntactically valid conceptual models, are prone to result in unintended domain representations. In other words, we are interested in configurations that when used in a model will typically cause the set of valid (possible) instances of that model to differ from the set of instances representing *intended state of affairs* in that domain [2]. We name here these configurations *Semantic Anti-Patterns*.

The contributions of this paper are two-fold. Firstly, we contribute to the identification of Semantic Anti-Patterns in Ontology-Driven Conceptual Modeling. We do that by carrying out an empirical qualitative approach over a model benchmark of 52 OntoUML models. In particular, we employ the visual simulation capabilities embedded in OntoUML editor [3]. Secondly, once these anti-patterns have been elicited, we extend the OntoUML editor with a number of features for: (a) automatically and proactively detecting anti-patterns in user models; (b) supporting the user in exploring the consequences of the presence of an anti-pattern in the model and, hence, deciding whether that anti-pattern indeed allows for unintended model instances; (c) automatically generating OCL constraints that excluded these unintended model instances.

The remainder of this paper is organized as follows: in Section 2, we briefly elaborate on the modeling language OntoUML and some of its ontological categories, as well on the approach for model validation via visual simulation embedded in the OntoUML editor; Section 3 characterizes the model benchmark used in this research; Section 4 presents the elicited Semantic Anti-Patterns with their undesired consequences and possible solutions; section 5 elaborates on the extensions implemented in the OntoUML editor taking into account these anti-patterns. Finally, Section 6 presents some final considerations of this work.

2   Model Validation via Visual Simulation in OntoUML

The OntoUML language meta-model contains: (i) elements that represent ontological distinctions prescribed by the underlying foundational ontology UFO; (ii) constraints that govern the possible relations that can be established between these elements reflecting the axiomatization of this underlying ontology. These two points are illustrated below using some ontological distinctions among the categories of object types (**Kind**, **Subkind** and **Roles**), trope types (**Relator**) and relations (**formal relations** and **material relations**). For an in depth presentation, formal characterization and empirical evidence for a number of the ontological categories underlying OntoUML, the reader is referred to [2].

In a simplified view we can state that: Kinds and Subkinds are types that aggregate all the essential properties of their instances and, for that reason, all instances of a given Kind/Subkind cannot cease to instantiate it without ceasing to exist (a meta-property known as *rigidity*). A Kind defines a uniform principle of identity that is obeyed by all its instances; Subkinds are rigid specializations of a Kind and inherit that principle of identity supplied by that unique subsuming Kind. A Role, in contrast, represents a number of properties that instances of a Kind have contingently and in a relational context. A stereotypical example can be appreciated when contrasting the Kind *Person*, the Subkinds *Man* and *Woman* (specializing Person) and the Role *Student* (also specializing Person).

A Relator is the objectification of a relational property (i.e., a complex relational trope) and is intimately connected to an event in which roles are played. Relators are existentially dependent on a multitude of individuals, thus, mediating them [2]. In other words, a relation of **mediation** is a particular type of existential dependence relation connecting a relator to a number of relata. Examples of relators are *Enrollments, Employments, Covalent Bonds* and *Marriages*. Relators are the foundation and truthmakers of the so-called material relations in the way, for instance, that the marriage between John and Mary founds (is the truthmaker of) the relation *is-married-to* between John and Mary (but also the relations *being-the-husband-of, being-the-wife-of*), or in the way that the *Enrollment* between Mick and the London School of Economics founds the relation *studies-at* between these two individuals. Contrary to material relations, formal relations hold directly between entities without requiring any intervening (connecting) individual. Examples include the relations of existential dependence and parthood but also *being-taller-than* between individuals.

Regarding characteristic (i) above, OntoUML incorporates modeling constructs that represent all the aforementioned ontological categories (among many others) as modeling primitives of the language. Regarding (ii), the meta-model embeds constraints that govern the possible relations to be established between these categories. These constraints are derived from the very axiomatization of these categories in the underlying foundational ontology. Examples include (among many others): a Role (as well as a Subkind) must be a subtype of exactly one ultimate Kind; a role cannot be a super-type of a Kind or a Subkind; a relator must bear mediation relations to at least two distinct individuals.

As a result of these constraints, as discussed in [2], the only grammatically correct models of OntoUML are ontologically consistent models. In other words, by incorporating ontological constraints in its meta-model, OntoUML proscribes the representation of ontologically non-admissible states of affairs in conceptual models represented in that language. However, as discussed in [5], the language cannot guarantee that, in a particular model, only model instances representing *intended state of affairs* are admitted. This is because the admissibility of domain-specific states of affairs is a matter of factual knowledge, not a matter of consistent possibility [1].

To illustrate this point, we will use for the remainder of the paper the running example presented in Fig.1. This model describes people's *roles* and relevant properties in the context of a criminal investigation. Some of roles may be the detectives that investigate the crime, other the suspects of committing the crime, but also witnesses that are interrogated by the detectives about the crime. Each investigation has a detective who is responsible for it. Detectives are ranked as officers and captains. Finally, since other relational properties are relevant in investigations, the model also represents parenthood and acquaintance ("person knows person") relations among people.

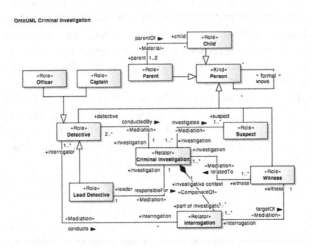

Fig. 1. Partial OntoUML model of the domain of criminal investigation

Capturing aspects of this domain, the model of Fig.1 does not violate ontological rules; it would have done so, for example, had we placed Suspect as a super-type of Person, or had we represented the possibility of a Suspect or Witness without being related to Criminal Investigation (we assume here a suspect is a suspect in the context of an investigation and so is a witness) [2]. These cases can be easily detected and proscribed by an editor such as the one proposed in [3]. One example is one in which the Lead Detective of an investigation is also a Suspect on that investigation. Another example is one in which a Detective interrogates himself. A third one is one in which someone is his own parent (or a parent of one of her parents). This simple and relatively small model fragment actually contains 13 cases of what we term Semantic Anti-Patterns, i.e., model fragments that when used, typically create a deviation between the set of possible and the set of intended state of affairs [2]. We will return to this point in sections 4 and 5.

Guaranteeing the exclusion of unintended states of affairs without a computational support is a practically impossible task for any relevant domain [1]. In particular, given that many fundamental ontological distinctions are modal in nature, in order to validate a model, one would have to take into consideration the possible valid instances of that model in all possible worlds.

In [4], the authors propose an automated approach for OntoUML that offers a contribution to this problem by supporting conceptual model validation via visual simulation. In the proposed tool, the models are translated into Alloy [6], a logic language based on set theory, which is supported by an analyzer that, given a context, exhaustively generates possible instances for a given specification and also allows automatic checking of assertions' consistency. The generated instances of a given conceptual model are organized in a branching-time temporal structure, thus, serving as a visual simulator for the possible dynamics of entity creation, classification, association and destruction. In [4], the modeler is then confronted with a visual representation of the snapshots in this world structure. These snapshots represent model instances that are deemed admissible by the ontology's current axiomatization. This enables modelers to detect unintended model instances (i.e., model instances that do not represent intended state of affairs) so that they can take the proper measures to rectify the model.

The comparison between admissible model instances, generated by the Alloy Analyzer, and the intended ones, obtained from domain experts or the conceptual model documentation, highlights possibly erroneous modeling decisions. The recording and categorization of these decisions for a set of OntoUML conceptual models served as a basis for identifying the semantic anti-patterns proposed in this paper. The process for empirically uncovering these anti-patterns is explained in section 3 below.

3   Empirically Uncovering Semantic Anti-patterns

The approach used in this work for the identification of the proposed set of anti-patterns was an empirical qualitative analysis. The idea was to simulate existing OntoUML conceptual models by employing the approach described in section 2. In a preliminary analysis reported in [7], we studied the recurrence of these anti-patterns across: (i) different domains; (ii) different levels of modeling expertise in Ontology-Driven Conceptual Modeling; (iii) models of different sizes, maturity and complexity.

In that study, we have first started with 9 models selected across the following areas: (1) a Conceptual Model that describes a Brazilian Health Organization; (2) a Conceptual Model that describes the Organizational Structure of Brazilian Federal Universities; (3) a Conceptual Model that describes a Domain of Online Mentoring Activities; (4) an Ontology representing the domain of Transport Optical Network Architectures; (5) an Ontology in the Biodiversity Domain; (6) a Heart Electrophysiology Reference Ontology; (7) an Ontology in the Domain of Normative Acts; (8) an Ontology of Public Tenders; (8) an Ontology in the Domain of Brazilian Federal Organizational Structures.

Regarding levels of expertise, we have classified as "beginners", those modelers with less than one year of experience with OntoUML and its foundations. In contrast, we classified as "experienced", those modelers that had worked with the language for two or more years and had applied the language in large-scale complex domains. In all the analyzed cases, the modelers involved in the creation of the models had a significant experience in traditional conceptual modeling approaches. In our first sampling of models, we had 4 models created by beginners (models 1-3, 9) and 5 models created by experienced modelers (4-8).

Finally, regarding scale and complexity, three of the investigated models were graduate final assignments (models 1-3), two of which were produced by modelers with vast experience in the respective domains (1-2); model (4) was produced by experienced modelers in an industrial project. Moreover, the modelers had access to domain experts as well as a supporting international standard of the domain (ITU-T G.805). Finally, the resulting ontology was published in a relevant scientific forum in the area of Telecommunications; Model (5) was developed in the Brazilian National Center for Amazon Research in collaboration with domain experts; Model (6) was published in a renowned international journal in the area of Bioinformatics in a special issue of Biomedical ontologies; Models (7-8) were produced in a large-scale industrial project for the Brazilian Regulatory Agency for Land Transportation (ANTT). The modelers had constant access to normative documentation and to domain experts; finally, model (9) was produced by a group of modelers in the Brazilian Ministry of Planning. The group was formed by experts in the domain who had a professional-level experience in traditional conceptual modeling. The size of these models varied from 15-31 classes (between 7-30 associations) for the models produced by beginners (models 1-3, 9) to 46-194 classes (between 29 to 122 associations) for those models produced by experienced researchers.

In what follows, we describe our strategy for identifying anti-patterns across this sample of models. For each of these cases, we started by simulating the model at hand using the approach described in the previous section. This process resulted in a number of *possible model instances* for that model (automatically generated by the Alloy Analyzer). We then contrasted the set of possible instances with the set of *intended instances* of the model, i.e., the set of model instances that represented intended state of affairs according the creators of the models. When a mismatch between these two sets was detected, we analyzed the model in order to identify which structures in the model were the causes of such a mismatch. Finally, we catalogued as anti-patterns those model structures that recurrently produced such mismatches, i.e., modeling patterns that would repeatedly produce model instances that were not intended ones. To be more precise, we considered as anti-patterns the error prone modeling decisions, which occurred in at least one third of the validated models. We carried out this simulation-based validation process with a constant interaction with the model creators (when available), or by inspecting the textual documentation accompanying the models otherwise.

In this first empirical study, we manage to identify 6 initial semantic anti-patterns. The occurrence of these anti-patterns in the studied models was 33.33% for two of the patterns (i.e., the anti-patterns appeared in 1/3 of the models), 66.67%, 77.78%, 88.89% and 100% (i.e., one of the anti-patterns appeared in all the analyzed models). The details of this studied are found in the following preliminary report [7].

This initial study gave us confidence that the adopted method could be used as a means for detecting these semantic anti-patterns. In the follow up study reported here, we manage to assemble a much larger benchmark of 52 OntoUML models. These models can be characterized as follows: (a) 61,53% of the models were produced by experienced modelers while 38,46% of them were produced by beginners; (b) the majority of these models (69,23 %) were graduated assignments at the master and PhD level produced as a result of a 60-hours OntoUML course. We have also that 21,15% of these models were results of graduate dissertations (MSc and PhD thesis) in areas such as Provenance in Scientific Workflow, Public Cloud Vulnerability, Software Configuration Management, Emergency Management, Services, IT Governance,

Organizational Structures, Software Requirements, Heart Electrophisiology, Amazonian Biodiversity Management, Human Genome. Finally, 7,69% of these models were produced in industrial projects in areas such as Optical Transport Networks, Federal Government Organizational Structures, Normative Acts, and Ground Transportation Regulation; (c) in terms of size and complexity, these models varied from a simple model in a graduation assignment containing 11 classes and 14 associations to an industrial model in the domain of Ground Transportation Regulation containing 3775 classes, 3566 generalization relations, 564 generalization sets and 1972 associations. The average number of classes and relations (generalization relations plus associations) when considering all models is 114.92, 169.26, respectively. If only industrial projects are considered these averages go up to 1.027 for classes and 388 for relations.

In order to analyze this new benchmark, we have implemented a set of computational strategies to automatically detect occurrences of these anti-patterns in OntoUML models (see discussion in section 5). By running these algorithms for our initial set of anti-patterns under this benchmark, we managed to refine and extend the initial set elicited in [7] to a refined set of anti-patterns. Table 1 below reports on these new anti-patterns whose automatic strategy of detection and correction have been incorporated in the OntoUML computational editor (see section 5). Among the anti-patterns presented in this new set, one of them is a refinement and extension of the existing STR anti-pattern, two of them are newly discovered anti-patterns, namely, TRI and RWOR. Moreover, RWOR have been generalized under the category RelOver together with the RBOS anti-pattern. Finally, the so-called PA (Pseudo-AntiRigid) anti-pattern from our original catalog was excluded from the analysis conducted here due to the fact that the detection of its occurrences cannot be performed algorithmically.

It is important to highlight that given the size of this new set of models, unlike in our previous study, we were not able to check for each occurrence of these anti-patterns (3612 occurrences!) whether they were always cases of model fragments that entailed unintended consequences. For this reason, in the analysis reported in table 1, each occurrence of an anti-pattern does not necessarily mean an unintended occurrence of the corresponding model fragment. However, in our previous empirical study, we could observe a very strong correlation between the high occurrence of these anti-patterns as model fragments and cases in which they were identified as unintended. In fact, that is exactly why they were identified as anti-patterns (as opposed to purely syntactic constraints) in the first place.

The anti-patterns represented in table 1 are discussed in section 5.

Table 1. Occurrences of Semantic Anti-patterns in the model Benchmark used

Semantic Anti-Patterns (SAP)	% of occurrences across models	Total # of occurrences
RS	46,15%	1435
IA	71,15%	725
AC	51,92%	155
RelOver (RWOR + RBOS)	30,7%	437
TRI	55,77%	685
BinOver (incl. STR)	48,07%	175

4   A Catalogue of Semantic Anti patterns

4.1   Relation Specialization (RS)

As depicted in **Fig. 2(a)**, the RS anti-pattern is characterized by the representation of a relation R between two types T1 and T2, such that their respective super-types ST1 and ST2 are also associated by a relation SR. It is important to highlight that ST1 and ST2 are not necessarily direct super-types (depicted in the figure by the sign "…") but also that they are not necessarily strict (proper) super-types. In fact, we can have cases in which T1 = ST1, T2 = ST2, and even a case in which T1 = T2 = ST1 = ST2, i.e., a case in which the model of fig 2(a) degenerates into a model with one type and two type-reflexive relationships R and SR between instances of this unique type. What we have found in our analysis is that there is usually some sort of constraint between R and SR overlooked by the modeler.   The solution for eliminating this potential source of problem (in the case the modeler in fact judges this to be one) is to include constraints on the relation between R and SR, thus, declaring R to be either a specialization, a subset, a redefinition or disjoint with relation SR. OntoUML has an in depth treatment of these relations as well as precise ontological guidelines for differentiating when each of these modeling alternatives should be used. An example of an occurrence of this pattern in Fig.1 is the following: we should guarantee that the Lead Investigator responsible for a Criminal Investigation is one of the Detectives conducting that Investigation.

4.2   Relation Between Overlapping Subtypes (RBOS)

The RBOS anti-pattern occurs in a model having two potentially overlapping (i.e., non-disjoint) types T1 and T2 whose principle of identity is provided by a common Kind ST, and such that T1 and T2 are related through a formal relation R as depicted in **Fig. 2(b)**. This problem frequently appears when T1 and T2 are roles, although it can also occur having T1 and T2 as subkinds. The problem here comes from the fact that an object may instantiate both T1 and T2 simultaneously. Occasionally, roles in relation R are played by entities of the same kind ST. However, it is frequently undesired that these roles are played by the same instance of ST. In case T1 = T2 and R is a binary relation this anti-pattern degenerates to a case of the *BinOver* pattern and, in the limit case in which T1, T2 and ST are identical, it degenerates to a particular case of BinOver termed *STR*. BinOver and STR are discussed in the sequel. Moreover, when the relation R in Fig. 2(b) is a material relation (not-necessarily a binary one), this anti-pattern configures a case of the RWOR anti-pattern explained in section 4.6. Possible rectifications of this anti-pattern include characterizing R as (non/anti)reflexive, (non/a)symmetric or (in/anti)transitive, or defining T1 and T2 as disjoint. For example, in Fig.1, we have the formal relation *parentOf* between the roles Child and Parent. Although the two roles in this relation must be played by instances of the same Kind (Person), they cannot be played by the same instance of Person for the same instance of the relation. In this case, the types T1 and T2 are not disjoint, since the same individual can play both these roles (i.e., someone can be a father of person x and son of person y) but not in the same relation instance. In this case, the solution is to declare relation *parentOf* as anti-reflexive, asymmetric and anti-transitive.

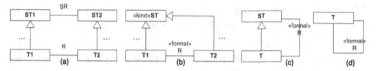

Fig. 2. Structural configuration illustrating the **(a)** RS, **(b)** RBOS, **(c)** BinOver, and **(d)** STR

4.3   BinOver and Self-type Relationship (STR)

The BinOver pattern occurs when the two association ends of a binary relations R can be bound to the same instance. A particular case of BinOver is the so-called Self-Reflexive *STR* anti-pattern. BinOver is configured by a relation R having one of its associations ends connected a type T and another of its association ends connected to a super-type ST of T as depicted in **Fig. 2(c)**. In case that ST=T, we have a particular case of BinOver termed Self-Type Relationship (STR) (see **Fig. 2(d)**). Type-Reflexive relations as they appear in these two configurations are usually overly permissive and typically should be constrained using the meta-properties that precisely characterize a formal binary relation such as (in/anti)transitive, (a/non)symmetric, (non/co)reflexive, total, trichotomous or euclidean. This anti-pattern occurs when R are formal relations. In case R is a material relation, this anti-pattern configures a case of the RWOR anti-pattern explained in section 4.6. In Fig. 1, this configuration appears in the relation "knows" between People. Notice that this relation is indeed a formal relation, since it can be reduced to an intrinsic property of the relata (in this case the knowledge of the knowers). In this domain, this relationship is reflexive, asymmetric (but not anti-symmetric) and intransitive (but not anti-transitive). In other domains, e.g., some social networks, this relation can in contrast be considered to be symmetric and transitive.

4.4   Association Cycle (AC)

This anti-pattern consists of three or more types $T1...Tn$ connected through an association chain $R1,2...Rn-1,n$ (where Rij connects type Ti with type Tj) in a way to form a cycle. In **Fig. 3.(a)**, T1, T2 and T3 form a cycle through the associations R1, R2 and R3. The possible constraints to be applied over this configuration are that these cycles should be reinforced to be either closed or open cycles. A OCL-like constraint having T1 as a reference (i.e., as an OCL context) for the case of closed cycles has the form (*self.T2.T3...Tn.T1.asSet()=self.asSet()*) and for the open cycle the form (*self.T2.T3...Tn.T1->excludes(self)*). In section 5, we discuss in detail an example from Fig.1 in which a close cycle must be guaranteed, namely, that a detective who conducts an interrogation that is part of an investigation must be one of the detectives of that investigation.

4.5   Imprecise Abstraction (IA)

As depicted in **Fig. 3(b)**, this anti-pattern is characterized when two types T1 and T2 are related through an association R with an upper cardinality in both ends greater than one, and at least one of the related types containing its own subtypes. The source of the inconsistency comes from the representation of a single, more abstract association between T1 and T2, instead of more concrete ones between T1 and T2's subtypes. In this case, there might be domain-specific constraints missing in this model referring to which subtypes of T2 an instance of T1 may be related. As an example, suppose that in **Fig.3(b)** an instance of T1 can only be related through relation R to instances of a particular STi, or that instances of T1 are subject to different cardinality constraints on R for each of the different subtypes STj. An example in the model of Fig.1 is the following: although a Criminal Investigation can have at least two Detectives, exactly one of them must be a Captain.

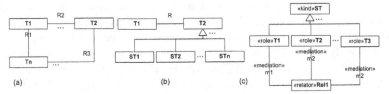

Fig. 3. Structural configuration illustrating the **(a)** AC, **(b)** IA and **(c)** RWOR

4.6   Relator with Overlapping Roles (RWOR)

The generic structure of the Relator With Overlapping Roles (RWOR) anti-pattern is depicted in **Fig. 3(c)**. It is characterized by a *Relator* (R1) mediating two or more *Roles* (T1, T2… Tn) whose extensions overlap, i.e. have their identity principle provided by a common *Kind* as a super-type (ST). In addition, the roles are not explicitly declared disjoint. This modeling structure is prone to be overly permissive, since there are no restriction for an instance to act as multiples roles for the same relator. The possible commonly identified intended interpretations are that: the roles are actually disjoint (disjoint roles), i.e., no instance of ST may act as more than one role for the same instance of a relator Rel1 (mutually exclusive roles); some roles may be played by the same instance of ST, while others may not (partially exclusive roles). An alternative case is one in which all or a subset of the roles in question are mutually exclusive but across different relators. An instance of RWOR in our running example is discussed in section 5.

4.7   Twin Relator Instances (TRI)

This anti-pattern occurs when a relator is connected to two or more «mediation» associations, such that the upper bound cardinalities at the relator end are greater than one. The problem associated with this anti-pattern is that it opens the possibility for two distinct instances of the same relator type to co-exist connecting the very same relata instances. We empirically found that the existence of these relator instances in this situation should frequently be subject to several different types of constraints. For instance, it can the case that there cannot be two different relator instances of the same type connecting the very same relata. An example in the domain depicted in Fig.1 could be: one cannot be the subject of a second criminal investigation as a suspect and be investigated by the same detectives that interrogate the same witnesses. There can be cases that the existence of these multiple relators instances are allowed but not simultaneously (e.g., a passenger can have more than one reservation for the same hotel but not for the same time period). In fact, there can be a number of variations of the cases above due to domain-specificity: (a) two or more relators of the same type can bind the same relata but these relators have to exist separated by a specific time interval from each other (e.g., contracts between the same employee and the same public institution can exist but only if separated by at least two-years from each other), or they can partially overlap but cannot be totally synchronized, etc.; (b) two or more relators of the same type have to vary in at least a specific subset of its roles (e.g., an employee can have more than one valid contract with the same employer at intersecting time intervals, however, not for the same position).

5   Anti-pattern Detection, Analysis and Elimination

In order to support the approach presented in Section 4, we developed a suite of plugins for validating OntoUML models that have been incorporated in the OntoUML editor (**Fig.4**). With the goal of supporting the entire process described in section 2, this tool supports a set of tasks. First, it allows for the automatic detection of anti-patterns in the model. Since we cannot know a priori which are the unintended situations (if any) that should be excluded from the model, the tool offers a visual simulation environment implementing the approach previously discussed. Finally, when the expert identifies the unintended instances to be excluded, the tool offers semi-automatic correction via the automatic generation of OCL constraints.

In what follows, in order to illustrate this process we use the domain model of Criminal Investigation depicted in Fig.1. Once a model is constructed or loaded into the OntoUML editor (**Fig.4.1**), the anti-pattern detection algorithms embedded in this tool can be activated (**Fig.4.2**). When analyzing the criminal investigation model of Fig.1, the detection algorithms identified 13 candidate occurrences of semantic anti-patterns (**Fig.4.3**): 1 occurrence each of RBOS and STR; 2 occurrences each of *AC*, *RS*, *RWOR* and *TRI*, and 3 occurrences of *IA*. In the following, due to lack of space, we elaborate an example of *AC*, and an example of RWOR in this model.

One identified *AC* is a cycle composed by Criminal Investigation, Detective, Interrogation and, again, Detective (with the respective associations). This possible occurrence of an anti-pattern is shown in the window depicted in **Fig.4.4**. In that window, the modeler can select the option of visualizing possible instances of the model in which the identified anti-pattern is manifested (button "execute with Analyzer"). One visual representation of an instance of this model produced with this functionality is depicted in **Fig.5**. In this instance, detective *Object9* conducts interrogation *Property7*, which is part of the Criminal Investigation *Property2*. However, *Object9* is not one of the detectives conducting Criminal Investigation *Property2*. In other words, the model allows for a representation of a state of affairs in which an interrogation that is part of a criminal investigation is conducted by a detective that is not part of that investigation. Let us suppose that the creators of that model do not intend such a state of affairs. The modelers can then request the editor for an OCL solution that would proscribe instances with this detected unintended characteristic (button "OCL solution" in Fig.4.4). In this case, the OCL constraint to be incorporated in the model (Fig.4.5) is the following:

```
context CriminalInvestigation
inv closedCycle:
self.interrogation.interrogator.investigation->asSet()= self->asSet()
```

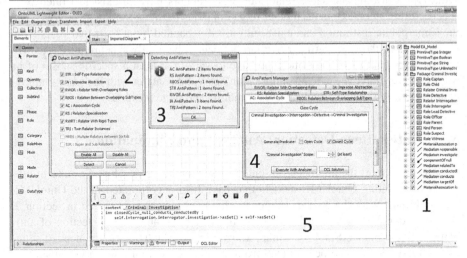

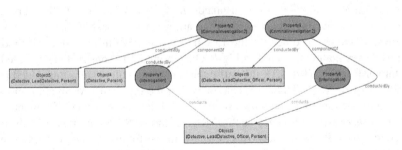

Fig. 4. Anti-Pattern detection and analysis capabilities incorporated in the OntoUML editor

Fig. 5. Possible interpretation of the *AC* identified in the Criminal Investigation model

An example of an identified RWOR anti-pattern involves criminal investigation as a relator that mediates the Roles Detective, Lead Detective, Suspect and Witness. As explained in Section 4, there are three types of possibly unintended instances that can be allowed by an occurrence of this anti-pattern. First, all roles are exclusive in the scope of a particular relator, which means that in each particular investigation the roles of suspect, witness, detective and lead detective are necessarily all instantiated by different people. Second, it may be the case that only some of these roles are exclusive in the scope of a particular relator, for example, the detective and the suspect are exclusive, but not detective and witness, or suspect and witness. Finally, it may also be the case that some of the roles are disjoint (across different relators). For example, suppose the constraint that detectives who participate in an ongoing investigation cannot be considered suspects in another investigation. Let us suppose that as a first action to rectify the model the modeler chooses to declare all roles as exclusive w.r.t. a given investigation. The set of instances of the resulting model, hence, includes the one depicted in **Fig.6**. By inspecting the model of Fig.6, the modeler can then realize that she perhaps over-constrained the model since, as a result of declaring all roles as exclusive, we have that the responsible for a given investigation (i.e., the lead detectives) is not considered as a participant of that investigation (i.e., one of its detectives). The modeler can then rectify the model again by choosing among a set of other alternative OCL solutions offered by the OntoUML editor. In **Fig.7**, we show the case in which the modeler chooses both to declare the roles of witness and suspect disjoint w.r.t. a given investigation (constraint on line 1 of the OCL code), as well as the roles witness and detective (line 4), but also to declare that the roles of detective and suspect should be disjoint across different investigations (line 7).

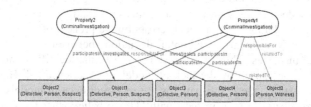

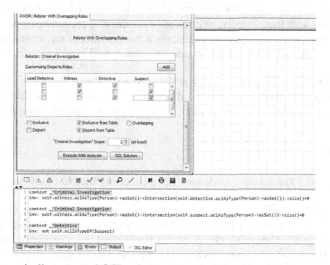

Fig. 6. Exclusive view of the roles in a criminal investigation

Fig. 7. Automatically generated OCL solutions to excluded unintended instances of RWOR

6   Final Considerations

This paper makes a contribution to the theory and practice of ontology-driven conceptual modeling by: (i) presenting a number of empirically elicited Semantic Anti-patterns that were identified as recurrent in a benchmark of conceptual models; (ii) presenting a computational environment that automates the process of supporting detection of anti-patterns, exploration of their consequence in individual models, formal rectification via the inclusion of pre-defined formal constraints. This computational environment is available in https://code.google.com/p/ontouml-lightweight-editor/.

Our approach is in line with authors both in the conceptual modeling and ontology engineering literature. Two representative examples of works in this area are [8] and [9], which discuss methods of detecting anti-patterns in OWL specifications via SPARQL queries. Although sharing the same general objective, our approach differs from these works in a number of important ways. Firstly, our approach is based on a much richer modeling language from the ontological point of view. As a consequence, the anti-patterns addressed by our approach are able to address more subtle ontological conditions such as, for example, the ones involving modality, identity principles as well as a richer ontology of material relations. Secondly, different from these approaches, our method does not aim at detecting general cases involving typical logical misunderstandings. In contrast, it focuses exactly on those cases that cannot be casted as modeling (grammatical) errors by the process of formal verification, and aims at identifying recurrent potential deviations between the sets of valid and intended model instances. Thirdly, for instance in [9], the identified anti-patterns are cases believed to be caused by the lack of modeling experience [9]. Here, as shown by our empirical study, these anti-patterns are recurrent even in models produced by experience researchers. In fact, in pace with [1], we believe that the repeated occurrence of these anti-patterns is an intrinsic feature of the disparity between the increasing complexity of our reference conceptual models and our limited cognitive capacities for dealing with that. Finally, in contrast with these approaches, besides automatic anti-pattern detection, our approach presents a computational environment for model analysis (via visual simulation) and systematic conceptual model rectification.

Acknowledgements. The authors are grateful to João Paulo Almeida, John Guerson and Pedro Paulo Barcelos for fruitful discussions in the topics of this article. This research was partially supported by the Lucretius ERC Advanced Grant # 267856.

References

1. Guizzardi, G.: Theoretical foundations and engineering tools for building ontologies as reference conceptual models. Semantic Web Journal 1, 3–10 (2010)
2. Guizzardi, G.: Ontological foundations for structural conceptual models. Centre for Telematics and Information Technology, University of Twente, The Netherlands (2005)
3. Benevides, A.B., Guizzardi, G.: A Model-Based Tool for Conceptual Modeling and Domain Ontology Engineering in OntoUML. In: Filipe, J., Cordeiro, J. (eds.) ICEIS 2009. LNBIP, vol. 24, pp. 528–538. Springer, Heidelberg (2009)
4. Benevides, A.B., et al.: Validating Modal Aspects of OntoUML Conceptual Models Using Automatically Generated Visual World Structures. Journal of Universal Computer Science 16, 2904–2933 (2010)
5. Koenig, A.: Patterns and Anti-Patterns. J. of Object-Oriented Programming 8 (1995)
6. Jackson, D.: Software Abstractions: Logic, Language, and Analysis. The MIT Press, Cambridge (2012)
7. Sales, T.P., Barcelos, P.P.F., Guizzardi, G.: Identification of Semantic Anti-Patterns in Ontology-Driven Conceptual Modeling via Visual Simulation. In: 4th International Workshop on Ontology-Driven Information Systems (ODISE), Graz, Austria (2012)
8. Vrandečić, D.: Ontology Validation, PhD Thesis, University of Karlsruhe (2010)
9. Roussey, C., et al.: SPARQL-DL queries for Antipattern Detection. In: Workshop on Ontology Patterns. CEUR-WS.org, Boston (2012)

Recall of Concepts and Relationships Learned by Conceptual Models: The Impact of Narratives, General-Purpose, and Pattern-Based Conceptual Grammars

Wolfgang Maass[1] and Veda C. Storey[2]

[1] Saarland University, 66123 Saarbrücken, Germany;
[2] University Plaza, Georgia State University, Atlanta 30302 United States
wolfgang.maass@iss.uni-saarland.de, vstorey@gsu.edu

Abstract. Conceptual models are the means by which a designer expresses his or her understanding of an envisioned information system. This research investigates whether modeling experts or novices differ in understanding conceptual models represented by textual descriptions in the form of narratives, by general-purpose conceptual modeling languages, such as entity-relationship models or by pattern-based conceptual modeling languages. Cognitive science theories on memory systems are adopted and a cued recall experiment carried out. The experimental results suggest that narratives cannot be underestimated during learning processes in information systems design. Furthermore, general-purpose conceptual modeling languages tend to lack capabilities for supporting template-based learning. The results are differentiated between subjects with at least basic conceptual modeling skills and novices.

Keywords: Conceptual modeling, conceptual patterns, design patterns, entity relationship diagrams, empirical study, knowledge structures, domain understanding, cued recall, template, experts, novices, narratives, chunks.

1   Introduction

Conceptual models are complex knowledge structures used by designers to represent integrated collections of concepts and relationships about application domains. The knowledge required to create effective conceptual models fall into two categories: 1) knowledge related to conceptual modeling grammars and associated techniques; and 2) knowledge about the domain being modeled. For knowledge related to conceptual modeling grammars, designers must know basic concepts and abstract modeling techniques, independent of a particular domain. Different types of designers create and use conceptual models, with experts being more likely to conceptualize and understand domain descriptions than novices [1].

In addition, knowledge structures are developed for some domains. For instance, reference models encompass knowledge structures that provide templates for large domains that can be instantiated by design teams. Alexander's well-recognized patterns [2] are smaller knowledge structures that can be used to express domain

E. Yu et al. (Eds.): ER 2014, LNCS 8824, pp. 377–384, 2014.

knowledge. Examples of patterns include place-transaction [3] and service-interaction [18]. Knowledge structures and patterns form larger conceptual groups, are referred to as chunks. Cognitive load theory emphasizes chunking as effective when considering many concepts and relationships simultaneously [4].

The objective of this research is to investigate design patterns as knowledge structures in conceptual modeling. Grouping stimuli by chunks by novices and experts, a recall experiment is carried out in which subjects who use a newly learned conceptual pattern language are compared to a control group. This research investigates two questions for experts vs. novices: (a) Do conceptual patterns improve the creation of a conceptual model? and (b) Do conceptual patterns improve recall of concepts and relationships? This study is part of more general research on shared understanding in design teams.

2   Related Research

Various conceptual modeling languages have been created including simple narrative text, entity-relationship diagrams, star diagrams, formal ontologies, business process models, use case descriptions, and object-oriented representations. Prior research has investigated such as ease of use [5], effectiveness, and efficiency of a conceptual modeling language [6]. Few studies, however, have empirically compared different kinds of conceptual modeling languages (narrative text, entity-relationship diagrams, and semantic patterns).

Understanding conceptual models relies on memory processes, called *chunking*, that enable the collection of pieces of information from conceptual models and merging of them into integrated mental representations [5]. Chunking mechanisms are basic for mental processes used by conceptual modeling. Conceptual models in textual descriptions provide little schematic structures, yet require processing of primitive stimuli. In contrast, conceptual models whose representation is based on generic conceptual grammars, such as Entity-Relationship Diagrams (ERD) [6], provide basic schematic structures, but the more complex conceptual modeling languages need to be learned by the user beforehand. Pattern-based conceptual languages provide higher-order semantic structures that encompass generic domain knowledge and can be reused in conceptual design. Mental representations of conceptual models can be derived by the following three learning processes:

1. Basic stimuli process: derivation of mental representations from unstructured conceptual models, such as textual representations.
2. General model process: derivation of mental representations from structured conceptual models based on general-purpose conceptual grammars, such as entity-relationship diagrams or class diagrams. Domain knowledge is inherently part of a conceptual model.
3. Template-guided model process: mental representations derived from patterns expressed by structured conceptual models with domain knowledge.

In investigations of whether entities and attributes are distinct items in individual's mental representations [7], entity-attribute pairs are related by a "hasAttribute" relationship. In contrast, most application domains include several kinds of relationships. Furthermore, natural language descriptions informally use several kinds of relationships to connect entities. As one moves from natural language descriptions to entity-relationship diagrams to semantic design patterns, the designer implicitly imposes additional structure. It is not clear, however, whether this additional structure leads to a positive effect on individual understanding [6].

This research explores whether an additional structure given by an entity-relationship diagram or a design pattern improves the creation of a conceptual model. An entity-relationship model is compared to a conceptual model created by a pattern language. The expectation is that the additional cognitive effort for deriving a mental representation from an entity-relationship model or from a pattern-based models is compensated for by more sophisticated mental representations [8].

The study uses a cued recall experiment to assess whether concepts and relationships in a conceptual model are: a) correctly remembered or b) incorrectly included in a conceptual model. This assessment was carried out for both novices and experts. Table 1 presents the hypotheses investigated.

Table 1. Hypotheses

	Description with expected outcome
H1a	Subjects will *recall more concepts and relationships* when they are learned via constructing entity-relationship diagrams than when they are learned via reading natural language narratives
H1b	Subjects will *recall more concepts and relationships* when they are learned via semantic patterns than when they are learned via constructing entity-relationship diagrams
H1c	Subjects will *recall more concepts and relationships* when they are learned via semantic patterns than when they are learned via reading natural language narratives
H2a	Subjects will *reject more added concepts and relationships* when they are learned via constructing entity-relationship diagrams than when they are learned via reading natural language narratives
H2b	Subjects will *reject more added concepts and relationships* when they are learned via semantic patterns than when they are learned via constructing entity-relationship diagrams
H2c	Subjects will *reject more added concepts and relationships* when they are learned via semantic patterns than when they are learned via reading natural language narratives
H3a	Subjects will *have less unknown concepts and relationships* when they are learned via constructing entity-relationship diagrams than when they are learned via reading natural language narratives
H3b	Subjects will *have less unknown concepts and relationships* when they are learned via semantic patterns than when they are learned via constructing entity-relationship diagrams
H3c	Subjects will *have less unknown concepts and relationships* when they are learned via semantic patterns than when they are learned via reading natural language narratives

3   Research Experiment

Treatments: Three different treatments were used in this study: 1) textual narratives (basic stimuli process); 2) entity-relationship diagrammatic (general model process) [9]; and 3) design patterns (template-guided model process).

Narratives are a natural form for describing situations of intended information systems using textual descriptions [10]. They are small stories that explicitly describe what happens if one or more actors perform in an anticipated manner. More formally, a situation describes which actors interact with one another or with services. Interactions can transfer information objects from one actor to another. An entity-relationship model is intended to adopt a "more natural view that the real world consists of entities and relationships. It incorporates some of the important semantic information about the real world" [9]. Entity-relationship diagrams (ERD) relate two entity sets by one relationship set ([9]. Conceptual design patterns capture larger knowledge structures in a schematic manner. They relate typed entities, such as information objects, roles, interactions, services, and physical objects, and define typed relationships between entities [11]. We use a pattern grammar that has been developed for the domain of human and service-oriented communication [11] (cf. Figure 2). For instance, the role interaction pattern has four typed variables (two roles, one information object, and one service) and one relationship (r(ole)-interacts). The role-interaction patterns represent any situation in which one role (sender) sends a message (information object) to another role (receiver) by using an interface service (e.g., a telephone). This pattern grammar was new to every subject and introduced before the experiment started.

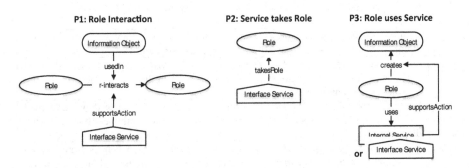

Fig. 1. Conceptual design patterns (selection) [11]

Experimental tasks and procedure: each subject was randomly assigned one of the three treatment groups in an online experiment: 0 (narrative), 1 (entity-relationship diagram), and 2 (pattern). Each experiment consisted of a model extraction phase, a distraction phase, and a recall phase. During the extraction phase for group 0, subjects were asked to read the textual description for an intended information system. Group 1 was asked to identify and mark as many entities and relationships as possible. Group 2 received the same instructions as Group 1 and, additionally, asked to identify and mark as many patterns as possible. During the distraction task a video (3 min.) was shown and subjects were asked three questions about this video. During the recall phase, 40 questions posed on whether concepts and relationships were present in the textual description (cf. Appendix). Subjects could answer 'yes,' 'no,' or 'don't know.' Three control questions were asked. At the beginning, group 1 and 2 refreshed their knowledge of ERD and were taught how to apply patterns of this particular grammar.

A total of 57 subjects (24 female and 33 male, age between 20 and 43) from universities and research institutions in Europe, Asia, and North America participated in the online experiment. Forty-two (42) subjects were students and 15 were professionals (referred to as experts). The subjects' backgrounds were from Computer Science (19), Information Sciences and Technology (17), Economics (5), and MIS (3).

4   Results

Overall 51% of all concepts and relationships were either correctly recalled or correctly rejected. 17% were incorrectly recalled or incorrectly accepted, although subjects could not decide on 32% of all concepts and relationships. Table 2 presents the descriptive statistics.

Table 2. Descriptive statistics ('0': group narratives, '1': group ERD, and '2': group pattern)

Groups		N	Mean	Std.Dev.	Std.Error
Correct concepts	0	13	6.38	2.142	.594
	1	15	4.80	2.210	.571
	2	14	5.93	2.556	.683
Correct Relationships	0	13	7.15	1.625	.451
	1	15	4.8ß	2.145	.554
	2	14	5.36	2.951	.789
Added Concepts	0	13	2.54	1.984	.550
	1	15	2.27	2.052	.530
	2	14	2.57	3.031	.810
Added Relationships	0	13	2.31	1.494	.414
	1	15	2.07	2.120	.547
	2	14	2.21	2.778	.743

Because of non-normality characteristics of all distributions found by our study, the non-parametric Kruskal-Wallis rank sum test was applied [12]. For differences between all three groups, the test became highly significant. However, the dyadic Kruskal-Wallis tests between two groups are only significant for incorrectly identified concepts and relationships. Therefore, we restricted our further analysis to subjects with basic skills (>3 on a 6 point scale) (n=29). For this subset, all three rank sum tests are significant on a 10% significance level due to small sample size. Based on the Wilcoxon rank sum H1b and H3b are accepted whereas H1a and H2c are rejected. The other hypotheses are not significant.

Table 3. Median values for groups and correct, incorrect and unknown items

	Median values for groups		
	0	1	2
Correct (0..2)	27	20.5	23
Incorrect (0..2)	3.5	7	9
Unknown (0..2)	10.5	17	8

5   Discussion

This research has investigated how two different types of conceptual modeling languages contribute to learning and recall. An underlying assumption was that, the more structured a conceptual language, the better the mental representations and, hence, the learning and recall results. However, the results suggest that natural language alone (here, written narratives) is much better suited to learning and recall than expected. Narratives are significantly more effective than general-purpose conceptual modeling languages with respect to recall of concepts and relationships. Pattern-based languages are not more effective than narratives. Pattern-based models more effectively support recall of correct items than general-purpose models. Stories told by narratives resemble those of patterns, supporting our initial assumption that patterns are useful for template-based cognitive processes. The research results indicate that general-purpose languages, such as ERD, provide less support for activating cognitive templates.

For incorrectly recalled items, narratives were even more efficient than pattern-based models. This result poses the question of whether pattern-based models result in expanding mental representations that add complementary items missing in the original description. Pattern-based models performed significantly better than general-purpose languages. This is surprising for a subgroup that has at least basic conceptual modeling skills with entity-relationship diagrams. Again, narratives appear to be at least as good as general-purpose models or pattern-based models.

Several results emerge. First, narratives are a very effective means for supporting cognitive learning processes and building mental representations about information systems. Narratives even exceed capabilities of conceptual models build by more structured conceptual grammars. Because structured conceptual models are necessary for building information systems, it can be concluded that narratives are substantial enhancements for learning processes and building mental representations.

Other research suggests that general-purpose grammars perform better on recall accuracy, whereas narratives and design patterns are expected to be less effective [13]. This research, however, found support for the competing assumption that pattern-based grammars, such as the one used in this study, exhibit improved learning processes. All of these results were found for subjects with at least basic conceptual modeling skills. Novices were not able to use structures and pattern codes provided by conceptual grammars.

6   Conclusion

This research has investigated whether learning processes are better supported by conceptual models based on general-purpose grammars or pattern-based grammars compared to natural language narratives. A cued recall experiment found evidence of significant differences between general-purpose grammars and pattern-based grammars with respect to correct and unknown items. Narratives provided efficient support for learning processes in the design of information systems. This study also showed that differences between novices and skilled modelers should be accommodated. Finally, theories from cognitive science, in particular memory theories, guided the study. This research is an initial attempt to obtain an understanding of cognitive processes and mental representations related to conceptual modeling.

References

1. Shanks, G.: Conceptual data modelling: An empirical study of expert and novice data modellers. Australasian Journal of Information Systems 4 (2007)
2. Alexander, C.: A Pattern Language: Towns, Buildings, Construction (1978)
3. De Groot, A.D., de Groot, A.D.: Thought and choice in chess. de Gruyter (1978)
4. Van Merrienboer, J.J., Sweller, J.: Cognitive load theory and complex learning: Recent developments and future directions. Educational Psychology Review 17, 147–177 (2005)
5. Batra, D., Hoffer, J.A., Bostrom, R.P.: Comparing Representations with Relational and Eer Models. Communications of the ACM 33, 126–139 (1990)
6. Parsons, J., Cole, L.: What do the pictures mean? Guidelines for experimental evaluation of representation fidelity in diagrammatical conceptual modeling techniques. Data & Knowledge Engineering 55, 327–342 (2005)
7. Weber, R.: Are attributes entities? A study of database designers' memory structures. Information Systems Research 7, 137–162 (1996)
8. Bodart, F., Patel, A., Sim, M., Weber, R.: Should optional properties be used in conceptual modelling? A theory and three empirical tests. Information Systems Research 12, 384–405 (2001)
9. Chen, P.: The Entity-Relationship Model–Toward a Unified View of Data. ACM Transactions on Database Systems 1, 9–36 (1976)
10. Kuechler, W., Vaishnavi, V.: So, talk to me: The effect of explicit goals on the comprehension of business process narratives. MIS Quarterly 30, 961–996 (2006)
11. Maass, W., Janzen, S.: Pattern-Based Approach for Designing with Diagrammatic and Propositional Conceptual Models. In: Jain, H., Sinha, A.P., Vitharana, P. (eds.) DESRIST 2011. LNCS, vol. 6629, pp. 192–206. Springer, Heidelberg (2011)
12. Kruskal, W.H., Wallis, W.A.: Use of ranks in one-criterion variance analysis. Journal of the American statistical Association 47, 583–621 (1952)
13. Parsons, J.: Effects of local versus global schema diagrams on verification and communication conceptual data modeling. Journal of Management Information Systems 19, 155–183 (2002)

Appendix: Questionnaire [Abbreviated]

C: concept. R: relationship, y: part of descriptions, e: extra entity (concept / relationship)

Ease of Use Modeling with a Particular CML (EoU-CML)
• Learning to use Entity-Relationship Diagrams (ERD) was easy for me
• Modeling with ERD is clear and understandable
Ease of Use Modeling with a Particular CML (EoU-CML)
• Learning to use Pre-Artifact Patterns (PAP) was easy for me
• Modeling with PAP is clear and understandable
Correct Concepts / Relationships [9]
• Mr. Jones is relationship manager [C][y]
• Mr. Jones manages financial portfolios [C][y]
Correct Concepts / Relationships [Total: 10]
• Total assets are discussed [C][y]
• Mr. Jones is adding todos [R][y]
Extra Concepts / Rels [Total: 10]
• Mr. Jones is a bank assistent [C][e]
• Mr. Jones manages family offices for clients [C][e]
Extra Concepts / Rels [Total: 10]
• Total assets are visualized [C][e]
• Mr. Jones assigns todos to his assistant [R][e]
Questionnaire: User Satisfaction with CM Understanding
• I am very *content* with my understanding of the requirements given by the narratives
• I am very *pleased* with my understanding of the requirements given by the narratives
• Overall, I am very *satisfied* with my understanding of the requirements given by the narratives
Questionnaire: User Satisfaction with CM Understanding [analogously]

Visual Maps for Data-Intensive Ecosystems

Efthymia Kontogiannopoulou, Petros Manousis, and Panos Vassiliadis

Univ. Ioannina, Dept. of Computer Science and Engineering, Ioannina, 45110, Hellas
{ekontogi,pmanousi,pvassil}@cs.uoi.gr

Abstract. Data-intensive ecosystems are conglomerations of one or more databases along with software applications that are built on top of them. This paper proposes a set of methods for providing visual maps of data-intensive ecosystems. We model the ecosystem as a graph, with modules (tables and queries embedded in the applications) as nodes and data provision relationships as edges. We cluster the modules of the ecosystem in order to further highlight their interdependencies and reduce visual clutter. We employ three alternative, novel, circular graph drawing methods for creating a visual map of the graph.

Keywords: Visualization, data-intensive ecosystems, clustered graphs.

1 Introduction

Developers of data-intensive ecosystems construct applications that rely on underlying databases for their proper operation, as they typically represent all the necessary information in a structured fashion in them. The symbiosis of applications and databases is not balanced, as the latter act as "dependency magnets" in these environments: databases do not depend upon other modules although being heavily depended upon, as database access is performed via queries specifically using the structure of the underlying database in their definition.

On top of having to deal with the problem of tight coupling between code and data, developers also have to address the disperse location of the code with which they work, in several parts of the code base. To quote [2] (the emphasis is ours): "Programmers spend between 60-90% of their time reading and navigating code and other data sources ... *Programmers form working sets of one or more fragments corresponding to places of interest* ... Perhaps as a result, *programmers may spend on average 35% of their time in IDEs actively navigating among working set fragments* ... , since they can only easily see one or two fragments at a time."

The aforementioned two observations (code-data dependency and contextualized focus in an area of interest) have a natural consequence: developers would greatly benefit from the possibility of jointly exploring database constructs and source code that are tightly related. E.g., in the development and maintenance of a software module, the developer is interested in a specific subset of the database tables and attributes, related to the module that is constructed, modified or studied. Similarly, when working or facing the alteration of the structure

E. Yu et al. (Eds.): ER 2014, LNCS 8824, pp. 385–392, 2014.

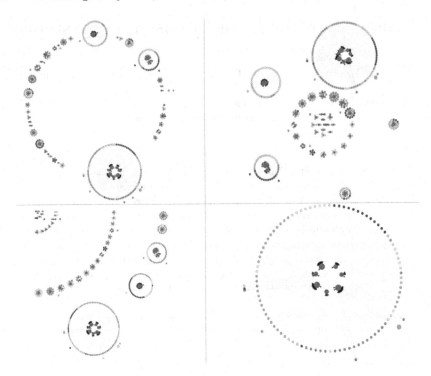

Fig. 1. Alternative visualizations for Drupal. Upper Left: Circular layout; Upper Right: Concentric circles; Lower Left: Concentric Arches. Lower Right: zoom in a cluster of Drupal.

of the database (e.g., attribute deletions or renaming, table additions, alteration of view definitions), the developer would appreciate a quick reference to the set of modules impacted by the change.

This *locality of interest* presents a clear call for the construction of a map of the system that allows developer to understand, communicate, design and maintain the code and its internal structure better. However, although (a) circular graph drawing methods have been developed for the representation general purpose graphs [11], [10], [6], and, (b) visual representations of the structure of code have been used for many decades [7], [4], [2], [3], the representation of data-intensive ecosystems has not been adequately addressed so far.

The research question that this paper addresses is the provision of a visual map of the ecosystem that highlights the correlation of the developed code to the underlying database in a way that supports the locality of interest in operations like program comprehension, impact analysis (for potential changes at the database layer), documentation etc.

Our method visualizes the ecosystem as a graph where all modules are modeled as nodes of the graph and the provision of data from a database module –e.g., a table– to a software module is denoted by an edge. To automatically detect "regions" of the graph with dense interconnections (and to visualize them accordingly) we cluster the ecosystem's nodes. Then, we present three circular graph drawing methods for the visualization of the graph (see Fig. 1). Our first method places all clusters on a embedding "cluster" circle, our second method splits the space in layers of concentric circles and our last method employs concentric arcs. In all our methods, the internal visualization of each cluster involves the placement of relations, views and queries in concentric circles, in order to further exploit space and minimize edge crossings.

2 Graph Layout Methods for Data-Intensive Ecosystems

The fundamental modeling pillar upon which we base our approach is the *Architecture Graph* $G(V, E)$ of a data-intensive ecosystem. The Architecture Graph is a skeleton, in the form of graph, that traces the dependencies of the application code from the underlying database. In our previous research [9], we have employed a detailed representation of the queries and relations involved; in this paper, however, it is sufficient to use a summary of the architecture graph as a zoomed-out variant of the graph that comprises only of *modules* (relations, views and queries) as nodes and edges denoting data provision relationships between them. Formally, a *Graph Summary* is a directed acyclic graph $G(V, E)$ with V comprising the graph's module nodes and E comprising relationships between pairs of data providers and consumers.

In terms of visualization methods, *the main graph layout we use is a circular layout.* Circular layouts are beneficial due to a better highlight of node similarity, along with the possibility of minimizing the clutter that is produced by line intersections. We place clusters of objects in the periphery of an embedding circle or in the periphery of several concentric circles or arches. Each cluster will again be displayed in terms of a set of concentric circles, thus producing a simple, familiar and repetitive pattern.

Our method for visualizing the ecosystem is based on the principle of *clustered graph drawing* and uses the following steps:

1. Cluster the queries, views and relations of the ecosystem, into clusters of related modules. Formally, this means that we partition the set of graph nodes V into a set of disjoint subsets, i.e., its clusters, $C_1, C_2, \ldots, C_n$.
2. Perform some initial preprocessing of the clusters to obtain a first estimation of the required space for the visualization of the ecosystem.
3. Position the clusters on a two-dimensional canvas in a way that minimizes visual clutter and highlights relationships and differences.
4. For each cluster, decide the positions of its nodes and visualize it.

2.1 Clustering of Modules

In accordance with the need to highlight locality of interest and to accomplish a successful visualization, it is often required to reduce the amount of visible elements being viewed by placing them in groups. This reduces visual clutter and improves user understanding of the graph as it applies the principle of proximity: similar nodes are placed next to each other. To this end, in our approach we use clustering to group objects with similar semantics in advance of graph drawing.

We have implemented an average-link agglomerative clustering algorithm [5] of the graph's nodes, which starts with each node being a cluster on its own and iteratively merges the most similar nodes in a new cluster until the node list is exhausted or a sued-defined similarity threshold is reached.

The distance function used in our method evaluates node similarity on the grounds of common neighbors. So, for nodes of the same type (e.g., two queries, or two tables), similarity is computed via the Jaccard formula, i.e., the fraction of the number of common neighbors over the size of the union of the neighbors of the two modules. When it comes to assessing the similarity of nodes of different types (like, e.g., a query and a relation), we must take into account whether there is an edge among them. If this is the case, the nominator is increased by 2, accounting for the two participants. Formally, the distance of two modules, i.e., nodes of the graph, M_i, M_j is expressed as:

$$dist(M_i, M_j) = 1 - \begin{cases} \dfrac{|neighbors_i \cap neighbors_j|}{|neighbors_i \cup neighbors_j|}, & if \; \nexists \; Edge(i,j) \\[3mm] \dfrac{|neighbors_i \cap neighbors_j| + 2}{|neighbors_i \cup neighbors_j|}, & if \; \exists \; Edge(i,j) \end{cases} \quad (1)$$

2.2   Cluster Preprocessing

Our method requires the computation of the area that each cluster will possess in the final drawing. In our method, each cluster is constructed around three bands of concentric circles: an innermost circle for the relations, an intermediate band of circles for the views (which are stratified by definition, and can thus, be placed in strata) and the outermost band of circles for the queries that pertain to the cluster. The latter includes two circles: a circle of *relation-dedicated queries* (i.e., queries that hit a single relation) and an outer circle for the rest of the queries. This heuristic is due to the fact that in all the studied datasets, there was a vast majority of relation-dedicated queries; thus, the heuristic allows a clearer visualization of how queries access relations and views.

In order to obtain an estimation of the required space for the visualization of the ecosystem, we need to perform two computations. First, we need to determine the circles of the drawing and the nodes that they contain (this is obtained via a topological sort of the nodes and their assignment to strata, each of which is assigned to a circle), and second, we need to compute the radius for each of these circles (obtained via the formula $R_i = 3 * \log(nodes) + nodes$). Then, the outer of these circles gives us the space that this cluster needs in order to be displayed.

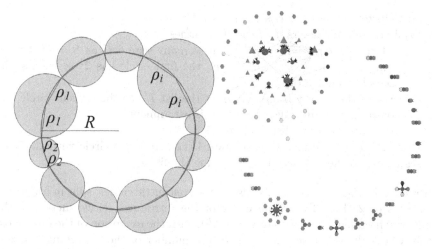

Fig. 2. Circular cluster placements (left) and the BioSQL ecosystem (right)

2.3 Layout of Cluster Circle(s)

We propose three alternative circular layouts for the deployment of the graph on a 2D canvas.

Circular Cluster Placement with Variable Angles. In this method, we use a single circle to place circular clusters on. As already mentioned, we have already calculated the radius r of each cluster. Given this input, we can also compute R, the radius of the embedding circle. We approximate the contour of the inscribed polygon of the circle, computed via the sum of twice the radius of the clusters by the perimeter of the embedding circle, which is equal to $2\pi * R$ (Fig. 2). We take special care that the layouts of the different clusters do not overlap; to this end, we introduce a white space factor w that enlarges the radius R of the cluster circle (typically, we use a fixed value of 1.8 for w). Then, $R = \sum_{i=0}^{|C|} \frac{2 * \varrho_i}{2\pi * w}$, where C is the set of clusters, and ϱ_i the radius of cluster i. As the arc around which each cluster will be placed is expanded, this leaves extra whitespace between the actually exploited parts of the clusters' arcs. Given the above inputs, we can calculate the angle ϕ that determines the sector of a given cluster, as well as its center coordinates (c_x, c_y) via the following equations:

$$\phi = 2 * \arccos\left(\frac{2 * R^2 - \varrho^2}{2 * R^2}\right), \; c_x = \cos\left(\frac{\phi}{2}\right) * R * w, \; c_y = \sin\left(\frac{\phi}{2}\right) * R * w \quad (2)$$

Concentric Cluster Placement. This method involves the placement of clusters to concentric circles. Each circle includes a different number of segments, each with a dedicated cluster. The proposed method obeys the following steps:

1. Sort clusters by ascending size in a list L^C
2. While there are clusters not placed in circles
   (a) Add a new circle and divide it in as many segments as $S = 2^k$, with k being the order of the circle (i.e., the first circle has 2^1 segments, the second 2^2 and so on)
   (b) Assign the next S fragments from the list L^C to the current circle and compute its radius according to this assignment
   (c) Add the circle to a list L of circles
3. Draw the circles from the most inward (i.e., from the circle with the least segments) to the outermost by following the list L.

Practically, the algorithm expands a set of concentric circles, split in fragments of powers of 2 (Fig. 3). As the order of the introduced circle increases, the number of fragments increases too ($S = 2^k$), with the exception of the outermost circle, where the segments are equal to the number of the remaining clusters. By assigning the clusters in an ascending order of size, we ensure that the small clusters will be placed on the inner circles, and we place bigger clusters on outer circles since bigger clusters occupy more space.

Radius Calculation. We need to guarantee that clusters do not overlap. This can be the result of two problems: (a) clusters of subsequent circles have radiuses big enough, so that they meet, or, (b) clusters on the same circle are big enough to intersect. To solve the first problem, we need to make sure that the radius of a circle is larger than the sum of (i) the radius of its previous circle, (ii) the radius of its larger cluster, and (iii) the radius of the larger cluster of the current circle. For the second problem, we compute R_i as the encompassing circle's periphery ($2 * \pi * R_i$) that can be approximated the sum of twice the radiuses of the circle's clusters. Then, to avoid the overlapping of clusters, we set the radius of the circle to be the maximum of the two values produced by the aforementioned solutions and we use an additional whitespace factor w to enlarge it slightly (typically, we use a fixed value of 1.2 for w).

$$R_i = w * \max \begin{cases} R_{i-1} + b_{i-1} + b_i \\ \\ \dfrac{1}{\pi} * \sum_{j=1}^{|C|} \varrho_j \end{cases} \tag{3}$$

where (a) b_α: is the rad of biggest cluster of circle α, and (b) ϱ_j: is the rad of cluster c_j which is part of C, where C is the set of clusters of circle i.

Clusters on Concentric Arches. It is possible to layout the clusters in a set of concentric arcs, instead of concentric circles (Fig. 3). This provides better space utilization, as the small clusters are placed upper left and there is less whitespace devoted to guard against cluster intersection. Overall, this method is a combination of the previous two methods. Specifically, (a) we deploy the clusters on concentric arches of size $\dfrac{\pi}{2}$, to obtain a more compact layout, and (b) we partition

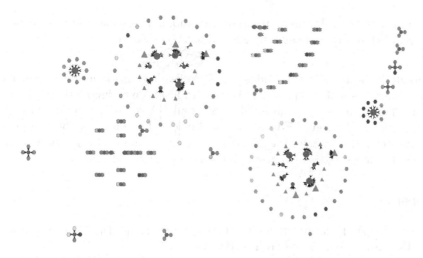

Fig. 3. Concentric cluster placement for BioSQL: circles (left), arcs (right)

each cluster in proportion to the cluster's size by applying the method expressed by equation (2).

2.4   Layout of Nodes inside a Cluster

The last part of the visualization process involves placing the internals of each cluster within the area designated to the cluster from previous computations. As already mentioned, each cluster is aligned in terms of several concentric circles: an innermost circle for relations, a set of intermediate circles for views and one or more circles for queries, as we previously stated at section 2.2. Now, since the radiuses of the circles have been computed, what remains to be resolved is the order of nodes on their corresponding circle. We order relations via a greedy algorithm that promotes the adjacency of similar relations (i.e., sharing the large amount of views and queries). Once relations have been laid out, we place the rest of the views and queries in their corresponding circle of the cluster via a traditional barycenter-based method [1] that places a node in an angle that equals the average value of the sum of the angles of the nodes it accesses.

3   To Probe Further

The long v. of our work [8] contains a full description of our method, along with its relationship to aesthetic and objective layout criteria and related experiments. Naturally, a vast area of research issues remains to be explored. First, alternative visualization methods with improved space utilization is a clear research area. Similarly, the application of the method to other types of data sets is also necessary. The relationship of graph metrics to source code properties potentially hosts interesting insights concerning code quality. Navigation guidelines (e.g., via textual or color annotation, or an annotated summary of the clusters of the graphs) also provide an important research challenge.

Acknowledgments. Prof. I. Fudos and L. Palios have made useful comments to an earlier version of this paper. This research has been co-financed by the European Union (European Social Fund - ESF) and Greek national funds through the Operational Program "Education and Lifelong Learning" of the National Strategic Reference Framework (NSRF) - Research Funding Program: Thales. Investing in knowledge society through the European Social Fund.

References

1. Battista, G.D., Eades, P., Tamassia, R., Tollis, I.G.: Graph Drawing: Algorithms for the Visualization of Graphs. Prentice-Hall (1999)
2. Bragdon, A., Reiss, S.P., Zeleznik, R.C., Karumuri, S., Cheung, W., Kaplan, J., Coleman, C., Adeputra, F., LaViola Jr., J.J.: Code bubbles: rethinking the user interface paradigm of integrated development environments. In: Kramer, J., Bishop, J., Devanbu, P.T., Uchitel, S. (eds.) ICSE (1), pp. 455–464. ACM (2010)
3. Caserta, P., Zendra, O.: Visualization of the static aspects of software: A survey. IEEE Trans. Vis. Comput. Graph. 17(7), 913–933 (2011)
4. DeLine, R., Venolia, G., Rowan, K.: Software development with code maps. ACM Queue 8(7), 10 (2010)
5. Dunham, M.H.: Data Mining: Introductory and Advanced Topics. Prentice-Hall (2002)
6. Halupczok, I., Schulz, A.: Pinning balloons with perfect angles and optimal area. J. Graph Algorithms Appl. 16(4), 847–870 (2012)
7. Johnson, B., Shneiderman, B.: Tree maps: A space-filling approach to the visualization of hierarchical information structures. In: IEEE Visualization, pp. 284–291 (1991)
8. Kontogiannopoulou, E.: Visualization of data-intensive information ecosystems via circular methods. Tech. rep., MT-2014-1, Univ. Ioannina, Dept. of Computer Science and Engineering (2014),
   http://cs.uoi.gr/~pmanousi/publications/2014_ER/
9. Manousis, P., Vassiliadis, P., Papastefanatos, G.: Automating the adaptation of evolving data-intensive ecosystems. In: Ng, W., Storey, V.C., Trujillo, J.C. (eds.) ER 2013. LNCS, vol. 8217, pp. 182–196. Springer, Heidelberg (2013)
10. Misue, K.: Drawing bipartite graphs as anchored maps. In: Misue, K., Sugiyama, K., Tanaka, J. (eds.) APVIS. CRPIT, vol. 60, pp. 169–177. Australian Computer Society (2006)
11. Six, J.M., Tollis, I.G.: A framework and algorithms for circular drawings of graphs. J. Discrete Algorithms 4(1), 25–50 (2006)

A Framework for a Business Intelligence-Enabled Adaptive Enterprise Architecture

Okhaide Akhigbe[1], Daniel Amyot[1], and Gregory Richards[2]

[1] School of Computer Science and Electrical Engineering, University of Ottawa, Canada
okhaide@uottawa.ca, damyot@eecs.uottawa.ca
[2] Telfer School of Management, University of Ottawa, Canada
richards@telfer.uottawa.ca

Abstract. The environments in which businesses currently operate are dynamic and constantly changing, with influence from external and internal factors. When businesses evolve, leading to changes in business objectives, it is hard to determine and visualize what direct Information System responses are needed to respond to these changes. This paper introduces an enterprise architecture framework which allows for anticipating and supporting proactively, adaptation in enterprise architectures as and when the business evolves. This adaptive framework exploits and models relationships between *business objectives* of important stakeholders, *decisions* related to these objectives, and *Information Systems* that support these decisions. This framework exploits goal modeling in a Business Intelligence context. The tool-supported framework was assessed against different levels and types of changes in a real enterprise architecture of a Canadian government department, with encouraging results.

Keywords: Adaptive Enterprise Architecture, Business Intelligence, Decisions, Goal Modeling, Information Systems, User Requirements Notation.

1 Introduction

Aligning business objectives with Information Systems (IS) to facilitate collecting, processing, storing, retrieving and presenting the different types of information organizations require has always represented a challenge. It has been observed that IS tend to be hard to use, are inflexible to the needs of the business, and fail to support or reflect the businesses they were designed to support; "*most information systems are technical successes but organizational failures*" [16]. Needless to say, CIOs of most companies agree that making IS simple and closely aligned to the business they support remains their uppermost priority today [21, 26].

The fundamental premise of an Enterprise Architecture (EA) is the alignment of the organization's business objectives with the IS that support them. Frameworks for EA design that enable alignment have been used for over 30 years [7], including the Zachman Framework for Enterprise Architecture, The Open Group Architectural Framework (TOGAF), the Federal Enterprise Architecture, and the Gartner Methodology [25]. Such frameworks and their companion methodologies, although used in

E. Yu et al. (Eds.): ER 2014, LNCS 8824, pp. 393–406, 2014.

over 90% of EA designs and implementations, do not seem to fully address the misalignment of IS to business objectives, especially from a decision-making viewpoint. These frameworks suggest that business objectives should be at the center of EA because these objectives define the information used to make decisions. However, the question of how the centrality of objectives allows organizations to adapt their architectures in the current dynamic business environment needs to be further explored. We recommend an adaptive architecture for the enterprise that links IS to business objectives, thus allowing for seamless co-evolution of the information structure. In such an architecture, the decisions made to achieve organizational business objectives should take priority in the design and implementation of IS structures. This is because these decisions influence the sourcing and subsequent use of information.

This paper introduces and illustrates a framework that links decisions regularly made by managers in achieving organization's business objectives to the IS providing the information utilized. This *Business Intelligence - Enabled Adaptive Enterprise Architecture* (BI-EAEA) framework consists of a model, a methodology and tool support [1]. The framework exploits goal, process, and indicator modeling and analysis in establishing links between an organization's business objectives and IS. It relies on the User Requirements Notation (URN) [4, 12] and jUCMNav [5] (a free Eclipse-based tool for analyzing and managing URN models), to model business scenarios, the stakeholders involved, their intentions in terms of organizational objectives, tasks they perform, and the IS that support these objectives. Processes and indicators measuring their performance (often obtained through Business Intelligence tools – BI) are captured, modeled and evaluated to anticipate and support architectural changes.

The rest of the paper is structured as follows: Section 2 provides the background on adaptive EA and highlights the need for the proposed framework. Section 3 discusses the methodology, types of changes that occur, and levels within the enterprise where adaptation is required. It also addresses tool support within jUCMNav for the framework. Section 4 presents the proposed model and illustrates its applicability. Section 5 discusses and evaluates the framework in a real-life case study. The paper concludes in Section 6 with a summary, limitations and future work directions.

2   Background

Information technology (IT) has transformed the way organizations deal with information used to make decisions, giving rise also to the use of different kinds of IS. Nonetheless, organizations still face the challenge of continually adapting to remain relevant in the face of changing business environments. The reality is that organizations are open systems that evolve through interaction with the environment around them [15]. To survive, some form of adaptation is often required (not necessarily automated). As the business adapts, the IS must also adapt and evolve its artifacts to meet new business demands either through a modification, deletion or an addition.

In providing a holistic view of the business, an EA should allow for maximal flexibility and adaptability [10]. In reality however, within the different domains of EA, there are different architectural practices and ways of addressing domain concerns.

These practices are characterized by varying degrees of maturity and different methods or techniques for handling the architecture. When changes in business objectives do occur, the resulting adaptive responses tend to be disparate, leading to local adaptations rather than to adaptations that serve the organization as a whole. This results from the heterogonous methods and techniques currently used in EA. Also is the lack of well-defined alignment between services delivered at every level of the organization, and of support for cross-organizational interaction [20, 30].

Current adaptive EA frameworks do not address these limitations. These frameworks focus on strategic assessment and adoption or decommissioning of technology in response to constantly changing business needs [9], while attempting to enable more adaptive IS, which in turn leads to organizational adaptability [29]. Others focus on the use of Service Oriented (SO) paradigms [20]. These SO approaches, while useful, do not directly solve the need to take a more holistic view where business objectives of stakeholders, decisions made by decision-makers, IS supporting processes and the relationships between them can be exploited for adaptability.

We propose an adaptive EA framework that enables a coherent view across the domains of the EA, while facilitating alignment of an organization's business objectives to daily operations and required information sources. This framework is modeled on a BI theme where information about business objectives and IS artifacts is continually gathered and delivered to decision makers for use in deciding on architectural changes. In its simplest form, BI is about getting data into a system to enable decision-making. BI helps organizations derive meaning from information and is especially useful in dynamic environments [19, 30] to support decisions (Fig. 1).

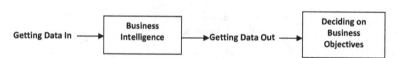

Fig. 1. Relationship between Business Intelligence and business objectives

The BI theme, therefore, refers to instrumenting of data used to make decisions. In this paper, the instrumentation relies on the use of URN and jUCMNav to better inform decision makers about the business objective, decisions to be made, the IS linkages, and the changes required as objectives and decision requirements evolve. The link from IS serving as information sources, to decisions made with information, and to the objectives the information is used to achieve, shows a clear opportunity to trace, monitor, and address change. This link also addresses the challenge of connecting insights from BI with enterprise decisions and actions as businesses evolve [19].

With this opportunity to trace, monitor and address change, the principles of business process modeling can be applied to show the relationships between the IS, decision makers, and objectives they achieve, as well as to show the changes and resulting responses (adaptation). URN is a modeling language that supports processes with Use Case Maps (UCM) [22, 28], goals and indicators with the Goal-oriented Requirement Language (GRL) [12], as well as goal evaluations based on strategies, i.e., initial satisfaction values of some elements in a goal model, including indicators potentially fed by external sources of information such as BI systems [3]. URN can also be tailored or profiled to a particular domain [2] through the use of metadata (name-value pairs for stereotyping or annotating model elements), URN typed links (between a pair of elements), and constraints in UML's Object Constraints Language (OCL) [27]. This set of characteristics of URN is quite unique among goal and business process modeling languages and it informs our choice of URN. In our BI/EA context, the use of URN enables one to model the relationships discussed above and observe and manage adaptation in terms of satisfaction levels of the IS, decisions, and business objectives.

3   BI-EAEA Approach

This section introduces the *Business Intelligence - Enabled Adaptive Enterprise Architecture* (BI-EAEA) framework, with its methodology, types of changes, and levels within the enterprise where adaptation is required. We also discuss tool support.

3.1   Phases and Steps of the Methodology

The BI-EAEA methodology consists of two phases ("As Is Scenario" and "To Be Scenario") and four steps (Fig. 2) and is iterative between the phases and their steps, as the business and architectural needs become clearer. The steps are in line with the evolution of an enterprise. The former phase represents the organization's EA as it currently exists and functions, while the latter indicates how the EA will be after the anticipated change due to the business or IS evolving.

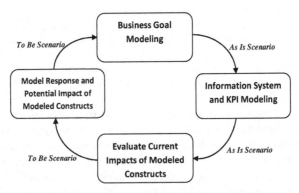

Fig. 2. Phases and steps of the BI-EAEA methodology

The first step (**Business Goal Modeling**) is to build the organization's business goals showing, with GRL, stakeholders and decision makers as actors (⌒⌒) with their goals (◯), softgoals (⌒⌒), tasks (◯, for decisions), and resources (□) utilized to meet business objectives. GRL links are also documented. In the second step (**Information System and KPI Modeling**), each IS that provides the information supporting decisions about the goals is modeled with a GRL resource. KPIs (⌒⌒) are used to model characteristics that indicate the performance level of the IS in alignment with business objectives of the organization. These KPIs are integrated with the GRL model of the IS. Evaluation strategies are developed to set context for evaluating KPIs.

In the thirds step (**Evaluate Current Impacts of Modeled Constructs**), each modeled IS is linked to the business goals using contributions ($\rightarrow$), indicating the extent to which the IS support business goals. This gives a depiction of the EA with links from business objectives to actions of decision makers to information utilized to meet the objectives. Each link is assessed to see the level of contribution or influence the source element has on the target. The satisfactions levels in GRL strategies are also checked to determine whether they are reflecting the "As Is Scenario" of the EA. Color feedback is used to assess satisfaction at a glance (the greener, the better).

In the fourth step of the methodology (**Model Response and Potential Impact of Modeled Constructs**), the anticipated "what-if" changes in the modeled business objectives, actions of decision makers and/or IS, are assessed to see the effects in the contributions to, or influence on, the satisfaction of other modeled entities, thereby indicating and informing the methodology users (typically an enterprise architect) of the anticipated changes in the EA, which allows for support as required.

3.2   Types of Changes and Enterprise Levels

The reasons for adaptation generally include responding to change in ways that make the new state more suitable for the revised/new use or purpose. In its application to EA, adaptation represents how the enterprise and architecture in place respond to various forms of changes (see below), which make the new EA more suitable:

- **Modifications:** Increase or decrease in importance or priority attributed to objectives, decision maker's actions, or IS.
- **Deletions:** Objectives have been achieved or are not needed anymore; decision makers are no longer involved; decision maker's actions are finished or are not needed anymore; or IS are decommissioned or have failed.
- **Additions:** Emergence of new objectives, decision makers, actions, or IS opportunity, with their importance or priorities.

We observe that instances of modifications, deletions, or additions occur in three levels within the organization, regardless of abstractions and consistent with the *goal-decision-information* (GDI) literature [24]. They are: in the business objectives of the organization (which we refer to as the *High level*), within actions of decision makers required to achieve these objectives (the *Decisions*), and lastly, in the IS that provide the information utilized in achieving these objectives (the *IS*). This representation can also accommodate many levels of abstractions for goals within the enterprise, an important consideration in performance analysis of EAs [6].

3.3   Tool Support: Pairwise Comparison of Business Objectives and IS

In addition to the complexity of processes within enterprises, we find techno-social and political paradigms to consider. These paradigms bring to the fore conflicts to be resolved among stakeholders whenever the issues of prioritizing objectives, taking actions, using information systems, or handling change arise in organizations. These conflicts, which relate to concerns about things such as context, interest, cost, relations, or structures, influence the importance and priority attributed to business objectives, decision, IS, and their relationships within the organization. The BI-EAEA framework uses the Analytic Hierarchy Process (AHP), in which factors are arranged in a hierarchical structure [24], to evaluate and identify the importance of levels and priorities. This approach helps accommodate and resolve the aforementioned concerns at play in enterprises by eliciting and aggregating quantitative measures for them. Although AHP has recently been used on goal models in other languages [14, 17], to our knowledge, this is the first use in GRL models, which support quantitative measures for contribution levels, indicator definitions, and actor importance levels. Different business objectives, decisions of actors, IS in place, as well as their priorities or influences, are compared against each other using AHP's pairwise comparison technique to get importance and contribution levels from stakeholders (e.g., architects), thus giving an agreeable representation of all concerns.

3.4   Tool Support: Well-Formedness Constrains

To ensure that models, including the organization's objectives and IS in place, together with their relationships, have been built correctly with respect to assumptions we make during analysis, they are checked against well-formedness rules that go beyond URN's basic syntax. These rules are constraints for GRL models designed in OCL and checked by jUCMNav [2]. BI-EAEA defines nine new OCL well-formedness rules in addition to a selection of 19 currently existing URN rules supported by jUCMNav. Examples of rules include "The elements of the Information System must not receive contributions from other actors" and "The sum of the importance values of the intentional elements of an actor must not be higher than 100". These 28 rules are part of a URN profile for Adaptive EA. Once models are created with the methodology from Section 3.1, they are checked against these rules to ensure conformity to the style expected for the analysis. jUCMNav reports violating model elements, if any.

4   Illustrative Example

To illustrate the BI-EAEA framework, we apply the approach to a business unit involved in administering grants within a large government organization. This is a highly dynamic business unit influenced by continually changing policies and a frequently evolving Information Technology landscape as new IS technologies emerge.

4.1   The As Is Scenario

The methodology starts out with the first phase, the "As Is Scenario", by modeling the organization's current business objectives, decision maker's actions and IS that provide the information utilized to achieve them, using the GRL notation.

In the **first step** of the methodology (Business Goal Modeling), based on the organization's priority, requirements and relative importance of respective goals, the corresponding process that satisfies high priority requirements and goals is selected as targets for modeling. In modeling the business goals of the organization, the extensive work that exists on modeling organizations using GRL and UCM (e.g., [22, 28]) provides a strong basis. From the process identified, the organization's business analysts model goals, softgoals, tasks and resources along with their links, current importance levels and priorities, for each selected process. The AHP pairwise comparison approach described in Section 3.3 is used for quantifying contribution levels and importance values of elements in actors.

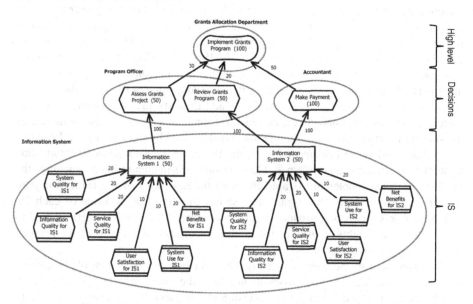

Fig. 3. GRL model example of a Grants Implementation Program

The top half of Fig. 3 illustrates a partial GRL model of the department's grants implementation program. The model contains the business objective of the organization represented as a softgoal Implement Grants Program with a 100 importance level (on a 0-100 scale). This is an objective of the actor Grants Allocation Department in the *High level* view of the model. The other stakeholders associated with this objective are the decision makers represented as actors, Program Officer and Accountant, in the *Decisions level*. Both actors have different tasks that they act upon utilizing different resources, to be defined in the next step. The tasks each have an importance level, summing up to 100 for each actor, in conformity to OCL rules as discussed in Section 3.4. Respective contribution weights are also illustrated, and they too sum up to 100 for each target intentional element.

The **second step** of the methodology is the modeling of the Information Systems (IS) themselves, including their KPIs. Ideally, the modeling procedure utilized in the previous step [22, 28] should be sufficient. However, the representation of IS in goal-modeling notations such as URN is mainly about the individual functions of an IS and its effects; they are not represented as whole entities, i.e., an accumulation of all functions with their resultant effects. We introduce a different way of modeling IS by representing them along the line of *"...how aligned the Information System is with the organization's business objectives, as it performs its required functions"*. Using the AHP pairwise comparison approach again, stakeholders can agree and model the individual IS as a whole and not based on their functions, in ways they agree the IS performance is in alignment to the organization's business objectives.

We use the performance characteristics that IS possess to do this. The former also indicate how IS are considered and judged to be of benefit by organizations. We therefore represent IS as GRL *resources* with *indicators* inside a single Information System actor. In providing information that is utilized to achieve goals, they act as resources. Indicators are used to quantify IS characteristics. With such indicators, we can show how well organizations perceive the IS to be performing and, in doing so, how they are meeting desired business objectives, a measure of the IS-objectives alignment. When business objectives change and adaptation is required, the modeler can observe how the IS currently performs and quantify the performance level required to meet the new objectives. For each information system, we use as indicators the six characteristics for measuring IS success described by DeLone and McLean [8].

As illustrated at the bottom of Fig. 3, the IS actor has two resources: Information System 1 and Information System 2. They provide information utilized to achieve the business objective Implement Grants Program through tasks of the actors Program Officer and Accountant. This figure also shows the six characteristics of each IS, which measures the IS performance level via weighted contributions. AHP is used to determine these weights, as well as the definitions of each indicator (i.e., their target, threshold, and worst case values).

The **third step** in the methodology is the evaluation or assessment of the current state of the modeled EA. Such assessment shows the satisfaction levels of the modeled business objectives, decisions of decision makers, and IS performing in line with business objectives.

First, the model is checked against the OCL rules described in Section 3.4 to ensure it was built correctly. Then, GRL strategies are used to evaluate the degree of satisfaction or dissatisfaction of the model elements. These strategies define a set of initial values for the leaf elements of the GRL model (in this case the KPIs), and the values are then propagated to the decisions and high level's intentional elements in order to compute their satisfaction levels, using a bottom-up quantitative propagation algorithm [3]. Fig. 4 illustrates the evaluated GRL model (indicating *IS*, *Decision*, and *High levels*) for the as-is situation, with values propagated from the KPI. It indicates the current satisfaction level of the organization and its IS, on a 0-100 scale.

For the KPIs, the GRL strategies also have the value sets defined: the "Target Value" (used to specify the target the KPI should attain), the "Threshold Value" (specifying the least acceptable value for the KPI), and the "Worst Value" (specifying the maximum value of dissatisfaction for the KPI). The strategy also defines the "Evaluation Value" (specifying the actual measured value of the KPI). These evaluation values can be entered for the KPIs in jUCMNav manually, imported through an Excel sheet (e.g., based on survey results), or derived and fed in from BI tools assessing the specific characteristics by the organization to generate a satisfaction value. Each indicator uses linear interpolation to compute a satisfaction level from an evaluation

(100 for target or better, 50 for the threshold, and 0 for the worst value or even worse). For example, if the target system use is 250 hours per month (hpm), with a threshold of 200hpm and a worst-case situation of 50hpm, then a measured usage of 225 hpm will result in a satisfaction of 75 (midway between the target and threshold) whereas a measured usage of 45 hpm will result in a satisfaction of 0 (below the worst value).

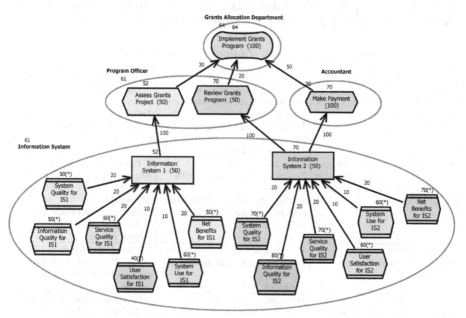

Fig. 4. Sample model showing current satisfaction levels of the IS, Decision Maker's and High Level

4.2   The To Be Scenario

The second phase of the methodology shows how the model responds to the needs for change in the enterprise. It also presents the adapted state, showing the impact of these changes. As described in Section 3.2, these adaptations are observed as modifications, deletions or additions in the three levels within the enterprise: the organization's business objectives (*High level*), actions of decision makers in achieving these objectives (*Decision level*), and the IS providing the information utilized (*IS level*).

Table 1, as part of the BI-EAEA methodology, provides a summary of identified changes and the steps the model takes to adapt to them, as well as corresponding responses based on automation in jUCMNav. Some of the automation steps take advantage of advanced jUCMNav features such as strategy differences, a constraint-oriented propagation algorithm, and contribution overrides [5]. For example, from Fig. 4, a decrease (modification) of the current evaluation value of the System Quality for IS2 KPI, contributing to Information System 2, will result in an update of its satisfaction value (say, from 70 to 30). This change in turn affects Information System 2 and its ability to support the Review Grants Program task of the Program Officer and the Make Payment task of the Accountant towards achieving the Grants and Allocation

Department's Implement Grants Program objective. By executing the As Is Strategy with values indicative of this change as fed by the BI system or entered manually, the BI-EAEA model shows the resultant impacts of the change on the EA. If the satisfaction of these actors becomes too low, this might trigger a reassessment of the suitability of Information System 2 and perhaps the analysis of an update or a replacement. Such options can again be modeled as modifications (the "To Be" system), with evaluations assessed and compared through what-if scenarios.

Table 1. Summary of types of adaptation and automated responses

Change Need	Adaptation	Automation in jUCMNav
Modification of importance level of a High level, Decision level or IS level modeled intentional element.	1) Locate goal, decision or IS. 2) Increase or decrease importance level as required. 3) Check the sum of importance levels. 4) Execute As Is Strategy.	2) Pairwise comparison to compute new levels [3, 5]. 3) OCL rule checks violation [2]. 4) jUCMNav evaluations to indicate impact [3].
Modification of the contribution weights to a High level, Decision level or IS level modeled intentional element.	1) Locate contribution. 2) Increase or decrease contribution link. 3) Check the sum of contribution links to goal, decision or IS. 4) Execute As Is Strategy.	2) Pairwise comparison to compute new values. Use of jUCMNav contributions overrides for new weights [5]. 3) OCL rule checks violation. 4) jUCMNav evaluations to indicate impact.
Modification of the KPIs definitions or current evaluations.	1) Change in KPI values as fed by BI System (or manual increase or decrease). 2) Execute As Is Strategy.	1) Feeds from BI systems [22]. 2) jUCMNav evaluations (quantitative GRL algorithm [3]) to indicate impact.
Modification of the desired satisfaction level of a High level, Decision level or IS level modeled intentional element.	1) Locate objective, decision or IS. 2) Increase or decrease satisfaction level as required. 3) Execute As Is Strategy.	2) OCL rule checks violation. 3) jUCMNav evaluations (Constraint-Oriented GRL Algorithm) to indicate impact.
Deletion of a High level, Decision level or IS level modeled intentional element (their importance and satisfaction levels as well).	1) Locate goal, decision or IS. 2) Remove goal, decision or IS from model (in a *copy* of the model). 3) Check the sum of importance levels of actor's intentional elements. Also sum of related destination contributions links if applicable. 4) Execute As Is Strategy.	3) Pairwise comparison to compute new values. OCL rule checks violation. 4) jUCMNav evaluations to indicate impact.
Deletion of contribution links to a High level, Decision level or IS level modeled intentional element.	1) Locate contribution. 2) Set contribution link to 0. 3) Check the sum of importance levels. 4) Execute As Is Strategy.	2) jUCMNav contributions override. 3) OCL rule checks violation. 4) jUCMNav evaluations to indicate impact.
Addition of an actor, or intentional element or their contributions to a High level, Decision level or IS level.	1) Include actor, goal, decision, IS (and characteristics) or contribution link (in a *copy* of the model). 2) Check that they are linked. 3) Execute As Is Strategy.	2) OCL rule checks violation. 3) jUCMNav evaluations to indicate impact.

5   Case Study

We have used the BI-EAEA framework to model a real-life Enterprise Architecture, namely the "Grants and Contributions Program" of a large department of the Government of Canada. Based on discussions with personnel of the department responsible for their enterprise architecture, on program descriptions, and on existing business process descriptions, and using the AHP-based approach described in Section 3.3, we developed the "As Is Scenario" model composed of the business goals, decisions, IS, and KPIs. We also collected realistic data to provide the model with an "As Is" strategy, enabling its evaluation. The jUCMNav size metrics indicate that the model, which represents the head and provincial offices involved in the program, is non-trivial. It is composed of 4 diagrams, 8 actors, 40 intentional elements (12 goals, 9 softgoals, 8 tasks, and 11 resources), 30 indicators, and 102 links. The model proved to conform to our 28 OCL rules. We then investigated one particular and likely "To Be Scenario", mainly based on a deletion, with the potential impact on the modeled constructs.

With the domain of adaptive EA relatively emerging, the work of Yu et al. [30], which proposes twelve key characteristics of an adaptive enterprise to gauge feasibility and effectiveness adaptive EA models should meet, was used to evaluate our methodology. To empirically measure and evaluate the BI-EAEA model, these twelve characteristics were operationalized as questions with a *Likert scale* styled response ranging from "All" to "None". The questions were administered to the personnel at the department (four senior enterprise architects) who were exposed to the model and the methodology. Their responses, summarized in Table 2 for all phases and steps of the methodology and the model's performance, are encouraging and show no apparent major weakness. Informal but very positive observations on our BI-EAEA framework were also provided by these senior enterprise architects:

- They liked the presence of the three levels; from experience, much time is spent working at the Decisions level, to adapt to changes in (and negotiate with) the High level and the IS level. The importance of the Decision level is often underestimated, yet this is where "magic happens", as they mentioned. The links between the three levels is where the real value of this framework rests.
- With the increasing need for numbers and quantities in organizations, the KPIs and satisfaction values could likely help accommodate this.
- There is a risk to spend much time documenting the "As Is" enterprise architecture in many approaches, and little value is seen in this from their experience. They liked BI-EAEA because investment in the modeling is minimal.
- The granularity of the IS could be changed too (and BI-EAEA could represent one or several functionalities or modules of a complex IS instead of the IS as a whole). The framework seems to accommodate this as well. This would also enable to better specify the links between particular IS functionalities and decisions, although at the cost of higher modeling effort.
- They liked that the URN-based modeling used reflects what is done informally right now. The framework can likely make this happen faster or more systematically, while providing a rationale for decisions. An earlier availability of EA models can also enable people to "disagree sooner", which can help avoid disappointments and failures in the long run.

- The models, with GRL strategies, could also be used as documentation trail for analysis and decisions.

Table 2. Evaluation of BI-EAEA characteristics (Yu et al. [30]) by enterprise architects

CHARACTERISTICS	MODEL RESPONSE					Weighted Average (Max: 5)
	All (76% - 100%)	Most (51% - 75%)	Some (26% - 50%)	Few (1% - 25%)	None (0)	
Diversity and Variability		3	1			3.75
Uncertainty and Commitment for known changes		3	1			3.75
Uncertainty and Commitment for unknown changes		2	2			3.50
Sensing and Effecting Change (known changes)	1	3				4.25
Sensing and Effecting Change (unknown changes)	1	2	1			4.00
Barrier to Change		3	1			3.75
Multiple Levels of Dynamics for documented change		3	1			3.75
Multiple Levels of Dynamics for ease of use of documented change		4				4.00
Dynamic Syst., Boundaries, Closure		4				4.00
Actor Autonomy and Alignment	1	2	1			4.00
Business-IT Alignment	1	2	1			4.00
Adaptiveness as a Business Requirement	1	1	2			3.75

6　Summary, Limitations and Future Work Directions

This paper discussed the Business Intelligence-Enabled Adaptive Enterprise Architecture (BI-EAEA) framework, which enables anticipation and support of architectural changes. The framework consists of a modeling language implemented as a profile of URN, a methodology, and tool support based on jUCMNav. The framework helps enterprises model the relationships between business objectives of important stakeholders, the decisions made by decision-makers in achieving these business objectives, the IS serving as sources of the information utilized by the decision makers, and indicators measuring six common performance aspects of these IS. Using GRL goal modeling and evaluation strategies within jUCMNav, these concepts and their relationships can be modeled and analyzed with the response and impacts of adaptation evaluated to further aid decision making in organizations. BI tools can be used both as means to feed the indicators enabling model analysis and as means to further visualize and distribute the analysis results.

Our BI-EAEA approach represents a significant step towards achieving adaptive EAs. BI-EAEA also stands out compared to common adaptive EA approaches [9, 20, 29] by a focus on goal and decision modeling, the systematic handling of various adaptations (caused by modifications, additions, and deletions at three levels of abstraction), and tool support for automating part of the adaptation analysis. BI-EAEA also conforms in part to the elements of the ISO/IEC/IEEE 42010 standard [14] required in the architecture viewpoints and the architecture description language (ADL).

However, several limitations were encountered along the way. We did not consider what triggers decisions as organizations decide about business objectives, but rather captured and treated decision as scenarios of "the business evolving". These scenarios were subsequently modeled adequately as adaptations. The construction of the questions used to evaluate the model did not have a comparison point for the result obtained. While we could have compared our results with an assessment of their current practices, informal discussions confirmed we presented a more rigorous and useful assessment compared to what they currently use.

For future work, since we covered only one case study, more enterprise architectures of different sizes and domains should be modeled and assessed, for generalization and to better understand the business situations that the framework can and cannot support. The department model explored here also did not take into consideration cost issues related to decisions, so a research question is whether cost aspects should be included in the model or handled separately. Although GRL was used here, some aspects of the framework could be transposable to other modeling languages, especially the Business Intelligence Model (BIM) [11] as it also covers actors, goals, indicators, and (limited) strategies. Better tool support in jUCMNav for automating pair-wise comparisons and AHP analysis (e.g., through generation of online comparison surveys) is something that would greatly enhance the usability of the methodology.

Acknowledgements. We thank the NSERC Business Intelligence Network for funding this project. Thanks also go to F. Pushelberg, A. Béchamp, E. Laliberté, N. Camacho, and S. Champagne for their time and support.

References

1. Akhigbe, O.S.: Business Intelligence - Enabled Adaptive Enterprise Architecture. M.Sc. thesis, Systems Science, University of Ottawa (2014),
   http://hdl.handle.net/10393/31012
2. Amyot, D., Yan, J.B.: Flexible Verification of User-Defined Semantic Constraints in Modelling Tools. In: CASCON 2008, pp. 81–95. ACM Press (2008)
3. Amyot, D., Ghanavati, S., Horkoff, J., Mussbacher, G., Peyton, L., Yu, E.: Evaluating Goal Models within the Goal-oriented Requirement Language. Int. J. Intell. Syst. 25(8), 841–877 (2010)
4. Amyot, D., Mussbacher, G.: User Requirements Notation: The First Ten Years, The Next Ten Years. Journal of Software 6(5), 747–768 (2011)
5. Amyot, D., Shamsaei, A., Kealey, J., Tremblay, E., Miga, A., Mussbacher, G., Alhaj, M., Tawhid, R., Braun, E., Cartwright, N.: Towards Advanced Goal Model Analysis with jUCMNav. In: Amyot, D., et al. (eds.) ER 2012 Workshops 2012. LNCS, vol. 7518, pp. 201–210. Springer, Heidelberg (2012)
6. Cardoso, E.C.S.: Challenges in Performance Analysis in Enterprise Architectures. In: 17th IEEE Int. EDOC Conference Workshops, pp. 327–326. IEEE CS (2013)
7. Cretu, L.G. (ed.): Designing Enterprise Architecture Frameworks: Integrating Business Processes with IT Infrastructure. Apple Academic Press (2014)

8. DeLone, W., McLean, E.: Information Systems Success Revisited. In: Proc. 35th Annual Hawaii International Conf. (HICSS 2002), vol. 8, pp. 2966–2976. IEEE CS (2002)

9. Gill, A.: The Gill Framework: Adaptive Enterprise Architecture Toolkit. Create Space Independent Publishing Platform (2012)

10. Hoogervorst, J.: Enterprise Architecture: Enabling Integration, Agility and Change. International Journal of Cooperative Information Systems 13, 213–233 (2004)

11. Horkoff, J., Barone, D., Jiang, L., Yu, E., Amyot, D., Borgida, A., Mylopoulos, J.: Strategic Business Modeling: Representation and Reasoning. Software & Systems Modeling 13(3), 1015–1041 (2012)

12. International Telecommunication Union: Recommendation Z.151, User Requirements Notation (URN) – Language Definition (October 2012)

13. ISO/IEC/IEEE 42010 Systems and Software Engineering - Architecture Description, 1st edn. (2011)

14. Kassab, M.: An integrated approach of AHP and NFRs framework. In: Seventh Int. Conf. on Research Challenges in Information Science (RCIS), pp. 1–8. IEEE CS (2013)

15. Kast, F.E., Rosenzweig, J.E.: Organization and Management: A Systems and Contingency Approach. McGraw-Hill (1985)

16. Laudon, K.C., Laudon, J.P.: Essentials of management information systems: Managing the digital firm. Prentice Hall (2005)

17. Liaskos, S., Jalman, R., Aranda, J.: On eliciting contribution measures in goal models. In: 20th Int. Requirements Engineering Conference, pp. 221–230. IEEE CS (2012)

18. Luftman, J., Brier, T.: Achieving and Sustaining Business-IT Alignment. California Management Review 42(1), 109–122 (1999)

19. Nalchigar, S., Yu, E.: From Business Intelligence Insights to Actions: A Methodology for Closing the Sense-and-Respond Loop in the Adaptive Enterprise. In: Grabis, J., Kirikova, M. (eds.) PoEM 2013. LNBIP, vol. 165, pp. 114–128. Springer, Heidelberg (2013)

20. Najafi, E., Baraani, A.: An Adaptive Enterprise Architecture Framework. In: Int. Summit and Conf. on Enterprises *as* Systems. Hoffman Estates, IL (2010)

21. Nash, K.S.: CIOs in Search of IT Simplicity. CIO (June 2012), http://bit.ly/1yZVbYT (retrieved January 24, 2013)

22. Pourshahid, A., Chen, P., Amyot, D., Forster, A.J., Ghanavati, S., Peyton, L., Weiss, M.: Business Process Management with the User Requirements Notation. Electronic Commerce Research 9(4), 269–316 (2009)

23. Prakash, N., Gosain, A.: An approach to engineering the requirements of data warehouses. Requirements Engineering 13(1), 49–72 (2008)

24. Saaty, T.L.: How to Make a Decision: The Analytic Hierarchy Process. European Journal of Operational Research 48(1), 9–26 (1990)

25. Sessions, R.: A Comparison of the Top Four Enterprise Architecture Methodologies. Microsoft (2007), http://msdn.microsoft.com/en-us/library/bb466232.aspx

26. Singh, S.N., Woo, C.: Investigating business-IT alignment through multi-disciplinary goal concepts. Requirements Engineering 14(3), 177–207 (2009)

27. Warmer, J., Kleppe, A.: The Object Constraint Language: Getting Your Models Ready for MDA, 2nd edn. Addison-Wesley, Boston (2003)

28. Weiss, M., Amyot, D.: Business Process Modeling with URN. IJEBR 1(3), 63–90 (2005)

29. Wilkinson, M.: Designing an 'Adaptive' Enterprise Architecture. BT Technology Journal 24(4), 81–92 (2006)

30. Yu, E., Deng, S., Sasmal, D.: Enterprise Architecture for the Adaptive Enterprise - A Vision Paper. In: Aier, S., Ekstedt, M., Matthes, F., Proper, E., Sanz, J.L. (eds.) TEAR 2012 and PRET 2012. LNBIP, vol. 131, pp. 146–161. Springer, Heidelberg (2012)

Modeling Organizational Alignment

Henrique Prado Sousa and Julio Cesar Sampaio do Prado Leite

Departamento de Informática, PUC-Rio, Rio de Janeiro, Brasil
hsousa@inf.puc-rio.br
www.inf.puc-rio.br/~julio

Abstract. In the world of business, even small advantages make a difference. As such, establishing strategic goals becomes a very important practice. However, the big challenge is in the designing of processes aligned with the goals. Modeling goals and processes in an integrated way improves the traceability among strategic and operational layers, easing up the alignment problem.

Keywords: Business process modeling; Goal modeling, BPM, KPI, i*, BPMN.

1   Introduction

Organizational alignment, a concept explored in organizational theory, has different patterns according to the viewpoint from which it is defined or from the standpoint of who define it [13]. According to Sender [14]: "Organizational alignment is the degree to which an organization's design, strategy, and culture are cooperating to achieve the same desired goals". It is a measurement of the agreement or relative distance between several ideal and real elements of organizational life. In the field of information systems, alignment has been researched in a more focused pattern, where the object of alignment is not the organization, but the relationship of IT processes with the organization needs [5]. Our work aims to fill a gap, that is; providing proper support for organizational alignment by means of conceptual models, since the work driven by the IT perspective, put more emphasis on the operational aspects. Studies [9], [12] believe that the lack of proper tools and notations to represent other layers, than the operational one, is a culprit on this limited approach. It could be also due to the inheritance of a historical workflow view and the consequent practice of, preferentially, working only at the "practical" details and analysis of the operational layer.

It is important to clarify that organization theory usually understand organizations in three decision levels: strategic, tactical and operational. As such, languages that focus just on processes leads to models focusing mainly on the operational decision level, whereas languages with more abstract concepts such as goals, are more apt to have models that deals with the other levels. Given this context, we frame organizational alignment as a way to have all three levels of decisions aligned, which of course may involve different patterns. As such, if models are used to help managing the organization alignment they need to have proper representations to different levels of decision. The invention of goal-oriented requirements engineering brought new

E. Yu et al. (Eds.): ER 2014, LNCS 8824, pp. 407–414, 2014.

capabilities for representing issues at the strategic and tactical level. Our contribution is the proposition of a conceptual model that seamless merges i* [18], Business Process Modeling Notation (BPMN) [10] and Key Performance Indicators (KPI) [2] as to produce a modeling language that addresses strategic, tactical and operational layers with explicit tracing among the levels. The merge of languages first addresses the lack of notations that support both process and goal modeling; second, maintains a more detailed traceability between the layers by using relationships in places where the languages intercept each other; and third, i* is used as the interconnection of the three layers, departing from the viewpoint of intentional actors. Actors, who may be agents, roles and positions, according to the i* ontology [18], are central since they link decision levels to organization structure. On top of that, we propose a new systematic way of using KPIs that helps evaluate business models alignment before performing them, and inserts an implicit link of traceability that helps identify crucial elements in the process. Providing a language with built in traces among different organizational decision levels contributes, we believe, towards organizational alignment.

2   GPI: A Result of Merging Different Languages

Sousa [17] departing from the works of [9], [12], and [16], surveyed and selected two languages (one from business process modeling and other for goal modeling) that offer better support to the process and goal modeling. In order to increase the capability of alignment analysis, the KPI element was integrated into the language with a proper representation. GPI (Goals, Processes and Indicators) is a proposal that merges, by explicit links, concepts of i*, BPMN, and KPI. The GPI proposal was implemented by reusing the Oryx [11], an open source tool. Oryx is an academic framework that permits the definition of new notations by using the Oryx language.

The main goal of the merger is to allow the construction of models, which explicitly answers the 5W2H questioning regarding organizations. Then, actors, pools (who/where), hardgoals, softgoals (why), resources, data object (what), process flow (when), tasks, activities (how), indicators (how much) are represented together with different associations among them, trough the implementation of traceability, leading to a built in alignment of indicators, processes and goals elements. We have approached the merger as follows: a) identify mappings between BPMN and i*, b) merge BPMN and i*, c) merging KPI into the union of i* and BPMN, forming GPI.

2.1   Mappings

In order to integrate the languages, we have mapped its elements. Other papers had already done some similar work, for example, [1] proposed a bi-directional mapping between i* and BPMN. However, it is hard to perform a perfect transformation between the proposals because of their significant differences. One difference we can mention is conceptual: i* offers a different vision, focusing on strategy and the relations of dependency between actors. BPMN present the sequence of activities (operational view) through a sophisticated workflow notation. Other important difference is that i* does not consider temporality, disabling the verification of **when** things happen, as such it is completely different from BPMN. Then each language has its specific contributions, making then strong when combined. Sousa [17] presents more details about i* and BPMN mappings considered in our proposal, and the changes applied in the notation in order to integrate them.

2.2   Merging i* with BPMN

The merging of i* and BPMN results on an architecture composed by the traditional goal and process layers, together with a new intermediate layer that is inspired in i*. This is the main difference of GPI. During the studies of alignment, we identify that not only elements to link the layers are needed, but also more details about actor's activities and its real correlation with organizational goals. Modeling languages usually resume information when linking different layers, thus lacking more expressive semantics about the links. It also does not offer resources to control the distance inserted by the abstraction applied in the models. Worse yet, our experience on business process modeling shows that organizations model their processes and goals a part, and also after everything is set up and being used. Macro and micro levels are modeled based on information extracted from different stakeholders, with different perspectives of business. Moreover, as bigger the company is, more far are the stakeholders of strategic and operational layers. The concern of alignment only appears at the end, when some answers could not be obtained just looking at the models.

The importance of the intermediate layer starts from the consideration that a process, in most of cases, reaches many sub goals in order to achieve the main one (or more). However, in order to verify alignment, it is necessary to have elements to be analyzed. This layer also permits the extraction of tacit knowledge when using the 5W2H framework as an analysis method. As such, it is possible to identify deviation of comprehension about: the role of the actor, the tasks he is performing, and what are his responsibilities inside the company. The 5W2H works by eliciting information from the viewpoint of actors, making the links between the layers more transparent [8]. GPI enforces a "meet in the middle" approach, considering the information obtained from the actor, it is possible to design a traceability link between the "lowest level goals" and "organizational goals"; and the "lowest level goals" and their "respective set of activities". We named these low-level goals as *Local goals*. Identifying and linking *Local goals* to organizational goals results in a decomposition that comes from low level and is extracted from the actor's viewpoint. These elements **meet in the middle** with high-level elements, improving traceability and helping to analyze the alignment. This is possible because of the detail of the connection **of each operational element** (how) and the respective business goal that **justifies** those actions in the processes (why). These elements, together, contribute to a more transparent model [8] that helps the alignment analysis. Fig. **1** shows the overall merging scheme, with the explicit pointers (as means-end) used for integration.

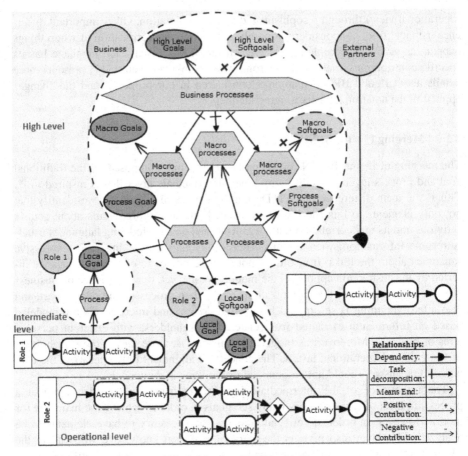

Fig. 1. Merging BPMN with i*

The i* model is "instantiated" in a manner to provide the necessary elements to GPI. In the higher level, i* is instantiated to represent business goals and macro process, considering the business as an actor (business view). Our merging approach maintains the syntax and semantics of both languages, and merges them using three mechanisms: the i* means-end link or contribution link [4], or the BPMN "assignment" (sign "+"), which denotes macro process. The basic merge is done at the i* task level, reflecting the fact that i* is a language suited for more abstract descriptions and that relies on tasks or ends, in a means-end relationship, to provide more concrete descriptions.

Note that the merging is performed over the detail of a given actor boundary, that is, the merging occurs within the i* SR (Strategic Rationale) model. Also note that the GPI language suggests the organization of goals following the levels of decision of an organization: strategic (high-level), tactic (macro), and operational (process goals and goals). The bottom of Fig. 1 shows the detail of the *Local goals* of "Role 1" and "Role 2". The example of "Role1" presents a *Local goal* linked (through means-end link) to a process that is detailed by an entire workflow (illustrated by two activities). In the case of "Role 2", *Local goals* are merged with BPMN by means-end and contribution links. Note that different set of activities are linked to specific *Local goals*. Worth noting is that this merge allows traceability between "why" and "how" at the operational layer. This is important because it links high level goals, actors and its activities, helping, for example, identifying responsibilities and propagation of impacts caused by problems or changes (impact analysis).

2.3   Merging KPI into the Union of i* and BPMN

Each organization goal requires that a set of conditions be satisfied or satisficed in order to reach goal achievement. The term "conditions" refers, for example, to the development of a product, a state of the process, the production of some information, start of a specific event, and any other thing reached from the performing of process, including quality goals. These conditions expected for one goal are defined by elements named as "Indicators".

The GPI business process layer maps a set of activities that must be performed in order to accomplish a process. It shows how acts are performed to produce the expected conditions in order to achieve the goals related to a given process. As such, indicators are defined according to goals in the goal layers of GPI (high level goals, macro goals, process goals and *Local goals*). It is understood that the indicators are gauged during process execution, showing whether the process has indeed produced the expected, which is defined though the indicators.

Therefore, indicators can be defined through the elements that are developed along the process execution. Assuming that the process produces the necessary information (*Critical resources*) for the indicators to be calculated, we can infer that: a) the indicators can be calculated. b) If the indicators are satisfied, one can assume that the process is effective.

Failing to produce an indicator or an indicator that misses the expected value or range of values, points to problems in goal achievement, **indicating a misalignment in the organization.**

3   An Example of GPI

The GPI proposal was evaluated through a systematic method as shown in [10]. In this work, we present a simpler example in order to facilitate comprehension. Fig. 2 exemplifies the relation of a business process, goals and its indicators in the "Integrated Diagram". The goals are defined from the viewpoint of the main actor (General attendant). The layer of macro goals and process was not considered in this case.

The General attendant has two goals: one consists on meeting the customers quickly, and other on maintaining the unsuccessful assistances rates less than 10%. The first goal has the indicator "Average response time" that calculates the average time of assistances. If the average is less or equal to the established time as "quickly", this goal is considered satisfied. In this case, the *Critical resource* is the average of time extracted from the assistance records. To verify the satisfaction of the hardgoal "Unsuccessful assistances be less than 10%" the indicator is "Percentage of unsuccessful attendance". The goal is met if the number of assistances is less or equal to 10% considering all the assistances registered. To satisfy these goals, the General Attendant must perform the task "Assist client". This task is executed by performing the process "Perform presence attendance to external customers" or "Perform telephone assistance to external customers". In the integration of models, the process "Perform presence attendance to external customers" was detailed. In this process, it is possible to identify the production of the *Critical resource* "Assistance recording", needed to calculate the indicator "Average response time", and also one of the resources needed to calculate the indicator "Percentage of unsuccessful attendance". But it is not possible to identify the *Critical resource* "Unsuccessful attendance". Then it is possible to conclude that the process is not able to produce the resources to verify if the goal "Unsuccessful assistances be less than 10%" is reached or not, what demonstrates the misalignment between the process and its goal.

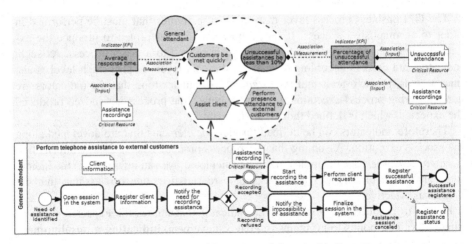

Fig. 2. The *Integrated Diagram* and the use of indicators

4   Related Work

The URN [6] is one of the most important proposals toward the goal and business process alignment. URN is composed by two languages: GRL (to model goals) and UCM (Use Case Map, to model business process). Comparing both proposal in terms of alignment between business process and goals, URN keeps the traceability between the layers through the "Realization link" that interconnect the goal with its respective process. GPI has two similar links (assignment and means-end links) that connect both layers, as show in Fig. 2. GPI also offers a relationship between a goal and a task, but in this case, representing a process activity. This link occurs at the lowest level, having different meaning from the relationship available in the URN.

The main difference between these languages is the intermediate layer proposed by GPI. This layer is responsible for increasing the traceability between the goal and processes layers by inserting a new activity in the modeling process that consists of investigating, from the actor's viewpoint, what are their goals inside the process they participate. These goals, called *Local goal*, links process and goals layers in a manner to make possible identify, for example, which activities, systems, roles and information are involved in satisfying a given objective in the highest strategic level.

Another important difference is that URN uses UCM to model business process, which was designed to model software scenarios, being adapted to model business process. Its graphical elements are very different from that usually adopted by business process notations, and there is a lack of important business elements like business rules and common artifacts used as input/output of activities. Conversely, BPMN is an international standard for business process modeling notation, widely used.

With respect to indicators, the KPIs proposal of GPI differs from others approaches [3], [7], [15] because it does not evaluate the process efficiency, but helps to evaluate alignment over business models. The use of KPI in GPI aims to demonstrate, in an early analysis (or, as we call, design runtime) what processes are necessary in order to achieve its goals. Our main concern is about defining the "inputs" to calculate the KPIs. These inputs implicitly represent what is expected (products) by the goals to be achieved by the process. The KPIs are not linked to the process, but to the goals, and they detail the goals by expressing what is necessary to satisfy them (or satisfice, in the case of softgoals). The quantification or qualification of how much the process is being performed, how goals and softgoals could be calculated and measured is not the concern of our approach. The analysis proposed does not cover the performance of process instantiation.

Central to our alignment proposal is the element *Critical resources*. They are elements that must be modeled as product of process (even if it is intermediate products). The identification of the absence of these key elements in the processes means that the related goals could not be measured and/or satisficed, what implies in the misalignment, because one element expected in the goal layer is not present in the operational layer. The existence of these elements in both goals and processes makes an implicit relationship that enables traceability between crucial activities, actors, systems and other element involved in the activity. With this, GPI improves the identification of weaknesses as well as the impact of possible changes in strategic goals.

5   Conclusion

Business process modeling is an important resource to the organizations, when it provides support for organizational analysis. One of such fundamental analysis is checking for organizational alignment. Our contribution is providing a language, where it is possible to model the strategic, tactic and operational levels in an integrated manner. The integration uses different levels of abstraction for goals upon which a strong tracing is provided. On top of that, the use of indicators makes it possible to check if desired results are being achieved in the design.

It is important to remember that the requirements engineering process may use business models as information sources in requirements elicitation [4], improving information system alignment. However, the organizational misalignment, if exists, will be propagated to the software. Therefore, it is proper to have early models aligned from the perspective of the organization.

Future work should trail three camps: evaluations of the GPI language/editor; application of GPI models in organizations, as to evaluate the use of GPI in modeling alignment problems (at the design time); and evaluation addressing monitoring of implemented processes according to the GPI design.

References

1. Alves, R., Silva, C.T.L.L., Castro, J.: A bi-directional integration between i* and BPMN models in the context of business process management: A position paper. ER@BR (2013)
2. Fitz-Gibbon, C.T.: Performance Indicators. Bera Dialogues, vol. 2, p. 111. Paperback (1990) ISBN-13: 978-1-85359-092-4
3. del-Río-Ortega, A., Resinas, M., Cabanillas, C., Cortés, A.R.: On the definition and design-time analysis of process performance indicators. Inf. Syst. 38(4), 470–490 (2013)
4. Fiorini, S.T., Leite, J.C.S.P., Macedo-Soares, T.L.V.A.: Integrating business processes with requirements elicitation. In: WETICE, pp. 226–231 (1996)
5. Haes, S.D., Grembergen, W.V.: Analyzing the Relationship Between IT Governance and Business/IT Alignment Maturity. In: International Conference on System Sciences (2008)
6. ITU-T, Recommendation Z.151, User Requirements Notation (URN) – Language Definition (November 2008), http://www.itu.int/rec/T-REC-Z.151/en (2012)
7. Kaplan, R., Norton, D.: The balanced scorecard-measures that drive performance. Harvard Business Review 70 (1992)
8. Leal, A.L.C., Sousa, H.P., Leite, J.C.S.P., Braga, J.L.: "Transparência Aplicada a Modelos de Negócio". In: Workshop em Engenharia de Requisitos, Brasil, pp. 321–332 (2011)
9. List, B., Korherr, B.: An evaluation of conceptual business process modelling languages. In: 21st ACM Symposium on Applied Computing, Dijon, France, pp. 1532–1539 (2006)
10. OMG, Business Process Model and Notation (BPMN), version 2.0 (2011)
11. Oryx, Site oficial Oryx, http://Oryx-project.org/research
12. Pourshahid, A., Amyot, D., Peyton, L., Ghanavati, S., Chen, P., Weiss, M., Forster, A.J.: Business process management with the user requirements notation (2009)
13. Powell, T.C.: Organizational Alignment as Competitive Advantage. Strategic Management Journal 13(2), 119–134 (1992)
14. Sender, S.W.: Systematic agreement: A theory of organizational alignment. Human Resource Development Quarterly 8, 23–40 (1997), doi:10.1002/hrdq.3920080105
15. Shamsaei, A., Pourshahid, A., Amyot, D.: Business Process Compliance Tracking Using Key Performance Indicators. In: International Workshop on Business Process Design (2010)
16. Sikandar-gani, S.B.: User Requirement Notation (URN). Graduate Student, Department of Electrical and Computer Engineering, Mississippi State University, MS, USA (2003)
17. Sousa, H.P.: Integrating Intentional Modeling to Business Modeling., Master's Dissertation, Departamento de Informática, PUC-Rio (2012) (in Portuguese)
18. Yu, E.: Modeling Strategic Relationships for Process Reengineering., Phd Thesis, Graduate Department of Computer Science, University of Toronto, Canada, pp.124 (1995)

Compliance with Multiple Regulations[*]

Sepideh Ghanavati[1], Llio Humphreys[2,3], Guido Boella[3], Luigi Di Caro[3],
Livio Robaldo[3], and Leendert van der Torre[2]

[1] CRP Henri Tudor, Luxembourg
{sepideh.ghanavati}@tudor.lu
[2] University of Luxembourg, Luxembourg
{llio.humphreys,leon.vandertorre}@uni.lu
[3] University of Torino, Torino
{guido,dicaro,robaldo}@di.unito.it

Abstract. With an increase in regulations, it is challenging for organizations to identify relevant regulations and ensure that their business processes comply with legal provisions. Multiple regulations cover the same domain and can interact with, complement or contradict each other. To overcome these challenges, a systematic approach is required. This paper proposes a thorough approach integrating the Eunomos knowledge and document management system with LEGAL-URN framework, a Requirements Engineering based framework for business process compliance).

Keywords: Requirements Engineering, Business Process Compliance, Legal Requirements, Multiple Regulations.

1 Introduction

Organizations need to comply with more regulations from different jurisdictions and domains due to the distribution of their services internationally. The cost of non-compliance is usually too high and can bring bad reputation to the organization. However, identifying relevant regulations, finding relevant provisions and complying with multiple regulations is not easy without specialist support. Although some official portals publish legislation online, Holmes[1] states that statutory law is not practically accessible today, even to the courts, since the law often exists in a patchwork of primary and secondary legislation, and there is no comprehensive law database with hyperlinks to enable the user, via a search engine, to find out all of the legislation on a particular topic.

Legal statements from different regulations may enforce the same rules, contain overlaps or even contradict each other. Sartor [21] explains the reasons as:

---

[*] **Acknowledgements.** Llio Humphreys is supported by the National Research Fund and Sepideh Ghanavati is supported by AFR - PDR grant #5810263, Luxembourg. Guido Boella is supported by the ITxLaw project funded by Compagnia di San Paolo.

[1] http://blog.law.cornell.edu/voxpop/2011/02/15/accessible-law/

E. Yu et al. (Eds.): ER 2014, LNCS 8824, pp. 415–422, 2014.
© Springer International Publishing Switzerland 2014

- a) the freedom of the legislator is limited only by procedural rules and new norms can be enacted that conflict with those already in force, with or without knowledge of norms that may be affected.
- b) the law has to deal with complex social contexts with conflicting interests. Balancing these interests are implemented through rules and exceptions. For unforeseen scenarios, the rule-exception hierarchy may not be explicit.
- c) legislation can be ambiguous. Traditional techniques of literal, systematic and teleological interpretation may lead to diverging results.

In this paper, we integrate Eunomos [4] with LEGAL-URN [7] to provide organizations with a method to find relevant regulations and then ensure compliance. Eunomos crawls the web collecting new regulations and translating them into legislative XML, then classifies the norms and relates them to existing legislation via similarity metrics and cross-reference analysis. When the relevant regulations are selected, the interaction between multiple legal statements are captured with the pairwise comparison algorithm of LEGAL-URN [8]. The detail about the integration of the two systems has been discussed in [2]. In Section 2, we discuss our method for business process compliance with multiple regulations and in Section 3 we analyze and discuss our method through a case study. Section 4 provides related work and Section 5 our conclusions and future work.

2   An Integrated Approach to Business Process Compliance with Multiple Regulations

We follow the steps proposed in LEGAL-URN framework [8] to ensure business process compliance with multiple regulations:

2.1   Step 1- Identify Relevant Regulations Based on the Business Process Domain

Finding Related Legislation Using Text Similarity: For each piece of legislation, Eunomos generates a list of the most similar pieces of legislation in its repository using Cosine Similarity. We avoid a naive solution of using an arbitrarily fixed cutoff k, where only the first k articles are considered relevant. Instead, we separate the truly similar articles from the rest by finding where the similarity values suffer a significant fall, following similar work in [5].

2.2   Step 2 - Identify Relevant Parts of the Regulations

Determining Topic of Legislative Articles: Eunomos contains a classification module to find which domains are relevant to the legislation, and to identify which domain each article belongs to, based on the well-known Support Vector Machines (SVM) algorithm [13]. Transforming text into vectors requires selection of suitable terms, and use of a weighting function as part of the frequency calculations. We use the Term Frequency-Inverse Document Frequency

(TF-IDF) weighting function as proposed in [20]. This function takes into account both the frequency of a term in a text and how the characteristic the term is of a particular class. In the literature, many systems improve on SVM and the entire bag of words, by using lists of stopwords and external resources such as WordNet to extract the lemmas. The drawback of such a general approach is that top-domain ontologies are unable to recognize and lemmatize many legal domain-specific terms. Our solution is to use a dependency parser called TULE [17] that performs a deep analysis over the syntactic structure of the sentences. Our classification module works reasonably well for classifying individual pieces of legislation as well as individual articles within legislation - which is useful for legislation that cover a range of different topics. The Eunomos user interface makes it possible to view only articles belonging to a selected domain. **Explicit and Implicit References:** The interaction between norms are often catered for by explicit references that clearly delineate norms that modify or override existing legislation. The Eunomos software uses the ITTIG CNR XM-Leges parser (http://www.xmleges.org/ita/) to automatically find references to articles in other legislation and create inline hyperlinks within the legislation text. A knowledge engineer can then look at each explicit reference and denote its type: whether it is merely a simple reference or in fact modifies or overrides existing legislation. For explicit references that are missed by the automatic parser due to irregular textual patterns, a knowledge engineer can make links manually. The manual approach is also used where legislation fails to mention which existing legislation it modifies or overrides. A list of similar legislation (see above) can help find legislation implicitly modified or overridden. The Eunomos functionality to add comments about legislation and all its paragraphs and articles is especially useful for implicit modifications.

2.3 Step 3 - Develop a Hohfeldian Model for Each Regulation

A tabular representation of norms facilitates both indexing and representation in diagrammatic form, and are present in both Eunomos and Legal-URN. Table 1 shows the key elements of an integrated Hohfeldian model with Eunomos [2]. Integrated Hohfeldian models are currently created manually, but we are working on information extraction techniques to semi-automate their creation. In [3], we extract active roles, passive roles and involved objects (e.g. risks, location) using syntactic dependencies and Support Vector Machines. The extracted dependencies are transformed into abstract textual representation in the form of triples, a level of generalization of the feature set that collapses the variability of the nouns involved in the syntactic dependencies. The task is, then, seen as a classification problem where each term has to be associated with a specific semantic label given its syntactic dependencies.

2.4 Step 4 - Pairwise Comparison between Multiple Regulations

We compare newly added regulations identified by Eunomos and modeled by an integrated Hohfeldian model with existing regulations in the system. This steps

Table 1. Integrated Hohfeldian Models

Fields	Meaning
Hohfeldian Modality	duty-claim, privilege-no-claim, power-liability, or immunity-disability
Responsible Actor	the addressee of the norm (e.g., director, employee)
Beneficiary	the beneficiary of the norm (e.g., customer
Violation	the crime or tort resulting from violation (often defined in other legislation)
Sanction	the sanction resulting from violation
Clause	the prevision reworded as necessary to aid comprehension
Precondition	todo
=Postcondition	todo
IsA Relation	todo
PartOf Relation	todo
Exception Relation	todo
Norm Identifier	hyperlink to relevant provision in the source document
Cross-reference	todo
Stakeholder	todo

involves comparing pairs of statements from different regulations to determine whether they are independent, similar, complementary, or contradictory. We perform the pairwise comparison method to compare the elements of the integrated Hohfeldian model of Statement$_i$ of the first regulation with Statement$_j$ of the second regulation (Part a of Figure 1 as follows:

Statement$_i$	Statement$_j$
A$_i$	A$_j$
Mv$_i$	Mv$_j$
∀i C$_i$	∀j C$_j$
∃i P$_i$	∃j P$_j$
∃i Ex$_i$	∃j Ex$_j$
∃i XR$_i$	∃j XR$_j$

HOHFELDIAN MODEL	LEGAL-GRL MODEL
ACTOR	ACTOR, EXPECTIONACTOR
MODAL VERB	OBLIGATION, PERMISSION STEREOTYPE
CLAUSE	INTENTIONAL ELEMENT
PRECONDITON	PRECONDITION INTENTIONAL ELEMENT
EXCEPTION	EXCEPTION INTENTIONAL ELEMENT
XREF	CROSSREFERENCE IE

a) Anatomy of Comparison   b) Mapping between Hohfeldian Model and Legal-GRL Model

Fig. 1. Legal Statements Comparison & Hohfeldian Model and Legal-GRL Mapping

Case 1 - There is nothing in common between the two statements.
Statement$_i$ is dealing with different issue from Statement$_j$. Thus, all of the "clauses" ("verb" and "action") and/or some of the "exception" parts of each statement are different from each other. However, "actor", "modal verb", "Precondition" and "XRef" may not necessarily be different. Two statements can be directed to the same actor, have the same type of modality and be related to the same cross-referenced statement but have different concerns.

Case 2 - Both statements are similar to each other. Statement$_j$ contains an "actor", "modal verb", "clause", "precondition", "exception" and "XRef" similar to those of Statement$_i$. In short, Statement$_i$ ≡ Statement$_j$.

Case 3 - One statement is complementary to the other statement.
Statement$_j$ and Statement$_i$ have their "actor" in common or complementary. Both statements have at least one "clause", 0 to many "precondition"(s), "exception"(s) or "XRef"(s) in common but each statement has at least one "clause"

and 0 to many "precondition"(s), "exception"(s) or "XRef"(s) in addition to the common parts . "Modal Verb" for both statements are not necessarily similar but they are also NOT contradicting each other. $Statement_i \cup Statement_j =$ $Statement_i + Statement_j - (Statement_1 \cap Statement_j)$

Case 3' - One statement is a subset of the other statement. This case is the subset of case 3. In case 3, both statements could have additional clauses, precondition, exception or XRef, while in this case, one of them has an additional clause, precondition, exception or XRef. ($Statement_i \cup Statement_j =$ $Statement_j$) or ($Statement_i \ cup \ Statement_j = Statement_i$).

Case 4 - One statement contradicts the other statement. $Statement_j$ is in conflict with $Statement_i$ when both statements have a common "actor" and the "modal verb" and "clause" of one statement is in contradiction with those of the other statement. If the "precondition"s or "exception"s of the statements contradict each other, there is a conflict.

2.5   Step 5 & 6 - Develop Legal-GRL and Organizational GRL and Business Process Models

Based on the result of the comparison in Step 4, first, the Legal-GRL models are created. The elements of integrated Hohfeldian models are mapped to the elements of the Legal-GRL models. Part b of the Figure 1 shows this mapping. Then, the impact of the new elements on organizational GRL and business processes are analyzed. We now discuss the solution for each case from the previous section and the changes that are needed for the business process.

Case 1 - Since the two statements have nothing in common, the second statement is modeled in Legal-GRL (as discussed in Section 2.2). Both Legal-GRL models are mapped to the GRL model of organization. Since there are additional legal goals and tasks, business processes have to be modified to include new legal activities or a new business process must be developed to reflect the new requirements. The detail of business process modeling with UCM is explained in [23].

Case 2 - Compliance with one statement ensures compliance with the other. To avoid non-compliance in the face of change, both statements are modeled in Legal-GRL. The two models are interlinked via traceability links. As both legal statements are similar, business processes are unaffected.

Case 3 &3' - To enable change management, we model both statements in Legal-GRL but link only one statement as well as the complementary part of the second statement to the organizational model. Where both statements are complementary, there are additional legal goals and tasks that the organization needs to satisfy. The business processes need to be modified to comply with the additional activities enforced by Legal-GRL. Where a legal statement is the subset of the other, we have two options: 1) $Statement_i$ from regulation 1 is the subset of $Statement_j$. In this case, the new legal statement contains more goals and tasks than the original one. In this case, a new business process model shall be introduced with new set of activities or the current business process models shall be modified to reflect the additional constraints. 2) $Statement_j$ is the subset of Statement$_i$. Here, all the goals and tasks of the new legal statements are covered by the original one. No changes are needed for the business processes.

Case 4 - Complying with the first statement results in non-compliance with the second, and vice versa. To resolve the conflict, it is necessary to consult a legal expert. Analysis may show business processes are impacted and require changes. With the integration of Legal-URN and Eunomos, it is possible to enable users to explore case law to determine which norms prevailed before.

3   Case Study

We outline the viability of our approach with a case study in the health care domain. Our task is to find relevant regulations that apply to business processes for collecting, using or disclosing of the patient data for fund raising and for improving health care. Starting with 11 articles from a regulation called Personal Health Information Act (PHIPA) [12], we use the Cosine Similarity methods to find two more regulations, Freedom of Information and Protection of Privacy Act (FIPPA) [19] and Quality of Care Information Protection Act (QCIPA) [11]. FIPPA contains four relevant articles and QCIPA contains three.

After creating Hohfeldian models for these articles and performing the pairwise comparison, we find that most new articles are either not relevant to PHIPA or are complementary. Thus, a hospital's business processes can easily be revised to ensure compliance with the new provisions and by introducing new processes. However, there are three genuine conflicts. However, Article 2 of QCIPA helps resolve the issue: *"In the case of a conflict with other acts or regulations, this act prevails."*. Thus, conflicting provisions from other regulations are marked as obsolete. The more detail of this case study is discussed in [7].

This small case study shows the effectiveness and importance of our methods in one jurisdiction, where the hierarchy of norms is made explicit in the text of the relevant legislation. There are more complex scenarios than this, where the hierarchy is resolved by analyzing the principles behind legislation or case law. The exception relation mechanism in the integrated Hofheldian model allows the relationship between norms to be viewed at a glance, while Eunomos's extensive annotation features allows complex issues to be explained in more detail. Moreover, since Eunomos enables legislation to be analyzed in multiple jurisdictions and multiple languages, more complex cross-border scenarios can be accommodated with our integrated solution.

4   Related Work

The problem of compliance with multiple regulations and potential conflicts was neglected in formal normative reasoning, as many assumed the position of legal philosophers such as Kelsen that normative conflicts within the same legal system do not exist [14]. This position was challenged by [1] which used logic to describe prioritization of norms. Some attention has been paid to contrary-to-duty obligations i.e. a conditional obligation arising in response to a violation of another obligation, particularly for compliance management [10].

While there has been much work about resolving conflicts in software requirements, up to now, very little work has been done to address issues related to compliance with multiple regulations. Maxwell et al. [18] identify, analyze and resolve conflicts in multiple regulations via analysis of cross-references. The conflicts are determined with a set of heuristics and a set of guidelines. Gordon et al. [9] use requirements watermarking to analyze differences and similarities between statements. They identify union disjoint and minimum watermarks. It is questionable whether the minimum watermark is practical, as it might remove applicable norms. Siena et al. [22] extend the Nómos Framework to capture variability in laws. They analyze the compliance,based on approach which includes situations, roles and six types of relations.

Perhaps the most thorough work on normative similarity is that of [16]. Provisions are tagged with the stems of noun phrases, legislative definitions or glossaries from reference books. The similarity analysis core takes as an input the parsed regulations and associated features, and produces a list of the most similar pairs of provisions. No explicit mechanism is provided for handling conflicts. Another promising NLP approach for identifying related statements is Recognizing Textual Entailment [6], which consists in deciding, given two text fragments (respectively called Text T, and Hypothesis H), whether the meaning of H can be inferred from the meaning of T. Relations between statements are classified as entailment, contradiction or null (i.e. irrelevant). EDICTS [15] includes as input the probabilities of entailment between certain words.

5   Conclusion

We have provided a method for compliance with multiple regulations using Eunomos and LEGAL-URN framework. Our method covers selecting relevant regulations for the business processes, representing them in a structured format, performing a pairwise comparison between multiple regulations and resolving sets of norms before applying them to business processes. A small case study presented a proof-of-concept of our approach. Our future work will involve investigating the EDICTS textual entailment system [15] to help analyze the relations between statements as a first step towards pairwise comparison. With the help of Eunomos, we aim to create semi-automatic algorithm for such comparison.

References

1. Alchourrón, C.E., Makinson, D.: Hierarchies of regulations and their logic. In: New Studies in Deontic Logic, pp. 125–148. Springer (1981)
2. Boella, G., Colombo Tosatto, S., Ghanavati, S., Hulstijn, J., Humphreys, L., Muthuri, R., Rifaut, A., van der Torre, L.: Integrating legalurn and eunomos: Towards a comprehensive compliance management solution. In: Proceeding of Artificial Intelligence and the Complexity of Legal Systems, AICOL (2014)
3. Boella, G., Di Caro, L., Robaldo, L.: Semantic relation extraction from legislative text using generalized syntactic dependencies and support vector machines. In: Morgenstern, L., Stefaneas, P., Lévy, F., Wyner, A., Paschke, A. (eds.) RuleML 2013. LNCS, vol. 8035, pp. 218–225. Springer, Heidelberg (2013)

4. Boella, G., Humphreys, L., Martin, M., Rossi, P., Violato, A., van der Torre, L.: Eunomos, a legal document and knowledge management system for regulatory compliance. In: ITAIS 2011, pp. 571–578. Springer (2012)

5. Cataldi, M., Schifanella, C., Candan, K.S., Sapino, M.L., Di Caro, L.: Cosena: A context-based search and navigation system. In: Proc. of the Int. Conf. on Management of Emergent Digital EcoSystems, p. 33. ACM (2009)

6. Dagan, I., Glickman, O.: Probabilistic textual entailment: Generic applied modeling of language variability (2004)

7. Ghanavati, S.: Legal-URN framework for legal compliance of business processes. Ph.D. thesis, UOttawa, Canada (2013), http://hdl.handle.net/10393/24028

8. Ghanavati, S., Amyot, D., Rifaut, A., Dubois, E.: Goal-oriented compliance with multiple regulations. In: Proceedings of 22nd IEEE International Requirements Engineering Conference, RE 2014 (to appear, 2014)

9. Gordon, D., Breaux, T.: Comparing requirements from multiple jurisdictions. In: RELAW 2011, pp. 43–49 (August 2011)

10. Governatori, G., Rotolo, A.: A conceptually rich model of business process compliance. In: Proc. of the 7th Asia-Pacific Conf. on Conceptual Modelling, pp. 3–12. Australian Computer Society, Inc. (2010)

11. Government of Ontario. Quality of Care Information Protection Act (QoCIPA) (2004), http://www.e-laws.gov.on.ca/html/statutes/english/elaws_statutes_04q03_e.htm (accessed January 2013)

12. Government of Ontario. Personal Health Information Protection Act (PHIPA) (2004, 2011), http://www.e-laws.gov.on.ca/html/statutes/english/elaws_statutes_04p03_e.htm#BK39 (accessed November 2012)

13. Joachims, T.: Text categorization with support vector machines: Learning with many relevant features. In: Nédellec, C., Rouveirol, C. (eds.) ECML 1998. LNCS, vol. 1398, pp. 137–142. Springer, Heidelberg (1998)

14. Kelsen, H., Paulson, B.L., Paulson, S.L.: Introduction to the problems of legal theory. Cambridge Univ. Press (1992)

15. Kouylekov, M., Negri, M.: An open-source package for recognizing textual entailment. In: ACL 2010, pp. 42–47. Assoc. for Computational Linguistics (2010)

16. Lau, G.T., Law, K.H., Wiederhold, G.: Similarity analysis on government regulations. In: Proc. of the 9th ACM SIGKDD, pp. 711–716. ACM (2003)

17. Lesmo, L.: The turin university parser at evalita 2009. In: Proc. of EVALITA, p. 9 (2009)

18. Maxwell, J., Antón, A., Swire, P.: A legal cross-references taxonomy for identifying conflicting software requirements. In: RE 2011, pp. 197–206 (2011)

19. Ministry of Health and Long-Term Care, Ontario. Freedom of information and protection of privacy act (2011), http://www.e-laws.gov.on.ca/html/statutes/english/elaws_statutes_90f31_e.htm#BK63 (accessed November 2012)

20. Salton, G., Buckley, C.: Term-weighting approaches in automatic text retrieval. Information Processing & Management 24(5), 513–523 (1988)

21. Sartor, G.: Normative conflicts in legal reasoning. Artificial Intelligence and Law 1(2-3), 209–235 (1992)

22. Siena, A., Jureta, I., Ingolfo, S., Susi, A., Perini, A., Mylopoulos, J.: Capturing variability of law with nómos 2. In: Atzeni, P., Cheung, D., Ram, S. (eds.) ER 2012. LNCS, vol. 7532, pp. 383–396. Springer, Heidelberg (2012)

23. Weiss, M., Amyot, D.: Designing and evolving business models with URN. In: Proc. of Montreal Conf. on Technologies (MCETECH 2005), pp. 149–162 (2005)

CSRML4BI: A Goal-Oriented Requirements Approach for Collaborative Business Intelligence

Miguel A. Teruel[1], Roberto Tardío[2], Elena Navarro[1], Alejandro Maté[2],
Pascual González[1], Juan Trujillo[2], and Rafael Muñoz-Terol[2]

[1] LoUISE Research Group,
Computing Systems Department,
University of Castilla - La Mancha, Spain
[2] Lucentia Research Group,
Department of Software and Computing Systems,
University of Alicante, Spain
miguel@dsi.uclm.es, {Elena.Navarro,Pascual.Gonzalez}@uclm.es,
{rtardio,amate,jtrujillo,rafamt}@dlsi.ua.es

Abstract. Collaborative Business Intelligence (BI) is a common practice in enterprises. Isolated decision makers have neither knowledge nor time required to gather and analyze all the information for making many decisions. Nevertheless, current practice for collaborative BI is still based on arbitrarily interchanging e-mails and documents between participants. In turn, information is lost, participants are missed, and the decision making task yields poor results. In this paper, we propose a framework, based on state of the art approaches for modelling collaborative systems and eliciting BI requirements, to carefully model and elicitate the participants, goals, and information needs, involved in collaborative BI. Therefore, we can easily keep track of all elements involved in a collaborative decision, avoiding losing information and facilitating the collaboration.

Keywords: Collaborative systems, business intelligence, requirements, *i**.

1   Introduction

For more than a decade, Business Intelligence (BI) has been focusing on providing better and more timely information to decision makers, in order to improve the decision making process. However, isolated decision makers can only make accurate, informed decisions within their expertise field and within a time window. When making a decision that requires going beyond one's expertise or beyond one's available time, decision makers collaborate with others who can cover their weaknesses. Imagine the situation where a CEO had to develop a statistical model to analyze customers' habits in order to explain the recent increase or drop in sales. It would require that the CEO had strong technical and statistical skills and ample time that would have to be subtracted from his other tasks. Such scenario seems unlikely and, yet, current practice and support for collaborative scenarios in BI is to let decision makers communicate and share data with others as they can by sending and receiving e-mails,

E. Yu et al. (Eds.): ER 2014, LNCS 8824, pp. 423–430, 2014.

excel files, and so on [1]. Unsurprisingly, information is lost, participants are missed, and, as a result, the decision making process yields poor results.

Recently, literature has been focusing on enabling support for collaborative decision making within BI platforms [7,1]. From sharing data [7] to creating virtual rooms [1], approaches try to provide tools that allow decision makers to share information in an easier and more ordered manner. However, until now, no approach has been proposed in order to allow designers to model the collaborative tasks and information to carry them out and, thus, provide adequate support for these tasks.

In this paper, we present CSRML4BI (Collaborative Systems Requirements Modelling Language for Business Intelligence), a goal-oriented framework that is an extension of our previous work, CSRML [8] (Collaborative Systems Requirements Modelling Language), to support BI systems requirements elicitation, along with a recent approach for modelling business intelligence requirements [6]. It allows us to carefully model and elicitate user requirements and participants involved in both isolated and collaborative BI.

The remainder of this paper is structured as follows: Section 2 presents the Related Work in collaborative BI and decision making, BI requirements modeling, and collaborative modeling. Next, Section 3 describes our framework, presenting the metamodel and introducing the new elements by means of the application of our proposal in a case study: a collaborative Smart City dashboard. Finally, Section 4 presents the conclusions and future works.

2   Related Work

In recent years, the amount of information available has been constantly increasing. Big Data and Open Data initiatives have favored the rise of collaborative BI [5], as it is increasingly difficult that a single decision maker or analyst has all the knowledge necessary to make a decision.

In a recent survey [5], several approaches on collaborative BI were analyzed, establishing two well-differentiated groups. The first comprises the approaches [1, 2] that understand collaborative BI as the enrichment of existing BI systems by communication tools. The second group refers the collaborative BI systems focused on *partnership in data* (PD), where external partners get involved in the data provision process. The approach proposed in [7] introduces the concept of *Business Intelligence Networks* (BIN). Under this scenario, each participant in the network can share and query information from other participants in the network by means of mappings between information schemata. While technical advances enable support for collaborative BI, they would greatly benefit from an approach that adequately captures the information system (IS) requirements in order to ensure that the system is adequately built.

In terms of collaborative system requirements modelling, in [8] the authors present CSRML, a language that provides additional expressive capabilities to *i** [9] so that analysts can specify the requirements of collaborative systems. However, it was designed for general collaborative systems and, thus, it lacks the detail provided by BI and data warehouse requirements modelling approaches, such as [6,4], also based on *i**. These approaches allow to specify the rationale of each decision maker, as well as the information that the BI system must store in order to support the decision making process. For instance, Horkoff et al. [4] propose a complete framework for BI system design based on *i** and focused on the modeling of strategic decisions and the indicators to support them. In spite of the advantages, this work does not cover the issue of collaborative BI, therefore cannot be applied on collaborative BI systems design. The same applies to the other approaches [6]. Summarizing, current advances in collaborative BI could benefit from a requirements language that captures the requirements of the IS including the collaborative aspects.

3   CSRML4BI

In this section, we present our framework CSRML4BI. It is a Goal-Oriented Requirements Engineering language designed for modeling collaborative BI requirements. Similarly to CSRML [8], it allows specifying collaborative tasks and groups of actors, while modelling the system from a decisional point of view, like *i** for data warehouses [6]. Additionally, CSRML4BI introduces new constructs in order to enable designers to elicitate and specify information requirements involving single or multiple decision makers collaborating between them. We can see these constructs in the CSRML4BI metamodel (surrounded by a red dashed line), illustrated in Fig. 1.

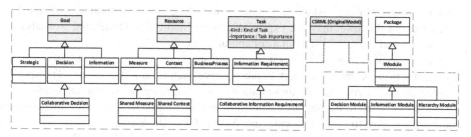

Fig. 1. CSRML4BI metamodel. Only extensions to the original CSRML metamodel are shown

In order to present the CSRML4BI a case study, namely a *Smart City Dashboard*, is used in the following. Smart City Dashboard citizens to analyze data and make decisions in a collaborative way in order to improve the public transport services focused on the urban bus. In the following sections, we will describe how we can model with CSRML4BI the requirements of this system

3.1   Actors and Groups

Taking into account that CSRML4BI has collaboration as one of its main cornerstones, *Actor* and *GroupActor* have been described in the language as follows:

- *Actor*: it is a user, program, or entity with certain acquired capabilities (skills, category, and so forth) that can play a role while it executes, uses devices or is responsible for actions. An actor can play one or more *roles* w.r.t. the IS being designed.

- *GroupActor*: it is a designator for a group composed of one or more actors whose aim is to achieve one or several common goals. By using this element, the representation of groups of users will be possible.

In the *Smart City Dashboard* there are several actors and groups involved. The "Council Member" and "Transport Representative" in our case study are grouped into the "Regional Transport Consortium". The members of the consortium collaborate at the same level, and thus have access to the same information in order to analyze it and make better decisions.

3.2   Roles

Actors can play one or more *Roles* when interacting with the system so that the same actor can be treated differently depending on the role it plays. A *Role* is a designator for a set of related tasks to be carried out. An actor playing a role can participate in individual or collaborative tasks (through *participation links*) and they can be responsible for the accomplishment of a goal (through *responsibility links*). Each relationship establishes a guard condition that must be fulfilled in order for the actor to play as the role. In our case study, the "Council Member" actor has only one role, whereas the "Transport Representative" actor can play two different roles.

The roles diagram describes the several ways that actors are involved in the system. The "Council Members" and the "Transport Representative" become "Consortium Decisions Makers" when they meet at the "Regional Transport Consortium". When playing this role, they are expect to use the Smart City Dashboard to analyze information and make decisions in a collaborative way.

Because some information owned by the transport companies is not initially available in the system, the "Transport Representative" actors can also act as "Transport Information Suppliers" sharing these data if it is required by the "Regional Transport Consortium". Therefore, they are responsible for sharing these data using their own company system to connect with the *Smart City Dashboard* system. This is represented in the role diagram by the guard condition "Company System".

3.3   Goals

Actors within the system can have one or more *Goals* to be fulfilled. As $i*$ states, a Goal answers "why?" questions. It describes a certain state of the world that an actor would like to achieve. However, a goal does not prescribe how it should be achieved. In BI requirements modeling, informational goals [6,4] are refined into several types, as opposed to traditional goals [8], resulting in *Strategic Goals, Decision Goals and Information Goals*. Given the increased number of goals, CSRML4BI simplifies the diagram by specifying only which *Actors* are responsible for achieving each *Strategic Goal*. The same actor is necessarily responsible for the rest of non-collaborative informational goals derived from them. This can be defined as follows:

- *Business Process (BP)*: it represents a business activity that decision makers wish to analyze in order to improve its results and, in turn, the business performance.

A business process can also be modeled by using specific business process notation, such as BPMN [10]. However, this is outside the scope of this research.

- *Strategic Goal (S):* it is a goal related to one or more decision makers aimed to improve a *Business Process* within the enterprise. It represents the highest level of abstraction in informational goals. It causes an immediate benefit for the organization when it is achieved.

- *Decision Goal (D):* it tries to answer the question "how can a strategic goal be achieved?", and represent decisions aimed to take actions that contribute to achieve the strategic goal. A decision goal does not represent the decision process itself, but the desire to make it possible. Decision goals only take place in the context of a strategic goal and do not provide a benefit for the organization on their own. It can be further specialized into *Collaborative Decision Goal.*

- *Collaborative Decision Goal (CD):* it is a *Decision Goal* that requires the *Collaboration* or *Coordination* of several *Actors* in order to be achieved. It represents decisions that must be made by a group, rather than by a single person.

- *Information Goal (I):* they try to answer the question "how can decision goals be achieved in terms of information required?", and their fulfilment helps to achieve one or more decision goals. Information goals only take place within the context of a decision goal.

The *BP* task in our *Smart City* case study is the "Public Transport". The "Regional Transport Consortium" group consider that "Minimize delays" at bus stops is a strategic goal that causes an immediate benefit to the improvement of the public transport. In order to achieve it, they need to make decisions about which actions should be taken to reduce delays in bus routes. For instance, to determine the number and location of the bus stops in a route is a decision goal, shown as "Set route stops" in Fig. 2, that has a direct impact on the possible delays. Since this decision requires collaboration between the members of the Regional Transport Consortium, we also mark it as CD (Collaborative Decision). We identified that two information goals are required to achieve this goal: "Unpunctual stops identified" and "Route duration analyzed".

3.4 Information Requirements and Context

In order to achieve the different information goals, decision makers need to perform certain analysis tasks using information provided by the IS. In our approach, we capture these special tasks by means of the refined task concept *Information Requirement,* allowing us to capture both the analysis tasks to be supported as well as the information that must be provided by the system being designed. Specifically, CSRML4BI identifies two kinds of information requirements:

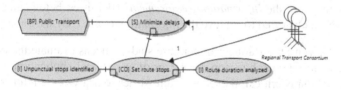

Fig. 2. Goals and information goals modelled in the transport scenario

- *Information Requirement*: it represents the analysis of information that the decision maker will carry out in order to achieve the corresponding *Information Goals*. It can be decomposed into other *Information Requirements, Contexts* and *Measures,* that must be recorded in order to support the decision making process. It can be further specialized into *Collaborative Information Requirement.*
- *Collaborative Information Requirement:* it is an *Information Requirement* that involves additional actors aside from the decision makers who require them in order to achieve their *Information Goals.* It can (i) simply denote the involvement of an additional actor with no additional consequences for the analysis, such as in the case of sharing information, (ii) specify a *Communication,* where one or more *roles* communicate between them, such as when a decision maker requests information from an analyst or a manager, (iii) specify a *Collaboration,* where all the *roles* involved interact with each other during the analysis, or (iv) specify a *Coordination,* where all the *roles* involved need to coordinate their analysis task.

In addition to tasks, *i** suggests to specify what *resources* a role needs to achieve a goal or execute a task. According to *i**, a *resource* represents the provision of some entity, physical or informational. In order to tailor this concept for collaborative BI systems, it has been specialized (see Fig. 1) into information resources as follows:

- *Context (C):* it represents information about a certain entity that needs to be captured and provided by the system in order to enable the analysis of the business process from a certain point of view. It can be aggregated into other *Contexts,* forming analysis hierarchies that will be implemented in the IS being designed. A *Context* can be further specialized into a *Shared Context.*
- *Measure (M)*: it represents numeric information that estimates in some way the performance of the business activity being studied and needs to be recorded in order to empower the analysis. It can be specialized into *Shared Measure.*
- *Shared Context (SC)*: It represents entity information that an *Actor* provides to the system, rather than captured by the system itself. Therefore, the existence of this information is a responsibility of the supplier.
- *Shared Measure(SM)*: It represents numeric information about a certain activity that an *Actor*s provides to the system. Its existence is responsibility of the supplier.
- *Awareness Resource:* It represents a perception need that helps a role to accomplish a task by providing the required awareness. It includes a set of attributes attached to a *participation link* between a role and a task. It shows all the Workspace Awareness features identified by Gutwin [3] that can be set with their importance according to the contribution they have to the accomplishment of a task.

All these concepts have been used for the specification of the Smart City Dashboard. With this aim, the *Information Requirements* (IR) listed below, and shown in Fig. 3, have been identified to achieve the *Information Goals* (IG) shown in Fig. 2:

- "Analyze Citizen Stop Rating": In our case study, citizens evaluate the occupation and punctuality of each bus stop, by means of an external application. Given that citizens' opinion is critical, the Consortium wishes to analyze the information provided by citizens. This information is represented by the measure "Average of

Punctuality Rating". The analysis also requires information about the "Stop" and the "Day"→"Month"→"Year" contexts. The consortium members require being aware of *who* is analyzing *what* stop in order to avoid conflicts. This awareness is specified by using an "Alert Panel" where all the added information is shown.

- "Analyze Service Information": the decisions makers of the Consortium have to analyze the information about the historical delays for each bus service to achieve the information goal "Unpunctual stops identified". However, the information resources about services are not initially stored in the BI system but they are owned by each transport company and need to be shared by the respective companies. Therefore, these resources are provided by the IR "Transport Information".

- "Analyze Transport Information": This IR encapsulates the task of analyzing the historical service information since it requires the participation of not only the analyst who is performing the task but also the information supplier "Transport Information Supplier", who is responsible for sharing and managing the shared information. The shared information is formed by the *Shared Contexts* (SC) "Service" and "Vehicle Type" (an aggregation of services), as well as the measure "Average Stop Delay" as *Shared Measure* (SM).

It is worth highlighting that the first IRs listed above are realized in a collaborative manner, so are modelled as Collaborative IR (CIR). The roles who collaborate in these IRs are the Consortium Decisions Makers, i.e. the Consortium members who use the dashboard system to make decisions about the public transport. Therefore, these CIRs capture the collaboration needed to execute the tasks for each *Decision Goal*, and establish the collaborative aspects that must be supported by the system. Furthermore, we have also noted how part of the information cannot be captured or stored by the system at hand, and, rather, it has to be provided by an external entity, such as the transport company. Thus, we are modelling here an inter-enterprise collaboration [7], where the actors involved share the information that is needed. As shown, we are able of identifying who is sharing the information, i.e. "Transport Information Supplier", as well as what information is being shared.

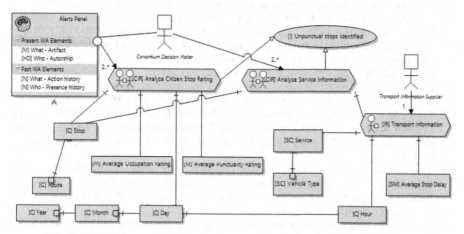

Fig. 3. Information requirements and their respective contexts in our scenario

4   Conclusions and Ongoing Work

Collaborative BI is a common practice in enterprises, although it is poorly supported by current tools. While recent proposals have been focusing on improving the technical support for performing collaborative tasks, they could greatly benefit from a requirements modelling approach that enables designers to specify the requirements of the collaborative system being designed. In this paper we have presented CSRML4BI, a goal-oriented framework for collaborative BI that allows us to model and identify (i) the decision making tasks that require collaboration across participants, (ii) the participants involved in a collaborative decision, and (iii) the information required or shared between them. We have shown the core elements involved in our framework and how they are applied to the specification of the Smart City Dashboard. Thanks to our framework, we obtain a clear view of the collaborative decisions to be supported by the BI system we can plan how to support them. Currently, we are working on improving the tool that includes graphical capabilities for the new elements introduced in CSRML4BI.

Acknowledgments. This work has been funded by the Spanish Ministry MINECO and by the FEDER funds of the EU under the project Grants insPIre (TIN2012-34003) and GEODAS-BI (TIN2012-37493-C03-03). It has also been funded by Spanish Ministry MECD (FPU scholarship, AP2010-0259).

References

1. Berthold, H., Rösch, P., Zöller, S., Wortmann, F., Carenini, A., Campbell, S., Strohmaier, F.: An architecture for ad-hoc and collaborative business intelligence. In: 2010 EDBT/ICDT Workshops, pp. 13–19. ACM (2010)
2. Devlin, B.: Collaborative Business Intelligence: Socializing Team-Based Decision Making. Business Intelligence Journal 17(3), 9–17 (2012)
3. Gutwin, C., Greenberg, S.: A Descriptive Framework of Workspace Awareness for Real-Time Groupware. Comput. Support. Coop. Work 11(3), 411–446 (2002)
4. Horkoff, J., Barone, D., Jiang, L., Yu, E., Amyot, D., Borgida, A., Mylopoulos, J.: Strategic business modeling: Representation and reasoning. Softw. Syst. Model., 1-27 (2012)
5. Kaufmann, J., Chamoni, P.: Structuring Collaborative Business Intelligence: A Literature Review. In: 47th Hawaii Int. Conf. on System Sciences (HICSS), pp. 3738–3747 (2014)
6. Mazón, J.-N., Pardillo, J., Trujillo, J.: A model-driven goal-oriented requirement engineering approach for data warehouses. In: Hainaut, J.-L., et al. (eds.) ER Workshops 2007. LNCS, vol. 4802, pp. 255–264. Springer, Heidelberg (2007)
7. Rizzi, S.: Collaborative business intelligence. In: Aufaure, M.-A., Zimányi, E. (eds.) eBISS 2011. LNBIP, vol. 96, pp. 186–205. Springer, Heidelberg (2012)
8. Teruel, M.A., Navarro, E., López-Jaquero, V., Montero, F., González, P.: CSRML: A Goal-Oriented Approach to Model Requirements for Collaborative Systems. In: Jeusfeld, M., Delcambre, L., Ling, T.-W. (eds.) ER 2011. LNCS, vol. 6998, pp. 33–46. Springer, Heidelberg (2011)
9. Teruel, M.A., Navarro, E., López-Jaquero, V., Montero, F., Jaen, J., González, P.: Analyzing the Understandability of Requirements Engineering Languages for CSCW Systems: A Family of Experiments. Inf. Softw. Technol. 54(11), 1215–1228 (2012), doi:10.1016/j.infsof.2012.06.001
10. White, S.A.: BPMN modeling and reference guide: understanding and using BPMN. Future Strategies Inc. (2008)

Embracing Pragmatics

Marija Bjeković[1,2,3], Hend*erik* A. Proper[1,2,3], and Jean-Sébastien Sottet[1,3]

[1] Public Research Centre Henri Tudor, Luxembourg, Luxembourg
[2] Radboud University Nijmegen, Nijmegen, The Netherlands
[3] EE-Team, Luxembourg, Luxembourg*
{marija.bjekovic,erik.proper,jean-sebastien.sottet}@tudor.lu

Abstract. In enterprise modelling, we witness numerous efforts to predefine and integrate perspectives and concepts for modelling some problem area, which result in standardised modelling languages (e.g. BPMN, ArchiMate). The empirical observations however indicate that, in actual use, standardising and integrating effect of such modelling languages erodes, due to the need to accommodate specific modelling contexts. Instead of designing yet another mechanism to control this phenomena, we argue it should first be fundamentally understood. To account for the functioning of a modelling language in a socio-pragmatic context of modelling, we claim it is necessary to go beyond a normative view often adopted in modelling language study. We present a developing explanatory theory as to why and how modelling languages are used in enterprise modelling. The explanatory theory relies on a conceptual framework on modelling developed as the critical synthesis of the existing theoretical work, and from the position of socio-pragmatic constructivism.

Keywords: Model, modelling language, language use, pragmatics.

1 Introduction

In the field of enterprise modelling, a number of *fixed* modelling languages, e.g. [31,32,23,53,17], is defined for creating models for different purposes. Most of these languages have the ambition to provide a standard way of modelling some problem area, for different uses and stakeholders. This promises to enable tool development and increase of productivity in modelling, to facilitate knowledge transfer and communication about the problem area, etc.

However, a growing empirical material indicates that, in actual use, the standardising effect of such modelling languages erodes. This can be observed in the emergence of dialect-like and/or light-weight variants of the original language, e.g. [55,29,13,7,1,34,27], and specific extensions of standards intended to deal with 'missing aspects', e.g. [23,8]. The empirical reports [1,7,27,29,37,55] suggest that such language variants emerge to compensate for the inability of fixed modelling languages to aptly fit specific modelling situations. In an extreme case, the practitioners favoured ad-hoc and semi-structured notations [29,1], despite the

---

* www.ee-team.eu

E. Yu et al. (Eds.): ER 2014, LNCS 8824, pp. 431–444, 2014.

loss of potential benefits. For instance, the preference of business architects for home-grown semi-structured models in early and creative phases of enterprise modelling is reported in [1], as they allow delayed commitment to syntax, and closer fit to the needed way of thinking.

While such compensatory strategies enable practitioners to overcome problems with modelling languages used, they also potentially lead to a redundant work. Moving from semi-structured models to more formal tasks, an additional effort is needed to enter them in a dedicated modelling tool. Likewise, more structured models need to be distilled into 'boxology'[1] to be communicated back to stakeholders [29]. This diminishes perceived benefits of using modelling languages, but also prevents further maturation of modelling practices.

In our view, the problem comes from the fact that language engineering efforts typically overemphasise the challenges of mechanical manipulation of models, and neglect the variety of contexts, users and purposes for which models need to be created. Adopting a utility-oriented perspective on modelling languages [33], we argue that this variety needs to be better understood and more explicitly accounted for in language engineering efforts.

We will argue that the value of a modelling language is inherently related to its use [33], and that the role of language in a wider socio-pragmatic context of modelling needs to be better fundamentally understood. To do so, we believe it is necessary to go beyond a strictly normative view often adopted in design and evaluation of modelling languages [46], and favour a broader perspective [14,49] in their studies.

The paper is part of an ongoing effort to develop an *explanatory theory* as to why and how fixed modelling languages are used within enterprise modelling. We present a matured version of initial ideas reported in [5,4]. This maturation refers to a clearer and explicit theoretical grounding of the framework, and evolved and consolidated reflection, supported with further theoretical evidence.

In the paper, we discuss our theoretical grounding in Section 2. Our fundamental view on modelling is presented in Section 3, Relying on this view, our theoretical understanding on the role of language in modelling is developed in Section 4. The next steps of this research are outlined in the conclusion.

2   Theoretical Grounding

Our research is motivated by a long-term desire to improve the design of enterprise modelling languages and frameworks, and to align them better with the needs of their (potential) users. Although fitting into a design-oriented research philosophy [19], in our research we do not aim at a design theory [18]. Our primary focus is on its *rigour cycle* [19], i.e. on an *explanatory theory* [18]. We expect that the explanatory theory feeds the knowledge base [19], and contributes to the foundation for a modelling language design theory.

---

[1] This term was used by one of the enterprise architects in exploratory interviews to refer to the informal diagrams created on the basis of more elaborated models for the purpose of stakeholder communication.

We justify the *relevance* of our research subject based on: (1) empirical reports on enterprise modelling practice, which identify the need to adapt modelling languages to specific modelling tasks, and pinpoint at the lack of such flexibility in existing modelling infrastructures [1,7,27,29,37,55]; (2) our own past experiences with UML [31], ArchiMate [23], i* [53] and e3Value [17] across different enterprise modelling tasks; (3) our observation of continuous extension and increasing complexity of ArchiMate and BPMN standards, contrasted to their practical usage [4].

In our research, we adopt an inherently *pragmatic orientation* on models and modelling languages. We see them as *means-to-an-end*, i.e. particular instruments that should provide some *value* when used for the intended goals by the intended users. We understand *models* as essentially means of representation of some socially constructed knowledge [45,51]. We understand *modelling* as the process of constructing, representing and sharing this knowledge between people involved, where communication has a fundamental role [12,22]. *Modelling languages* are studied primarily from the perspective of their utility [33] for constructing, representing and sharing this knowledge (through models) by the people involved in modelling. Such an orientation on the phenomena of modelling is strongly related to our choice of *epistemological* and *ontological position* of socio-pragmatic constructivism [51].

The explanatory theory is developed by combining *analytic* and *interpretative research*. As for the analytic part, the theory relies on our conceptual framework on modelling (Section 3), which is developed through a critical synthesis of the selected theoretical work [39,36,12,22,33,42,25]. Given the space limitation, the details of this synthesis won't be elaborated in the paper. Furthermore, our theoretical understanding of language functioning in modelling is grounded in functional linguistics [11,10], cognitive linguistics [16], cognitive science [48] and semiotics [40]. The presently developed theoretical synthesis is then coupled with a number of interpretative case studies. They should serve both as a preliminary evaluation of the theory, and the source for its further maturation.

Although some elements of the theoretical framework are general, and thus applicable to conceptual modelling, we empirically study the functioning of modelling languages only within enterprise modelling, and the empirical evaluation of the theory will only take place in this context. Therefore, we presently restrict the *application domain* of our theory to enterprise modelling.

3   A Fundamental View on Modelling

3.1   Model Definition

Our general model definition is inspired by [39,36,12,41]. In our view:

> A **model** is an artefact acknowledged by the observer as representing
> some domain for a particular purpose.

By stating that a model is an **artefact**, we exclude *conceptions* [12], or so-called mental models, from the scope of this definition. Conceptions are *abstractions* of the world under consideration, adopted from a certain perspective, and share this property with models. However, a conception resides in the mind of a person holding it, and as such is not directly accessible to another human being. To communicate the conception, it has to be externalised. While conceptions reside in mental space, models are necessarily *represented* in physical/material space. This being said, we do consider conceptions to be fundamental to modelling. This point is elaborated later in the section.

The **observer** in our definition refers to the group of people consisting of model creators and model audience. On one extreme, it can refer to the entire society, on the other extreme, to the individual. Though it may not be the general rule, it is very often the case, in an enterprise modelling context, that model creators are at the same time its audience. We take the position that the observer is the essential element in modelling. The discussion in the rest of this section provides support for this claim.

A **modelling situation** is *at least* characterised by the wider context to which a modelling effort relates (e.g. particular organisation, project), the involved observer and goals of modelling. Though the goals of modelling are not necessarily restricted to the goal of model creation[2], our immediate focus is on the latter goals, i.e. on model purpose.

Similarly to [12], we define **domain** as any 'part' or 'aspect' of the world *considered relevant by the observer* in the given *modelling situation*. The term *world* here refers to 'reality', as well as to possible worlds [15,52,28][3].

The **purposefulness** dimension of models is present in most model definitions, and is often considered as the main discriminant of the model value [39,36,41]. However, the notion of purpose is rarely defined, and its role in the modelling process is scantly discussed in the research. Based on [42,36,39], we currently understand **purpose** as aggregating the following interrelated dimensions:

(1) the **domain** that the model pertains to, and
(2) the intended **usage** of the model by its intended **audience**.

In other words, the reason why an observer creates a model in the first place is to enable some *usage* of that model (e.g. analysis, sketching, execution, contracting etc.) by its intended *audience* (e.g. business analysts, business decision-makers, enterprise architects, process experts, etc.).

3.2   Modelling Process and Role of Purpose

To discuss the role of purpose in the modelling process, we propose to identify its three essential streams: (see Figure 1): *abstraction*, *manifestation*, and *evaluation*. Though these streams are typically interrelated and not clearly differentiated in a real modelling process, this distinction is kept for analytic purposes.

---

[2] Particularly, organisational learning, achieving consensus/commonly agreed knowledge on a topic, are very important in enterprise modelling efforts [7,6].

[3] Even more, the domain of a model can be another model as well [39].

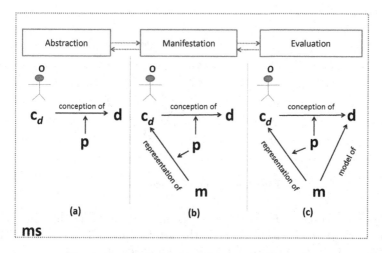

Fig. 1. Essential streams of the modelling process

Let us consider the proposed streams in a modelling situation **ms** involving an *individual* observer **O**, and the purpose **p**. This is illustrated in Figure 1. We assume here that **O** is aware of **p**, i.e. of intended use and intended audience of the model to be created, and more or less aware about the (possible) domain **d**.

Abstraction refers to the stream in which the observer **O** delimits the relevant 'aspects' of the world under consideration (i.e. domain **d**)[4]. The identification of relevant and *abstracting away* from the irrelevant 'aspects' of the world yields the observer's *conception of the domain* c_d and the relationship *conception of* (see Figure 1a). Note that c_d is in itself an *abstraction* of the considered domain, though not yet externalised at this point. It is also important to underline that the mechanism of abstraction, lying at the core of human cognitive capacities [44], is always *relative* to the cognitive task at hand [44,36]. So, in a modelling situation **ms**, c_d depends on the observer's judgement of the relevance of some 'aspects' of the world, relative to the wider context of **ms**, and the purpose **p**. In other words, we assume that the purpose **p** influences the creation of the relation *conception of*, as illustrated in Figure 1a.

As pointed out in [39], strictly speaking, the selection of relevant 'aspects' of the world does not always follow the purposefulness criterion. In our work, we assume that the observer tends to *purposefully* conceive the domain[5].

Manifestation refers to the externalisation of c_d in the physical space. The observer **O** tries to shape an artefact (i.e. model-to-be) **m** in such a way that

---

[4] In conceiving the domain, the observer is not limited to using only his/her senses to *perceive* [12] and interpret 'reality'. S/he uses all his/her cognitive abilities, including creativity or imagination, particularly when conceiving possible worlds [15].

[5] We exclude from consideration the potential conscious *political intentions* underlying the observer's judgement.

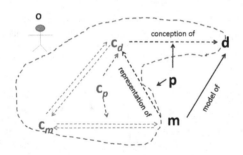

Fig. 2. Aligning of conceptions

it adequately *represents*, for the purpose **p**, his/her c_d. From this emerges the *representation of* relationship between the artefact **m** and the c_d. The Figure 1b illustrates both this relationship and the influence of **p** on it.

At this point, it should be noted that the observer's understanding of the purpose **p** is essentially a conception as well, i.e. the conception of the purpose of the model-to-be c_p. Even more, the observer **O** also forms the conception of the model-to-be, c_m. This is illustrated in Figure 2. The heart of modelling thus actually consists in the gradual alignment of these three conceptions (i.e. c_d, c_p, and c_m) by **O**, in parallel with the very shaping of the artefact **m**. Therefore, potentially neither of conceptions is completely stabilised before the artefact **m** is shaped in a satisfactory manner. The alignment of the three conceptions is driven by the observer's evaluation of the *fitness-for-purpose* of the artefact **m**.

Evaluation refers to the evaluation of the *fitness-for-purpose* **p** of the produced artefact **m** by the observer **O**. The adequacy of the *representation of* relationship is here at stake, but also, by transitivity, that of c_d and *conception of* relationship (see Figure 1c). We embrace the view of [25,36] that *fitness-for-purpose* primarily refers to the utility of the artefact for the intended purpose. The observer's judgement of artefact's utility involves trade-off between the expected value of using the model for the intended purpose and costs involved in its creation [6,36]. When **m** is judged as *fit* for **p**, it comes to be acknowledged, by the observer **O**, as the model **m** for **p**. It is only at this point that the relationship *model of* comes into being. Given the previous discussions, it is obvious that the **p** is central for establishing the *model of* relationship, as illustrated in Figure 1c.

Collaborative Modelling. When it comes to a collaborative modelling situation, an observer consists of a group of **n** human actors involved in modelling, and supposed to *jointly* observe some domain **d** and come up with its model m_d, for the purpose **p**. The great challenge in collaborative modelling consists in the fact that each participant forms its own conception of the domain c_d, of the model taking shape c_m, and of its purpose c_p. In order to reach a shared view on the **d**, **p** and **m**, the co-alignment of potentially **n**×**3** conceptions has to take place. This is indeed considered as a critical step in collaborative modelling, where all the discussions and negotiations about the model take place [35,7].

Artefact, Representation, Model. We would like to draw the reader's attention to the distinction we make between the notions of *artefact, representation* and *model.* In modelling, an observer can theoretically use *any* artefact (e.g. graphics, tangible object) as *sign*[6] when externalising his/her conception of the domain. In that context, the observer attributes to the artefact the function of *representation* of his/her conception [36]. Being a *model* is also a function of an artefact, a special case of the representation function [36]: the *model* function is attributed to the artefact only after the observer's judgement that the created artefact represents some domain adequately for a particular purpose. For an artefact to act as a model, the observer's judgement is absolutely essential. Prior to this judgement, an artefact acts still only as a representation, which, at some point of time, may or may not be fit for the given purpose.

Purposefullness as Essential. The purpose thus influences all the key steps of modelling in a non-trivial way. It is, at the same time, the main factor in judging the value of a created model. This influence is usually implicit in the modelling process. In line with [36,41], we take the position that it should be made explicit when creating and using models. At least the model creator should be aware of the intended usage and audience of the model. Explicitly considering the purpose may facilitate the alignment of conceptions in modelling, and making value judgements about the model explicit. Furthermore, it can also aid in understanding the model by the users not originally involved in its creation.

4   Role and Use of Enterprise Modelling Languages

Based on the elaborated view on modelling, we argue that language used in modelling has a *twofold function*:

1. *Linguistic function* - The language used in a modelling situation should facilitate framing the discourse about a domain and shaping the observer's conception of a domain [21,33]. With this respect, a fixed/standard modelling language provides a preconceived *linguistic structure*, a specific classification of concepts to be used in the discourse about the world [12]. This primarily relates to the *abstraction* stream of modelling (see 3.2).
2. *Representational function* - The language used in a modelling situation should facilitate expressing the conceived domain in a purposeful model. With this respect, a fixed/standard modelling language provides a preconceived *representation system*, relating primarily to the *manifestation* stream of modelling (see 3.2).

Traditionally, modelling language design and evaluation studies focus on the study of its *representation system*, overemphasising the challenges of its mechanical manipulation. These studies adopt a strictly normative view on modelling languages. While this view allows for the effective treatment of the representation system, it also disregards the variety of contexts, users and purposes that

---

[6] Even more, the artefacts used may have their primary function very different from the function they are given in modelling.

this system is intended to serve. Such a narrow focus is, in our view, due to the lack of fundamental consideration of language functioning in conceptualisation and communication activities of modelling, i.e. of the linguistic function of the modelling language. Inspired by e.g. [14,49,21,42], we build our understanding of the linguistic function in the present section. We then use this understanding to discuss the phenomena of interest in our research, i.e. the potential causes of the modelling language adaptation in its use in enterprise modelling situations.

4.1   Representational Function

As already stated, representational studies typically conceive the modelling language as a purely *representation system* of a *normative character*, which provides constructs and rules to be respected when creating representations. The representation system is usually defined in terms of abstract syntax, semantics and notation (i.e. concrete syntax) [24]. At least its abstract syntax has to be known *prior* to developing tools that implement manipulations over the representation system. For the needs of machine readability, both its abstract syntax and semantics need to be a priori *formally* (i.e. precisely and unambiguously) defined. This is usually achieved using mathematics.

While a *normative* (and *formal*) specification of the representation system is a prerequisite for obtaining predictable results from its mechanical manipulations [3,24], the assumption that these properties, required for purely technical manipulation, have to hold in the use of modelling languages across different modelling situations has to be questioned. For instance, projecting a *normative* character to the language is typical for language standardisation efforts. The standardised definition of a modelling language is expected to, on its own, increase the clarity of communication, and act as a common language across various modelling situations and audiences. Similarly, the influence of symbol's visual appearance and 'labels' (natural language words naming the syntactic constructs) on the (standard) language understanding and, consequently, on the creation of conceptions is not seriously taken into consideration. Although necessary for technical purposes of models, the normative perspective on the modelling language is untenable in the realm of its human use, as it denies the principles of socio-cognitive functioning of languages [51,16,11,10], as well as of the inter-subjective nature of conceptual knowledge [50,45].

More fundamentally, the normative perspective on modelling languages reflects, even if implicitly, a positivist orientation on the phenomena of *knowledge* and *language* [50,12,28]. Its underlying assumption is that the reference between language symbols and entities (already present) in the real-world can be established independently of a human mind and wider socio-pragmatic context in which the language is situated. These assumptions are furthered in the work of [46], prescribing (presumed universal) ontological constructs for representation systems modelling real-world phenomena. This approach reduces semantic phenomena to (presumably objective [49]) *referential type of meaning* [42], while the need for the formal specification of semantics further cuts it down to just a syntactic representation, i.e. *syntactic semantics*.

4.2   Linguistic Function

To properly understand the functioning of the modelling language in modelling, it is however necessary to go beyond this strictly normative view. This first of all concerns the need to better understand the linguistic function of modelling languages. We propose to do so through grounding in functional linguistics [11,10], cognitive linguistics [16], cognitive science [48] and semiotics [40] (in line with the adopted paradigm of socio-pragmatic constructivism).

According to socio-pragmatic constructivism, human cognition is always situated in a social context of shared practices and culture. Language emerges from, and is continuous with, *socially and culturally situated cognition* [16]. Its primary purpose is to objectify and communicate experiences among members of a community [49,16,10]. *Structurally*, language organises and stores knowledge in a way that reflects the needs, interests and experiences of individuals and cultures [16]. This knowledge is organised in terms of idealised conceptual/linguistic structures [9], reflecting the world as constructed by a community. *Functionally*, language mediates the processes of reality construction and cognition[7]. Finally, language is constantly *revised*, following the evolution of experiences and knowledge of the community, and depending on the *communicative usefulness* of pre-existing linguistic structure [16,11].

Consequently, *common language* is grounded in common practices, i.e. communities of practice, as it is *"only in such communities that objectifications by means of language develop a stable yet not fixed meaning that enables the members of respective community to communicate effectively and efficiently."* [49, pg.4307]. Different communities thus imply different 'realities' and languages [51].

As for the *meaning phenomena*, semantics is not considered as having an objective nature, i.e. the world is not objectively reflected in the language [49,16]. The meaning of linguistic expressions (i.e. symbols) arises in *their actual use*, within a particular *communication situation* and *purpose*. The very act of attributing meaning to linguistic expressions is context-dependent[8]. This act of human judgement actually establishes the *reference* between a symbol and its referent [50], which implies that the reference itself only arises in the particular communication context [11]. The role of pre-existing and idealised structures accumulated in the language (as spoken within a particular community) is to make the act of conceiving and encoding a conceptualisation in a linguistic expression (i.e. attributing meaning to it) cognitively more efficient [38]. We refer to this perspective on meaning as *pragmatic semantics*.

We argue that, when used in the abstraction stream in a modelling situation, the preconceived linguistic structure embedded in the modelling language is used according to the discussed principles of natural language functioning[9]. These

---

[7] This view is in line with the weak formulation of *linguistic relativity* hypothesis [43].

[8] The pervasiveness of communication background [48] or context [10,11] for linguistic meaning is thoroughly discussed in e.g. [10,48,11].

[9] Different authors have pointed at the relevance of linguistics in studying modelling languages, e.g. [12,14,20,41]. Some empirical support for this may also be found in the study of use of BPMN constructs in [55].

principles are not artificially imposed but intuitive to any human being, as they are profoundly rooted in the organisation and functioning of a human cognitive apparatus [16]. It can thus be assumed that these principles cannot be easily overridden by the rules of a normatively defined artificial language.

The preconceived linguistic structure embedded in the modelling language thus primarily has an *instrumental role* in shaping the discourse and conceiving the domain (in cognitively efficient and communicatively useful) way. In other words, the *value* of such linguistic structure depends primarily on its *utility* for the mentioned tasks. However, the modelling language is typically imposed onto the modelling situation from the outside, and is not rooted the wider socio-pragmatic setting of the modelling situation. This suggests that a preconceived linguistic structure of a modelling language will not be able to effectively and efficiently support a wide variety of modelling situations. It is therefore natural to expect an intuitive human tendency to adapt the linguistic structure so that it matches the pragmatic focus of modelling [20].

4.3 Variety in the Use of Enterprise Modelling Languages

In our view, this understanding of linguistic function is in particular relevant for an enterprise modelling effort. This effort typically aims to describe, understand or alter the existing (primarily) social structures and practices of the enterprise, e.g. by creating new strategy, services, processes, architectures, introducing new technologies etc. Reaching the consensus and shared understanding of the modelled phenomena among stakeholders is often mentioned in the literature as the key factor of success of enterprise modelling projects [7,37]. For these reasons, we believe an adequate linguistic structure in the abstraction stream of an enterprise modelling situation is crucial in conceiving of enterprise 'reality' through models. In other words, there will be an intuitive tendency to adapt the modelling language, in case the provided support is not effective and/or efficient. In the following, we explore some potential causes affecting the adaptation of the used linguistic structure (i.e. abstraction variety), and, consequently, of the used representation system (i.e. manifestation variety).

Abstraction Variety. The major challenge in using any modelling language, imposed from the 'outside' onto the modelling situation, consists in the fact that it is most likely not grounded in common practices of the observer. To act as, or override an existing, *common language*, the imposed linguistic structure has to be first made sense of, i.e. it has to be *situated* within the actual enterprise modelling situation. This can be a challenging task.

First of all, many factors are likely to affect a general understanding of the linguistic structure by the observer: his/her preconceptions [33], his/her abstraction capacity [47], level of expertise and experience with the given modelling language, modelling language complexity, etc. While these factors are discussed in detail in [4], we would like to only underline here that their inadequate handling increases the likelihood of *cognitive overload* [2] of the observer (especially but not only of non-modelling-experts [1,29]), when s/he *only* tries to understand the language. Consequently, the remaining cognitive resources in working memory [2] may be insufficient to focus on the primary modelling task. Humans will intuitively tend to avoid such a situation, by simplifying the language used [55,13], or even dropping the standard language in favour of a home-grown language actually grounded in an existing organisational practice [1,29].

Secondly, given *the lack of situatedness* of the linguistic structure, the latter is also likely not to cover all topics (i.e. knowledge) relevant for intended modelling situations. Indeed, the topical relevance is highly situation-dependent: different topics may be relevant for different enterprises, even in different transformation projects of the same enterprise. New topics may also become relevant as the result of the evolution of the enterprise. It is thus nearly impossible to a priori incorporate all potential topics in a preconceived modelling language. We discussed that the drive to adapt/extend the used linguistic structure to increase its communicative usefulness will be present. The compensatory strategies such as e.g. using tags, notes, additional models, etc. to compensate for 'missing aspects' may emerge in the absence of language/tool flexibility [34,27,8].

Manifestation Variety. Although not clearly separable from the previous discussion, we presently focus on challenges of using the language's representation system to create a *purposeful* representation, i.e. model. As discussed in Section 3, model purpose has the essential role in creating the representation, and in evaluating its utility. As model is created to *enable* some usage by some audience, specifically human audience, the *cognitive effectiveness* [30] of created representations for human communication should be optimised. The inadequate language support increases the costs of model creation, but it can also affect the usability of the model for the intended purpose. This is quite likely to happen when using representation systems overly tuned towards technical purposes of models. Consequently, there will be a drive to adjust such representation systems, e.g. to simplify or use just enough constructs. This reflects the intuitive human attitude to maintain a *pragmatic focus* [20] in their linguistic communication [11,16]. In our view, this underlines the emergence of informal and light-weight variants in explorative phases and for models oriented towards communication with stakeholders [7,13]. In line with [30], we also suggest that, within the same linguistic structure, multiple representational variants can be expected to occur (and should exist), each rooted in intended (classes of) model purposes.

5   Conclusion

In this paper, we have argued that the phenomena occurring in the actual use of modelling languages requires a fundamental understanding. With regards to enterprise modelling, our research offers a broader perspective in which the (modelling) language is studied as tightly related, in terms of its structure and functioning, with the practices and culture of the community it serves. From this stance, we argued that the 'dialectisation' of enterprise modelling languages is due to the crucial role of their linguistic function in these efforts.

To deepen the understanding of suggested factors affecting the effectiveness of the linguistic function, a number of interpretative case studies is foreseen. Within each case, we plan to conduct in-depth interviews, observations and analysis of the relevant artefacts (models, languages) used. Thus obtained empirical insight should allow for preliminary evaluation of the theoretical framework and for its further theoretical elaboration.

At least from a theoretical point of view, we expect that our framework contributes to language engineering efforts with insightful guidance. We believe that, at least in enterprise modelling, both representational and linguistic function of modelling languages should be carefully balanced and adequately accommodated in language engineering. With this respect, potentially more evolutionary [28] and flexible approaches to language engineering might be advised in the light of practical needs for language support. Indeed, a growing interest in these approaches within different academic communities may be observed, e.g. [26,30,54]. Such ideas will be evaluated in the empirical evaluation in our future work.

References

1. Anaby-Tavor, A., Amid, D., Fisher, A., Bercovici, A., Ossher, H., Callery, M., Desmond, M., Krasikov, S., Simmonds, I.: Insights into enterprise conceptual modeling. Data Knowl. Eng. 69(12), 1302–1318 (2010)
2. Bannert, M.: Managing cognitive load-recent trends in cognitive load theory. Learning and Instruction 12, 139–146 (2002)
3. Bézivin, J.: On the unification power of models. SoSym 4(2), 171–188 (2005)
4. Bjeković, M., Proper, H.A., Sottet, J.-S.: Enterprise Modelling Languages - Just Enough Standardisation? In: Shishkov, B. (ed.) BMSD 2013. LNBIP, vol. 173, pp. 1–23. Springer, Heidelberg (2014)
5. Bjeković, M., Proper, H.A.: Challenges of modelling landscapes: Pragmatics swept under the carpet? In: Third International Symposium, BMSD, pp. 11–22 (2013)
6. Bommel, P.V., Hoppenbrouwers, S., Proper, H., Roelofs, J.: Concepts and Strategies for Quality of Modeling. In: Innovations in Inf. Syst. Modeling. IGI Publishing (2008)
7. Bubenko Jr., J.A., Persson, A., Stirna, J.: An Intentional Perspective on Enterprise Modeling. In: Intentional Perspectives on Information Systems Engineering, pp. 215–237. Springer (2010)
8. Chiprianov, V., Alloush, I., Kermarrec, Y., Rouvrais, S.: Telecommunications Service Creation: Towards Extensions for Enterprise Architecture Modeling Languages. ICSOFT (1), 23–28 (2011)
9. Cienki, A.: Frames, Idealized Cognitive Models, and Domains. In: Geeraerts, D., Cuyckens, H. (eds.) The Oxford Handbook of Cognitive Linguistics, pp. 170–187. Oxford University Press (2010)
10. Clark, H.: Arenas of Language Use. University of Chicago Press (1993)
11. Cruse, A.: Meaning in Language: An Introduction to Semantics and Pragmatics. Oxford Textbooks in Linguistics. Oxford University Press (2011)
12. Falkenberg, E.D., Hesse, W., Lindgreen, P., Nilsson, B.E., Oei, J., Rolland, C., Stamper, R., Van Assche, F., Verrijn-Stuart, A., Voss, K.: FRISCO - A Framework of Information System Concepts. Technical report, IFIP WG 8.1 (1998)
13. Fernández, H.F., Palacios-González, E., García-Díaz, V., Pelayo, G., Bustelo, B.C., Sanjuán Martínez, O., Cueva Lovelle, J.M.: SBPMN – An Easier Business Process Modeling Notation for Business Users. Computer Standards & Interfaces 32(1), 18–28 (2010)

14. Frank, U.: Evaluating Modelling Languages: Relevant Issues, Epistemological Challenges and a Preliminary Research Framework. Technical Report 15, University Koblenz-Landau, Germany (1998)
15. Frank, U.: Towards a Pluralistic Conception of Research Methods in Information Systems Research. Technical Report ICB-Research Report No.7, University Duisburg-Essen (2006) (revised version)
16. Geeraerts, D., Cuyckens, H. (eds.): The Oxford Handbook of Cognitive Linguistics. Oxford University Press (2010)
17. Gordijn, J., Akkermans, H.: Value based requirements engineering: Exploring innovative e-commerce ideas. Requirements Engineering Journal 8(2), 114–134 (2003)
18. Gregor, S.: The nature of theory in information systems. MIS Quarterly 30(3), 611–642 (2006)
19. Hevner, A.R.: The three cycle view of design science. SJIS 19(2) (2007)
20. Hoppenbrouwers, S., Wilmont, I.: Focused Conceptualisation: Framing Questioning and Answering in Model-Oriented Dialogue Games. In: van Bommel, P., Hoppenbrouwers, S., Overbeek, S., Proper, E., Barjis, J. (eds.) PoEM 2010. LNBIP, vol. 68, pp. 190–204. Springer, Heidelberg (2010)
21. Hoppenbrouwers, S., Proper, H., Reijswoud, V.V.: Navigating the Methodology Jungle – The communicative role of modelling techniques in information system development. Computing Letters 1(3) (2005)
22. Hoppenbrouwers, S.J.B.A., Proper, H.A(E.), van der Weide, T.P.: A Fundamental View on the Process of Conceptual Modeling. In: Delcambre, L.M.L., Kop, C., Mayr, H.C., Mylopoulos, J., Pastor, Ó. (eds.) ER 2005. LNCS, vol. 3716, pp. 128–143. Springer, Heidelberg (2005)
23. Iacob, M.E., Jonkers, H., Lankhorst, M., Proper, H., Quartel, D.: ArchiMate 2.0 Specification. The Open Group (2012)
24. Karagiannis, D., Höfferer, P.: Metamodels in Action: An overview. In: ICSOFT (1) (2006)
25. Kaschek, R.: A semantic analysis of shared references. In: Ng, W., Storey, V.C., Trujillo, J.C. (eds.) ER 2013. LNCS, vol. 8217, pp. 88–95. Springer, Heidelberg (2013)
26. Kimelman, D., Hirschman, K.: A Spectrum of Flexibility-Lowering Barriers to Modeling Tool Adoption. In: ICSE FlexiTools Workshop (2011)
27. Kort, C., Gordjin, J.: Modeling Strategic Partnerships Using the e3value Ontology: A Field Study in the Banking Industry. In: Handbook of Ontologies for Business Interaction, pp. 310–325. IGI Global (2008)
28. Lyytinen, K.: Ontological Foundations of Conceptual Modelling by Boris Wyssusek – a Critical Response. SJIS 18(1) (2006)
29. Malavolta, I., Lago, P., Muccini, H., Pelliccione, P., Tang, A.: What Industry Needs from Architectural Languages: A Survey. IEEE Trans. Soft. Eng. 39(6), 869–891 (2013)
30. Moody, D.: The "Physics" of Notations: Toward a Scientific Basis for Constructing Visual Notations in Software Engineering. IEEE Trans. Soft. Eng. 35(6), 756–779 (2009)
31. OMG: UML 2.0 Superstructure Specification – Final Adopted Specification. Technical Report 03–08–02 (August 2003)
32. OMG : Business Process Model and Notation (BPMN), Version 2.0 (January 2011)
33. Proper, H.A., Verrijn-Stuart, A.A., Hoppenbrouwers, S.: On Utility-based Selection of Architecture-Modelling Concepts. In: APCCM 2005, pp. 25–34 (2005)
34. Recker, J.: Opportunities and constraints: the current struggle with BPMN. Business Proc. Manag. Journal 16(1), 181–201 (2010)
35. Rittgen, P.: Negotiating models. In: Krogstie, J., Opdahl, A.L., Sindre, G. (eds.) CAiSE 2007. LNCS, vol. 4495, pp. 561–573. Springer, Heidelberg (2007)

36. Rothenberg, J.: The Nature of Modeling. In: Artificial Intelligence, Simulation & Modeling, pp. 75–92. John Wiley & Sons, Inc., USA (1989)
37. Sandkuhl, K., Lillehagen, F.: The Early Phases of Enterprise Knowledge Modelling: Practices and Experiences from Scaffolding and Scoping. In: Stirna, J., Persson, A. (eds.) PoEM. LNBIP, vol. 15, pp. 1–14. Springer, Heidelberg (2008)
38. Schmid, H.J.: Entrenchment, Salience, and Basic Levels. In: Geeraerts, D., Cuyckens, H. (eds.) The Oxford Handbook of Cognitive Linguistics, pp. 117–138. Oxford University Press (2010)
39. Stachowiak, H.: Allgemeine Modelltheorie. Springer, Berlin (1973)
40. Stamper, R., Liu, K., Hafkamp, M., Ades, Y.: Understanding the roles of signs and norms in organizations - a semiotic approach to information systems design. Behaviour & Information Technology 19(1), 15–27 (2000)
41. Thalheim, B.: The Theory of Conceptual Models, the Theory of Conceptual Modelling and Foundations of Conceptual Modelling. In: Handbook of Conceptual Modeling, pp. 543–577. Springer (2011)
42. Thalheim, B.: Syntax, Semantics and Pragmatics of Conceptual Modelling. In: Bouma, G., Ittoo, A., Métais, E., Wortmann, H. (eds.) NLDB 2012. LNCS, vol. 7337, pp. 1–10. Springer, Heidelberg (2012)
43. Tohidian, I.: Examining Linguistic Relativity Hypothesis as One of the Main Views on the Relationship Between Language and Thought. Journal of Psycholinguistic Research 38(1), 65–74 (2009)
44. Tuggy, D.: Schematicity. In: Geeraerts, D., Cuyckens, H. (eds.) The Oxford Handbook of Cognitive Linguistics, pp. 82–116. Oxford University Press (2010)
45. von Braun, H., Hesse, W., Andelfinger, U., Kittlaus, H.B., Scheschonk, G.: Conceptions are Social Constructs - Towards a Solid Foundation of the FRISCO Approach. In: ISCO, pp. 61–73 (1999)
46. Wand, Y., Weber, R.: On the deep structure of information systems. Inf. Syst. J. 5(3), 203–223 (1995)
47. Wilmont, I., Barendsen, E., Hoppenbrouwers, S., Hengeveld, S.: Abstract Reasoning in Collaborative Modeling. In: HICSS, pp. 170–179. IEEE Computer Society (2012)
48. Winograd, T., Flores, F.: Understanding Computers and Cognition - A New Foundation for Design. Ablex Publishing Corporation (1986)
49. Wyssusek, B.: Ontology and ontologies in information systems analysis and design: A critique. In: AMCIS, pp. 4303–4308 (2004)
50. Wyssusek, B., Schwartz, M., Kremberg, B.: The Philosophical Foundation of Conceptual Knowledge a Sociopragmatic Approach. In: Supplementary Proceedings of the 9th Int. Conf. on Conceptual Structures, pp. 189–192 (2001)
51. Wyssusek, B., Schwartz, M., Kremberg, B.: Targeting the Social: A Sociopragmatic Approach Towards Design and Use of Information Systems. In: Information Resources Management Association Int. Conf., pp. 832–835 (2002)
52. Wyssusek, B.: On Ontological Foundations of Conceptual Modelling. SJIS 18(1) (2006)
53. Yu, E.: Towards Modelling and Reasoning Support for Early-Phase Requirements Engineering. In: 3rd IEEE Int. Symposium on Req. Engineering, pp. 226–235 (1997)
54. Zarwin, Z., Bjeković, M., Favre, J.M., Sottet, J.S., Proper, H.: Natural modelling. Journal of Object Technology 13(3), 1–36 (2014)
55. Muehlen, M.z., Recker, J.: How Much Language Is Enough? Theoretical and Practical Use of the Business Process Modeling Notation. In: Bellahsène, Z., Léonard, M. (eds.) CAiSE 2008. LNCS, vol. 5074, pp. 465–479. Springer, Heidelberg (2008)

From Needs to Services: Delivering Personalized Water Assurance Services in Urban Africa

Kala Fleming and Komminist Weldemariam

IBM Research Africa
Nairobi, Kenya
{kalaflem,k.weldemariam}@ke.ibm.com

Abstract. With rapid urbanization, a changing climate and increasingly strained centralized water systems, individuals and businesses across urban sub-Saharan Africa face unreliable water supplies, escalating water costs and health risks (e.g., from poor sanitation facilities or slow adoption of new practices). These deficiencies and risks are unevenly distributed over space and time. In some cases, low-income households may spend up to 20 percent of monthly income on water while others in the same geography may never see water prices that exceed one percent of household income. Several web/mobile applications have been launched in an attempt to address these deficiencies and risks. However, these applications are generally designed in a top-down manner and consequently fail to deliver personalized services. Furthermore, in many developing countries, these applications follow the *develop-and-deploy* paradigm. This implies that the end-user's needs and goals are often neglected prior to the actual development of the system. This paper presents part of our ongoing work to model, analyze and develop personalized water services using goal-oriented requirements engineering techniques. We focus on conceptual modeling in order to identify the requirements needed to design a system for personalized water assurance services. Our modeling and analysis follows a bottom-up approach that starts from interactive engagement with the water ecosystem to the use of goal-oriented approaches for the analysis and design of requirements for personalization.

Keywords: Water scarcity, Assurance, Water services, Goal-oriented requirements engineering, Conceptual modeling.

1 Introduction

Across sub-Saharan Africa, urban residents face chronic water scarcity from intermittent and unreliable piped water supplies [1,2]. The patterns of scarcity and general water insecurity that result are unevenly distributed over space and time and are linked to factors such as income [3] and the presence of alternative permanent water infrastructure (water kiosks and boreholes for example). In some cases, low-income households that depend on water kiosks may spend up to 20 percent of monthly income on water [4,5] while others in the same geography with

E. Yu et al. (Eds.): ER 2014, LNCS 8824, pp. 445–457, 2014.
© Springer International Publishing Switzerland 2014

access to boreholes may never see water prices that exceed one percent of household income. Water scarcity is also linked to the many operations and management challenges facing centralized water distribution systems [6]. Sabotage of the piped system and meters, intimidation of meters readers, leaky pipes and the potential for cross-connections from broken sewer pipes are just a few of the challenges that thwart efforts to ensure full coverage and consistent water supply.

The challenges that thwart efforts to provide fully centralized supply, twenty-four hours per day, seven days per week in urban areas, drives the development of complex water ecosystems. Within these ecosystems, a range of actors take on the responsibility for ensuring water supply (e.g., boreholes drillers, water resource agency, delivery vendors, consumers) with different levels of requirements and complexity. Given this complexity, in our previous work [7], we evaluated a number of existing water scarcity tools, techniques and processes from three perspectives: *resource stewarding* capabilities—enable monitoring and management of water resources in order to ensure sustainable supply, *value enhancing* capabilities — enable water intensive industries to increase efficiency and productivity, and *enabling responsible resource consumption* — provide individuals, businesses and other users with current and relevant information on quality and supply (e.g., when and at what price is water available for consumption?). We found that these tools generally employed a global approach to water scarcity and lacked bottom-up details that captured each individual's exposure to water scarcity which can be influenced by factors such as inadequate infrastructure, institutional constraints and social conflicts. As a result, local decision makers continue to lack an integrated and easy-to use platform that offers more than screening level information on the activities occurring within their watersheds and communities. Furthermore, these tools do not provide personalized water service delivery mechanisms for end-users.

Several developing regions around the world have introduced ICT-based information systems. These systems predominantly focus on compiling descriptive information about water points and serving up summary statistics and information such water price and availability. For example, *m-Maji* a "mobile-for-development" project, designed for undeserved communities in Kibera, an informal settlement in Nairobi, Kenya [4] provides residents with a list of the nearest registered and approved water vendors. The resident then decides which vendor is most suitable and walks to the water-point to fill their jerrycans. The system should have allowed many new vendors to enter the market, allowing more competition (to drive prices down) and increased access. However, the realities of Kibera have limited viability of the services offered by *m-Maji*. For example, many long-standing water cartels control the water market and new entrants are not easily introduced. It also turns out that potential users of *m-Maji* such as business owners require water delivery and rely on mobile jerrycan vendors for their supply. So on several fronts, we see the limitations of the *develop-and-deploy* paradigm and the waste that occurs when the actual needs and real challenges (e.g., personalization) of the ecosystem are not considered.

Public sector inefficiencies and increasing interest in a new wave of public administration termed the "digital era of governance" provide an opportunity to rethink urban water assurance [8]. Reconceptualizing the scarcity that results from intermittent water coverage as a last mile problem where information technology supplements the piped infrastructure to assure delivery of water services at the neighborhood and household level provides a progressive path to tackling chronic water insecurity. We have also seen that several social entrepreneurial approaches that predominantly target the very poor might provide clues on a how an enhanced range of water assurance services might be delivered to a broader segment of urban residents.

The goal of this paper is to address the above challenges by developing and demonstrating conceptual models for delivering *personalized water assurance services* in urban Africa using methodologies rooted in considering context relevance. Thus, we seek to understand the following three research questions:

1. How can technology be integrated to improve water monitoring and management capability of both individual consumers and water managers?
2. How do we enable continuous assessment of water scarcity risk over space and time at community and household levels?
3. What are the minimum requirements to properly specify the water environment to determine viability of a decentralized water assurance services?

The information and data required to address these questions is scattered throughout the entire ecosystem. Addressing the challenges outlined above requires a clear understanding of the water ecosystem starting from the identification of strategic dependencies as a means to designing personalized water services. Goal-oriented techniques (e.g., [9]) in requirements engineering can be used to understand the needs of actors through modeling their intentions, dependencies and expectations to be met by a system-to-be or by a new release of an existing system. On Question 3, while water scarcity concerns serve as a prerequisite for any water assurance program, we need to better understand which water scarcity situations would drive demand for an assurance program. In general, individual water use and consumption patterns are poorly understood and better data collection approaches are required to untangle influences from related factors such as location, income, socio-demographics, and the water environment.

The remainder of the paper is organized as follows. The next section presents the methodology we followed to derive use cases and provides example use cases. The conceptual model for water assurance is presented in Section 3. In Section 4, based on the results of conceptual modeling, we describe an example of how the system can be used to improve water monitoring capability in an urban area and we present a framework for continuous assessment of water scarcity risk. We conclude with a discussion and description of future work in Section 5.

2   Methodology and Use Cases

In this section, we first describe the methodology followed for the development of personalized water assurance services. We then present real-world use cases and their conceptual models using a goal-oriented approach. The use cases were obtained while working with the water ecosystem in Nairobi, Kenya.

2.1   Methodology

We organize the requirements elicitation and analysis process for designing personalized water assurance services in four steps. (i) *contextual inquiry*—interviews and focus group discussion to understand the context of water usage, the value chain in the ecosystem, and the delivery channels/methods; (ii) *use case definition* —based on real-world scenarios, we defined a number of use cases for each actor in the ecosystem; (iii) *conceptual modeling* —based on a goal-oriented approach we modeled and analyzed the use cases and derived fine-tuned needs and requirements; (iv) *mapping (from conceptual models to services)* —the requirements and scenarios are mapped to personalized water assurance services.

For (i), we used the contextual inquiry method (e.g., see in [10]) which emphasizes interviewing individuals in their context. For our inquiry, the process began with the investigation of the domain to quickly understand hierarchical relationships, organizational structures and constraints and spatio-temporal variations in needs of the water ecosystem in Nairobi, Kenya. We then identified the information needs of stakeholders involved in water supply-chain processes - from water harvesting and storage suppliers, delivery vendors, to intensive water consumers.

A number of contextual inquiries with local stakeholders and end-users were conducted. Specifically, a number of discussions with borehole service companies, the water resource agency, delivery vendors and consumers were conducted. For example, the delivery vendors were asked to give their opinions about their specific situation, needs and challenges. Moreover, we organized a mini focus group discussion with selected boreholes driller agencies and delivery vendors.

We also explored different design space dimensions including, for example, concerns such as literacy levels, existing infrastructure support and the feasibility of the technology to be applied. The assumptions and context information about the domain attributed in each dimension can influence the definition of goals and strategies and can lead to a set of fine-grained requirement models for personalized services.

At the end of our contextual inquiry process, we asked ourselves questions like: What are the external stakeholders in the water community dealing with (e.g., public entities, commercial companies, etc)? What is working well in the water harvesting from different water-points, monitoring, pricing (across different socio-demographic factors), and distribution and what is not working well and what would the stakeholders like to do about it? Regarding water scarcity risk monitoring, what are the data sources/types (e.g., remote sensing data, call centers and social medial) that the water agencies use for data processing and risk estimation. Furthermore, a focus group discussion was also organized to identify how a new system could support the critical situations identified and hence develop technological scenarios to be further evaluated with domain experts and stakeholders. In what follows, based on the result of our contextual inquiry, we present real-world use cases.

2.2 Use Case Definition

We begin with a condensed scenario that describes Elizabeth, an individual dealing with chronic water shortages.

Scenario: Elizabeth, a 30 year old resident in Nairobi, Kenya, lives in an apartment complex in Langata, a mixed low to middle income section of the city. She faces chronic water shortages that are exacerbated during the dry months. She has enrolled in a new water assurance program to reduce the annoyances and cost caused by her last minute and ongoing scrambles to find water. Her apartment receives water from the piped system no more than two times per week. Each apartment in the complex is equipped with a storage tank that is filled with piped water when available. Residents are responsible for ensuring the tank in continuously supplied with water. If the tank runs low because the piped system has not provided water, a delivery truck is ordered to supply water from the nearest borehole. Some delivery trucks may also supply piped water obtained from other areas of the city where the piped system is more reliable. As a part of the assurance program, Elizabeth's smart phone is able to monitor the water level in the tank, provide a comparison of prices on offer from nearby water vendors, and request delivery from a water vendor. A Water Assurance Advisor serves as Elizabeth's point of contact for any issues with water delivery vendors and recommends water alternatives she may want to consider in the future. The Advisor can monitor tank levels, quantity of water delivered and all logistics information related to the delivery. The Advisor also has access to weather, groundwater and piped system data and can anticipate one week ahead if piped system shortages are likely and has ongoing awareness on the status of groundwater levels.

From the scenario, we derive use cases for Elizabeth, the Water Assurance Advisor, and the Water Delivery Vendor. As described in [11], Elizabeth is a *resource (water) consumer* who simply wants to know that water will be available when she opens the tap and that it will not make her sick once she consumes it. The Water Assurance Advisor and the Water Delivery Vendor are *value enhancer* actors that depend on water to provide value for their profit-driven businesses.

Elizabeth (Water Consumer). From the scenario described, we see that Elizabeth will need to order water via the Water Assurance Advisor and allow the Advisor access to information on her water tank levels. Additionally, initiation of the assurance services will require input from Elizabeth. For example, after Elizabeth receives a low level tank alert, she much decide how to respond. She either initiates automated service delivery from one particular vendor, or the lowest cost vendor, or manually orders water service as needed. Once water is delivered she has the option to rate the quality of the delivery service.

Assurance Advisor (Value Enhancer). The Water Assurance Advisor will use general information on the water environment and water scarcity risk estimates developed via analytics from several data sources to personalize water assurance services for Elizabeth at a competitive cost. Personalized services arising from the the scenario above include: recommend the best vendor, anticipate shortage risks, and ensure fast delivery.

Water Delivery Vendor (Value Enhancer). The Water Delivery Vendor receives orders and confirms delivery once the order has been fulfilled.

Given these use cases, we demonstrate the strategic dependencies between Elizabeth, the Water Assurance Advisor and the Water Delivery Vendor in the following section.

3   Conceptual Modeling and Analysis

We applied goal-oriented requirements engineering techniques [12] to understand, model and analyze the use cases for personalized water assurance services. More specifically, in our water assurance conceptual framework, *water consumers* and *value enhancers* are modeled as strategic actors with goals, beliefs, abilities and commitments [9,11]. They depend on each other for goals to be achieved, tasks to be performed and resources to be furnished. By depending on someone else, an actor may achieve goals that would otherwise be unachievable. However, a dependency may bring along vulnerabilities since it can fail despite social conventions such as commitments. The explicit representation of goals allows the exploration of alternatives through means-ends reasoning.

Figure 1 shows the strategic dependencies between the *water consumer* and the two *value enhancer* actors, expresses what the actors want from each other, and thus identifies a network of dependencies. The resource consumer, seeking options for water assurance, **Orders Water** through the Assurance Advisor and depends on the Water Delivery Vendor to **Get Water** as promised after dispatch. The Assurance Advisor **Recommends Vendors** and **Dispatches Vendors** based on a collaborative risk rating score that considers location, source water quality and price. The Water Scarcity Risk Monitoring System facilitates collaborative risk scoring, allowing the Assurance Advisor to detect changes in the water environment. In locations and at the times of the years where the potential for contaminated shallow wells might occur the Advisor would have a lower confidence in selecting water vendors with proximity to those locations.

One key concern that emerges from modeling and analysis of the strategic dependencies is that guaranteeing quantity and quality to the individual water consumer is premised on being continually aware of the local water environment. By water environment, we mean an information set that comprises (at least initially) rainfall, water resources and built infrastructure such as boreholes. For example, since the Assurance Advisor dispatches a vendor to the water consumer, the Advisor has ultimate responsibility for addressing any last mile concerns regarding quality or quantity. This means the Advisor will need to have

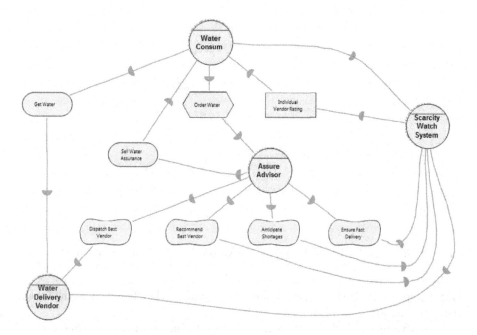

Fig. 1. Strategic Dependency Model for Key Water Assurance Actors

high confidence about the likely water sources the vendor will use, maintenance habits for the supply truck and the quality of the water delivered to the customer. Notice that both *quantity* and *quality* of individual water consumer are modeled as soft-goals (not shown in Figure 1).

When rainfall is scarce, water price increases may motivate water vendors to take shortcuts. In Nairobi, Kenya, for example, there are stories of exhauster vehicles for sewage being refurbished into water tankers in response to soaring demands at the peak of the 2009 drought [6]. To the extent that mobile water delivery via tanker trucks is implemented as the primary strategy for water assurance, there must be an underlying monitoring infrastructure that informs on the concomitant risks. While proceeding with strategic dependencies, we extended the diagrams incrementally by adding more specific actor and dependencies which come out form a means-ends analysis of each goal.

In Figure 2, we show the strategic rationale model for the Water Scarcity Risk Monitoring System. Whereas the strategic dependency model in Figure 1 focused in on the relationships between actors, the strategic rationale model provides support for modeling the reasoning of each actor about its intentional relationships. In the approach derived from the scenario to personalize water assurance, mobile water delivery is the base option in the *water consumer's* water services decision set. The water consumer relies on the Assurance Advisor to make the best judgment on vendors and associated water prices. The profit-driven Assurance Advisor depends on the domain awareness and predictive analytics capabilities of the

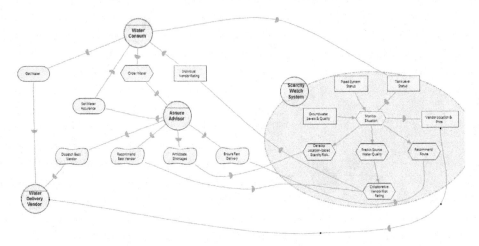

Fig. 2. Strategic Rationale Model for the Water Scarcity Risk Monitoring System

Water Scarcity Risk Monitoring System to help make the "best" decisions for the water consumer.

By analyzing strategic rationale models, we obtained the rationale (fine-grained requirements) for the solutions adopted for the design and implementation of personalized services as system-to-be. Using the goal-oriented terminology, we modeled the possible alternative ways of accomplishing a goal for the system as well as for delivery channels relevant to the individual context. Our usage of contextual inquiry with design space dimensions for evaluating the alternative choices revealed three important insights: to explore non-functional concerns such as quality and quantity of water distributors, social relationships, trust related to, e.g., price points, monitoring activities, and data collection and acquisition for analytics service; ii) to explore concerns related to organizational and social activities that influence the design of system for water dispatching; iii) to explore various parameters for water scarcity risk monitoring and estimation algorithms.

4   Personalized Water Assurance Services

Based on our detailed requirements analysis (Section 3) and by investigating expert finding techniques in requirements engineering, we identified initial subsystems that will support the delivery of personalized water assurance services. These services are developed in an application that supports data aggregation and visualization to understand the water environment (City Forward) and risk monitoring to anticipate changes in the water environment.

4.1   City Forward Mapping

Maintaining ongoing domain awareness of the water environment at the neighborhood and household level is a key requirement that emerged from goal modeling.

To fulfill this requirement, we extended an existing application, City Forward [13], which was designed to serve as a general aggregator to accommodate African urban water data.

Using Nairobi, Kenya as a test case, we captured the key elements needed to specify the urban water environment - boreholes, the piped system, rainfall, population and income along with aquifer and administrative boundaries (Figure 3). The borehole database was designed to capture key attributes such as location, elevation, date drilled, water levels, and owner. Nairobi's nearly 4,000 boreholes were loaded and visualized as shown in Figure 3. The drill date and water level records collected each time a borehole is drilled provide an updated snapshot of the state of the aquifer in a particular location. This insight is particularly important since an increasing number of boreholes signals that more water will be withdrawn from the system. Eventually, this may lead to a situation where the total withdrawals exceed the total being replenished by rainfall, and consequently declining borehole yields. In some areas of the city, water levels are falling as fast as 14 meters per year and boreholes are running dry sooner than expected [14]. When linked to rainfall information and details of the aquifer type, the system can alert on borehole water levels and infer water quality. As boreholes get deeper, the potential for poor water quality may increase (in Kenya, iron and fluoride are the biggest concerns). Shallow wells are not yet being captured by the system (because the data is not yet available), but could be integrated using a database design that mirrors the implementation for boreholes. Shallow wells are more susceptible to microbial contamination and are predominantly found in low income locations.

4.2   Water Scarcity Risk Monitoring

The quality of the piped system, groundwater availability and water quality are key and interconnected factors influencing water availability and water scarcity risks across African communities. Because each factor tends to be poorly monitored, aggregate risks are poorly understood. To deliver forecasts on shortages, new community level risk profiles must be generated as changes occur in factors such as the number of boreholes, rainfall, the piped water system or the population. The analytics required for risk monitoring are performed in a separate sub-system that shares the inputs aggregated via the City Forward interface.

In Figure 4 we provide a high-level view of the proposed architecture for the risk monitoring system in three phases: disparate data collection and cleaning, data synthesis, and risk estimation. This architecture follows from the requirements generated during conceptual modeling. We envisage continuously updated data from various sources to ensure ongoing domain awareness and accurate water scarcity risk predictions. The backend data processing phase accepts disparate data types (e.g., remote sensing data, call centers and social medial) and transforms them to common data and object models. The data and object models are then passed to various analysis and learning engines (e.g., sentiment analysis, text analysis and spatio-temporal models). In the risk estimation phase, risk factors are modeled and combined to produce the risk profiles.

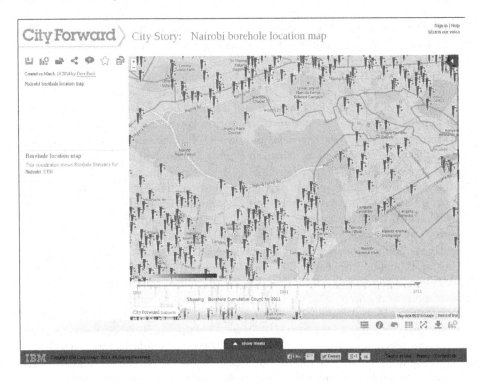

Fig. 3. Borehole Visualization for the Langata Section of Nairobi

Using Nairobi, Kenya, again as a test case, initial community-level risk profiles were developed by considering four factors: presence of piped supply, declining yield from boreholes, borehole density, potential for the presence of contaminated shallow wells. The potential for the presence of contaminated shallow wells was estimated by linking the ease of accessing shallow groundwater (based on aquifer type) and rainfall. Shallow wells are hand dug to depths of roughly 30 meters and found in aquifers with weathered rock and quaternary sediments [15]. Water levels in shallow wells are directly influenced by variations in precipitation. The opening section of a March, 2012 Kenyan news article captures the dynamics of rainfall, groundwater, and the persistent potential for contamination in low-income slum areas [16]:

Prolonged water shortage exposes Kosovo residents in [the] Mathare slum to health risks. They rush, queue and fetch water from a source they believe is clean.

Grace Mueni, a resident of the area says, *Ni kisima kwa sababu maji yanatoka chini." (It is a borehole because the water comes from underground). Heaps of hazardous wastes surround this water source thereby exposing harm not only to human health but also to the environment.*

According to a resident, George Kadima, *the water was mainly used for building purposes but this changed due to the increase in the cost of living. There is a queue here when there is water shortage in this area. The water is fetched until the source dries up forcing us to wait until it fills up to continue fetching again.*

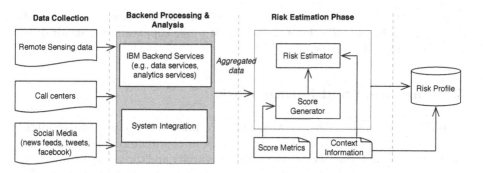

Fig. 4. High-level view of the Conceptual Framework for Water Scarcity Risk Monitoring

A reference set of *low*, *medium* and *high* risk communities was developed based on the four factors. A community with no or limited piped system access, limited borehole density and high potential for the presence of contaminated shallow wells was rated as having high water scarcity risk. A community with no or limited piped system access, high borehole densities, declining borehole yields and low potential for contaminated shallow wells, was considered to have medium water scarcity risk, while a community with significant piped supply, high borehole densities, no indication of declining yields and low potential for contaminated shallow wells, was considered to have low risk. In our approach, deep boreholes are considered to serve as protective infrastructure for a community, while shallow wells are unprotected and assumed to pose an ongoing risk if filled with water. In the story snippet above, although the water point was referenced as a "borehole" by the resident, it was more likely an unprotected well.

The Mathare and Kangemi low-income sections of Nairobi were included in the reference set as locations with high water scarcity risk. In these communities, the piped system is limited or non-existent, borehole densities are low and the potential for contaminated shallow wells is high. The Karen and Langata areas of Nairobi were included in the reference set as locations with medium water scarcity risk given the declining borehole levels and limited or non-existent piped water supply. While these locations are relatively high income and average more than 200 boreholes per square km, declining water levels signal higher access costs for consumers if groundwater continues to be the primary water source. Lavington and Westlands were included in the reference set as locations with relatively low water scarcity risk. These are high income areas with significant piped presence, high borehole densities and borehole water levels do not yet appear to be declining.

This preliminary rating of reference communities in Nairobi (Kenya) provides a framework for profiling community-level water scarcity risk across a range of urban spaces. The underlying benefit to value-enhancer actors who have the potential to drive sustainable water management is significant. The Water Assurance Advisor monitors changes in these indicators to anticipate changes in water scarcity risk. Declining borehole yields in the Langata area of Nairobi might signal the potential for a tightening of water supplies available for delivery and rising water prices.

5 Conclusion and Future Work

Water scarcity in sub-Saharan Africa is more influenced by inadequate infrastructure than an absolute lack of water. Lack of coordination and cooperation between actors in the water ecosystem drives scarcity and threatens use and management of shared resources. Water ecosystem actors need relevant tools that can help them understand and anticipate changes in the water environment.

We presented a conceptual framework for water assurance where information technology supplements piped infrastructure to assure delivery of water services at the neighborhood and household levels. In the scenario and use cases discussed, a mobile Water Delivery Vendor, dispatched via a Water Assurance Advisor, was ultimately responsible for assuring the quantity and quality requirements of an urban apartment dweller. Ongoing awareness of the water environment and capability to anticipate changes in the water environment, by the Water Assurance Advisor, enables service delivery.

Given the system described, we can imagine other scenarios in the future that will also require a well-informed Water Assurance Advisor. For example, urban business also face chronic water scarcity, but due to varying quantity and quality requirements may have additional viable options in their water services portfolio. Just like an apartment dweller, a business may desire delivery of water with quality fit for consumption purposes. But the business may also leverage recycled wastewater to supplement other processes. In this implementation of the Water Assurance Advisor, the range of on-site options would be optimized first with arrangements for mobile water delivery as needed. In the situation where many urban business are co-located, a coordinated water trading arrangement might emerge to meet the varying needs of the businesses.

Acknowledgments. We thank the IBM Interactive Experience team in Chicago, Illinois for their continued support to extend City Forward.

References

1. Bryl, V., Giorgini, P., Mylopoulos, J.: Africa-ebbing water, surging deficits: Urban water supply in sub-saharan africa. Requir. Eng. 14(1), 47–70 (2009)
2. Naughton, M., Closas, A., Jacobsen, M.: The future of water in african cities: Why waste water? In: Diagnostic of Urban Water Management in 31 Cities in Africa, Companion Volume (2012)
3. Un-Habitat. State of the world's cities: 2008/2009: harmonious cities. Earthscan; UN-HABITAT (2008)
4. M-maji, http://mmaji.wordpress.com

5. Usaid: Can water meters ease kenya's supply woes?, http://www.usaid. gov/news-information/frontlines/water-neglected-tropical-diseases/ can-water-meters-ease-kenyas-supply

6. Tsukada, R., Hailu, D., Rendtorff-Smith, S.: Small-Scale Water Providers in Kenya: Pioneers or Predators (2011)

7. Fleming, K., Weldemariam, K., Wangusi, N., Stewart, O.: Monitoring Water Scarcity Risk in Africa. In: Proceedings of the 29th Annual ACM Symposium on Applied Computing, SAC 2014, Coimbra, Portugal, March 24-28, pp. 567–569 (2014)

8. Purao, S., Seng, T.C., Wu, A.: Modeling citizen-centric services in smart cities. In: Ng, W., Storey, V.C., Trujillo, J.C. (eds.) ER 2013. LNCS, vol. 8217, pp. 438–445. Springer, Heidelberg (2013)

9. Bresciani, P., Perini, A., Giorgini, P., Giunchiglia, F., Mylopoulos, J.: Tropos: An agent-oriented software development methodology. Autonomous Agents and Multi-Agent Systems 8(3), 203–236 (2004)

10. Beyer, H., Holtzblatt, K.: Contextual design. Interactions 6(1), 32–42 (1999)

11. Yu, E.: Agent-oriented modelling: Software versus the world. In: Wooldridge, M.J., Weiß, G., Ciancarini, P. (eds.) AOSE 2001. LNCS, vol. 2222, pp. 206–225. Springer, Heidelberg (2002)

12. Dalpiaz, F., Giorgini, P., Mylopoulos, J.: Adaptive socio-technical systems: A requirements-based approach. Requir. Eng. 18(1), 1–24 (2013)

13. Ibm city forward, http://cityforward.org/wps/wcm/connect/CityForward_en_ US/City+Forward/Home

14. Kenya water resources management agency, http://www.wrma.or.ke/index. php/about-us/departments-79/technical-coordination/ground-water/ nairobi-metropolitan-borehole-study.html

15. Keraita, B., Ramesh, V., Pavelic, P., Giordano, M., Rao, T.: Groundwater availability and use in Sub-Saharan Africa: A review of 15 countries. International Water Management Institute, IWMI (2012), http://www.iwmi. cgiar.org/Publications/Books/PDF/groundwater_availability_and_use_in_ sub-saharan_africa_a_review_of_15_countries.pdf

16. Water or health,what first?, http://m.news24.com/kenya/MyNews24/ Water-or-healthwhat-first-20120322

Modeling Claim-Making Process in Democratic Deliberation

Ye Tian and Guoray Cai

College of Information Science and Technology
Pennsylvania State University, PA, USA
{yxt157,cai}@ist.psu.edu

Abstract. Online deliberation is a promising venue for rational-critical discourse in public spheres and has the potential to support participatory decision-making and collective intelligence. With regard to public issues, deliberation is characterized by comparing and integrating different positions through claim-making, and generating collective judgments. In this paper, we examine the claim-making process and propose a conceptual model to manage the knowledge entities (claims, issues, facts, etc.) in claim-making and their relationships. Extending prior works in argumentation models and issue-based information systems, our model is especially capable of depicting the formation and evolvement of collective judgments in deliberation context.

Keywords: Claim-making, online deliberation, collective intelligence.

1 Introduction

A great challenge of modern organizations is to make decisions leveraging collective knowledge and wisdom of the crowd (stakeholders) [1]. Social web technologies generated an incredible breadth of publicly available content (personal experiences, positions on public issues, etc.) and created unprecedented opportunities to collect and share personal ideas for collective action for the community. However, as Gruber [2] argued, existing social web technologies helped us to achieve *collected* intelligence ("what *you and I* think"), which is far from the grand vision of *collective* intelligence ("what *we* think") [3], where ideas are highly connected and mutually informed. Collective intelligence emerges from the process of evolving isolated knowledge nuggets towards a higher order of complex thought, problem-solving, and integration of shared individual knowledge [4].

The construction of collective intelligence requires certain type of communications in a community. The key characteristics of such communications are dialog [5], deliberation [3], and the marriage between the two [6]. Deliberative dialogs are characterized by a desire to understand all views and reach outcomes which are rationally identified as optimal for a given issue, i.e. to *think* together and discover where the collective mind might lie. This involves listening deeply

E. Yu et al. (Eds.): ER 2014, LNCS 8824, pp. 458–465, 2014.

to other viewpoints, exploring alternative perspectives, and seeking for collective judgments.

One of the most powerful ways to think together is to use reasoned claims to state one's position on an issue [7]. Supported by evidence, claims help to externalize private ideas and personal judgments for public inspection and evaluation. Collective claims towards an issue, which are fully justified and acknowledged, are sought in deliberation to inform subsequent decision-making [8]. The construction of such claims involves careful evaluation of different perspectives and an integration of evidence that is scattered in the minds of the individuals.

A conceptual model is needed to formally represent the claim-making process in deliberation context, especially reflecting the evolvement from personal ideas to collective judgments. Although prior models [9–11] are able to provide a detailed structure of argumentation within a single claim or the trade-off of different claims towards an issue, they are not capable of describing the development from individual claims to collective ones. As an extension to these models, our model reflects this development process by capturing the relations between claims (revision, synthesis, etc.)

In the rest of this paper, we first conceptualize the claim-making process in deliberation context (Sec. 2), followed by a formal definition of our model (Sec. 3). In Sec. 4 we discuss the applicability of prior models in capturing the claim-making process in deliberation.

2   Understanding Claim-Making in Deliberation

The following scenario is representative of the claim-making behavior in deliberation.

Scenario. The local borough is planning to replace the coal-burning system of the local power plant with a high-pressure pipeline of natural gas, in order to meet a new air pollution reduction requirement set by EPA (Environmental Protection Agency. The city council has received a proposal to install a gas pipeline that goes through a residential neighborhood. A community discussion forum collected the following conversation online.

Molly: *I cannot think of running a high-pressure gas line through my neighborhood without any hazard. It reminds me what happened with the explosion of an unpressurized pipeline that caused multiple deaths and destruction in Allentown a few months ago.*

Joe: *Well, the exploded pipeline was installed in around 1960, even before the construction standards were set. Today they have much stronger material for the pipes, which essentially eliminates failures. So I believe the pipeline is totally safe.*

Molly: *I agree that the safety goal is more workable now. Even though, the danger is still there no matter how small it is. I would say sticking with coal isn't wrong, though.*

Matt: *Coal won't work; it doesn't meet the new EPA standards on air pollution. But switching to gas is also expensive – the government can do pretty much work with 48 million dollars!*

Claim is defined as a falsifiable proposition meant to be supported with evidence [12]. In support of a claim, *facts* are used to serve as evidence, which are usually statistics, professional knowledge, personal experience or other types of objective truth [13]. *Warrant* is a proposition given to indicate the bearing on a claim of some provided facts, and to prove that starting from those facts, the step towards the claim is a legitimate one [9]. With their legitimacy established by warrant, facts act as the evidence that support the original claim. Fig. 1 (a) shows the argumentation of a claim extracted from the scenario above.

Deliberation starts from an *issue* that receives concern from the public, for which collective decision is sought. Note that an issue may consist of sub-issues that address different aspects of the issue. In the scenario above, the issue of building gas pipeline could be addressed from sub-issues such as necessity, feasibility, routing, etc.

Given an issue, the participants in deliberation tend to have intrinsic principles, concerns or preferences that lead them to take positions. We refer to this characteristics as *values* [14,15]. In the scenario, although Matt was aware of the safety of pipeline, he was not in favor of the decision, mainly for cost concern. Through exchanging ideas and understandings during deliberation, the participants clarify and negotiate the discrepancy of individual values and seek *shared values* that are reflected in their collective judgments.

Toulmin's argumentation model [9] and the issue-based information system (IBIS) [10] can be used to analyze and structure the claim-making behavior in this scenario. Examined with Toulmin's argumentation model, the claim-making process involves stating one's opinion, backing up it with facts, and establish legitimacy of the facts towards the claim (Fig. 1a); examined with the IBIS model, alternative options of the issue are presented, and each of them is analyzed from both upsides and downsides (Fig. 1b).

The limitation of these models lies in that Toulmin's model assume the knowledge involved in claim-making to be clearly defined and acknowledged in advance, while the IBIS model assumes that the different positions are juxtaposed and mutually exclusive. However, these assumptions are not valid in deliberation, where the claim-making process has a more complex pattern:

– In deliberation, the evidence needed to generate well-informed claims is scattered in the minds of the individuals, rather than being clear and acknowledged by every individual. Typically the participants are randomly sampled from the community, each having different background in terms of ethnicity, education and occupation [16]. This results in remarkably diversified knowledge background among the participants. For example, the fact about the

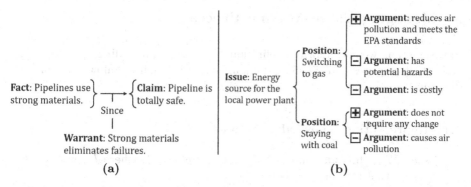

Fig. 1. (a) The argumentation structure of one claim made in the scenario, analyzed with Toulmin's model. (b) Information extracted from the scenario with IBIS model.

advanced installment technology is used to support the claim "gas pipeline is safe", and this fact is known to Joe, but not to Molly. When Joe shared this information, Molly's position changed.

– The claims made by the participants are usually informed by and linked to earlier claims, rather than independent and isolated from each other. Before deliberation, the participants take their initial positions out of their personal value and preferences [6,14]. For example, Molly opposes the idea of building a gas pipeline, because the suggested route was close to her home. In this stage, the claims made by participants are supported by evidence that is unshared and local to themselves. During deliberation, the participants share their judgments of the issue and provide supporting evidence through claim-making. In the light of newly available evidence or being aware of other existing values, people make new claims as revision or reformation of existing claims [17].

As a result of these characteristics of claim-making, the claims in deliberation are changing and evolving. During deliberation, individual knowledge is shared, meshed and integrated, while personal values are externalized and negotiated. With this process, lower-order claims are revised, reformed and synthesized to evolve into higher-order ones that reflect collective thoughts. Eventually, deliberation produces collective claims that take full consideration of the information possessed by the participants and reflect their shared values.

A model for deliberative knowledge should be able to capture the incremental introduction of knowledge, and the relations between claims that contribute to their evolvement. To address these challenges, our model handles the relation *between* claims, in addition to capturing the argumentation structure *within* a single claim.

3   Managing Claim-Making Process

In this section, we give a formal definition of our model, including the knowledge artifacts it captures and the claim-making action it handles, followed by an E-R diagram.

3.1   Representing Knowledge Artifacts

- *Issues.* We define an issue as $i = \langle id, description, I \rangle$, where I denotes a set of issues that are the sub-issues of i.
- *Claims.* A claim is denoted as $c = \langle id, position, time, p, i, F, V \rangle$ where *position* specifies the position expressed in the claim, *time* marks its time of creation, p is the proposer, i is the issue to which c is addressed, F is the set of facts that supports c, and V is the set of values that are expressed in c.
- *Facts and values.* Fact f is defined as $f = \langle id, content, type, time, source \rangle$, where $type \in \{knowledge, personal experience, statistics, other\}$, and *source* could be participant, news agency, government official, etc. We capture the description of a value $v = \langle id, description \rangle$. Set of facts and values are denoted as F and V, respectively.

We also define a participant of deliberation as $p = \langle id, name, age, description \rangle$ and the set of participants P for further reference.

3.2   Representing Claim-Making Actions

- *Proposing a claim.* When stating an initial opinion towards an issue i, a claim $c = \langle id, position, time, p, i, F, V \rangle$ is generated. Extra facts may be adduced to serve as evidence to further strengthen the claim: $c' = \langle id', position, time', p, i, F', V \rangle$.
- *Revising a claim.* In the light of some newly-introduced evidence or being aware of values held by other people, one may revise a pre-existing claim c. By revision, they may refine the expression of a claim with assessment of the evidence, and generate a new claim $c' = \langle id', position', time', p', i, F', V \rangle$.
- *Synthesizing a claim.* An important step in building towards collective judgment is mitigating the difference among a group of claims and synthesizing them [8], as Molly's second statement shows. A new claim c is generated based on the common ground of a set of pre-existing claims C, addressing different positions of them and combining the values of them.
- *Decomposing a complex claim.* The *position* of a complex claim c may contain evaluations/judgments of different aspects, each of them targeted on a different sub-issue, and driven by different value. We define a sub-claim $c' = \langle id', position', time, p, i', F', V' \rangle$ to decompose the original claim. Different from a synthesized claim, a claim with sub-claims is essentially a part of a complex claim, proposed by the same participant.

3.3 E-R Diagram

We schematize the knowledge artifacts and the claim-making process as an E-R diagram, shown in Fig. 2. In translating the claim-making actions into the relations between claims, we introduce $revision(c_i, c_k)$, $synthesis(c, C)$ and $sub\text{-}claim(c_i, c_k)$ relations.

Using this model, we revisit the excerpt of deliberation shown in the scenario in Sec. 2, structure and visualize the claim-making process in Fig. 3.

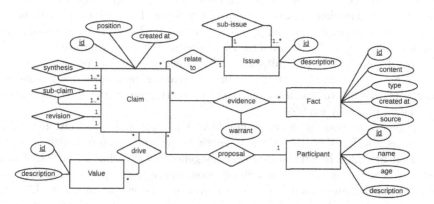

Fig. 2. An E-R diagram for the claim-making model

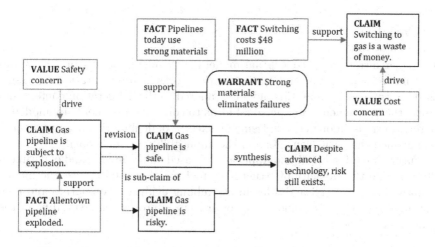

Fig. 3. Extracted knowledge entities and relations from the scenario

4 Related Works

In this section, we discuss the applicability of prior models in capturing the claim-making process in the context of deliberation.

Toulmin's model [9] provides a detailed anatomy within the argumentation process of one claim. It defines a variety of semantic elements (data, claim, warrant, modality, rebuttals, etc.), from which we adopted the basic claim-warrant-fact structure. The Toulmin model is widely used to structure the argumentation in science and politics [18,19]. However, it assumes that the elements in the argumentation of a claim as static and clearly presented. It is therefore unable to capture the time dimension of deliberation and the evolvement of claims.

IBIS model [10] and its extensions [20,21] treat the deliberation process as issue-centered. Given an issue, IBIS captures a group of options towards it [22], each of which is further argued in terms of upsides and downsides. In IBIS-based models, the purpose of argumentation is to evaluate the alternative options and choose a single option as the final decision; therefore it is appropriate for human-centered design [12,23]. Its limitation is that it assumes the options are mutually exclusive and presented all at once. In deliberation, new options dynamically emerge as revisions to existing ones, partially overlapping with each other rather than being mutually exclusive.

The generic/actual argument model (GAAM) [11] models the decision-making process as a series of clearly-defined generic statements, each of which contains slots that are filled in with actual findings generated in deliberation. GAAM is useful in structuring decision-making process where the steps towards the final decision can be predefined [24]. In deliberation, the claims made in different stages towards the final decision are proposed by participants in the light of available information at that stage, rather than predicted of predefined.

5   Conclusion

This paper introduces a conceptual model for the claim-making process in online democratic deliberation. Extending prior works in argumentation and issue-based information system, this model is tailored to the deliberation context and depicts the evolvement from personal ideas to collective judgments by modeling the relationships among claims. Using an excerpt of deliberation as our scenario, we explained the basic elements and the applicability of our model.

A future direction is to build applications based on the model, and experimentally evaluate the capacity of structuring real social web data with the model. By observing the users' activities in assembling evidence, comparing and contrasting claims, etc., we could move towards an improved understanding of the claim-making process.

References

1. Garrido, P.: Business sustainability and collective intelligence. The Learning Organization 16(3), 208–222 (2009)
2. Gruber, T.: Collective knowledge systems: Where the Social Web meets the Semantic Web. Web Semantics: Science. Services and Agents on the World Wide Web 6(1), 4–13 (2008)

3. Landemore, H., Elster, J.: Collective Wisdom: Principles and Mechanisms. Cambridge University Press, New York (2012)
4. Gavious, A., Mizrahi, S.: Information and Common Knowledge in Collective Action. Economics and Politics 12(3), 297–319 (2000)
5. Ellinor, L., Gerard, G.: Dialogue: Rediscover the Transforming Power of Conversation. John Wiley & Sons, New York (1998)
6. McCoy, M.L., Scully, P.L.: Deliberative Dialogue to Expand Civic Engagement: What Kind of Talk Does Democracy Need? National Civic Review 91(2), 117–135 (2002)
7. Knobloch, K.R.: Public Sphere Alienation: A Model for Analysis and Critique. Javnost-The Public 18(4), 21–38 (2011)
8. O'Doherty, K.C.: Synthesising the outputs of deliberation: Extracting meaningful results from a public forum. Journal of Public Deliberation 9(1) (2013)
9. Toulmin, S.E.: The Uses of Argument. Cambridge University Press (1958)
10. Kunz, W., Rittel, H.W.J.: Issues as Elements of Information Systems. Technical Report 131, Institute of Urban and Regional Development, University of California at Berkeley (1970)
11. Yearwood, J.L., Stranieri, A.: The generic/actual argument model of practical reasoning. Decision Support Systems 41(2), 358–379 (2006)
12. McCrickard, D.S.: Making Claims: Knowledge Design, Capture, and Sharing in HCI. Morgan & Claypool (2012)
13. Burkhalter, S., Gastil, J., Kelshaw, T.: A Conceptual Definition and Theoretical Model of Public Deliberation in Small Face-to-Face Groups. Communication Theory 12(4), 398–422 (2002)
14. Carpini, M.X.D., Cook, F.L., Jacobs, L.R.: Public Deliberation, Discursive Participation and Citizen Engagement: A Review of the Empirical Literature. Annual Review of Political Science 7(1), 315–344 (2004)
15. Cai, G., Yu, B.: Spatial Annotation Technology for Public Deliberation. Transactions in GIS 13, 123–146 (2009)
16. Philipsen, G.: Speaking culturally: Explorations in social communication. SUNY Press (1992)
17. Dutwin, D.: The Character of Deliberation: Equality, Argument and the Formation of Public Opinion. International Journal of Public Opinion Research 15(3), 239–264 (2003)
18. Lowe, D.G.: Co-operative structuring of information: the representation of reasoning and debate. International Journal of Man-Machine Studies 23(2), 97–111 (1985)
19. Tweed, C.: Supporting Argumentation Practices in Urban Planning and Design. Computers, Environment and Urban Systems 22(4), 351–363 (1998)
20. McCall, R.J.: PHI: A conceptual foundation for design hypermedia. Design Studies 12(1), 30–41 (1991)
21. Conklin, J., Begeman, M.L.: gIBIS: A Hypertext Tool for Exploratory Policy Discussion. ACM Transactions on Information Systems 6(4), 303–331 (1988)
22. Fischer, G., Lemke, A.C., McCall, R., Morch, A.I.: Making Argumentation Serve Design. Human-Computer Interaction 6(3), 393–419 (1991)
23. Carroll, J.M., Moran, T.P.: Introduction to This Special Issue on Design Rationale. Human-Computer Interaction 6, 197–200 (1991)
24. Yearwood, J.L., Stranieri, A.: Deliberative discourse and reasoning from generic argument structures. Ai & Society 23, 353–377 (2009)

Creating Quantitative Goal Models: Governmental Experience

Okhaide Akhigbe[1], Mohammad Alhaj[1], Daniel Amyot[1], Omar Badreddin[2], Edna Braun[1], Nick Cartwright[1], Gregory Richards[1], and Gunter Mussbacher[3]

[1] University of Ottawa, [2] Northern Arizona University, [3] McGill University
okhaide@uottawa.ca, malhaj@sce.carleton.ca,
damyot@eecs.uottawa.ca, Omar.Badreddin@nau.edu,
eawbraun@gmail.com, ncart@sympatico.ca,
richards@telfer.uottawa.ca, gunter.mussbacher@mcgill.ca

Abstract. Precision in goal models can be enhanced using quantitative rather than qualitative scales. Selecting appropriate values is however often difficult, especially when groups of stakeholders are involved. This paper identifies and compares generic and domain-specific group decision approaches for selecting quantitative values in goal models. It then reports on the use of two approaches targeting quantitative contributions, actor importance, and indicator definitions in the Goal-oriented Requirement Language. The approaches have been deployed in two independent branches of the Canadian government.

Keywords: AHP, Compliance, Contributions, Decision Making, Enterprise Architecture, GRL, Indicators, Quantitative Values.

1 Introduction

Goal modeling offers a way of structuring requirements according to their contribution towards achieving the objectives of various stakeholders. Goals can be decomposed and linked, and trade-offs can be evaluated when stakeholder objectives are conflicting. Common goal modeling languages include *i** [28], Tropos [7], KAOS [25], the Goal-oriented Requirement Language (GRL) [11], and the Business Intelligence Model (BIM) [10]. Each language comes with different sets of concepts and analytic capabilities. Most languages however have a *contribution* concept, used to indicate how much a goal model element influences, positively or negatively, another model element. *Qualitative* contribution scales often specify the level of sufficiency of the positive/negative contribution (sufficient, insufficient, or unknown), leading to a handful of possible contribution value combinations. Such coarse-grained qualitative scales are useful in a context where little information is known about the domain, or when there is uncertainty about the exact degree of contribution.

A recent trend in such languages is to support *quantitative* contribution scales, with numerical values. Such finer-grained scales enable modelers and analysts to better differentiate between the contributions of alternatives to higher-level objectives. However, whereas agreeing on the positive negative nature of a contribution is often

E. Yu et al. (Eds.): ER 2014, LNCS 8824, pp. 466–473, 2014.

easy, deciding on valid contribution/importance values on a quantitative scale is not trivial, especially when different groups of stakeholders are involved.

There are many generic and domain-specific group decision-making approaches. This paper presents our experience using some of these approaches to create quantitative GRL goal models at two different departments of the Canadian government. Section 2 provides background on GRL and defines some key quantification challenges. Section 3 identifies seven generic and domain-specific group decision approaches for selecting quantitative values in goal models. Section 4 presents our experience using consensus to derive indicators from regulations and generating legal models for compliance, while Section 5 illustrates our experience using the Analytic Hierarchy Process (AHP) for contribution, importance and indicator values in enterprise architecture goal models. Section 6 discusses lessons learned and Section 7 our conclusions.

2   Background and Goal Modeling Challenges

Both quantitative and qualitative techniques in goal modeling are accommodated adequately in the Goal-oriented Requirement Language – GRL, one of the sub-languages of the User Requirements Notation (URN), whose standard was revised in 2012 [11]. GRL has four primary elements: *intentional elements* (goals, softgoals, tasks, resources, and beliefs), *indicators*, *intentional links*, and *actors* (basically various forms of stakeholders, or the system itself, which contain intentional elements).

Goals can be achieved fully whereas *softgoals* are usually satisfied (or "satisficed") to a suitable extent. *Tasks* represent solutions and may require *resources* to be utilized [4]. Intentional links connect elements in a goal model: *decompositions* allow elements to be decomposed into sub-elements through AND/OR/XOR relationships, *contributions* model desired impacts of elements on other elements qualitatively or quantitatively, *correlations* describe side effects rather than impacts, and *dependencies* model relationships between actors. The quantitative scale used in GRL to describe contribution weights goes from −100 (break) to +100 (make). For simplicity in this paper, whatever applies to contributions also applies to correlations.

In GRL, a *strategy* captures a particular configuration of alternatives and satisfaction values in the GRL model by assigning an initial qualitative or quantitative satisfaction level to some intentional elements in the model. A GRL *evaluation algorithm* disseminates this information to other intentional elements of the model through their links and computes their satisfaction level [3]. Strategies can be compared to each other to facilitate the identification of the most appropriate trade-off amongst conflicting stakeholders' goals. When evaluating the degree of satisfaction of goals, the qualitative approach uses measures such as "satisfied", "partially satisfied", "denied", or "undetermined". This scale may be too coarse-grained or vague in some decision-making contexts, and hence GRL also supports a *quantitative scale* that ranges from −100 (denied) to 0 (neutral) to +100 (satisfied). jUCMNav [5], an Eclipse tool for URN modeling and analysis, further supports a satisfaction scale more intuitive in some application areas, ranging from 0 (denied) to 50 (neutral) to 100 (satisfied).

Indicators allow real-life values to be the basis for goal model evaluations. A conversion function translates the real-world value of the indicator into a GRL quantitative satisfaction value. This conversion can be done through linear interpolation by comparing the real-life value against target, threshold, and worst-case values for that indicator, or through an explicit conversion table. Real-life values in indicators can be fed manually in a strategy (to explore what-if scenarios) or from external data sources (e.g., sensors or BI systems), turning the GRL model into a monitoring system.

GRL was selected in the two government projects presented here because 1) it is a standardized modeling language (a genuine concern for government agencies), 2) it supports quantitative evaluations, 3) it supports strategies and numerous propagation algorithms, with color feedback, 4) it supports indicators, which can be fed from external data sources, 5) it can be profiled to a domain (through URN metadata and URN links) while remaining within the boundaries of the standard, 6) good tool support is available (jUCMNav), 7) GRL had been successfully used in many projects, and 8) local expertise was readily available at the time these projects were done.

Like many other goal-oriented modeling languages, GRL has several limitations with respect to the use of decomposition links [21, 22], the lack of modularity [19, 22], or the cognitive fitness of its graphical syntax [20]. However, the main challenges of interest in this paper relate to the quantification of the model (contributions, indicators, and importance values): "what do the numbers mean" or "where are the numbers coming from" [14, 22]. Very often in GRL, it is more important to compare evaluation results of different strategies when making a decision than to focus on the exactitude of the values of a single evaluation. Also, decisions are not always very sensitive to values, and this is why jUCMNav also supports value ranges ([min, max]) for sensitivity analysis [5]. Yet, precision in quantitative values is still desirable, especially when multiple stakeholders are involved.

For the creation of goal models, there is an emerging trend in trying to use systematic approaches for reaching agreements on quantitative values, especially for goal contributions. In particular, the Analytic Hierarchy Process (AHP) technique [23] is used to take into consideration the opinions of many stakeholders, through surveys based on pairwise comparisons. In the last few years, relative contribution weights have hence been computed with AHP for $i*$ models by Liaskos et al. [16], for models using the Non-Functional Requirements framework by Kassab [13], and for models in a proprietary goal modeling language by Vinay et al. [27]. In all cases, these approaches targeted relative contributions, without support for negative contributions, for under-contributions (sum of relative contributions to a target element being less than 100%), or for over-contributions (sum greater than 100%). Although an AHP-based approach is useful when constructing goal models, it does not necessarily eliminate the need for validation and conflict detection, e.g., with questionnaires [9, 12].

When compared to related work, this paper focuses on the creation of quantitative goal models in a different and standardized language (GRL). Not only are contributions covered, but so are indicators and the importance of intentional elements. This paper also reports on the industrial application of two group decision approaches in two different departments of the Government of Canada, in real projects.

3   Group Decision Approaches for Goal Modeling

We have identified and evaluated seven approaches divided into two groups: generic and domain specific. Other approaches exist to support group decisions or multiple criteria decision analysis [26]. However, after a first filtering exercise, we limited ourselves to those that are suitable in a GRL context (e.g., without fuzzy values). The first five approaches are generic whereas the last two are specific to GRL models in the domain of regulatory compliance, which was studied in one of our two projects:

- **Equal Relative Weights (ERW):** All contributions targeting the same intentional element have equal weights, neglecting the fact that some contributors might be more important than others. This approach does not require any discussion.
- **Round-Table Discussion and Consensus (RTD&C):** A focus group method where experts are assembled in a dialog setting. Groupings of related choices, contained in models, are put up on a screen, and the experts are asked to discuss and assign relative weights to each choice in each grouping.
- **Delphi Process (DP)** [17, 18]: A method used to reach consensus amongst a group of experts. Participants answer short questionnaires and provide reasons for their answers through several rounds. After each round, an anonymous summary of the responses is provided to the participants.
- **Analytic Hierarchy Process (AHP)** [23]: A structured technique for organizing and analyzing complex decisions using pair-wise comparisons.
- **Approximate Weighting Method – Rank Order Centroid (ROC) Weights** [2]: Objectives are ordered from most to least important, and a number of different formulas are used to assign relative weights.
- **Relative Weights Derived from Regulatory Penalties (RP):** Relative weights for regulations within the models are assigned according to the *penalties* attached to each regulation (i.e., the more severe the penalty associated with a violation of a regulation, the higher it will score in terms of contribution).
- **Relative Weights Derived from Frequency of Inspection Requirements (FIR):** Relative weights for regulations within the models are assigned according to the *frequency* at which inspectors are required to check for compliance with a given regulation, and to the level of investigation associated with each regulation.

These seven approaches were evaluated according to criteria relevant in our context (Table 1). RTD&C and DP require face-to-face meetings (FF), while the other approaches do not (AHP can be done in a face-to-face or virtual meeting (VM), or through surveys). RTD&C, DP, and AHP also allow group thinking and require preparation. RTD&C is more susceptible to peer pressure. All approaches allow for record keeping. The last three criteria were all assessed qualitatively using High, Medium, or Low. In general, the assessment divides the seven approaches into two groups with similar results. The first group (RTD&C, DP, and AHP) requires high or medium preparation and meeting time, yields high accuracy, but offers low precision. The second group needs low preparation and meeting time, but is not as accurate even though precision is high. The ERW approach has the lowest accuracy.

Table 1. Comparison of group decision approaches

Criteria	Group Decision Approaches						
	RTD&C	DP	AHP	ERW	ROC	RP	FIR
Setting	FF	FF	FF/VM	VM	VM	VM	VM
Peer Pressure	Yes	No	No	No	No	No	No
Record Keeping	Yes	Yes	Yes	Yes	Yes	Yes	Yes
Group Thinking	Yes	Yes	Yes/No	No	No	No	No
Anonymity	No	Yes	Yes	Yes	Yes	Yes	Yes
Time	Medium	High	High/Low	Low	Low	Low	Low
Precision	Low	Low	Low	High	High	High	High
Accuracy	High	High	High	Low	Medium	Medium	Medium

4   Experience Using Consensus

In our work with a government regulator, we used GRL to model goals and indicators for regulations in order to support inspection-based measurement of compliance and performance [6, 24]. We needed to insure high accuracy while minimizing time spent in meetings, so we selected RTD&C. As anonymity was not a concern, we encouraged discussions in order to learn from domain experts. This work was performed on two separate sets of regulations with two different sets of clients.

For the first clients, the objective was to convert a set of *management-based regulations* to outcome-based regulations and derived goal models. Management-based regulations direct regulated organizations to engage in a planning process that targets the achievement of public goals, while offering regulated parties flexibility as to how they achieve these goals [8]. In our RTD&C meetings, each regulation was displayed on screen and read out loud. Participants then discussed what indicator was needed together with evaluation questions that would reliably measure whether the desired outcome had been achieved. How to score different levels of compliance was also discussed. The meetings' progress was initially very slow but the speed picked up as participants got comfortable with the process.

For the second clients, we decided to use RTD&C again to derive inspection/evaluation questions from a large set of *prescriptive regulations* imposing specific actions rather than specifying desired outcomes. Prescriptive regulations are more complex because why actions exist is not always apparent. However, because the modeling team had gained experience working with the first clients, progress was much faster and smoother. Each regulation was projected and read, and the participants decided the desired outcome(s), relevant indicators, and inspection questions. For weighting the indicators, the group selected RTD&C over Delphi mainly because of lower preparation time. The assignment of relative weights was relatively faster because the regulations were dealt with in groups. In general, both experiments were successful. The rigor of the process and documentation were useful and compelling, particularly for questions asked later by people not involved in the actual process.

5   Experience Using AHP

The second set of experiments involved the use of GRL models to support decision making during adaptation of enterprise architectures (EA) at a different Canadian government department [1]. The rationale was that Information Systems (IS) in the enterprise provide the information utilized by decision makers in achieving organizational objectives. The EA goal model produced showed links from IS to decisions made by decision makers, and then to business objectives, providing opportunities to trace, monitor, and address change at the architecture level. In addition, the health of each information system was monitored through the use of six quality-oriented indicators. Herein, quantification is mainly required in three places: for contribution levels, for importance values, and for indicator definitions. The EA GRL model covering the main and provincial offices had 4 diagrams, 8 actors, 40 intentional elements (12 goals, 9 softgoals, 8 tasks, and 11 resources), 30 indicators, and 102 links.

In order to determine the contribution/importance/indicator quantities, we had access to four senior and busy enterprise architects. We had little time yet we wanted accuracy. As we were not looking for a face-to-face learning opportunity, we decided to use a virtual approach based on AHP. Given that for any element in the GRL model, we only had up to six contributions, pairwise comparison was deemed to be feasible; $n(n-1)/2$ comparisons are needed for n elements to compare, so there was a maximum of 15 questions to ask per element. Questionnaires targeting the required quantities were administered to the senior architects. The data obtained was analyzed using pairwise comparison to obtain values, normalized over a 0-100 scale in the model.

The GRL model was used to assess various adaptation scenarios of the enterprise architecture. The four architects evaluated the approach after the project through questionnaires, with positive feedback. Only one criterion pertained to the quantification itself (business-IT alignment), with a good result (4.0/5). The questionnaires were also seen as quick and easy to use, and the resulting quantities were reasonable.

6   Lessons Learned

Based on formal and informal discussions and observations on our GRL-based quantification approaches, we learned the following:

- Quantification of GRL goal models is practical, and many approaches can be used.
- Government departments are facing increasing demands for numerical values and quantities to support program decisions. Current approaches, while useful, do not provide the necessary rigor, whereas our GRL-based approach with indicators helps accommodate the need for objectivity and precision.
- In the first department, RTD&C enabled very effective knowledge transfer from the subject matter experts to the team. An unintended side-effect was hence an improved understanding of regulations and models in both groups.
- Even for large EA models, AHP and pairwise comparisons are feasible because local decisions only require a few (often 2 or 3) elements to compare.
- The preparation of slides in the first approach took time, but the discussions that took place among the facilitators brought out some misunderstandings that needed to be clarified. Since then, we have partially automated the creation of such views.

7   Conclusions and Future Work

In this paper, we demonstrated the feasibility and effectiveness of quantification approaches for goal models based on experience gained at two departments of the Government of Canada. We focused on the use of relative weights with consensus in regulatory compliance and on the use of AHP in enterprise architectures. We also introduced the use of AHP to compute contribution and importance levels in GRL models for the first time. Feedback was positive in both places, with many lessons learned.

There are obvious limitations to our results. First, we collected data as we were developing and experimenting with the group decision approaches and with the modeling styles themselves. These two aspects should be better separated in the future. Second, we used two approaches that appeared to fit the tasks, however, this does not mean that they are optimal. Our results merely suggest that quantification of goal models is feasible in the policy/regulation contexts explored.

Liaskos et al. [15] indicate further research questions related to quantification that should be considered in the future. In addition, there is a need to consider confidence and uncertainty in the quantities that are "agreed" on.

Acknowledgements. This work was supported in part by NSERC's Business Intelligence Network. We also thank the many collaborators and visionary people at the Government of Canada for their participation and support.

References

1. Akhigbe, O.S.: Business Intelligence - Enabled Adaptive Enterprise Architecture. M.Sc. thesis, Systems Science, University of Ottawa (2014),
   http://hdl.handle.net/10393/31012
2. Ahn, B.S.: Compatible weighting method with rank order centroid: Maximum entropy ordered weighted averaging approach. EJOR 212(3), 552–559 (2011)
3. Amyot, D., Ghanavati, S., Horkoff, J., Mussbacher, G., Peyton, L., Yu, E.: Evaluating Goal Models within the Goal-oriented Requirement Language. International Journal of Intelligent Systems 25(8), 841–877 (2010)
4. Amyot, D., Mussbacher, G.: User Requirements Notation: The First Ten Years, The Next Ten Years. Journal of Software 6(5), 747–768 (2011)
5. Amyot, D., et al.: Towards Advanced Goal Model Analysis with jUCMNav. In: Castano, S., Vassiliadis, P., Lakshmanan, L.V.S., Lee, M.L. (eds.) ER 2012 Workshops. LNCS, vol. 7518, pp. 201–210. Springer, Heidelberg (2012)
6. Badreddin, O., et al.: Regulation-Based Dimensional Modeling for Regulatory Intelligence. In: RELAW 2013, pp. 1–10. IEEE CS (2013)
7. Bresciani, P., Perini, A., Giorgini, P., Giunchiglia, F., Mylopoulos, J.: Tropos: An Agent-Oriented Software Development Methodology. Autonomous Agents and Multi-Agent Systems 8(3), 203–236 (2004)
8. Coglianese, C., Lazer, D.: Management - Based Regulation: Prescribing Private Management to Achieve Public Goals. Law & Society Review 37(4), 691–730 (2003)

9. Hassine, J., Amyot, D.: GRL Model Validation: A Statistical Approach. In: Haugen, Ø., Reed, R., Gotzhein, R. (eds.) SAM 2012. LNCS, vol. 7744, pp. 212–228. Springer, Heidelberg (2013)

10. Horkoff, J., Barone, D., Jiang, L., Yu, E., Amyot, D., Borgida, A., Mylopoulos, J.: Strategic Business Modeling: Representation and Reasoning. Software & Systems Modeling 13(3), 1015–1041 (2012)

11. International Telecommunication Union, Recommendation Z.151 (10/12), User Requirements Notation (URN) – Language Definition. Geneva, Switzerland (2012)

12. Jureta, I., Faulkner, S., Schobbens, P.-Y.: Clear justification of modeling decisions for goal-oriented requirements engineering. Requirement Engineering 13(2), 87–115 (2008)

13. Kassab, M.: An integrated approach of AHP and NFRs framework. In: Seventh Int. Conf. on Research Challenges in Information Science (RCIS), pp. 1–8. IEEE CS (2013)

14. Letier, E., van Lamsweerde, A.: Reasoning about partial goal satisfaction for requirements and design engineering. Software Engineering Notes 29(6), 53–62 (2004)

15. Liaskos, S., Hamidi, S., Jalman, R.: Qualitative vs. Quantitative Contribution Labels in Goal Models: Setting an Experimental Agenda. In: iStar 2013. CEUR-WS, Vol. 978, pp. 37–42 (2013)

16. Liaskos, S., Jalman, R., Aranda, J.: On eliciting contribution measures in goal models. In: 20th Int. Requirements Engineering Conference (RE), pp. 221–230. IEEE CS (2012)

17. Lilja, K.K., Laakso, K., Palomki, J.: Using the Delphi method. In: Technology Management in the Energy Smart World (PICMET), pp. 1–10. IEEE CS (2011)

18. Linstone, H.A., Turoff, M.: The Delphi method. Addison-Wesley (1975)

19. Maté, A., Trujillo, J., Franch, X.: Adding semantic modules to improve goal-oriented analysis of data warehouses using I-star. JSS 88, 102–111 (2014)

20. Moody, D.L., Heymans, P., Matulevičius, R.: Visual syntax does matter: improving the cognitive effectiveness of the i* visual notation. Req. Eng. 15(2), 141–175 (2010)

21. Munro, S., Liaskos, S., Aranda, J.: The Mysteries of Goal Decomposition. In: iStar 2011. CEUR-WS, vol. 766, pp. 49–54 (2011)

22. Mussbacher, G., Amyot, D., Heymans, P.: Eight Deadly Sins of GRL. In: iStar 2011. CEUR-WS, vol. 766, pp. 2–7 (2011)

23. Saaty, T.L.: A scaling method for priorities in hierarchical structures. Journal of Mathematical Psychology 15(3), 234–281 (1977)

24. Tawhid, R., et al.: Towards Outcome-Based Regulatory Compliance in Aviation Security. In: 20th Int. Requirements Engineering Conference (RE), pp. 267–272. IEEE CS (2012)

25. van Lamsweerde, A.: Requirements Engineering: From System Goals to UML Models to Software Specifications. Wiley (2009)

26. Velasquez, M., Hester, P.T.: An Analysis of Multi-Criteria Decision Making Methods. International Journal of Operations Research 10(2), 56–66 (2013)

27. Vinay, S., Aithal, S., Sudhakara, G.: A Quantitative Approach Using Goal-Oriented Requirements Engineering Methodology and Analytic Hierarchy Process in Selecting the Best Alternative. In: Aswatha Kumar, M., et al. (eds.) Proceedings of ICAdC. AISC, vol. 174, pp. 441–454. Springer, Heidelberg (2012)

28. Yu, E.: Towards Modelling and Reasoning Support for Early-Phase Requirements Engineering. In: 3rd Int. Symp. on Requirements Engineering, pp. 226–235. IEEE CS (1997)

Author Index